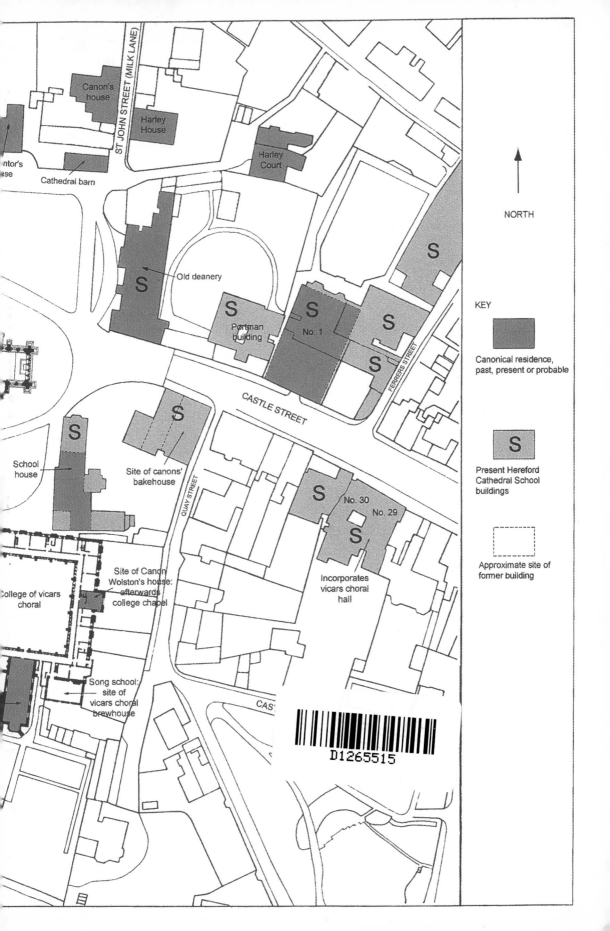

Canon's
house

Harley
House

ST JOHN STREET (MILK LANE)

Harley
Court

ntor's
use

Cathedral barn

NORTH

KEY

Canonical residence,
past, present or probable

S

Present Hereford
Cathedral School
buildings

Approximate site of
former building

S

Old deanery

S

Portman
building

S

No. 1

S

S

FERRERS STREET

S

CASTLE STREET

S

School
house

Site of canons'
bakehouse

QUAY STREET

S

No. 30

No. 29

S

College of vicars
choral

Site of Canon
Wolston's house:
afterwards
college chapel

Incorporates
vicars choral
hall

Song school:
site of
vicars choral
brewhouse

CAST

D1265515

HEREFORD CATHEDRAL

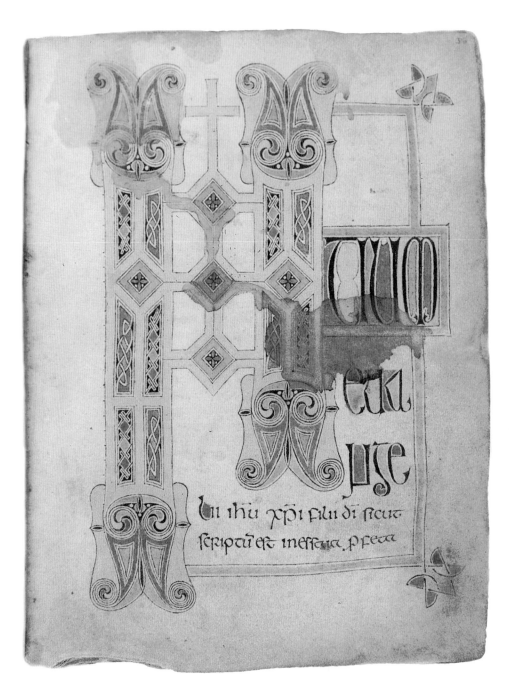

Fig. i. Hereford Gospels, eighth century: the oldest artefact in the cathedral, and the only item still in place to have survived the destruction of the Saxon cathedral in 1055. Opening page of St Mark's gospel. (HCL, MS P.I.2, fol. 36r.)

Hereford Cathedral

A History

EDITED BY

GERALD AYLMER AND JOHN TILLER

THE HAMBLEDON PRESS

LONDON AND RIO GRANDE

Published by The Hambledon Press, 2000
102 Gloucester Avenue, London NW1 8HX (UK)
PO Box 162, Rio Grande, Ohio 45674 (USA)

ISBN 1 85285 194 5

A description of this book is available from the
British Library and The Library of Congress

Typeset by Carnegie Publishing, Lancaster,
and printed on acid-free paper and bound
in Great Britain by Cambridge University Press

Contents

Illustrations ix
Illustration Acknowledgements xx
Abbreviations xxi
Contributors xxiii
Acknowledgements xxv

Preface xxvii
Robert Willis

Introduction xxix
John Tiller

PART I THE HISTORY OF THE FOUNDATION

1   Diocese and Cathedral before 1056 3
    Simon Keynes

2   Athelstan to Aigueblanche, 1056–1268 21
    Julia Barrow

3   The Later Middle Ages, 1268–1535 48
    Robert Swanson and David Lepine

4   Reformation to Restoration, 1535–1660 87
    Stanford Lehmberg with Gerald Aylmer

5   Restoration to Reform, 1660–1832 109
    Howard Tomlinson

6   From Victorian to Modern Times, 1832–1982 156
    Philip Barrett

7   The Closing Years of the Second Millennium 184
    John Tiller

PART II ARCHITECTURE AND FURNISHINGS

8   The Architectural History of the Medieval Cathedral Church   203
     R. K. Morris

9   The Architectural History of the Cathedral since the Reformation 241
     David Whitehead

10   The Restoration of the Modern Cathedral   286
     Michael Reardon

11   The Close and its Buildings   293
     Ron Shoesmith

12   The New Library Building   311
     John Tiller

13   The Stained Glass   314
     Paul Iles

14   The Medieval Tombs and the Shrine of Saint Thomas Cantilupe   322
     Nicola Coldstream

15   The Brasses and Other Minor Monuments   331
     Sally Badham

16   The Decorative Ironwork   336
     Jane Geddes

17   The Bells   342
     John Eisel

18   The Woodwork   345
     Philip Dixon

19   The Post-Reformation Tombs   350
     Roger Bowdler

PART III MUSIC AND WORSHIP

20   Music before 1300   363
     John Caldwell

21   Music and Liturgy, 1300–1600   375
     John Harper

22   Music and Liturgy since 1600   398
     Paul Iles

23   The College of Vicars Choral   441
Philip Barrett

24   The Three Choirs Festival   461
Anthony Boden

25   The Organs   470
Roy Massey

26   The Ornaments: The Textiles   493
Wendy Toulson

27   The Ornaments: The Plate   500
Joan Williams

PART IV LIBRARY AND ARCHIVES

28   The Library   511
Joan Williams

29   The Hereford Gospels   536
Richard Gameson

30   The Archives   544
Brian Smith

31   Mappa Mundi   557
P. D. A. Harvey

PART V THE SCHOOL AND THE HOSPITALS

32   The Cathedral School before the Reformation   565
Nicholas Orme

33   The Cathedral School since the Reformation   579
Egerton Parker

34   St Ethelbert's Hospital, Hereford   599
David Whitehead

35   St Katherine's Hospital, Ledbury   610
Joe Hillaby

36   The Present and the Future   628
      John Tiller

Appendix 1: The Constitution of Hereford Cathedral in the Thirteenth
      Century   633
      Julia Barrow

Appendix 2 Office Holders at Hereford Cathedral since 1300   637
      G. Aylmer, J. Barrow, R. Caird, D. Lepine, H. Tomlinson

Appendix 3 Cathedral Charities   649
      Rosalind Caird

Glossary   650

Index   652

Illustrations

Plates

I   Hereford Gospels, eighth century: opening page of St John's gospel.

IIa   Opening page of the thirteenth-century statutes.

IIb   Title page of the Laudian statutes, 1636.

IIc   Hereford Cathedral from the south by J. M. W. Turner, 1794.

IIIa   Hereford Cathedral from the headmaster's garden, 21 May 1799: watercolour by James Wathen.

IIIb   East view of the remains of the old chapter house, 9 July 1799: watercolour by James Wathen.

IVa   Hereford breviary, 1262–68: from the office for the feast of St Ethelbert.

IVb   Wycliffite English translation of the Bible, early fifteenth century.

IVc   Late thirteenth-century stained glass in one of the windows on the south side of the Lady chapel.

V   The great north window in the north transept: stained glass by John Hardman, 1864.

VIa   Tomb of Joanna de Bohun, died 1327, Lady chapel.

VIb   Tomb attributed to Peter, Lord Grandisson, died 1358, Lady chapel.

VIIa   Tomb of Bishop Charles Booth, died 1535, north nave aisle.

VIIb   Effigies of Alexander and Anne Denton, 1566, south transept.

VIIIa Medieval manuscript miniature painting: St Mark, winged and with a lion's head, as a medieval scribe, in a twelfth-century gospel book.

VIIIb Medieval manuscript miniature: baptism of a child in a large font: fourteenth-century painting in a thirteenth-century law book.

VIIIc Medieval manuscript miniature: deathbed scene, with scribe writing will, in a thirteenth- to fourteenth-century law book.

VIIId Elaborate marginal decoration by hand in an early printed book: law dictionary by Petrus de Monte, Nuremberg, 1476.

Between pages 436 and 437

IXa The cloister of the college of vicars choral from the tower: school house is in the foreground to the left.

IXb College hall, college of vicars choral.

Xa, b Tiles of *c.* 1500 and late medieval stained glass in the chapel of St Katherine's Hospital, Ledbury.

Xc Coloured decoration discovered by the architect L. N. Cottingham on the arch at the end of the south nave aisle leading to the south transept.

XI Watercolour by Joseph Carless of the nave in 1833.

XII View of the nave during the opening service of the Three Choirs Festival, 18 August 1991.

XIIIa The Gilbert Scott altar frontal, 1873, framed in the Lady chapel.

XIIIb The Limoges enamel reliquary of Thomas Becket, early thirteenth century.

XIV Hereford Cathedral from the north west, summer 1999.

XV Opening of the new library building, 3 May 1996.

XVI Mappa Mundi: the medieval map of the world.

Plans

Hereford Cathedral Close	endpapers
Hereford Cathedral in the later middle ages	84–85
Hereford Cathedral in 1815	199
Hereford Cathedral, 1999	205
Cathedral area from Isaac Taylor's plan of Hereford, 1757	302

Figures

Plan of Hereford Cathedral Close endpapers

i Hereford Gospels, eighth century: opening page of St Mark's gospel ii

ii Eastern nave, tower and south transept from the Dean Leigh library xix

1 Fourteenth-century statue of St Ethelbert 11

2 Charter of Cuthwulf, bishop of Hereford, issued 840–52 13

3 A record of proceedings at a meeting of the shire-court of Hereford, between 1016 and 1035, entered in a blank space at the end of the Hereford Gospels 17

4 A record of the eastern boundary of the diocese of Hereford, made by Bishop Athelstan in the first half of the eleventh century 18

5 Posthumous (early fourteenth-century) tomb of Bishop Robert the Lotharingian, south choir aisle 24

6 South transept interior, east elevation 28

7 One of six Romanesque capitals from the presbytery arch of the Norman cathedral 31

8 Chapter seal impression, *c.* 1190 32

9 Charter of Dean Ralph, *c.* 1135–58 33

10 Romanesque font, south side of nave 35

11 Tomb of Bishop Peter of Aigueblanche, died 1268, with the tomb of Dean John of Aigueblanche in the foreground: north transept, looking south east 44

12 Displaced architectural stones and carvings from the medieval cathedral in St John's walk 47

13 Cast of dean and chapter seal impression, dated 1394, with the cathedral's joint patrons St Mary and St Ethelbert 55

14 The rebus of Precentor John Swinfield, died 1311, on his tomb in the retrochoir 57

15 Retrochoir looking north, with south-east transept and the tomb of Bishop Lewis Charlton to the right 58

16 The late medieval chapter house, built between 1364 and 1382: reconstruction of the interior drawn by the antiquary William Stukeley in 1721   62

17 The memorial brass of Dr Richard Rudhale, died 1476, archdeacon of Hereford and residentiary canon   66

18 Dean Thomas Chandler, died 1490, presenting a copy of his book to his patron Bishop Beckington of Wells   68

19 Bishop Audley's chantry chapel, probably built between 1516 and 1524   70

20 Cast of the seal impression of Bishop Thomas Cantilupe, 1275–82   72

21a, b Indulgences to visitors to Thomas Cantilupe's shrine offered by Bishop Drokensford of Wells in 1318 and Archbishop Becknor of Dublin in 1320   74

22 A roll of indulgences offered to pilgrims to Thomas Cantilupe's shrine dating from just after his canonisation in 1320   75

23 Posthumous tombs of bishops, south choir aisle   77

24 Lady chapel interior   81

25 Plan of Hereford Cathedral in the later middle ages, *c.* 1280–1540, showing location of altars, chapels, images and other features   84–85

26 Detail of the fragments of the memorial brass of Precentor William Porter, died 1524   88

27 John Whitgift, archbishop of Canterbury 1583–1604   94

28 Effigy from the tomb of Bishop Herbert Westfaling, died 1602, north transept   95

29 Seventeenth-century engraving of the tomb of Robert Bennett, bishop of Hereford 1603–17, north choir aisle   97

30 Matthew Wren, bishop of Hereford 1634–35   99

31 Title page of a Civil War pamphlet giving an account of the taking of the city of Hereford on 18 December 1645   101

32 The 'Croft' pulpit, south-east transept   103

33 Seventeenth-century engraving of Hereford Cathedral from the north west   108

34 Herbert Croft, dean of Hereford 1644–61, bishop of Hereford 1662–91   110

35 Tomb slabs of Bishop Herbert Croft, died 1691,
    and Dean George Benson, died 1692, joined by clasped hands:
    south-east transept   121

36 Portrait of Francis Webber, dean of Hereford 1756–71   130

37 'A View of the West Tower and Front of Hereford Cathedral taken
    on the morning of the 17th of April 1786', drawn by James Wathen   138

38 'The North West View of Hereford Cathedral, as it appeared
    the 18th April 1786', drawn by James Wathen   139

39 South-east view of Hereford Cathedral, 9 August 1794,
    showing scaffolding on the tower: watercolour by James Wathen   142

40 The north transept furnished with pews for the parish
    of St John the Baptist   143

41 Portrait of Canon John Napleton as master of St Katherine's Hospital,
    Ledbury, in 1817   153

42 Dean John Merewether in 1848   157

43 Renn Dickson Hampden, bishop of Hereford 1848–68   161

44 Tomb of Dean Richard Dawes, died 1867, north-east transept   163

45 Early photograph of the Lady arbour, c. 1858–60   164

46 Opening of the Dean Leigh library, 1897   167

47 Oldrid Scott's design for the present west front, completed 1908   168

48 Bishop and chapter, c. 1920   170

49 Herbert Hensley Henson, bishop of Hereford 1918–20,
    in the garden of the bishop's palace   172

50 Royal visit, April 1957   178

51 Chapter meeting, summer 1999   187

52 Proposed sale of Mappa Mundi, 16 November 1988   192

53 Bishop John Oliver celebrating the 10.00 a.m. eucharist
    at the tower crossing on Whitsunday 1999   198

54 Plan of Hereford Cathedral in 1815   199

55 Plan of Hereford Cathedral, 1999   205

56 Gilbert Scott's reconstruction of the Romanesque choir   209

57 Crypt interior, looking south west   211

58	Choir interior, looking north east	213
59	North transept interior, looking north east	215
60	South transept interior, looking south	217
61	Inner north porch doorway	220
62	Inner north porch, arch sculpture detail	221
63	Tower, detail	223
64	Nave, north arcade, east bay, in 1841	223
65	Chapter house yard, looking south west	228
66	Fan-vaulted springer stone on the site of the chapter house	228
67	Booth porch exterior from the north east	230
68	Nave interior, eastern bays	233
69	Watercolour of 1731, showing the medieval cathedral	242
70	Bishop Bisse's choir panelling	251
71	The east end of the choir *c.* 1841	251
72	The 1735 design by Francis Smith of Warwick for a new west window with cast iron tracery	253
73	View of the ruined west end of Hereford Cathedral 'as it appeared in 1786 and 1788', drawn by James Wathen	260
74	The south aisle of the nave showing Wyatt's plaster vault	262
75	View of the cathedral from the south west *c.* 1840	263
76	View of the cathedral from the north east in 1833	264
77	A sketch of the south choir aisle in 1819	266
78	The unrestored Lady chapel	268
79	The Lady chapel east wall propped up at the instigation of Dean Merewether	269
80	Merewether's conjectural scheme for the restoration of the Lady chapel	272
81	The Scott/Skidmore screen in situ from the south, 1890	277
82	A mid nineteenth-century drawing by C. Radclyffe of the Lady arbour	282
83a, b	Plan and elevation of Sir Arthur Blomfield's proposed design for a new chapter house, *c.* 1890	283

84   Stonemason working on a ballflower detail for the tower, 1984   288

85   Foliate capital for the Lady chapel, 1999   291

86   Plan and elevation of the bishop's chapel, printed London, 1738   295

87   The stone-lined cellar found during the 1993 excavations
      on the site of the new library building   297

88   The cathedral barn including the remains of a thirteenth-century hall 301

89   A section of the plan of Hereford by Isaac Taylor, 1757,
      showing the cathedral and Close   302

90   The fourteenth-century first floor hall inside 20 Church Street   303

91   The entrance porch to the college of vicars choral   309

92   New library building, 1996, and the Dean Leigh library, 1897   312

93   The reading room in the new library building   313

94   Tomb of Sir Richard Pembridge, died 1375, south side of nave   326

95   Tomb of Bishop Richard Mayew, died 1516, south choir aisle   327

96   Shrine of St Thomas Cantilupe, north transept   329

97   Early fourteenth-century incised cross slab, north-east transept   332

98   Relief cross slab, late thirteenth century, north-east transept   332

99   Brass figure of St Ethelbert, made by 1287, from the indent
      in the Cantilupe shrine, north transept   333

100   Brass to Bishop John Trillek, died 1360, floor of choir   334

101   Brass to unknown civilian, once part of a cross brass   335

102   Lock plate of door to Bishop Audley's chapel   337

103   The choir screen by Sir George Gilbert Scott and Francis Skidmore   340

104   King Stephen's Chair   347

105   Misericord: a cat with a viol, and a goat with a lute   349

106   Detail of the roof of St John's walk   349

107   Effigy of Bishop Robert Bennett, died 1617, with the effigy of
      Bishop Giles de Braose, died 1215, beyond, north side of choir   353

108   Half effigies of William and Mary Evans, died 1659 and 1668.   355

109   Bust of James Thomas, died 1757   355

110   Gothic monument to Richard Jones Powell,
      died 1834, in south cloister   356

111 Detail of the effigy of Bishop James Atlay, died 1894, north transept 358

112 Detail of the monument to George Robertson Sinclair,
organist, died 1917, south-east crossing pier 359

113 Hereford breviary, 1262–68: two antiphons for St Ethelbert 372

114 Transcript of the two antiphons for St Ethelbert
from the Hereford breviary 373

115 Stanbury chapel, interior 380

116 Booth porch upper chamber, interior 381

117 Choir and nave, looking west 383

118 Portrait of John Bull, organist 1582–86 396

119 Organ book in the hand of Henry Hall, organist 1688–1707 405

120 Thomas Bisse, chancellor 1716–31 409

121 Samuel Sebastian Wesley, organist 1832–35 417

122 George Townshend Smith, organist 1843–77 421

123 The earliest surviving music scheme, 1851 423

124 Sir Frederick Arthur Gore Ouseley, precentor 1855–89 425

125 Langdon Colborne, organist 1877–89 428

126 Dr Roy Massey rehearsing with the choristers
in the song school, 1999 439

127 The choir in the choir stalls during the 10.00 a.m. eucharist,
Whitsunday 1999 440

128 Seal impression of the college of vicars choral, 1413 445

129 Cloisters of the college of vicars choral,
looking north up the east alley 446

130 Drawing and description of the college from Thomas Dingley's
'History from Marble', 1684 453

131 William Felton, vicar choral 1741–69 455

132 Lewis Maxey, vicar choral 1768–1820 456

133 John Constable, butler to the college 1783–1828 457

134 Philip L. S. Barrett, 1947–98, the last vicar choral, in the choir stalls 460

135 The nave of Hereford Cathedral during a performance
of *Messiah*, 1837 465

136   Scene at Hereford Cathedral during the Three Choirs Festival, 1897   467

137   Three Choirs Festival, Hereford 1933: Sir Ivor Atkins,
      Dr Percy Hull, Herbert Sumsion, Sir Edward Elgar   468

138   Contemporary print of the restored choir, *c.* 1863   475

139   George Robertson Sinclair at the organ in 1909   484

140   The present organ console   487

141   Medieval and Reformation vestments: effigies of Bishop John
      Stanbury, died 1474, and of Bishop George Coke, died 1646   497

142   Detail of the Gilbert Scott altar frontal, 1873   499

143   Ted Pannell, head verger 1978–85, with the
      seventeenth-century dean's mace   503

144   Processional cross, fifteenth century   507

145   Silver chalice and paten found in the tomb
      of Bishop Richard Swinfield, died 1316   508

146   The chained library in the Lady chapel: drawing *c.* 1841   516

147   Memorial to Thomas Thornton in Ledbury church   517

148   Title page of the library donors' book, 1611   519

149   Francis Tebbs Havergal, 1830–90, vicar choral and deputy librarian   526

150   The chained library in the new library building, 1996   535

151   Hereford Gospels: page of St John's gospel   539

152   Hereford Gospels: opening page of St Matthew's gospel   541

153   Detail of the archive capsules in the muniment room
      in the lower Dean Leigh library, 1970   548

154   Archives register, 1665–1751   550

155   The muniment room above the north transept, *c.* 1860   552

156   Canon W. W. Capes, keeper of the archives 1904–14   553

157   Honorary cathedral librarians Penelope and F. C. Morgan
      with Canon H. A. V. Moreton in 1955   555

158   Detail of Mappa Mundi: the Mediterranean   559

159   A medieval teacher with clerical students: miniature painting in a
      late thirteenth- or early fourteenth-century manuscript
      in the cathedral library   571

160   View of the ruined west end of the cathedral in 1786,
      showing the Music Room   583

161   School house, west front   587

162   F. H. Tatham, headmaster 1875–90   589

163   No. 1, Castle Street, former headmaster's house, with
      the Portman building on the left   592

164   The old deanery   595

165   The interior of the extended Gilbert library, opened 1998   597

166   The north-west corner of the cathedral Close, the site
      of St Ethelbert's Hospital from 1225 to the mid sixteenth century   601

167   The Castle Street façade of the new St Ethelbert's Hospital
      designed by Robert Jones in 1805   605

168   The garden front of the new St Ethelbert's Hospital
      with the River Wye   607

169   Seal impression of St Katherine's Hospital, Ledbury,
      thirteenth century.   614

170   Chapel and hall of St Katherine's Hospital   619

171   St Katherine's Hospital: painted overmantel with portrait
      of Bishop Hugh Foliot   625

172   St Katherine's Hospital: the 1866 northern wing, from the west   627

Fig. ii. Eastern nave, tower and south transept from the Dean Leigh library.

Illustration Acknowledgements

The editors and publisher wish to thank the following for their kind permission to reproduce figures and plates:

His Grace the Archbishop of Canterbury 27; Sally Badham 100,101; The Bodleian Library, Oxford, 16, 130; John Caldwell 114; Dean and Chapter of Hereford endpapers, ii, 1, 2, 5–11, 13–15, 17, 19–24, 26, 28–30, 32–35, 37, 38, 40–47, 49, 51, 53–65, 67, 68, 71–82, 83b, 84–86, 89, 92–99, 103–112, 115–17, 120, 122, 123, 125–29, 131–38, 140–47, 149, 153–56, 160–65, 169, 170, pls IIa, b, V, VIa, b, VIIa, b, IXa, b, Xc, XII-XV; Dean and Chapter of Hereford and the Hereford Mappa Mundi Trust i, 3, 31, 113, 119, 148, 150–52, 158, 159, pls I, IVa, b, VIIIa-d, XVI; Rector and Fellows of Exeter College, Oxford 36; Jane Geddes 102; Hereford City Library 39, 69, 70, 83a; Hereford Times 157; Herefordshire Heritage Services (Hereford Museum and Art Gallery) pl. IIc; Herefordshire Record Office pls IIIa, b; J. G. Hillaby 171, 172, pls Xa, b; Mr K. James 48, 124; David Lepine 25; Roy Massey 139; R. K. Morris 12, 66; Faculty of Music, University of Oxford 118; PA News Photo Library 52; Master and Fellows of Pembroke College, Cambridge 4; Royal College of Music 121; Ron Shoesmith 87, 88, 90, 91, pl. IVc; Mrs J. Steel pl. XI; Master and Fellows of Trinity College, Cambridge 18; Vivian of Hereford 50; David Whitehead 166–68.

Photographers

Anon., rephotographed by F. C. Morgan 136; Anon., rephotographed by G. W. Taylor 45, 46, 49, 50, 81, 103, 125, 137, 139, 149, 155, 156, 162; Barry Batchelor 52; W. H. Bustin, rephotographed by G. W. Taylor 48, 124; Jane Geddes 102; J. G. Hillaby 171, 172, pls Xa, b; Miss T. Holland 50; Ken Hoverd 87, 88, 90, 91, pls IIIa, b, IVc; F. C. Morgan 8, 16, 20, 33, 47, 56, 64, 71, 83b, 86, 146, 153, 169; R. K. Morris 12, 66; T. E. Seed, rephotographed by G. W. Taylor 122; G. W. Taylor endpapers, i, ii, 1–3, 5–7, 9–11, 13–15, 17, 19, 21–24, 26, 28–32, 34, 35, 37–44, 51, 53–55, 57–63, 65, 67–70, 72–80, 82–85, 89, 92–99, 104–13, 115–17, 119, 120, 123, 126–29, 131–35, 138, 140–45, 147, 148, 150–52, 154, 158–61, 163–65, 170, pls I, IIa, b, IVa, b, V, VIa, b, VIIa, b, VIIIa-d, IXa, b, Xc, XI, XII, XIIIa, b, XIV, XV, XVI; David Whitehead 166–68.

Abbreviations

Bannister, *The Cathedral Church of Hereford*	A. T. Bannister, *The Cathedral Church of Hereford: Its History and Constitution* (London, 1924).
BL	British Library
Bradshaw and Wordsworth, *Statutes of Lincoln Cathedral*	H. Bradshaw and C. Wordsworth, eds, *Statutes of Lincoln Cathedral* (3 vols, Cambridge, 1892–97).
Capes, *Charters*	W. W. Capes, *Charters and Records of Hereford Cathedral* (Hereford, 1908).
DNB	Dictionary of National Biography
New DNB	New Dictionary of National Biography
EEA, vii	J. Barrow, ed., *English Episcopal Acta*, vii: *Hereford, 1079–1234* (Oxford, 1993).
FHC	Friends of Hereford Cathedral Annual Reports
The Hereford Breviary	W. H. Frere and L. E. G. Brown, eds, *The Hereford Breviary*, Henry Bradshaw Society, 26, 40, 46 (3 vols, London, 1904–15).
HCA	Hereford Cathedral Archives
HCL	Hereford Cathedral Library
HRO	Herefordshire Record Office
Jebb and Phillott, *The Statutes of the Cathedral Church of Hereford*	J. Jebb and H. W. Phillott, eds, *The Statutes of the Cathedral Church of Hereford, promulgated AD 1637* (Oxford, 1882).

Marshall, *Hereford Cathedral*	G. Marshall, *Hereford Cathedral: Its Evolution and Growth* (Worcester, [1951]).
Mynors and Thomson, *Catalogue*	R. A. B. Mynors and R. M. Thomson, *Catalogue of the Manuscripts of Hereford Cathedral Library* (Cambridge, 1993).
NLW	National Library of Wales
PRO	Public Record Office
RCHME, *Herefordshire*	Royal Commission on the Historical Monuments of England, *An Inventory of the Historical Monuments in Herefordshire* (3 vols, London, 1931–34).
S + number	Reference to charters in P. H. Sawyer, *Anglo-Saxon Charters: An Annotated List and Bibliography* (London, 1968).
TWNFC	*Transactions of the Woolhope Naturalists' Field Club*
Whitehead, *Medieval Art at Hereford*	D. Whitehead, ed., *Medieval Art, Architecture and Archaeology at Hereford*, British Archaeological Association Conference Transactions, 15 (Leeds, 1995).
Willis, *Survey of the Cathedrals*	B. Willis, *A Survey of the Cathedrals of York, Durham, Carlisle, Chester, Man, Lichfield, Hereford, Worcester, Gloucester, and Bristol* (London, 1727).

Contributors

Gerald Aylmer, Fellow of the British Academy, Honorary Fellow of St Peter's College, Oxford

Sally Badham, art historian, Leafield, Oxfordshire

Philip Barrett, formerly Vicar Choral, Hereford Cathedral; died 1998

Julia Barrow, Senior Lecturer in Medieval History, University of Nottingham

Anthony Boden, writer, formerly Administrator of the Gloucester Three Choirs Festival

Roger Bowdler, historian, English Heritage

Rosalind Caird, Archivist, Hereford Cathedral

John Caldwell, Professor, Faculty of Music, University of Oxford

Nicola Coldstream, art historian, London

Philip Dixon, Reader in Medieval Archaeology, University of Nottingham

John Eisel, retired archaeologist, Hon. Librarian, Central Council of Church Bell Ringers

Richard Gameson, Reader in Medieval History, The University of Kent, Canterbury

Jane Geddes, Lecturer in the History of Art, University of Aberdeen

John Harper, Director General, The Royal School of Church Music, and RSCM Research Professor in Christian Music and Liturgy, University of Wales, Bangor

Paul Harvey, Professor Emeritus of Medieval History, University of Durham

Joe Hillaby, Honorary Research Fellow, University of Bristol

Paul Iles, Canon Precentor, Hereford Cathedral

Simon Keynes, Elrington and Bosworth Professor of Anglo-Saxon in the University of Cambridge, and Fellow of Trinity College

Stanford Lehmberg, Professor of History Emeritus, University of Minnesota

David Lepine, Head of History, Dartford Grammar School

Roy Massey, Organist and Master of the Choristers, Hereford Cathedral

Richard Morris, Reader in the History of Art, University of Warwick

Nicholas Orme, Professor of History, University of Exeter

Egerton Parker, formerly Head of History, Hereford Cathedral School

Michael Reardon, Architect, Hereford Cathedral

Ron Shoesmith, Consultant Archaeologist, Hereford Cathedral

Brian Smith, lately Secretary, Royal Commission on Historical Manuscripts

Robert Swanson, Reader in Medieval Church History, University of Birmingham

John Tiller, Canon Chancellor, Hereford Cathedral

Howard Tomlinson, Headmaster, Hereford Cathedral School

Wendy Toulson, freelance textile conservator, Kington, Herefordshire

David Whitehead, historian, Hereford

Joan Williams, Librarian, Hereford Cathedral

Robert Willis, Dean, Hereford Cathedral

Acknowledgements

Gerald Aylmer and John Tiller

The first sight of a book is normally its cover. We are indebted to Fiona Field, an artist who has done many studies of Hereford Cathedral and who is the mother of a former head chorister, for her gift of an original painting for the cover of this book. She reveals the spirit of the place today in a way which no photograph could do. Most historic paintings and prints also show a rather different building from the one which actually exists at the start of the third millennium.

The contents of the book have been put together by three overlapping teams; first, the authors themselves, nearly all of whom were already associated with the cathedral or had previously worked on its records. Their enthusiasm for the project has been a source of constant encouragement to the editors and has enabled us to achieve our target of a publication date in the millennium year.

Secondly, although only two names appear on the title page, the editing of this book has been very much a cooperative enterprise. We have worked with an editorial committee which has met seventeen times since March 1995 and attended to a mass of detailed work on the text and the illustrations. In addition to ourselves the members were: Philip Barrett (until his death in April 1998), Julia Barrow, Rosalind Caird (from 1998), Paul Iles, Brian Smith, Howard Tomlinson and Joan Williams. We pay tribute to Philip Barrett who was vicar choral at Hereford from 1976 until 1986. His detailed knowledge was invaluable to the committee and his death a very considerable loss. Fortunately the texts for his own contributions to the book were completed shortly before he died, although not finally revised, and they therefore represent his last published work.

The third team consisted of the library staff at the cathedral. Joan Williams, the librarian, acted as secretary to the committee, tracked down innumerable references for authors, coordinated the whole process of choosing the illustrations, and then worked through the entire completed text to ensure uniformity of presentation and accuracy of references; all this in addition to writing her own chapter on the library and then, for good measure, dropping everything and writing a piece on the cathedral plate in the space of a few days when it became apparent at the last minute that we would be without an author for this. We acknowledge her unstinting dedication to our project. During her time as acting archivist Marion Roberts made an important contribution as research assistant to the authors and prepared a helpful bibliography. Since arriving as archivist in November 1997, Rosalind Caird has unravelled several mysteries thrown up by accounts written by different authors, made the book more authoritative than previous texts, for example on the dating of the Laudian statutes, and written up the information on the capitular charities, as well as collating and completing the list of office holders. Her extensive grasp of the detail of the cathedral's history, as represented in the archives, has been acquired in a remarkably short space of time and has benefited our work enormously. Jane Barton, the library secretary, has kept in touch with the authors, photocopied reams of paper and managed all the files of the text on the computer. Keeping up with the latest versions (and even reading some of the disks sent in) has required great skill. Ken Turner, a volunteer helper in the library for many years, has enabled normal services to the public to continue while other staff were preoccupied with the book. Finally, Gordon Taylor, a local photographer with many years' experience of taking pictures in and of the cathedral, has been indispensable in his work on assembling a good coverage of illustrations for this volume.

The book has greatly benefited from generous financial help from a number of sources. The working expenses of the committee and the authors, two day-conferences for authors, administration and research costs, photocopying and the costs of photography and copyright fees have all been met with grants from Sir Paul Getty and the Scouloudi Foundation. Two further grants, one from the Howard Bulmer Charitable Trust, and the other from the Greene Settlement in memory of Nicholas Moore (who was formerly a member of the cathedral's Fabric Advisory Committee), have been used to enable the volume to include a generous section of colour plates. We are thankful that by these means a subject of such visual richness has received worthy illustration.

Many other people have aided our labours in a variety of ways. Some who have assisted with particular chapters are acknowledged by the authors concerned in the relevant places. More general acknowledgement needs to be given to Miss D. S. Hubbard, Record Office Manager, and the staff of the Herefordshire Record Office; Mr R. Hill, Senior Librarian, and the staff of the Hereford City Reference Library; Ms Annie Evans and the staff of the Hereford SPCK Bookshop; the Revd Stephen Evans, Warden of Ecton House, Northamptonshire; and Mr Stephen Challenger and the accounts staff at the cathedral. The whole cathedral staff and volunteers have 'owned' this project and done much in individual ways to help it forward.

Preface

Robert Willis

I do not believe that there are many establishments in English history with a more varied life than that of a cathedral. From music to libraries, from liturgy to architecture, from education to archaeology, a cathedral's life involves so many disciplines. It is played out against the backcloth of the political and cultural history of the nation and at the centre is the fascination of the interaction of the members of chapter. This interaction has proved a fitting topic for many novelists, not least the Trollopes of both the nineteenth and twentieth centuries, but here is the story not in fiction but in fact. I remember only too well the first time I read Philip Barrett's pamphlet about Dean Merewether and his tussles with his chapter about the possession of the seal, thinking this was much more colourful history than any novelist would paint, and Lord John Russell's letter to the dean is one of the great letters of a prime minister in English history. It is one of our sadnesses that Philip, whom I remember as a fellow ordinand at Cuddesdon in the late 1960s already fascinated by cathedral history, has not lived to see the completion of this venture. Happily though his contribution is complete.

The members of the chapter have been privileged to receive from time to time sections of research for this volume as they were written and our understanding of our own cathedral foundation has grown accordingly. To take simply one example: the history of the music of the cathedral, which our precentor, Canon Paul Iles, has shared with us as he engaged in his task. Each member of chapter became fascinated with the characters involved in the story and details which piece by piece fitted into place. Canon B. H. Streeter wrote of his discoveries about the cathedral library earlier this century that they were like a detective story with new clues being discovered day by day. The story of the music was just the same as new facts were discovered. Each of us would read the chapters that we had been given and talk over the fascinating discoveries which had been made about the make up or practices of the choir in the nineteenth century. We all know that this wealth of detail about what was simply one section of our cathedral life could not possibly all be included in the book and that a distillation of this scholarship would have to occur, but it demonstrated the sure foundations of research on which each chapter was based. It was exactly the same for every section of the history.

Not only are we beginning a new millennium but we are also beginning a completely new chapter in the life of English cathedrals with passing of the Cathedrals Measure. The distinction which we have long held dear between old foundations, which were never monasteries; new foundations, which having been monasteries were reformed at the Reformation, and parish church cathedrals will all be swept away. With the introduction of new statutes for each cathedral there will be a degree of similarity in cathedral government which has never been known before. All the more reason then to protect within that new context that which makes Hereford distinctly Hereford, and perhaps there can be no better way of highlighting that than the publication of this history of what it has meant to be one of the nine old foundations for over 1200 years.

Introduction

John Tiller

As one of the most ancient of our cathedral foundations, Hereford Cathedral has a past which reflects most of the aspects of the religious life of our nation over thirteen centuries, apart from the monastic. The interaction of individuals and communities centred on this place has revealed a wide range of personalities and human foibles, often combining great vision, courage and endeavour with self-interest, idleness, quarrelsomeness and discontent. Architecturally the present building is a composition of many elements representing a wide variety of styles from the twelfth century onwards, and containing many notable features, some of them of national importance. The total effect is not one of bits and pieces, but an exceptionally attractive whole which combines to an unusual extent both intimacy and grandeur. Few visitors leave without impressions of warmth and awe, openness and mystery, friendliness and transcendence.

The history which has contributed to this rare combination gives evidence of another odd conjunction. As the following pages will show, Hereford Cathedral has had its fair share of dramatic events and colourful characters, and yet there is a sense of tranquil continuity which has enveloped both cathedral and city down the ages. Being 'off the beaten track' may be part of the explanation for the survival of several major national treasures. These include the late thirteenth-century Mappa Mundi, the only complete wall map of the world surviving from the middle ages; the Cantilupe shrine, one of very few original shrines of medieval saints in England to have survived the Reformation; and the seventeenth-century chained library, by far the largest collection of books in the world to be seen still chained to their original presses. Even the advent of modern tourism has so far left Hereford relatively unscathed. The city has never had a London Road (or a by-pass for that matter), and Herefordshire remains largely devoid of dual carriageways. The cathedral guides know that booked coach parties are likely to arrive late because drivers are unaware of the slow pace of local traffic.

Against this apparently peaceful backcloth there have been dramatic moments.

Four dates which every Hereford schoolchild should know about the cathedral are: 1055, when the building, clergy, books and treasures were destroyed by Saxon rebels and their Welsh allies; 1320, when Bishop Thomas Cantilupe, who had died in 1282, was declared a saint; 1645, when the town was under siege in the Civil War and a disturbance took place in the cathedral; and 1786, when the west front of the building collapsed. Visible links with each of these episodes remain today, and fresh evidence continues to come to light. With the first is associated the gift to the cathedral by Bishop Athelstan of the gospel book now known as the Hereford Gospels.[1] The sword recovered from the archaeological excavation in 1993 also belongs to this period.[2]

For a brief while in the fourteenth century Hereford became a major place of pilgrimage because of the reputation of Thomas Cantilupe. The surviving shrine was probably spared at the Reformation because by then it no longer housed the saint's remains, a new shrine having become the focus of the cult.[3] Recently an account roll in the cathedral archives has been identified as the record of Cantilupe's last journey, to appeal to the pope against his excommunication by the archbishop of Canterbury, in 1282. From this it has been possible to plot the exact route he took.[4]

To the Civil War belongs the stirring encounter commemorated on the present west wall of the cathedral, and by the survival of what is now known as the Croft pulpit, being the one in use at the time of the incident.[5] Eloquent testimony to the conflict is also borne by the ruins of the once exquisite chapter house.[6] The foreshortening of the cathedral following the disaster of 1786 has given it what has been described by one modern writer as its 'chubby' appearance.[7] When it was rebuilt the nave was left one bay shorter, with the result that, even were the south-west cloister now to be completed along its western range, it would no longer 'fit' the cathedral.[8]

The continuity of life at Hereford which has endured through all upheavals is not just related to the cathedral's geographical location. It is given substance by the ongoing administration of a secular cathedral of the 'old foundation'. Having been governed by a dean and chapter since early times, the capitular body did not share in the fate of those which were monastic communities at the time of their dissolution under Henry VIII. In their new, post-Reformation guise the ex-monastic cathedrals retained a place of singular authority for their deans as

1. See below, Chapter 29, p. 542.
2. Now on display in the Mappa Mundi and chained library exhibition.
3. See below, Chapters 3 and 14, pp. 71–76 and pp. 328–30.
4. HCA, R 745/1.
5. See below, Chapter 4, pp. 100–1 and

fig. 32.
6. See below, Chapters 4, 5, 8, 9 and 11, pp. 102, 113, 227–29, 246 and 308.
7. Adam Hopkins, *Daily Telegraph*, 28 March 1998.
8. See below, Chapter 9, pp. 259–65 and fig. 54.

successors to the former priors, whereas the nine 'old foundation' cathedrals, including Hereford, were communities of equals, each enjoying the income from their individual prebends as well as, for the residentiary canons, a share in the common fund.[9]

There has therefore been, apart from the lapse during the Commonwealth in the seventeenth century, one basic constitution for Hereford Cathedral since the middle ages, expressed in a succession of statutes relating it to changing circumstances. Few other institutions can claim such length of existence without radical alteration. The fact that now, at the end of the twentieth century, it has just undergone the first major change in its constitution is in itself sufficient reason for marking the end of an era with this publication.

Under the Cathedrals Measure (1999), all cathedral chapters have been enlarged to include lay persons, and all chapters have become accountable to a council representing the interests of diocese, city, county and wider church. Furthermore, Henry VIII's 'new foundation' style of government has now spread everywhere, since no chapter decisions can be made in the absence of the dean unless subsequently ratified by him or her.

One of the recent events which undoubtedly influenced the General Synod of the Church of England in reforming the administration of cathedrals was the attempt by the dean and chapter of Hereford to sell their Mappa Mundi in 1988–89. The impact of this decision is described in the following pages,[10] but among the consequences for all cathedrals it is important to note not only the new measure just mentioned, but also the introduction for the first time of a national scheme of government grants for the restoration of cathedral fabric. Research by the media at the time of the proposed sale of Mappa Mundi to meet a financial crisis revealed that many other cathedrals were in similar straits in struggling to carry out urgent repairs. In this respect Hereford was a catalyst for change which was desperately needed.

In Hereford, of course, two further positive outcomes of the Mappa Mundi affair were the construction of the new building to house the library and exhibition, made possible by means of a gift from Sir Paul Getty, and the endowment by the National Heritage Memorial Fund of a capital sum for the cathedral, to be administered by the Mappa Mundi Trustees. This had the effect of widening the scope of lay involvement in cathedral affairs even before the passing of the measure, and something of the contribution which has been made by the trustees is recorded below.[11]

The controversy into which Hereford was plunged at the end of the 1980s was

9. See below, Appendix 1, pp. 633–36.   11. Ibid., pp. 194–96.
10. See below, Chapter 7, pp. 190–93.

not unprecedented. There had been the removal of the Scott/Skidmore screen in the sixties (now the subject of a grand restoration scheme at the Victoria and Albert Museum), which affords an example of the impact of the liturgical movement on many English cathedrals in the post-war period. However, as with the earlier removal of the chained library from the Lady chapel and the latter's restoration as a place of worship, the immediate reason for change was the urgent need of restoration.[12] Controversy also occurred over the appointment of a bishop not universally acceptable to the dean and chapter in both the nineteenth and twentieth centuries.[13]

The review of these and other episodes offered by the authors in this volume enables us to gain a fresh perspective on some hitherto accepted judgements. For example, the chapters on the eighteenth century contribute to a widespread recovery by recent historians of a more favourable verdict on the state of the Church of England in that era. The refurbishment of the choir is here seen to have been part of a coherent liturgical approach, however strange to later minds influenced by Victorian ecclesiology.[14] Again, the place of Dean Merewether as the great restorer of the cathedral is here put into a more balanced narrative.[15] Some new heroes emerge from previous obscurity, a notable example being Canon Napleton.[16] Nearly all of the authors had worked on the records of the cathedral before contributing to this volume. The result is a comprehensive treatment derived from many years' research.

As Hereford Cathedral enters the new millennium, it is encouraging to look back on a record of stirring times out of which something spiritual and enduring has been woven into the fabric of the peaceful Herefordshire countryside. Archbishop Randall Davidson is reputed to have told Herbert Hensley Henson, when the latter was appointed bishop of Hereford in 1917, that Hereford was 'a poor little country place'.[17] Nevertheless it is here that such issues as the call to holiness, the nature of the clerical state, the place of the monarchy in the church, the link between faith and education, and the use of art and music in the service of religion, have all been contested in a place which Henson himself later described as 'intensely local in feeling and interest'.[18] It is remarkable how often Hereford has felt the national pulse and found its own destiny.

12. See below, Chapters 6, 9 and 28, pp. 179–80, 268–69 and 524.
13. See below, Chapter 6, pp. 160–61, 171.
14. See below, Chapters 9 and 22, pp. 249–50 and 408–9.
15. See below, Chapters 6 and 9, pp. 156–61 and 265–74.
16. See below, Chapter 5, pp. 150–54.
17. H. H. Henson, *Retrospect of an Unimportant Life* (3 vols, London, 1942–50), i, p. 212.
18. Ibid., p. 271.

PART I

The History
of the Foundation

Diocese and Cathedral before 1056

Simon Keynes

The origins of the church of Hereford lie hidden in the obscurity of the history of the west midlands in the last quarter of the seventh century. Following the early stages of the Germanic invasions and settlement of Britain, in the fifth and sixth centuries, the people who established themselves west of the River Severn (and east of the River Wye) came to be known as 'westerners' of some kind (presumably in relation to other Anglian peoples), and, later, as the Magonsætan ('dwellers at the stomach(s)', or, more probably, 'the Maund-dwellers').[1] We should like to know more about the relationship which developed between the Anglian settlers and the native British population, though we may well be disposed to imagine that it involved gradual assimilation as opposed to sustained oppression, and continuity as opposed to cataclysm. It is likely, at the same time, that the incomers became familiar with Christianity as much through association with the British in their own region as through the preaching of any missionaries who came from outside to work among them. The names given to or adopted by peoples tend as a matter of convenience to express a collective sense of identity, and to conceal many deeper complications; so in the case of the 'westerners', or Magonsætan, we should perhaps be thinking in terms of the emergence in the seventh century of a people of mixed Welsh and Anglian stock, with social, political and economic structures which were distinctively their own.

If we may trust the information contained in some rather late hagiographical sources, the ruler of the 'westerners', or Magonsætan, in the 650s was a certain

---

1. See F. M. Stenton, *Anglo-Saxon England* (3rd edn, Oxford, 1971), pp. 46–48; K. Pretty, 'Defining the Magonsæte', in S. Bassett, ed., *The Origins of Anglo-Saxon Kingdoms* (Leicester, 1989), pp. 171–83 and 277–79; and P. Sims-Williams, *Religion and Literature in Western England, 600–800*, Cambridge Studies in Anglo-Saxon England, 3 (Cambridge, 1990), pp. 39–53. For the 'westerners', see below, n. 9; for discussion of the name 'Magonsætan', see M. Gelling, *Signposts to the Past: Place-Names and the History of England* (London, 1978), pp. 101–5, and Sims-Williams, *Religion and Literature*, p. 40. I am grateful to Professor G. E. Aylmer and Dr Julia Barrow for their most helpful comments on a draft of this chapter.

Merewalh; and although he is said to have been a son of Penda, king of the
Mercians (*c.* 630–55), and thus a brother of Peada, ruler of the Middle Angles
(d. 656), Wulfhere, king of the Mercians (658–75), and Æthelred, king of the
Mercians (675–704), it is possible that he was in fact a member of a local ruling
family who became 'attached' in later tradition to the Mercian royal dynasty.[2]
Merewalh married a Kentish princess called Eormenburga or Æbba (Domneva).
Among his sons by an earlier marriage were Merchelm and Milfrith, both of whom
appear to have been active as rulers of the Magonsætan in the late seventh century;[3]
and among his daughters by Eormenburga were Mildburg (St Milburga), abbess of
Much Wenlock, and Mildthryth (St Mildred), abbess of Minster-in-Thanet.[4] Merewalh himself is said to have been converted to Christianity by a Northumbrian
priest called Eadfrith, and was credited with the foundation of religious houses at
Leominster (Herefordshire) and at Much Wenlock (Shropshire), and perhaps others
elsewhere;[5] his son Milfrith was credited with the foundation of the church of
Hereford.[6] It has long been assumed that the episcopal see for the Magonsætan was

2. For different views of the rulers of the Magonsætan, see F. M. Stenton, 'Pre-Conquest Herefordshire' (1934), in D. M. Stenton, ed., *Preparatory to Anglo-Saxon England* (Oxford, 1970), pp. 193–202, at 194–95; H. P. R. Finberg, 'The Princes of the Magonsæte', in his *The Early Charters of the West Midlands* (2nd edn, Leicester, 1972), pp. 217–24; and Sims-Williams, *Religion and Literature*, pp. 47–49. For the suggestion that Merewalh was in fact of native British origin, see Pretty, 'Defining the Magonsæte', pp. 175–77 and 183.

3. The evidence is preserved in the form of the purported 'Testament of St Mildburg', incorporated in the late eleventh-century *Vita S. Milburgae* attributed to the hagiographer Goscelin of Saint-Bertin. See S 1798–99, in H. P. R. Finberg, 'St Mildburg's Testament', in *Early Charters of the West Midlands*, pp. 197–216, at 202–3.

4. D. W. Rollason, *The Mildrith Legend: A Study in Early Medieval Hagiography in England*, Studies in the Early History of Britain (Leicester, 1982).

5. On the early history of the religious house at Leominster, see J. Hillaby, 'Early Christian and Pre-Conquest Leominster: An Exploration of the Sources', *TWNFC*, 45 (1987), pp. 557–685; see also Sims-Williams, *Religion and Literature*, pp. 55–56.

6. On the early history of Hereford, see D. A. Whitehead, 'The Historical Background to the City Defences', in R. Shoesmith, *Hereford City Excavations*, ii, *Excavations On and Close to the Defences*, Council for British Archaeology Research Report, 46 (London, 1982), pp. 13–24, at 13–15, and R. Shoesmith, 'The Origins and Growth of Hereford', ibid., pp. 88–94, at 90–94; see also R. Stone and N. Appleton-Fox, *A View from Hereford's Past* (Little Logaston, 1996), pp. 4–9. For traditions concerning the origins of the church, see the Hereford *Passio S. Æthelberhti regis et martyris*, chapter 15, in M. R. James, ed., 'Two Lives of Saint Ethelbert, King and Martyr', *English Historical Review*, 32 (1917), pp. 214–44, at 244, and Gerald of Wales, *Vita regis et martyris Æthelberti*, chapter 12, in James, 'Two Lives of Saint Ethelbert', p. 231; see also J. Barrow, 'A Lotharingian in Hereford: Bishop Robert's Reorganisation of the Church of Hereford, 1079–1095', in Whitehead, *Medieval Art at Hereford*, pp. 29–49, at 30.

established on the site of Hereford Cathedral from the outset, presumably *c.* 680.[7] The possibility has been raised, however, that the see had been established initially elsewhere — for example on the site of St Guthlac's in Hereford, or at Leominster, or at Ledbury (near Hereford), or at Lydbury North (Shropshire) — and was only moved to its present site during the course of the eighth century.[8] Ecclesiastical arrangements were doubtless as flexible in the late seventh and early eighth centuries as they remained thereafter, and could always be changed in response to political considerations and pastoral needs; but the strongest reasons for persisting in the presumption that the see of the 'westerners' was established on its present site at Hereford, in the late seventh century, are the quality of its location within the town and the fact that the see is not *known* to have been elsewhere at any time before the end of the eighth century, when it was certainly at Hereford.

The compiler of the earliest surviving set of Anglo-Saxon episcopal lists, representing a view of the English church formulated probably at Canterbury in the late eighth or early ninth century, named the first in the line of the bishops of the 'westerners' (if thus we may represent the obscure term used to denote the bishops of the Magonsætan at Hereford), as a certain Putta, who would appear to have flourished in the last quarter of the seventh century.[9] According to Bede (writing in 731), Æthelred, king of the Mercians, had ravaged Kent in 676, and destroyed the see of Rochester; whereupon Putta, bishop of Rochester, sought help from Seaxwulf, bishop of the Mercians (probably at Lichfield), and was granted 'a church and a small estate'.[10] Bede does not feel the need to explain in this context where Putta's new church was located, and says of him simply that 'he served God in this church and went round wherever he was invited, teaching church music'; indeed, it is by no means certain that Putta retained episcopal status, and it is only the link with Seaxwulf which might encourage the supposition

7. E.g. William of Malmesbury, *De gestis pontificum Anglorum*, book iv, chapter 163, in N. E. S. A. Hamilton, ed., *Willelmi Malmesbiriensis monachi de gestis pontificum Anglorum libri quinque*, Rolls Series, 52 (London, 1870), p. 298. See also Bannister, *The Cathedral Church of Hereford*, pp. 14–16; and *EEA*, vii, p. xxvii.

8. For discussion of these possibilities, see D. A. Whitehead, 'Historical Introduction', in R. Shoesmith, *Hereford City Excavations*, i, *Excavations at Castle Green*, Council for British Archaeology Research Report, 36 (London, 1980), pp. 1–6, at 3–4; Sims-Williams, *Religion and Literature*, pp. 90–91, and *EEA*, vii, pp. xxvi–xxviii.

9. For a general account of Anglo-Saxon episcopal lists, see M. Lapidge and others, eds, *Blackwell's Encyclopedia of Anglo-Saxon England* (Oxford, 1999), pp. 170–71. On the 'westerners' ('Uuestor E[…]'), see discussion by Sims-Williams, *Religion and Literature*, pp. 40–43.

10. Bede, *Historia ecclesiastica gentis Anglorum*, book iv, chapter 12, in B. Colgrave and R. A. B. Mynors, eds, *Bede's Ecclesiastical History of the English People*, Oxford Medieval Texts (Oxford, 1969), p. 369. For Bishop Seaxwulf, see S. Keynes, *The Councils of Clofesho*, Brixworth Lecture, 1993 (Leicester, 1994), pp. 33–35.

that he was accorded a role somewhere within the extended 'Mercian' domain. A charter issued in the early 680s, under the political dispensation of Æthelred, king of the Mercians, was attested by Archbishop Theodore, by a bishop called Putta, and by Bosel, bishop of Worcester;[11] so there can be little doubt that a Bishop Putta was active in the west midlands at about this time, presumably as bishop of the Magonsætan. The question arises whether the former bishop of Rochester had been established by Seaxwulf as an assistant for himself in the west midlands, and so was soon to be found moving in the same world as the king who had been instrumental in his ejection from Kent; or whether it is easier to presume that there were two contemporary bishops of the same name, one operating under Seaxwulf in the west midlands and another from Rochester established by Seaxwulf elsewhere. Against the identification stands the silence of Bede, and the assumption that he would have made more of Putta's later career had there been more to make of it; in favour of the identification stands a wish to economise with contemporary bishops called Putta, and the association of both with Seaxwulf, bishop of the Mercians. It has to be admitted that the majority of modern commentators prefer one Putta at Rochester and another Putta among the Magonsætan;[12] it has also been suggested that Putta's name was placed falsely at the head of the episcopal list for Hereford, by a person at Lichfield eager for reasons of his own to push the origins of the see back into the late seventh century, and that the only genuine bishop of that name was Putta of Rochester.[13] The possibility remains, however, that Putta of Rochester had given assistance to Seaxwulf, beyond the Severn, without being formally established as bishop; and that if we make some allowance for Bede's ignorance of ecclesiastical arrangements in certain parts of the country, and adopt a more relaxed understanding of the sense in which Putta might have come to be regarded in retrospect as a bishop of the Magonsætan, it may be that the erstwhile bishop of Rochester should be re-installed as the first in the line of the bishops of Hereford.[14]

11. S 1167: W. de G. Birch, ed., *Cartularium Saxonicum* (3 vols, London, 1885–93), no. 57; D. Whitelock, ed., *English Historical Documents, c. 500–1042*, English Historical Documents, 1 (2nd edn, London, 1979), no. 57, p. 484.

12. C. Plummer, ed., *Venerabilis Baedae opera historica* (2 vols, Oxford, 1896), ii, p. 222; Stenton, 'Pre-Conquest Herefordshire', p. 193 n. 3; J. M. Wallace-Hadrill, *Bede's 'Ecclesiastical History of the English People': A Historical Commentary*, Oxford Medieval Texts (Oxford, 1988), pp. 149–50; Sims-

Williams, *Religion and Literature*, pp. 88 and 97–98; *EEA*, vii, p. xxv.

13. J. G. Hillaby, 'The Origins of the Diocese of Hereford', *TWNFC*, 42 (1976), pp. 16–52, and idem, 'Leominster and Hereford: The Origins of the Diocese', in Whitehead, *Medieval Art at Hereford*, pp. 1–14. On this view, the first 'genuine' bishop of the Hereford line was Tyrhtil.

14. See also, in the same spirit, C. N. L. Brooke, 'The Diocese of Hereford, 676–1200', *TWNFC*, 48 (1994), pp. 23–36, at 26–27.

By the time of his death, *c.* 690, Bishop Seaxwulf was responsible for the spiritual care of the Mercians, the men of Lindsey and the Middle Angles; and although steps may have been taken during his lifetime to formalise arrangements within this sprawling diocese, it was later understood (by the compiler of the episcopal lists) that the five-fold division of the see emerged after Seaxwulf's death. There were two bishoprics for the 'Mercians' (in fact the Mercians and the Middle Angles), at Lichfield and at Leicester; one for the men of Lindsey, at a place unknown; one for the Hwicce, at Worcester; and one for the 'westerners', probably at Hereford.[15] Putta himself was regarded as the first of the bishops of the 'westerners', after Seaxwulf, though other evidence suggests that he may not in fact have outlived his notional predecessor.[16] The bishops who presided over the diocese of Hereford in the eighth and ninth centuries acknowledged the political authority of the Mercian kings, and (in theory) their activities cannot be understood except in relation to the changing political fortunes of their Mercian overlords. Unfortunately, little is known of the bishops themselves beyond their names; for while we are relatively well-informed about their neighbours at Worcester, the muniments which would have covered the history of the church of Hereford in this period have not chanced to survive. We are reduced, therefore, to the frustrating process of fastening on a few unrelated scraps of evidence, and otherwise to an exercise in tracing the appearances of successive bishops of Hereford among the attestations in charters of the Mercian kings.[17] In the early eighth century, Bishop Tyrhtil sold an estate of fifty hides at Fulham (Middlesex) to Wealdhere, bishop of London, 'that by these benefits willingly conferred on the church I may be able to purge the guilt of my sins and obtain the remedy conferred by the divine goodness'.[18] It may follow that Tyrhtil was a man of East (or Middle) Saxon origin, and that he had been appointed to his office by the king of the Mercians. Tyrhtil's successor Torhthere left scarcely a trace of his existence; but Torhthere's successor Walhstod did marginally better. At the end of his work, Bede had occasion to enumerate all of the bishops holding

15. R. I. Page, 'Anglo-Saxon Episcopal Lists, Part III', *Nottingham Mediaeval Studies*, 10 (1966), pp. 2–24, at 5–6, 10–11 and 15–16. On the conception of the 'Mercian' bishoprics, see also Keynes, *The Councils of Clofesho*, p. 25 n. 105.

16. According to John of Worcester, Putta died in 688; see R. R. Darlington and P. McGurk, eds, *The Chronicle of John of Worcester* (3 vols, Oxford, 1995-), ii, p. 150; but it is not clear on what authority, if any, this is based.

17. The attestations of the bishops in question (Tyrhtil, Torhthere, Walhstod, Cuthberht, Podda, Acca, Headda, Aldberht, Esne, Ceolmund and Utel, in the eighth century; and Wulfheard, Beonna, Eadwulf, Cuthwulf, Mucel, Deorlaf, Cynemund and Edgar, in the ninth) are displayed in tabular form in S. Keynes, *An Atlas of Attestations in Anglo-Saxon Charters, c. 670–1066*, University of Cambridge, Department of Anglo-Saxon, Norse and Celtic (1998), tables 3, 6, 8, 13 and 14 (covering Mercian charters from *c.* 670 to *c.* 920).

18. S 1785: Whitelock, ed., *English Historical Documents*, no. 62, p. 488.

office in 731, and described Walhstod as 'bishop of the peoples who dwell west of the river Severn'.[19] Bede's failure specifically to identify the location of the see encourages the suspicion that the see was not yet firmly located at Hereford; but since his main concern was to list the bishops of each kingdom or people, it is quite possible that he was able in this context to take the location of the see for granted. Perhaps the most important figure among the early bishops was Cuthberht, bishop of Hereford 736–40, and archbishop of Canterbury 740–60.[20] Two Latin verses composed by Cuthberht as bishop of Hereford were incorporated in a collection of occasional verses assembled in the mid eighth century by Milred, bishop of Worcester (*c.* 745–75). A copy of this collection, written probably at Worcester in the mid tenth century, came to be preserved at Malmesbury Abbey, where it was used by the historian William of Malmesbury in the twelfth century and by the antiquary John Leland in the sixteenth.[21] One of the poems appears to have been inscribed or embroidered on a set of cross-cloths which had been begun by Bishop Walhstod, left unfinished at his death, and then completed by Cuthberht;[22] the other poem appears to have been inscribed on a marble tomb in which Cuthberht had placed the mortal remains of three bishops (Tyrhtil, Torhthere, Walhstod), a sub-king (*regulus*) called Milfrith and his wife Cwenburh, and a certain Osfrith, son of Oshelm.[23] The implication in the second case seems to be that the three bishops, and Milfrith, Cwenburh and Osfrith, had lain in separate graves in the church at Hereford until placed by Cuthberht in a grand tomb befitting their distinction, perhaps in connection with some major alterations within the church; but of course that is little more than speculation. Cuthberht's distinction on a larger stage arises from his role, as archbishop of Canterbury, in collaborating with Æthelbald, king of the Mercians, in the reform of the English church in the 740s. He presided over a church council held at *Clofesho* in 747; and, if we may assume that he was himself responsible for planning the programme of reform promulgated on that occasion, he can be seen to have responded in his own distinctive way to the abuses which had arisen in the opening decades of the eighth century.[24]

19. Bede, *Historia ecclesiastica*, v, 23, in Colgrave and Mynors, eds, *Bede's Ecclesiastical History*, p. 559.

20. On Cuthberht, see N. Brooks, *The Early History of the Church of Canterbury: Christ Church from 597 to 1066* (Leicester, 1984), pp. 80–83, and Sims-Williams, *Religion and Literature*, pp. 337–39.

21. M. Lapidge, 'Some Remnants of Bede's Lost *Liber Epigrammatum*' (1975), reprinted in his *Anglo-Latin Literature, 600–899* (London, 1996), pp. 357–79 and 510–12; Sims-Williams, *Religion and Literature*,

pp. 328–59; D. N. Dumville, 'English Square Minuscule Script: The Mid-Century Phases', *Anglo-Saxon England*, 23 (1994), pp. 133–64, at 148–49.

22. Sims-Williams, *Religion and Literature*, pp. 340–41, with translation, p. 340 n. 50.

23. Ibid., pp. 341–2, with translation, p. 342 n. 58, see also Chapter 26, p. 493.

24. See Keynes, *The Councils of Clofesho*, pp. 5–6; and S. Keynes, 'The Reconstruction of a Burnt Cottonian Manuscript: The Case of Cotton MS Otho A. I', *British Library Journal*, 22 (1996), pp. 113–60, at 135–39.

Hereford was a frontier town; and its bishops in the eighth century would have been especially concerned about the ever-present danger of incursions of Welshmen from across the border. There is known to have been trouble during the reigns of Coenred, king of the Mercians (705–9),[25] and Æthelbald, king of the Mercians (716–57);[26] and matters seem to have been brought to a head during the reign of King Offa (757–96), finding expression first in a battle at Hereford in 760, and then in expeditions conducted by Offa into Welsh territory in 778, 784 and 795.[27] It was Offa, of course, 'who terrified all the neighbouring kings and provinces around him, and who had a great dyke built between Wales and Mercia from sea to sea';[28] and it may be that the dyke had the intended effect of discouraging the Welsh from mounting further raids across the border into English territory. Yet while the centre of Offa's power always remained in the Mercian heartland, at Tamworth and Lichfield (Staffordshire), and reached from there over the dependent provinces of Lindsey, the Hwicce, the Magonsætan and the Middle Angles, his political influence extended much further afield, over East Anglia, Essex, Surrey, Sussex and Kent. For reasons or in circumstances that are now obscure, Offa had Æthelberht, king of the East Angles, beheaded in 794.[29] The story told in the *Passio S. Æthelberhti regis et martyris*, composed probably at Hereford in the early twelfth century, was that the young King Æthelberht had come to the royal estate at Sutton (Herefordshire) in order to obtain the hand of Offa's daughter Ælfthryth in marriage, and that he was treacherously killed by a certain Winberht, acting on the instructions of Offa's wicked queen, Cwenthryth. At first, the king's body was thrown into the marshes by the River Lugg, but soon its location was miraculously revealed to a certain Byrhtferth, who with his friend Ecgmund translated the body from the marshes to the place called *Fernlage* (later called

25. Felix, *Vita S. Guthlaci*, chapter 34, in B. Colgrave, ed., *Felix's Life of Saint Guthlac* (Cambridge, 1956), p. 108.

26. For relations between Ithel ap Morgan and King Æthelbald, said to have involved much fighting around Hereford and the River Wye, leading eventually to the re-establishment of peace, see J. G. Evans, *The Text of the Book of Llan Dâv Reproduced from the Gwysaney Manuscript* (Oxford, 1893), p. 192. See also W. Davies, *Wales in the Early Middle Ages* (Leicester, 1982), p. 113; and Sims-Williams, *Religion and Literature*, p. 52.

27. J. Williams ab Ithel, ed., *Annales Cambriae*,

Rolls Series, 20 (London, 1860), pp. 10–11. For further discussion, see J. E. Lloyd, *A History of Wales from the Earliest Times to the Edwardian Conquest* (3rd edn, 2 vols, London, 1939), i, pp. 197–201, and Sims-Williams, *Religion and Literature*, p. 53.

28. Asser, *Vita Ælfredi regis Angul-Saxonum*, chapter 14, in S. Keynes and M. Lapidge, *Alfred the Great: Asser's 'Life of King Alfred' and Other Contemporary Sources* (Harmondsworth, 1983), p. 71.

29. *Anglo-Saxon Chronicle*, s.a. 794, in Whitelock, ed., *English Historical Documents*, p. 167: citations by year (*s.a.*) are to the corrected dates in this edition.

Hereford), on the River Wye.[30] It is not immediately clear how to account for the development of the cult of St Æthelberht at Hereford, or indeed when it developed.[31] Perhaps he was genuinely the innocent victim of political subterfuge, and perhaps there were men in Hereford who had a special interest in promoting the cult, whether for the benefit of the church, or in subtle defiance of the political establishment in Mercia, or in competition with the pretensions of St Guthlac's minster in Hereford, or (at a later stage) to rival the development of similar royal cults elsewhere in England.[32] Whatever the case, Æthelberht's feast day (20 May) was registered in several eleventh-century calendars and litanies, and the church at Hereford, originally dedicated to St Mary, was by the end of the tenth century dedicated additionally to the East Anglian king (fig. 1).[33]

The ninth-century bishops of Hereford appear but sporadically in the historical record. When Wulfheard made his profession of faith to Æthelheard, archbishop of Canterbury, *c*. 800, he styled himself (or was styled) 'gratia Dei humilis Hereford-ensis ecclesie episcopus';[34] when he attested a special decree issued by the council

30. The earliest version of the legend is represented by the *Passio S. Æthelberhti regis et martyris*, in Cambridge, Corpus Christi College, MS 308; the text is printed in James, ed., 'Two Lives of St Ethelbert', at pp. 236–44, and translated by E. C. Brooks, *The Life of Saint Ethelbert King and Martyr, 779 AD–794 AD* (Bury St Edmunds, 1996), pp. 28–38. Osbert de Clare's *Vita S. Æthelberti*, preserved in Gotha, Landesbibliothek, MS I.81, fos 30r–39r, has not been printed. Gerald of Wales's *Vita regis et martyris Æthelberti* was preserved in Cotton MS Vitellius E vii (destroyed in 1731), and is preserved in Cambridge, Trinity College, MS B.11.16 (255), fos 77v–102r, between lections on St Mary and miracles of St Thomas of Hereford; the text is printed by James, ed., 'Two Lives of St Ethelbert', pp. 222–36, and translated by Brooks, *The Life of Saint Ethelbert*, pp. 40–58.

31. The church at Hoxne, Suffolk, was dedicated to St Æthelberht in the first half of the tenth century: see S 1526 (D. Whitelock, ed., *Anglo-Saxon Wills* (Cambridge, 1930), no. 1).

32. For further discussion of the circumstances behind the development of the cult of St Æthelberht, see A. Thacker, 'Kings, Saints and Monasteries in Pre-Viking Mercia', *Midland History*, 10 (1985), pp. 1–25, at

16–18; D. Rollason, *Saints and Relics in Anglo-Saxon England* (Oxford, 1989), p. 122; P. A. Hayward, 'The Idea of Innocent Martyrdom in Late Tenth- and Eleventh-Century English Hagiology', in D. Wood, ed., *Martyrs and Martyrologies*, Studies in Church History, 30 (Oxford, 1993), pp. 81–92, at 90–91; and P. Hayward, *Kingship, Childhood and Martyrdom in Anglo-Saxon England* (forthcoming).

33. F. Wormald, ed., *English Kalendars before AD 1100*, Henry Bradshaw Society, 72 (1934), pp. 34 (BL, Cotton MS Nero A ii), 76 (Cambridge, University Library, MS Kk. v. 32), 188 (Cambridge, Corpus Christi College, MS 422), 202 (Oxford, Bodleian, MS Hatton 113), 216 (Cambridge, Corpus Christi College, MS 391), 244 (Vatican, MS Reg. Lat. 12), 258 (Oxford, Bodleian, MS Douce 296); M. Lapidge, ed., *Anglo-Saxon Litanies of the Saints*, Henry Bradshaw Society, 106 (London, 1991), pp. 143 (BL, MS Arundel 60), 163 (BL, Cotton MS Galba A xiv), 205 (BL, Harley MS 2904), and 297 (Vatican, MS Reg. Lat. 12).

34. M. Richter, ed., *Canterbury Professions*, Canterbury and York Society, 67 (1973), pp. 4–5, no. 4. For professions by later ninth-century bishops of Hereford, see ibid., nos 16 (Eadwulf), 25 (Mucel), and 24 (Deorlaf).

Fig. 1. Fourteenth-century statue of St Ethelbert, rediscovered in *c*.1727, when it was thought to represent Richard II. It was restored to its probable original position to the south of the high altar in *c*.1840. See Oxford, Bodleian, MS Willis 47, fos 167–68; F. T. Havergal, *Fasti Herefordenses* (Edinburgh, 1869), p. 110.

of *Clofesho*, on 12 October 803, he was called 'Herefordensis ecclesiae episcopus'.[35] It was at the same council of *Clofesho*, in 803, that Wulfheard, bishop of Hereford, and Deneberht, bishop of Worcester, aired their grievances over the rights due from the minsters at Cheltenham and Beckford (Gloucestershire). Both minsters were in the diocese of Worcester, but had been given some thirty years previously to the church of Hereford; Wulfheard denied that any refection had ever been given to Worcester, by himself or by his predecessors, in respect of the minsters; Deneberht produced testimony to the opposite effect; and the archbishop urged a compromise. The record of this dispute, and its settlement, was preserved at Worcester, and is cast in terms which may not do full justice to Wulfheard's

---

35. Birch, ed., *Cartularium Saxonicum*, no. 312.

case;[36] moreover, one should bear in mind that it is not likely to represent an isolated instance of the conflicts of interest which arose between neighbouring dioceses. According to the episcopal lists, Wulfheard was succeeded by a certain Beonna, who would appear to have been another 'Mercian' appointee. The person of that name who as abbot of *Medeshamstede* (Peterborough) was evidently a significant figure on the Mercian stage, in the late eighth and early ninth centuries, seems suddenly to disappear from view *c.* 805; and while we may wonder what became of him in the interim, it is possible that the Beonna known to have been elected bishop of Hereford at a council of *Clofesho* in October 824, and who held office until *c.* 830, was the same person.[37] A charter issued in the name of Cuthwulf, bishop of Hereford, some time between 840 and 852, is the earliest episcopal act of a bishop of Hereford which has the distinction of surviving in what would appear to be its original form (fig. 2).[38] It records how the bishop and his community leased an estate on the River Frome to a certain Ealdorman Ælfstan, for three years, at an annual render of a cask of beer, a vessel of honey, a plough-beast, one hundred loaves of bread, a sheep and a pig, with reversion to the minster at Bromyard (Herefordshire). The wealth of detail is a reminder of what we have lost; and in the person of Ælfstan we encounter someone who in his service to successive Mercian kings, and in his relationship with the churches of Hereford and Bromyard, was probably a person useful to know in the second quarter of the ninth century.[39] It is only more so the pity that we have no idea how the bishops of Hereford fared at the hands of those who might be expected to have coveted their property in these troublous times, whether the Welsh, or the Vikings, or the Mercians, or the West Saxons.

In the late ninth century Hereford and its diocese passed from the authority of the kings of the Mercians into the newly conceived 'kingdom of the Anglo-Saxons' (initially under Alfred the Great, and thereafter under his son Edward the Elder); and from 927 the bishops would have found themselves on the western boundary of the 'kingdom of the English'.[40] It was probably at about this time that Hereford-shire, as such, came into being, as a territory administered from Hereford though

36. S 1431: Birch, ed., *Cartularium Saxonicum*, no. 309; see also Sims-Williams, *Religion and Literature*, pp. 138–39.

37. Keynes, *The Councils of Clofesho*, pp. 36–37 and 47.

38. S 1270: Birch, ed., *Cartularium Saxonicum*, no. 429; Capes, *Charters*, pp. 1–2; S. Keynes, ed., *Facsimiles of Anglo-Saxon Charters* (Oxford, 1991), no. 3. The charter was presented to the cathedral in the 1890s, and may have been preserved formerly in the archives of a religious house other than Hereford itself.

39. Ealdorman Ælfstan appears as a witness in Mercian charters from 831 to 852: see Keynes, *Atlas of Attestations*, table 17.

40. For these political developments, see S. Keynes, 'England, 900–1016', in T. Reuter, ed., *The New Cambridge Medieval History*, iii, *c. 900–c. 1024* (Cambridge, 1999), pp. 456–84.

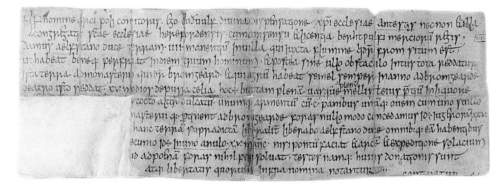

Fig. 2. Charter of Cuthwulf, bishop of Hereford, issued 840–52. (HCA, 4067.)

not yet extending beyond the River Wye into the former Welsh kingdom of
Ergyng (Archenfield);[41] and the bishops themselves would have continued to play
their largely unknown part in affairs of church and state. The historian William
of Malmesbury, writing in the 1120s, affords a clear indication of Hereford's place
in Anglo-Welsh relations during the reign of King Æthelstan (924–39):

> The princes of the Northwalians, that is, the Northern Britons, he compelled
> to meet him in the city of Hereford and, after a spell of reluctance, to change
> their minds and surrender. He thus brought into effect what no king before
> him had presumed even to contemplate: they were to pay him by way of
> annual tribute twenty pounds of gold and 300 pounds of silver, and to hand
> over by the count 25,000 oxen, besides as many as he might wish of hounds
> that with their keen scent could track down the lairs and lurking-places of
> wild beasts, and birds of prey skilled in pursuing other birds through empty
> air.[42]

41. For the kingdom of Ergyng, see Davies, *Wales in the Early Middle Ages*, pp. 93, 101 and 102. The anomalous position of Ergyng in the early tenth century is suggested by the fact that when a Viking force captured Cyfeiliog, bishop of Archenfield, in 914, he was ransomed by King Edward for £40: see *Anglo-Saxon Chronicle*, s.a. 914, in Whitelock, ed., *English Historical Documents*, p. 194. For the situation in the mid eleventh century, see G. R. J. Jones, 'Early Historic Settlement in Border Territory: A Case-Study of Archenfield and its Environs in Herefordshire', in C. Christians and J. Claude, eds, *Recherches de géographie rurale: hommage au Professeur Frans Dussart* (2 vols, Liège, 1979), i, pp. 117–32, and F. Thorn and C. Thorn, eds, *Domesday Book*, xvii, *Herefordshire* (Chichester, 1983), Introductory Notes 1–2 and 4 [unpaginated].

42. William of Malmesbury, *Gesta regum Anglorum*, book ii, chapter 134.5, in R. A. B. Mynors, R. M. Thomson and M. Winterbottom, eds, *William of Malmesbury: Gesta regum Anglorum/The History of the English Kings*, i (Oxford, 1998), pp. 214–16.

The River Wye was established as the frontier;[43] and the various rulers of the Welsh people regularly attended meetings of the king's council convened in England.[44] It is a reasonable assumption that the successive bishops of Hereford in the first half of the tenth century (Edgar, Tidhelm, Wulfhelm and Ælfric) would have played some part in the unfolding process of accommodation between the English and the Welsh; but in truth little is known of them beyond the fact that they were regularly in attendance at the king's court.[45] Matters may have been more complicated in the 950s and 960s, when the bishop of Hereford is conspicuous only by his absence; though it is possible that a certain Wulfric, who attested charters of King Edgar between 958 and 970, may have belonged to the line.[46] Another bishop of whom we could wish to know more was Æthelwulf (Athulf), formerly a 'brother' of the Old Minster, Winchester,[47] who was bishop of Hereford for over forty years, from *c.* 970 to *c.* 1015, and who like his eighth- and ninth-century predecessors might well have been instrumental in upholding political and social order in times of great stress.[48] One should add that the will of a certain Wulfgeat of Donington (Shropshire), drawn up *c.* 1000, includes bequests to St Æthelberht's (Hereford), St Guthlac's (Hereford), Leominster and Bromyard, and serves to remind us in this way that the ecclesiastical landscape in Hereford-shire contained more features than the episcopal see alone.[49] The church of St Guthlac at Hereford appears to have been founded in the eighth century (if not before), and there is good reason to believe that it was still flourishing in the

43. William of Malmesbury, *Gesta regum Anglorum*, ii, 134.6, in Mynors and others, eds, *William of Malmesbury: Gesta regum Anglorum*, p. 216. A legal text known as *Dunsæte*, which may date from the tenth century, represents an attempt to regulate relations between the English and the Welsh.

44. For the appearances of Welsh 'sub-kings' in Anglo-Saxon charters, see Keynes, *Atlas of Attestations*, table 36.

45. See Keynes, *Atlas of Attestations*, tables 33 (Edward the Elder), 37 (Æthelstan), 41 (Edmund), 44 (Eadred).

46. See Keynes, *Atlas of Attestations*, table 54. The first charter attested by Wulfric is S 677 (Birch, ed., *Cartularium Saxonicum*, no. 1040; Whitelock, ed., *English Historical Documents*, no. 109), dated 958, by which King Edgar granted an estate at Staunton on Arrow, Herefordshire, together with a house in Hereford, to his thegn Ealhstan.

Ten years later, in 968, King Edgar granted an estate in Derbyshire to Bishop Wulfric (S 768), which might be taken to suggest that Wulfric's interests actually lay elsewhere; and the difficulty remains that Wulfric is not included in the extant episcopal lists for Hereford.

47. S. Keynes, ed., *The 'Liber Vitae' of the New Minster and Hyde Abbey, Winchester*, Early English Manuscripts in Facsimile, 26 (Copenhagen, 1996), p. 87.

48. For Æthelwulf's appearances in charters, see Keynes, *Atlas of Attestations*, tables 54 (Edgar) and 60a–b (Æthelred). Interestingly, he rose steadily in the order of precedence, and by the end of his life was regularly in third place.

49. S 1534 (Whitelock, ed., *Anglo-Saxon Wills*, no. 19), preserved at Worcester. For the church in the west midlands, see also D. Hill, *An Atlas of Anglo-Saxon England* (Oxford, 1981), p. 160 (map 254).

tenth.[50] The minster at Bromyard is known to have been in existence in the mid ninth century, and on this (albeit flimsy) evidence may have enjoyed a continuous existence, in some form, into the late tenth century and beyond.[51] Leominster is also reputed to have been an ancient foundation; but although the evidence is tenuous, there is some reason to believe that it may have become a nunnery of special importance in the tenth and eleventh centuries, with particular connections to the royal family.[52]

50. For St Guthlac's, see Whitehead, 'Historical Introduction', pp. 1–5; Shoesmith, *Hereford City Excavations*, i, *Excavations at Castle Green*, pp. 55–56, and R. Shoesmith, *Hereford City Excavations*, ii, *Excavations On and Close to the Defences*, Council for British Archaeology Research Report, 46 (London, 1982), pp. 13–15 and 88–94. See also Thacker, 'Kings, Saints and Monasteries in Pre-Viking Mercia', pp. 5–6; *EEA*, vii, p. xxix; and Barrow, 'A Lotharingian in Hereford', p. 44 n. 42.

51. For its existence in the mid ninth century, see above, p. 12. The pre-Conquest minster at Bromyard does not seem otherwise to have left any trace of its existence.

52. For the early history of Leominster, see B. R. Kemp, 'The Monastic Dean of Leominster', *English Historical Review*, 83 (1968), pp. 505–15, at 505–7, and Hillaby, 'Early Christian and Pre-Conquest Leominster', pp. 563–86. For King Æthelstan and Leominster, see ibid., pp. 626–28. For the suggestion that Leominster was re-founded as a nunnery in the tenth century, from Shaftesbury, see D. Bethell, 'The Making of a Twelfth-Century Relic Collection', in G. J. Cuming and D. Baker, eds, *Popular Belief and Practice*, Studies in Church History, 8 (Cambridge, 1972), pp. 61–72, at 65–66. It has also been argued, most convincingly, that the prayer-book which survives as BL, Cotton MS Nero A ii, fos 3–13 and Cotton MS Galba A xiv was written, *c.* 1030, for use at Leominster. For the text, see B. J. Muir, ed., *A Pre-Conquest English Prayer-Book BL MSS Cotton Galba A xiv and Nero A ii (fos 3–13)*, Henry Bradshaw Society, 103 (1988); and for exposition of its Leominster connections,

see G. H. Doble, 'The Leominster Relic-List', *TWNFC*, 31 (1942), pp. 58–65, at 61–62, extended decisively by Hillaby, 'Early Christian and Pre-Conquest Leominster', pp. 628–54, and Hillaby, 'Leominster and Hereford', pp. 6–8. The case turns on the inclusion of St Eadfrith, above, p. 4, in the calendar (26 October) and in the litany ('Entferth') (Muir, ed., *A Pre-Conquest English Prayer-Book*, pp. 12, 126), on the inclusion of St Hemma, first abbot of Leominster, in the calendar (25 May), in the litany, and in a special prayer (ibid., pp. 7, 126, 190), and on the inclusion of a mysterious St Æthelmod (? = 'Æthelred', whose resting-place was at Leominster) in the calendar (9 January) and with 'Entferth' and Hemma in the litany (ibid., pp. 3, 126); note also the inclusion of special prayers for St Æthelberht, ibid., p. 23, and St Mildburg, ibid., pp. 187, 188. Another striking feature of the prayer-book is the inclusion of material with royal associations: a poem on King Æthelstan, ibid., pp. 18–20; a prayer for King Æthelred's soul, ibid., p. 122; and prayers for St Edward, ibid., p. 185, St Ælfgifu, ibid., p. 189, and ? King Edgar, ibid., p. 192. In 1046 Earl Swein abducted Eadgifu, abbess of Leominster: see *Anglo-Saxon Chronicle*, MS C, *s.a.* 1046, and Darlington and McGurk, eds, *Chronicle of John of Worcester*, ii, p. 548. By 1066 the nunnery and its substantial endowment was in the possession of Queen Edith: see Great Domesday Book, fol. 180rv, in Thorn and Thorn, eds, *Domesday Book*, xvii, *Herefordshire*, section 1.10a–38, and Hillaby, 'Early Christian and Pre-Conquest Leominster', pp. 586–600.

Æthelwulf was succeeded by Æthelstan, who was bishop of Hereford from *c.* 1015 until his death on 10 February 1056.[53] The southern part of the west midlands (Herefordshire, Worcestershire, Gloucestershire) was apparently much favoured by Danish incomers during the reign of King Cnut (1016–35), perhaps in particular by members of the rank and file of the Danish army who had wished to stay in England, and Æthelstan would thus have become accustomed to dealing with a mixed Anglo-Scandinavian population.[54] We see him on one occasion in a shire-meeting at Worcester, maintaining his ownership of part of an estate at Inkberrow (Worcestershire), which he had bought previously during the reign of King Æthelred, against a claimant who seems to have been in dispute with the person who had sold the land to the bishop in the first place; and we are treated in this connection to a delightful image of the contending parties riding round the boundaries of the disputed estate, as a result of which procedure the bishop was able to establish that he was indeed the rightful owner of the land.[55] Another record affords a glimpse of Æthelstan's involvement in proceedings at a shire-meeting held at Aylton, near Hereford. 'There were present Bishop Æthelstan and Earl Ranig and Edwin, the earl's son, and Leofwine, Wulfsige's son, and Thurkil the White; and Tofi the Proud came there on the king's business, and Bryning the sheriff was present, and Æthelgeard of Frome and Leofwine of Frome and Godric of Stoke and all the thegns of Herefordshire.' A dispute had arisen between a mother and her greedy son over some land at Wellington and Cradley in Hereford-shire. 'Then the bishop asked whose business it was to answer for his mother, and Thurkil the White replied that it was his business to do so, if he knew the claim.' It turned out that Thurkil did not know the claim (or said he did not); so three thegns were despatched to go to the mother, at Fawley, in order to ascertain what her position might be. The mother was evidently determined to disinherit her son, and declared her wish to grant all her land and possessions to her kinswoman Leofflæd, wife of Thurkil the White; whereupon she told the thegns to make an announcement to this effect at the shire-meeting. The thegns

53. For Æthelstan's appearances in charters, see Keynes, *Atlas of Attestations*, tables 60b (Æthelred), 66 (Cnut, etc.), and 72 (Edward the Confessor).
54. S. Keynes, 'Cnut's Earls', in A. R. Rumble, ed., *The Reign of Cnut: King of England, Denmark and Norway* (London, 1994), pp. 43–88, at 60–61 and 80.
55. S 1460: A. J. Robertson, ed., *Anglo-Saxon Charters* (2nd edn, Cambridge, 1956), pp. 162–65, no. 83, and 411–13. There were

three copies of the record: one at St Mary's, Worcester, 'to which the estate belongs' (suggesting that there were further compli-cations); one at St Æthelberht's, Hereford; and one with those 'in whose possession the estate is'. The surviving copy, BL, Cotton Charter viii 37, in E. A. Bond, *Facsimiles of Ancient Charters in the British Museum* (4 vols, London, 1873–78), iv, 14, was presumably (though not necessarily) derived from the Worcester archive.

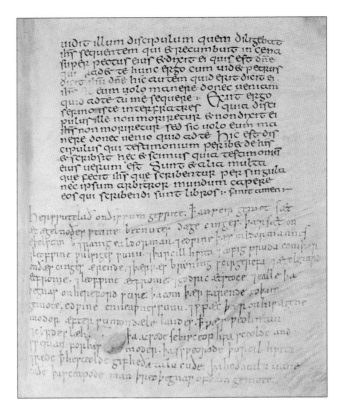

Fig. 3. A record of proceedings at a meeting of the shire-court of Hereford, held at Aylton, Herefordshire, during the reign of King Cnut, 1016–35, entered in a blank space at the end of the late eighth-century Hereford Gospels. (HCL, MS P.1.2, fol.134r.)

did as they had been asked to do, and Thurkil the White asked all those present to ratify the bequest. Thurkil then 'rode to St Æthelberht's minster', at Hereford, and with the consent of all had a record of the proceedings entered in a gospel-book (fig. 3).[56] It also happened at about the same time that Leofflæd's brother purchased some land at Mansell (Herefordshire) from another man, 'with the cognisance of Earl Swegn and Bishop Æthelstan and Thurkil the White and Ulfketel the sheriff and all the thegns of Herefordshire and the two communities at St Æthelberht's minster and at St Guthlac's'. Again, the record was entered in a blank space in a gospel-book.[57] The gospel-book used on both of these occasions is the book now

56. S 1462: Robertson, ed., *Anglo-Saxon Charters*, pp. 150–53, no. 78, and 399–402; Whitelock, ed., *English Historical Documents*, no. 135, from HCL, MS P.1.2, fol. 134rv. For the manuscript, see N. R. Ker, *Catalogue of Manuscripts Containing Anglo-Saxon* (Oxford, 1957), p. 156, no. 119; for a facsimile, see E. M. Thompson and others, eds, *The New Palaeographical Society: Facsimiles of Ancient Manuscripts* (1903–12), pl. 234 (a),

showing the latter part of the text on fol. 134v. For further discussion, see P. Stafford, 'Women and the Norman Conquest', *Transactions of the Royal Historical Society*, 6th series, 4 (1994), pp. 221–49, at 241–42.

57. S 1469: Robertson, ed., *Anglo-Saxon Charters*, pp. 186–87, no. 99, and 435, from HCL, MS P.1.2, fol. 135r. For a facsimile, see Thompson and others, eds, *New Palaeographical Society*, pl. 234 (b).

known as the 'Hereford Gospels', written in the late eighth century.[58] It was, in fact, standard practice in the tenth and eleventh centuries to use blank spaces in a church's liturgical books for recording matters of this kind. Yet one could not wish for a better indication of the continued respect in the eleventh century for the church's role as protector of order in local society; and it is especially interesting to see how eager were these laymen to avail themselves of this form of security.

Bishop Æthelstan himself caused a formal record to be made of the eastern boundary of his diocese, apparently in connection with a dispute between himself and the bishop of Worcester, and had a copy of the record entered in an evangeliary belonging to his church (fig. 4).[59] He is otherwise known to have been responsible for the building of 'the glorious minster' at Hereford, probably in the 1020s or 1030s. In 1055 the outlawed and disaffected Earl Ælfgar, with some Welsh and Irish supporters, appeared at Hereford and was opposed there by Earl Ralph 'the Timid' and an English army. A chronicler sympathetic to Ælfgar's cause reported the outcome of events in a way which manages to obscure responsibility for what was evidently conceived as a disaster for the English in general:

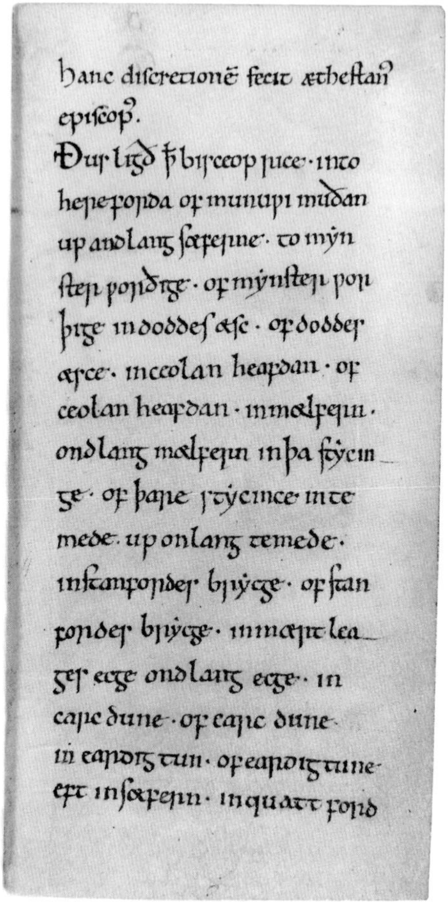
hanc discretionē fecit æthestan
episcop.
Ðus ligð þ bisceop rice into
hereforda of munuwi muðan
up andlang sæferne. to myn
ster worðige. of mynster wor
þige in doddes æsc. of doddes
æsce. in ceolan heafdan. of
ceolan heafdan. in mælfern.
ondlang mælfern in þa stycin
ge. of þare stycince in te
mede. up onlang temede.
in stanforder brycge. of stan
forder brycge. in mæres lea
ges ecge ondlang ecge. in
caric dune. of caric dune
in earnigtun. of earnigtune
eft in sæfern. in quatt ford

Fig. 4. A record of the eastern boundary of the diocese of Hereford, made by Bishop Æthelstan in the first half of the eleventh century, entered in an evangeliary belonging to the church. (Cambridge, Pembroke College, MS 302, fol. 8r.)

58. R. A. B. Mynors and R. M. Thomson, *Catalogue of the Manuscripts of Hereford Cathedral Library* (Cambridge, 1993), pp. 65–66.

59. S 1561, from Cambridge, Pembroke College, MS 302, fol. 8r. For the manuscript, see Ker, *Catalogue of Manuscripts Containing Anglo-Saxon*, pp. 125–26, no. 78; for a facsimile, see Thompson and others, eds, *New Palaeographical Society*, pl. 238 (b). For further discussion, see Finberg, *Early Charters of the West Midlands*, pp. 225–27; and Sims-Williams, *Religion and Literature*, pp. 43–46.

Before any spear had been thrown the English army fled because they were on horseback, and many were killed there – about four or five hundred men – and they killed none in return. And then they went back to the town and burnt it with the glorious minster which Æthelstan the venerable bishop had had built. They stripped and robbed it of relics and vestments and everything, and killed the people and some they carried off.[60]

Another chronicler, overtly hostile to Ælfgar, was more direct: 'and Earl Ælfgar sought the protection of Gruffudd (ap Llywelyn] in Wales; and in this year Gruffudd and Ælfgar burned down St Æthelberht's minster and all the city of Hereford'.[61] It emerges that Bishop Æthelstan had gone blind in the early 1040s, and had been assisted by Tremerig, called 'the Welsh bishop', who died soon after the devastation of the see in October 1055.[62] Bishop Æthelstan himself died on 10 February 1056, on his estate at Bosbury (Herefordshire); according to a Worcester chronicler, 'his body was taken to Hereford, and buried in the church which he himself had constructed from the foundations'.[63]

The destruction of Bishop Æthelstan's 'glorious minster' at Hereford, in 1055, was presumably the event which accounts for the almost total absence of records pertaining to the history of the church in the eighth, ninth, tenth and first half of the eleventh centuries; for although some books did survive the conflagration (notably the 'Hereford Gospels' and Bishop Æthelstan's evangeliary), it is striking that the sequence of extant records begins almost pointedly in the later 1050s.[64] The account of the lands belonging to the church of Hereford, in Domesday Book, shows nonetheless that the bishops had accumulated a sizeable endowment, amounting to 300 hides;[65] and while the loss of the bulk of Hereford's pre-Conquest documentation means that we cannot reconstruct let alone understand the process of its endowment, we may suspect that it was a process which involved a combination of enterprise and initiative on the part of successive bishops, and a mixture of piety, patronage and opportunism on the part of the

60. *Anglo-Saxon Chronicle*, MS C, *s.a.* 1055. Cf. *Anglo-Saxon Chronicle*, MS D, *s.a.* 1055, and Darlington and McGurk, eds, *Chronicle of John of Worcester*, ii, pp. 576–78.

61. *Anglo-Saxon Chronicle*, MS E, *s.a.* 1055. For exposition of the Welsh connection, see K. L. Maund, *Ireland, Wales, and England in the Eleventh Century*, Studies in Celtic History, 12 (Woodbridge, 1991), pp. 129–36.

62. *Anglo-Saxon Chronicle*, MSS CD, *s.a.* 1055; Darlington and McGurk, eds, *Chronicle of John of Worcester*, ii, p. 578. It may be significant that Æthelstan does not attest

charters of Edward the Confessor after 1048.

63. *Anglo-Saxon Chronicle*, MSS CD, *s.a.* 1056; Darlington and McGurk, eds, *Chronicle of John of Worcester*, ii, pp. 578–80.

64. S 1101 and 1102: F. E. Harmer, *Anglo-Saxon Writs* (Manchester, 1952), pp. 227–31, nos 49–50.

65. Great Domesday Book, fos 181v–182v, in Thorn and Thorn, eds, *Domesday Book*, xvii, *Herefordshire*, section 2; see also Barrow, 'A Lotharingian in Hereford', p. 30, and below, pp. 25–27.

local population.[66] No less intriguing are the arrangements made at Hereford for the support of the clergy and the organisation of the church's estates; though in this case we can learn something by extrapolation from the arrangements implicit in the Domesday survey.[67] Nor does it come as a surprise to find that Earl Harold was able to encroach upon the church's property in Herefordshire and in Worcestershire, perhaps because he was able to take advantage of Æthelstan's declining powers, or perhaps in the wake of Æthelstan's death.[68] Æthelstan was succeeded briefly by Leofgar, who was Earl Harold's priest (d. 16 June 1056); Leofgar was followed by Ealdred, bishop of Worcester, who held Hereford in plurality until 25 December 1060, when he became archbishop of York; and Ealdred was replaced at Hereford by Walter, who was Queen Edith's priest. The impression of a revival of the fortunes of the church after the Norman Conquest, especially under the direction of Robert the Lotharingian (1079–95), is doubtless real enough;[69] but even so, the activities and achievements of their English predecessors, shrouded as they may be in the impenetrable obscurity of a period for which so little documentation survives, are not beyond recovery if we are prepared to make up for the loss by exercising our powers of historical imagination.

66. Some of Hereford's benefactors are commemorated in the obit book of the cathedral, Oxford, Bodleian, MS Rawlinson B 328 (S.C. 11667), printed in R. Rawlinson, *The History and Antiquities of the City and Cathedral Church of Hereford* (London, 1717), supplement, pp. 1–31. For example, Wulviva (Wulfgifu) and Godiva (Godgifu), cited more accessibly by Capes, *Charters*, p. iii, are registered under 15 January. Walter Map tells a story to the effect that King Edmund Ironside gave Ross on Wye to Hereford, M. R. James, ed., *Walter Map: De Nugis Curialium/Courtiers' Trifles*, rev. C. N. L. Brooke and R. A. B. Mynors (Oxford, 1983), p. 430; but perhaps it should be set beside the story to the effect that Alnoth gave Lydbury to Hereford, ibid., pp. 158, 350.

67. On these matters, see especially Barrow, 'A Lotharingian at Hereford'. Arrangements at Hereford might be compared usefully with arrangements at Wells and elsewhere: see S. Keynes, 'Giso, Bishop of Wells (1061–88)', *Anglo-Norman Studies*, 19 (1997), pp. 203–71, at 249–51.

68. On Hereford's recovery of lands taken by Harold, see C. Lewis, 'The Norman Settlement of Herefordshire under William I', *Anglo-Norman Studies*, 7 (1985), pp. 195–213, at 199.

69. See Barrow, 'A Lotharingian at Hereford', and below, pp. 23–27.

2

Athelstan to Aigueblanche, 1056–1268

Julia Barrow

Between the late eleventh and the mid thirteenth century the community of clergy serving Hereford Cathedral acquired the institutional features which it was to retain for the rest of the middle ages and beyond: the title of chapter with the legal implications of corporate authority; the appearance of the dean and other dignitaries; and a considerable degree of independence from the bishop. These changes were taking place in most cathedrals throughout Latin Christendom over this period: some, particularly the establishment of a hierarchy of cathedral dignitaries, had begun much earlier on the Continent and were introduced into England following the Norman Conquest. Normandy, where such hierarchies were relatively new also, acted as a conduit for ideas from the rest of France.[1] Other changes, notably the idea that those clerics who shared in the endowments of the cathedral, the canons, should – at least theoretically – form the body of electors to choose the bishop, grew out of the papal reform movement of the eleventh century.[2]

Surviving sources for Hereford are few at the outset of this period but plentiful by the end. As a consequence it makes sense to break up the story into three sections: first, the years from 1056 to 1131, very poorly documented, but significant in the history of the cathedral as the first period when Hereford was opened up to continental influences; secondly, the years 1131 to 1240, for which sources survive in some quantity and in which the chapter first began to claim a degree of independence from the bishop; and thirdly the pontificate of Peter of Aigueblanche (1240–68), in which tensions between different factions within the chapter made it necessary to take stock of the latter's institutional structure, leading to the composition of the earliest set of Hereford's cathedral statutes.

1. Cf. D. Spear, 'L'administration épiscopale normande: archidiacres et dignitaires des chapitres', in P. Bouet and F. Neveux, eds, *Les évêques normands du XIe siècle* (Caen, 1995), pp. 81–102.

2. Cf. C. Morris, *The Papal Monarchy: the Western Church from 1050 to 1250* (Oxford, 1989), pp. 224–26.

By the middle of the eleventh century the diocese of Hereford was long-established, but lacking political influence and not in any way notable for cultural achievements. The cathedral was served by a community of clerks: in other words, it had escaped the process of conversion to monasticism which had been undergone by the cathedrals of Canterbury, Sherborne, Winchester and Worcester in the tenth and eleventh centuries.[3] Becoming monastic was only an option for those cathedrals rich enough to afford to support a large community of monks: Hereford was too poor to do so, and moreover its bishops may not necessarily have viewed monasticisation as desirable. At the same time, Hereford had also escaped moves under way in some English cathedrals of the mid eleventh century towards a more structured form of clerical life with *vita communis* (common life, with a shared refectory and sometimes also a shared dormitory). Yet, if not alive to new religious ideas, Hereford's cathedral community was respected in its locality, as is clear from the will of Wulfgeat of Donington,[4] and from the inclusion of two shire court judgements in the cathedral gospel book.[5]

The 1050s were a period of tension in the Welsh Marches. Crisis struck when, on 24 or 25 October 1055, Gruffudd ap Llywelyn sacked Hereford. Three canons, Eilmar, Ordgar and Godo, with Eilmar's four sons, were killed defending the doors of the cathedral, which itself was burnt.[6] The damage is hard to quantify: there is no evidence of any rebuilding of the cathedral as such before the early twelfth century. However, it is clear that much was lost. Only one book, the cathedral gospel book, survived; the other books and the relics of St Ethelbert were destroyed,[7] or robbed.[8] Bishop Athelstan, now very old, survived, but died early in the following year. To replace him Edward the Confessor appointed Leofgar, a chaplain of Earl Harold, a cleric so warlike that he refused to shave off his moustache until he became a bishop. On 16 June 1056 he undertook a revenge attack on

3. J. Barrow, 'English Cathedral Communities and Reform in the Late Tenth and the Eleventh Centuries', in D. Rollason, M. Harvey and M. Prestwich, eds, *Anglo-Norman Durham, 1093–1193* (Woodbridge, 1994), pp. 25–39.

4. S 1534: D. Whitelock, *Anglo-Saxon Wills* (Cambridge, 1930), no. 19.

5. S 1462, 1469: A. J. Robertson, ed., *Anglo-Saxon Charters* (2nd edn, Cambridge, 1956), pp. 150–53, 186; see above, pp. 16–18.

6. According to John of Worcester, in R. R. Darlington and P. McGurk, eds, *The Chronicle of John of Worcester*, Oxford Medieval Texts (3 vols, Oxford, 1995-), ii, p. 576,

seven canons were killed on 24 October; Oxford, Bodleian, MS Rawlinson B 328, fol. 42v, gives obits for Canon Eilmar, his colleagues and his sons under 25 October; cf. also D. Whitelock, D. C. Douglas and S. I. Tucker, eds, *The Anglo-Saxon Chronicle: A Revised Translation* (London, 1961), pp. 130–31 (CDE); for discussion cf. F. M. Stenton, 'Pre-Conquest Herefordshire', in D. M. Stenton, ed., *Preparatory to Anglo-Saxon England* (Oxford, 1970), pp. 193–202, at 200.

7. Darlington and McGurk, eds, *Chronicle of John of Worcester*, ii, pp. 576–79.

8. Whitelock, Douglas and Tucker, eds, *The Anglo-Saxon Chronicle*, pp. 130–31 (CD).

the Welsh but was killed in battle at Glasbury together with several cathedral canons.[9]

Decisive action was now taken to secure the peace in Herefordshire: the main roles were taken by Harold Godwinson, who organised the defences and in 1057 took over the earldom of Hereford, and by Ealdred, bishop of Worcester, who assumed temporary responsibility for the see of Hereford.[10] Meanwhile Edward the Confessor confirmed to the cathedral clergy jurisdiction over their lands:[11] this did not mean that they had separate rights as a community vis-à-vis the bishop but that, in a vacancy, they represented the latter.[12] The new bishop, appointed in 1061, was Walter, the queen's chaplain and one of a large group of Lotharingian clerics imported into England by Cnut and Edward the Confessor. Walter was a shadowy character whose life is poorly recorded.[13] It is likely that he did nothing to restore morale in the diocese and it is evident that he did little to build up the resources of the bishopric, damaged by warfare and by the loss of lands to Harold before 1066 and to Norman settlers afterwards: Walter's successor, Robert, was careful to point out in the Domesday returns of the church the difference between the values of the estates at Walter's death and in 1086.[14]

With the consecration of Robert in 1079 the fortunes of the diocese and of the cathedral revived (fig. 5). Robert, another Lotharingian cleric, had been trained in the cathedral school at Liège, one of the best schools in the Empire, and had perhaps been invited to England by William I in the early 1070s, when the higher echelons of the English church were being purged of Anglo-Saxons.[15] He would have brought to his new post knowledge of how a major imperial cathedral operated; at the same time he cooperated with the views of Lanfranc, archbishop of Canterbury (1070–89), about how to alter the structures of the English church. In line with Lanfranc's reforms, Robert appointed the first ever archdeacon in

9. Ibid., p. 132 (CD); Darlington and McGurk, eds, *The Chronicle of John of Worcester*, ii, p. 580.

10. Ibid., ii, p. 580.

11. S 1101: F. E. Harmer, *Anglo-Saxon Writs* (Manchester, 1952), no. 49; the term *prestes* in the ME version of the writ probably represents OE *preostas*, 'clerks'.

12. E. U. Crosby, *Bishop and Chapter in Twelfth-Century England: A Study of the Mensa Episcopalis* (Cambridge, 1994), p. 278.

13. J. Barrow, 'Walter, Bishop of Hereford', in *New DNB* (forthcoming), and, on Lotharingian clergy in England, cf. F. Barlow, *The English Church, 1000–1066* (2nd edn, London, 1979), pp. 81–84, 156–58; S. Keynes, 'Giso, Bishop of Wells (1061–88)', in C. Harper-Bill, ed., *Anglo-Norman Studies*, xix, *Proceedings of the Battle Conference 1996* (Woodbridge, 1997), pp. 203–71.

14. J. Barrow, 'A Lotharingian in Hereford: Bishop Robert's Reorganisation of the Church of Hereford, 1079–1095', in Whitehead, *Medieval Art at Hereford*, pp. 29–47.

15. J. Barrow, 'Robert the Lotharingian, Bishop of Hereford', in *New DNB* (forthcoming).

Fig. 5. Posthumous (early fourteenth-century) tomb of Bishop Robert the Lotharingian, south choir aisle.

the diocese of Hereford, Heinfrid, who first occurs in 1085;[16] he also began to acquire books for the cathedral, though not as yet the full range of works in canon law and patristics which Lanfranc wished each major church to possess.[17]

While these innovations were clearly inspired by Lanfranc, Robert drew on the traditions of his homeland in building his episcopal chapel (fig. 86). This was a square, two-storeyed edifice in which each floor served as a chapel, but the two were interconnected, with the top floor serving as a gallery; it was similar to chapels at Speyer and elsewhere in the Empire and was dedicated to two saints, Katherine and Mary Magdalene, as yet rarely chosen for church dedications in England.[18]

16. C. N. L. Brooke, 'The Archdeacon and the Norman Conquest', in D. E. Greenway, C. J. Holdsworth and J. E. Sayers, eds, *Tradition and Change* (Cambridge, 1985), pp. 1–19, especially 17.

17. Cf. Mynors and Thomson, *Catalogue*, p. 14 (HCL, MS O.II.7) and pp. 15–16 (HCL,

MS O.II.9); for Lanfranc, see N. R. Ker, *English Manuscripts in the Century after the Norman Conquest* (Oxford, 1960), pp. 7, 10.

18. On the architecture, see R. Gem, 'The Bishop's Chapel at Hereford: The Roles of Patron and Craftsman', in S. Macready and

The chaplains serving the chapel (the four chaplains who occur on the cathedral manors in Domesday) were clearly members of the cathedral community since they shared in cathedral revenues.[19] The inability of the bishops to provide endowments for the chapel as a separate institution, which may have been Robert's original intention, meant that the most practical solution was to give the chapel to the chapter; in the late twelfth century Bishop William de Vere gave the chapel of St Mary Magdalene to the chapter,[20] while in 1233 Bishop Hugh Foliot handed over St Katherine's.[21] Another Lotharingian fashion which Robert brought with him to England was an interest in computation, which led him to write a short commentary on the ideas of Marianus Scotus, an Irish chronicler living in the Empire, about the dating of the Incarnation. Into this commentary Robert inserted a short description of the Domesday Survey, for which he had perhaps been a commissioner.[22]

Domesday Book is our principal source for Robert's attempts to remodel the cathedral community. The returns for the estates of the church of Hereford in Domesday were probably drafted by Robert and can be read as his view of how things ought to function. The entry for the church in the Herefordshire section of Domesday is headed 'land of the church of Hereford',[23] and, after a short list of urban property and waste manors, the remaining manors are prefixed by the heading 'These lands belong to the canons of Hereford'. This suggests that Robert wanted to stress, at least publicly, the rights of the cathedral clergy, while preserving his own rights as bishop, which would have been harmed by a division. Nonetheless, most of the manors listed were treated by subsequent bishops as their own demesne, so it is unlikely that in practical terms the canons had much influence over them.

Robert also created small tenancies for individual members of the cathedral community, evidently embryonic prebends, though not termed such: about two-thirds of the holdings formed the basis of the later prebends, though the remainder were reassimilated into the episcopal demesne and replaced by other holdings

F. H. Thompson, eds, *Art and Patronage in the English Romanesque*, Society of Antiquaries Occasional Papers, new series, 8 (1986), pp. 87–96; on dedications cf. A. Binns, *Dedication of Monastic Houses in England and Wales, 1066–1216* (Woodbridge, 1989), pp. 26–27.

19. Barrow, 'A Lotharingian in Hereford', pp. 33–34.
20. *EEA*, vii, no. 198.
21. Ibid., no. 343, either 1232 or 1233.
22. W. Stevenson, 'A Contemporary Description of the Domesday Survey', *English Historical Review*, 22 (1907), pp. 72–84; H. Loyn, 'William's Bishops: Some Further Thoughts', in R. A. Brown, ed., *Anglo-Norman Studies*, x (Woodbridge, 1988), pp. 223–35.
23. A. Farley, ed., *Domesday Book seu Liber Censualis Willelmi Primi Regis Angliae* (2 vols, London, 1783), i, fol. 181c. The entry in the Gloucestershire section is also headed 'Land of the Church of Hereford' (i, fol. 165a), but in Shropshire and Worcestershire, 'Land of the Bishop of Hereford' (i, fos 252b, 174b).

created out of the cathedral estates or granted by outsiders. Of the clerical holdings listed in Domesday Book, one of the four at Bartonsham, the three holdings at Withington (Church Withington, Ewithington and Withington Parva), one of the two clerical holdings at the gate of Hereford (Eigne), one of the clerical holdings at Hinton, the holding at Huntington, two of the clerical holdings at Moreton on Lugg (Moreton Magna and Moreton Parva), one of the clerical holdings at Pyon, the clerical holding at Preston, one of the clerical holdings at Woolhope and two of the clerical holdings at Putson survived as prebends.[24] The terms used in Domesday to refer to the cathedral clergy holding these tenancies are clerks, episcopal clerks and chaplains, so hitherto they have usually not been identified with members of the chapter.[25] However, since the total number of clerks, chaplains and episcopal clerks in Domesday Book is twenty-nine excluding Bishop Robert's clerk William in Shropshire, while 150 years later the total number of canons was twenty-eight excluding the archdeacon of Shropshire, who was not automatically expected to hold a prebend, and since we know that in the intervening period four prebends were alienated and another three (Moreton and Whaddon, Wellington and the prebend of the penitentiary) were established,[26] the identification seems fairly certain. Robert's only surviving charter, his grant of Holme Lacy to Robert de Lacy in 1085, lists several clerics simply as *de hominibus episcopi* whom we know from the cathedral obit book to have been canons. At the head of the list in the witnesses to the charter comes Robert's brother, Gerard, identifiable with the Dean Gerard who occurs in the cathedral obit book: thus the deanery at Hereford was probably established by Robert. Further down the list, Liwin, another cleric, is probably identifiable with the Dean Liwin who occurs in the obit book; presumably he succeeded Gerard in office.[27] The appearance of the earliest dean by the 1080s shows that Robert was *au fait* with developments in other English cathedrals, such as Lincoln and York where deans were in post by the early 1090s.[28] What he does not appear to have introduced is any form of *vita communis*, though some Lotharingian bishops (Giso of Wells and Walcher of Durham) did this; at Hereford,

24. Barrow, 'A Lotharingian in Hereford', pp. 38–40; the list cited there should be amended to point out that Overbury, part of the prebend of Gorwell and Overbury, is within the parish of Woolhope: see W. N. Yates, 'The Dean and Chapter of Hereford, 1240–1320' (unpublished University of Hull MA thesis, 1969), p. 86.

25. M. Jones, 'The Estates of the Cathedral Church of Hereford, 1066–1317' (unpublished Universty of Oxford B.Litt. thesis, 1958), p. 41; cf. J. H. Round, 'Introduction to the Herefordshire Domesday', in W. Page, ed., *Victoria History of the County of Hereford* (London, 1908), i, p. 282.

26. J. Barrow, 'A Lotharingian in Hereford', pp. 37, 41.

27. *EEA*, vii, no. 2; Oxford, Bodleian, MS Rawlinson B 328, fos 49v (Gerard's obit), 45r (Liwin's obit).

28. D. E. Greenway, 'The False *Institutio* of St Osmund', in Greenway, Holdsworth and Sayers, eds, *Tradition and Change*, pp. 77–101, at 84.

however, the provision of separate tenancies for individual members of the chapter tends to suggest otherwise.

After Robert's death in 1095, successive bishops up to the consecration of Robert de Béthune in 1131 are poorly documented. We therefore have only a limited opportunity to assess how much they influenced the development of the chapter. Nonetheless, two of them seem to have had a considerable impact. Bishop Gerald (1096–1100) was probably responsible for introducing the Use of Hereford to Hereford;[29] as Edmund Bishop showed, it is based on the Use of Rouen,[30] and Gerald before his elevation to the see had been precentor of Rouen Cathedral and thus the person responsible for the organisation of services there. Gerald's successor, Reinhelm, elected 1100 but only consecrated in 1107, was described in the cathedral obit book as *fundatoris ecclesiae*:[31] clearly therefore it is to him that we owe the new Romanesque cathedral, which forms the core of the structure surviving today (fig. 6).[32] Here again Hereford was undergoing an experience shared by almost all English cathedrals of the late eleventh and early twelfth century, though rather later than the rest: the rebuilding of Winchester was begun by Walkelin in 1079, Worcester by Wulfstan in 1084, Durham by William of St-Calais in 1093, Norwich by Herbert Losinga in 1096.[33]

From the start of the 1130s the documentation for our subject expands. The cathedral chapter emerges as a force in its own right and not merely as an appendage of the bishops. However, the latter exercised strong influence over the development of the chapter and a brief summary of their individual contributions is necessary here to provide a chronological framework for what follows. Robert de Béthune (1131–48), a former schoolmaster who had studied under William of Champeaux and Anselm of Laon, had become an Augustinian canon at Llanthony in the Black Mountains and subsequently prior of that house; a strict disciplinarian, he expected his cathedral chapter to obey him (fig. 23).[34] His pontificate largely coincided with the Anarchy and many of his actions as bishop were a response to the impact of warfare. The community at Llanthony was driven from its priory in 1135 and

---

29. *EEA*, vii, p. xxxv.

30. E. Bishop, *Liturgica Historica* (Oxford, 1918), pp. 276–300; the links between Hereford and Rouen were also noted by A. T. Bannister, 'Origin and Growth of the Cathedral System', *Church Quarterly Review*, 104 (1927), pp. 95–96.

31. Oxford, Bodleian, MS Rawlinson B 328, fol. 43r, under 28 October, though he probably died on 27 October: cf. *EEA*, vii, p. xxxvi.

32. For the site, see J. Blair, 'The Twelfth-Century Bishop's Palace at Hereford', *Medieval Archaeology*, 31 (1987), pp. 59–72, at 71.

33. R. Gem, 'English Romanesque Architecture', in G. Zarnecki, J. Holt and T. Holland, eds, *English Romanesque Art, 1066–1200* (London, 1984), pp. 27–40.

34. J. Barrow, 'Robert de Béthune', in *New DNB* (forthcoming).

Fig. 6. South transept interior, east elevation.

sought Robert's protection; together with Miles of Gloucester, he set up a second home for them outside Gloucester in 1136. Then in 1139 Geoffrey Talbot and Miles, using the cathedral as a fortress, besieged forces loyal to Stephen in Hereford Castle, and Robert, who supported Stephen, had to withdraw to Shropshire, while the dean of Hereford, Ralph, was expelled from the city by the besiegers.[35] A brief truce between Robert and Miles allowed the foundation of St Guthlac's priory on episcopal land beyond Bye Gate in Hereford in 1143;[36] following Miles's death at the end of the year conditions in the diocese steadily became more peaceful.

The process of stabilisation continued under Robert's successor, Gilbert Foliot, a Cluniac monk who had risen to be abbot of Gloucester.[37] Gilbert encouraged local landowners to make grants to the cathedral.[38] He also gave more authority to the chapter, stressing in some of his charters that transactions had been made with their consent.[39] In 1163 he was translated to the diocese of London. His successor, a distinguished Parisian theologian of English extraction, Robert de Melun,[40] was in office for so short a time (1163–67) that he had no chance to set his imprint on the diocese, and since his death occurred at the height of the Becket dispute the see remained vacant until 1174, four years after Becket's death, when a new archbishop of Canterbury had been consecrated and the vacant sees could be filled.

The choice of the new bishop of Hereford, Robert Foliot (1174–86) was a diplomatic compromise: Robert was a kinsman of Gilbert Foliot who also happened to have been a supporter of Thomas Becket.[41] As archdeacon of Oxford (1151–74) he had become a highly experienced canon lawyer, and as bishop he corresponded frequently with Pope Alexander III, seeking rulings on contentious issues. He was also a connoisseur of fine craftsmanship, testimony to which can be found in the timber hall of the episcopal palace of Hereford, which he commissioned in 1179.[42]

35. A. Morey and C. N. L. Brooke, eds, *The Letters and Charters of Gilbert Foliot* (Cambridge, 1967), no. 2.

36. *EEA*, vii, nos 19, 21. St Guthlac's, probably founded in the eighth century, was, by *c.* 1000, a church staffed by secular clerics (see pp. 14–15 above). At the request of Gloucester Abbey, Robert de Béthune united it in 1143 with a small priory (St Peter's) in Hereford belonging to Gloucester and the new foundation, the Priory of SS Peter, Paul and Guthlac (usually simply called St Guthlac's) was moved to a new site outside the walls.

37. A. Morey and C. N. L. Brooke, *Gilbert Foliot and his Letters* (Cambridge, 1965), pp. 96–98, 188–201, 267–71.

38. Barrow, 'A Lotharingian in Hereford', pp. 37, 41.

39. Morey and Brooke, *Gilbert Foliot*, pp. 200–1.

40. *EEA*, vii, pp. xli–xlii and literature there cited.

41. J. Barrow, 'Robert Foliot', in *New DNB* (forthcoming).

42. J. Blair, 'The Twelfth-Century Bishop's Palace at Hereford'; for the date, see D. Haddon-Rees, D. Miles and J. Munby, 'Tree-Ring Dates', *Vernacular Architecture*, 20 (1989), pp. 46–47; see also below p. 296–97.

Both Robert and his successor, William de Vere (1186–98), were generous benefactors to the chapter. William, brother of the first earl of Oxford, had been an
Augustinian canon and clerk of works at Henry II's prestigious refoundation of
Waltham.[43] He may have begun the rebuilding of the choir (fig. 7). He tried to
build up the chapter's communal revenues, which were necessary to top up the
variable, often meagre, incomes provided by the prebends,[44] and he recruited many
canons with scholarly and literary interests, including Gerald of Wales and the
Anglo-Norman poet Simon (Simund) de Freine.[45]

   After William's death the canons tried to secure the election of one of their
number, Walter Map. It was as far as we can tell the first time they had tried to
propose a candidate, a real sign of their growing independence; however, before
they could obtain Richard I's approval, he died.[46] John had quite different plans
for the see. To show favour to William de Braose, lord of Brecon and the most
powerful figure in the southern Welsh marches, he made his son Giles bishop of
Hereford. Giles, who appears to have lacked experience of ecclesiastical affairs at
his consecration, made up for this by employing a large group of highly educated
household clergy, most of whom sooner or later entered the chapter.[47] Since he
was much in demand as a papal judge-delegate and an arbitrator in ecclesiastical
disputes, Giles cannot have lacked ability.[48] However, when relations between his
family and King John broke down irrevocably in 1208, he was forced to flee to
France, where he remained until 1213. On his return he spent some time cam-
paigning against John and the latter's allies in the Welsh Marches. The stresses this
imposed perhaps led to his early death, shortly after he had been forced to make
peace with John, in November 1215.

   The diocese remained vacant for about a year; the chapter wished to elect their
dean, who had been one of Giles' clerks, Master Hugh de Mapenore, but had to
wait until after John's death to be able to do so.[49] Hugh's two immediate successors,
Hugh Foliot (1219–34) and Ralph de Maidstone (1234–39), were likewise members
of the chapter before election, though in their cases royal favour as much as the
will of the chapter helped to secure their election.[50] Both Hugh Foliot and Ralph

43. J. Barrow, 'A Twelfth-Century Bishop and
    Literary Patron: William de Vere', *Viator*,
    18 (1987), pp. 175–89.
44. *EEA*, vii, nos 196–202.
45. See below at nn. 109, 111, 126–28, 130.
46. D. L. Douie and D. H. Farmer, eds, *Magna
    Vita Sancti Hugonis*, Oxford Medieval
    Texts (2nd edn, 2 vols, Oxford, 1985), ii,
    pp. 131–32.
47. *EEA*, vii, p. lix; J. Barrow, 'Giles de

    Braose', in *New DNB* (forthcoming).
48. Cf. C. R. and M. Cheney, eds, *The Letters
    of Pope Innocent III: A Calendar* (Oxford,
    1967), nos 340, 546, 551, 559, 560, 778;
    EEA, vii, nos 275, 287; J. Barrow, ed.,
    St Davids Episcopal Acta, 1085–1280 (Cardiff,
    1998), app. I–III.
49. *EEA*, vii, pp. xlvi–xlvii.
50. Ibid., p. xlix; J. Barrow, 'Ralph de Maid-
    stone', in *New DNB* (forthcoming).

Fig. 7. One of six Romanesque capitals from the presbytery arch of the Norman cathedral, now mounted on the west wall of the retrochoir.

de Maidstone improved details of the organisation of the chapter: Hugh extended to the cathedral dignitaries the right already enjoyed by prebendaries to have a year of grace, a year's payment of income to their executors on their decease. Ralph established the office of penitentiary,[51] before resigning the bishopric to become a Franciscan in 1239.

The term *capitulum* first occurs under Robert de Béthune in 1134.[52] While it is possible that it was used earlier than this at Hereford, it is certain that Robert encouraged the canons to act as a clearly defined body. Several of Robert's charters, even though none of them was actually for the cathedral, were addressed to the dean and chapter.[53] Nonetheless, his attitude to the canons was domineering. When Dean Ralph disagreed with Robert not long after the latter had appointed him, Robert went to Pisa to obtain a papal privilege which ordered the canons to be

51. *EEA*, vii, no. 340; the earliest penitentiary occurs 1234 x 1239, HCA, 1409.

52. *EEA*, vii, no. 17; fairly early in English terms for a cathedral chapter: cf. R. E. Latham, ed., *Dictionary of Medieval Latin from British Sources, Fascicule 2: C* (Oxford, 1981), p. 272, *s.v.*, para. 6, though cf. also F. Barlow, ed., *English Episcopal Acta*, xi, *Exeter, 1046–1184* (Oxford, 1996), no. 8 of 1100 x 1102.

53. *EEA*, vii, nos 16, 18, 20, 28, 37, 57.

Fig. 8. Chapter seal impression, *c.* 1190. (HCA, 233; HCL, neg. 810.)

obedient to their bishop.[54] The cause of the dispute was, very probably, Robert's high-handed action in bestowing four cathedral prebends on the canons of Llanthony when they were given their new site just outside Gloucester.[55] Ralph receives a bad press from Robert's biographer, William de Wycombe,[56] but by the 1140s he and Robert appear to have been reconciled.[57] From the 1140s Ralph and the chapter started to issue their own charters and use their own communal seal, an important step towards independence from the bishop (figs. 8, 9).[58]

As in other cathedrals the dean and chapter steadily built up rights of jurisdiction: the dean had archidiaconal rights within the city of Hereford and its suburbs, the dean's peculiar.[59] Since, in the late middle ages, the subdean's duties were limited to acting as the dean's official in his peculiar, rather than, as elsewhere, standing in for him at cathedral services, it is possible that references to subdeans from the late twelfth century point to the dean's peculiar existing at that date.[60] More important in the twelfth century was the definition of the chapter's

54. Capes, *Charters*, pp. 6–7; W. Holtzmann, ed., *Papsturkunden in England*, Abhandlungen der Gesellschaft der Wissenschaften zu Göttingen, philosophisch-historische Klasse, new series, 25; third series, 14–15, 33 (3 vols, Berlin, 1930–52), ii, p. 152, no. 15.
55. *EEA*, vii, no. 36; Morey and Brooke, eds, *Letters and Charters of Gilbert Foliot*, no. 327.
56. H. Wharton, *Anglia sacra* (2 vols, London, 1691), ii, p. 312; for discussion, see J. Barrow, 'Robert de Béthune', in *New DNB*, where it is argued that William was wrong to state that Robert deposed Ralph.
57. Morey and Brooke, eds, *Letters and Charters of Gilbert Foliot*, no. 2.
58. Capes, *Charters*, pp. 10–11; by contrast, a charter issued by the canons in 1132 uses

the word chapter to denote where they met rather than themselves as a body, ibid. pp. 7–8.
59. See below, n. 135.
60. For early subdeans see HCA, 233 of 1187/8 x mid 1190s and 870 of *c.* 1225 x 1230 (Master Aldred and Peter); Oxford, Balliol College, MS 271, fol. 77r, of 1195 (Roger); C. R. and M. Cheney, eds, *Letters of Pope Innocent III*, no. 964 (W.); on the office, see R. G. Griffiths and W. W. Capes, eds, *The Register of Thomas de Cantilupe, Bishop of Hereford, AD 1275–82*, Cantilupe Society (Hereford, 1906), p. 2 n. 2, and K. Edwards, *The English Secular Cathedrals in the Middle Ages* (2nd edn, Manchester, 1967), p. 153.

Fig. 9. Charter of Dean Ralph, *c.* 1135–58: contract between the dean and chapter and Hervey de Mucegros respecting a millpond at Preston. (HCA, 1088.)

property rights, first the prebends. Although Robert the Lotharingian had defined the total number of these, the endowments were not all firmly fixed and the properties making up the prebends could be allocated to other purposes. For example, in 1177 Canon William de Stokes received money from Onibury in Shropshire as his prebend, but this was obviously a temporary arrangement as there is no subsequent reference to a prebend there;[61] likewise Hugh Foliot transformed a prebend consisting of land at Pyon and Woolhope (evidently a survival of the clerical holdings there in Domesday) by giving land from the episcopal estates, first at Wellington and at the Hazle near Ledbury and later at Gorwell.[62] In this way the chapter was able to absorb some of the land at Pyon into its manor there, one of the four manors (Woolhope, Pyon, Preston and Norton) which were traditionally regarded as its own common property. Under Robert the Lotharingian these manors had between them provided holdings for six canons, but during the twelfth century the chapter was anxious to treat the manors as the nucleus of its common fund, rather than as prebendal holdings. However, they were unable to remove the latter completely, as shown by the prebends of Piona Parva, Norton, Cublington (from Preston-on-Wye) and Gorwell and Overbury (Overbury is within Woolhope). The four prebends lost through Robert de Béthune's generosity to Llanthony (lands at The Moor and Holmer, just outside Hereford) were partly made up through the establishment of two prebends (Moreton and Whaddon in Gloucestershire, and Wellington) by knightly families under Gilbert Foliot, and through the creation of a non-stipendiary prebend for the penitentiary by Ralph de Maidstone.[63] It is likely also that Gilbert was responsible for turning Hunderton and perhaps also Inkberrow into prebends, probably to replace prebends originally created on chapter manors.[64]

The values of the Hereford cathedral prebends varied widely, but tended to be

61. *EEA*, vii, no. 159.
62. Ibid., nos 337, 341.
63. Barrow, 'A Lotharingian in Hereford', pp. 37–41.

64. Ibid., p. 37 and cf. Morey and Brooke, eds, *The Letters and Charters of Gilbert Foliot*, no. 314.

much lower than those available at Lincoln, Salisbury or Wells.[65] Thus it was necessary to find ways of supplementing prebendal revenues, and Hereford shared in a development common to all the English secular cathedrals in the second half of the twelfth century: building up common funds to provide income (known as commons) which could be divided among all the canons, or more particularly among those declaring themselves willing to reside at their cathedrals for extended periods of time. Offering to perform continuous residence did not bind prebendaries to a cathedral throughout the whole year: thirty-six weeks was the requirement at Hereford.[66] The main source of commons at Hereford consisted of the four manors held by the chapter communally – Woolhope, Norton, Pyon and Preston – to supervise which it appointed two bailiffs from among the canons, who are first attested in the late twelfth century.[67] The income was distributed in three separate sets of payments, great commons for residents, lesser commons for all canons, and quotidian commons (bread, ale, or grain in lieu of ale); in addition mass pence were given to those who attended services. These are first described in detail in Peter of Aigueblanche's chapter statutes of the mid thirteenth century,[68] but had begun earlier, for reference to payments of bread and ale occurs first in 1195,[69] and to the chapter's barn (from which the grain was presumably distributed) in the early thirteenth century.[70] The chapter had a communal oven from the 1180s,[71] and a communal bakehouse in Castle Street by the early thirteenth century.[72] A chapter brewhouse is mentioned c. 1200.[73] Such payments, and the limited value of Hereford prebends, ensured that the absenteeism rate among canons was fairly low until the middle of the fourteenth century;[74] although records for attendance do not exist before the 1290s, it is possible to form some idea of absenteeism for earlier periods by counting up the number of canons with offices or other duties elsewhere. Over the period from the 1160s to the 1230s at least twenty canons fell into this category,[75] which suggests that the proportion of absentee canons may not have been dissimilar to that of the 1290s, when a quarter of the chapter did not reside.

65. Cf. T. Astle, S. Ayscough and J. Caley, eds, *Taxatio ecclesiastica Angliae et Walliae Auctoritate Papae Nicholai IV, circa AD 1291* (London, 1802), pp. 168–70, 181–82 and 199–200 for prebends at Hereford and Wells; for values of prebends at Lincoln and Salisbury, see D. E. Greenway, ed., *John Le Neve, Fasti ecclesiae Anglicanae, 1066–1300*, iii, *Lincoln* (London, 1977) and iv, *Salisbury* (London, 1991), throughout.

66. Bradshaw and Wordsworth, *Statutes of Lincoln Cathedral*, ii, p. 49.

67. HCA, 1091; for a list see M. Jones, 'The Estates of the Cathedral Church of Hereford', p. 246; see also Bradshaw and Wordsworth, *Statutes of Lincoln Cathedral*, ii, p. 50.

68. Ibid., pp. 47–48, 51–52.

69. *EEA*, vii, no. 200.

70. Ibid., no. 257 of 1200 x 1215.

71. Capes, *Charters*, p. 26.

72. HCA, 505; Oxford, Bodleian, MS Rawlinson B 329, fol. 132r.

73. Capes, *Charters*, p. 37.

74. Edwards, *English Secular Cathedrals*, p. 74.

75. Barrow, 'A Lotharingian at Hereford', p. 46 n. 88.

Fig. 10. Romanesque font, south side of nave.

Running a cathedral was a complex operation involving a wide range of activities and duties, such as the organisation of services and music, the provision of lighting, the safe-keeping of relics and vessels and the training of young clerks. These duties were usually devolved to dignitaries, chapter officials who held endowed offices called dignities. Medieval English secular cathedrals tended to have at least four of these: the dean in charge of discipline; the precentor in charge of services and chant; the chancellor in charge of the school; and the treasurer in charge of vestments, relics, sacred vessels and, not least, lighting (one of the most expensive items in an ecclesiastical budget).[76] Presumably for financial reasons, the endowment of dignities often proceeded slowly;[77] at Hereford, the emergence of a complete set took over a century. Although, as we have seen, deans existed from the late eleventh century, the earliest datable occurrences of a cantor (precentor) and a treasurer come in 1132; nonetheless, it is likely that there had been a treasurer already slightly earlier, for one is recorded in an early twelfth-century hand in the

76. D. E. Greenway, 'The False *Institutio* of St Osmund', pp. 77–101.
77. Ibid, p. 82.

Durham *Liber vitae*.[78] Only from the late 1180s does the cantor appear with the more formal title precentor,[79] suggestive of the existence of a deputy, a succentor. This office is not recorded at Hereford until the mid thirteenth-century statutes, which spelled out the duties attached to it.[80] Hereford was likewise slow to endow a dignitary to supervise the cathedral school, even though it is likely that there was a school by at least the 1130s.[81] No one occurs with the title master of the schools, and the earliest canon to be called chancellor, Master Nicholas *divinus*, seems to have been given the title quite unofficially in a single charter; at any rate, his entry in the cathedral obit book calls him a theologian, a canon and a priest.[82] Possibly there was no formally endowed chancery until the 1190s, when William de Vere appointed his nephew Henry to the dignity; however, an unidentifiable chancellor, Ranulf, probably of the twelfth century, occurs in the cathedral obit book.[83]

Because canons were often absent (even resident canons did not have to reside all the year round) it was necessary to employ vicars (vicars choral) to ensure that services could be regularly and adequately performed. The earliest reference to vicars is in a charter of Bishop Robert Foliot.[84] At this stage they may well have been employed on a casual basis by absent canons, but, before the end of the twelfth century, Bishop William de Vere ensured the endowment of posts for two vicars by setting up a confraternity arrangement with the Norman abbey of Cormeilles. Perhaps with the inducement of help in case of litigation, a potential problem for French abbeys with English possessions, the abbey turned all its property in Herefordshire into a prebend of Hereford Cathedral, with the abbot as prebendary. Since he would only be able to appear in Hereford very occasionally, the abbey provided funds for two vicars choral.[85] A similar confraternity scheme was set up between Hereford and the Norman abbey of Lire by Bishop Hugh de Mapenore,[86] providing another two vicars. Another six posts for vicars were endowed in 1237 by Bishop Ralph de Maidstone when he gave the church of Diddlebury to the chapter.[87] Canon Roger de Calkeberge, who died in the mid thirteenth century, after 1239, endowed another vicarage,[88] probably to assist his kinsman

78. *EEA*, vii, no. 55; 'Rodbertus de Herefordia parvus secretarius istius ecclesie', in A. H. Thompson, ed., *Liber vitae ecclesiae Dunelmensis: A Collotype Facsimile of the Original Manuscript*, Surtees Society, 136 (1923), fol. 23r.
79. Cf. *EEA*, vii, no. 182.
80. Bradshaw and Wordsworth, *Statutes of Lincoln Cathedral*, ii, p. 63.
81. Hugh *grammaticus*, mentioned, perhaps already dead, in HCA, 1095: Capes, *Charters*, pp. 7–8.
82. HCA, 233; Oxford, Bodleian, MS

Rawlinson B 328, fol. 53r.
83. *EEA*, vii, nos. 201–2 of 1195 x 1198; Oxford, Bodleian, MS Rawlinson B 328, fol. 4v.
84. *EEA*, vii, no. 149 of 1174 x 1183.
85. Ibid., no. 188 and cf. no. 250.
86. Ibid., no. 305 of 1216 x 1219.
87. Capes, *Charters*, pp. 74–75; Bradshaw and Wordsworth, *Statutes of Lincoln Cathedral*, ii, p. 74.
88. Oxford, Bodleian, MS Rawlinson B 328, fol. 15r.

Ralph de Calkeberge, the first appointee. Hereford was relatively slow to provide posts for vicars and chaplains, and was unusual in securing their employment through specific endowments administered by the dean and chapter, for normally in English secular cathedrals canons were responsible for paying their own vicars, as for example at Salisbury where, by the early thirteenth century, all canons, whether resident or not, were expected to employ vicars to assist with their choir duties.[89]

Thanks to charters and the thirteenth-century cathedral obit book we know the names of about 308 canons and dignitaries at Hereford between the late eleventh century and 1300. In many cases we know no more of them than their names, but these can be a useful form of evidence in trying to form a picture of the geographical and social origins of the members of the chapter. Over the period from the 1140s to the 1170s it was becoming increasingly common for clerics to use by-names, often toponyms or inherited family names, themselves sometimes toponyms, which allow us to make some guesses about their backgrounds. Even in the period before the 1140s, when by-names were rare, we can say something about family background from the form of the given name. For example, of the three canons killed in 1055, while two bore Anglo-Saxon names (Eilmar and Ordgar), one apparently had a continental Germanic one (Godo), though this is probably a thirteenth-century misreading of the Anglo-Saxon name Goda.[90] Among the clerics (almost certainly all canons) who witnessed Robert the Lotharingian's single surviving charter, four had continental Germanic names (Gerard, Robert's brother, Ansfrid, Heinfrid the archdeacon and William) and four had Anglo-Saxon ones (Alfward, Alcwin, Liwin, Sæwulf).[91] In the early years of the twelfth century, we find one canon with a Danish name (Ketelbern, 1101 x 1102) and three with continental Germanic ones (Walter, 1101 x 1102, and Durand and Erchemar of 1107 x 1115).[92] By the early years of the twelfth century Anglo-Saxon names were generally declining in popularity among families in England of Anglo-Saxon origin, so the dominance of French names in this period cannot necessarily tell us much about the composition of the chapter.[93]

Once by-names start to be used in the middle decades of the twelfth century we have more information. Of the over sixty canons who occur between 1131

89. D. E. Greenway, ed., *Fasti ecclesiae Anglicanae 1066–1300*, iv, *Salisbury*, p. xxxv; for discussion, see Edwards, *English Secular Cathedrals*, p. 267.

90. Oxford, Bodleian, MS Rawlinson B 328, fol. 42v.

91. *EEA*, vii, no. 2.

92. J. H. Round, ed., *Calendar of Documents Preserved in France Illustrative of the History of Great Britain and Ireland, AD 918–1206* (London, 1899), no. 1138; Oxford, Balliol College, MS 271, fol. 93v.

93. A. Williams, *The English and the Norman Conquest* (Woodbridge, 1995), p. 204.

and 1163 we know that nine came from families settled in Herefordshire and the Welsh border area, chiefly the de Cliffords, who provided three canons, while Master Ralph of Ledbury was also local.[94] Three canons were kinsmen of Bishop Gilbert Foliot,[95] one, Master Ranulf fitz Erchemar, was the son of a former dean, two bore names of towns outside the west midlands (Masters Hugh of Northampton and William of Salisbury), and Dean Ralph is described by William de Wycombe as *alienus* (foreign).[96] Already under Bishop Robert de Béthune there are canons bearing the *magister* title, suggestive of a completed period of study at a higher school; the number of *magistri* grew steadily up to the early thirteenth century, when it stabilised at just under half the total.[97]

From the 1170s we are on surer ground. Geographically, slightly under half the canons came from Herefordshire and surrounding areas (Worcestershire, Gloucestershire, Shropshire, south-east Wales), while the remainder tended to come from either south-eastern England or the midlands.[98] Few canons came from the Continent until the 1240s, when the patronage of Bishop Peter of Aigueblanche brought in a sizeable influx from Savoy.[99] Social origins are much harder to determine; we can usually only do this where canons bear inherited family names (e.g. Clifford, Foliot, Lacy, Vere). We can be certain, however, that hardly any came from the aristocracy and that many canons came from knightly families, of varying degrees of status. Several came from local knightly families, though it is noticeable that only a minority of Herefordshire knightly families were represented. Some canons bearing the names of small villages can be presumed to belong to the minor gentry (we have some evidence to support this in the case of Hugh de Mapenore),[100] and it is likely that most canons bearing the names of towns came from burgess families, though some of them might instead have been sons of royal officials living in towns.

The geographical and social mix can be explained by looking at how canons were recruited. Prebends were in the gift of the bishop, or, in episcopal vacancies,

94. Master Hugh de Clifford; Master Geoffrey de Clifford; Robert de Clifford; Gilbert d'Evreux (Devereux family); David de Aqua; Nicholas de Chandos; Master Robert de Clare; William Parvus; probably also Master Hugh de Hungeria, whose name is reminiscent of Hongreye Street in Hereford (now St Owens Street). (Material being compiled by J. Barrow for forthcoming Hereford *Fasti*.)

95. Morey and Brooke, *Gilbert Foliot*, p. 199, but add Richard Foliot.

96. Wharton, *Anglia sacra*, ii, p. 312.

97. J. Barrow, 'Education and the Recruitment of Cathedral Canons in England

and Germany, 1100–1225', *Viator*, 20 (1989), pp. 117–38, at 134.

98. J. Barrow, 'The Canons and Citizens of Hereford, 1160–1240', *Midland History*, 24 (1999), pp. 1–23.

99. W. N. Yates, 'Bishop Peter de Aquablanca (1240–1268): A Reconsideration', *Journal of Ecclesiastical History*, 22 (1971), pp. 303–17; J. P. Chapuisat, 'Le chapitre savoyard de Hereford au XIIIe siècle', in *Sociétés savantes de la Province de Savoie, congrès de Moutiers* (Moutiers, 1966), pp. 43–51.

100. *EEA*, vii, p. xlvii, and cf. BL, Cotton MS Domitian A iii, fos 82r–83v, 148v–149r.

of the king. It was in the interests of both bishops and kings to further the careers of clerics with administrative abilities, preferably with a higher education. In particular, bishops were expected to reward the senior clerks in their households: over thirty canons of Hereford in the period up to 1240 had begun their careers as episcopal clerks.[101] Since the bishops in this period tended not to be of local extraction (Hugh de Mapenore was the only exception), they were not especially inclined to show favour to local families. By contrast they could show favour to their own families, though in practice the only bishops to do this extensively before 1240 were the Foliots, who between them admitted twelve relatives into the chapter.[102]

Several of the canons appear to have had private means in addition to their prebendal incomes, and they could add to their resources by renting out property in the city: two canons of the late twelfth and the early thirteenth centuries, Roger fitz Maurice and Elias of Bristol, did this on a large scale.[103] However, all canons prepared to reside were expected to live in houses large enough to offer hospitality and to give lodgings to junior clerics. The earliest canon's house to be mentioned is that of Dean Erchemar, who died before 1127, which was inherited by his son, also a canon, and by his grandson.[104] Up to the end of the twelfth century references to canons' houses suggest that they were built of flimsy materials and that the sites (sometimes illegal, as when Archdeacon Walter Foliot encroached on royal land or when Archdeacon Peter built his house on the cathedral graveyard) were more important than the buildings,[105] but from *c.* 1200 onwards the latter seem to have gained in durability. From this point canons began to leave their houses to the cathedral, so that they could be given, by the bishop, who had them in his gift, to succeeding canons. A stock of prebendal houses began to be built up, mostly in Castle Street, which was one of the most sought after streets in medieval Hereford.[106] There was no attempt to create a Close or to insist that canons should live as near as possible to the cathedral.

101. Barrow, 'The Canons and Citizens of Hereford', p. 7.

102. Henry Banastre, Geoffrey Foliot, two Hugh Foliots, two John Foliots, Ralph Foliot, Richard Foliot, Simon Foliot, Thomas Foliot (precentor and then treasurer), Walter Foliot, William Foliot. However, Robert Foliot, the future bishop, probably owed his prebend to royal presentation, and a second Thomas Foliot obtained a prebend by papal provision in 1241. (Material being compiled by J. Barrow for forthcoming Hereford *Fasti*.)

103. For Roger, cf. HCA, I, 113, 156, 411, 590, 792, 963, 972, 1282, 1284, 1363, 1526, 1692, 1694, 2182; for Elias, cf. ibid., 122, 160, 494, 518, 734, 751, 861, 869, 893, 959–72, 974, 976, 978, 980–92, 1085, 1112, 2005, 2048.

104. Morey and Brooke, eds, *The Letters and Charters of Gilbert Foliot*, no. 311; *EEA*, vii, nos 123, 168, 199.

105. J. H. Round, ed., *The Great Roll of the Pipe for the Twenty-Third Year of the Reign of King Henry the Second, AD 1176–1177*, Pipe Roll Society, 26 (1905), p. 56; *EEA*, vii, no. 151.

106. Oxford, Bodleian, MSS Rawlinson B 329, fos 129r, 130v, 132r; B 328, fol. 20v.

Documentation of Hereford cathedral's liturgy in the period before Aigueblanche's pontificate is poor. Service books in the middle ages were all too liable to be destroyed once they had outlived their usefulness. We owe the preservation of Hereford's single most important liturgical manuscript, the Hereford breviary (HCL, MS P.IX.7), compiled between 1262 and 1268, to the fact that when it ceased to be useful to the cathedral it was handed down to the parish church at Mordiford.[107] About thirty years later, probably soon after 1298, the cathedral's obit book was compiled.[108] Both, however, preserve much older material. Hereford was fairly traditional in its observances, and, until the late thirteenth century, unadventurous about new developments. The principal local saint's cult, that of St Ethelbert, was furthered, but less actively than the cults of many of Hereford's rivals. Three lives of Ethelbert were written in the twelfth century, none with a large circulation: an anonymous one in the early twelfth century; one written by Osbert de Clare for Gilbert Foliot; and one by Gerald of Wales which was probably commissioned by William de Vere in the 1190s.[109] William himself wrote a Life of St Osyth and encouraged her cult at Hereford;[110] Osyth, who had no Hereford connections, was the patron saint of the Augustinian priory of Chich, where William had been a canon before entering Waltham Abbey. More esoteric was Canon Simon de Freine's choice of St George as the subject of a saint's life in Anglo-Norman verse.[111] Here too William, who had been to the Holy Land, is likely to have commissioned the work, doubtless as propaganda for the Third Crusade.[112] Perhaps rather short-sightedly, the cathedral chapter failed to develop this cult further. By contrast, Ethelbert maintained a modest local following; his feast, 20 May, the starting date of Hereford's major annual fair, was also the term day for payment of peppercorn rents.[113] However, the

107. Mynors and Thomson, *Catalogue*, pp. 124–25; see also pp. 369–74 and pl. IVa.

108. Oxford, Bodleian, MS Rawlinson B 328. The second last canon recorded in the main hand of this manuscript is apparently William Rufus, who died 14 April 1277 (fol. 13v), while a canon who died 1279 is not recorded. The last entry in the main hand is for the canon Master Alan de Creppinge, who died 1297 (fos 7r-v). R. Rawlinson published the obit list as an appendix to his *History and Antiquities of the City and Cathedral Church of Hereford* (London, 1717), but many of his readings are incorrect.

109. For the anonymous *Life* and the one written by Gerald, see M. R. James, ed., 'Two Lives of St Ethelbert, King and Martyr', *English Historical Review*, 32 (1917), pp. 214–44, with translations by E. C. Brooks, *The Life of Saint Ethelbert King and Martyr* (Bury St Edmunds, 1996), pp. 28–38 and 40–58; Osbert's is preserved in Gotha, Landesbibliothek MS I.81.

110. Barrow, 'A Twelfth-Century Bishop', pp. 178, 185; Mynors and Thomson, *Catalogue*, p. 124.

111. 'Vie de St Georges', in J. E. Matzke, ed., *Les oeuvres de Simund de Freine*, Société des anciens textes français (Paris, 1909), pp. 61–117.

112. Barrow, 'A Twelfth-Century Bishop', p. 187.

113. Barrow, 'The Canons and Citizens of Hereford', p. 9.

lack of relics meant that it was hard to make the cult attractive to pilgrims. Hereford, until the growth of the Cantilupe cult at the end of the thirteenth century, was at a disadvantage compared with, for example, Worcester with its cult of Wulfstan.

Other means of building up contacts with the lay community were more fruitful. Inhabitants of Hereford and its locality were encouraged to make grants to the cathedral and to have their names inserted into the obit book so that prayers could be said for them; over 130 Hereford citizens did so over the twelfth and thirteenth centuries. Comparison with contemporary charters shows, unsurprisingly, that it was the better off citizens who did so.[114] In addition the cathedral housed the parochial altar of St John.[115] This parish covered a small area in the centre of the town, but, since its outlying fragments lay beyond the other urban parishes,[116] the latter must have been carved out of its original area. Its existence is only first clearly attested in the person of William, canon and chaplain of St John, in the early thirteenth century,[117] but supporting evidence for its antiquity is shown by the cathedral's monopoly of intramural burials, successfully maintained from at least the early twelfth century, and potentially a valuable source of revenue, since the cathedral received burial fees.[118]

Outreach into the urban community was also, and perhaps more effectively, undertaken through the establishment of St Ethelbert's Hospital by Canon Elias of Bristol in about 1225.[119] Hereford already had no fewer than three hospitals, but Elias was keen to have one under the aegis of the cathedral chapter to improve its standing in the city; he may perhaps also have worried about competition from the Franciscans, newly arrived in Hereford.[120] Numerous donations were secured from inhabitants of Hereford and the surrounding countryside.[121] Not to be outdone, Bishop Hugh Foliot set up a hospital dedicated to St Katherine at Ledbury by 1231.[122] Both hospitals were placed under the control of the dean and chapter, and both increased the contacts between the cathedral and local communities through charitable work for the poor and the infirm.

114. Ibid.
115. G. Rosser, 'The Cure of Souls in English Towns before 1000', in J. Blair and R. Sharpe, eds, *Pastoral Care before the Parish* (Leicester, 1992), pp. 266–84, at 271.
116. Map of parish boundaries *c.* 1800, reconstructed from eighteenth-century maps, in M. D. Lobel, ed., 'Hereford', in *Historic Towns*, i (London and Oxford, 1969), map 6.
117. HCA, 159, 494, 1273, 1275.

118. J. Barrow, 'Urban Cemetery Location in the High Middle Ages', in S. Bassett, ed., *Death in Towns* (Leicester, 1992), pp. 78–100, at 81.
119. Capes, *Charters*, pp. 57–59; the hospital existed by 1226: cf. ibid., p. 61.
120. Lobel, 'Hereford'.
121. These form the bulk of the earlier thirteenth-century charters in HCA.
122. *EEA*, vii, no. 348, and cf. no. 342. See also below, Chapters 34 and 35.

The cathedral ran a school from at least the 1170s if not the early twelfth century.[123] Hereford provided a congenial atmosphere for writers and scholars, partly because several of its bishops attracted scholars and writers to their households, and partly because Herefordshire and the Welsh Marches were unusually fertile areas for Anglo-Norman literature, Romanesque sculpture and the study of science.[124] Arabic science appears to have been brought to Hereford by Roger of Hereford, a protégé of Bishop Gilbert Foliot when the latter was bishop of London. While his name suggests that he did not live in Hereford permanently, we know that he was in Hereford on 13 September 1178, when he drew up a set of astronomical tables for its meridian.[125] Possibly Roger was responsible for kindling the interest in astronomy and other branches of science displayed by Canon Simon de Freine in a Latin poem written to Gerald of Wales, perhaps about 1195, to encourage him to settle at Hereford.[126] The poem praises Hereford for fostering the seven liberal arts, especially astronomy, and other studies, in particular medicine and geomancy, an Arabic form of divination. Simon's interest in medicine surfaces also in his Anglo-Norman verse version of Boethius's *Consolation of Philosophy*, the *Roman de philosophie*, into which he inserts a description of the symptoms of dropsy.[127] A knowledge of medicine was one of the qualities of the young Master Robert Grosseteste underlined by Gerald of Wales when recommending him as a clerk to Bishop William de Vere in 1194–95.[128] In about 1200, an Italian medical text, the *Prose Salernitan Questions*, was copied at Hereford with off-colour references to the sexual proclivities of some of Bishop Giles de Braose's clerks, including the future bishop Master Hugh de Mapenore.[129]

The canons of Hereford in the twelfth and early thirteenth centuries included

123. Above, nn. 81–82, and see below, Chapter 32, p. 567.
124. Summarised by M. Clanchy, *England and its Rulers, 1066–1272* (Oxford, 1983), pp. 177–79; see also e.g. G. Zarnecki, *Later English Romanesque Sculpture, 1140–1210* (London, 1953); M. D. Legge, *Anglo-Norman Literature and its Background* (Oxford, 1963), pp. 85–95, 183–85; and nn. 125–26 below.
125. C. S. F. Burnett, 'Mathematics and Astronomy in Hereford and its Region in the Twelfth Century', in Whitehead, *Medieval Art at Hereford*, pp. 50–59; R. W. Hunt, 'English Learning in the Late Twelfth Century', *Transactions of the Royal Historical Society*, 4th series, 19 (1936), pp. 19–42. J. C. Russell, 'Hereford and Arabic Science in England about 1175–1200', *Isis*, 18 (1932–33), pp. 14–25, requires correction on many points.
126. Most of the poem is printed in J. S. Brewer, J. F. Dimock and G. F. Warner, eds, *Giraldi Cambrensis opera*, Rolls Series, 21 (8 vols, London, 1861–91), i, pp. 382–84; the section listing subjects studied at Hereford was printed in Hunt, 'English Learning', pp. 36–37.
127. Matzke, ed., *Oeuvres de Simund de Freine*, pp. 25–26, lines 681–86.
128. Brewer, Dimock and Warner, eds, *Giraldi Cambrensis opera*, i, p. 249; R. W. Southern, *Robert Grosseteste: The Growth of an English Mind in Medieval Europe* (2nd edn, Oxford, 1992), p. 65.
129. B. Lawn, *The Salernitan Questions* (Oxford, 1963), p. 34; B. Lawn, ed., *The Prose Salernitan Questions* (London, 1979), p. 6.

among their number several literary figures, the most distinguished of whom were Master Walter Map, author of *De nugis curialium*, who was probably given a prebend by Gilbert Foliot, and Gerald of Wales (Master Gerald de Barri), who owed his prebend almost certainly to William de Vere. Though neither of these two resided in Hereford permanently both were frequent visitors, Hereford forming a useful resting place on journeys from the Welsh Marches eastwards. Walter included several Shropshire and Herefordshire legends in his *De nugis*, and Gerald gave copies of his works on Ireland to the cathedral chapter, and corresponded frequently with Hereford canons.[130] One of Gerald's friends at Hereford was Canon Simon de Freine, who as we have seen wrote Latin and Anglo-Norman verse. While none of Simon's works can be said to display much merit, his Anglo-Norman works do illuminate one of the trends of the period, the attempt to disseminate ideas available in Latin to a wider audience of French-speaking laymen and laywomen.

The central years of the thirteenth century were a significant period for the cathedral chapter. The institutional shape of the chapter was codified in the first surviving set of statutes and the pattern of recruitment into the chapter changed dramatically as over twenty Savoyard clerics became canons. Both developments were initiated by the bishop during these years, Peter of Aigueblanche (fig. 11).

Peter was a younger son of a cadet branch of the Briançon family in Savoy. He had begun his career as clerk to William of Savoy, bishop-elect of Valence, and uncle of Henry III's bride Eleanor of Provence. When Henry married Eleanor in 1236 Peter made his first visit to England and evidently made a favourable impression on Henry, for on William's death in 1239 he returned to England and entered the king's service. His family background and linguistic skills made him especially appropriate as a diplomat in southern France and Spain, particularly useful to Henry in his campaigns in Poitou and in his negotiations with the king of Castile. As a consequence, Peter spent more than half his pontificate outside England, mostly in southern France. When he was actually in England he was frequently absent from his diocese, employed in collecting taxes on behalf of the papacy and Henry III.[131] Naturally this did not make him a popular figure, especially in rich Benedictine monasteries such as St Albans, where Matthew Paris described Peter as diseased, deformed by a polyp in his nose and exuding a stench

130. Walter Map, *De nugis curialium*, ed. M. R. James, C. N. L. Brooke and R. A. B. Mynors (Oxford, 1983), pp. 154–59, 350–51, 370–71; Brewer, Dimock and Warner, eds, *Giraldi Cambrensis opera*, i, pp. 382–87, 409–19; Giraldus Cambrensis, *Speculum duorum*, ed. M. Richter and others (Cardiff, 1974), pp. 156–67.

131. T. F. Tout, 'Peter of Aigueblanche', *DNB*, xv, pp. 946–51, which requires updating on some matters; cf. Yates, 'Bishop Peter de Aquablanca', pp. 303–17; N. Vincent, 'Peter of Aigueblanche', *New DNB* (forthcoming).

Fig. 11. Tomb of Bishop Peter
of Aigueblanche, died 1268,
with the tomb of Dean John of
Aigueblanche in the
foreground: north transept,
looking south east.

of sulphur.[132] Peter's foreign background aroused antagonism in the increasingly
chauvinistic England of the thirteenth century.

Many able bishops of the period were, however, absentees like Peter. Recent
reappraisals of his pontificate, based on the documentation which survives from his
diocesan administration, show that he took his duties seriously.[133] Relations between
him and the cathedral chapter were mostly harmonious and Peter's ideas for the
latter were constructive. Even his diplomatic duties could prove useful to the
chapter, as when he made use of his stay at Lyon in 1245 to obtain confirmation
from Innocent IV for the chapter for some of their regulations, for example a rule

132. H. R. Luard, ed., *Mattaei Parisiensis, monachi
      sancti Albani, chronica majora*, Rolls Series,
      57 (7 vols, London, 1872–83), v, p. 510.

133. Yates, 'Bishop Peter de Aquablanca', cor-
      recting the views of W. W. Capes (Capes,
      Charters, pp. xix–xxi) and A. T. Bannister
      (Bannister, *The Cathedral Church of Hereford*,
      pp. 47–56).

restricting commons to resident canons and another fixing the number of canons at twenty-eight.[134] Only once, in 1252, was there a serious falling out between them: Peter, who had accused the dean and chapter of intruding themselves without authorisation into the church of Baysham (now Sellack), then tried to claim rights of visitation in the dean's peculiar and the churches belonging to the chapter, but judgement went against him in the papal curia and he accepted it. The final decision was an opportunity for the dean and chapter to obtain a confirmation of their sources of income (tithes, mills, rents, churches and manors) and their jurisdiction within their own churches and the dean's jurisdiction within his peculiar.[135]

On several issues of importance Peter gave the chapter his support. Throughout his pontificate he and the chapter, together with the Hereford Franciscans, tried to prevent the Dominicans from building a convent on land which they had been given in the city. This necessitated extensive litigation at the papal curia.[136] Similarly, he and the chapter faced sporadic unrest from those inhabitants of Hereford living in the king's fee rather than the episcopal one, who were hostile to the privileges enjoyed by the latter, such as exemption from the jurisdiction of royal officials. Likewise they disliked the control the bishop had over the annual fair of St Ethelbert, an enterprise from which the dean and chapter benefited, as they received the tithes. Peter was able to obtain agreement from the citizens to accept the status quo in 1262.[137] Peter was also generous to the chapter, bestowing seven carucates which he had bought in the manor of Holme Lacy in 1256 to set up obit distributions for himself, his kinsmen and his friend Prior Bernard of Champagne, who had been murdered at the cathedral in 1252.[138] Above all, it was during Peter's pontificate that the cathedral liturgy was overhauled, and a full set of cathedral statutes was drawn up.[139] Peter was certainly influential in both these

134. Capes, *Charters*, pp. 80–81; W. H. Bliss and J. A. Twemlow, eds, *Calendar of Entries in the Papal Registers Relating to Great Britain and Ireland: Papal Letters, 1198–1492* (14 vols, London, 1893–1960), i, pp. 223, 229.

135. Capes, *Charters*, pp. 93–101, esp. 95–101; cf. Yates, 'Bishop Peter de Aquablanca', pp. 309–10.

136. HCA, 1349, 1330, 1343; cf. Yates, 'Bishop Peter de Aquablanca', p. 309; W. N. Yates, 'The Attempts to Establish a Dominican Priory at Hereford, 1246–1342', *Downside Review*, 87 (1969), pp. 254–67.

137. Griffiths and Capes, eds, *The Register of Thomas Cantilupe*, pp. 91–93; Yates, 'Bishop Peter de Aquablanca', p. 309; for the grant of tithes from the fair to the chapter see *EEA*, vii, no. 198.

138. Griffiths and Capes, eds, *The Register of Thomas Cantilupe*, pp. 128–31; Peter was less generous in his will, giving the chapter a mitre and paying his debts: C. E. Woodruff, ed., *The Will of Peter de Aqua Blanca, Bishop of Hereford (1268)*, Camden Miscellany, 14 (London, 1926), item 3, pp. 2, 7–8.

139. See nn. 107–8 and 134 above. Judging by the entries in Bliss and Twemlow, eds, *Calendar of Entries in the Papal Registers: Papal Letters*, i, pp. 223, 229, Peter was issuing statutes on separate aspects of the life of the chapter in 1245–46, and it was only later that they were consolidated into a single text, edited in Bradshaw and Wordsworth, *Statutes of Lincoln* Cathedral, ii, pp. 44–85.

developments. He obtained papal confirmations of various chapter regulations in 1245–6, and these formed the basis of the first full compilation of chapter statutes which were issued between the very end of December 1246 and Peter's death in 1268 (plate IIa).[140] Furthermore, when he was setting up a collegiate church dedicated to St Katherine at Aiguebelle in Savoy in the 1260s, he laid down that the Use of Hereford should be followed, and took a strong interest in Aiguebelle's statutes.[141] Clearly Peter thought it desirable for the chapter to have a comprehensive set of rules.

The amicability between Peter and the chapter can, of course, partly be attributed to the fact that, of the thirty canons he is known to have collated to prebends during his episcopate, twenty were Savoyards. Of these four were his nephews, John, James, Aymo and Aymeric, on whom he bestowed dignities. This example of nepotism is no different from the behaviour of the Foliots and modest compared with that of Bishop Richard Swinfield at the end of the thirteenth century, but the importation of Savoyards on a large scale aroused some animosity, given the competition for benefices in the thirteenth-century English church.[142] Peter and the Savoyard canons were an obvious target for Simon de Montfort's supporters, who captured them in May 1263 and imprisoned them at Eardisley.[143] There was violence on a more personal level too, including the murder of Bernard in 1252 and threats against Dean Anselm in 1255, but sometimes the divisions were not purely national, as when the canon Richard of Montvernier conspired with some English accomplices to attack the brother of a royal clerk in 1257.[144] Within the chapter itself relations between the English and the Savoyard canons, equally balanced in numbers, were at least outwardly harmonious: Giles of Avenbury, for example, agreed to demotion in giving up the deanery which Peter then bestowed on Anselm of Clermont.[145] Real antagonism showed itself after Aigueblanche's death, when his successors tried to eject some of the Savoyards from the chapter.

Aigueblanche's pontificate was a formative period for Hereford cathedral chapter. In particular his statutes gave it a clearer institutional structure. Not all aspects of

140. See Appendix 1 below, pp. 633–36, on the constitution of the cathedral.
141. Woodruff, ed., *The Will of Peter de Aqua Blanca*, p. vii. I have not been able to consult F. Mugnier, *Les savoyards en Angleterre au XIIIe siècle et Pierre d'Aigueblanche, évêque d'Hereford* (Chambéry, 1891). The collegiate church of St Katherine's was also dedicated to St Mary Magdalene, thus sharing the dedication of the episcopal chapel at Hereford.
142. Yates, 'Bishop Peter de Aquablanca',

pp. 310–11, who wrongly describes the influx of Savoyards as 'grossly exaggerated'; Chapuisat, 'Le chapitre savoyard de Hereford au XIIIe siècle', pp. 43–51.
143. Yates, 'Bishop Peter de Aquablanca', p. 306, who points out that the attack on the bishop was principally because he supported Henry III.
144. Chapuisat, 'Le chapitre savoyard de Hereford au XIIIe siècle', pp. 46–47.
145. Yates, 'Bishop Peter de Aquablanca', pp. 312–13.

Fig. 12. Displaced architectural stones and carvings from the medieval cathedral in St John's walk.

the canons' activities were covered, but rules were laid down concerning issues of central importance such as admission, residence, payment of commons (largely though not completely restricted to resident canons), the right of canons to jurisdiction in their own prebends and households, arrangements for the estates of deceased canons, the duties of the dignitaries and the behaviour of canons and vicars choral in choir. The statutes and the Hereford breviary show a new spirit of institutional confidence within the cathedral.

3

The Later Middle Ages, 1268–1535

Robert Swanson and David Lepine

The years between 1268 and 1535, between the deaths of Bishops Peter of Aigueblanche and Charles Booth, are an important part of Hereford Cathedral's history. The canonisation of Thomas Cantilupe in 1320 temporarily made Hereford one of England's leading pilgrimage sites. The cult immediately affected the shape of the cathedral, providing the money for extensive building. St Thomas of Hereford contributed to the cathedral's life through to the Reformation, ensuring its centrality in the life of the diocese, and its place in national spiritual life.[1] While thus integrated into the nation, and into the wider catholic church, Hereford remained distinct, as demonstrated by the retention of the Use of Hereford, and by the idiosyncracies of the cathedral's constitution.[2]

The late middle ages were years of change and upheaval for the English and international church. Some events barely touched the diocese: despite their international repercussions, the Great Schism of 1378–1417, or the Council of Basle in 1431–49, were remote concerns. The papacy's lengthy sojourn in Avignon in the fourteenth century affected the destination of petitions, correspondence and money, but little else. Nearer home, the diocese and the cathedral endured the economic crises of the period: years of famine from 1315–22 which undermined agricultural revenues; the Black Death of 1348–49 which killed between a third and a half of England's population (and presumably that of the diocese);[3] and later plague visitations. Their impact fundamentally transformed relations between

---

1. For liturgical impact, see P. Barrett, 'A Saint in the Calendar: The Effect of the Canonization of St Thomas Cantilupe on the Liturgy', in M. Jancey, ed., *St Thomas Cantilupe, Bishop of Hereford: Essays in his Honour* (Hereford, 1982), pp. 153–57; also below, Chapter 21, pp. 388–89.

2. Below, Chapter 21, pp. 375–77; K. Edwards, *The English Secular Cathedrals in the*

Middle Ages (2nd edn, Manchester, 1967), p. 133.

3. For the impact of the Black Death in the diocese, especially on its clerical population, see W. J. Dohar, *The Black Death and Pastoral Leadership in the Diocese of Hereford in the Fourteenth Century* (Philadelphia, Pennsylvania, 1995), pp. 37–55. See also below, Chapter 35, p. 617.

landlords and tenants, and drastically changed the economic value of appropriated rectories. The revolt of Owain Glyndwr in Henry IV's reign compounded these upheavals, bringing ruination to benefices across the diocese.[4]

Spiritual changes also took hold. The Franciscans and Dominicans established priories at Hereford, not without causing problems. New spiritual trends subtly changed the demands on the church and had to be accommodated. Some also had to be resisted: from 1380 England was home to Lollardy, its own brand of heresy, associated (at least by its opponents) with the thought of the Oxford academic John Wyclif. The heresy's impact was immediate within the diocese, and in the cathedral,[5] which was the site of two major heresy trials, of William Swynderby in 1391 and of Walter Brut in 1393.[6] In the 1530s, also, changes were felt: Booth died in the early stages of the Reformation, shortly before the heavy hand of Henry VIII's commissioners fell on the cathedral to jolt it into a new world.

At first glance, these years are well documented. The chief records are the cathedral archives: numerous accounts survive, from various officials, plus an important collections of additional muniments. Elsewhere, the run of episcopal registers begins with Thomas Cantilupe's and continues (with some gaps and incompleteness)

4. For the late medieval economy in general, see J. L. Bolton, *The Medieval English Economy, 1150–1500* (London and Totowa, NJ, 1980), chs 6–7; J. Hatcher, *Plague, Population, and the English Economy, 1348–1530* (London and Basingstoke, 1977). For changes affecting the church, see R. N. Swanson, *Church and Society in Later Medieval England* (rev. edn, Oxford, 1993), pp. 214–15; idem, 'Standards of Livings: Parochial Revenues in Pre-Reformation England', in C. Harper-Bill, ed., *Religious Belief and Ecclesiastical Careers in Late Medieval England* (Woodbridge, 1991), pp. 151–71; R. R. Davies, *The Revolt of Owain Glyn Dwr* (Oxford, 1997), pp. 115, 117, 230–31, 235, 247. For the impact on churches, see J. H. Parry, ed., *Registrum Roberti Mascall, episcopi Herefordensis, AD MCCCCIV–MCCCCXVI*, Canterbury and York Society, 21 (London, 1917), pp. 20–21. Affected churches were not taxed in the fifteenth century: J. H. Parry, ed., *Registrum Edmundi Lacy, episcopi Herefordensis,* *AD MCCCCXVII–MCCCCXX*, Canterbury and York Society, 22 (London, 1918), pp. 67, 69; A. T. Bannister, ed., *Registrum Thomas Spofford, episcopi Herefordensis, AD MCCCCXXII–MCCCCXLVIII*, Canterbury and York Society, 23 (London, 1919), p. 13.

5. Dohar, *Black Death*, pp. 142–45; J. A. F. Thomson, *The Later Lollards, 1414–1520* (Oxford, 1965), pp. 24, 31–32, 40–42, 47–48. For a heretic's penance in the cathedral in 1509, see A. T. Bannister, ed., *Registrum Ricardi Mayew, episcopi Herefordensis, AD MDIV–MDXVI*, Canterbury and York Society, 27 (London, 1921), p. 110.

6. For the full record, W. W. Capes, ed., *Registrum Johannis Trefnant, episcopi Herefordensis, AD MCCCLXXXIX–MCCCCIV*, Canterbury and York Society, 20 (London, 1916), pp. 231–411: for events in the cathedral pp. 257, 261, 359. In each case the date of the cathedral trial (3 October, the morrow of St Thomas) is unlikely to be a coincidence.

throughout the period.[7] However, these are less informative than might be hoped. As the records of outsiders concerned with the whole diocese, dealings with the dean and chapter do not loom large in their contents.

This seeming wealth of evidence is deceptive: while plentiful, the records are often frustrating. The accounts are particularly problematic. Their number, the infuriating gaps, and the sheer complexity of the Hereford accounting system, often combine to defy analysis. The muniments can fill holes, but they usually supply information only about an outcome, revealing nothing of the background. The most lamentable losses affect the chapter act books, of which the first survivor begins only in 1512.[8] This makes much of the chapter's early internal history and the minutiae of chapter life irrecoverable and largely unfathomable. The loss undermines any attempt to construct lists of minor clergy for the cathedral: it is unlikely that any like those for Exeter can be recreated.[9] Also missing is information on the dean and chapter's legal administration: their peculiar jurisdiction is a gaping void in the bishopric's administrative history.[10]

The accounts therefore provide the main source for the cathedral's internal life, and can often compensate for the loss of the chapter act books. The circumstances of their generation necessarily make them introspective; while much can be recovered from them, they do have defects. Much remains to be unravelled and all analyses of the cathedral finances are still provisional. The other muniments also await proper investigation. Many of them concern lands and appropriated rectories, the mainstays of the cathedral finances. Scattered from Shropshire to Berkshire, these resources were obviously of prime concern to the dean and chapter.

Despite the necessary reliance on the financial records, they are often opaque sources. This is largely due to the cathedral's administrative organisation, justifiably judged 'among the most complicated in use at any English secular cathedral'.[11] It is not just that there were numerous officials (who were often minor cathedral clergy rather than residentiary canons). The division of responsibilities, indeed the nature of the responsibilities, is often elusive, as the system changed over time;

7. For details, D. M. Smith, *Guide to Bishops' Registers of England and Wales: A Survey from the Middle Ages to the Abolition of Episcopacy in 1646*, Royal Historical Society, guides and handbooks, 11 (London, 1981), pp. 95–101.

8. HCA, 7031/1: because of the poor condition of the original volume, this is referred to from the modern manuscript transcript, P. G. S. Baylis, ed., 'Hereford Cathedral Chapter Act Book, vol. 1' (3 vols, 1969–70),

cited hereafter as HCA, Baylis, with the folio numbers of the original.

9. For vicars choral, see below, Chapter 23. For Exeter, N. Orme, *The Minor Clergy of Exeter Cathedral, 1300–1548: A List of the Minor Officials, Vicars Choral, Annuellars, Secondaries and Choristers* (Exeter, 1980).

10. Dohar, *Black Death*, p. 40. Occasional documents do survive from these courts, e.g. HCA, 2753.

11. Edwards, *Secular Cathedrals*, p. 242.

there are no all-encompassing central statements.[12] Even with something as central to the cathedral's existence as the shrine of St Thomas, the financial history cannot be fully reconstructed. Evidence is incomplete and intermittent, with details appearing first in the fabric accounts, then migrating to those of the clavigers. The final evidence on receipts is a summary mention in the *Valor ecclesiasticus* of 1535.[13]

Amidst all this uncertainty, the one statement which is close to a balance sheet appears in the *Valor ecclesiasticus*, with a papal taxation return for 1291 also providing a useful summary. Both returns have their defects, and with changes to the endowment and funding of the cathedral over the intervening years are not strictly comparable; but they do offer a rough basis for assessing the cathedral's changing fortunes.

The 1291 *Taxatio* indicates common fund receipts of around £365, with some £155 derived from spiritualities (mainly income from appropriated churches) and the rest from the manors.[14] In addition, the combined income of the dignitaries and prebendaries was in the region of £200. Their individual values varied considerably, depending on their specific endowments. The precentorship was the most valuable post, worth £25 14s. 5d. At the other extreme was the prebend held by Alan de Creppinge, Pratum Minus, which amounted to one truss of hay, worth 2d. a year.[15]

In 1535 the figures are different. The common fund's total clear value was £423 17s. 2¼d., with the overall total before deductions being £518 0s. 4¾d. (Over a third of this sum, £190 17s. 1¼d., reflects the value of grain received in kind.) The individual prebends and dignities are again separately recorded, with the precentorship now being worth £21 19s. 5d. Pratum Minus had crept up to a massive 16d. (but, as in 1291, this excluded small commons). Episcopi was actually worthless, its sole receipts being the commons.[16]

For all its seeming detail, the *Valor* simplifies the cathedral's finances. The canons' resources were many, scattered and various. Their property holding was complex, comprising a mixture of appropriated churches, lands and rent charges. Administration was equally complex, although for the larger properties and the tithes of churches usually simplified by a policy of leasing. Virtually all the income was made available for division among the residentiaries, from the offerings and money received from sales of heriots to the receipts from the sale of the profits

12. Ibid., pp. 242–43.

13. R. N. Swanson, 'Devotional Offerings at Hereford Cathedral in the Late Middle Ages', *Analecta Bollandiana*, 111 (1993), p. 94.

14. S. Ayscough and J. Caley, eds, *Taxatio ecclesiastica Angliae et Walliae auctoritate P. Nicholai IV, circa AD 1291* (London, 1802),

pp. 157, 168.

15. Ibid., pp. 168–70. The canons' incomes would be increased by the allowance for their little commons.

16. J. Caley and J. Hunter, eds, *Valor ecclesiasticus* (6 vols, London, 1810–34), iii, pp. 5–11.

of Hereford mill. The latter exemplify the small scale and miscellaneous nature of some revenues, for they included not only the sales of grain, received as mill tolls, but also the sales of eels (and the occasional salmon) caught at the mill weir.[17]

Similar in scale was a miscellaneous amalgam of rent-charges and petty receipts intended to fund obits and chantries, for which the chapter essentially acted as trustee. Characteristic was the collection of small rents recorded in the early fourteenth-century cartulary of William de la Hay's chantry, accumulated during his life and by his executors after death, and held by the chapter to the use of the vicar serving the chantry.[18] Very different were the manors and appropriated churches, which provided most of the canons' income.

A detailed history of chapter revenues from 1268 to 1535 cannot be attempted here. The general trend was downward, matching that for manorial and rectorial incomes across the country, especially in the period after the Black Death. The chapter had to acknowledge and respond to the new circumstances, as did individual canons and the other cathedral clergy.[19]

While all canons received little commons and some of the other dues (including the mass pence if they attended services),[20] most of the income was channelled to the residentiaries. Even if, compared to other cathedrals, 'at Hereford both the common fund and the prebends were exceptionally poor',[21] the residentiaries' incomes were not negligible. The *Valor ecclesiasticus* shared their dues among seven people, allowing each £68 11s. 1d., which was certainly not insignificant. However, this was not a stable (or in fact equal) annual income. The wide range of sources meant that incomes varied from year to year. As the central accountant commented in 1409: 'no canon knows the amount of his portion due to him until after the final account of the year is given, and then each canon holds himself content with whatever the portion then assigned to him, whether more or less'.[22] Values and revenues changed annually, depending on receipts, and on how many people were entitled to a share. Some receipts were unpredictable, like the oblations in the cathedral, the value of heriots sold (effectively a form of death duty), and the profits from the mills. Distribution rates also changed: those for mass pence, for instance, altered considerably. They were initially entered at 4d. per mass, but went into a lasting decline in the fifteenth century. By the 1450s the payment was 1¼d. a mass, and under Henry VIII less than 1d.[23] The real value of the grain

---

17. HCA, 2400–5.
18. Oxford, Bodleian, MS Jones 23.
19. For the trends, see above, n. 4. For links between the economic changes and the changing number of residentiaries, see Edwards, *Secular Cathedrals*, p. 74.

20. Ibid., p. 43.
21. Ibid., p. 267.
22. Capes, *Charters*, pp. 264–65; Edwards, *Secular Cathedrals*, p. 243.
23. HCA, R 437, R 488, R 556, R 575.

payments was also variable. The *Valor ecclesiasticus* valued the wheat and barley of the common fund respectively at 8½*d*. and 2½*d*. per bushel;[24] but the price was not static. In the mill account of 1412–13, wheat sold at 6*d*. or 6½*d*. a bushel; in that of 1508–9, it ranged from 4*s*. to 6*s*. 6*d*. a quarter (6*d*. to 9¾*d*. a bushel).[25]

Rental incomes also changed, as shown by the rents of the common fund, comprising rents and rent charges from properties within Hereford and rents, pensions and other income from outside the city. The picture appears generally healthy in the early fourteenth century;[26] but by mid century difficulties are evident: the chapter properties in Castle Street were being let at reduced rents, which fell further after the Black Death.[27] The fifteenth century reveals further problems, with rents in decline and often unpaid, and with properties apparently in decay. In both city and countryside, there was a lack of tenants.[28] The chapter's 'internal market' also caused difficulties for individual accountants. The receiver of common rents thereby confronted a classic pincer effect: despite his falling income, he still had to support the obits funded from rent charges by transfers to another cathedral official.

Farms of the larger properties, the rectories and manors, also declined. In 1450–51 the tithe farm of Sellack and Baysham produced £6 6*s*. 8*d*., having previously been worth over £12. By 1477–78 the figure was £6, by 1528–29 £5.[29] The practical value of these properties might be upheld to some degree by demanding payment in grain rather than cash, to supply the canons' commons. Accordingly, leases stipulate deliveries of wheat and barley to the cathedral to provide the commons allowances, sometimes without any mention of a cash payment.[30]

Blunt non-payment was also a problem. As early as 1319–20 a general threat of excommunication was issued for arrears of the common rents. (Similar threats were also made later in the period.) In 1456–57, Marjorie Holand was eighteen years behind in rent payments of 4*s*. 6*d*. a year; while Ralph Baskervyle owed £6 8*s*. 0*d*. for rent unpaid for sixteen years.[31] Clerics were equally reluctant payers: by Michaelmas 1536 the vicar of Peterstow owed £19 6*s*. 8*d*. for pension unpaid for twenty-nine years.[32] Sometimes the complexity of the chapter's city holdings defeated the accountant. A comment in 1327–28 hints at poor recording of locations and tenants' names;[33] in the mid fifteenth century unpaid rents (or, more likely,

24. Caley and Hunter, eds, *Valor ecclesiasticus*, iii, p. 5.
25. HCA, 2402, 2405.
26. E.g. HCA, R 124–25.
27. HCA, R 135–40.
28. HCA, R 160 records a lack of takers at Clehonger in 1456–57; R 164, for 1468–69, mentions a shortage of tenants at Holme Lacy and elsewhere.
29. HCA, R 488, R 515, R 568.
30. E.g. HCA, 1846, 1882.
31. HCA, R 160; see also J. H. Parry, ed., *Registrum Johannis Gilbert, episcopi Herefordensis, AD MCCCLXXV–MCCCLXXXIX*, Canterbury and York Society, 18 (London, 1915), pp. 7–8, 12–13.
32. HCA, R 575.
33. HCA, R 126–27.

rent charges) appear with the comment *nescitur ubi iacet* – 'whereabouts unknown'.[34] However, some non-payments were accounting fictions. In the common rent accounts the steward and bailiff had their rents remitted; the chapter sometimes gave a tenancy at a reduced rent; occasionally a property was held by a vicar serving a chantry as part of his income.[35]

The continued receipt of payments in kind is a notable aspect of Hereford's late medieval accounts. All went to the keeper of the canons' bakehouse, much then being redistributed as part of the canons' commons. Some was sold, but not much. Some went to lesser clergy and cathedral dependents, including vicars in the appropriated churches. The wheat for the communion wafers at the cathedral derived from these receipts, as did the grain for the simnels on St Milburga's day (23 February). Finally, a considerable amount was actually baked, to provide loaves for the canons, the vicars and others.[36]

At the centre of the cathedral's life, and therefore of its history, were the canons, particularly the residentiaries. They were the chief beneficiaries of the endowments; they were responsible for their oversight and administration, and for their transmission to the next generation in good condition.[37] They had to defend the cathedral, its rights and properties, against foes, intruders, and aggressors – sometimes among their own ranks.

The Hereford chapter, like those of the other eight secular cathedrals, was dominated by members of the higher clergy, the elite of the late medieval church. Able and established clerics, they were highly educated with successful careers in the service of the church or crown by the time they became canons. Possession of a canonry was a highly desirable reward and mark of status, much sought after by ambitious clerks. The right to appoint canons and dignitaries, with the exception of the dean who was elected by the chapter, lay with the bishop. However, both the king and the pope were able to encroach on this and the composition of the chapter was partly determined by them. For the aspiring canon there were in practice four principal routes to a canonry: collation by the bishop, royal grant,

34. E.g. HCA, R 160.
35. E.g. HCA, R 125, special reductions; R 160 (and following accounts), 51s. 4d. allowed to John Dore, celebrant at the altar of Holy Cross, for his tenement in Milkelane.
36. E.g. HCA, R 630. Although there is solid evidence for the baking, there are no signs of communal brewing: presumably the canons organised that individually.

37. Members of the chapter (or their executors) who did not maintain their properties might face claims for dilapidations: Parry, ed., *Reg. Mascall*, pp. 45–46, 91; A. T. Bannister, ed., *Registrum Caroli Bothe, episcopi Herefordensis, AD MDXVI–MDXXXV*, Canterbury and York Society, 28 (London, 1921), pp. 68–69; HCA, 3186 (unfoliated, see fos 1v–2, 4v–5r); HCA, Baylis, i, fos 63v–64r.

provision by the pope and by exchange
of benefices.[38] Access to all four routes
lay through the networks of patronage
and kinship that were such a central
feature of medieval society. Appointment by the bishop was the commonest
route, especially after 1400 when the
direct intervention of the king and
the pope at Hereford virtually ceased.
Though the bishops' registers record
episcopal collation as the normal method
of appointment, there was considerable
pressure from popes, kings and lay
magnates, as well as ambitious clerics,
to grant canonries.

Royal interventions were largely
confined to the periods when the see
was vacant, during which the king took
over the bishop's rights of patronage.
At Hereford these vacancies were
usually short, lasting a few months, but
they enabled the king to promote some
of his leading officials. Royal influence
also extended to papal provisions, many
of which were made at the king's request. Bishops found it hard to resist
royal requests and the presence of many

Fig. 13. Cast of dean and chapter seal impression,
dated 1394, with the cathedral's joint patrons
St Mary and St Ethelbert. It shows the Virgin and
child, and beneath a broken effigy of St Ethelbert
holding his severed head. (HCA, 6460.)

royal clerks among the chapter suggests their status contributed significantly to
their appointment. Papal influence on the composition of the chapter was smaller
than the crown's and confined to the fourteenth century, with provisions reaching
a peak in the half century after 1325. Hereford, however, received fewer provisions
than other cathedrals, even ones of comparable size and status, a reflection of its
relative poverty and remoteness.[39] Exchange was the only route to a canonry that
did not need the active support of a patron, though in theory the bishop's approval
was necessary to effect one. Once in possession of a benefice, a cleric could
exchange it for a canonry. This tended to be done either by ambitious clerics for

38. For a fuller discussion of methods of
    appointment see D. N. Lepine, *A Brother-*
    hood of Canons Serving God: English
    Secular Cathedrals in the Later Middle Ages
    (Woodbridge, 1995), chapter 2.

39. J. R. Wright, *The Church and the English*
    Crown, 1305–34 (Toronto, 1980), pp. 278,
    282.

immediate career advantage, sometimes for financial gain, or by those anxious to settle at the cathedral.

Although Hereford was a relatively small and often disturbed diocese on the Welsh Marches, the cathedral drew many canons from within it.[40] The chapter reflected the strong sense of place and loyalty to it widely felt in the later middle ages. Nearly a third (31 per cent) of those with known geographical origins (some two-thirds of canons) came from the diocese of Hereford. The strength of the cathedral's influence is clearer still from a regional analysis: 42 per cent came from the Severn and Wye valleys, the counties of Herefordshire, Worcestershire, Gloucestershire, Shropshire and Monmouthshire. This commitment to the mother church was strongest among the residentiaries, nearly two-thirds of whom (61 per cent) were from the diocese and three-quarters from the Severn and Wye valleys. Canons from outside the diocese originated from the rest of the country fairly evenly, with larger numbers, as might be expected, coming from the larger dioceses of Lichfield, Lincoln and York. Yet even these scarcely account for 10 per cent each. Foreign canons were rare, except in the mid thirteenth century, and confined to a handful of French and Italians. Welshmen were more numerous, and there were more canons from Wales than from Yorkshire. These aspiring clerics looked to Hereford and England for advancement and a third of them were appointed by the two Welsh bishops of Hereford, John Trillek (1344–60) and John Trefnant (1389–1404).[41] The main exception to this general pattern occurred when a bishop from outside the diocese brought his own men with him. The most contentious was Bishop Peter of Aigueblanche (1240–68), who filled the chapter with canons from Savoy, his birthplace.[42] Bishop Swinfield (1283–1317) appointed a large contingent of sixteen southerners from his native Kent; and Bishop Spofford (1422–48) more modestly introduced seven from Yorkshire having connections with St Mary's Abbey, York, where he was abbot before becoming bishop.[43]

40. The methods used for ascertaining the geographical origins of canons are set out in D. N. Lepine, 'The Origins and Careers of the Canons of Exeter Cathedral 1300–1455', in C. Harper-Bill, ed., *Religious Belief and Ecclesiastical Careers in Late Medieval England* (Woodbridge, 1991), pp. 88–92.

41. Trillek came from Monmouthshire, A. B. Emden, *A Biographical Register of the University of Oxford to 1500* (3 vols, Oxford, 1957–9), iii, p. 1906; and Trefnant from the diocese of St Asaph, W. E. Lunt and E. B. Graves, eds, *Accounts Rendered by Papal Collectors in England, 1317–78*, Memoirs of

the American Philosophical Society, 70 (Philadelphia, Pennsylvania, 1968), p. 422.

42. See above, Chapter 2, p. 46.

43. Swinfield's appointments were his kinsmen Gilbert, John (fig. 14) and Richard, Robert Canterbury, Thomas Cobham, Simon Faversham, Stephen Gravesend, Robert Icklesham, Richard Nonnington, Hamo Sandwich, William Sarden, John Selling, Roger Sevenoaks, Henry Shorne, Stephen Thaneto and John Winchelsea. Spofford's appointments were William Beford, William Hambald, Thomas Makeblith, Nicholas Mallon, Richard Martin, Henry Newton and Richard Rotherham.

Fig. 14. The rebus of Precentor John Swinfield, died 1311, on his tomb in the retrochoir, showing a pun on his name with swine feeding on acorns. The pigs are painted with the arms of the dean and chapter.

Though we know relatively little about their social origins, it is clear that the chapter was mainly drawn from the upper, landowning levels of medieval society. A handful were born into baronial families, especially local ones from the diocese; members of the Charlton, Mortimer and Talbot families were a significant presence in the fourteenth century.[44] Those from the lesser aristocracy, from the ranks of knight, esquire and gentleman, were a larger and more influential group. Some came from prominent and politically active families. More typical were the sons of local families, few of whom were unrepresented in the course of the later middle ages, among them the Barres, Baskervilles, Burleys, Caples, Chaundoses, Delaberes, Hacluits, Pembridges, Vaughans, Whitneys and

44. Five members of the Charlton family were canons between 1317 and 1385: Griffin, Humphrey, Lewis, Thomas and William. Lewis and Thomas later became bishops: J. M. Horn, ed., *John le Neve, Fasti ecclesiae Anglicanae, 1300–1541*, ii: *Hereford Diocese* (London, 1962), pp. 1, 14, 15, 17, 40, 50. Three members of the Mortimer family became canons between 1273 and 1332 including Edmund (d. 1304) who resigned his prebend on inheriting the lordship of Wigmore in 1282 (ibid., pp. 17, 19, 24; Emden, *Oxford*, ii, p. 1316). The Talbot influence lasted longer, from 1300 to 1417 when four members of the family were canons, Horn, ed., *Le Neve, Fasti, 1300–1541*, ii: *Hereford*, pp. 6, 9, 41, 44, 46, 50.

Fig. 15. Retrochoir looking
north, with south-east transept
and the tomb of Bishop Lewis
Charlton to the right.
J. Britton, *The History and
Antiquities of the Cathedral
Church of Hereford* (London,
1831), plate V.

Walwayns.[45] Their membership strengthened the local roots of the cathedral and
reinforced its standing in the diocese. Less prominent landowners, what might be
described as the parish gentry of the Severn and Wye valleys, were also plentiful:
William Sheynton (d. 1367) held the manor of Sheinton near Much Wenlock; and
William Huntlowe took his name from the Gloucestershire village of Huntley
where his family owned land.[46] Several from this background were non-aristocratic
and were small-scale landowners or tenant farmers, the franklins and yeomen as
they came to be called. Those from an urban background also came largely from
its upper levels, the merchants and master craftsmen who made up the ruling

45. Laurence and Richard de la Barre, Edward
    Baskerville, Simon Burley, William Caple,
    Richard Chaundos, Thomas Chaundos
    senior and junior, William Delabere,
    Thomas Hacluit, Thomas Pembridge,
    Hugh Vaughan, Baldwin Whitney,

Nicholas Walwayn (Walwen) (ibid.,
    passim).
46. *Calendar of Inquisitions Post Mortem and
    Other Analogous Documents Preserved in the
    Public Record Office*, xii: *Edward III* (Lon-
    don, 1938), no. 168; HCA, 257.

oligarchy. John Rosse (d. 1332), later bishop of Carlisle, was the son of Roger le Mercer of Ross-on-Wye and Hugh Webbe, the brother of Archdeacon William Webbe (d. 1523), was a Hungerford draper.[47] Until the early sixteenth century relatively few seem to have come from Hereford families, but by this time the ruling oligarchy and chapter had close ties and the Benlloyde, Chipnam and Marbulle families were members of both. None of the chapter is known to have come from a non-landowning or poor urban background.

As the cathedral was one of the most important educational centres in the diocese, it is not surprising to find that its chapter was highly educated. Although, unfortunately, almost nothing is known about the early education of the canons, all would have received a grounding in Latin and many went on to university; two-thirds of the canons had a university education. Furthermore, the proportion of graduates rose during the later middle ages and it was increasingly rare for non-graduates to be appointed after 1450. More than half the graduates gained a higher degree, with nearly 30 per cent having doctorates. Many had spent long periods of their early life at university, as a higher degree required a minimum of ten years' study. Their choice of discipline was strongly practical with law dominating: 45 per cent of graduates studied either civil or canon law. For the ambitious cleric there were many opportunities in royal and diocesan administration for the legal graduate. Theologians were relatively few and far between and, before the sixteenth century, were scarce among the residentiaries. The overwhelming majority of graduates studied at Oxford, reflecting its strong links with the west of England from where it recruited many of its students; only a handful attended Cambridge or foreign universities.

By the time they received their prebends most Hereford canons, as many as two-thirds, were experienced administrators in the service of either the crown or the church. Service to the king, which occupied over a quarter of the chapter, ranged from the relatively humble 'king's clerk', whose duties are unknown, to trusted diplomats and senior office holders.[48] Many of the non-resident canons were royal civil servants who had only a nominal connection with the cathedral. Some, however, on retirement brought their experience to the Close. After more than twenty years' service first in Wales in the 1280s, and later in the household of Queen Isabella, Hugh Leominster (d. 1327) was resident at Hereford for the last eight years of his life.[49] Over a third of canons were ecclesiastical civil servants.

47. Emden, *Oxford*, iii, pp. 1590–91; PRO, PROB 11/21, fol. 15r.

48. For further discussion of this see Lepine, *Brotherhood of Canons*, pp. 83–86.

49. W. Brown, ed., *The Register of Thomas of Corbridge, Lord Archbishop of York, 1300–1304*, Surtees Society, 138, 141 (2 vols, Durham and London, 1925–28), i, p. 272; W. W. Capes, ed., *Registrum Ricardi de Swinfield, episcopi Herefordensis, AD MCCLXXXIII–MCCCXVII*, Canterbury and York Society, 6 (London, 1909), p. 444; HCA, R 408–13.

Diocesan administrators were usually amongst the first to be rewarded with canonries by grateful bishops; virtually all senior office-holders gained prebends. At Hereford 20 per cent of the chapter were in the bishop's service and as many as three-quarters of them entered residence, demonstrating their strong commitment both to the diocese and cathedral. Humphrey Ogle started as Bishop Booth's chaplain in 1518, became a canon in 1521 and was appointed vicar general in 1526.[50] While vicar general he usually managed to spend four or five months a year at the cathedral and was fully resident after leaving office.[51] Some 15 per cent of canons were employed elsewhere in the church by other bishops, the archbishops of Canterbury and York, or the pope. Many, often the most able (like their counterparts in the royal civil service), had little to do with the cathedral. Magnate service was a third type of employment open to ambitious clerics, though it was not as widely practised by Hereford canons as royal and ecclesiastical service. Senior clergy were commonly chosen to serve in positions of trust, as executors and trustees in land transactions. Resident canons had particularly close associations with the leading families of the diocese. John Prat (d. 1416) settled at Hereford in 1390 and remained there for the rest of his life, serving as a trustee of William Beauchamp, lord of Abergavenny, and as Sir Thomas Walwayn's executor.[52]

The success of Hereford canons in their careers can be measured in the number of benefices they held. Most had acquired several by the time they had gained their prebends, ranging from parish churches to prebends in other cathedrals or collegiate churches. They were successful pluralists holding at least one other benefice as well as their Hereford canonry. The most prominent held several canonries and a series of parish churches, from which they derived a considerable income. Christopher Plummer (fl. 1490–1536) is typical of them: as a royal chaplain he collected four cathedral canonries, six rectories and a prebend at Windsor.[53] For many, half the chapter, their Hereford prebend was the high point of their career and they gained no other cathedral canonries. John Bridwode's career was spent in loyal service to the Mortimer earls of March, from whom he received his first benefice, Old Radnor, in 1363.[54] It was probably at their request that he gained a papal provision to a Hereford canonry in 1371, which brought him the

50. A. B. Emden, *A Biographical Register of the University of Oxford, AD 1501–1540* (Oxford, 1974), p. 423; Bannister, ed., *Reg. Bothe*, p. 52.

51. HCA, R 566–76.

52. J. Duncumb, *Collections towards the History and Antiquities of the County of Hereford* (8 vols, Hereford and London, 1804–1915), ii, p. 63; Capes, ed., *Reg. Trefnant*, p. 30.

53. Plummer is not listed as a canon in Horn, ed., *Le Neve, Fasti, 1300–1541*, ii: *Hereford*, but occurs in 1500–1 and 1501–2 (HCA, R 540–41). His career is set out in Emden, *Oxford*, iii, p. 1487.

54. J. H. Parry, ed., *Registrum Ludowici de Charltone, episcopi Herefordensis, AD MCCCLXI–MCCCLXX*, Canterbury and York Society, 14 (London, 1914), p. 66.

prebend of Hampton in 1375.[55] He remained at Hereford and in the service of the Mortimers until his death in 1388.[56]

The reputation of non-resident canons, many of them leading ecclesiastical and royal administrators, has generally been low. To their critics they appear as absentee drones, readily taking the income of their prebends but contributing little in return. While this is true for some, the detail of the Hereford accounts enables us to see a more complete picture. Nearly half (42 per cent) of non-residents visited the cathedral, most taking the trouble to be installed personally. Even the busy and distinguished canon lawyer William Lyndwood travelled to Hereford in 1423–24 on his appointment, despite his commitments in the service of the archbishop of Canterbury and the king that year.[57] A handful practised what amounted to partial residence, regularly spending up to three months a year at Hereford.[58] Though many non-residents had little to do with the cathedral, the chapter found them useful as it was able to seek advice from senior and influential officials. The presence of Richard Martin on the Council of the Marches in 1473, and twenty years later of John Arundel and John Argentine in the household of Prince Arthur, based at Ludlow, was no doubt helpful in pursuing the chapter's interests.[59]

The community of resident canons formed the core of the cathedral: leading the worship, supervising the administration and dispensing hospitality. During the thirteenth century all chapters made a clear distinction between residents and non-residents, accepting the fact that a significant proportion of the chapter would be absent on royal or ecclesiastical business. Residence and participation in the liturgy was encouraged by setting aside part of the chapter's resources, the common fund, to make special payments to residentiaries. At Hereford these were set out together with the minimum requirements for residence in the statutes of 1264.[60] To qualify for full residence a canon had to be present for thirty-six weeks a year (the sixteen weeks' absence could not be taken consecutively) and to attend

55. Bridwode is not listed in Horn, ed., *Le Neve, Fasti, 1300–1542*, ii: *Hereford*, but was granted a papal provision on 26 March 1371 (Lunt and Graves, *Accounts of Papal Collectors*, pp. 424, 497) and occurs as a canon from 1375 to 1387/8 (HCA, R 442–52).

56. He acted as feoffee in 1374, BL, MS Harley 1240, fos 46v–47, and as executor in 1383, Parry, ed., *Reg. Gilbert*, p. 117.

57. Emden, *Oxford*, ii, pp. 1191–93; HCA, R 475.

58. Robert Bygge, for example, attended 164 masses at Hereford in 1532–33, fifty-one in

1533–34, sixteen in 1534–35, ninety-four in 1535–36, ninety-one in 1536–37 and twenty-two in 1537–38, HCA, R 571–77.

59. Emden, *Oxford*, ii, p. 1236; ibid., i, pp. 50–51. Argentine is not listed in Horn, ed., *Le Neve, Fasti, 1300–1541*, ii: *Hereford*, but occurs as a canon from 1498/9–1500/1, HCA, R 537–40. For his career see A. B. Emden, *A Biographical Register of the University of Cambridge to 1500* (Cambridge, 1963), pp. 15–16.

60. These are discussed in Edwards, *Secular Cathedrals*, chapter 1.

Fig. 16. The late medieval
chapter house, built between
1364 and 1382: reconstruction
of the interior drawn by the
eighteenth-century antiquary
William Stukeley in 1721.
(Oxford, Bodleian, MS Top. gen.
d.13, fol. 24v; HCL, neg. 146.)

matins each day. These were amongst the most rigorous requirements at any
cathedral. In return residentiaries received 'greater commons', payments of bread
and money allocated from particular estates. In addition they were entitled to 'little
commons' – a share of bread, grain and 20s. a year – and 'mass pence' which
were also available to non-resident canons. Residentiaries also shared the distributions
of the surplus income from the chapter's common fund.[61]

Residence flourished from the 1270s to the 1330s when between a third and
half the chapter, ten to fourteen canons, were resident.[62] In peak years there were
sixteen or seventeen canons present in the Close, and occasionally twenty in
the 1290s. This was a period of economic prosperity and vigorous activity in the

61. Above, pp. 51–52.
62. The methods used for calculating residence levels and the particular problems encountered at
    Hereford are set out in Lepine, *Brotherhood of Canons*, pp. 199–200.

cathedral, when it was an important pilgrim shrine, as well as a time of major rebuilding. Some decline occurred in the 1340s, before the Black Death, when numbers fell to ten or eleven. These levels were sustained until the beginning of the fifteenth century. Further decline set in during the mid 1410s, after which it was unusual for there to be more than a quarter of the chapter, seven canons, resident. From the 1420s to the 1540s there were normally at least four canons in residence and eight or nine in good years. The 1420s to the early 1450s were difficult years with only four or five resident, but for the next forty years, until the early 1490s, there was often a quarter of the chapter present. There was another lean period from the mid 1490s for a decade, when there might only be three residentiaries, followed by some recovery after 1505 to between six and eight. Apart from a temporary falling off in the later 1520s, this was sustained through the 1530s. Residence was by no means moribund at Hereford on the eve of the Reformation. By comparison with other cathedrals, residence levels at Hereford were healthy but not outstanding.[63] Overall, almost a third of the chapter entered residence, though for much of the fifteenth and early sixteenth centuries the average was a quarter. Hereford never reached the sustained high levels found at Exeter and Wells, matching instead the moderate levels found at Lincoln, Salisbury and Lichfield, but avoiding the persistently low levels of St Paul's and York.

Residence was not entered into lightly. It required a formal request to and acceptance by the chapter, and the payment of an entry fine of 100 marks; it also involved considerable obligations of hospitality. Those who chose to become residentiaries made a major commitment to the cathedral that for some spanned decades and generally lasted until they died. When John Grene died in 1472 he had been resident for fifty years.[64] While few could match such an extraordinary commitment, many spent long periods in the Close; a quarter of all residentiaries, most of them from the Severn and Wye valleys, resided for at least twenty years. In addition it was common to find canons present for almost the whole year. Successive deans set an example that was rarely equalled at other cathedrals: non-residents occupied the deanery for only twenty-five years from 1310 to 1541.[65]

The residentiaries of later medieval England have been seen by some as the forerunners of Barchester, living comfortable, complacent and undistinguished lives in the Close; the 'good vianders' indulging in 'superfluous belly cheer' complained of by Archbishop Cranmer in 1539.[66] Though harsh and an oversimplification this view has at least a grain of truth. They certainly lived comfortably and expansively,

63. Ibid., pp. 95–100.
64. HCA, R 472–508.
65. Thomas Felde (1404–19), James Goldwell (1462–63), Oliver King (1491), Reginald West (*c.* 1503–*c.* 1507), and Thomas Wolsey

(*c.* 1509–12).
66. J. E. Cox, ed., *Miscellaneous Writings and Letters of Thomas Cranmer*, Parker Society (Cambridge, 1846), pp. 396–97.

reflecting both their birth and their status as canons. An open and liberal lifestyle was necessary to fulfil the duty of hospitality, an important obligation of residence. Dressed in their best scarlet gowns with fur-lined hoods and accompanied by a small retinue, they made a striking impression.[67] Their houses were substantial buildings with halls for entertaining, private rooms and a chapel; several halls still survive inside later buildings.[68] From their wills we can picture the luxury that made their lives comfortable, the silver cups and spoons on their tables, the tapestries on their walls, the cushions and fine covers on their beds. A household of four to six servants was thought necessary to maintain the lifestyle considered appropriate to the dignity and status of a residentiary; in larger households they would be liveried. Archdeacon William Webbe's was unusually large with fifteen at his death in 1523. The presence in it of three members of leading gentry families of the diocese and a kinsman of the bishop indicates the high standing in the community enjoyed by canons.[69]

To medieval residentiaries there was no contradiction between their lifestyles and their religious duties. They had a religious vocation and a genuine, if utterly conventional, piety which they expressed by entering residence and increasing 'divine worship'. As well as the private devotions in their chapels, they worshipped in the cathedral regularly; the accounts show that many attended over 300 masses a year. Some canons were aware of and contributed to new liturgical and devotional developments. John Leche, a residentiary from 1480–90, observed the feast of the Visitation of the Blessed Virgin Mary.[70] By the early sixteenth century newer Christocentric devotions such as the Five Wounds and the Name of Jesus were practised.[71] There were preachers and pastors (sermons were regularly given on feast days); Hugh Charnock's skill as a preacher was recognised in an indulgence offered to all who heard him; Robert Geoffrey was repeatedly appointed to hear confessions as a parish priest in Devon.[72] Two canons gave up residence for a more rigorous regime in a religious house: Nicholas Hereford in 1417 for the austerities of the

---

67. William Burghill's best gown was crimson lined with scarlet, PRO, PROB 11/22, fol. 77.

68. Canons' houses and households are discussed in Lepine, *Brotherhood of Canons*, Chapter 6; see also below, Chapter 11, pp. 299–304.

69. PRO, PROB 11/21, fol. 15r. William Mayew, a kinsman of Bishop Mayew and two members of leading Herefordshire gentry families, Eustace Walwayn and James Baskerville, both styled gentleman, are listed as members of his household.

70. R. W. Pfaff, *New Liturgical Feasts in Later Medieval England* (Oxford, 1970), pp. 46–47, 50–51.

71. David Walker, PRO, PROB 11/31, fol. 302; and William Burghill, PRO, PROB 11/22, fol. 77.

72. Bannister, ed., *Reg. Bothe*, p. 207; Geoffrey was regularly appointed a penitentiary from 1450–55: G. Dunstan, ed., *The Register of Edmund Lacy, Bishop of Exeter, 1420–55: Registrum Commune*, Canterbury and York Society, 60–63, 66 (5 vols, 1963–72), iii, pp. 65, 99, 138, 164, 194, 206.

Charterhouse at Coventry, and Thomas Chipnam in 1516 for St Mary's Southwark.[73] The conservative religious outlook of residentiaries is evident in their devotion to saints: the Virgin Mary, St Anne and St Katherine were the most popular. William Lochard promoted the cult of St George in his chantry chapel in the 1430s but he also venerated the cathedral's own saints, St Ethelbert and St Thomas.[74] This local pride was expressed on the eve of the Reformation in the memorial brasses of William Porter and Edmund Frowcester, both of which included images of the cathedral's saints (fig. 26).[75] Education was a particular concern at Hereford and the statutes encouraged residentiaries to take study leave.[76] As well as training future generations in their households during their lifetimes, an unusually high proportion made provision for education in their wills. The beneficiaries included kinsmen, servants, cathedral clergy, godchildren, the city and the diocese. Dean Frowcester singled out two of the most promising choristers.[77]

The resident chapter at Hereford was never as distinguished as the community of scholars which flourished at Salisbury in the first half of the fifteenth century. Its membership was much more modest and mainly drawn from able local men engaged in diocesan administration. However, though it was remote, it was not entirely a provincial backwater, and some outstanding figures came to Hereford. In the early fourteenth century the saintly James Berkeley (d. 1327), a future bishop of Exeter around whom an unofficial posthumous cult grew, was resident for a decade, and the chronicler Adam Murimuth was a frequent visitor in the 1320s and briefly resident in 1333.[78] Chancellor Nicholas Hereford's experience was wider than most. When a student at Oxford he took up Wyclif's ideas for which he was condemned in 1382, suffering two periods of imprisonment. After his recantation and absolution in 1391 he returned to Hereford and took an active part in rooting out Lollardy.[79] The resident community in the half century after 1450 shows the chapter at its best, a body of conscientious and learned ecclesiastics. Richard Rudhale's career exemplifies their qualities, rooted in his native diocese but acquiring much wider experience with which he enriched life in the Close. A local man from near Ross-on-Wye, he studied first at Oxford and later at Padua, graduating

73. Emden, *Oxford*, ii, pp. 913–15; ibid., i, p. 418.

74. *Calendar of the Patent Rolls, Henry VI* (6 vols, London, 1901–10), iii, p. 549; PRO, PROB 11/3, fos 202v–203v.

75. RCHME, *Herefordshire*, i, p. 106.

76. This was still practised in the early sixteenth century. The first surviving chapter act book contains several examples, HCA, Baylis, i, fos 28v, 46r.

77. PRO, PROB 11/23, fol. 56r.

78. Berkeley was at Hereford from 1313–24, HCA, R 410–13. For his career see Emden, *Oxford*, i, pp. 174–75, and for his cult N. I. Orme, 'Two Saint-Bishops of Exeter: James Berkeley and Edmund Lacy', *Analecta Bollandiana*, 104 (1986), pp. 403–18. Adam Murimuth spent time at Hereford from 1324/5 to 1333/4, HCA, R 413–19. For his career see Emden, *Oxford*, ii, pp. 1329–30.

79. Ibid., ii, pp. 913–15.

Fig. 17. The memorial brass of Dr Richard Rudhale, died 1476, archdeacon of Hereford and residentiary canon, south-east transept. The cathedral library contains his law books, many with his annotations.

with a doctorate in canon law in 1442 (fig. 17).[80] While in Italy he collected, commissioned and partly copied legal texts, several of which survive in the cathedral library today. Rudhale was an inveterate annotator of his books, often highlighting points that supported his view against the opinions of fellow residentiaries.[81] Unusually, he broke off residence from 1458 to 1460 to study further before returning to diocesan administration. His last years were spent at Hereford where he died in 1476. In death, as in life, he was both loyal and generous to the cathedral, giving £40 to the vicars, paying for repairs to St Katherine's chapel, presenting his legal texts to the library and commemorating its saints on his memorial brass. A loyal episcopal servant, it is perhaps fitting that he chose to be buried in front of the bishop's throne.[82] John Home, another native of the diocese, also brought wider intellectual horizons to the Close, having served as secretary to Humphrey, duke of Gloucester, the leading patron of humanism in the mid fifteenth century.[83] Dean Thomas Chandler was the most outstanding scholar to reside at Hereford. A distinguished humanist and skilled artist, he

80. Ibid., iii, p. 1603. For his origins see Duncumb, *Collections*, iii, p. 165.
81. Mynors and Thomson, *Catalogue*, pp. 49–50, 53–54, 56–57, 60–61, 75.
82. PRO, PROB 11/6, fol. 179; RCHME, *Herefordshire*, i, p. 106.
83. F. T. Havergal, *Monumental Inscriptions in the Cathedral Church of Hereford* (London, Walsall and Hereford, 1881), p. 40. For his geographical origins see HCA, 3200.

wrote several books and was chancellor of Oxford University before his election as dean in 1481 (fig. 18).[84]

Much of the residentiaries' time was taken up with running the chapter's affairs. The chapter was an important and privileged corporation with extensive estates and other interests to be protected and advanced. This could be both time-consuming and troublesome and involved a good deal of travelling and litigation. While most of the daily administration was carried out by competent and trusted members of the minor clergy, residentiaries were expected to hold the more senior offices and supervise them. Music flourished at Hereford in the early sixteenth century. The first chapter act book shows that particular care was taken to regulate and promote it.[85] Two musical canons, both of whom had studied music at Oxford, played a major part. John Mason, an active composer, some of whose motets have survived, was resident from 1525 until his death in 1548.[86] William Chell, a local man from the Malverns, owed his career entirely to the chapter. Beginning as a vicar choral in 1518, he was appointed succentor by 1526 and canon in 1533.[87] After their deaths most residentiaries were buried in the cathedral; many established obits or chantries and virtually all were benefactors in their wills. Amongst the most generous was William Lochard who, as well as founding a chantry, gave £100 for the glazing of a window and a gold 'tablet' of the Virgin and the Trinity to St Thomas's shrine.[88] In their loyalty and generosity they acknowledged the importance of the cathedral in their lives, as the focus of their devotion and the source of their income and status.

The canons, and the cathedral they served, did not exist in splendid isolation. The cathedral was, after all, the bishop's official seat. As bishop succeeded bishop, so the cathedral played its part in diocesan affairs. Relations with the bishops were generally good, with canons often acting as vicars general during episcopal absences.[89] The litigious Bishop Trefnant was more assertive than most, and there were clashes when the chapter felt that its status was under threat.[90] Most bishops found a last

84. Emden, *Oxford*, i, pp. 398–99.
85. HCA, Baylis, i, fos 10r, 36r, 37r, 39r, 65r. On music in the cathedral at this point, see also below, Chapter 21, pp. 389–93.
86. Emden, *Oxford, 1501–40*, pp. 386, 657; see also Chapter 21, p. 390.
87. HCA, Baylis, i, fos 14r, 38v; Emden, *Oxford, 1501–40*, p. 115; Bannister, ed., *Reg. Bothe*, p. 304. See also below, Chapter 21, p. 390.
88. PRO, PROB 11/3, fos 202v–203v.

89. E.g. A. T. Bannister, ed., *Registrum Ricardi Beauchamp, episcopum Herefordensis, AD MCCCCXLIX–MCCCCL*, Canterbury and York Society, 25 (London, 1919), p. 1; A. T. Bannister, ed., *Registrum Johannis Stanbury, episcopi Herefordensis, AD MCCCCLIII–MCCCCLXXIV*, Canterbury and York Society, 25 (London, 1919), p. 15; Bannister, ed., *Reg. Mayew*, p. 53.
90. Edwards, *Secular Cathedrals*, p. 108; Capes, ed., *Reg. Trefnant*, pp. 51–100; Bannister, ed., *Reg. Mayew*, pp. 96–97.

Fig. 18. Dean Thomas Chandler,
died 1490, presenting a copy of
his book to his patron Bishop
Beckington of Wells. A leading
humanist scholar, Chandler spent
the last decade of his life at
Hereford and was buried in the
south-east transept.
(Cambridge, Trinity College,
MS R.14.5, fol. 8v.)

resting place within the cathedral, if they had not, like William Courtenay, been
promoted elsewhere or, like Thomas Spofford, retired to a monastic life. Maintaining
the fiction that bishopric and cathedral were a unity, despite the earlier division
of the resources, the dean and chapter exercised their right and duty to approve
a range of episcopal actions, including leases and the appointment of officials.[91]

91. Capes, *Charters*, pp. xxiii–xxiv, 217–19; A. T. Bannister, ed., *Registrum Reginaldi Boulers, episcopi
    Herefordensis, AD MCCCCXLI–MCCCCLIII*, Canterbury and York Society, 25 (London, 1919),
    pp. 14–25; Bannister, ed., *Reg. Spofford*, pp. 142, 167, 173, 191–92; Parry, ed., *Reg. L. de Charleton*,
    pp. 41, 46–47; HCA, 1159, 2755; HCA, Baylis, i, fos 1v, 4r–v, 7v–8r, 13r, 23r, 25r, 28r, 30v–31v,
    32v, 34r, 38r, 65v, 66v, 69r–v, 70v, 71r–v, 72r–73r. Cf also HCA, 3185: capitular ratification of
    the introduction of the feast of St Raphael within the diocese. The bishop in a sense reciprocated
    this oversight in his control of the allocation and maintenance of the canonical houses: Edwards,
    Secular Cathedrals, p. 124.

Whether assent was ever refused is unknown; it is unlikely to have been recorded. The chapter also had custody of the archives and regalia of the see during vacancies, receiving them from one bishop for transmission to his successor.[92]

The bishops still technically appointed the canons (subject to assorted external influences), but too direct interference could draw protests.[93] They were also occasionally asked to arbitrate disputes within the chapter, despite regulations to keep such disputes for internal resolution.[94] In general, though, episcopal intervention was minimal. The right to visitation was virtually extinguished: although fifteenth-century bishops tried to assert it, with papal backing, they failed, and the canons in their turn appealed to papal support for their own claims to exemption.[95] Yet the bishops were not excluded from the cathedral: they had to be enthroned. They might return to preach or to participate in services. On such occasions, they could even claim commons.[96]

While concerned about their relations with the bishop, the canons had also to oversee the lesser clergy in the cathedral. Here the sources prove particularly difficult: these minor clergy are much more elusive than the canons. Only with the appearance of the chapter act book in the sixteenth century can something approaching a decent picture be reconstructed. Hereford had few minor clergy, the *Valor ecclesiasticus* listing only six petty canons, the vicars choral, a subtreasurer and subchanter, and a number of chantry priests (several of whom doubled up as vicars choral). Before 1500, detailed information is limited. A light penetrates the shadows in 1407, with a tax return identifying the unbeneficed clergy (no cathedral returns survive for the clerical poll taxes of 1377–81). This names the twenty-one vicars choral then in post, and the clerics attached to the altars of St John, St Katherine and Mary Magdalene.[97] Striking in the St John's list is the name of a monk, Brother William. He is not a unique occurrence: in June 1395 the Benedictine William Spernore was a clerk of the chapel of St Mary when his fellow chapel clerics helped to clear him of a charge of adultery with a local woman.[98]

Control of the minor clergy was time-consuming, with disciplinary problems requiring frequent attention.[99] The chapter was an influence in many clerics' careers.

92. Bannister, ed., *Reg. Bothe*, pp. 10–11.
93. For appointment processes, see above pp. 54–56. For protest against episcopal interference, see e.g. HCA, Baylis, i, fos 71v–72r.
94. Capes, *Charters*, p. 170; Banister, ed., *Reg. Mayew*, pp. 181–85, 228–29; Edwards, *Secular Cathedrals*, p. 124.
95. Ibid., pp. 132–33; Bannister, ed., *Reg. Spofford*, p. 102; Bannister, ed., *Reg. Bothe*, pp. 130–32; HCA, Baylis, i, fol. 30r–v.

In fact, Bishop Beauchamp may have held a visitation in 1450: Bannister, ed., *Reg. Beauchamp*, p. 11.
96. Dohar, *Black Death*, p. 18; Bannister, ed., *Reg. Boulers*, pp. 16–17; but cf. Bannister, ed., *Reg. Spofford*, p. 46.
97. PRO, E 179/30/21.
98. HCA, 1492.
99. HCA, Baylis, i, fos 13v, 16v, 18r, 29v, 32r, 40r–41r, 46r, 61v, 64r–65r, 68v, 69v, 70v, 73v.

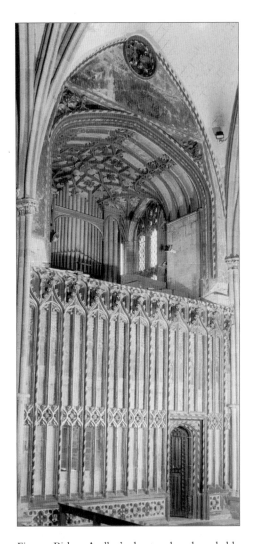

Fig. 19. Bishop Audley's chantry chapel, probably built between 1516 and 1524. Audley began his career as a canon of the cathedral in 1464 before becoming its bishop in 1492.

It gave ordination titles throughout the period, presumably mainly to cathedral clerics. The chapter also offered further patronage, but limited in extent.[100] As few prebends had appropriated churches, individual canons could not appoint to prebendal vicarages. The chapter had some advowsons collectively, but the leases of its appropriated rectories stipulated that the presentation to the vicarage was not among the devolved rights.[101] The patronage of churches specifically tied to dignities was retained by those dignitaries. Exercise of this patronage is noted in the first act book, particularly for the choral vicarages: sometimes there were disagreements over the candidates.[102]

While personnel figure largely in the records, the cathedral's prime function was spiritual, as a powerhouse of prayer and the bishopric's devotional centre. That spiritual life is rarely recorded: the administrative sources usually take it as read. One oddity was that the parish church of St John was actually located within the cathedral, even though the parochial services were disrupted by (and disrupted) the services in the cathedral choir.[103] Other sporadic references include notes of special celebrations at the Conversion of St Paul (25 January), St Laurence (3 February), Trinity (a movable feast), and the Commemoration of St Paul (30 June), with payments for choral 'repetitions' or antiphons appearing across the

100. Dohar, *Black Death*, pp. 110–11; HCA, Baylis, i, fol. 73r.
101. E.g. HCA, 3168.
102. HCA, Baylis, i, fos 24r, 28v–29r, 59r–60r, 61r. For an attempt to settle the patronage

problem, ibid., fos 69v–70r.
103. Above, Chapter 2, p. 41; Capes, ed., *Reg. Trefnant*, pp. 20–21; *Calendar of the Patent Rolls, Henry V* (2 vols, London, 1910–11), i, p. 226; Bannister, ed., *Reg. Bothe*, p. 365.

centuries.[104] Concern for the quality of liturgical performance appears in a statute of 1388 (reiterated in 1524) which required each canon to contribute 40s. to the provision of copes.[105] A hint on performance appears in the bakery accounts of Richard II's reign, with the vicar of St John receiving 1d. a day for 'ruling' the choir, while four vicars who played horns and harps (*cornulens et lirens*) each received 2d. a day.[106] One annual event on Holy Innocents' Day (27 December) was the appointment of a boy bishop, who received appropriate commons in the accounts.[107] Special liturgical events are occasionally mentioned. In December 1368, Bishop Lewis Charlton ordered prayers in the cathedral for the soul of Lionel of Clarence (one of Edward III's sons), offering forty days' indulgence to the participants. The prayers were also to be said throughout the diocese.[108]

Such post-mortem commemoration was an important element in the cathedral's life. The *Valor ecclesiasticus* notes the several chantries then functioning, and names their founders. Others may have already collapsed. Also important was the round of obit celebrations, which once a year offered masses and prayers for whoever had endowed the commemoration.[109] These were coordinated by a cathedral officer, but no accounts survive.[110] Some obits were perpetual, others short-term. In 1418 the dean and chapter undertook to celebrate an obit for John Hereford, archdeacon of Hereford, who had remitted a claim to £25 lent to them. That obit was to cost 10s. a year, until the expenditure had totalled £25.[111]

A key influence on the cathedral during these years was the canonisation of Thomas Cantilupe in 1320; to a great extent the late medieval period concides with Cantilupe's celestial career after his death in 1282. (How different Hereford's history would have been if Cantilupe had been buried where he died, at Ferento

---

104. They begin in the accounts for oblations and heriots, e.g. HCA, 2409, and continue in the account of mass pence, e.g. HCA, R 515. The cost increased from 14d. in the early fourteenth century to 20d. in the fifteenth.

105. HCA, 3186 (unfoliated, at fos 3r-v).

106. HCA, R 630.

107. The relevant entries in the accounts are abstracted in D. N. Klausner, ed., *Records of Early English Drama: Herefordshire, Worcestershire* (Toronto, Buffalo and London, 1990), pp. 100–13. On boy bishops, see S. Shahar, 'The Boy Bishop's Festival: A Case-Study in Church Attitudes towards Children in the High and Late Middle Ages', *Studies in Church History*, 31 (1994), pp. 243–60; T. N. Cooper, 'Children, the Liturgy, and the Reformation: the Evi-

dence of the Lichfield Cathedral Choristers', ibid., pp. 267–68.

108. Parry, ed., *Reg. L. de Charleton*, p. 49.

109. On obits, see C. Burgess, 'A Service for the Dead: the Form and Function of the Anniversary in Late Medieval Bristol', *Transactions of the Bristol and Gloucestershire Archaeological Society*, 105 (1987), pp. 183–211. Hereford's annual round is recorded in HCA, 2030A. Names are sometimes noted elsewhere, for instance in accounts of the common rents, with other identifications in e.g. HCA, R 135.

110. The collector of obits is mentioned in e.g. HCA, R 160, R 194; also in the annual lists of minor officers in HCA, Baylis, i.

111. HCA, 2060. For other obit foundations, Capes, *Charters*, pp. 171–72, 181–82, 196; HCA, Baylis, i, fol. 45r-v.

Fig. 20. Cast of the seal impression of Bishop Thomas Cantilupe, 1275–82. (HCA, 6460; HCL, neg. 102.)

in Italy!) The return of his bones to Hereford provided a focus for a cult. Soon miracles were reported – and encouraged – at the tomb. Visitors from across the midlands, and further afield, reported cures and visions. Local women used his mantle to secure an easy birth.[112] Not everyone favoured the new cult – attempts were made to ascribe one miracle to Bishop Robert de Béthune, rather than to Cantilupe,[113] but Bishop Thomas finally prevailed. At first, the attraction was tentative: the papal *Taxatio* of 1291 valued the wax offered at the tomb (not yet a formal shrine) at £13 6s. 8d., but added the canny rider that this sum should not be considered secure annual revenue as (like modern stock market investments) the return could go up or down.[114]

In the short term, it went up. A concerted campaign lobbied the papacy to secure Cantilupe's canonisation. The formalities were duly initiated, with obstacles being overcome and witnesses questioned.[115] 1320 saw Cantilupe confirmed as a member of the heavenly host.[116] Diverted to the cathedral fabric fund, the shrine offerings were a major support for the building works.[117] Pilgrims left other

112. J. van Bolland and others, eds, *Acta sanctorum, Octobris*, i (Antwerp, 1765), p. 697.

113. Ibid., p. 698. Offerings at Béthune's tomb are recorded to 1332–33: HCA, 2412–13, 2437.

114. Ayscough and Caley, eds, *Taxatio*, p. 157. See also B. Nilson, *Cathedral Shrines of Medieval England* (Woodbridge, 1998), p. 160.

115. R. C. Finucane, *Miracles and Pilgrims: Popular Beliefs in Medieval England* (2nd edn, Basingstoke, 1995), pp. 173–88. See also Bolland and others, eds, *Acta Sanctorum*, pp. 610–705 (but see the strictures in Finucane, *Miracles and Pilgrims*, pp. 173, 175–77); R. C. Finucane, 'Cantilupe as

Thaumaturge: Pilgrims and Their Miracles' and P. H. Daly, 'The Process of Canonization in the Thirteenth and Early Fourteenth Centuries', in M. Jancey, ed., *St Thomas Cantilupe*, pp. 137–44 and 125–35. See also comment in S. Menache, *Clement V*, Cambridge Studies in Medieval Life and Thought, 4th series, 36 (Cambridge, 1998), pp. 175–77.

116. Capes, *Charters*, pp. 190–94.

117. P. E. Morgan, 'The Effect of the Pilgrim Cult of St Thomas Cantilupe on Hereford Cathedral', in M. Jancey, ed., *St Thomas Cantilupe*, pp. 146–50; Nilson, *Cathedral Shrines*, p. 138.

votive offerings, including several silver ships (Cantilupe regularly rescued ships at sea).[118] The pilgrimage traffic affected Hereford's economy and those of the pilgrim routes: Worcester Cathedral shrines gained some £10 a year from the passing trade in odd farthings, halfpennies and pennies – between 2400 and 9600 people along that one route.[119]

Securing popular recognition of Cantilupe's sanctity was a lengthy process, assisted by grants of indulgence for visitors made by several bishops (fig. 21a, b).[120] With the canonisation, the chapter mounted a nationwide collecting campaign to build the shrine, exploiting all available marketing techniques with considerable sophistication. Backed by royal and archiepiscopal letters of commendation,[121] the collectors toured England, bearing schedules indicating the spiritual rewards on offer. As well as the papal indulgence, these amounted to 600 trentals (recitations of thirty masses), twenty-two years of pardon, 22,000 masses a year, 15,000 psalters annually, and a total of Paternosters and Aves which 'no one knows except for God alone' (fig. 22).[122] Overall receipts are unknown, but the one surviving account records £45 4s. 2½d. from collections in the archdeaconry of Norfolk.[123] While expenses would have been considerable, this suggests that a substantial sum reached Hereford as a result of this enterprise.

Yet, in the way of cults, the initial momentum did not last. In 1336 the papal collector was told to alter the tax assessment for wax collected at the shrine, as offerings had fallen considerably.[124] The cult was boosted by the translation of Cantilupe's relics in 1349, which set them in a new location, added a further

118. On votives, see Finucane, 'Cantilupe as Thaumaturge', p. 144. For silver ships, see Bolland and others, eds, *Acta sanctorum*, pp. 667, 673, 678, 680, 683 (and for a wax ship, p. 677).

119. Ibid., p. 584.

120. HCA, 1421–26, 1428, 1430–31, 1433, issued at various dates between 1285 and 1328. This is not the full range of indulgences offered: John Dalderby of Lincoln also made a grant in 1320 of forty days of pardon, Lincoln, Lincolnshire Archives Office, Ep. Reg. III, fol. 263r. See also Finucane, *Miracles and Pilgrims*, p. 5.

121. HCA, 1435, 1444. The royal letters also direct that unlicensed collectors falsely claiming to be collecting for the shrine should be arrested, and their receipts be turned over to the legitimate collector: HCA, 1435, printed from another copy in T. Rymer, *Foedera* (20 vols, London,

1704–35), iii, pp. 863–64; see also *Calendar of the Patent Rolls, Edward II* (5 vols, London, 1894–1904), iii, p. 526.

122. Copies of these mass-produced publicity schedules survive in HCA, 1447, 3214. I assume that they were for this enterprise, although the papal indulgence does not match any of the known indulgences granted to the cathedral. It is possible that they are publicity for other collections, for which see below, p. 78.

123. HCA, 1446.

124. W. H. Bliss and others, eds, *Calendar of Entries in the Papal Registers Relating to Great Britain and Ireland: Papal Letters, 1198–1492* (18 vols, London and Dublin, 1893–1989 in progress), ii, *1305–42*, p. 531: the yearly amount offered was now less than six pounds – presumably in value rather than weight, but still a drop of over 50 per cent since 1291.

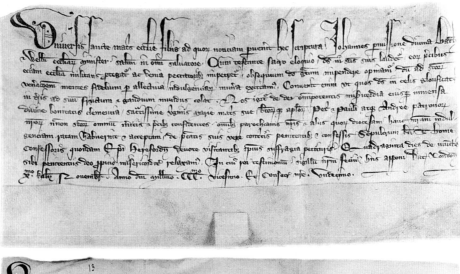

Fig. 21a, b. Indulgences to visitors to Thomas Cantilupe's shrine offered by Bishop Drokensford of Wells in 1318 and Archbishop Becknor of Dublin in 1320. (HCA, 1428, 1427.)

feast to the cathedral and diocesan calendars and, with further papal indul-gences, gave an extra incentive to devotion and donation.[125] Yet recorded offerings

125. For the shrine and translation, Dohar, *Black Death*, pp. 59–60; Finucane, *Miracles and Pilgrims*, p. 179. For the additional indulgence, see Bliss and others, eds, *Calendar of Entries in the Papal Registers: Papal Letters*, iii, *1342–62*, p. 512. The sponsors of the translation had sought a plenary indulgence for those attending the event itself: the pope allowed much less, W. H. Bliss, ed., *Calendar of Entries in the Papal Registers Relating to Great Britain and Ireland: Petitions to the Pope, 1342–1419* (London, 1896), p. 163. On the lead-up to the translation, and the 'makeshift' shrine of the 1320s, see Nilson, *Cathedral Shrines*, pp. 21, 46–8.

Fig. 22. A roll of indulgences offered to pilgrims to Thomas Cantilupe's shrine dating from just after his canonisation in 1320. (HCA, 1447.)

were under £3 in 1383–84, under £2 in 1386–87 (but the figures may be unreliable).[126] Cantilupe retained his liturgical significance at Hereford, with a motet being composed in his honour *c.* 1415.[127] The cult re-emerges from the shadows

126. Morgan, 'Effect of the Pilgrim Cult', pp. 151–52; Nilson, *Cathedral Shrines*, pp. 138, 160. For a bequest in 1381, Parry, ed., *Reg. Gilbert*, p. 24.

127. B. Trowell and A. Walthey, 'John Benet's "Lux fulget ex Anglia – O pater pietatis – Salve Thoma": The Reconstruction of a Fragmentary Fifteenth-Century Motet in Honour of St Thomas Cantilupe', in M. Jancey, ed., *St Thomas Cantilupe*, pp. 159–80; also below, Chapter 21, p. 388.

as shrine revenues reappear intermittently from the mid fifteenth century, supplemented by notices in the first chapter act book. Worth almost £23 in 1478–79, it fell to around £10 a year under Henry VIII, plus wax donations. This was a significant drop from the early days, but the receipts were still respectable, matching for instance those at the Holy Blood of Hailes.[128] The cult was abruptly terminated when the Henrician commissioners destroyed the shrine in 1538.

The cathedral's other cults were less prominent (fig. 23). The £10 entered in the *Valor ecclesiasticus* for devotional receipts was derived from Thomas Cantilupe and (unhelpfully) 'other saints'.[129] St Ethelbert remained an uncharismatic presence: devotion to him has left scant evidence, although his depiction on canons' tombstones shows that he was not altogether forgotten. From 1292 to 1348 a series of accounts details receipts of oblations, but their provenance and stimulus is never identified.[130] A Holy Cross had a reputation as a healing site in the late thirteenth century.[131] The naming of altars is suggestive, but inconclusive. Medieval cults could be very short-lived. Henry VI's, although national, lacked stamina. The king was commemorated at Hereford, with a collecting box (if not an image) in his honour. Recorded offerings were relatively insignificant.[132] Lesser devotions included the cult of St George. In June 1418, Bishop Lacy granted forty days' indulgence to contributors to his light and to donors to the construction or repair of his image.[133] Other major late medieval devotions were mainly Marian or Christocentric. A pietà was set up in 1446–47;[134] devotion to Jesus appears with mention of a chantry at the north door, probably established in the late fifteenth century.[135] The personal devotions of the canons mirrored these general trends.[136]

The interlinking of indulgences, Cantilupe's cult and the fabric fund raises the issue of how building works were funded over the period. Cantilupe's cult alone would have provided insufficient income, as would other expedients such as the allocation of a share in the commons.[137] The precise funding mechanisms remain elusive, but there are suggestive hints. Indulgences and collections clearly played a part. In 1355 the bishop promised to appoint a collector for the fabric fund to tour the diocese, and to secure a batch of indulgences from his fellow bishops at the imminent

128. Swanson, 'Devotional Offerings', pp. 93–102 (to which should be added HCA, R 369a). For the wax receipts, see Caley and Hunter, eds, *Valor ecclesiasticus*, iii, p. 8. See also the discussion and figures in Nilson, *Cathedral Shrines*, pp. 160–1, 221, 239.

129. Caley and Hunter, eds, *Valor ecclesiasticus*, iii, p. 5.

130. HCA, 2406–50.

131. Bolland and others, eds, *Acta sanctorum*, p. 632.

132. Swanson, 'Devotional Offerings', pp. 96–97; Nilson, *Cathedral Shrines*, p. 221.

133. Parry, ed., *Reg. Lacy*, p. 28.

134. HCA, 2370.

135. Swanson, 'Devotional Offerings', p. 97 (the reference to the papal register at n. 15 may be a misidentification).

136. See above, pp. 64–65.

137. Morgan, 'Effect of the Pilgrim Cult', pp. 145–46; Nilson, *Cathedral Shrines*, p. 138.

Fig. 23. Posthumous tombs of bishops, south choir aisle. A temporary unofficial cult grew up in the late thirteenth and early fourteenth centuries at the tomb of Bishop Robert de Béthune, died 1148 (second from right).

parliament.[138] Questorial licences may regularly have stipulated (as they did elsewhere) that collections for the cathedral fabric had precedence over all others.[139] In March 1523 Bishop Booth granted a forty-day indulgence for participation in prayers offered on Sundays throughout the diocese for the cathedral's benefactors.[140] In Lichfield diocese, similar prayers offered for members of the fraternities of St Chad (linked to Lichfield Cathedral) and St Mary (associated with Coventry Cathedral) were for supporters of the respective fabrics;[141] this ties in

138. HCA, 2453.

139. J. H. Parry, ed., *Registrum Johannis de Trillek, episcopi Herefordensis, AD MCCCXLIV–MCCCLXI*, Canterbury and York Society, 8 (London, 1912), pp. 77–78; see also HCA, 2453.

140. Bannister, ed., *Reg. Bothe*, p. 138.

141. R. N. Swanson, 'The Priory in the Later Middle Ages', in G. Demidowicz, ed., *Coventry's First Cathedral: The Cathedral and Priory of St Mary* (Stamford, 1994), p. 153; idem, *Catholic England: Faith, Religion and Observance before the Reformation* (Manchester, 1993), pp. 218–20.

with formal fraternities established to support cathedral fabric funds elsewhere.[142] One mention of a 'fraternity of the whole bishopric' in 1291 is insufficient evidence for the existence of a similar organisation in Hereford diocese;[143] but references in the fabric accounts to activities of penitentiaries and breviators, and to the issue of indulgences, hint at some formal mechanism.[144] They resemble equally uninformative hints in the fabric accounts of York Minster, where penitentiaries functioned alongside formal quests.[145]

The contexts affecting the cathedral were many and varied. As landholders, the dean and chapter exercised secular jurisdiction, even if only at manorial level. Some of their claims were more extensive, but still relatively minor. In the hundred rolls and *Quo warranto* proceedings under Edward I, the chapter claimed the assize of bread and ale in various places. In the latter proceedings they also claimed rights of warren and pleas of the crown in Bullinghope, Norton Canon, Pembridge, Pyon and Weobley. Whether these were formally acknowledged is unclear: they were challenged but no outcome is recorded.[146]

An immediate focus of jurisdictional interest was Hereford itself. The chapter fee centred on the cathedral and the Close, and extended beyond in scattered blocks and tenements. This gave the city a complex jurisdictional map with adjacent houses under different authorities, providing the basis for long-running conflict between the cathedral and urban authorities of a kind characteristic of towns with divided lordship, and perhaps particularly of those having a substantial ecclesiastical presence. Clashes over precedence and power flared throughout the period, often starting with minor incidents, blowing up into skirmishes and rhetorical claims, and ending in vague compromises which really settled nothing. Landmark arbitrations, as in 1410, could not eliminate intransigence. Yet, for all their hot air and heated tempers, these disputes appear somewhat ritualised affairs, often between people who knew each other well and were economically interdependent.[147] The cathedral authorities were also touchy about the invasion of their privileges by

142. Ibid., p. 202; L. S. Colchester, ed., *Wells Cathedral Fabric Accounts, 1390–1600* (Wells, 1983), pp. 6, 10, 17, 22–23, 29, 36; A. M. Erskine, ed., *The Accounts of the Fabric of Exeter Cathedral, 1279–1353*, Devon and Cornwall Record Society, new series, 24, 26 (2 vols, Torquay, 1981–83), ii, p. xi.

143. Capes, *Charters*, p. 163.

144. HCA, 2369–70.

145. York Minster Library, E3/1–43.

146. W. Illingworth, ed., *Rotuli hundredorum temp. Hen. III et Edw. I* (2 vols, London, 1812–18), i, p. 186; idem, ed., *Placita de quo warranto temporibus Edw. I, II et III* (London, 1818), p. 272.

147. G. Rosser, 'Conflict and Political Community in the Medieval Town: Disputes between Clergy and Laity in Hereford', in T. R. Slater and G. Rosser, eds, *The Church in the Medieval Town* (Aldershot, Brookfield, Vermont, Singapore and Sydney, 1998), pp. 21–42.

royal officials, notably the sheriff of Herefordshire. Attempts to make arrests within the Close were strongly resisted.[148]

The chapter's spiritual jurisdiction was defended with equal persistence. The cathedral, like every consecrated building, served as a sanctuary.[149] The dean maintained his peculiar jurisdiction in and around Hereford, running his own courts to deal with matters under spiritual jurisdiction. Evidence of this activity as ordinary is fragmentary,[150] although his duty to hold triennial visitations is reflected in the 73s. 4d. which the *Valor ecclesiasticus* records as due in procurations. He also received 12s. p.a. for synodals.[151] Sometimes the jurisdiction was slackly enforced: at least one bishop reprimanded the dean for failing to prosecute cases with due vigour.[152]

Some of the cathedral's other prerogatives were also challenged, notably its status as the sole burial place for the city and surrounding countryside.[153] This was staunchly defended. Presumably the chapter's concern was partly monetary, but money was probably less of an incentive than the sense of duty to maintain the right for its own sake. The jealous concern is reflected in several battles fought against subject parishes and their incumbents seeking autonomy.[154] (Such clashes appear across England, usually between parishes and dependent chapelries;[155] Hereford's chief difference was the relative status of the adversaries.) In the early fourteenth century Allensmore's first bid for autonomy led to the cathedral permitting local burials of children and paupers, but no others. 'Inadvertently' the parishioners buried some of the greater and wealthier inhabitants as well, generating disputes. An agreement of 1348 allowed general burial, provided that the funeral profits went to the cathedral rather than the local church.[156] More striking was the long-running dispute between the chapter and Roger Side, vicar of St Peter's in Hereford.[157] He started conducting funerals and receiving the profits, so the chapter took him to court. Despite their much greater resources, in Side they found their match for endurance. Initiated in

---

148. Bannister, ed., *Reg. Spofford*, p. 62.
149. Parry, ed., *Reg. Lacy*, pp. 9–11.
150. A few indications of activity survive, e.g. HCA, 3150. See also Edwards, *Secular Cathedrals*, p. 153.
151. Caley and Hunter, eds, *Valor ecclesiasticus*, iii, p. 4.
152. Bannister, ed., *Reg. Beauchamp*, pp. 8–9.
153. Michael Franklin, 'The Cathedral as Parish Church: The Case of Southern England', in D. Abulafia, M. Franklin and M. Rubin, eds, *Church and City, 1000–1500: Essays in Honour of Christopher Brooke* (Cambridge, 1992), pp. 182–83.
154. Capes, *Charters*, pp. xxx–xxxi.
155. R. N. Swanson, 'Parochialism and Particularism: The Disputed Status of Ditchford Frary, Warwickshire, in the Early Fifteenth Century', in M. J. Franklin and C. Harper-Bill, eds, *Medieval Ecclesiastical Studies in Honour of Dorothy M. Owen* (Woodbridge, 1995), pp. 242–57.
156. HCA, 3157–58; Capes, ed., *Reg. Trefnant*, pp. 129–31.
157. Briefly treated in S. H. Martin, 'The Case of Roger Side versus the Dean and Chapter of Hereford', *TWNFC*, 35 (1955–57), pp. 156–62; Dohar, *Black Death*, pp. 82–86.

the deanery courts in 1362, the case went to the archbishop of Canterbury's court of Arches, and thence to the papal curia (at the time wandering between Avignon and Rome). The papal courts found for Side in 1376, but appeals by the dean and chapter fruitlessly extended proceedings to 1382. Despite the papal decree, acknowledging funerary autonomy for St Peter's, Side's victory was not quite complete. After so much argument and parchment, it all ended in compromise, with the cathedral saving face by receiving most of the candles offered at funerals in St Peter's, but the incumbent retaining two plus the cash oblations. Even into the fifteenth century, the chapter was exercising its control over burials, but not always insisting that they be held in Hereford: in 1477–78 they received 12*d*. for a licence to bury William Derlynge at Morton rather than Pipe.[158]

The chapter's status faced a more insidious challenge from the friars, whose privileged position often undermined settled arrangements for cure of souls.[159] The Franciscans seemingly caused no problems; but there was a running battle with the Dominicans from their arrival in the 1250s through to the early fourteenth century.[160] This was partly about income from the lands they were to occupy, with rents and tithes due to the chapter; partly it concerned threats to the cathedral's monopoly on burials and receipt of funerary and mortuary offerings. The Dominicans did pay rent (later eliminated by an exchange), and the chapter insisted on payment of the canonical portion of funeral offerings as established by the papal bull *Super cathedram*.[161] The practical concern about the effect of the Dominican presence appears in the chapter's resistance to a proposed expansion of the priory, which would have blocked Frog Lane. This would prevent access to chapter properties, make distraint for unpaid rents impossible and inevitably mean a loss of income.[162] Nevertheless, the Dominicans gained their extension, with royal support. While relations with the friars appear to have been generally amicable thereafter, problems about burials with the Dominicans flared up again in 1435.[163] In 1511 a complaint made by the Convocation of Canterbury to the pope about the privileges of the friars and the Hospitallers appears in the bishop's register, but nothing ties this directly to events in Hereford.[164]

158. Capes, *Charters*, pp. 258–59; HCA, R 515.
159. For a general discussion of these tensions, R. N. Swanson, 'The "Mendicant Problem" in the Later Middle Ages', in P. Biller and B. Dobson, eds, *The Medieval Church: Universities, Heresy and the Religious Life*, Studies in Church History Subsidia, 11 (Woodbridge, 1999), pp. 217–24.
160. On the rows with the Dominicans at Hereford, see Capes, *Charters*, pp. xxxiv–xxxvii; W. N. Yates, 'The Attempts to Establish a Dominican Priory at Hereford,

1246–1342', *Downside Review*, 87 (1969), pp. 254–67; idem, 'The Hereford Dominicans: An Unknown Document', *Archivum fratrum praedicatorum*, 41 (1971), pp. 157–73.
161. Capes, *Charters*, pp. 197–98, 221–22; HCA, 1334.
162. HCA, 1336; see also 1335.
163. Bannister, ed., *Reg. Spofford*, pp. 206–7 (the dispute seems to centre on episcopal rights to oblations, even though members of the chapter were present: compare ibid., p. 46).
164. Bannister, ed., *Reg. Mayew*, pp. 50–52.

Fig. 24. Lady chapel interior.

Beyond jurisdictional concerns, the cathedral obviously had considerable economic impact. In Hereford itself, the constant building provided employment for numerous craftsmen, as did the decoration of the cathedral. Its liturgical needs (in wax, vestments, incense, wine) sustained trade and industry. Such needs were not always met locally: wine was also purchased at Leominster.[165] Conversely, there were sales, sometimes also far afield. In 1446–47 scrap bell metal was sold to a Bristol bellfounder.[166] Some of the chapter's grain imported into Hereford presumably filtered out into the wider economy; the multure of the mills was occasionally sold to bakers.[167] The personal spending of the residentiaries, as fairly well-off individuals with disposable income, also had an effect.

The chapter estates also provided opportunities for profit. The leasing out of demesnes and appropriated churches demands further and more detailed research,

165. HCA, R 194.
166. HCA, 2370.
167. HCA, 2405.

but it is likely that one possible seedbed of capitalism was in lessees' exploitation of such ecclesiastical resources.[168] Certainly the farming of tithes, with relatively low costs and almost guaranteed profit, had considerable potential. For the dean and chapter, however, a policy of leasing out resources was not without dangers. Entering into a lease was one thing; actually securing the rent another. It was often difficult to obtain payment, especially in the hard economic circumstances of the fifteenth century.[169] The safest course was to grant the leases to fellow canons, whose income from the common fund could be seized to cover unpaid rent.[170] However, non-clerics were also involved, the potential problems of non-payment being circumvented by bonds to observe the terms of the lease.[171]

Although relatively remote, Hereford Cathedral and its chapter remained part of the wider realm, and of that even wider entity of the catholic church, under papal headship: the establishment and support for the cult of Cantilupe demonstrates that integration forcibly enough. Integration also appears in other ways. The chapter itself had an international component with the inclusion of the French abbots of Lire and Cormeilles as nominal prebendaries (at least until the fifteenth century), even if their participation in cathedral business was seemingly limited to the appointment of their vicars choral.[172] At a national level, the chapter and its members contributed to royal taxes (not always on time).[173] As already noted, the crown influenced appointments to canonries;[174] kings also sought to influence decanal elections.[175] The chapter was separately represented in fourteenth-century parliaments and was still naming proctors for sessions under Henry VIII.[176] As the convocation of Canterbury emerged as the main clerical consultative and tax-granting

---

168. On benefice farming, see Swanson, *Church and Society*, pp. 238–42.
169. For action to evict a non-paying farmer, see HCA, 2370.
170. E.g. HCA, 1180, 1846.
171. E.g. HCA, 1882, 1905, 3167, 3183–84.
172. Edwards, *Secular Cathedrals*, p. 258; above, Chapter 2, p. 36. In the fifteenth century, patronage of the Cormeilles vicar passed to Fotheringhay College, that of the Lire vicarage to Sheen: HCA, Baylis, i, fos 33r (but in this case the chapter seemingly exercised the nomination, see fol. 31v), 71r, 72v. So tenuous were the abbots' links with the cathedral that they do not appear in Le Neve's *Fasti*. Indeed, to call them prebendaries may be technically wrong, as they had no claim on the

cathedral's resources.
173. E.g. A. T. Bannister, ed., *Registrum Thome Myllyng, episcopi Herefordensis, AD MCCCCLXXIV-MCCCCXCII*, Canterbury and York Society, 26 (London, 1920), pp. 119–22; Parry, ed., *Reg. Trillek*, p. 368. In 1522 they also contributed £40 to a forced loan: HCA, Baylis, i, fol. 31v.
174. See above, p. 55.
175. HCA, Baylis, i, fos 47r-v.
176. *Rotuli parliamentorum* (6 vols, London [1783]), i, pp. 190–91; J. H. Denton and J. P. Dooley, *Representatives of the Lower Clergy in Parliament, 1295–1340*, Royal Historical Society Studies in History, 50 (Woodbridge, 1987), pp. 44, 104, 106; Parry, ed., *Reg. Trillek*, p. 13; HCA, Baylis, i, fol. 62v.

body around 1350, representation there presumably became more important and parliamentary representation merely nominal. The sixteenth-century proctors for parliament and convocation were often identical.[177]

Subjection to Canterbury's metropolitan authority also brought contacts with the archbishop, chiefly during the vacancies of the see of Hereford. Then the archbishop claimed spiritual jurisdiction in the diocese, appointing keepers of the spiritualities (sometimes these were members of the chapter) and holding visitations.[178] The canons resisted archiepiscopal visitation of the cathedral as forcefully as they resisted those of their own bishop, even when threatened with excommunication and interdict.[179] At other times, however, the chapter was happy to exploit the archbishop's powers, appealing to his courts against challenges to their rights and jurisdiction.[180]

Links with the papacy were much like those with Canterbury. Papal jurisdictional claims entangled the chapter in their skeins. They contributed to papal taxes and contributed annually to the procurations claimed by the papal collector in England.[181] The chapter fought – sometimes against its own members – in the papal courts, maintaining proctors to conduct its business there.[182] The papacy had its uses: it was, after all, Pope John XXII who canonised Thomas Cantilupe and papal indulgences were integral to the strategy for exploiting that canonisation.

While geographically remote, the papacy had local power. The prior of Wormsley, as papal conservator of the cathedral, could be appealed to if the chapter felt threatened.[183] In the fourteenth century, papal provisions affected the chapter's composition.[184] Later, the papacy continued to affect careers by granting dispensations for pluralism and non-residence.[185] From 1515 to 1529 Wolsey's status as papal legate *a latere* gave him a peculiar status within and over the church, which made his power irresistible. He appointed once to a cathedral prebend, while his court was also appealed to to resolve internal disputes.[186]

Much of this medieval regime was shattered as Henry VIII constructed a new English church after breaking with Rome. Change was already presaged in the *Valor ecclesiasticus* in 1535, drawn up to assess new taxes. In 1538 Cantilupe's shrine

---

177. HCA, Baylis, i, fos 61v–62r, 65v.
178. I. J. Churchill, *Canterbury Administration* (2 vols, London, 1933), ii, pp. 261–62.
179. Ibid., i, pp. 237–39; Capes, *Charters*, pp. xxiv–xxv, 145–46, 256–58; HCA, 1550–51; HCA, Baylis, i, fos 75v–76r.
180. HCA, 3204; HCA, Baylis, i, fol. 217v.
181. E.g. HCA, 2636.
182. E.g. Capes, *Charters*, pp. 159–60; Capes,

ed., *Reg. Trefnant*, p. 92.
183. HCA, 1551, 2847.
184. See above, p. 55.
185. E.g. Bliss and others, eds, *Calendar of Entries in the Papal Registers: Papal Letters, xi, 1455–64*, pp. 681–82; xviii, *Pius III and Julius II, Vatican Registers, 1503–13, Lateran Registers, 1503–8*, no. 531.
186. HCA, Baylis, i, fos 39v, 61r.

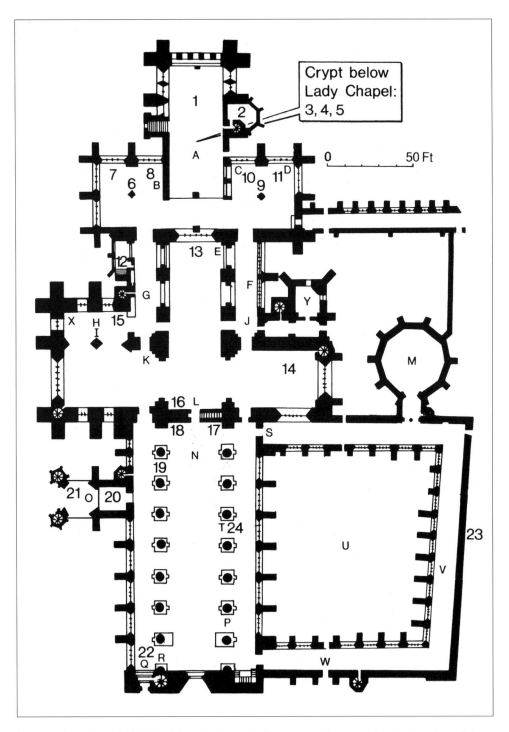

Fig. 25. Plan of Hereford Cathedral in the later middle ages, *c.* 1280–1540, showing location of altars, chapels, images and other features.

Plan of Hereford Cathedral in the Later Middle Ages, *c.* 1280–1540
Key (with first and last recorded dates to 1540) [1]

Altars and Chapels

1. Lady chapel, altar of St Mary, early C13; later a joint dedication with St Thomas Cantilupe, 1516
2. Audley chapel, St Mary, 1516 x 1524
3. Altar of the Holy Trinity, second half C13, 1518
4. Unidentified altar, 1518
5. Altar of St Anne, 1379, 1518
6. Chapel of St James, 1346, 1544
7. Altar of St James and St Margaret, 1346, 1536; a joint dedication, 1453
8. Altar of St Stephen, second half C13, 1536
9. Chapel of St John the Evangelist and St Michael, 1364, 1536
10. Altar of St John the Evangelist, 1364, 1536
11. Altar of St Michael, 1364, 1536
12. Stanbury chapel, St Mary and St Gacianus, 1478, 1536
13. High Altar, St Mary; a joint dedication with St Ethelbert, 1320
14. St Anne's chapel and altar, 1319, 1446
15. Unidentified altar, 1320
16. Altar of the Holy Cross in the pulpitum, 1287, 1536
17. Altar of St John the Baptist (parochial altar), late C13, 1536
18. Altar of the Holy Cross (Much Cross), 1536, 1538
19. Altar of St Nicholas, 1230 x 1254, 1536
20. Chapel of St Mary over the north door, 1366, 1536; called the Greenhouse, 1536
21. Proposed altar of St Saviour/Holy Name of Jesus, 1518
22. Chapel and altar of St George, 1441, 1536
23. Double chapel of St Katherine and St Mary Magdalene with altars of St Katherine and St John the Baptist, and St Mary Magdalene, 1200 x 1219, 1536
24. Altar of St Mary on the south side, 1315

Images and other Features

A. Shrine of St Thomas, 1349–1550
B. St Anthony, 1533
C. St John the Evangelist, 1416–17
D. Blessed Virgin Mary, 1383
E. St Ethelbert, 1514
F. Collecting box at the tomb of Robert de Béthune (d. 1148), 1300–1, 1332–33
G. St Katherine's aisle, 1476, 1526
H. Shrine of St Thomas, 1287–1349
I. St Thomas's head, 1457–58, 1493
J. St Anne's aisle, 1499
K. St Katherine, 1496
L. Pulpitum, 1287, 1536
M. Chapter house, 1364 x 1382, 1540
N. Crucifix, 1515
O. Jesus image, 1518
P. Font, 1494
Q. St George, 1418
R. Annunciation of Blessed Virgin Mary, 1524
S. Holy Trinity, 1511
T. Blessed Virgin Mary, 1368
U. Our Lady's arbour, 1469, 1513
V. Cloisters, 1412 x *c.* 1490
W. Library, 1412 x 1478–79
X. North treasury, 1406
Y. South or sub treasury, 1406, 1511

Features with unidentified locations

Altar of St Agatha and St Agnes, early C14, 1536
Altar of St Andrew, 1536
Altar of St Francis, 1272 x 1290
Altar of St Helen, early C14
Altar of St Peter and St Paul, 1547
Altar of St Thomas of Canterbury, second half C13
Chapel of St Richard, 1383–84
Collecting box of Henry VI, 1490–91, 1508–9
Image of Our Lady of Mercy, 1446–47

Note: the late medieval choir contained ten stalls against the pulpitum and forty-eight stalls placed in the two western bays of the crossing, dating from *c.* 1340–50.

1. Compiled by D. N. Lepine and drawn by T. P. Smith, with contributions from John Harper, Richard Morris, Ron Shoesmith, Joan Williams and the late Philip Barrett. (Ground plan based on that in Willis, *Survey of the Cathedrals.*)

was destroyed, while the abolition of indulgences and the elimination of masses
for souls challenged much of the cathedral's liturgical rationale. The late middle
ages had been times of change, even occasionally of trauma, but the cathedral's
spiritual function had continued unquestioned. As Henry VIII asserted himself as
Supreme Head of the English Church, as England slowly experienced Reformation,
change was unavoidable.

4

Reformation to Restoration, 1535–1660

Stanford Lehmberg with Gerald Aylmer

The period from the Reformation to the Restoration was a difficult one at Hereford. Many of the changes dictated by the reformers were unpopular with the conservative clergy and people of the city. Lengthy and bitter disputes between the bishops and the dean and chapter, primarily over the issue of episcopal visitations, characterised the late sixteenth and early seventeenth centuries. The Civil War brought puritan armies into Hereford, where in a famous confrontation they encountered Dean Croft. During the Interregnum (the years of the Commonwealth and Oliver Cromwell's protectorate) cathedral services ceased and cathedral clergy lost their positions. Hereford Cathedral, however, was less badly damaged than many of the cathedral churches, and the institution stood ready to be revived upon the restoration of the monarchy in 1660.

The initial phases of the Reformation had little impact at Hereford. Thomas Cranmer, who was to favour radical reform in the church, was consecrated archbishop of Canterbury in 1533, the year in which parliament repudiated the jurisdiction of the pope when it passed the Act in Restraint of Appeals.[1] Henry VIII divorced Catherine of Aragon and married Anne Boleyn in the same year. But at Hereford, as in most dioceses, these events produced no significant change, other than the required deletion of references to the pope from missals and other service books. The chief Henrician bishops of Hereford were conservatives who opposed significant reform. Charles Booth, builder of the north porch of the cathedral, died in 1535, before pressure for change manifested itself (plate VIIa). Following the brief episcopate of Edward Fox (1535–38), who was sympathetic to reform but much involved at court, his successor John Skip, despite having been Anne Boleyn's chaplain, preached against innovations and alterations and later

---

1. D. MacCulloch, *Thomas Cranmer* (New Haven and London, 1996), emphasises the radical nature of Cranmer's policies more than earlier studies. See also S. Lehmberg, *The Reformation Parliament, 1529–1536* (Cambridge, 1970), pp. 163–76.

Fig. 26. Detail of the fragments of the memorial brass of Precentor William Porter, died 1524, originally in the nave, now mounted as a mural in the south-east transept.

opposed the introduction of the first Book of Common Prayer.[2] Nor is there any indication that the cathedral clergy were eager to alter their traditional forms of worship.

The campaign against shrines was the first innovation to affect the cathedrals. The King's chief minister Thomas Cromwell condemned shrines and images in sets of injunctions issued in 1536 and 1538. At Hereford these strictures affected the veneration of St Thomas Cantilupe, the thirteenth-century bishop credited

2. Ibid., pp. 244–45; E. W. Ives, *Anne Boleyn* (Oxford, 1986), pp. 311–12. Edmund Bonner, the notorious Marian bishop of London, was elected bishop of Hereford in 1538 but translated to London before he could be consecrated.

with performing many miraculous cures. Observance of his feast days, 25 August and 2 and 25 October, continued well into the sixteenth century. Offerings at the shrine, however, had fallen off well before its official condemnation. In 1532 the dean and chapter blamed the dilapidation of their buildings on the decline of revenue from St Thomas's shrine; they suggested, rather feebly, that they offset this by allowing themselves twelve additional weeks a year free from the responsibility of providing hospitality.[3] An undated list of items removed from the shrine at Hereford probably belongs to 1538. It includes 'an image of the Trinity of gold with a diadem on his head with grene stones and rede, one oche on his breste with v. stones and iij. perles', as well as 'tables' (i.e. probably tablets) of gold and gems, one of which showed Jesus and Our Lady. There was also a crucifix with emeralds and pearls and an Agnus Dei with a chain of gold and fifteen rings.[4]

The shrine itself seems to have survived until the reign of Edward VI: in March 1547 the dean and chapter received a letter from Bishop Bonner ordering that all shrines and images be pulled down, and on 9 May 1550 they agreed to remove them.[5] In the end it was only the monument in the Lady chapel that was destroyed. The original tomb in the north transept escaped, probably because it was no longer associated with devotion to the saint, although its delicate beauty was marred when the heads of the figures contained in its lower stage were defaced. According to a long tradition some relics of St Thomas were rescued by the faithful and taken in procession through the city streets in 1610, in the hope of warding off the plague. Some of them later found their way to Roman Catholic religious houses at Downside and Belmont.[6]

Two acts of parliament, the first passed shortly before the death of Henry VIII and its successor shortly after the accession of Edward VI, ordered the dissolution of chantries throughout the realm on the grounds that prayers for the dead were ineffectual and chantry endowments might be put to better use by the state. At Hereford, however, chantry masses for the dead had been sung by the vicars

3. HCA, 7031/1, fol. 68v; cf. F. Heal, *Hospitality in Early Modern England* (Oxford, 1990). On the cult of Thomas of Hereford see Chapter 3 above; also M. Jancey, ed., *St Thomas Cantilupe, Bishop of Hereford: Essays in his Honour* (Hereford, 1982), and E. Duffy, *The Stripping of the Altars: Traditional Religion in England, 1400–1580* (New Haven and London, 1992), p. 48.

4. J. S. Brewer, J. Gairdner and R. H. Brodie, eds, *Letters and Papers, Foreign and Domestic, of the Reign of Henry VIII* (23 vols in 38, London, 1862–1932), xiii, pt 2, no. 1208.

5. HCA, 7031/1, fos 98r, 102v.

6. E. M. Jancey, *St Thomas of Hereford* (Hereford, 1978), pp. 18–19. In 1841 a processional cross adorned with symbols of the Evangelists was discovered in the groining of the central tower, together with several small crucifixes, fragments of alabaster carvings, and remnants of a small fourteenth-century shrine. It is not clear when these were hidden away, but 1538 seems a likely date. See the drawing and description in F. T. Havergal, *Fasti Herefordenses* (Edinburgh, 1869), pp 146–47, and below, Chapter 27, p. 506.

choral, and it was argued that related revenues should remain the property of the college. Rather surprisingly, this view prevailed; in this matter, as in some others, Hereford fared better than most other cathedrals.[7] The beautiful chantry chapel of Bishop John Stanbury in the north choir aisle remained, although masses at its altar must have ceased (fig. 115), and Stanbury's alabaster tomb continued to stand near it, although the figures in its gothic arches were decapitated. In addition to the vicars choral, some other members of the cathedral establishment profited from funds gathered by the collector of mass pence. In 1541, for instance, the dean and another eighteen priests divided £40 14*s*. 1¾*d*., their individual payments varying from 28*s*. 9*d*. to 2*d*.; it appears that the cost of a mass was literally a penny. These payments ceased under Edward but were revived under Mary, their total for 1558–59 being £54.[8]

The introduction of the first Book of Common Prayer in 1549 must have brought substantial change. It became illegal, for instance, to sing anthems or motets with Latin texts, thus (if one followed the letter of the law) necessitating a scramble for new liturgical music. The failure of the act books to note the coming of English language services may be significant; very likely the cathedral clergy, like Bishop Skip, disliked the new service book and were reluctant to abandon their traditional observances. The act books do record the introduction of the more radically Protestant second Prayer Book, with the note that it was brought into use on 2 November 1552.[9]

Continuing to ordain radical policies, in November 1550 Edward VI's privy council issued a demand that stone altars be removed from churches throughout England and replaced by 'honest wooden tables' orientated tablewise east and west, not north and south, in the main body of the church.[10] The dean and chapter were notified of the order in December.[11] Similar requirements were written into the 1552 Prayer Book. Once again the sources do not reveal exactly what was done at Hereford, and once again it may be that compliance was grudging or incomplete; we know that in many cases there was reluctance to dismantle the traditional altars and that some were hidden away, to be brought back into use when Mary I came to the throne.[12]

This reversion to Catholic practice was not long delayed, for the young king died in July 1553. At Hereford, Mary's reign began with the deprivation of Bishop

7. P. Barrett, *The College of Vicars Choral at Hereford Cathedral* (Hereford, 1980), p. 16; cf. S. E. Lehmberg, *The Reformation of Cathedrals* (Princeton, NJ, 1988), pp. 105–9.

8. HCA, R 578, R 582a.

9. HCA, 7031/1, fol. 114.

10. MacCulloch, *Cranmer*, p. 458.

11. HCA, 7031/1, fol. 105v.

12. Cf. Duffy, *Stripping of the Altars*, pp. 556, 583. An earlier historian of the cathedral, A. T. Bannister, wrote that 'everything would seem to have gone on in the old way without interruption', *The Cathedral Church of Hereford*, p. 84.

John Harley, the chaplain to the duke of Northumberland, who had been given the see of Hereford following the death of Bishop Skip in 1553. His replacement was the reliably conservative Robert Parfew or Wharton, a former Cluniac monk who was translated from St Asaph.[13] The removal of married clergy from the cathedral staff, in accordance with articles sent to all dioceses by Bishop Bonner, took place in 1554.[14] Those deprived included the precentor John Barlow, and three prebendaries, Thomas Carpenter, Edward Welsh, and Rowland Taylor. A further married priest was inhibited from performing the sacraments, and there were proceedings against married clergy who served in cathedral benefices rather than in the cathedral church itself. Interestingly enough, a few of these were former monks.[15] The Bull of Julius III reconciling England to the Church of Rome was recorded in the act book for 1554, as was the fact that prayers were said daily for the queen, who was thought to be pregnant, in January 1555. Rather curiously, the dean, Hugh Coren, was granted three years' leave for study: one wonders if he was uncomfortable at Hereford in the midst of the Counter Reformation and, perhaps as a token of appreciation, he gave the chapter a cope worth 40 shillings.[16] In 1556 Cardinal Pole, Mary's archbishop of Canterbury, conducted a visitation of the cathedral, his expenses being paid by the canons and prebendaries, but we do not know what he found or what changes he may have decreed.[17]

With Elizabeth's accession the Marian changes were reversed and once again the deprivations began. Parfew had died conveniently in September 1557; Thomas Reynolds had been nominated as his successor but was not consecrated and was deprived in 1559. Elizabeth's choice as bishop of Hereford was John Scory, a former Dominican friar who had adopted strongly reformed views, married, and risen under Edward VI to be bishop of Rochester, then Chichester. He had also served as a chaplain to both Cranmer and Ridley. Although he renounced his wife under Mary, he fled abroad to join the Marian exiles, and like many of them he enjoyed promotion upon returning to his native land. His work was cut out for him at Hereford, for upon arriving he found that all but one of the canons were 'dissemblers and rank papists', and even the sextons were 'mortal enemies to this [reformed] religion'. So were members of the city council. Indeed Hereford had become a magnet for disaffected conservatives: 'priests and such like enemies

---

13. Parfew's enthronement on 9 May 1554 is noted in HCA, 7031/1, fol. 133. The first six months of Mary's reign may have been a time of confusion or disarray at Hereford, since there are no entries in the act book for the period from October 1553 to March 1554.

14. Presumably Bonner, as bishop of London, acted in place of the archbishop of Canterbury, for Cardinal Pole was not consecrated until 1556.

15. HCA, 7031/1, fos 125–133.

16. HCA, 7031/1, fos 140v, 142.

17. HCA, 7031/1, fol. 147v.

of the church', he wrote, 'find a safe asylum here ... and are maintained and feasted as if they were God's angels.'[18]

In 1559 royal injunctions were sent to Hereford by three university professors who had been appointed the queen's visitors. Specific to Hereford rather than being a copy of injunctions sent generally throughout the realm, these included a number of obvious points: sermons were to be preached regularly; the clergy were to avoid adultery and fornication; they were to pray for the queen; they were to keep hospitality and relieve the poor. Two copies of the English Bible were to be set up in the choir, one for the ministers and one for lay people, and Erasmus's *Paraphrases* were to be provided as well. The cathedral was also charged to make a yearly inventory of vestments and plate.[19]

Following the enactment of the Elizabethan religious settlement all clergy throughout the realm were required to swear the oath of supremacy, and the Marian priests who refused to do so were deprived. At Hereford the conservatives who lost their positions included the dean, Edmund Daniel, the new precentor, William Chell, and five of the canons, one of them a son of Bishop Parfew.[20] But the new appointments did not bring good relations with the bishop. When Scory proposed to hold his own episcopal visitation of the cathedral, the dean and chapter told him that he had no constitutional right to do so; the beleaguered bishop vented his bitterness in a letter to Sir William Cecil, denouncing the cathedral church as 'a verie nursery of blasphemy, whoredom, pryde, superstition and ignorance', and complaining that it was 'exempted from my ordinary jurisdiction and under the jurisdiction of none that I know of'. Cecil himself wrote to the queen seeking letters authorising the bishop to visit the cathedral, 'whereby that church shall be purged of many enormities', but without success.[21]

Bishop Scory's desire to renovate the bishop's palace so that he might reside at Hereford a good part of the year, unlike his predecessors, aroused further contention. The cathedral clergy held that they could not agree to this unless they were able to convene a meeting attended by all the prebendaries, which they allegedly found impossible. Frustrated once again, Scory had to abandon the project, although he had 'bespoken my carpynder and mason and prepared tymbor and other necessaries for the buyldinge'.[22]

18. Bannister, *The Cathedral Church of Hereford*, pp. 85–86.
19. HCA, 5755: a typescript copy of Cambridge, Corpus Christi College, MS 120, fol. 516.
20. HCA, 7031/1, fos 153v, 155v. Daniel had been installed as dean in July 1558, only a few months before Mary's death: HCA, 7031/1, fol. 152.
21. Bannister, *The Cathedral Church of Hereford*, pp. 86, 177–78, quoting State Papers Domestic, Elizabeth I, in the Public Record Office; HCA, 7031/1, fos 157–59, correspondence with Archbishop Parker concerning the proposed visitation.
22. HCA, 7031/2, fos 6–7; Bannister, *The Cathedral Church of Hereford*, p. 87.

A number of entries in the act books confirm the bishop's view that all was not well at the cathedral. In March 1567 the vicars choral were admonished not to frequent houses of ill repute or associate with women of suspect character.[23] A year later the petty canons and deacons were ordered not to walk about, talk or read books during services but rather apply themselves wholly to the psalmody, and not to go into the city alone, but only with a companion. Prebendaries were admonished to keep hospitality and the keeper of the library was told to make a list of all the books remaining in the library (perhaps an admission that some had been lost).[24] In 1578 one of the vicars choral, Clement Lewys, was accused of having a woman in his chambers; when her husband came looking for her he denied that she was there, but she was found hiding in a coal house under a stair. He was admonished, and another vicar was warned to stop haunting taverns and suspect places.[25]

A more serious dispute arose just before Christmas 1579, when a vicar choral, Richard Madox, was charged with speaking contemptuous words against the dean. The act book records:

> That he the foresaid daye ... departed the Chore before the tyme of sayinge the Letanye, leavinge the Chore unserved. And after that Day beinge called by the seid Deane, and charged with the premisses, and also with often goinge withoute licence to Gloucester, the seid Madocke answered sayinge the seid Dean sayed not trewe, sayinge also, he was as good as the seid Dean in everie respecte, further sayinge that he wold serve hym for that & other thinges in the Storre Chambor.

The dean countered by threatening to deprive him, but in fact Madox remained and was admitted to a prebend in 1581.[26]

Claiming that he was in purgatory at Hereford, Scory sought promotion to the see of Norwich, but without success. He did obtain a commission for a special visitation in 1582. This was not conducted by Scory himself, but by John Whitgift, later archbishop of Canterbury, in his capacity as bishop of the neighbouring diocese of Worcester, and it resulted in a set of statutes for the cathedral, published under the queen's authority in 1583 (fig. 27).[27] The promulgation of new statutes under these conditions was most unusual; the cathedrals that had been served by monks received new statutes following the dissolution of the monasteries, thus becoming known as cathedrals of the new foundation, but

23. HCA, 7031/2, fol. 11.
24. Ibid., fol. 73v.
25. Ibid., fol. 79.
26. Ibid., fos 82–83, 88v.
27. HCA, 4642 is a set of articles and answers relating to Whitgift's visitation. The answers are generally short and positive, although it is admitted that sometimes sermons are not delivered because of the lack of qualified preachers.

Fig. 27. John Whitgift,
bishop of Worcester 1577–83,
archbishop of Canterbury
1583–1604.

the old secular cathedrals like Hereford generally went on under their medieval constitutions.

The Elizabethan statutes for Hereford decreed the size of the cathedral establishment: six residentiary canons, each to be in residence for six full months, twelve vicars choral, four sub-canons, one of whom was to be the organist, and seven choristers. They provided that only holders of an MA should be appointed prebendaries or canons, that persons convicted of any great offence be banished without hope of return; that the holy communion should be celebrated monthly; that a sermon lasting an hour or thereabouts should be delivered each Sunday; that there should be biblical lectures; and that the library and school be properly cared for and governed. Each canon was to spend a sixth of his income on repairs to buildings, so long as this was needed. Rather surprisingly, the statutes did not clarify the jurisdiction of the bishop; instead of confirming his right to conduct a visitation they referred the resolution of problems to a triumvirate composed of the bishops of Hereford and Worcester and the dean of

Fig. 28. Effigy from the tomb of Bishop Herbert Westfaling, died 1602, north transept.

Worcester.[28] It may well be that this unique arrangement reflected the inability of the bishop and chapter to agree on a simpler statement. With some modifications these statutes remained in force until the nineteenth century except, as will be seen, for the years 1646–60.

Scory died in 1585 and was followed by Herbert Westfaling, who served almost all the rest of Elizabeth's reign, dying himself in 1602 (fig. 28). A descendant of German immigrants, Westfaling had been educated at Christ Church, Oxford, and was a prebendary there as well as chancellor of St Paul's before being elevated to the episcopate. In 1582 he had published *A Treatise of Reformation in Religion*. A man of unimpeachable integrity and less irascible than Scory, he enjoyed better relations with the cathedral clergy, but his attempts to conduct visitations were no more successful. One was proposed in 1585 but was immediately prorogued, and was again postponed in 1588 and 1589.[29] Visitation inquiries, however, were sent to the college of vicars choral by the dean and chapter in October 1588, and some interesting answers survive. Bartholomew Mason, one of the vicars choral, wrote that 'the prayer in the church is verie orderlye and in due tyme sayd and songe by the vicars, but the deacons are verie much absent'. Sometimes the vicars depart before the end of common prayer, but only if their 'necessary occasions' require it. No one is a common swearer, blasphemer, sorcerer or incontinent; no one is a 'common ribald, rayler, drunkard, scoffer, gamester, sower of discord, or

28. HCA, 1553; Bannister, *The Cathedral Church of Hereford*, pp. 88–92.

29. HCA, 7031/2, fos 116v, 121v, 131, 135.

goeth excessive in apparell their wives or famylies'. The choristers are properly instructed (some other respondents disagreed with this view), but their surplices are 'soe rent' that they cannot be worn. The library [of the vicars choral] is well kept but contains only 'ould bookes ... to little proffit of anye, for that the most parte doe not understand the lattine tonge; but if anie of your worships do want any of the said bokes, we would verie gladlie exchaunge [them] for some newe writers, whereby we might be occupied in godlye study'. The worst problem was the absence of the organist, who had not been present for a year.[30] Another set of replies by vicars choral contains William Hosier's very honest response to a query about the effect of services on those who attended: 'Our singinge and songes is as it is in all other cathedral churches, but what devocion or pyetie it stirres up in the myndes of the hearers I knowe not'.[31]

In 1598 Westfaling tried again to hold a visitation and was again resisted. The dean and chapter maintained that the bishop might correct heresies held by canons but that they themselves should deal with all other matters. Westfaling countered that he was the bishop of the cathedral church as well as the rest of the diocese and quoted Paul's letter to the Corinthians to prove that he had god-given power to 'admonish, exhorte, reprove, excommunicate and absolve', preach and administer the sacraments. 'The staffe or rodde of discipline God hath undoubtedly gyven to all trewe bishops', he concluded: but the visitation did not take place.[32]

There are fewer charges of misconduct late in Elizabeth's reign than there had been earlier, but a warning about suspect religious views, images and pictures sent to the vicars choral in 1586 suggests that conservatism still prevailed.[33] William Hosier wrote optimistically that 'there hath bene dissentions and controversies amongest us ... but they are appeased and all reconsiled'.[34]

James I's bishops made little impact at Hereford. A local initiative to secure the appointment of the dean, Charles Langford, failed, and the king nominated Robert Bennett, another reformer who found the diocese full of recusants and traditionalists who expressed contempt for his efforts (fig. 29). Bennett died in 1617 and was followed by Francis Godwin, earlier the bishop of Llandaff, but Godwin, evidently frustrated by conditions at Hereford, left affairs there in the hands of the dean and

30. HCA, 3395. The absentee organist was Thomas Warrock, but his predecessor, the more famous John Bull, was also frequently away from the cathedral. See Watkins Shaw, *The Succession of Organists* (Oxford, 1991), p. 133.

31. HCA, 4588, answers to articles of enquiry, visitation of the college of vicars choral by the dean and chapter, 1595–96.

32. HCA, 7031/2, fos 98–99.

33. Ibid., fol. 123v.

34. HCA, 4588. In fact Hosier was over-optimistic. In June 1600 the chapter registrar complained that Hosier had called him 'old doting fool' and said 'hee should be hanged, ere he should paie anye tithes in his parisshe of Holmer'; Hosier was suspended until they were reconciled. HCA, 7031/3, p. 5, chapter acts, 26 June 1600.

Fig. 29. Seventeenth-century engraving of the tomb of Robert Bennett, bishop of Hereford 1603–17, north choir aisle. (HCL, B.3.6.) Only the base and the effigy remain today: see fig. 107.

chapter and spent his time in literary work at his manor of Whitbourne. His works included an annotated list of the bishops of England, Latin annals of the reigns of Henry VIII, Edward VI and Mary I, and the fanciful *Man in the Moon* (1638). Several members of the Jacobean chapter, on the other hand, made significant contributions. Edward Doughtie, dean from 1607 to 1616, had been chaplain for the English expedition to Cadiz in 1596; he returned with at least nineteen books from the Jesuit library there, some of which are still in the cathedral library.[35] His colleague Miles Smith, a prebendary since 1580, was one of the leaders in James I's new translation of the Bible. He specialised in the Old Testament (as early as 1596 he had published *Certain Plaine Notes upon Every Chapter of Genesis*)

---

35. See below, Chapter 28, p. 518 n. 35. Doughtie's election was recorded in HCA, 7031/3, p. 53, chapter acts, 23 December 1607.

and was also a notable preacher, a number of whose sermons were printed. Smith was consecrated bishop of Gloucester in 1612 but continued to hold his prebend at Hereford until his death in 1624.[36] Richard Montagu, the noted controversialist and theologian, followed Doughtie as dean in 1616 but exchanged the position for a canonry at Windsor the next year. Montagu was later bishop of Chichester and then of Norwich; he became famous for his tract *A Gagg for the New Gospell? No: A New Gagg for an Old Goose* (1624), and was accused of popery and Arminianism, charges from which he attempted to clear himself in *Apello Caesarem* (1625).[37]

A charming account of Hereford during the reign of Charles I forms part of the travel diaries of three military officers from East Anglia who toured the western counties in 1634. Their leader, Lieutenant Hammond (we do not know his Christian name), described the monuments, library and chapter house, which contained 'forty-six old pictures, curiously drawn', of Christ and the twelve apostles, as well as several kings and two women who had donated manors to the cathedral. The vicars choral entertained Hammond and his friends in their library, 'wherein (after we had freelie tasted of their choral cordiall liquor) we spent some time till the bell call'd us away to cathedrall prayers. There we heard a most sweet organ, and voyces of all parts, tenor, counter-tenor, treble and bass; amongst that orderly snowy crew of queristers, our landlord-guide did his part in a deep and sweet diapason.'[38] They were less enthusiastic about Gloucester, Worcester, Bristol and Wells.

A number of very brief episcopates marked the reign of Charles I at Hereford. When Godwin died in 1633 William Juxon was nominated as his successor, but was translated to London before he could be consecrated. As is well known, Juxon received Charles's last words on the scaffold; he himself ended his life as archbishop of Canterbury, 1660–63. In March 1634 Augustine Lindsell was translated from Peterborough to Hereford, but he died later the same year and was succeeded by Matthew Wren, a rising high churchman who was master of Peterhouse, Cambridge, and dean of Windsor (fig. 30). Like Lindsell, Wren made little impact at Hereford, for he was translated to Norwich in 1635 and then to Ely in 1638. Theophilus Field came to Hereford from St David's in December 1635 but died in June 1636. He is commemorated in the cathedral by an appealing monument, as is his successor, George Coke (fig. 141). Translated to Hereford from Bristol, Coke finally provided

36. His right to hold a prebend is noted in HCA, 7031/3, p. 100, chapter acts, 25 June 1624.

37. On Montagu see P. White, *Predestination, Policy and Polemic* (Cambridge, 1992), pp. 215–55; S. Lehmberg, *Cathedrals under Siege, 1600–1700* (Exeter, 1996), pp. 130–31; P. Barrett, 'Richard Montagu: An Early Seventeenth-Century Dean and Archdeacon', *FHC*, 44 (1978), pp. 25–32.

38. BL, Lansdowne MS 213, fos 332–34; printed in L. G. Wickham Legg, ed., *A Relation of a Short Survey of 26 Counties Observed in a Seven Weeks' Journey begun on August 11, 1634, By a Captain, a Lieutenant, and an Ancient, All Three of the Military Company in Norwich* (London, 1904), pp. 82–83. See also, Lehmberg, *Cathedrals under Siege*, pp. xxiv–xxviii.

some continuity, for he lived another ten years. Almost all of these bishops tried to hold visitations. When the chapter resisted Lindsell's attempt in 1634 he appealed to Archbishop Laud, who wrote to the dean and chapter that they must accept the jurisdiction of the bishop and acknowledge his right to hold triennial visitations. Lindsell actually initiated a visitation in October, but died before it could be completed. Wren too tried to hold a visitation, but few of the cathedral clergy attended it and the bishop left Hereford before anything could be accomplished. In May 1636 Field obtained a commission granting him power to hold a metropolitical visitation as a representative of the archbishop, not in his own episcopal capacity, but again death intervened.

Fig. 30. Matthew Wren, bishop of Hereford 1634–35. (HCL, B.3.83.)

New statutes were, however, promulgated under the king's authority in May 1636 (plate IIb). It was evidently Wren who prompted Laud to undertake this revision. Although based on the Elizabethan statutes these incorporated provisions from the medieval *Consuetudines*. They reduced the residentiaries' term of residence from six months to thirteen weeks, and required the presence of two rather than three canons at any one time. Laudian policies can be seen behind the requirement that the celebrant, epistoler and gospeller be vested in copes for the holy communion and that every member of the cathedral clergy should wear a surplice and hood at services. All were to bow at the name of Jesus and make obeisance to the dean as well as the altar when entering the choir. When the bishop was present, two candles were to be lighted at his throne. Perhaps most important, the interpretation of doubtful points was placed in the hands of the bishop of Hereford alone and his right to conduct a visitation finally confirmed, although the possibility of an appeal from the diocesan to the archbishop of Canterbury was recognised.[39] Although the issue was finally settled, no visitation took place until 1677.

39. The Laudian statutes are summarised in Bannister, *The Cathedral Church of Hereford*, pp. 94–96. They were printed in 1882 with an English translation in Jebb and Phillott, *The Statutes of the Cathedral Church of Hereford*, in which they were erroneously dated 1637; this error – presumably caused by a misinterpretation of the regnal year – is found as early as the eighteenth century in the annotations to the copy of the statutes signed by the dean and residentiaries on

The chapter act book breaks off following an entry for 7 May 1622 and records do not resume until August 1660. Our knowledge of events from Charles's reign and from the Interregnum is therefore based on other sources. For those who served in the cathedrals, or simply loved them, the choice between the churchmanship of Charles and Laud and the puritanism of Cromwell and the New Model Army was obvious. If the king fell, the cathedrals would follow.[40] It is interesting to note that the House of Commons, while debating the Root and Branch Bill, received a petition from Herefordshire favouring the retention of episcopacy and cathedral establishments.[41]

In the autumn of 1642, shortly after the war began, Hereford was occupied by a parliamentary army commanded by the earl of Stamford. One of his sergeants, Nehemiah Wharton, a former London apprentice, has left us a vivid account of what happened on 7 October.

> Sabbath day, about the time of morninge prayer, we went to the Minster, when the pipes played and the puppets sang so sweetely that some of our soldiers could not forbeare dauncing in the holie quire; whereat the Baalists were sore displeased. The anthem ended, they fell to prayer, and prayed devoutly for the kinge, the bisshops, etc., and one of our soldiers, with a loud voice said, 'What! neiver a bit for the Parliament?' which offended them much more. Not satisfied with this humane service, we went to the divine, and passing by, found shops open and men at wirke, to whom we gave some plaine exhortations; and went to hear Mr Sedgwick, who gave us two famous sermons, which much affected the poore inhabitants, who wonderinge said they neiver heard the like before, and I beleeve them. The Lord move your harts to commiserate the distressers, and to send them faithfull and painfull ministers; for the revenues of the Collidge will maintain many of them.[42]

Sentiment in Hereford was primarily royalist, and in December Stamford's men were forced to abandon the city. The following April Waller held Hereford for a month, but then withdrew. The royalists successfully resisted an attack by the Scottish army in the summer of 1645, but that December Colonel Birch gained control of the city for parliament (fig. 31). Herbert Croft, who had become dean

note 39 continued
1 September 1636 (HCA, 7044/8). The articles of enquiry for the abortive visitations of Bishops Coke and Wren are printed in K. Fincham, ed., *Visitation Articles and Injunctions of the Early Stuart Church*, Church of England Record Society, 1 and 5 (2 vols, Woodbridge, 1994–98), ii, pp. 115, 129.

40. On these issues see J. Morrill, *The Nature of the English Revolution* (London, 1993), and Lehmberg, *Cathedrals under Siege.*

41. Printed in J. and T. W. Webb, *Memorials of the Civil War in Herefordshire* (2 vols, London, 1879), ii, p. 337.

42. Bannister, *The Cathedral Church of Hereford*, p. 97, reprinted from *Archaeologia*, 35 (1853), pp. 309–34.

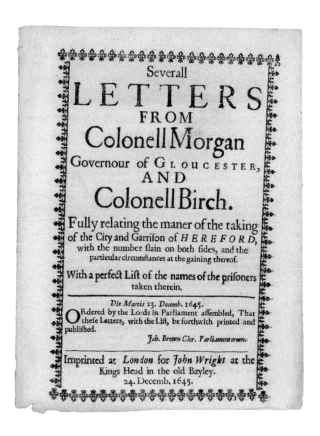

Fig. 31. Title page of a Civil War pamphlet giving an account of the taking of the city of Hereford by Colonel John Birch and Parliamentary army on 18 December 1645. (HCL, X.13.2/16.)

of the cathedral in 1644, tangled with the parliamentary army. A member of an old gentry family, Croft is an interesting figure because in his youth he had converted to Catholicism: his father, a Roman Catholic who ended his life as a Benedictine monk at Douai and wrote a number of controversial tracts, had sent him to study at a Catholic college on the Continent, and he spent some time in Rome. After returning to England he was brought back to the Church of England following conversations with Thomas Morton, bishop of Durham. When confronted by the parliamentary soldiers, Dean Croft mounted the cathedral pulpit and, according to a contemporary account, 'inveighed boldly and sharply against sacrilege'. Some of the soldiers present, perhaps feeling the prick of a guilty conscience, began to mutter against him and prepared to fire on him, but Birch prevented them from doing so.[43] The pulpit from which Croft defended the cathedral is still to be seen (fig. 32), and a roundel on the present west front of the cathedral commemorates the confrontation.

Croft was ejected from the deanery, and his other ecclesiastical holdings were

43. Bannister, *The Cathedral Church of Hereford*, pp. 98–99.

confiscated. His elder brother having died, he inherited the family estates and lived quietly during the Interregnum, mainly as a guest of Sir Rowland Berkeley at Cotheridge in Worcestershire; following the Restoration he was to return to Hereford as bishop.[44] Others were less fortunate. Bishop Coke was sent to the Tower in 1641 and was again imprisoned in 1645; he lost all his property and died in 1646. Coke's sons Richard, chancellor of the cathedral, and John, a prebendary, also lost their livings, as indeed did all the canons, prebendaries and vicars choral.[45]

Hereford Cathedral suffered less than many of its sister cathedrals. The hardest hit were Lichfield and Carlisle. Both were the object of sieges, and when they were over Lichfield had lost its famous three spires, Carlisle several bays of its nave. The lead roof of the chapter house at Hereford had been stripped off in 1645; the building was not restored after 1660 and was to be demolished by the order of the then bishop in the next century. Between 1647 and 1650 the dean's properties were sold off for little more than £1000, probably less than they were worth, and Colonel Birch is said to have made a large profit on his purchase of the bishop's lands. These included six manors as well as the episcopal palace. Tenements in Worcester and Lambeth were sold to others. The total received from these sales was £8,850 9s. 3½d.[46] In addition, a London tavern owned by the cathedral, the Labour-in-Vain near Old Fish Street, was sold for £544. The fabric of the cathedral itself remained substantially intact and it was to become a centre for puritan preaching in the years which followed.

The clergy of Hereford cathedral were somewhat less well educated during this period than those at most other cathedrals. Relatively few of the Tudor canons are known to have held university degrees. Educational qualifications improved markedly under the Stuarts; 35 per cent of the clerics for whom information is available held an MA, and a further 35 per cent a doctorate. But 12 per cent had no university connection. Only Llandaff, Bangor and Exeter ranked lower. Most of those who did attend university were at Oxford; as one might expect, relatively few studied at Cambridge. Hereford was also unusual in that most of the cathedral clergy had been born in the shire itself: 72 per cent of the men born in Herefordshire

44. On Croft see A. L. Moir, 'Some Deans of Hereford', *FHC*, 32 (1966), pp. 11–13; A. G. Matthews, ed., *Walker Revised* (Oxford, 1948), p. 296; O. G. S. Croft, *The House of Croft of Croft Castle* (Hereford, 1949), pp. 94–104. Bishop Croft married Ann, the daughter of Jonathan Brown, dean of Hereford. Their only child, also named Herbert, was created a baronet in 1671. The bishop and the baronet together restored the family residence, Croft Castle.

45. Matthews, ed., *Walker Revised*, pp. 191–96. A number of the cathedral clergy were restored to office in 1660.

46. R. Rawlinson, *The History and Antiquities of the City and Cathedral-Church of Hereford* (London, 1717), pp. 1–4.

Fig. 32. The 'Croft' pulpit, south-east transept: probably made during the campaign to pew the nave in *c.* 1617.

who went on to hold cathedral appointments served at Hereford itself, with only the remaining 28 per cent being called to more remote cathedrals.[47] The possibility that the chapter at Hereford was inbred and isolated is perhaps confirmed by the fact that its members published fewer books than those at most other places. The London puritans no doubt regarded Hereford as one of the 'dark corners of the realm' which the gospel had not penetrated.

It is not easy to sort out the details of finance at Hereford. Individual members of the chapter received income from their own estates, so that there was no comprehensive annual accounting. The most useful records are the rolls kept by the clavigers (literally the keepers of the cathedral keys), which give some idea of

47. Lehmberg, *Reformation of Cathedrals*, p. 232; idem, *Cathedrals under Siege*, pp. 96–97, 100–2.

expenditure on repairs.[48] There are also accounts of the collector of common rents of the dean and chapter.[49] In each case income remaining at the end of the year was distributed to residentiary canons. To select a few examples, each of the six residentiaries received 14*s*. 10*d*. from the collector of common rents in 1538, 21*s*. 2*d*. in 1590. The 'dividend' distributed by the clavigers in 1593 was £20 16*s*. 8*d*. for each canon. It remained at about that level until 1641, the last account before the war, when it amounted to £28 14*s*. 8*d*. The fact that such distributions were possible suggests that revenues were adequate to keep the cathedral and its associated structures in repair, to give occasional alms to students and poor persons, to augment some inadequate stipends, and to pay for such incidental expenses as the 'bonefire made in token of joye and thankesgyvinge for delyvery of her Ma[jes]tie out of her enemyues handes' at the time of the Spanish Armada.[50] Another interesting payment dating from 1588 was £1 13*s*. 9*d*. to a carpenter 'for making a backe for a new seate for the gentlemen of the citie, on promise that he make it lower, [so] that the people may see the pulpit and heare the better'.[51] This shows that both ordinary people and members of the civic hierarchy came to hear sermons in the cathedral.

There is very little direct evidence about the value of the prebends to indicate the probable wealth of the dean and individual canons during this period. Shortly after the establishment of republican rule in 1649 the government of the Commonwealth abolished deans and chapters of cathedrals. The capitular lands and other prebendal properties, notably the tithes of many parishes, were ordered to be surveyed and valued, with a view either to their sale or to their being used to augment the incomes of deserving parochial clergy and school teachers.[52] These surveys (either the originals, or contemporary copies) were handed over to the Anglican church after the Restoration and survive in Lambeth Palace Library.[53] Anyone expecting that this will enable us to give accurate money values for prebendal incomes is, however, bound to be disappointed. The surveys show that the prebendaries of Hereford enjoyed the rents from great tithes (of corn or grain) from several of the richest parishes in the central area of the county around the city, and from numerous other parishes further afield including a few in other counties, even outside the boundaries of the diocese. These rents were measured by volumes

48. These survive as HCA, R 584–608 and HCA, 2384–85.
49. For the Tudor period these are HCA, R 170–98. They include revenue from thirteen manors.
50. According to HCA, R 591, the bonfire cost 40*s*. Ringing on the Queen's birthday was cheaper, only 2*s*. being paid.
51. HCA, R 588, fabric roll.

52. C. H. Firth and R. S. Rait, eds, *Acts and Ordinances of the Interregnum, 1642–1660* (3 vols, London, 1911), ii, pp. 81–104 (30 April 1649).
53. J Houston, *Catalogue of Ecclesiastical Records of the Commonwealth, 1643–1660 in the Lambeth Palace Library* (Farnborough, 1968); Lambeth Palace Library, MS COMM XIIa/10, fos 82–170, 181–217.

(not weights) of grain: for example, every canon residentiary was to receive one quarter (equal to eight bushels or sixty-four gallons) of good quality wheat and one sum (or 'some', equal to fourteen bushels or 112 gallons) of oats yearly from the manor of Woolhope. Wheat was valued at 3s. 6d. a bushel, oats at 12d.; in the few instances where they appear, rye was priced at 2s. 6d. and barley at 2s. a bushel. So in theory the cash value can be worked out. In the case of Norton Canon every qualified prebendary was entitled to eight bushels of wheat and seven of oats yearly; but, most unusually, he could if he so wished take payment in cash instead, the wheat to be valued at the second highest price paid in Hereford market during the month of February, and the oats at the best market price. This is the only instance recorded of any kind of hedge against inflation, comparable to the famous 'corn rents' act of the 1570s for the colleges of Oxford and Cambridge.[54]

Many of the capitular properties were let on long leases (in one case for ninety-nine years from the reign of Edward VI), and in the vast majority of cases the surveyors recorded that the actual or potentially improvable value was greatly in excess of the existing rent. The financial implications of these long leases emerge very clearly from a survey of miscellaneous holdings of the dean and chapter and the treasurer and chaunter of the cathedral covering over twenty parishes. The existing cash rents were reckoned at a total of £323 19s. 6d. per annum and the corn rents to be worth another £119 4s. 0d., but the potential improvements when all the present leases had expired was set at the staggering total of £1164 0s. 11d. a year, less only £59 for the cathedral's schoolmaster and his usher, the two sextons and a scholar at Oxford. Where the prebend included a rectory, the payment of a stipend to the vicar represented a further deduction. All this is in line with what is known more generally about the church as a landowner during the generations preceding the Civil War.[55] We can safely say that the prebendaries of Hereford enjoyed a modest competence; but as landlords they were doing less

54. For a recent attempt to describe this measure and to assess its importance see G. E. Aylmer, 'The Economics and Finances of the Colleges and the University *c.* 1530–1640', in J. McConica, ed., *The History of the University of Oxford*, iii: *The Collegiate University* (Oxford, 1986), pp. 534–44.

55. See C. Hill, *Economic Problems of the Church from Archbishop Whitgift to the Long Parliament* (Oxford, 1956); J. Youings, 'Landlords in England, part C: The Church', in J. Thirsk, ed., *The Agrarian History of England and Wales*, iv: *1500–1640* (Cambridge, 1967), pp. 355–56; F. Heal, 'Economic Problems of the Clergy', in F. Heal and R. O'Day, eds, *Church and Society in England: Henry VIII to James I* (London, 1977), ch. 5; R. O'Day and F. Heal, eds, *Princes and Paupers in the English Church, 1500–1800* (Leicester, 1981), especially ch. 8, R. O'Day and A. Hughes, 'Augmentation and Amalgamation: Was there a Systematic Approach to the Reform of Parochial Finance, 1640–1660?'

well and their tenants correspondingly better than was the case with improving
lay landowners and their tenants, particularly from the 1590s to the 1630s. In this,
as in other ways, the Restoration settlement of 1660 and after was to mark both
a return to old ways and a new beginning.

From 1645 the puritan *Directory for Public Worship* had by law replaced the Book
of Common Prayer as the liturgical basis for all religious services, whether in
cathedrals, parish churches or chapels.[56] And the next year the Long Parliament
legislated to provide 'preaching ministers' for the city and county of Hereford.
The three cathedral preachers were to receive a stipend of £150 per annum each,
plus rent-free accommodation in one of the decanal or canonical residences.
During their time off from cathedral duties they were to preach in country
churches round about the city.[57] The three original ministers appointed seem likely
to have been presbyterians. George Primrose (1610s–95) came of a Scottish medical
family with court connections; he was an Edinburgh graduate who had also studied
at the French Huguenot seminary in Saumur. William Lowe (*c.* 1603–80) matricu-
lated at Oxford but graduated from Emmanuel College, Cambridge. Samuel Smith
(1610s–85) was likewise a Cambridge graduate (from Trinity College). William
Voyle (*c.* 1594–1674) first appears as the 'intruded' vicar of St Peter's, Hereford,
and joined the cathedral team later; he was the sole Oxford graduate among them.
By contrast Richard Harrison was said to be a baptist; he was appointed in 1652,
to replace Lowe, who may have refused to take the Engagement (the Commonwealth's loyalty oath), which many presbyterians held to be incompatible with
the monarchist (though of course not royalist) affirmations in the Solemn League
and Covenant of 1643–44. Finally Richard Delamaine, who replaced Samuel Smith
from 1652/3 to 1654, perhaps for the same reason, was allegedly even more
heterodox. The son of a mathematician and himself a land surveyor, he was
denounced in an anonymous pamphlet (written from a conservative but puritan
rather than Anglican standpoint) as a seeker, and an admirer of the German mystic
Jacob Boehme; he was said to be a doctor (of what is not clear) but never to
have been ordained; he was also portrayed as a sycophantic client of various
leading puritan and republican radicals under the Commonwealth. Small wonder
that he was too advanced for Hereford: he was removed from his post at the
cathedral and Smith restored in June 1654 (by which time the Protectorate
government of Oliver Cromwell had repealed the Engagement).

Delamaine appears, however, to have retained control of St Ethelbert's Hospital
until his death in 1657. He argued tenaciously, citing documents from Elizabethan
times down to 1646, to show that the mansion house, or almshall, of the hospital

---

56. Firth and Rait, eds, *Acts and Ordinances*, i,   57. Ibid., i, pp. 840–41 (28 March 1646).
    pp. 582–607 (4 January 1644/5).

belonged with the mastership of St. Ethelbert's and was not attached to the treasurership of the cathedral. The house, so he maintained, had therefore been wrongly disposed of as a possession of the dean and chapter; by the time that he staked his claim, in November 1654, it had been resold twice and was then occupied by the well-known sequestrator, Silas Taylor. Yet in March 1657, not long before his own death, Delamaine leased the house to the son of the last royalist master, or *custos*, of the hospital. His widow (who was by then remarried) reassigned the lease in the following year. After the Restoration, in November 1660, the newly appointed master of the hospital (who was one of the residentiary canons) leased the house back to the eventual assignee of the Delamaine lease. His case, that the house did not automatically pass with the cathedral treasurership, had apparently prevailed. When Delamaine made his will in April 1657, he clearly still had associates, perhaps even friends, in the county; two Herefordshire gentlemen and one cleric were asked to act as overseers of his will, which was witnessed by the parliamentarian physician, Dr Bridstock Harford. The only real property mentioned was land which he had bought in Buckinghamshire; in their capacity as trustees, the overseers were to raise £200 for Delamaine's only daughter, and to see to the provision for his only son. They and his wife were made jointly responsible for the religious education and upbringing of the two children, but in what confession or denomination is not stated. There is little indication of radicalism, let alone revolutionary zeal, here. The hostile pamphlet evidence of three years earlier can neither be disregarded, nor yet accepted uncritically. Whether the other three or four preaching ministers all remained in post from the Protectorate to the Restoration is not entirely clear. If so, the cathedral must have been the setting for a positive plethora of puritan sermons. All the survivors were put out of their places in 1660, and none of them appears to have qualified themselves for other church livings by accepting the Uniformity Act of 1662.[58]

58. *DNB*, 'Richard Delamaine the Younger' (the entry may confuse the careers of father and son); 'Samuel Smith' (apparently eliding or confusing two puritan divines of this name: a very understandable error); A. G. Matthews, *Calamy Revised* (Oxford, 1934), pp. 250 (Harrison), 329 (Lowe), 399 (Primrose), 448 (Smith), 504 (Voyle) – the most reliable source (does not include Delamaine because he did not survive to be extruded after 1660); *Impostor Magnus: Or The Legerdemain of Richard Delamain, now Preacher in the City of Hereford* (London, 1654), prelims and pp. 1–31. See D. Wing, *Short-Title Catalogue, 1641–1700* (3 vols, London, 1972–88; 2nd edn, London, 1994), i, p. 105. This work and A. W. Pollard and G. R. Redgrave, *Short-Title Catalogue, 1475–1640* (London, 1946; 2nd edn, 3 vols, London, 1976–91) may also be consulted, in either the original or the revised editions, for works by members of the Primrose family, the two Richard Delamaines, and (hopefully) the correct Samuel Smith; HCA, 6442/2, Delamaine's case concerning St Ethelbert's, and HCA, 4494, the original leases relating to the same; PRO, PROB 11/267, sig. 316.

Fig. 33. Seventeenth-century engraving of Hereford Cathedral from the north west. W. Dugdale, *Monasticon Anglicanum* (London, 1718), p. 292. (HCL, B.3.2, neg. 126.)

One of the frustrations of writing cathedral history is that dissension and controversy are recorded while the satisfactory progress of daily life goes unnoticed; or, to put it another way, 'the evil that men do lives after them; the good is oft interred with their bones'. This may seem particularly true in the case of Hereford Cathedral during the years between the Reformation and the Restoration. While we cannot ignore the problems, we should set against them the sense that prayer and praise were regularly offered, most often with dignity and sincerity; that the chapter remained a community of canons serving God; that great music like that of Hereford's own John Bull was sung; that visitors like Lieutenant Hammond were entertained hospitably; and that the great building survived, an inspiration for the future as well as in its own time. Many awaited the 'happy return of the church' in 1660 with eager anticipation.

5

Restoration to Reform, 1660–1832

Howard Tomlinson

The essential dimension of the church's restoration lay in the provinces. As an historian has written: 'In the dioceses and shires which lay beyond White-hall, Westminster and the Savoy, the re-establishment of the church of England was a living reality before either parliament or convocation had chance to legislate on church affairs'.[1] In no place was this reality more apparent than in the cathedrals, where chapters had to be re-established first if the bishops needed to fill the fourteen vacant sees were to be canonically elected. The speed by which this was accomplished is testimony to the king's recognition of the importance of an episcopally governed church as an essential support for monarchy. Within a month of the king's triumphant entry into his capital, on 29 May 1660, the first decanal appointments were being made.[2] Soon complete chapters had been restored, particularly in those cathedrals nearest London, and by mid July the chapters at Peterborough and Canterbury had held their first meetings.[3] Others quickly followed and these included the gatherings on 7 August at Norwich and on 8 August at Hereford, the first general chapter in the city for nearly fifteen years.[4]

It is clear, however, that business had been transacted several weeks before the

1. R. A. Beddard, review article on Gilbert Sheldon, *Historical Journal*, 19 (1976), p. 1010. This chapter could not have been written without the support of the Governors of Hereford Cathedral School who granted me sabbatical leave 1997–98, and the master and fellows of St Peter's College, Oxford, who elected me to a school-teacher fellowship, Hilary Term, 1998. I am indebted to both institutions.

2. Robert Creighton of Wells was appointed on 29 June and was among the first of the new deans: see L. S. Colchester, ed., *Wells Cathedral: A History* (Shepton Mallet, 1982), p. 160.

3. I. M. Green, *The Re-Establishment of the Church of England, 1660–1663* (Oxford, 1978), pp. 67, 72.

4. Ian Atherton and others, eds, *Norwich Cathedral: Church, City and Diocese, 1096–1996* (London, 1996), p. 558; HCA, 7031/3, p. 183. Although the Hereford acts for the period have disappeared, the fabric account had been last signed in 1645 (HCA, 2379) at what was probably the last chapter meeting before the Restoration.

formally constituted chapter meetings of midsummer 1660, not least in the eight foundations where the dean had survived the wilderness of the Interregnum years. At Peterborough, for example, Dean Cosin had been 'invited thither by the prebendaries and divers tenants of the church who desired to renew their leases', and had taken possession of the cathedral in July 'to the great satisfaction of the whole city'.[5] A similar situation may have occurred even earlier at Hereford: Dean Croft, who having inherited his brother's estates had spent much of the revolutionary years as the guest of a neighbouring squire, would have been in a much easier position than the exiled Cosin to reclaim both his inheritance and his cathedral. The family's papers having disappeared, so much is speculation. How-

Fig. 34. Herbert Croft, dean of Hereford 1644–61, bishop of Hereford 1662–91. (HCL, B.3.81.)

ever, the earliest surviving Restoration document in the cathedral archives – the king's circular warrant of 22 June 1660, requiring deans and chapters to reduce all leases from three lives to twenty-one years – makes it likely that Dean Croft was busy about cathedral affairs well before that first meeting with his surviving canons (fig. 34).[6]

Nevertheless, the 8 August meeting was of crucial importance as it enabled the dean to begin the task of filling the depleted ranks of his staff and to start the process of reconstruction. Although the precentor, the chancellor and twelve prebendaries, led by John Pember, had survived the Interregnum,[7] the dean represented the sole element of continuity among the residentiaries, and as a canon of Windsor it is probable that

5. R. A. Beddard, 'The Restoration Church', in J. R. Jones, ed., *The Restored Monarchy, 1660–88* (London, 1979), p. 163.
6. HCA, 7031/3, p. 621. Croft explained, in a letter to Canon Watts more than a decade later, the advantage of this change for the church: '[In] my long experience ... in several churches, as Worcester, Windsor, Hereford ... we clearly found that the profits arising from leases for years was seven times greater than from leases for

lives', HCA, 1152.
7. Bannister, *The Cathedral Church of Hereford*, p. 101. Francis Coke was precentor and Richard Coke chancellor. Neither were residentiaries. Bannister suggests nine prebendaries survived but it is clear from the lists in Willis, *Survey of the Cathedrals* pp. 556ff, that at least twelve (including Croft but excluding James Rawlins of Putston Major who died in 1660) survived until the Restoration.

he was the key emissary with the court with regard to the impending capitular appointments. These were speedily accomplished. Before the end of August, the five vacancies had all been filled (largely, as elsewhere, by men with strong local connections),[8] and the offices of claviger, master of the library and master of the fabric had been shared out among the new brethren.[9] Fourteen prebendaries were also installed between 7 August and 24 September.[10] The men had thereby been put in place for the belated election of Nicholas Monck, brother of the general who had helped bring about the Restoration, as the new bishop of Hereford.[11] By the end of 1660 Dean Croft might well have echoed Bishop Duppa's remark of early May: 'Never was there so miraculous a change as this, nor so great things done in so short a time'.[12] But this was only the beginning. The personnel, including important minor staff like the verger, the sexton and the keeper of the canon's bakehouse,[13] had largely been established, but the cathedral's services, fabric, rights and procedures were less easily restored.

The resumption of cathedral worship may be briefly mentioned here. A service was undoubtedly held to herald the king's return in May, for the clavigers' accounts record retrospective payments of 10s. to the bell-ringers, 5s. 'to the drums and trumpets' and £3 5s. 0d. to the Hereford poor on the same day.[14] At this time the cathedral may still have been in the hands of non-royalist clergy, in which case the Book of Common Prayer would not have been used at this service. Nevertheless, it is evident that public worship according to the pre-war prayer book was quickly re-established thereafter. Indeed, the little evidence in the surviving accounts of prayer books being purchased (although £1 3s. 0d. was paid by Michaelmas 1660 'for two common prayer books for the choir')[15] supports Hutton's suggestion that in conservative communities 'existing prayer books were simply … dusted down and re-used, if indeed they required dusting'.[16] It comes as no surprise, moreover, to find that the new dean, Dr Hodges, whose appointment following Croft's elevation as bishop of Hereford was in recognition of his services as chaplain

8. Green, *Re-Establishment of the Church*, pp. 67–68.

9. HCA, 7031/3, pp. 183, 185, 186, 188, re appointments of Benson, Phillips, Watts, Seddon ('Seden') and Good and elections of officers.

10. Willis, *Survey of the Cathedrals*, pp. 556ff.

11. On 8 December 1660, HCA, 7031/3, p. 195. Monck was consecrated on 13 January 1661, HRO, AL 19/18, fol. 176v. He never visited the diocese.

12. Quoted by Beddard, 'Restoration Church',

p. 155.

13. Richard Stallard and James Drewry were appointed verger and sexton, respectively, on 8 August. Roger Cocks was appointed keeper of the bakehouse on 30 August. HCA, 7031/3, p. 183; 2909.

14. HCA, R 609, clavigers' account, 1660–61.

15. Ibid.

16. Ronald Hutton, *The Restoration: A Political and Religious History of England and Wales, 1658–1667* (Oxford, 1985), p. 172.

to the House of Lords,[17] had purchased eleven copies of the new prayer book for the cathedral's use soon after the passing of the Act of Uniformity in May 1662.[18] The clavigers' accounts also indicate that the regular celebration of holy communion at major festivals, as well as on the first Sunday of every month as the Laudian statutes required, was soon established.[19]

The re-establishment of the cathedral's choral tradition was inevitably accomplished with greater difficulty, given the time that had elapsed since the singing of the choir's last pre-Restoration service, which may have been performed before Charles I himself.[20] A generation might have been insufficient to have brought about either a comprehensive settlement or a reformed church, but it was time enough to have broken the line of musicians that had served the cathedrals of Caroline England. Nevertheless, attempts were quickly made to revive this tradition, and among the early chapter appointments were those for the admission of vicars choral and organist.[21] It also became the organist's responsibility to train the choristers, who, not surprisingly following the break in tradition, needed encouragement 'when they began to sing alone in the choir'.[22] The rebuilding of the organ was not completed until after the middle years of the decade; prior to this, the choir depended for accompaniment on a cornet played by 'one Mr Birch' and an organ loaned by a Mr Stallard.[23]

Hereford Cathedral itself escaped the worst excesses of the revolutionary period. As well as the destruction caused by the sieges at Lichfield and Carlisle, already

17. The House of Lords made recommendations for 'some good ecclesiastical preferment' for Hodges on 30 July and 4 December 1661. Bishop Monck died on 17 December and Croft was nominated to the bishopric on 27 December, elected 19 January and enthroned (by proxy) on 18 February 1662, *Hereford Cathedral News*, 34 (1956), pp. 7–8. Hodges was installed as dean (also by proxy) on 10 February, and admitted as a full residentiary (his greater residence being dispensed with) on 19 February 1662, HCA, 7031/3, pp. 210–11.

18. HCA, R 610, £4 3s 0d. for eleven common prayer books 'sent unto us by Mr Dean'. It is possible that Hodges originally purchased twelve copies, keeping one for himself. See Phillips's draft account 'for twelve common prayer books to Dr Hodges', ibid., accounts, 1661–62. The prayer books seem to have cost 7s. 6d. each.

19. 9s. 3d. was spent on communion bread and wine for Christmas Day 1660 and the Sunday following. For the years 1661–66 these sums were spent on the communion (both kinds) each year: £3 5s. 11d.; £3 5s. 11d.; £4 3s. 10d.; £3 12s. 2d.; £5 2s. 2d. The sexton was allowed 1s. per annum for 'washing the communion table linen'.

20. See Anthony Adams's petition on behalf of his son, HCA, 7031/3, p. 224.

21. HCA, 7031/3, p. 192, 27 September 1660. In 1661 the organist, John Badham, received £6 'by reason of his poverty and necessity' and thereafter a yearly salary of £12, augmented occasionally by casual payments – as in 1665–66 when he was given 10s. 'for encouragement for making an anthem', HCA, R 610.

22. In 1660 they were given an extra 2s. 6d. for their efforts, HCA, R 609.

23. HCA, R 610, payments of £2 to Birch, £6 to 'Dic Stallard', and several to Mr Taunton, the organ-maker.

mentioned, Canterbury, for example, was in a 'sad, forlorn and languishing condition' and Exeter may have been unserviceable.[24] Nevertheless, Hereford had also suffered depredations. The chapter house, having been stripped of its lead to strengthen the garrison, was significantly weakened, and the cathedral's windows, statues and brasses were badly damaged by the Scottish Covenanters.[25] Indeed, by 1660 the cathedral was certainly in a worse state than it had been during the civil wars for, following the sale of dean and chapter lands in 1649, there was no money to make substantial repairs to its fabric. The poor state of the building is made clear in the king's warrant of 23 November 1660, deferring royal rents to the chapter's use because the church had become 'very ruinous through the disorders of the late ill times'.[26] This situation had begun to be remedied several months earlier, however, after George Benson's elevation as a canon residentiary and his consequent election as master of the fabric – an auspicious appointment, for Benson, as a minor canon, had signed the last pre-Restoration fabric account and thus provided another vital element of continuity with the old order.[27] For more than three years, as holder of the office, the direction of the rebuilding was in Dr Benson's capable hands.

The people of Hereford must have witnessed some remarkable scenes in the decade that followed, as the interior of their cathedral was slowly transformed by the returning of treasures safely preserved during the revolution; the obtaining of covers, furniture, fittings, vestments and vessels for the seemly conduct of worship; the renewing of windows, and the repair and redecoration of other parts of the interior. Sadly, the patchy nature of the sources enables only a rough sketch, rather than a complete picture, to be drawn. Some indication of the scale of activity in the months after the Restoration, however, may be gathered from the large amounts spent on the fabric: £295 15s. 8d. from 8 August 1660 to Michaelmas 1661, exceeding the general account for the period by over £60.[28] In the next two years the expenditure (perhaps £175) was smaller, and even less appears to have been

24. Above, p. 102; Green, *Re-Establishment of the Church*, pp. 75–76.

25. Above, p. 246; R. Rawlinson, *The History and Antiquities of the City and Cathedral-Church of Hereford* (London, 1717), p. vii.

26. HCA, 2265. Also see the chapter's submission to Sancroft of *c*. November 1670: 'By the late war, our fabric was ruined, some of our bells sold, our fair organ utterly spoiled, all our ornaments defaced and taken away, our records and many deeds lost ...', Oxford, Bodleian, MS Tanner 147, fol. 94r.

27. HCA, 7031/3, pp. 183, 185, 188; David Whitehead, 'A Goth among the Greeks: The Architecture of Hereford Cathedral in the Eighteenth Century', *FHC*, 57 (1981), p. 21.

28. The surviving fabric accounts for 1660–63 are not itemised on the expenditure side, and those for 1663–64, 1665–66 and after 1667 (until 1681) are missing. Neither have I come across a contemporary description of the rebuilding. For other cathedrals, see Green, *Re-Establishment of the Church*, pp. 74–76.

spent from 1663–65,[29] so that by June 1665 the chapter was complaining about 'the present ruins and wants' of the cathedral.[30] This slow process of refurbishment was directly related to the cathedral's financial straits. Although Dr Benson had done wonders in raising over £235 for necessary repairs in his first term in office – receipts were from a variety of sources and included the traditional fabric rents and burial fees, as well as over £200 in extraordinary tithes, and other one-off payments like the £25 for the admission of the five new residentiaries – by Michaelmas 1661 his account was in deficit by nearly £75. This funding gap widened by more than £50 in the following two years and increased each year thereafter.[31] It was eventually bridged by loans from the dean and chapter, including £120 from Benson himself, who also gave £20 as a 'free gift towards the organ'; fines on those dignitaries who had continued to lease in lives rather than years; and by £180 in gifts, described in the 1664–65 accounts as 'donations by the nobility, gentry and people of Hereford and Shropshire towards the repair and necessary ornamentation of the cathedral church of Hereford'. Heading the list of benefactors was John, Viscount Scudamore, with £100, followed by Bishop Croft, who gave £40.[32] As we shall see, it was a story which was to be repeated in later generations.

The recovery of the cathedral's rights went hand in hand with the restoration of its lands, both of which took some time to complete. The Convention Parliament of 1660 had laid down general principles about repossession of confiscated crown and church lands, but it had failed to pass a measure to deal with the problem, thereby leaving the initiative entirely with the king and his servants. The recovery of capitular land, therefore, took place piecemeal, but in general accord with Charles II's own wishes that churchmen should favour purchasers and old tenants in sealing their leases, those ejected receiving compensation as laid down in the Commons guidelines, with any disputes being referred to the arbitration of a specially established royal commission.[33] The only case of appeal

29. It is not clear exactly how much was spent on the fabric, as opposed to fees and other payments. £53 14s. 3d. seems definite for 1661–62, and possibly c. £120 for 1662–63: HCA, 2380, 2381. For 1663–64 some fabric payments are included on the clavigers' account: e.g. £22 10s. 0d. to 'James Jaggard' for glazing windows, and £15 to Rowland Andrews, the carpenter. About £130 of the £193 0s. 2d. on the debit side of the 1664–65 fabric account was for repayment of loans: HCA, R 610, 2382. Also see Oxford, Bodleian, MS Tanner 147, fos 83r–83v, for an account of

disbursements in the early 1660s.
30. HCA, 7031/3, p. 243, 26 June 1665.
31. HCA, 2379–81, fabric accounts, 1660–63.
32. HCA, R 610, 1663–64, clavigers' account for Benson's gift and repayment; 7031/3, p. 233, 5 June 1664, for same repayment; 7031/3, p. 243, 26 June 1665, for loans from the dean and chapter out of their petty commons; 7031/3, pp. 246, 247, for fines; 2382, fabric account, 1664–65, for the list of donors. Scudamore's gift was received on 30 December 1664, HCA, 7031/3, p. 237.
33. Hutton, *Restoration*, pp. 139–42.

in the cathedral archives is that of Frances Hall, whose husband had purchased the lease of the manor of Norton Canon for over £700 'in the late troubles', and had spent more than £170 on another estate near Hereford. This suggests that the commissioners did their work fairly in that the dean and chapter was enjoined to treat her claim favourably, assist her in the recovery of arrears and grant no further leases on the properties for the time being.[34] What is also clear, however, is that the dean and chapter was equally determined to assert and defend its own rights, over £76 being paid in lawsuits for this purpose in the opening years of the Restoration.[35] Its defence of title, however, could be placed in jeopardy by the lack of historical record. The chapter's defence of its claim to the Llangarron estate, for example, was undoubtedly weakened by its ignorance of the appellant's right to the title and the incomplete nature of its own documentation.[36]

It was of paramount importance, therefore, for both the cathedral's archives to be traced and its record-keeping, not least its knowledge of land holdings, to be improved. The £3 15s. 0d. spent by the restored chapter in 1660 'for getting and carrying records from London' and the £3 paid to the Gloucester gentleman 'skillful in old court and chancery hand' show its determination to resurrect its past, but manuscripts like the pre-war act books proved beyond recovery.[37] Nevertheless, something could be done to improve its custodianship of records. One key order in this respect was that of 5 June 1664, requiring all prebendaries within twenty miles to give bond that they had not set any lease contrary to statute. Future leases, moreover, were to be first authorised by the dean and chapter.[38] This resulted in a plethora of surveys being taken, giving the chapter some indication of the nature of the estates held by cathedral dignitaries.[39] Not only were terriers made anew. Further acts stipulated where the act book itself should be kept and

34. HCA, 5232, petition and report, 2 March 1661.
35. Oxford, Bodleian, MS Tanner 147, fol. 83.
36. HCA, 5234, case papers, 12 July 1666. Also see Oxford, Bodleian, MS Tanner 147, fol. 94r, chapter report to Sancroft c. November 1670.
37. HCA, R 609; Oxford, Bodleian, MS Tanner 147, fol. 83v. On 16 September the chapter formally recorded that some act books had been lost in the civil wars. These may well have been among the manuscripts taken by Silas Taylor, HCA, 5748, extract from W. Nicolson, *The English Historical Library* (London, 1714), pp. 130–31.

38. HCA, 7031/3, p. 231; also p. 236 re future leases.
39. There are a number of these terriers extant. See (in chronological order), HCA, 2326, 2344, 2355, 2341, 2361, 2319, 2359, 2322, 2363–65, 2329. The earliest is dated 20 June, the latest 29 September 1664, most being submitted within the two month deadline. Even in 1670, it was admitted that 'only with much difficulty can the canons find out what, or on what unlawful conditions, leases are set'. Oxford, Bodleian, MS Tanner 147, fol. 94v, for this and other uncomplimentary chapter comments about the prebendaries' neglect.

when and how it should be examined.[40] Matters were not helped by there being
no settled room for chapter business, meetings being occasionally held in the library
or at a canon's house as well as the chapter house, which was described in
September 1670 as 'the now accustomed chapter house'.[41] The appointment of the
redoubtable Abraham Seward as chapter clerk from September 1672 was further
to transform the organisation of business and the maintenance of records, Seward
being given a little room within the library to 'enter the acts of chapter ... and
keep the records committed to his charge 'till further conveniencey be found out
for him'.[42]

It is not without significance that a new dean was installed just days before the
appointment of an energetic chapter clerk, thereby ensuring that the recovery of
the 1660s would be sustained.[43] It also inaugurated a twenty-year partnership between
dean and bishop without parallel in the early modern history of the cathedral. For
Dean Benson was a protégé of Bishop Croft, the dean owing his appointment as
archdeacon of Hereford and his place as canon residentiary in 1660 to the bishop's
patronage. The first obvious manifestation of their close alliance was the episcopal
visitation of 1677. The background to the visitation and the visitation itself are
worth describing in some detail because they illustrate the tensions which could
exist between Close and palace, and further indicate how far the cathedral's fortunes
had recovered in the quarter century since the Restoration.

The Laudian statutes had importantly placed the interpretation of disputes in
the hands of the bishop of Hereford, who was appointed 'visitor and ordinary
judge of this church'.[44] In December 1662, within the year of Croft's election,
forty-six detailed articles were presented for answer by each member of the dean
and chapter 'by virtue of their oath'. Watts and Sherborne led the opposition to
the presentation and the chapter then promulgated a decree against all episcopal

40. HCA, 7013/3, p. 206, 23 October 1662;
p. 221, 9 September 1663.
41. HCA, 7013/3, pp. 185, 230, 242, for library
meetings, 8, 29 August 1660, 5 June 1664,
26 June 1665; p. 228, for meeting in the
precentor's house, 8 December 1663;
p. 280, for 29 September 1670 meeting.
The chapter house was cited as the place
of meeting more frequently than anywhere
else in this period. It is not at all clear
whether the 'now accustomed chapter
house' is indeed the old pre-war building.
Some fifty years later the chapter had definitely moved to the present canons' vestry,
Willis, *Survey of the Cathedrals*, plan.
42. HCA, 7031/3, p. 303, 27 March 1673. Also

see p. 316, re recording of leases; p. 358,
26 June 1678 re custody of act book;
p. 397, 3 December 1681, re entries for
Tomson's gift. It is no coincidence that
following Seward's appointment there is
a new regularity in the act book's
appearance.
43. Benson was elected by general chapter on
10 September 1672; Seward assumed the
office of chapter clerk on 12 September
'until Mr Wall shall have his business decided by Mr Dean and Mr Watts', HCA,
7031/3, pp. 295–97. For Pauncefoot Wall,
see HRO, BG 11/17/5, fol. 36.
44. Bannister, *The Cathedral Church of Hereford*,
p. 96.

visitations. The bishop's power of visitation was further disputed in 1668 by Dean Hodges on the grounds that it was contrary to the ancient statutes, and again the bishop withdrew.[45] By the third time of asking in 1677, five years after his friend's elevation as dean, all resistance had crumbled and Bishop Croft completed the first full episcopal visitation in the cathedral's history.

The visitation was nothing if not thorough and took almost a year to complete.[46] Sixty general articles, covering every aspect of cathedral life, were issued, together with fourteen further articles concerning the administration of Ledbury Hospital. Before the end of the year the bishop had promulgated twenty-six injunctions which were followed by seven further and final orders on 4 April 1678.[47] Three injunctions refer to preaching and worship at the cathedral. All preachers were to be licensed; the lecturer was always to preach at his appointed times and only such sermons 'as may most tend to the instruction of all persons, especially the younger clergy [in the] fundamental parts of religion'; and the college was to ensure that morning prayer was read by the vicars choral and not by the deacons, the vicars being enjoined 'constantly [to] frequent' the service.[48] Others relate to the organist, John Badham, who was required to 'be diligent in performing his duty', including teaching choristers 'to play on the organ or some other instrument'. In return, Badham was to receive his agreed salary of £12 p.a., which the chapter resolved to do '*salva conscientia*'.[49] The organist was also to be paid for setting 'the song books ... into a good and perfect order', the books having first been 'pricked by some careful person who is skilful in music'.[50] Order was brought to other aspects of cathedral life: a fees table, for example, was to be displayed in the chapter house and a catalogue made and an account rendered of all library books.[51]

45. Bannister, *The Cathedral Church of Hereford*, pp. 101–2; HCA, 1565, 1662 articles (endorsed 2 August: see 2 December in the actual document); 6247 (Cove MS), pp. 52, 54, re the 1662 and 1668 resistance.

46. The process started with the inhibition of 16 April 1677, served on the cathedral two days later 'by affixing the same upon the door of the choir', and was completed by the issuing of the final order on 4 April 1678. HRO, AL 19/18, pp. 250r, 270v.

47. There are complete sets of the visitation papers among the diocesan records and in the cathedral archives, HRO, AL 19/18, fos 253v–259r, 263v–268r, 270v–272r; HCA, 1575, 1579. The injunctions of 23 August and 11 September (only) were copied into the act book, HCA, 7031/4 (end).

No individual replies to the 1677 articles have survived.

48. HCA, 1579, visitations, 1677, p. 8, injunctions, nos 1, 5, 12, 16.

49. Ibid., nos 2, 6; p. 10, answers of the dean and chapter, no. 2. The chapter eventually agreed to pay £5 arrears of salary, as well as the £12, ibid., p. 12, no. 4.

50. Ibid., p. 8, injunctions, no. 4; p. 12, further injunctions, no. 1. Badham was assisted in the first task by Robert Griffiths, one of the vicars choral.

51. Ibid., p. 8, injunctions, no. 4; p. 12, further injunctions, no. 2. The chapter replied that the catalogue had been 'already taken' and that the account would be provided at the subsequent general chapter, ibid., p. 10, answers, no. 8.

Parochially, improvements were to be made to the regularisation of preaching and the repair of chancels; more vicars were to be placed in benefices within seven miles of the city. Estate problems to be remedied included the dubious leases at Lugwardine, Woolhope and Yarkhill rectories, as well as those made on terms other than twenty-one years (except where statute permitted), and the failings of miscreant tenants who had unlawfully felled trees at Kempley or had neglected to pay their corn rents elsewhere.[52] Further injunctions relate to the visitation and rents of Ledbury Hospital, the use of fabric fines and the churchyard passage of carts bound for the college without fine.[53] The number and range of these injunctions should be compared with the multifarious responsibilities of the canons – the twenty-one chapters of the Laudian statutes contained over 150 orders – so it can be fairly concluded from the evidence of Bishop Croft's only visitation that the cathedral was in safe hands.

The final phase of the cathedral's restoration took place in the decade before the 1688 Revolution. It was a period of faithful administration and some prosperity. Although there were occasional squabbles and examples of errant preaching among some prebendaries,[54] as well as indications that not all of Croft's more serious complaints had been put right (one notable instance being his warning to the chapter about a rumour that the fabric fund was still being alienated 'from the ancient use to ... private profits'),[55] there is also much evidence of a more business-like and modern approach to cathedral governance. This is apparent, for example, not only from the act book's appearance, its greater order perhaps reflecting the development of a proper agenda at chapter meetings, but also from its increasing use of English.[56] The recorded acts of the period further suggest that the chapter

52. Ibid., pp. 8–9, injunctions, nos 3, 11; p. 11, orders and injunctions, no. 4 re parishes; pp. 8–9, injunctions, nos 9, 10, 13–15, 17; p. 11, orders and injunctions, no. 5 re leases. City tenements were allowed a maximum thirty-year lease and were usually let for twenty-nine years, ibid., p. 8, injunctions, no. 10; p. 11, orders and injunctions, no. 3 re tenants' failures.

53. Ibid., p. 9, injunctions, nos 18, 19; p. 11, orders and injunctions, no. 7; p. 12, further injunctions, no. 5 re the hospital; pp. 12–13 re fabric fines. The large fines from Shinfield and Swallowfield were always to be used for the fabric; the others could be divided after a £79 debt had been repaid to St Katherine's Ledbury and a stock of £100 had been established for emergencies.

Ibid., p. 12, further injunctions, no. 3 re carts.

54. See HCA, 7031/3, pp. 346, 348, re the quarrel over stalls and the 40s. 'mulcting' of Prebendary Lewis.

55. HCA, 7031/3, pp. 411–12, 18 June 1683. Only part of the Swallowfield fine was accredited to the fabric account for that year, HCA, R 614.

56. The greater orderliness is apparent in the thematic recording of business transactions. During Giles Ganderton's tenure as chapter clerk, c. 8 November 1705 to 4 May 1707, the acts revert to Latin. Thereafter, English is generally used, except for initial headings and appointments. The last Latin entry is that for 8 November 1733, HCA, 7031/4, p. 157.

continued to assert its responsibilities, whether they concerned individual rights like the 'hebdomadariship'; its own corporate duties over voting, confidentiality, residence or attendance – the lead in the latter instance being taken by Dean Benson who in January 1677 had promised to attend all general chapters 'if possibly he can ...',[57] as well as 'any ... like necessary occasion'[58] – or the traditional defence of its landed rights.[59] Careful watch continued to be kept over the conduct of worship. In December 1680 attempts were made to ensure that there would always be three vicars on each side of the choir for the Sunday evening service. Fifteen months later the chapter tried to remedy the 'several defects in the choir and vacancies by reason of infirmities of body', by the insistence that on the vacancy of a vicar choral only 'a scholar graduate' would be admitted 'if within the two months he may be had out of either of the universities'.[60] The chapter was later sufficiently alert to protect the interests of a newly elected vicar in his probationary year.[61] Its wider pastoral concerns are also indicated by its ready response to Archbishop Sancroft's appeal for the relief of repressed Huguenot ministers and the £6 given to the city corporation 'as a free gift ... towards the losses sustained by the late lamentable fires in ... Hereford'.[62]

The extent to which the cathedral had recovered from its hand to mouth existence of the early 1660s may be gauged from the evidence of the accounts, largely complete for the final ten years of Dean Benson's life, 1681–91. These reveal a cathedral in robust health, with receipts averaging £440 p.a. on the clavigers' account and payments only £304 p.a., the £136 difference being the average dividend shared among the six residentiaries each year.[63] The masters of the fabric for the period were also good stewards, their surpluses averaging out

57. HCA, 7031/3, pp. 327, 340, 9 December 1675, 9 January 1677, re the five supernumerary weeks above the two months residence period and 'the settling of the hebdomadariship' (rights with the canon in residence unless the dean present); p. 389, 4 December 1680, for the important act re voting.
58. HCA, 7031/3, p. 341.
59. HCA, 7031/3, pp. 483–84, 4 December 1690, suit between the vicar of Woolhope and the dean and chapter and James Gregory, concerning the lease of the rectory and tithes. Gregory spent £140 18s. 9d. on the suit at the Exchequer and Lords, half of which was to be paid by the prebendaries (£3 15s. 0d. each).
60. HCA, 7031/3, p. 389, 4 December 1680;

p. 400, 8 March 1682; p. 402, ratification by general chapter, 26 June 1682.
61. HCA, 7031/3, p. 463, 29 July 1687, re the annulling of an act of the college stopping his pay. For the chapter's concern for the college in general, see its visitation articles of the early 1690s, HCA, 7031/3, pp. 157–58.
62. HCA, 7031/3, p. 420, 4 December 1683 (£5 p.a. was subscribed for the Huguenots); p. 441, 16 June 1685.
63. HCA, R 612, 614–19; 7036/1 (for 1690–91). The total receipts, payments and dividends for the ten-year period were: £4407 12s. 6d.; £3044 12s. 6d., and £1363. Although Dean Benson lived on until September 1692, the 1691–92 account has been ignored as it was the first to be signed by Dean Tyler.

at £120 p.a. Their accounts recorded a deficit only for 1682–83, but just once (in 1688–89) did annual expenditure on the fabric exceed £100, the annual norm running at £63. The major works of renovation had clearly been completed by this time, the only sizeable payments being made to William Griffiths for new leads and other plumbing work.[64] The 1680s then were generally a time of routine maintenance, the repairs being conducted under the watchful eye of the sexton, John Silvester, himself a skilled craftsman.[65] There was also occasional adornment of both cathedral and Close. Over £40 was spent in 1683, for example, 'for making the wall, gravelling the walks and planting the trees in the churchyard', and thousands of tiles were bought in three successive years (1685–88) from a Huguenot artisan, 'monsieur the tiler', who had presumably established business in the Hereford area following his exile from France.[66] Details of the finest work of the period, however, are not to be found in the cathedral accounts, for Renatus Harris's great organ of 1686 was built by the generosity of the local people and accounted for separately. The total cost of £720 exceeded the amount spent on the fabric for the whole ten-year period by some £80, the exquisitely carved and gilded baroque organ case alone costing more than the average expenditure in any one year.[67] This wondrous work was a constant reminder to all worshippers that the cathedral had been triumphantly restored at last. It was the apogee of Dean Benson's career (plate XI.).

His earthly triumph, however, was to be short-lived, for in less than three years he was to experience the pain of a revolution which not only changed the face of his church but also resulted in his son, Samuel, being deprived of his offices of archdeacon of Hereford, prebendary of Warham and canon residentiary, and vicar of Sellack, for his refusal to abjure his oath to James II and swear a new oath of allegiance to William and Mary. Samuel was one of eleven ordained clergy in the diocese to lose his living, the only others from the cathedral to do

64. HCA, R 612, 614–15; 7020/2/1; 7036/1 (for 1688–89). Surpluses were generally credited on the following year's account, although when the balances were large, as in the mid 1680s, money could be transferred to other accounts. See e.g. HCA, 7031/3, p. 466, 2 December 1687, re the transfer of £100 to the senior claviger. For payments to Griffiths of £49 18s. 2d. (1685–86), £39 13s. 2d. (1687–88) and £41 9s. 10d. (1689–90), see HCA, 7020/2/1.

65. Whitehead, 'A Goth among the Greeks', p. 23.

66. HCA, R 614, account 29 November 1683; 7020/2/1, re payments of 10 guineas,

£1 18s. 6d. (for 1000 tiles), and £3 4s. 8d., 1685–88. In 1688 the tiler was styled 'Richard Monsieur'.

67. Over £400 was given by local gentry and others, and more than £100 by members of the foundation. Bishop Croft's £40 was the largest donation; the £20 gifts of the dean and Sir Timothy Baldwyn the next largest. Renatus Harris received £515 for the organ, Giles Campion £100 for gilding and painting and Rowland Andrews £70 for carving the case. For the full account and list of benefactors, see W. E. H. Clarke, 'Hereford Cathedral Organ', *TWNFC*, 24 (1921–24), pp. 43–48.

Fig. 35. Tomb slabs of Bishop
Herbert Croft, died 1691, and
Dean George Benson, died
1692, joined by clasped hands:
south-east transept.

so being the chancellor, Joseph Harvey, and the prebendary of Moreton Parva,
Thomas Martin.[68] Apart from these quickly remedied deprivations (Adam Ottley,
Samuel's successor, was elected residentiary before 1690 had ended and all other
diocesan vacancies had been filled by May 1691),[69] and the brief disruption caused
by the abandonment of the March 1689 chapter, the 1688 Revolution did not
seriously affect cathedral life.[70] Dean Benson and Bishop Croft, too, survived the
Revolution, but they were able to serve their church for only a few more months,
the bishop dying, aged eighty-eight, on 18 May 1691, and his friend the dean
fifteen months later, aged seventy-eight. It is fitting that their friendship was
posthumously symbolised by the joining of hands on their tombstones
(fig. 35),[71] for theirs had been a glorious partnership, not the least of their
achievements springing from Bishop Croft's determination to admit only those

68. J. H. Overton, *The Nonjurors: Their Lives,
Principles and Writings* (London, 1902),
pp. 471–96. See HCA, 7031/3, p. 482,
for the installation of Francis Jauncey in
Martin's place, 12 August 1690.

69. HCA, 7031/3, pp. 484–85 (and also for
Hugo Lewis's installation as prebendary, 18
December 1690, following Benson's deprivation). For the other institutions and
collations, see HRO, AL 19/19, fol. 111r,

Baldwyn to Oxenden, 4 May 1691.

70. HCA, 7031/3, pp. 471–72. The chapter was
successively adjourned from 6 December
1688 and next met on 25 June 1689.

71. Croft's inscription reads: *In vita conjuncti*,
Benson's: *In morte non divisi*. For a description, see Rawlinson, *History*, pp. 98–99. For
the scriptural allusion, see 2 Samuel 1:23. I
am indebted to Canon John Tiller for this
reference.

who lived within the diocese to the dignity of prebendary.[72] Yet they must have prepared to meet their maker with a sense of world-weariness. Bishop Croft, who made his will on 4 January 1689, during the dark days of the century's second revolution, can speak for them both:

> This is my last will and testament. Jacob said: 'Few and evil have the days of my life been'; but I say many and evil have the days of the years of my life been. For we Christians, whom our blessed saviour, Jesus, hath both by himself and his holy apostles so fully assured that we shall enjoy his gracious and glorious presence after our death, should think every day a year 'till we arrive at that blessed enjoyment, and especially in these evil days wherein we have lived to see such sad revolutions and dismal catastrophies ...[73]

Within thirty years of the Restoration the cathedral's course had been set; its fabric had been fully restored; its statutes had been successfully reimplemented; its business methods had been tested and refined, and its rightful place as the mother church of the diocese had been re-established. Even the turmoil of the Revolution, as we have seen, proved no more than a tremor from which it quickly recovered. In the near century from the deaths of Croft and Benson until the fall of the west front, on Easter Monday 1786, it was to experience no similar upheaval. That is not to say, however, that the cathedral and its chapter fell into a torpor throughout this period, still less that the details of its history 'are of trifling importance'.[74] Bannister's 'settled centuries' may seem settled from what came before and what went on afterwards, but to those residentiaries who lived through them the late seventeenth and eighteenth centuries would have been far from a period of slumber.

Indeed, the period coinciding with John Tyler's deanship (1692–1724) has been characterised as one of 'rage' between Tory and Whig, which in church terms was reflected in the vehement controversies between high and low churchmen. These heated debates could easily spill over into a cathedral close, as they did at Norwich during Humphrey Prideaux's time, when party intruded into all aspects of cathedral life.[75] It would be surprising indeed if Hereford had entirely escaped such strife, even given the vastly contrasting political complexions of the two cathedral cities. The extant evidence, however, is slim. We do know that under the moderate Whig dean (named another Wat Tyler by the high churchman and

---

72. One result was a more active, because more local, chapter, as indicated by the attendance of every residentiary at six successive November audits, 1682–87.
73. HCA, 7005/1, p. 210.
74. Bannister, *The Cathedral Church of Hereford*, p. 101.
75. Ian Atherton and Victor Morgan, 'Revolution and Retrenchment: The Cathedral, 1630–1720', in Atherton and others, eds, *Norwich Cathedral*, pp. 563–75.

antiquary, Browne Willis)[76] one other Whig, Richard Smalbroke, was brought in as a canon residentiary in 1710. This was accomplished 'by the option of the Archbishop of Canterbury', Smalbroke having been his chaplain, and through the means of the bishop's prebend, styled the 'golden prebend' because it gave the fortunate prebendary an automatic right to a seat on chapter.[77] Destined for even higher office, Smalbroke was a learned and energetic cleric, responsible for some significant additions to the chained library during his period as master.[78] As the negligent vicars choral found to their cost when they failed to attend choir service and sermons, he was also zealous in reforming abuse and may have been a difficult colleague to work with.[79] Smalbroke had once fallen foul of Bishop Humphreys. He later crossed swords with the admittedly intemperate Browne Willis, after openly criticising him in a sermon in Llandaff Cathedral. His Tory colleague, Adam Ottley, senior residentiary and also bishop of St David's, may have been implicated in Smalbroke's pulpit polemic, and the handover between the old bishop's executor and the new bishop, following Ottley's death and Smalbroke's own elevation to the St David's see, was by no means a smooth one.[80]

Only one indication of these divisions under Dean Tyler occurs in the cathedral archives. This relates to the election of the bishop of Hereford's brother, Dr John

76. For Willis's vituperative comments on Tyler as bishop of Llandaff, see NLW, Ottley papers, no. 1789, Willis to Ottley, 25 February 1720; and other letters in the series relating to Tyler's alleged neglect.

77. Willis, *Survey of the Cathedrals*, p. 571; Oxford, Bodleian, MS Willis 81, fos 49r, 50r. The bishop's prebendaries from 1660 to the mid eighteenth century were successively: Thomas Good, Philip Lewis, Thomas Rogers, Richard Smalbroke and Robert Breton. On Good's death in 1678 Bishop Croft (who succeeded in maintaining his right of patronage against Thomas Seddon, despite Seddon's support from the king himself) had argued that the golden prebend, although worth only £80 p.a., was 'the best and only considerable thing in my gift as bishop', M. A. E. Green, F. H. B. Daniell and F. Bickley, eds, *Calendar of State Papers, Domestic Series, of the Reign of Charles II* (28 vols, London, 1860–1939), xx, p. 199, Croft's petition, May 1678. (I am indebted to Professor Gerald Aylmer for this reference.) Also see HCA, 7031/3, pp. 352–56, for Lewis's installation as a residentiary and Seddon's protest (17 May), and the king's

letter (2 June 1678) withdrawing Seddon's claim until the next vacancy.

78. HCA, 7020/1/1 (end), library accounts, 1699–1730; whereas under Smalbroke's immediate predecessors, Thomas Rogers (1699–1709) and Adam Ottley (1709–13), purchases were mainly for the choir. They spent in their respective periods in office: £28 14s. 10d. (Rogers); £19 5s. 3d. (Ottley); £121 11s. 0d. (Smalbroke). See below, Chapter 28, pp. 522–23.

79. HCA, 7031/4, p. 23, 4 March 1714. The vicars were made to 'own the hebdomadary's power' when a 3d. per day fine was levied for non-attendance. The chapter then remitted the fine on promise of future good behaviour.

80. NLW, Plas-yn-Cefn collection, nos 2754–55, Tyler to Humphreys, 3, 6, January 1712; Ottley papers, no. 1857, Willis to Ottley, 29 May 1722; Willis, *Survey of the Cathedrals*, pp. 500–1; NLW, Ottley papers, nos 3034–53, for the difficulties between Ottley's nephew and Smalbroke. It was not until April 1727 that a stone was laid on Bishop Ottley's grave at Abergwili, NLW, Ottley papers, no. 3385.

Hoadley, as a residentiary canon in 1722–23, following William Watts's death. In one of the few instances in the act books where votes are recorded,[81] we find the chapter split three to two between the candidatures of Hoadley and one Dr John Davies, prebendary of Withington – the Whig phalanx of Tyler and Smalbroke, together with Hugh Lewis, little more than two weeks before his death, voting for Hoadley, and the Tory Bishop Ottley, with Robert Morgan, voting for Davies. As a result, a stalemate ensued, the statutes declaring 'nothing ... of force or validity' unless it was agreed by at least the dean and three residentiaries. The chapter therefore initially agreed to an appeal to John Hoadley's brother, as bishop – hardly an impartial arbiter – 'reserving to any person that shall think himself aggrieved' leave to make a further appeal to Archbishop Wake of Canterbury. A few days later, however, Ottley and Morgan argued against this decision because Bishop Hoadley himself had not accepted the appeal 'in the form proposed';[82] and with Dr Lewis's death there remained 'no more colour for that question concerning a statutable majority'. This argument was ignored and nine days later Tyler, styling himself bishop of Landaff, dean and president of the chapter, and 'having tried all reasonable methods for the sake of peace, and finding his endeavours ineffectual', declared John Hoadley duly elected as a canon residentiary. Even this executive action failed to produce the desired result immediately, for Ottley and Morgan, protesting that the dean had again acted unconstitutionally, finally agreed to an appeal to the bishop. Not surprisingly the appeal failed, as did a further appeal to Archbishop Wake. It was appropriately left to Dr Smalbroke to report the archbishop's dubious interpretation of the statutes to chapter on 2 May 1723:

> That as in the election of a residentiary canon the concurrence of the dean and two of the residentiaries is sufficient to make a good election, so in all other matters where suffrages are required, when the chapter is full, the concurrence of the dean and three is necessary and requisite to a statutable determination.

Dr Hoadley was then admitted to his first residency, being elected a full residentiary on 13 June following completion of the statutory forty-day period of continuous residence.[83]

81. For two other instances re an incumbency and a vicar choral election, see HCA, 7031/4, p. 458, 1 August 1766; 7031/5, fos 224v, 227, 1783–84.
82. For Hoadley's view of the appeal, see his letter to Ottley of 27 November 1722, NLW, Ottley papers, no. 1696.
83. For the whole affair, see HCA, 7031/4, pp. 84–89, 91, 92, 95; Oxford, Bodleian, MS

Willis 47, fos 160–61, and 72, fos 128–29, Trahern to Willis, 22 December 1722. John Evans's election could then take place, the chapter being careful to ask the bishop's 'advice, assistance and concurrence toward confirming and settling the said election' in that 'necessary impediments' had prevented the election within the six month statutory period. HCA, 7031/4, pp. 92–93, 13 June 1723.

Although, as with any fellowship, there are indications of sniping about other matters (Browne Willis observed to Ottley in mid February 1721, for example, that everyone at Oxford and elsewhere was 'scandalised' at Dean Tyler's 'Charles the Martyr' sermon of the 30 January),[84] these are not commonly recorded. It is also important to emphasise that the dispute over Hoadley's election was more about statutable procedures than churchmanship,[85] and that there are many more recorded instances of the chapter working together as a corporate body, even in this period of party conflict. For example, in March 1714 eighteen rules covering all aspects of chapter business – voting procedures, election to office, the examination and proper registration of leases, the ordering of repairs, and even mundane concerns like the laying of gravestones – were passed at general chapter. Significantly, it was also required that at the beginning of each subsequent chapter, the acts of the previous meeting should be read out and that 'so many of the statutes, standing rules and orders of chapter [that] concern the members of the church in general be read once every year ... at a general chapter'. Such orders were a sensible attempt to enforce collective chapter responsibility, as well as to reform cathedral procedures: not least the agreement to levy a £5 fine against any residentiary who either pre-engaged his vote or disclosed 'any set act of chapter'.[86] One of the March 1714 acts again reflects badly on the attitude of some vicars choral, the sub-chanter being enjoined to 'keep a roll of those that make default of attending the divine service and sermon'. In the following years the chapter continued to try to ensure that worship was regularly and properly conducted.[87]

The chapter was further prepared to defend its own privileges when the foundation's authority was being threatened by another corporation. On Tuesday 16 May 1704, for instance, there was a violent disturbance in the Close when the city officers 'together with a great multitude with clubs, staves and spittles or shovels entered the churchyard of the said cathedral church, and in an obstinate and rude manner opened the grave of one John Thomas Owen who was interred therein the day before according to the rites and ceremonies of the Church of England'. The body was then 'exposed to public view', and the county coroner

---

84. NLW, Ottley papers, no. 1825, letter 17 February 1721.

85. This is made clear in Bishop Hoadley's letter to Ottley of 27 November 1722: 'I am informed there is ... no complaint of one part of the chapter against the other, but that a dispute has arisen whether the dean and two can make a statutable election'. NLW, Ottley papers, no. 1696.

86. HCA, 7031/4, pp. 24–25. The fine clause implies, of course, that previously there had

been 'leaks' and divisions among the residentiaries.

87. E.g. HCA, 7031/4, pp. 39–40, 56, 57, 62, re failures to ring the prayer bell (for 5 a.m. prayers!), read morning prayers, neglect of duty in the choir and other misdemeanours, June 1716, November 1719. For some later examples of vicars' neglect, see HCA, 7031/4, pp. 182–83, 230, 247, 283, 342, 368–69, 331–32; 7031/5, pp. 91–96, 109–10, 112–14.

conducted an inquest in the cemetery before an especially summoned jury. The
city clearly thought it had right on its side, as the Welshman had drowned in the
Wye, within its liberties, and had been buried 'without any view or inquisition
taken'. Yet the youth was a servant of Bishop Humphreys and had died within
a stone's throw of his palace. The unauthorised exhumation was also a flagrant
breach of the cathedral's 'just rights'. The chapter and bishop immediately agreed
to proceed against the corporation; it was not until June 1705 that peace was
eventually restored, without recourse to law. It was a testing time in the normally
harmonious relationship between church and city, a relationship which had already
been strained by the city's attempt to levy taxes on the college for the repair of
Wye bridge, and the consequent arrest, in full surplice, of Barnabas Alderson, a
vicar choral.[88] Cathedral and palace worked closely together in these disputes, but
a few years later it was Dean Tyler himself who defended his chapter against
Bishop Humphreys over the proposed election of Dr Lewis to the important
position of cathedral lecturer.[89]

By the mid eighteenth century, when a senior residentiary could report that
the Hereford chapter 'had been unanimously in the interest of the government for
near thirty years',[90] any party strife had long since disappeared from the cathedral
Close. This period of Whig dominance coincided with a marked decrease in the
length of tenure of successive deans. In the fifty years following Tyler's death in
1724, seven deans of Hereford were appointed, whereas there were only two –
Benson and Tyler himself – in the preceding half century. Three of these seven,
moreover, were elevated to bishoprics: Clavering to Peterborough, Cresset to Landaff
and Egerton to Bangor. In the second quarter of the century, in particular, the
deanery of Hereford was seen in Whig circles as a stepping stone to greater episcopal
office, the see of Landaff having already become the preserve of successive deans
of Hereford, it being held *in commendam* by Deans Tyler, Clavering and Harris
continuously from 1706 until 1736. There then occurs a break until Dean Cresset's
election as bishop of Landaff in 1749, although he did not retain the deanery with
the see. Cresset was delighted with his promotion, which enabled him to be seen

88. HCA, 7031/3, p. 555, 23 May 1704;
    7008/1, pp. 21ff, re taxation dispute;
    pp. 54–56, 67–69, re the disputed burial and
    accommodation. For the city's side of these
    disputes, see HRO, HLC O/U 185, A/1,
    pp. 143, 148, 149, 161, 170, common coun-
    cil minutes, 4 December 1703; 16, 29 May
    1704; 16 January, 8 June 1705. In July 1707,
    the bishop controversially suspended Alder-
    son, 'upon a vehement suspicion and fame
    of adultery and of being very disorderly

and quarrelsome', HCA, 7008/1, p. 280.
89. NLW, Plas-yn-Cefn collection, nos 2750–
    57, letters from Tyler to Humphreys, 29
    December 1711 to 12 January 1712. The
    praelector's (or lecturer's) office conferred
    the right to the next residentiary's place.
    Dr Lewis was subsequently elected despite
    the bishop's misgivings, HCA, 7031/3,
    p. 608.
90. BL, MS Egerton 1714, fol. 199r, Breton to
    countess of Portland, 11 June 1750.

in parliament 'as a steady and hearty friend to our happy establishment'; but this may not have been the case with earlier deans, Landaff sharing Carlisle's distinction in the earlier years of the century as being the most dilapidated cathedral in the kingdom, as well as one of the poorest sees.[91] The fact that there was no habitable palace at Landaff, too, may have meant that Dean Tyler preferred living even in the rambling medieval deanery in Hereford to living in his see.[92]

Despite this, the decanal ties between Hereford and Landaff also had the effect of drawing other residentiaries like Watts, Smalbroke and John Evans, who were also appointed to offices *in commendam* in the neighbouring Welsh see, away from the Hereford diocese. As two of these three canons were archdeacons of Llandaff, as well as Hereford residentiaries, the effect could not have been entirely marginal, even though Browne Willis regarded these English canons as being entirely complacent in their attitudes towards the Welsh church.[93] Nor did the Welsh connection end at Llandaff. Adam Ottley held his residentiaryship with the bishopric of St David's for the last ten years of his life (1713–23), although he kept his promise to Bishop Croft that he would resign as archdeacon of Shropshire on gaining a living requiring a residence 'in any distant place'.[94]

The practice of holding Welsh sees with Hereford deaneries or residentiaryships died out as the century progressed. Dean Cresset, as we have seen, resigned the Hereford deanery on his promotion to Llandaff in 1749, as did Dean Egerton (while keeping his stall) when translated bishop of Bangor seven years later at the advanced age of thirty-four.[95] With the loosening of the Welsh connection, however, came

91. Norman Sykes, *Church and State in the Eighteenth Century* (Cambridge, 1934), pp. 360, 364–65; NLW, Ottley papers, nos 1735, 1814, 1872, Willis to Ottley, 7 June 1716, 16 January 1721, 26 December 1722.

92. For the huge size of the deanery prior to Dean Cresset's 1737 alterations, see HRO, HD 6/42, ground-plan and reports. The deanery was described as 'a very ancient, decayed, irregular building, much larger than is either necessary or convenient ...' Tyler died, aged ninety-one, 'at the deanery of Hereford', and was buried in the lower south transept of the cathedral, Oxford, Bodleian, MS Willis 81, fol. 28r.

93. Watts was archdeacon of Llandaff from 1707, Smalbroke treasurer from 1712 and Evans archdeacon from 1722. For Willis's antipathy, see NLW, Ottley papers, nos 1821, 1827, undated letters (*c*. January/ February 1721).

94. NLW, Ottley papers, no. 1633, Croft to Ottley, n.d. (but before March 1687). For Ottley's appointment to St David's, see the fascinating correspondence in the NLW, Ottley papers, nos 1479, 1499, 1564, 1611, 1620, 1622, letters, 23 October 1712 to 29 January 1713.

95. Egerton's career is a good illustration of how rapidly a well-connected Whig could rise in the eighteenth-century church. Appointed prebendary of Cublington in 1746, at the age of twenty-four, just before the death of his father, who was bishop of Hereford, he was installed dean of Hereford at the age of twenty-eight, translated from Bangor to Lichfield in 1768, and then to Durham in 1771, when he finally resigned his prebendaryship. Despite his youth, Egerton's appointment as dean was welcomed by the chapter, not least because he had a living within the diocese

a tightening of the already strong Oxford axis: Deans Clavering (1724–29), Webber (1756–71) and Wetherell (1771–1807) were also respectively canon of Christ Church, rector of Exeter College and master of University College; and Joseph Browne, a residentiary canon 1752–67, was provost of Queen's College from 1756 to 1767.

Bishop Croft's strict policy of only choosing locally beneficed clergymen as prebendaries had broken down under his successors. Yet there were clearly better pickings from the royal stalls at Westminster, Windsor and Worcester than from those at Hereford, where the revenues of even the richest prebend, Moreton Magna, were meagre and where the bishop's rather than the monarch's prebendal patronage held sway.[96] Consequently, in Hereford many prebendaries and most residentiaries – who, after all, as the chapter itself admitted, were 'only prebendaries ... appointed to residence'[97] – were still beneficed locally in the richer chapter livings.[98] This was of importance for the cathedral. One reason for the chapter declaration of December 1768 that Woolhope and Fownhope vicarages should be regarded as one living was not simply the need for 'competent provision' for a senior cleric, but also the belief that residentiaries 'should be so situated as to attend the several chapter meetings with ease and convenience', the cathedral's business having been 'greatly prejudiced and interrupted for want of a sufficient number to supervise the same'.[99] In 1782 the dean and chapter resisted the vicars' claim for exclusive rights over presentations within seven miles of the city for exactly the same reason.[100] Similarly they had earlier appealed to the archbishop of Canterbury against the diocesan's jurisdiction over canonical houses which had been given to 'simple prebendaries' rather than to residentiaries as had been the custom.[101]

note 95 continued
(at Ross-on-Wye), and would 'easily from thence be at every chapter to attend the business of the church ...', BL, MS Egerton 1714, fol. 199r, Breton to countess of Portland, 11 June 1750.

96. A valuation of £24 p.a. was attached to this stall in *c.* 1662, NLW, MS Bude 30. Only Bartonsham and Bullinghope were valued above £20 p.a. at this time. A century later royal stalls at Windsor, Westminster and Worcester were worth £450, £300 and £200 p.a. respectively: Sykes, *Church and State*, p. 149. For Bishop Croft's successful defence of his patronage against the king's candidate in 1678, see above, note 77.

97. HCA, 7031/5, fol. 213r, 3 October 1782.

98. See HCA, 7031/5, pp. 19, 21–22, fol. 233v, for examples of presentations to Woolhope,

Fownhope, Lidney (in the Gloucester diocese), 29 March 1769; and to Lugwardine and Upton Bishop, 24 March 1785.

99. HCA, 7031/5, p. 6, 19 December 1768. James Birt was presented to the livings on 8 March and 12 April 1769, HCA, 7031/5, pp. 19, 23.

100. HCA, 7031/5, fol. 213r, 3 October 1782, re Madley.

101. HCA, 7031/4, pp. [474–84], 25 August, 2 October, 12 November, 8, 29 December 1767; 7031/5, pp. 7, 17–18, 31, 41, 53, 19 December 1768 to 18 August 1770. Archbishop Cornwallis heard the case, unlike his predecessor Archbishop Secker who, in refusing to hear it, acted unconstitutionally (according to the Laudian statutes) as the chapter tactfully pointed out. There seem to have been

As those many acts recording residential elections also make clear, the chapter took its residential duties seriously, even during the smallpox outbreak in the summer of 1736.[102] The two months period of continuous residence was generally conscientiously kept throughout the period. The general level of chapter attendance at ordinary meetings, too, was commendable, although there are obvious exceptions. Thomas Whishaw, Bishop Hoadley's brother-in-law, was one – he may have found life sweeter in Salisbury (where he was also a canon) than in Hereford, especially after his 1736 residence in a diseased city – and Joseph Browne, both absent and infirm for most of the last seven years of his life, another.[103] In the 1760s indeed the chapter suffered badly from absences and infirmities. In September 1765 Robert Breton, who had been a residentiary for over forty years, the longest period of the century, was given leave, at his own expense, to find a deputy because at his age (he was in his mid seventies) 'it was not safe for him to frequent church during his residence as the statutes require'.[104] Earlier in the year, Humphrey Whishaw's gout had caused the chapter meeting to be adjourned to his own house.[105] More serious than these ailments, however, were the absences of Dean Webber, whose primary concern throughout his deanship was his college rather than his cathedral (fig. 36).[106] Nevertheless, extended absences among residentiaries

two canonical houses in the Close in regular use in the eighteenth century prior to 1767, three from 1767 to 1776 and four from 1776 to 1830, HCA, 5093. Four had been in use in the late 1660s: see Oxford, Bodleian, MS Tanner 147, fol. 83v, re payments totalling £430 for repairs etc. to Sherborne's, Watts's, Good's and Benson's houses.

102. HCA, 7031/4, p. 168, 25 June 1736. Thomas Whishaw agreed to undertake Evans's residence as it would have been 'dangerous to bring his family hither in August and September'.

103. Whishaw, for example, was absent from chapter meetings from 10 November 1738 until his resignation on 24 March 1740, just before his residence was about to begin. Browne's absences from meetings (although not necessarily from residence) have been noted for the following periods: 24 May 1754 to 25 June 1755, 15 April 1760 to 5 May 1764, 23 May 1764 to death (June/July 1767), HCA, 7031/4, passim. He was described as 'old and infirm' as vice-chancellor of Oxford in the 1760s: L. S. Sutherland and L. G. Mitchell, eds,

The History of the University of Oxford, v: *The Eighteenth Century* (Oxford, 1986), p. 154.

104. HCA, 7031/4, p. 444, 16 September 1765. I know of no other instance where this happened.

105. Ibid., p. 438, 6 February 1765. He was also under doctor's orders not to attend chapter meetings in the summer of 1756, HCA, 5636, letter to Moore, 3 August 1756. He was, however, a much more devoted servant of Hereford Cathedral than his brother Thomas.

106. The chapter was rightly unsympathetic with his argument that he could not manage the four months residence that the Hereford statutes required the master of Ledbury Hospital to undertake, because six months was 'a vast deal more time than the Exeter statutes would allow its rector', HCA, 7031/4, p. 402, Webber to the chapter, 5 November 1761; see pp. 401–4, 407, for the chapter's response and Webber's subsequent resignation from the hospital. Whishaw's comment in 1765 that 'the dean is seldom here' should also be noted, HCA, 1543, answer no. 34.

were the exception rather than the rule. The careful registering in the act books of proxy votes from the late seventeenth century onwards is further suggestive of concern for the conduct of business, as are the sixty or so proxies to have survived for the period 1718–61.[107] Most of these are formal legal documents, but the few extant letters of proxy do not all read like lame excuses. On the other hand, Canon Breton's missive to his friend from the delights of Weston-under-Penyard in the summer of 1760 was – perhaps understandably from a canon with a working lifetime of service behind him – more carefree:

> we will put off dining etc. you till this day (Tuesday) seven night, by which time Nanny Johnson will be back from Hereford with the ladies, who I shall send in my chariot to Harewood's Inn, where a post-chaise … is to meet them. So that you see I can't come to the chapter on Thursday, nor is there any need of it as you have my proxy and Leigh being there. Besides, Mr Clarke of Capel has sent word he will be with me to-morrow by dinner, and I imagine he will stay till Saturday.[108]

Fig. 36. Portrait of Francis Webber, dean of Hereford 1756–71.

Some idea of the state of the eighteenth-century cathedral may be gleaned from the surviving records of visitations (or intended visitations) by three bishops: Humphreys, Bisse and Beauclerk. These records are sadly incomplete given the distinct processes of proclamation, return, citation, charge, administration of articles and exhibition of collations, together with the final answers and injunctions, required by an eighteenth-century visitation.[109] Bishop Humphreys may not have completed his visitations for only his articles survive: significantly Bishop Beauclerk in 1765 did not require Humphreys's orders to be written up in the act book (as he did for other visitations). Nevertheless, by comparing the extant 1703 and 1710 articles, some indication of

107. HCA, 5636.
108. Ibid., Breton to Jones?, 5 August 1760.
109. HCA, 1571, method of proceeding in visitations, n.d.

Humphreys' growing concerns about the 'sufficiency' of the deacons, the recording of leases and terriers and the registering of patents can be appreciated. Moreover, a clause about boys being called to account for playing in the cathedral and its environs on Sundays and holy days is wholly new in 1710.[110] Bishop Bisse also asked some new questions in his sixty articles of 1716:

> Are there always two [canons resident] and do they, after their residence is settled resort unto their benefices? ... Are the choristers before and after divine service and sermon kept diligently at the grammar school; or such as have not natural capacities fit for that are they kept at the writing school ... and before all are they diligently instructed in the church catechism and trained up to such further knowledge of pious and divine matters ... to the initiating them to a holy Christian conversation all their life afterwards? ... Hath anything been granted in lease within these fifty years which ... was never demised before, and are all rent grants now greater by a third part than they were fifty years before the making of your statutes?[111]

The dean and chapter responses have not survived, but the difficulty of answering such questions truthfully can be imagined. Nevertheless, it appears from what was not said in Bishop Bisse's injunctions that he was satisfied with many of the answers he received. He did require the act of Dean Benson's time (4 July 1687), cancelling bonds and installation fines, to be 'erased from the chapter book', and ordered that every dignitary should give security for his office before 26 March 1717. By that date also a fees table was to be prepared and accounts rendered of the value of college and hospital revenues and the nature of prebendal estates, terriers being made of each 'corps' before Michaelmas 1718 and every seventh year thereafter. Remarkably, the bishop's only stated worry about ministry or worship was the failure of preachers to say the bidding prayer, as expressed in the fifty-fifth canon, when 'exciting the people to pray' before sermons. Final orders required chapter observance of annual visitations to the college and hospitals, and triennial visitations of churches within their jurisdiction. In the dean's absence, four residentiary canons, Chancellor Thomas Bisse (the bishop's brother) and nine vicars undertook to observe the injunctions 'in every particular'.[112] It is reasonable to cast doubt on whether these admirable intentions were ever fully implemented.

By far the fullest records survive for Bishop Beauclerk's visitation to the cathedral

---

110. HCA, 1568 (1703), 1569 (1710); see also articles 19/17, 22 and 24/25 in the two documents, and article 23 for the comment on the boys. In general terms the 1710 articles are written in plainer English. Fifty-two articles were issued in 1703 and

fifty-three in 1710.

111. HCA, 1579, pp. 15, 16, 18, nos 8, 18, 31.

112. Ibid., pp. 22–23, 24, injunctions, 28 September, 2 October 1716. See HCA, 1570, for the promises of observance, and 7031/4 (end) for the act book copy of the orders.

in 1765. Importantly, three of the residentiaries' answers, one counter-response and a summary of complaints are extant, as well as the summons, articles and injunctions.[113] Richard Moore's postal list also survives and gives a fascinating insight into both the process of visitation and the principal summer residences of the prebendaries at that time. During the eight-day period, 25 July to 2 August 1765, the chapter clerk sent out thirty-five copies of Beauclerk's articles to the cathedral dignitaries. Twenty-two were living within (or near) the diocese; three in London; four (including Dr Browne) in Oxford; two in Yorkshire; and one each at Windsor, Canterbury, Hanworth (Middlesex) and near Liskeard, the place where presumably Dean Webber took his holiday that year.[114] They all received quite long missives, the bishop's sixty-three articles running to three printed pages, to which responses were required by 17 September. The articles bear a close resemblance to those of 1716, except that rubrics concerning the sermon prayer and preachers' licences were omitted and 'fifty years' was the preferred time for rental comparisons. New clauses were added about the 'mulcting' of defaulting preachers, the distribution of wheat for the minor canons and sextons and 'petty commons' for the prebendaries, the disposal of chapter livings, and the observance of funeral rites and 'the injunctions of former visitors'.[115] Far more revealing, though, are the answers of Canons Breton, Russell and Whishaw, and the responses they evoked.[116] Of the three residentiaries, Breton was the most evasive. Indeed, he was charged by the palace itself with being 'equivocal' and not responding properly to fifteen articles, a charge he vigorously denied.[117] This venerable archdeacon was clearly not overawed by his aristocratic diocesan. Whishaw's attitude, on the other hand, was more reverential and his answers better considered.

113. In chronological order: HCA, 1557, summons, 29 May 1765; 5599, Breton's printed copy of sixty-three articles; 1543, 5125, 5599, Whishaw's, Breton's and Russell's answers, n.d.; 1573, summary, n.d.; 1554, 1555, 5599, 7031/4 (end), injunctions, 1765–66.

114. This could have been Menheniot, although the name is difficult to decipher. For the list, see HCA, 5599. Compare the thirty-four dignitaries on the 1765 visitation list, HCA, 1572. Clack, the organist, received the extra copy from the chapter clerk.

115. HCA, 5599, nos 13, 14, 17, 18, 32, 35, 43, 46, 55, 63. The 1716 requirement for setting out of fees, and registering counter-parts of leases and 'perfect terriers' in the archives, was abandoned in 1765 (cf.

articles nos 20/19, 31/30 for 1765/1716 articles respectively, HCA 5599; 1579, pp. 16–18). Otherwise the articles are virtually identical.

116. These are the only replies we have to visitations in this period, apart from those of the vicars choral and Digby Cotes's response (see note 118 below). For some vicars' responses (from 1698, including those of 17 September 1765), see HCA, 6247 (Cove MS), pp. 61ff.

117. HCA, 1547, episcopal complaints against Breton, n.d.; HCA, 5599, Breton's endorsement on the printed articles. Canon Jones was charged with failing to answer seven articles properly; he was also required to explain his answer to article 6 about the sacraments, HCA, 1544.

Russell, too, responded conscientiously, particularly with regard to his mastership of St Katherine's, Ledbury.

Certain faults were acknowledged, however reluctantly, and these complaints were then collated by the palace. Some cathedral windows needed mending, the state of its floor was 'indifferent' and it was not kept free from dust; there was one observation about the sacrament not having been administered on two occasions, yet more about the attendance of the vicars and their lack of voice and musicianship; the sub-chanter neglected his duty through ill-health; chorister surplices were often dirty and their behaviour disorderly; prayer books were dilapidated and anthem and service books 'in an indifferent order and but few in number'; the lecture was not well attended and not read according to statute; wheat for the minor canons and sextons may not have been equally divided and the prebendaries' petty commons paid late, no option being given for compounding grain for money; canonical houses were not visited and their inventories were not regularly renewed, and visitations to the school and St Ethelbert's hospital were also lax; Bishop Croft's 1677 orders regarding the disposal of chapter livings and the college's use of the churchyard had been ignored, and ignorance was pleaded about later bishops' injunctions.[118] Against such criticisms should be set the fact that thirty of the sixty-three articles elicited no adverse comment, or even no comment at all. While silence may be variously interpreted as approval, indifference or ignorance – Whishaw himself freely admitting that his absence at his country cure for between five and seven months of the year meant that he did not know whether each member of the church received communion on the first Sunday of every month as the statutes required – it does seem from the fragmented evidence that the cathedral's worship was tolerably well conducted and its affairs reasonably administered at this time.

Bishop Beauclerk's private opinions are not recorded, but it is apparent from his injunction of 14 November 1765 that he wished the orders of his predecessors to be 'faithfully observed' and registered in the act books of both cathedral and college because 'the greatest part of the foundation' was unacquainted with them, the assertion being proved when Croft's seven articles of April 1677 were later 'discovered' and also duly recorded. Beauclerk's other orders of 26 June 1766 reflect the points of substance of the earlier responses. They concerned the state of the fabric, the qualifications of the vicars choral, the condition of the prayer and choir books, the preaching of prebendaries and minor repairs to Dr Browne's outhouses and the college. His penultimate injunction answered the vicars' call for

---

118. HCA, 1573, n.d., for the collated note of complaints. As well as the answers of the residentiaries and vicars (notes 111 and 114 above), see also HCA, 1544 for the brief response of Digby Cotes to the bishop, 16 September 1765.

a ruling about presentation to chapter livings. Prebendaries were to be promoted only to those benefices which 'on account of their value or distance' could not 'be conferred on the vicars choral'.[119] This ruling provoked a learned protest from one residentiary (John Jones) that it was an infringement upon dean and chapter rights and 'contrary to both the statutes and practice of the church'. Canon Jones's scholarship won the day for shortly afterwards the bishop informed the chapter that his opinion was only a 'point of equity' and not 'a statutable interpretation of a doubtful statute'.[120] This might not have been the end of the matter for, as Beauclerk's warrant to his vicar general of 8 November 1766 indicated, although personally indisposed because of parliament's sitting, he wished 'further to proceed in the business of visiting our cathedral'.[121] No other record of this proposal exists, however, and it seems probable that after 1766 episcopal visitations of the cathedral were laid to rest (at least for this period), unlamented by all concerned.

One of the most vital routines in the cathedral's year was that surrounding the audit, held annually within the first two weeks of November. The occasion was presided over, at least at the beginning of the century, by the dean, the lead being set by John Tyler who attended three out of every four audits during his deanship (1692–1724). Thereafter, with the notable exception of John Egerton, who never missed an audit when dean (1750–55), the dean's attendance was more spasmodic.[122] Nevertheless, it was usual for most other residentiaries, together with the chapter clerk as auditor, to be present to explain, pass and sign the several accounts presented to them by the high bailiff and collector of common rents; the keeper of the canons' bakehouse, who discharged three accounts (for corn and money); the master of St Katherine's Hospital; and the foundation's other officers – the masters of the fabric and library, and the clavigers (senior and

119. That is vicarages or rectories above £8 or 10 marks p.a. (according to the king's book of 1534) respectively and more than seven miles from Hereford, or any vicarage or rectory more than twenty miles from the city.

120. See HCA, 7031/4 (end) for Beauclerk's injunctions and Jones's contrary opinion; HCA, 7031/4, p. 459, for the bishop's response to Jones, 19 September 1766; and HCA, 1545, 1554, 1555, 1557, 5599, for other copies/drafts of the injunctions.

121. HCA, 1546, warrant to Browne, Willim and Woodcock.

122. It is significant that all Tyler's eight absences (1706–8, 1712–13, 1716, 1718, 1721) came after his appointment as bishop of Llandaff in August 1706. Thereafter the attendances of successive deans were as follows: Clavering, one out of five; Harris, three out of seven; Cresset, two out of eight; Castle, none out of one; Egerton, five out of five; Webber, seven out of fifteen; Wetherell, five out of fifteen (for this period). HCA, R 620; 7020/1/1–2, passim. See also Breton's comment to the countess of Portland about 'the many inconveniences arising from having a dean who lives at a remote distance, and is never there more than two months in a year, and very often not at all, as was the case of all the four last deans' (Clavering, Harris, Cresset, Castle), BL, MS Egerton 1714, fol. 199r, 11 June 1750.

junior).[123] After the completion of these solemnities, which normally took two days, came the revelries of the audit dinner, limited in November 1777 to one public dinner on the Thursday of audit week,[124] and the audit chapter meeting at which the chapter officers were elected for the following year.

The clavigers were, literally, the key keepers, for they discharged most of the cathedral's wealth. The unbroken set of clavigers' accounts for this period are a model of order and uniformity, the methods of accounting varying little from the beginning to the end of the period. Over the near century (1690–1785) receipts averaged £468, disbursements £320 and dividends £148 (or over £24 for each residentiary) p.a. The decade by decade average shows a remarkably static pattern (the second decade apart) for the first fifty years, and a gradual increase in receipts and dividends from 1750, reflecting the increase in rental fines from the mid century onwards, itself a reflection of rising prosperity, increasing land values and improvements in chapter valuations. Overall, a residentiary was likely to be more than £10 p.a. better off in the 1770s and 1780s than at the beginning of the century, although the exceptional years of 1772–74, 1777–78 and 1781–82, where individual dividends exceeded £45 (and in the latter year £63), were partly compensated by a share of little over £13 in 1778–79, the leanest year of the period, and less than £19 in 1783–84. An eighteenth-century canon of Hereford was not likely to get rich from the share of the profits of a residentiaryship alone.[125]

The 'fabric' accounts (a misnomer as by no means all the money raised on this account was spent on the cathedral's fabric) relate a similar story, which was to end in more tragic circumstances. The comparable yearly averages for the period 1690–1785 are annual receipts of £270, expenditures of £162 and balances of £123.[126] Certain observations may be made with regard to these accounts. The revenues included casual sums like the £5 paid by each residentiary on his admittance, the £50 gift from the duke of Chandos, the high steward, in 1720–21, and windfall sales of old timber from the chapter estates of Canwood, the Frith

123. For a summary of these accounts, 1699–1715, see HCA, 5714. The pricker's account (for mulcts?) is listed (without figures) until 1713, after which it presumably fell into disuse.

124. HCA, 7031/5, p. 157, 15 November 1777.

125. These figures have been calculated from the yearly clavigers' accounts for the period 1690–1785, HCA, 7020/1/1–2, passim. The dividend, of course, was not the only source of income for a residentiary, their tithes being more valuable than the share

by the late eighteenth century. See Brian Trueman, 'The Administration of Hereford Cathedral, 1776–86', *FHC*, 42 (1976), p. 29.

126. Extrapolated from HCA, 7020/2/1–2. The 'non fabric' items included: fees (£30 plus in the 1760s, £40 plus by the mid 1770s); organ maintenance; music and choir books; Madley chancel repairs; loan interest repayments, etc. The detailed references in this paragraph are all from these accounts, unless otherwise indicated.

and Ridgehill, which raised £130 in 1719–20 and over £300 in 1772–73. By their very nature, however, such sums could not be relied on. More regular income came from rents, which brought in over £30 p.a. from the mid century. Fees were charged for cathedral vaults (£2), other 'stacks' (£1) and gravestones (10s.), and burials in the bishop's cloister or Lady arbour doubled in price to 13s. 4d. and 6s. 8d. respectively after November 1741, but even in a 'good' year not much more than £15 might be raised from these sources. Much more important were the fines on the renewal of leases on the Shinfield and Swallowfield estates in Berkshire and Wiltshire, which increased steadily as the century progressed: those at Shinfield (on seven-year renewals) doubling from £150 to £300 by the mid century, and then, after Smith's survey, increasing to £725 in 1773–74; and at Swallowfield increasing from £60 or £70 to a swingeing £362 10s. 0d. (on a twelve-year renewal) in 1719–20, and then to a steady £210 (on seven-year renewals) in the 1740s and 1750s, and to £540 by the end of the period. Such five-fold and ten-fold increases from between about 1700 and 1780 do not suggest negligence on behalf of the dean and chapter. The problem was that these fines came in spasmodically (every second and fifth year for much of the century) and this did not help sustain a regular programme of repair for the cathedral, even if the need had been recognised. Moreover, such cash injections were totally inadequate to maintain such a large building, let alone provide for occasional adornment.

In this light, the thousands of pounds spent by successive chapters through the century on projects like the new peal of bells (1697–98), the Bisse altarpiece and choir refurbishments (1718–22), the central spire alterations (1725–30), the new west window and north aisle repairs (1735–38), the regilding of the choir (1752–53) and the rebuilding of the organ (1772–74) should be seen as major achievements. Not surprisingly, by the mid century, the fabric account was unable to cope with the demands that were being made upon it, so that expenditure exceeded revenue in twenty out of the thirty years from 1740–70. Borrowings of over £1000 (1765–85), largely from the residentiaries themselves at 3 to 4 per cent interest, only provided temporary relief, and it was not until significant adjustments were made to the Swallowfield and Shinfield fines in 1770 and 1773 respectively that the fund was returned to a more even, if not entirely stable, keel. During this time, too, £200 from the 1772 balance was invested in South Sea stock, which, while it was a distinctly unprofitable capital investment, at least provided the fund with an additional annual income of around £8 p.a. for five years. It is a supreme irony that the fall of the west front occurred during a period when more 'fabric' money – over £5000 in the fifteen-year period, 1771–85 – was being spent than ever before, and at a time when the chapter was more alive than it had ever been to the necessity of securing its fabric fund on an adequate basis.[127] This was at some personal cost to the residentiaries themselves who lent over £800 between 1765 and 1785 to try to preserve the fabric.[128]

Indeed, chapters throughout the century had endeavoured to preserve the west front. The restoration of the great perpendicular west window in the mid 1730s has already been mentioned, but concern was also shown for its maintenance. From 1752 the chapter was aware of the 'alterations and repairs' that needed to be made to the west end; and in 1763, following the demolition of the western range of the south-west cloister, a buttress was built 'at the north west corner of the church' and an inside wall erected 'for securing the building'. Thirteen years later, Dean Wetherell commissioned James Pearce, an Oxford builder, to survey 'the state of the west tower and other parts of the cathedral'. Perhaps as a result of the survey, Thomas Symonds was appointed surveyor of the fabric in September 1777. In November 1781 he was ordered to repair the western tower, 'agreeably to a plan exhibited by him to the chapter', at a sum not exceeding £200, exclusive of the cost of the stone and ironwork. Symonds was to be sacked five years later, following the fall, but at the time the chapter seemed pleased enough, he being given an *ex gratia* payment of £18 7s. 0d. in 1783 for 'superintending the work'.[129] The truth is that, whatever Symonds had tried to do to shore up the decaying structure, nothing short of the dismantling of the entire tower could have saved the west front, such had been the neglect over the previous centuries.

When the crash occurred at about 6.30 p.m. on 17 April 1786, Easter Monday, it may not have occasioned such a surprise. Nine days earlier stone from inside the roof had started flaking away, and, as James Wathen's drawing indicates, substantial diagonal cracks were clearly visible on the outside of the façade before the fall (fig. 37). Certainly the footman of Dr Luntley, who was entertaining his fellow vicars in his Old College residence on the evening of the 17th, did not disturb his master with the fateful news for several hours, until the dinner party was drawing to a close.[130] Nor did the event make headline news. On the Thursday of the same week, the incident was reported on in the *Hereford Journal* towards

127. See HCA, 5695, for the adjusted fabric figures and an account of the loans. The South Sea capital stock was worth £26 12s. 0d. less in 1777, when it was sold, than in 1772.

128. HCA, 5695. Whishaw loaned £300 (and left a £72 legacy); Woodcock, £200; Birt, £150; Russell, £100. For a more hostile interpretation, see Truman, 'Administration', pp. 33–35.

129. HCA, 7031/4, p. 253, 6 May 1752; 7031/5, fol. 206, 13 November 1781; fol. 243v, 9 November 1786; Whitehead, 'Goth among the Greeks', pp. 30ff. *Gentleman's Magazine*, 57 (1787), p. 958, gives a hostile view of Symonds's work.

130. The story is told by William Cooke in his biographical memoirs of the college, 1660–1832, HCA, 7003/4/4, entry no. 62 on Luntley. I am indebted to Revd Philip Barrett for this reference.

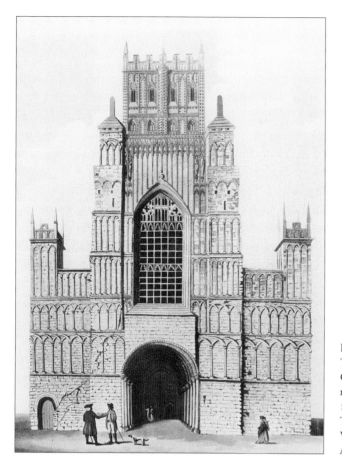

Fig. 37. 'A View of the West Tower and Front of Hereford Cathedral taken on the morning of the 17th of April 1786 (on which Day the Tower fell)', drawn by James Wathen, printed London, 12 April 1788. (HCL, B.3.15.)

the bottom of the third page, sandwiched between an advertisement for a delivery man and an article on the market price of oxen, as follows:

> last Monday afternoon … all that beautiful and magnificent structure [the west tower] fell down, and with it a part of the body of the church. We are happy to find that no person has received any hurt, [n]or has any damage been done to any of the buildings near it, except the music room, which is considerably injured … The ruins, though awful, afford a pleasing view, especially to behold the statues of kings and bishops resting one upon the other (figs 38, 73, 160).[131]

131. *Hereford Journal*, 16, no. 820, 20 April 1786. I am indebted to Dr Heather Tomlinson for transcribing the reference for me.

Fig. 38. 'The North West View of Hereford Cathedral, as it appeared the 18th April 1786', drawn by James Wathen, printed London, May 1789. (HCL, B.3.17.)

Some may have viewed the ruins of the cathedral's west front with romantic detachment, but those responsible for its stewardship could afford no such self-indulgence. For quite apart from immediate practical difficulties, the fall imposed an immense financial strain on a relatively poor foundation, the repercussions of which were to be felt throughout the period.

Such was the scale of the disaster, it would have taken a great visionary to have seen the opportunities presented by the pile of rubble on that fateful Monday evening. Gibbons Bagnall, the canon in residence in April 1786, although formerly the cathedral school's headmaster, was probably not one of these. With the aid of hindsight, however, we can put the event into a proper perspective; we can now see that the fall had a number of beneficial consequences. For it not only resulted in the eventual securing of a building which at times seemed on the verge of complete collapse, but it also accelerated reforms in land management which had been set in motion during the previous decade. Other changes, too, like the reordering of the cathedral's interior and its churchyard, stem directly from 1786. These local improvements are mirrored by the intermittent renewal of elements of the national church in this period.[132] In 1832, however, the pace of change quickened, both in Hereford and in the country at large: the installation of a radical dean through the good offices of a radical Whig government, fresh from its Reform Bill triumph, led to both a local assault on customary practice within Hereford Cathedral itself and a national attack against capitular 'privilege' among all cathedral and collegiate foundations. Nevertheless, the significant developments under Dean Merewether after 1832 should not disguise the real achievements of his more conservative predecessors in the forty-six years after the 'very real calamity' of 1786.[133]

There were many moments of crisis during the cathedral's rebuilding from the first 'lead watch' on the night of 17–18 April 1786 to the memorable chapter declaration of 26 June 1796 requesting the resumption of 'evening choir prayers' following completion of 'the repairs of the church'.[134] The full story of the cathedral's restoration will be told elsewhere. It is sufficient here to mention some of the problems the chapter faced from a situation that was far worse than it had been in 1660, and as bad as it could have been from any Cromwellian bombardment. First, there was the obstacle of an elderly bishop (Beauclerk), nearing the end of a forty-year episcopate, who at best lacked sympathy for the cathedral's enormous task and at worst was downright obstreperous.[135] Once he had finally died in November 1787, and Wyatt's design for a shortened nave had been agreed upon by Bishop Butler, Beauclerk's successor but one (his immediate successor, John Harley, having lasted but a few weeks), there were the ever-present dangers accompanying the repair of a crumbling building, as illustrated by the fatal accident of January 1790 when the collapse of scaffolding killed three workmen and injured others. This in itself caused damage to the great organ which had to be taken down.[136] Above all, there were the financial strains imposed by the most expensive building project that had been undertaken in several centuries.

The impression given by the financial accounts and other extant records is a familiar one: a chapter living from hand to mouth in response to ever spiralling costs. Wyatt had originally reckoned, in a vague estimate of June 1788, that these

132. For an excellent summary, see G. F. A. Best, *Temporal Pillars: Queen Anne's Bounty, the Ecclesiastical Commissioners and the Church of England* (Cambridge, 1964), pp. 185–209.

133. The phrase is used in the chapter's 1792 parliamentary petition, HCA, 5695/6.

134. HCA, 5702, payment, 18 April 1786 of 2s. each to John Williams, Thomas Jones, Rowland Jones and William Maddox for 'one night each watching the lead'; 7031/5,

fol. 325v, 25 June 1796.

135. Beauclerk's refusal to countenance any plan which would not 'cover the same ground on which it [the cathedral] originally stood' resulted in an appeal to Archbishop Moore of Canterbury. For this testy correspondence, see HCA, 7031/5, fos 242v, 246v, 247r, 247v, letters 4 September 1786, 24, 30 January, 19 March 1787.

136. See the report in *Gentleman's Magazine*, 60 (1790), p. 172, 30 January.

would be no more than £6500, plus 'near a thousand pounds' if a spire was built. This compares with a final cost (to the end of 1796) of over £16,650.[137] Even the former amount could only have been met by 'substantial aid' from a public subscription. By mid August 1788, the bishop, the dean and chapter and some other dignitaries had responded magnificently by advancing £1600. This made a promising start to the subscription campaign, and through direct solicitations – to the county's great and good, to rich London and Marches bankers and to not impecunious bishops, canons and other clergy throughout the kingdom – as well as regular public appeals in the columns of the *Hereford Journal*, over £5000 was raised in less than six months. Several hundred pounds more were subscribed over the course of 1789. Dr John Napleton, the new bishop's prebend and canon residentiary, used the occasion of the three choirs meeting that September, in 'a plain, affecting and impressive address', to pay 'a proper compliment to the munificent subscriptions for the raising the ancient temple where he was preaching out of its ruins'.[138] Such munificence, however, could not match the continued outlay. This was approaching £10,000 by March 1792 when the chapter, again doubtless relying on Dr Napleton's energy and expertise, successfully petitioned for a further £4000 to be raised by a private act of parliament (ironically in accord with a statute designed to promote the residence of parochial clergy), repayment being secured 'by mortgage of their other estates'.[139] Even this parliamentary enactment could not prevent further borrowings 'on bond', totalling £3300, and a private advancement of £1200 by the residentiaries themselves. These sums, together with a loan from the Ledbury Hospital account, a sale of investments surplus to requirements on the fabric account (this time realising a near £100 profit), and a second subscription in 1793 for work on the tower (which in the absence of the spire was considered essential 'to the dignity of the building ... as well as ornamental to the surrounding country') covered the total rebuilding costs. It is little wonder that at the end of it all

---

137. Unless otherwise indicated, the following account is based on the collection of papers relating to the rebuilding in HCA, 5695.

138. *Gentleman's Magazine*, 60 (1790), p. 150, report on his sermon of 9 September 1789. The subscriptions give some idea of the relative wealth/generosity of the twelve deans and chapters that contributed: £105 was given by Canterbury, Westminster; £100 by Christ Church, Durham, St Paul's, Windsor; £50 by Bristol, Exeter, Norwich, Winchester, Worcester; £30 by Rochester, HCA, 5695/13.

139. HCA, 7031/5, fol. 287r, act, 24 March 1792. All non-residentiary dignitaries were to contribute towards paying off the principal and interest at a collective rate of £28 for every £100 borrowed, 'according to the emoluments annexed to the stall of each member, to be ascertained by the bishop of Hereford', HCA, 7031/5, fol. 287v. Copies of the 1792 *Act to Enable the Dean and Chapter to Rebuild the West End of Hereford Cathedral* are in HCL and HCA, 7020/2/4, fabric account book, 1796–1814.

Fig. 39. South-east view of Hereford Cathedral, 9 August 1794, showing scaffolding on the tower: watercolour by James Wathen. (Hereford City Library, Pilley Collection, 2328, fol. 3v.)

Mr Lane, the chapter clerk, received an increased fee, 'as a reward for extraordinary services under singular circumstances'.[140]

The church 'appeared very neat' when the cathedral received its guests on Monday 16 September 1795, towards the end of a glorious harvest, for the opening service of the three choirs. It was indeed a very different building from the 'ruins' of six years earlier, and most of the major works had been completed. Wyatt's castellated 'Gothic' west front had been finished even before the previous meeting, but since then the nave itself had been renewed; its roof (as well as those of its transepts) had been arched and lowered and its floor paved; the south transept, which had also been in danger of falling, had been secured; and the tower spire had been taken down, two small pinnacles having been added at each tower corner and all scaffolding removed.[141]

The cathedral's seating, too, had been reordered. In the choir some seating had been reserved for dignitaries' families, although apart from the north gallery pews, temporarily reserved for cathedral school scholars, 'all the rest of the seats and

140. HCA, 7031/5, fos 335r-v, act, 11 November 1796. He was to receive 2s. in the pound from both copyhold fines and north transept pew rents, during the chapter's pleasure. The increase was also

for his other services. See below, pp. 148, 151.

141. The progress of the works can be traced in *Gentleman's Magazine*, 61 (1791), p. 865; 63 (1793), p. 179; 65 (1795), p. 785.

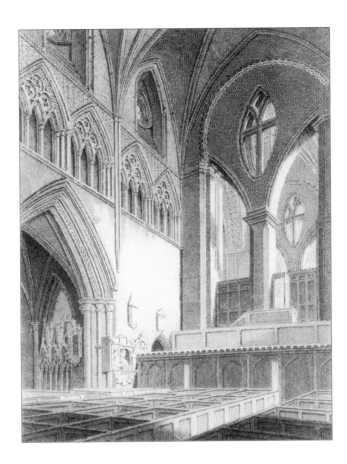

Fig. 40. The north transept
furnished with pews for the
parish of St John the Baptist,
showing the 'oxeye' masonry
supporting the crossing, early
nineteenth century.
(HCL, B.5.204.)

the body of the choir and the galleries [were to] remain unappropriated'. Locks
on all stalls, however, had been renewed. Earlier in the summer of 1795, new
seats in the north entrance of the choir had been set aside for the mayor and
corporation, and at other times 'for the ladies of the city and neighbourhood and
strangers'. During the music meeting itself these were reserved for the residentiaries
and their guests.[142]

The vexed problem of how to deal with the parish of St John the Baptist
was less easily solved. When the west front fell, the parochial service was removed
to the choir, until in November 1794 its ministers and church wardens were
given a year's notice to move, the dean and chapter hoping 'that by then the
parishioners would have prepared the north transept for divine service'. It was an
optimistic forecast, and in the succeeding months the parish fiercely resisted the
order on the grounds of its inconvenience and cost. Eventually a compromise
was reached, the chapter insisting on the move to the north transept – 'the south

142. HCA, 7031/5, fos 305v, 312r, 313v, acts, 13 November 1794, 16 July, 11 August 1795.

transept being the consistory court and the library necessarily limited to its proper uses'[143] – but agreeing to pay for the pulpit, desk, communion table and a certain number of seats, the cost of which was to be defrayed by a pew rent. For good measure, the chapter pointed out that the scheme was 'very ineligible to them after the large expenses incurred in the reparation of the cathedral'. Before the end of July 1795, work was begun on transforming the north transept 'according to Mr Potter's plan', although it was not opened for parish worship until Sunday 19 June 1794 (fig. 40).[144]

The cathedral was now gradually taking its modern shape, although the nave had not yet been pewed.[145] Not the least sign of modernity was the public display in November 1797 of the following visitors' notice (possibly the first in the cathedral's history): 'The dean and chapter desire all persons to refrain from talking or walking in the cathedral during divine service. The sextons will show them places in the choir.'[146]

The limiting of burial and reordering of the churchyard was an indication that the Close too was beginning to take on a familiar form. Although it was a task that was not completed until after the 1795 choral meeting, James Wyatt in his original report of June 1788 had observed that the gradual raising of the churchyard's level over the centuries, 'by its being the common and only burying place of the whole city of Hereford', had prevented proper drainage and resulted in a weakening of the foundations.[147] Little more than two years later, the chapter, anxious no doubt to prevent any further undermining of the new foundations, and acutely conscious of other risks, sent this solemn declaration to all incumbents within the city and its suburbs:

> The dean and chapter … having very seriously considered the present state of the minster churchyard and that of the Lady Arbour (the only places of interment in the populous city); how greatly crowded they are and have long been with bodies; how highly indecent it is and improper to observe the many putrid limbs continually thrown out and exposed to public view; and

143. At that time the library was housed in the Lady chapel.
144. HCA, 7031/5, fos 305v, 307v, 310v–11r, 312v, 324v, acts, 13 November 1794, 24 March, 25 June, 23 July 1795, 12 May 1796.
145. There is a suggestion, however, that the parish worshipped in the nave before 1786: *Gentleman's Magazine*, 65 (1785), p. 78.
146. HCA, 7031/5, fol. 341r, act, 9 November 1797. This was soon followed by a further notice in the north transept ordering that one of the sextons and the beadle attend every service, 'to take care that no person injure any part of the cathedral or disturb the congregation', HCA, 7031/5, fol. 352r, November 1800. These formed part of the standing regulations re 'the good order of the churchyard and precincts' which were to be 'hung in the library', HCA, 7031/5, fol. 349v, 4 June 1800.
147. HCA, 5695/3, report, 2 June 1788.

how great reason there is to apprehend that some contagious distemper may arise to the endangering the health and even the lives of the inhabitants, have found it absolutely necessary to declare that from and after the twenty-fifth day of March 1791, no bodies can be admitted for sepulchre here except of those who shall happen to die within the precincts of the cathedral.[148]

The deadline was later extended by some eighteen months to give time for Bishop Butler to consecrate the ground 'for the burying of the dead in the several parishes within the city', but the chapter held firm to its resolve.[149] The consequence of this resolution for the fabric fund was no small matter. To compensate for its loss, burial fees were increased more than five-fold, to ten guineas for interment in the cathedral and five guineas anywhere else within the precincts: rates which were soon further increased to twenty guineas in the restructured north transept and seven guineas in the Lady arbour.[150] Attempts were also made to improve behaviour and limit activities within the Close. Boys were banned 'from playing at all in the walks or within the rails at cricket, bandy [an early form of hockey] or any other diversion that may endanger the passengers or the windows of the cathedral', and 'military muster, parade or exercise' in the churchyard was also forbidden – a reminder that this was a period of war with France. Correspondingly, a sexton was ordered to patrol the close at least twice daily 'to lock the gates and turn out all the boys except the college school boys'; iron railings were placed before the new west end 'to exclude all nuisances' and an iron fence around the whole churchyard. Later, wrought iron gates were erected at the churchyard's eastern end and post and rails on the western side to obstruct 'carriages from being driven over the graves'. Nuisances, however, continued and were to continue.[151] Finally efforts were made to landscape and illuminate the Close. The churchyard was at last levelled in 1796; at the beginning of the new century, trees were planted at the north end of the music room; and, before the period ended, gas lamps were placed in the precincts, in part paid for by the paving

148. HCA, 7031/5, fol. 277r, act, 11 September 1790.

149. HCA, 7031/5, fos 281r, 282v, acts, 24 March, 25 June, 27 August 1791.

150. HCA, 7031/5, fos 286r, 291v, 342r, acts, 10 November 1791, 8 November 1792, 17 April 1798. Before the end of the period, the fees had increased again to fifteen, ten and seven guineas for burials in the cathedral, Lady arbour and 'oates churchyard' respectively, HCA, 7031/18, p. 163, act, 9 November 1820.

151. HCA, 7031/5, fos 335r, 337v, 338v, 352v, 353v, acts, 10 November 1796, 16 May, 26 June 1797, 2 December 1800, 21 January 1801. The ineffectiveness of some of these measures may be gathered from the further act of 27 September 1831 requiring the chapter clerk to employ someone to prevent noise and games being played in the churchyard. The city beadle was later employed at £8 p.a., HCA, 7031/18, pp. 319, 320, acts, 27 September, 17 October 1831.

and lighting commissioners.[152] The city and its cathedral were emerging into a more recognisable world.

The financial legacy of 1786 was felt long after these attempts were made to secure and manicure the churchyard. Indeed, given the extent of the loans which totalled nearly £9000, well over half the rebuilding costs, and the cathedral's importunate state, it could not have been otherwise, as the chapter itself acknowledged when instructing its solicitor to draft a loan bond which would indemnify executors in the event of a residentiary's death.[153] The dean and canons, however, could not be so indemnified and were personally responsible for the capital and interest repayments. It was a liability that the residentiaries did their best to discharge but the odds were heavily stacked against them. The annual returns from the fabric estates were insufficient to service the debt, which amounted to *c.* £696 p.a. in 1796 and reached a peak of more than £826 p.a. in 1815, during the high interest years of the French Revolutionary wars, let alone pay off the capital or sustain the cost of maintaining the cathedral.[154] Some progress was made in the 1790s when income from the fabric estates increased substantially. In 1793 the annual additional reserved rent of £75 5s. 0d. on the Swallowfield estates represented an increase of £60 (over the eight-year period) on the last renewal fine (of £540) in 1784. The following year on the Shinfield estate a record renewal fine of £1247 (an increase of some £500 on 1787) was set 'at the request of the lessee as an equivalent for an additional reserved rent'.[155] This paid off the residentiaries' substantial loan with £47 to spare. Other small loans, such as the £48 to the Ross Bank, were also discharged but the debts continued to mount. A timely act of parliament of 1798, empowering ecclesiastical bodies to sell their estates for the purpose of purchasing

152. *Gentleman's Magazine*, 66 (1796), p. 607, 24 June report on the 'outrage' of levelling the churchyard; HCA, 7031/5, fol. 352v, 2 December 1800; 7031/18, p. 232, act, 6 November 1825. £56 9s. 3d. was paid by the cathedral for the gas lights; thereafter, £12 p.a., HCA, 7020/2/3, accounts, 1825–27.

153. HCA, 5695/27, n.d. (*c.* October 1794). This appears to have been a cost-saving proposal to avoid the necessity, in that eventuality, of a new bond having to be drawn up. James Poole advised the chapter that it would be impossible to avoid the execution of another bond in such circumstances and added: 'I think it will be better for all parties that a distant day be fixed on for payment ...' Also see 5695/23,

re Poole's draft of a mortgage following the private act, 27 July 1792.

154. Unless otherwise indicated, the following is based on the collection of rebuilding papers, the 1819 act and the fabric accounts, HCA, 5695, 6269/2, 7020/2/2–3.

155. I.e. an extraordinary fine rather than an increased annual rent (as at Swallowfield), which would have been the chapter's preference, as is indicated by the chapter clerk's letter to Alexander Cobham of 14 October 1794, HCA, 5695/18. The fabric estate fines/rents are best set out in the hebdomadary's book, HCA, 7007/1, pp. 658, 659. Also see the act of 25 June 1792, HCA, 7031/5, fol. 289r, re Shinfield and Swallowfield.

land tax, enabled the chapter (after an abortive attempt to sell Shinfield two years earlier) to sell the Swallowfield estates for £11,000.[156] Following the payment to the government of *c.* £3200 in lieu of land tax on the remaining fabric estates, this left a little over £7799 to be invested in the 3 per cent consolidated stock, one or two points lower than the rates on the chapter mortgages and bonds.

Continued borrowings, therefore, were the inescapable consequence, and much of this again came from the residentiaries themselves. Despite some capital repayments, from 1800 to 1803, £2580 was owed to chapter members by 1811 and £2755 (plus a further £1600 accredited as a 'mortgage' debt) by 1819, by which time three of the reverend gentlemen (Drs Ford, Morgan and Napleton) had died. This is quite apart from the £1401 14*s.* 0*d.* raided from the trustees – themselves! – of the Philpott, Thomson and Croft charities. All told, the accumulated debt had reached a staggering £8576 14*s.* 0*d.* by 1819. A further private act of parliament in that year enabled the chapter to apply the money invested in the consolidated stock and the sums gained from the sale of its properties in Broad Cabbage Lane (Church Street), described as being 'very ancient ... much dilapidated' and producing 'a very small rental ...', towards paying off this crippling and ever increasing burden.[157] This was gradually accomplished, but even the sizeable sums raised from the statutory transfer and property sales, and the far less substantial sum from the prebendaries own sinking fund,[158] were insufficient to clear the debt. Interest payments averaged over £380 p.a. between 1820 and 1832, and negative balances on the fabric account were recorded in all but two of those years. The rebuilding was still being paid for, even unto the third generation, despite all the residentiaries' efforts in the intervening years.

From the closing decades of the eighteenth century the chapter was also intent on improving the management of its estates. As the visitations – and, indeed, Dr Morgan's survey of *c.* 1720 – had shown, knowledge of the exact nature of the

156. I have not been able to find any details of the Swallowfield sale, but for the attempt to sell Shinfield in 1796 and 1799, see HCA, 5695/9, 16, 20, 26. That it was not sold is clear from the continued fine entries in the hebdomadary's book.

157. These properties are described in the second schedule of the 1819 Act. They comprised nine 'dwelling houses' (some of which were shops) and occupied 11,270 square feet. Some of these tenements were sold (for £645) in 1819–20, others (for £315) in 1826–27, HCA, 7020/2/3. It is clear from the annotations on the cathedral copy of the statute (HCA,

6269/2) that the house fronting Castle Street and the one in the churchyard (comprising 995 and 2442 square feet respectively) were not sold.

158. In November 1821 a general tax of 5 per cent for the residentiaries and 2½ per cent for the other prebendaries was established on prebendal estates. £147 10*s.* 0*d.* had been raised by this means four years later, and in 1831 it was decided to pay off Miss Holt, a fabric creditor, who held £600 in bonds in 1819, if she refused to lower her interest rates. HCA, 7031/18, pp. 183–84, 229–30, 323, 324, acts, 8 November 1821, 10 November 1825, 10 November 1831.

cathedral's land holdings had been imprecise.[159] Even as late as 1769–70, the chapter acquired a transcript of 'Oliver's' parliamentary survey from Lambeth Palace Library, but the usefulness of a 120-year-old account of dean and chapter lands can be doubted.[160] Of more long-term consequence was the important act of 9 November 1775 requiring, prior to the renewal of any lease, a professional surveyor rather than the tenant himself to undertake 'a survey terrier and estimate of the value thereof'; the survey, and all 'ancient terriers', being entered into a book provided for the purpose. The residentiaries' election tithes were also to be surveyed in a similar manner.[161] From the hebdomadary's book, as it became known, it is evident that T. Smith of Shrivenham was one of the land surveyors employed by the chapter in the late 1770s to survey its own tithes.[162] The use of such professionals soon became normal practice, and surveyors were employed by the chapter in the 1780s to measure and map the hospital estates.[163] Although there are many other factors at work, one explanation of the marked rise in renewal fines on the cathedral's leasehold estates from *c.* 1780 is the chapter's direct employment of professional agents to ascertain their real value, rather than customary reliance on the uncertain evidence of 'ancient terriers' or the findings of its own tenantry.[164] Copyhold rents, too, increased in this period, the dean and chapter ordering a survey to be made of all its copyhold lands in June 1792, and the chapter clerk being rewarded four and a half years later in part because of his 'laborious and successful investigation of the manorial rights of the church, as appears by the increase of the copyhold fines'.[165] Mention should further be made of the chapter's decisions in the same period 'to take no fine on the renewal of certain of their larger estates' and to substitute an 'additional reserved rent' in lieu on an annual

159. HCA, 7029 (end), especially Morgan's list of 'particulars which nobody accounts for as I find'; see above, p. 131, for the visitation evidence.

160. HCA, 7031/5, pp. 36, 43, acts, 9 November 1769, 13 February 1770; 7007/1, p. 388; 7020/1/2, 1769–70 account, re payment of £8 9s. 0d. for the survey; 7006/1, copy of the actual survey.

161. HCA, 7007/1, p. 1, copies of the act. An earlier act of 31 August 1769 tried to enforce tenants (under penalty) to submit new terriers for comparison 'with the ancient terriers in the archives'. That the chapter had to employ a surveyor for this purpose some six years later shows the reluctance of tenants to comply. See HCA, 7031/5, pp. 34, 133, for the original acts.

162. HCA, 7007/1, pp. 329ff.

163. HCA, 7031/5, fos. 218r, 233v, acts, 12 April 1783, 24 March 1785.

164. The renewal fines, from the late seventeenth to the mid nineteenth centuries, for all chapter estates are listed alphabetically (from Breinton to Woolhope manors) in the hebdomadary's book, HCA, 7007/1, pp. 637–63. The significant fine increases, of course, are also a reflection of the general rise in agricultural prosperity in the late eighteenth century. A complicated formula existed for ascertaining renewal fines. See N. Yates and P. A. Welsby, eds, *Faith and Fabric: A History of Rochester Cathedral, 604–1994* (Woodbridge, 1996), pp. 79ff, and HCA, 7016, pp. 184–85; see HCA, 7017, list 25 March 1717, for Hereford tables.

165. HCA, 7031/5, fos 289r, 335r, acts, 25 June 1792, 19 November 1796.

basis; these terms being profitably imposed in 1792–93 on the governors of Guy's Hospital, the lessees of Llangarron, as well as on the tenants of the Swallowfield estates.[166]

It is probable that the deans of Hereford were not the driving force behind such improvements. The most long-serving, Nathan Wetherell, dean for thirty-six years (1771–1807), certainly presided over the key period of change when most of these initiatives, to say nothing of the rebuilding, took place. He was a reformer by nature, moreover, and has been described as 'a remarkably vigorous and far-seeing' vice-chancellor of Oxford, who was not only responsible for the reform of Convocation, the Bodleian statutes and the university's dress code, but also can claim the credit for the city's 1771 improvement act, which as far as Oxford's geography is concerned marked 'the end of the middle ages'.[167] Wetherell's very preoccupation with Oxford, however, makes it unlikely that he would have made the same impact on his cathedral. Indeed, as we have seen, he had a worse attendance record at pre-1786 audits than his predecessor and fellow Head of House. Although this marginally improved in the later period – he favoured four consecutive months (August to November) in residence every other year and therefore attended every other audit between 1790 and 1804 – extended absences must have meant that for Wetherell, as for Webber, Hereford became a poor second to his *alma mater*. For George Gretton who was made dean in 1809, after over a year's interregnum, following the successive deaths of Wetherell in 1807 and Leigh (who never came into residence) in 1809, the opposite was the case. As the first dean to be beneficed locally (at Upton Bishop) for over a hundred years, his presence was very much felt in chapter in his early years in office. Perversely, this seems to have lessened his influence, Gretton losing out in 1809–10 in an appeal to the archbishop of Canterbury over a disputed praelector's election, Archbishop Sutton unusually declaring the election of Hugh Morgan (the dean's candidate) 'null and void'.[168] A little later, the dean was in a minority of one when he was elected senior claviger by the five other residentiaries, a dispute which

166. HCA, 7031/5, fos 296r–297v, June 1793; HCA, 7007/1, pp. 650, 659. The Shinfield lease was also converted (at least in part) in the early nineteenth century, HCA, 7007/1, p. 658.

167. Sutherland and Mitchell, eds, *History of the University of Oxford*, v, pp. 215, 219–24.

168. On the grounds of academic ineligibility, Morgan not having spent 'seven whole years in the study of theology' following his admission as an Oxford MA. For details of this complicated dispute, which casts light on both the position of lecturer and the nature of theological studies at the universities, see HCA, 7031/6, pp. 75–76, 77–78, 85, 86–103, 14 November 1809–24 March 1810. Napleton, as bishop's prebend, then took over the lectureship, preaching thirty-one lectures between 21 April 1810 and 21 September 1812 (when he was over seventy), until Clutton was finally elected (twice!), in the dean's absence, in January 1813, HCA, 7031/6, pp. 127, 128, 7, 9 January 1813; HCA, 6434, fos 27–28.

rumbled on for two years (1812–14), only this time to be settled (by Bishop Luxmoore) in Gretton's favour.[169] After these momentous disputes the dean's authority may never have fully recovered, although his attendance record in the last two and a half years of his life (1818–20) was remarkable, and he certainly took the initiative in forwarding the 1819 parliamentary act.[170] Thereafter Deans Carr, Mellish and Grey followed in quick succession. Although Carr's presence is evident from 1820 to 1823, after his election in 1824 as bishop of Chichester, which he held *in commendam* with Hereford for three years, the deans once again become more remote figures until Edward Grey's translation in 1832 as bishop of Hereford, nicely mirroring Croft's elevation over 170 years previously, institutes a new era. The inescapable conclusion from this survey of the late Georgian deans is that we have to look below the first rank for the architect of the cathedral's 'age of improvement'.

John Napleton's name has already been mentioned in connection with his 1789 Three Choirs sermon, delivered little more than a month after he had been admitted to full residency.[171] The appointment of one of the century's best Oxford tutors, as well as a conservative reformer who had written a penetrating critique of the failings of his university's examination system, to Hereford's 'golden' prebend was Bishop Butler's most inspired act of patronage.[172] It was also one which was amply repaid over the next twenty years, for Napleton more than anyone in this period was to mould the shape of the modern cathedral. As his protégé and biographer, W. J. Rees, wrote after Napleton's death in 1817: 'He became an active and eminently efficient member of the chapter. At the time of his promotion, the cathedral being in a state of dilapidation and about to undergo very extensive repairs, he contributed much to its restoration by his attention and perseverance.' Rees further claimed that Napleton was pre-eminent among all his colleagues as a man of business and land management:

169. HCA, 7031/6, pp. 126, 142, acts 'electing' Clutton, 14 November 1812, 11 November 1813; pp. 155–84, petition, appeals and the bishop's judgement, 19 January to 10 November 1814.

170. HCA, 7031/18, p. 127, 23 February 1819, the chapter approving, retrospectively, Gretton's sealing of a petition to the House of Lords for a private act.

171. See HCA, 7031/5, fos 266v–67r, 268r, 268v, re Napleton's installation and admission, 9 May to 5 August 1789. By this time a canon who was serving his first residence, after he had performed his 'exercises' of four English and four Latin sermons, but prior to his full admission, was given leave 'to ride out of the liberties ... frequently during the time of his said residence on account of his health ...' – thereby circumventing the statutes' requirement for continuous residence within the city for the first forty days unless there was 'extraordinary cause'.

172. See Sutherland and Mitchell, eds, *History of the University of Oxford*, v, p. 6, for the observation about Napleton as tutor; and pp. 568–69, 615–18, for his university proposals.

Having a readiness in conducting business seldom equalled, the other members of the chapter found him so eminent in that respect that they, in great measure, gave up the management of their concerns to his superintendence. In this department therefore nothing was left undone towards their improvement, and accordingly the revenues of the canonries, during what might be called his administration, were advanced one fourth and that principally through his ability and perseverance.[173]

These judgements, of course, come from an acolyte, and underestimate both the support of Wetherell himself and the contributions made by Napleton's colleagues. With the notable exception of Henry Ford (1803–13), who was concurrently principal of Magdalen Hall, and was described posthumously as having been 'of infirm health',[174] most residentiaries of the period were beneficed locally, and most appear to have been conscientious in their duties. James Lane too, judging by the chapter's successive tributes and pay increases in November 1796, June 1803 and April 1809 – the latter at a time when 'the business of these offices has, from well known temporary circumstances, been more burthensome these eighteen years past than it has been in times preceding, and probably than it will be … in many years to come' – was an outstanding auditor and chapter clerk.[175]

Despite this, there is little doubt that it was Napleton who was the supreme influence. Evidence of his energy and handiwork is everywhere apparent. His record of attendance at the November audits, for example, was without parallel: he missed only two (in 1798 and 1816) in nearly thirty years, his last attendance being a few days before his death, and alternated with Wetherell as hebdomadary at these meetings during the 1790s and early 1800s, then acting alone as hebdomadary every year from 1805 to 1809.[176] It was Napleton to whom people deferred with regard to the possible sale of Shinfield in December 1799, and it was he who prosecuted successful appeals against the vicars choral in 1795–96 and the 'election'

173. HCA, 6434, fos 17, 51–52, manuscript memoir of Napleton's life.

174. See Gretton's observation that Ford had 'claims of indulgence on the ground of infirm health, and of favour from the amicable qualities of his heart, in addition to those of his academical avocation …', HCA, 7031/6, p. 168, 4 June 1814. Ford's attendances at meetings are certainly spasmodic, although he does undertake the offices of senior and junior claviger (1802–8), master of the fabric (1808–12) and master of the library (1812 to death in 1813).

175. HCA, 7031/5, fol. 335, 11 November 1796; 7031/6, p. 20, 25 June 1803; p. 70, 7 April 1809. In 1809, the stipend of 'these united offices' was augmented to £60 p.a. for twelve years, with a recommendation that it should be continued to Lane's 'representatives' in case of his decease within that time. Following Lane's death in 1813, Theophilus Lane was elected 'chapter clerk, head bailiff, receiver and auditor' on 12 August 1813, HCA, 7031/6, p. 139.

176. HCA, 7020/1/2–3, clavigers' accounts, 1789–1817.

of an unqualified praelector in 1809–10.[177] As master of Ledbury Hospital, he also undertook to defend dean and chapter interests in the court of Exchequer in a long law suit for alleged breach of trust, which eventually was also successful. Well might Napleton's biographer further claim that his election as master of the hospital in 1801 was a 'circumstance which proved of great advantage to the charitable foundation', for he doubled the stipends of the poor hospitallers and prepared the ground for the building of the new almshouses. John Napleton's death in the early hours of Tuesday 9 December 1817 brought this tribute from the *Hereford Journal*: 'He was indeed a man in whom the profound and elegant scholar, the sound divine, the exemplary Christian, the ardent friend and generous philanthropist were most eminently combined'. Over 500 people attended his funeral the following week, his great friend, George Cope, who was soon to become a cathedral benefactor in a different sense, almost breaking down during the burial service (fig. 41).[178]

Napleton was a reformer, but he belonged to that cast of late Georgian churchmen whose instincts were essentially conservative. In his attack on the 'lifeless, unedifying formalities' of the Oxford degree exercises, he made this illuminating remark which encapsulates his philosophy of progress: 'This is an age of improvements as well as of extravagancies: if it sometimes proposes alterations unnecessary and excessive, it sometimes presents us too with schemes that are rational and laudable'.[179] He acutely analysed Oxford's examining deficiencies but, as an historian of the university has observed, his remedies were 'somewhat paltry ... for a deep-seated disease'.[180] The same, too, might be said *apropos* Napleton and Hereford. He would go no further than 'rational and laudable reform', which for him included improvements to the cathedral and its charities, but did not go beyond the boundaries of the Laudian statutes which governed its foundation. Still less did he wish to see innovation in the national church. In doctrine he was staunchly orthodox; in matters of establishment, he was mindful of 'the mischief attending groundless innovations in religion and civil government'. In particular, he thought Catholic pleas for 'privileges' could not be granted 'without hazard to the state'. The

---

177. HCA, 5695/17, unsigned letter to a 'Mr Morgan', 6 December 1799; 7031/5 fos 309, 312–14, 315, 326–22, 326–33, 25 June 1795 to 16 August 1796; 7031/6, pp. 75–76, 85–103, 4 November 1805 to 24 March 1810. Both appeals went, in different circumstances, to the primate.

178. HCA, 6436, passim; 7031/6, pp. 80, 108, 185, acts, 21 November 1809, 17 September 1710, 3 January 1814 [recte 1815] re Ledbury. For Cope's will, 5 April 1820, see

HCA, 7007/1, pp. 157–59. Cope died on 5 September 1821, and was buried in 'surplice, scarf and band' in Booth's outer porch. His bequests (not all to the cathedral) amount to over £4500, including £200 for the institution of an eighth chorister and £500 towards a stained glass window.

179. Quoted by V. H. H. Green in Sutherland and Mitchell, eds, *History of the University of Oxford*, v, p. 616.

180. Ibid., p. 618.

Fig. 41. Portrait of Canon John Napleton as master of St Katherine's Hospital, Ledbury, in 1817: possibly the portrait by A. W. Devis, mentioned in the 'Memoir' of Napleton's life by W. J. Rees (HCA, 6434, p. 29), or a copy of it. This portrait was presented to St Katherine's by Lady Tulloch, Napleton's great-niece, in November 1892, and it now hangs in college hall.

parliamentary petition he prepared against such claims in January 1813 also illustrates the conservative stance of the cathedral and the Hereford diocesan clergy for whom he spoke:

> we conceive that no subject of a sovereign independent state can equitably claim to be admitted to offices of authority therein, while he acknowledges a spiritual dependence on any foreign state or potentate; that such admission is contrary to the principles of national union and the policy of nations; that it has generated disorder and calamity in this and other countries, and is carefully avoided as a solecism in governments. We think that other tenets of the Roman Catholic church render the ministers thereof unfit to be legislators and ministers under a king and over a nation professedly and legally Protestant, and engaged by constitutional stipulations and settled convictions so to continue ...[181]

181. HCA, 6434, fos 74–75.

The petition was the forerunner of a flood of even fiercer 'loyal addresses' submitted to king and parliament by Napleton's successors in the new reign.[182] These deplored 'the open, shameless avowal and extensive propagation of infidelity and blasphemy', and predicted that 'perpetual agitation and disputes' would inevitably follow Catholic emancipation. The Protestant succession itself would be endangered and 'the pure and mild doctrines of the established church' would give way 'to a religion abounding in superstition, bigotry and intolerance, inimical alike to religious and civil liberty'.[183]

To men of such persuasion, the repeal of the Test and Corporation Acts in 1828 and the Roman Catholic Relief Act of 1829 came as a mortal blow. But worse was to follow, for accompanying the agitation over parliamentary reform, which culminated in the great bill of 1832, were demands that the church should also be reformed. As one Durham prebend wrote to the dean of Christ Church in the summer of 1831: 'It appears to be morally certain that as soon as the reform bill is disposed of an attack will be made on dean and chapters and as certain that Durham will be its first object ...'[184] The prophecy was half accurate. The attack, indeed, was not long in coming, but it was not simply Durham that was singled out for attention: Hereford and all other cathedral, as well as collegiate, foundations were to be subjected to assault.

Ironically, it was the church itself which formally started the move to put its cathedral house in order. Archbishop Howley's plea in the House of Lords on 23 March 1832 for a full enquiry into church revenues inescapably led three months later to the formation of an ecclesiastical commission with extensive powers to investigate the finances of the whole ecclesiastical system. Bishops had been used to making returns to the privy council about their dioceses since the early nineteenth century, but now capitular and collegiate clergy were to be subject to the greater indignity of an inquisition.[185] The conservative churchmen of Hereford could not now temporise. And when the older residentiaries returned to their cathedral in

182. At least six cathedral petitions were submitted to parliament against Roman Catholic emancipation in the 1820s, the first three being drafted by Morgan, Carr and Clutton, respectively, HCA, 7031/18, pp. 167–69, 24 March 1821; pp. 193–94, 21 May 1822; p. 246, 27 February 1827; p. 260, 4 March 1828; p. 261, 19 April 1828; p. 268, 17 March 1829. Other 'loyal addresses' to the king expressed similar sentiments, HCA, 7031/18, pp. 165–66, 22 December 1820; pp. 246–48, 10 February 1827.

183. HCA, 7031/18, pp. 168–69, 24 March 1821.

184. Quoted in Best, *Temporal Pillars*, p. 275. The wealth of Durham, given its mining estates, was prodigious, the 'golden' prebend alone being worth *c.* £2000 p.a. in the 1830s: P. Virgin, *The Church in an Age of Negligence: Ecclesiastical Structure and Problems of Church Reform, 1700–1840* (Cambridge, 1989), pp. 61–62.

185. Best, *Temporal Pillars*, pp. 270ff, provides an admirable summary of these reforms. For the episcopal returns stemming from Sir William Scott's non-residence act (including the bishop of Hereford's dilatoriness in 1807), see ibid., p. 200.

the late summer of 1832, only weeks after the installation of a dean who was to prove more vigorous than any of his predecessors, their worst fears would have been confirmed. For waiting for their attention were twenty-two printed articles sent from 44 Parliament Street, the new office of the ecclesiastical revenue commissioners – articles demanding detailed replies to questions covering every aspect of the cathedral's revenue and establishment. They would then have known, had they not realised before, that the days of gradual 'improvements' were over and that a new radical age had dawned.[186]

186. Copies of these articles, together with the chapter replies, can be found in HCA, 7012/1 and 7012/2.

From Victorian to Modern Times, 1832–1982

Philip Barrett

The year 1832 was a key date in the history of Hereford Cathedral, as indeed it was for all English cathedrals. Voices were being raised in the press and in parliament calling for the removal of all cathedral endowments and their conversion into parish churches. It was being urged that the money from the cathedrals would be better spent on providing new churches for the urban populations being created by the industrial revolution, rather than on giving a comfortable and indolent security to a small group of privileged clergy. Pressure for reform was to lead eventually to the Dean and Chapter Act of 1840, which limited the number of residentiary canonries in each cathedral and transferred surplus endowments to the newly-formed Ecclesiastical Commissioners.[1]

In May of 1832, the dean of Hereford, the Honourable Edward Grey, was nominated for the see of Hereford by his brother, the prime minister Earl Grey, who was at that time struggling with an episcopal bench in the House of Lords reluctant to pass his crucial Reform Bill. Grey's successor as dean was John Merewether, aged thirty-five and 'a valued friend' of William IV (fig. 42).[2] Merewether had been incumbent of Hampton in Middlesex and chaplain to Queen Adelaide when she was duchess of Clarence. He was also deputy clerk of the closet. There was much for a young and vigorous new dean to do. The cathedral itself was still in the dilapidated, uncared for condition which F. E. Gretton found in about 1810.[3] Both the vicars choral and the choristers were irregular in their

1. O. Chadwick, *The Victorian Church* (2 vols, London, 1966), i, p. 137. For a general account of the cathedral, see P. L. S. Barrett, 'Hereford Cathedral in the Nineteenth Century', *FHC*, 52 (1986), pp. 12–37.

2. For Merewether, cf. P. L. S. Barrett, 'John Merewether, Dean of Hereford, 1832–50', *FHC*, 43 (1977), pp. 23–39.

3. F. E. Gretton, *Memory's Harkback through Half-a-Century* (London, 1889), pp. 1–20.

Fig. 42. Dean John
Merewether in 1848.
(HCL, B.3.78.)

attendance and had been reprimanded for being absent without leave.[4] Services
were regularly disturbed by noise both inside and outside the cathedral.[5] Unfortunately, Merewether brought an arrogant and ambitious personality to address
these and other problems, and the result, not surprisingly, was a period of conflict
as the dean clashed both with his chapter and with the vicars choral in pursuit
of his own aims.

One of Merewether's first tasks was to find a new cathedral organist. Dr John
Clarke-Whitfeld was old and ill and the youthful Samuel Sebastian Wesley was
appointed in his place. Wesley was twenty-one and had been Merewether's organist
at Hampton.[6] The poor standard of worship in the cathedral offended the dean.
He described it as 'a disgrace, a blot to the Church – from the insufficiency, the

4. HCA, 7031/18, pp. 267, 319, 337, chapter
   acts, 3 March 1829, 27 September 1831, 14
   February 1832.
5. Ibid., pp. 319, 380, 27 September 1831, 8
   November 1832.

6. Ibid., pp. 356, 365, 16 June, 10 July 1832;
   W. Shaw, *The Organists and Organs of
   Hereford Cathedral* (2nd edn, Hereford,
   1988), p. 21.

coldness, and the meagreness of its choral performances'.[7] For two years Merewether bided his time, but by July 1834 he had lost patience with some of the slack ways of the cathedral. On 19 July there was not a single vicar choral present at evensong, so Merewether fined them 2s. 6d. each.[8] Canon Hobart, the canon-in-residence, was absent from evensong the previous day and also found himself faced with a demand for a fine. The succentor was chided by the dean for being absent from his stall for the previous three weeks and the prebendaries were instructed to fulfil their preaching turns in person and not to rely on deputies. Despite protests from the vicars choral, Merewether continued to fight for better attendance from both them and the choristers and to exhort them to observe the statutes strictly. In 1835 Bishop Grey held a general visitation of the cathedral. The injunctions which he subsequently issued included a requirement to restore the daily morning service which had lapsed, and to repair the college chapel so that the lectures required by the statutes could be read there. Merewether used these injunctions to further his efforts to discipline and regenerate the vicars choral.[9]

The proposals of the Ecclesiastical Commissioners for the reform of cathedrals were resisted at Hereford, as elsewhere. In 1837 Theophilus Lane, the chapter clerk, wrote to the archbishop and to the commissioners on behalf of the dean and chapter protesting against them.[10] Merewether himself took an independent line in a letter of 30 January 1837, in which he regretted 'the present state of opposition between the Ecclesiastical Commission and Cathedral Bodies as most unconstitutional and most detrimental to the Church'.[11] Under the act of 1840, all the residentiary canons at Hereford were to be appointed by the bishop, their number was limited to four, and the estates attached to the individual prebendal stalls were gradually to be taken over by the Commissioners. The vicars choral were to be reduced until there were only six, which produced fresh difficulties in the provision of services. Merewether proposed a drastic solution in 1846 whereby all the vicars choral should resign and the college be disbanded; the idea

7. HCA, 7031/19, p. 103, chapter acts, 31 March 1837.

8. HCA, 7031/18, p. 441, 9 August 1834. The exchange of letters in July and August 1834 may all be found in HCA, 7031/18, pp. 454ff, 1834. The lower parts of the choir were sustained by the vicars choral, all of whom (except one, a bass) held livings in or near the city. Their duties in their parish churches prevented them from attending the 11 a.m. Sunday service in the cathedral. See J. S. Bumpus, *A History of English Cathedral Music* (2 vols, London,

[1908]), ii, pp. 374–75.

9. HCA, 7031/19, pp. 24–27, chapter acts, 28 July 1835; HCA, 7003/1/5, pp. 336–38, vicars choral acts, 9 July 1835.

10. London, The Church of England Record Centre, Church Commissioners Files, 3189, Theophilus Lane to Ecclesiastical Commission, 2 January 1837.

11. Ibid., J. Merewether to Ecclesiastical Commission, 30 January 1837; see P. L. S. Barrett, *Barchester: English Cathedral Life in the Nineteenth Century* (London, 1993), p. 19.

was resisted. Gradually a solution was found by the employment of lay clerks in addition to the vicars choral.[12]

A controversy of a more local nature was developing at Hereford at just the same time as Lane and Merewether were writing to London. Merewether complained that the rest of the chapter had decided matters in his absence and he took over the custody of the chapter seal.[13] The canons appealed to Bishop Grey.[14] When Grey raised the matter with him, Merewether said that it all arose from 'the culpable laxity with which the affairs of the Cathedral Church have been administered and the utter neglect of the provisions of the statutes and laudable customs of the said Cathedral Church'.[15] He claimed that the statutes clearly indicated that the seal could be used only in the presence of the dean.[16] Merewether had been insulted by one of the canons and, in the absence of an apology, had walked out of a chapter meeting. The behaviour of the canons in involving the bishop had caused him 'indignation and disgust'. His efforts to reform the cathedral had been met by determined opposition:

> Is it because I was not content with the plain reading of the Morning Service by one vicar which *no residentiary ever attended* and the evening chaunting *by two only* on that sacred day, but have pressed the re-establishment of both in their regular and proper mode, and have myself assisted by reading the lessons at those services? ... Is it because by my efforts and perseverance the Chaunts, the Choral Services and the Anthems in the morning and evening daily service have been restored whereas when I first came amongst them they had been content with having only on Wednesdays and Fridays a chaunt through the psalms and services, and to suffer the evening service of every day of the week to be hurried through without an anthem and only one monotonous chaunt throughout the psalms? ... Is it because I have reminded some members of the body that both they and their families have largely, very largely, benefitted by its profits, have advocated the performance of duty before the indulgence of luxury, and the necessary demands of the Church before the gratification of family requirements?

The canons were furious when they heard about this letter and composed a joint reply on 24 May regretting that 'the Dean's sense of honour is as dormant and as extraordinary as his sense of duty'.[17] Each canon also wrote separately to

12. HCA, 7031/20, pp. 72, 137–41, chapter acts, 25 June 1846, 26 June 1848; HCA, 7003/1/6, pp. 77–83, vicars choral acts, 18 and 20 April 1846.
13. HCA, 7031/19, p. 84, chapter acts, 24 January 1837.
14. Ibid., p. 87, 3 February 1837.
15. Ibid., p. 96, 31 March 1837.
16. The Laudian statutes do not justify such a claim; see Jebb and Phillott, *The Statutes of the Cathedral Church of Hereford*, pp. 22–23.
17. HCA, 7031/19, pp. 103–4, 134, chapter acts, 1 and 8 August 1837.

the bishop. Canon Matthews's letter of 1 June occupies more than forty pages in the act book. The dispute between Merewether and the canons over the custody of the chapter seal continued to smoulder over the years causing a rift which was exacerbated as fresh subjects were found over which they quarrelled.[18] Merewether also took matters into his own hands with the restoration of the fabric. In 1835 the dilapidated music room was demolished, the Lady arbour landscaped and the end of the remaining cloister enhanced by an archway. In 1835 and 1836 the dean presented a scheme to the chapter for remodelling the choir, involving dismantling the Bisse screen and opening up the east end, but he encountered opposition. From 1837 Merewether was excavating around the Lady chapel, which led to a dispute with Canon Clutton.[19]

After these quarrels the canons formally complained to Bishop Musgrave that Merewether was absent too frequently. It was 'gross and wilful neglect of duty'. Merewether said that he was at court, helping in the preparations for Queen Victoria's coronation, and produced a royal dispensation from residence.[20] Later there were disputes over the election of a praelector, over presentations to St Katherine's Hospital, Ledbury, and St Ethelbert's Hospital, Hereford, and over seats for the families of the dean and canons.[21] Then in 1842 Merewether found that the cathedral itself was about to collapse and initiated repairs which took twenty-one years to complete.[22] Under the direction of the architect Lewis Nockalls Cottingham, work was begun to stabilise and repair the central tower and crossing, followed by work on the Lady chapel and choir. The deanery was also rebuilt with financial help from Queen Adelaide.[23]

In 1847 Merewether played a key role in the attempt to prevent Dr Renn Dickson Hampden, the Regius Professor of Divinity at Oxford, from being appointed bishop of Hereford (fig. 43). Most of the chapter refused to support Merewether's protest and so he wrote a long letter on his own behalf to the prime minister, Lord John Russell, saying that he had read Hampden's writings and had found them 'heretical, dangerous and objectionable'. The prime minister replied on Christmas day with extreme brevity and informed Merewether: 'Sir, I have had the honour to receive your letter of 22nd inst., in which you intimate to me your intention of violating the law'.[24] Merewether may also have been motivated by personal reasons since he had long felt aggrieved at being overlooked

18. For details, see Barrett, 'John Merewether', pp. 31–34.
19. HCA, 7031/19, pp. 338–41, chapter acts, 18 April 1838.
20. Ibid., pp. 351, 355, 369, 29 June, 3 July, 13 August 1838.
21. Ibid., pp. 374–539, 22 August, 4 Sept-

ember, 30 October 1838, 1 and 16 January, 21 February, 25 October 1839, 17 January, 19 February, 5 March 1840, 20 April 1842.
22. See below, Chapter 9, pp. 267–68.
23. HCA, 3596.
24. Barrett, 'John Merewether', pp. 37–38.

Fig. 43. Renn Dickson
Hampden, bishop of Hereford
1848–68. (HCL, B.8.7.)

for preferment to a bishopric because of what he thought were political reasons resulting from his friendship with Queen Adelaide.[25] On the day of the election Merewether was outvoted. Hampden was therefore duly elected and consecrated as bishop. But Merewether maintained his opposition to the end, and refused to attend the enthronement. The chapter refused to receive the protest which he sent to them via the chapter clerk.[26]

Merewether died in the spring of 1850. He was succeeded as dean in 1850 by Richard Dawes, 'a sound, faithful and earnest churchman', whose innovative educational reforms while he was vicar of King's Somborne in Hampshire had attracted wide attention.[27] By the time Merewether died, the interior of the cathedral was still not yet fully restored and it was said to be 'a scene of chaotic disorder'. Dawes was thought to be the 'man of energy and resolution' that was needed to

25. HCA, 3596, *A Statement of Circumstances of the Late King's Wishes in Respect of the Dean of Hereford* (privately printed, c. 1842).
26. HCA 7031/20, pp. 127, 133, chapter acts,
28 December 1847, 27 April 1848.
27. W. C. Henry, *A Biographical Notice of the Late Very Rev Richard Dawes, Dean of Hereford* (London, 1867).

complete the work. He continued raising the funds for the restoration of the cathedral and provided 'frank, refined and generous hospitality' at the deanery. During his time the architect George Gilbert Scott completed the restoration of the cathedral, which was reopened at a magnificent service on 30 June 1863. After the reopening Sunday evening services were held in the nave and became very popular. The crowd of people waiting in the north porch before the doors were opened was said to be 'not unlike that at the pit door of a theatre', and with the great *corona lucis* and the standard gas lamps lit with more than 500 jets of gas, the scene was said to be 'of more than Oriental magnificence'.[28]

Dean Dawes died in 1867 (fig. 44) and his successor was the Honourable George Herbert, vicar of Clun. Herbert is a rather shadowy figure, but following the work of restoration undertaken by his two predecessors he was able to tell the committee set up by the Lambeth meeting of deans in 1872 that the cathedral 'has already been rendered fairly efficient and useful without any help from Parliament and if left alone will no doubt increase in usefulness and popularity still more'.[29] Although he presided over various changes in the cathedral during his twenty-seven years at Hereford, the main impetus for them came from others in the cathedral.[30]

The latter part of the nineteenth century witnessed a widespread increase in antiquarian interests, and a number of figures at Hereford played a part in promoting these. The most significant were John Jebb, Sir Frederick Ouseley, Lord Saye and Sele, and Francis Havergal. Jebb was appointed prebendary in 1858, served as praelector and finally became a residentiary canon from 1870 until his death in 1886. Sir Frederick Ouseley was appointed precentor whilst a non-residentiary in 1855, but became a residentiary in 1886, three years before his death. Both men were deeply committed to the ceremonial and liturgical revival of the Church of England along the lines promoted by the Ecclesiological Society. In 1843 Jebb published a study on the liturgy in cathedrals, advocating a return to what he saw as authentic practices. This, in conjunction with a volume of choral responses and litanies which he edited using original early music sources including a number of manuscripts found at Hereford, were very influential in the choral revival in both cathedral and parish churches throughout the country.[31] Sir Frederick Ouseley founded the choral college of St Michael near Tenbury Wells in 1856 to promote and practise his own ideals of daily sung services, and brought his influence to

28. *Hereford: Cathedral, City and Neighbourhood* (3rd edn, Hereford, 1867), pp. 26–27.
29. *Hereford Times*, 20 April 1850.
30. HCA, 5685.
31. J. Jebb, *The Choral Service of the United Church of England and Ireland: An Enquiry* into the Liturgical System of Cathedral and Collegiate Foundations of the Anglican Communion (London, 1843); idem, *The Choral Responses and Litanies of the United Church of England and Ireland* (London, 1847).

Fig. 44. Tomb of Dean Richard Dawes, died 1867, north-east transept.

bear on the music and liturgy of the cathedral.[32] Through the combined influence of Jebb and Ouseley the eucharist was celebrated weekly and many changes were made to the style and content of the services.[33]

Interest in historical tradition was further promoted by the long serving canon, Lord Saye and Sele, who was a residentiary from 1840 to 1887. A keen antiquarian, he was president of the Hereford Natural History, Philosophical, Antiquarian and Literary Society. As master of the library he encouraged and supported his deputy, F. T. Havergal, in his researches and efforts to preserve and record the historical artefacts of the cathedral.[34] Perhaps the most colourful figure in the Close in his time, Lord Saye and Sele delighted to give dinner parties before the winter soirées of the society. Both Dean Dawes and Lord Saye and Sele would fall asleep during sermons, the latter covering his face with a handkerchief soaked in eau-de-cologne.[35]

The lengthy restoration of the cathedral during the 1840s and 1850s not only displaced cathedral worship but also that of St John's parish. Serious consideration was given to building a separate church near Harley Court but this came to

32. W. Shaw, ed., *Sir Frederick Ouseley and St Michael's Tenbury* (Birmingham, 1988).
33. Barrett, 'Hereford Cathedral in the Nineteenth Century', p. 33.
34. See below, Chapter 28, pp. 525–27.
35. W. J. Humfreys, *Memories of Old Hereford* (Hereford, [*c.* 1925]), pp. 5, 10–15.

Fig. 45. Early photograph of the Lady arbour, *c.* 1858–60, during Scott's restoration of the cathedral. (HCL, B.3.37.)

nothing. A proposal by the dean for the use of the Lady chapel in 1854 was opposed, but later accepted by the chapter, although this did not come into effect until the cathedral was reopened in 1863.[36] Services which served the outlying, detached parts of the parish were also regularly held at Blackmarstone and Burcott Row.[37] In 1872 the chapter discussed a new site for the vicarage in the close, and when Alfred Capel was appointed vicar in 1877 he was given temporary accommodation in Church Street until a suitable house could be found. After several moves he came to live in King Street, but no permanent vicarage was established.[38] In the early years of the twentieth century the position of the parish became increasingly eroded as the dean and chapter wished to have proper control of the Lady chapel, and the detached portions of the parish were felt to be unworkable. In 1917, for the first time, the dean rather than a vicar choral was appointed incumbent, and in 1918 the boundaries of the parish were reviewed and reduced

36. HCA, D 858/6/1, vestry minutes, 9, 19 March, 2 April 1849; HCA, 7031/20, p. 294, chapter acts, 27 May 1854.

37. HCA, D 858/5/5, 9, St John's parish,

reports and accounts, 1866, 1903.

38. HCA, 7031/22, pp. 9, 16, 18, 231, chapter acts, 21 February, 3 May, 6 June 1872, 17 November 1877.

to the cathedral precincts only.[39] Since that time the deans have been instituted to the parish after installation as dean.

Throughout the Victorian era links between the cathedral and the city were close, and a cordial relationship prevailed. For example, in January 1841 Dean Merewether attended a public meeting at which the mayor presided. This meeting, held following a heavy snowfall and a severe frost, established 'a subscription for the relief of the poor in this inclement season'. The dean and chapter gave £10 to the fund.[40] A few weeks later, Merewether took the chair at a general meeting of the mechanics' institution in the city. The members resolved to celebrate their anniversary with a procession to the cathedral, to hear the dean preach a sermon. Just after this, Merewether attended a public meeting, chaired by the mayor, to form a society 'for Aiding the Industrious'. When another public meeting was held in November of the same year, to celebrate the birth of the Prince of Wales, he suggested that there should be a subscription for the relief of the poor and a dinner for them in the workhouse.[41]

In November 1850 the dean and chapter received a petition signed by the mayor and 140 inhabitants of the city asking for an alteration in the times of services,[42] while in the following year, after the dean and chapter had spent £200 in laying out the Close, the city council passed a vote of thanks 'for the great improvements they had carried out in the Close, improvements which the Commissioners feel are as much a credit to the city as they are satisfactory to the inhabitants'.[43] In 1861 Dean Dawes was authorised by the chapter to arrange with the mayor for a policeman to patrol the Close from 6 p.m. until 11 p.m. each evening.[44] In 1870 the town council was asked to water the walks in the Close.[45] In 1885, when a new special constable was sworn in by the city magistrates for the cathedral precincts, his duties included keeping order and preventing 'prostitutes and other improper characters loitering in the Close' each evening, and helping to blow the organ at cathedral services.[46]

Hereford, like many other cathedrals, became something of a tourist attraction during these years of the expansion of railway travel. In 1876 the cathedral was open each weekday from 9 a.m. to 6 p.m. There was no compulsory fee but visitors were asked to contribute not less than 6*d.* each. The vergers and sextons,

39. HCA, D 858/6/1, vestry minutes, 4 April 1918, 25 April 1919; D 858/10/3, scheme for new parish boundary, 15 April 1919.
40. *Hereford Times*, 16 January 1841.
41. Ibid., 27 November 1841.
42. HCA, 7031/20, p. 206, chapter acts, 14 November 1850.
43. Ibid., p. 239, 8 December 1851; P. E. Morgan, 'The Cathedral Close', *FHC*, 42 (1976), p. 18.
44. HCA, 7031/21, p. 6, chapter acts, 25 March 1861.
45. Ibid., p. 411, 25 June 1870.
46. HCA, 7007/1, p. 454, quoted in Barrett, *Barchester*, p. 28.

who were employed by the dean and chapter to show visitors around the cathedral, were forbidden to accept gratuities. Two years later visitors were *required* to pay 6*d.* each.[47]

The dean and chapter were well served at this time by their chapter clerk, J. H. Knight. When he died in 1890 they paid tribute to his work over the previous twenty-five years and set on record 'his scrupulous fidelity, his consistent integrity, his excellent judgment and ability in transacting their business'. He was, they said, 'ever friendly, ever patient and considerate'.[48] By the time Knight died most cathedrals had commuted their estates to the Ecclesiastical Commissioners in return for a fixed income, later exchanged again for estates which were supposed to provide a guaranteed income. The great agricultural depression in the 1880s and 1890s severely affected many cathedrals, but Hereford was less affected than many. Although the dean and chapter opened negotiations about the commutation of their estates in 1866, and agreed to the proposed terms five years later, in fact the matter was left in abeyance and the original estates were retained until the 1930s.[49]

In 1894 the Honourable James Wentworth Leigh succeeded Dean Herbert. Leigh had been vicar of Leamington and was married to an American lady, Frances Butler, the daughter of the actress Fanny Kemble. Hensley Henson described Leigh as 'generally popular':

> He belonged to the traditional type of dean. Well born and well bred, with a good presence, a hearty manner, and a kindly disposition, he was everywhere welcome. Even his zeal for total abstinence was condoned as a harmless eccentricity and it was counterbalanced by his prominence as a Freemason.[50]

Leigh found the cloisters in a terrible condition:

> they had been used as outhouses for coal, mowing machines, festival platforms and all sorts of rubbish; the windows were in a decaying state and the roof was pronounced in a dangerous condition.

He constructed a two-storey building on the site of the west cloister, completed in

47. HCA, 7031/22, pp. 185, 261, chapter acts, 4 July 1876, 14 November 1878. The vergers were not well paid. In 1868 the verger was paid £65 p.a. and the two sextons £50 each. They were allowed 10 per cent of visitors' fees, and installation fees: see London, Church of England Record Centre, Church Commissioners file, 32508. For the duties of the verger in 1874, see HCA, 7031/22, pp. 87–88, chapter acts, 9 May 1874.

48. HCA, 7031/23, p. 108, chapter acts, 17 April 1890.

49. HCA, 7031/21, p. 257, chapter acts, 25 June 1866; 7031/22, p. 4, 11 December 1871; see G. F. A. Best, *Temporal Pillars: Queen Anne's Bounty, the Ecclesiastical Commissioners, and the Church of England* (Cambridge, 1964), pp. 459–60.

50. H. H. Henson, *Retrospect of an Unimportant Life* (3 vols, London, 1942–50), i, p. 272.

Fig. 46. Opening of the Dean Leigh library, 1897. Dean J. W. Leigh is sixth from the left, Bishop John Percival fourth from the right and Frederick Temple, archbishop of Canterbury, second from the right. (HCL.)

1897, as a new home for the library (fig. 46). He also engaged Oldrid Scott to rebuild the west front of the cathedral in 1908, following damage from an earthquake in 1896 and widespread feeling that Wyatt's restoration had been unsatisfactory (fig. 47).[51]

For nearly all of the time Leigh was dean, the bishop of Hereford was John Percival. A former headmaster of Clifton College, Percival had a national reputation in the field of education, and in both politics and theology was a liberal.[52] Having inherited a largely high church and conservative chapter, Percival became determined to use his patronage to bring together a group of brilliant scholars who would improve the intellectual interests of the diocesan clergy. But this policy eventually created a rift between cathedral and diocese. The first of these appointments, installed in 1904, was W. W. Capes, a Hampshire incumbent and distinguished medieval historian. As keeper of the archives, he edited and published several episcopal registers and cathedral records during his eleven years on the chapter, and did much

51. J. W. Leigh, *Other Days* (London, 1921), pp. 223–24, 228–29.
52. W. Temple, *The Life of Bishop Percival*

(London, 1921); J. Potter, *Headmaster: The Life of John Percival, Radical Autocrat* (London, 1998).

Fig. 47. Oldrid Scott's design
for the present west front,
completed 1908.
(HCL, neg. 1014.)

to support the cathedral school.[53] In 1909 A. T. Bannister was installed as a canon
residentiary, having already been a prebendary. Bannister had only one lung and
preached with difficulty, but he was a fine scholar, producing among other works
a history of Hereford Cathedral. After he became precentor in 1916 he always gave
each chorister a newly-minted half-crown at Christmas.[54] A few months after
Bannister's installation, Hastings Rashdall accepted Percival's invitation to join the
chapter. He was a distinguished Oxford don who shared Percival's liberal theological
outlook. He had a European reputation as the leading historian of medieval
universities. Percival wanted Rashdall and Bannister to train a few ordinands, while
lodged at the palace, but the scheme attracted only five students and was ultimately
unsuccessful.[55] A. L. Lilley was the next canon to arrive, early in 1912, becoming
archdeacon of Ludlow in the following year. He was 'certainly a liberal and certainly
distinguished'. This appointment was much criticised in both the church press and
local newspapers. One incumbent in the diocese told the *Hereford Times* that the
laity were alienated and the clergy out of touch with the bishop.[56] Then, when

53. Henson, *Retrospect of an Unimportant Life*, i,
    p. 271. See below, Chapter 30, pp. 552–53.
54. HCA, Barrett (uncatalogued), letter of
    F. R. W. Blackler, 28 February 1996.
55. Temple, *Life of Bishop Percival*, pp. 304–
    6.
56. Ibid., p. 336; *Hereford Times*, 9, 16 and 23
    December 1911.

Capes died in 1914, Percival appointed another liberal theologian and Oxford don, B. H. Streeter. He was well known as a New Testament scholar and, like Rashdall, it was expected that he would keep only three months' residence in Hereford during the university vacations. Percival planned for him to lecture and preach in the diocese in addition to his cathedral duties, but this appointment was roundly condemned by Archdeacon E. H. Winnington-Ingram.[57] In fact, Streeter proved to be an asset to the chapter. A tall, gaunt man, with a long, pointed beard (which he would pull, chuckling to himself, when he preached), he had long feet with boots which turned up at the end, and altogether he looked rather like an oriental mandarin.[58] He was largely responsible for the restoration of the chained library, and he remained at Hereford until 1935 (fig. 48).[59]

In his biography of Percival, Temple has shown that it was only in his later years that his appointments provoked opposition. He quotes a letter from Percival to Archdeacon Winnington-Ingram:

My stalls were filled with High Churchmen during my first ten years, and I myself appointed the highest of them, and no one uttered a word of complaint. Now, when I have looked on for twenty years and seen Liberal Churchmen, however distinguished, relentlessly boycotted and passed over with depreciation and detraction almost everywhere, and have thought it necessary in the interest of the Church to do something to prevent this freezing out of Broad Churchmen and the narrowing of our National Church into a sect, there is raised this outcry ... but I shall be justified in the long run.[60]

Hensley Henson, describing the chapter as he met them on succeeding Percival as bishop in 1917, paid tribute to their scholarly distinction, but questioned whether it was their theology which distanced them from the clergy and laity of the diocese:

The Hereford diocese did not provide a favourable soil for the experiment [Percival] attempted. [The canons] were regarded by the townsfolk with more respect than affection. Hereford was not unconscious of their distinction, but doubtful of their efficiency. In the case of Rashdall and Streeter, the two most intellectually eminent of the quartet, their frequent absenteeism, their unfamiliarity with rural problems and points of view, and their lack of local connexions, were specially criticized.[61]

There were two other controversial episodes shortly before the First World War.

---

57. Temple, *Life of Bishop Percival*, pp. 342–45.

58. HCA, Barrett, letter of Blackler, 28 February 1996; personal communication from the late Miss Scott.

59. See below, Chapter 28, p. 530.

60. Temple, *Life of Bishop Percival*, p. 345.

61. Henson, *Retrospect of an Unimportant Life*, i, pp. 271–72.

Fig. 48. Bishop and chapter, *c.* 1920. Left to right: Archdeacon A. L. Lilley, Dean R. Waterfield, Canon B. H. Streeter, Bishop M. Linton Smith, Prebendary A. B. Wynne-Willson, Precentor A. T. Bannister, J. Bateman, mace-bearer.

In June 1911, Percival decided to hold a communion service in the cathedral to mark the anniversary of the coronation, to which nonconformists were invited. Two days before the service was due to take place, the general chapter presented a remonstrance to Dean Leigh, who said that he had not realised the nature of the service. Percival was angered by this move, as he had been when objections were raised in the upper house of the convocation of Canterbury.[62] The second controversy concerned the Athanasian Creed. On Easter Day 1912, Percival remarked to Bannister as they left the cathedral after matins, 'How terrible it sounded – those innocent choir boys repeating those awful words, "without doubt he shall perish everlastingly"'. Bannister relayed his views to the chapter, who decided to discontinue the use of the Athanasian Creed.[63] The four minor canons (all that remained of the college of vicars choral) sent a formal objection to Percival on the grounds that this proposal violated both the cathedral statutes and their ordination declaration. The chapter

62. HCA, 7031/23, p. 453, chapter acts, 26 June 1911; *Chronicle of Convocation: Record of Proceedings of the Convocation of Canterbury* (1911), session 8, 4 May, Upper House, pp. 246–56.

63. Temple, *Life of Bishop Percival*, pp. 306–7; HCA, 7031/23, p. 473, chapter acts, 14 November 1912. The date of 30 November given by Temple is incorrect.

then amended their decision, so that on days when the Athanasian Creed was appointed to be said, this would take place at a plain matins at 8 a.m., to be followed by a sung matins at the usual hour.[64] Despite an appeal from the bishop, the minor canons boycotted sung matins on Christmas Day, and Percival wrote to his son: 'We had a beautiful service at 11 a.m. without either minor canon or Athanasian Creed'.

On the first Sunday after the outbreak of war in August 1914, a great service of intercession was held, attended by some three thousand soldiers, boy scouts and nurses. The cathedral 'was full from end to end' and many others could not get in. Dean Leigh gave a short but much appreciated address. Local camps for troops were established and Rashdall spoke at recruitment meetings. His wife visited soldiers' wives and established a club for munition workers. They took as lodgers two Belgian refugees.[65] War bonuses were paid to the lay clerks remaining at home and increased payments were made to both the women cleaners at the cathedral.[66] The main local effect of the National Mission in 1916 was to diminish the congregation at the cathedral, as people went to hear the special preachers in the parish churches. Dean Leigh rejected Rashdall's suggestions for special lessons and psalms, but appropriate prayers were read from the pulpit after the third collect.[67]

In 1917 Rashdall was appointed dean of Carlisle and was succeeded as residentiary canon by Archdeacon Winnington-Ingram. It was said of him that he was 'in aspect, manner and type of churchmanship an old-fashioned High Churchman, rigidly orthodox and severely loyal to the requirements of formal duty'.[68] Later that year, Hereford hit the national headlines when Hensley Henson, the dean of Durham, was appointed to succeed Percival (fig. 49). He too had a reputation for theological liberalism, and opposition to his appointment went far beyond the bounds of the diocese, being led by Bishop Gore of Oxford. The editor of the *Church Times* of the day lived in Hereford and orchestrated the opposition, enlisting the support of the *Hereford Times*.[69] Four of the Hereford prebendaries declined to vote for Henson at his election by the chapter on 4 January 1918. Furthermore, Archdeacon Winnington-Ingram and three other prebendaries protested against the method of election according to law.[70] But in the end the opponents of Henson did not prevail and he duly became bishop of Hereford.

64. HCA, 7031/23, p. 475, chapter acts, 2 January 1913.
65. P. E. Matheson, *The Life of Hastings Rashdall* (London, 1928), pp. 152–55, 159; Leigh, *Other Days*, pp. 250–51.
66. HCA, 7031/24, pp. 4, 18, 23, chapter acts, 26 June 1916, 25 June, 3 January 1918.
67. Matheson, *Life of Hastings Rashdall*, pp. 160–61.
68. Henson, *Retrospect of an Unimportant Life*, i, p. 271.
69. Ibid., i, p. 224; see G. K. A. Bell, *Randall Davidson, Archbishop of Canterbury* (2 vols, Oxford, 1935), ii, pp. 851–82.
70. HCA, 7031/24, pp. 29–30, chapter acts, 4 January 1918.

Fig. 49. Herbert Hensley Henson, bishop of
Hereford 1918–20, in the garden of the bishop's
palace. (HCL.)

Soon after the First World War ended, the chapter considered various requests for war memorials. An offer to erect a memorial crucifix in the Close was declined, though there was persistent pressure for a county war memorial to be placed there. Various other proposals, including a memorial in the Lady chapel to Old Herefordians killed in action and a reredos in the crypt, were accepted.[71]

Dean Leigh retired in 1919 after twenty-five years as dean and was succeeded by Reginald Waterfield (fig. 48), formerly principal of Cheltenham College and more recently archdeacon of Cirencester and Cheltenham. Waterfield was an imposing dean. He had 'great spiritual powers as well as administrative gifts which gave an impressive dignity to the cathedral services, which were conducted with the utmost reverence and orderliness'. He was punctilious in his attendance at the daily offices and insisted on being escorted to the cathedral by a verger.[72] To the choristers, even in the 1936, he seemed 'very old and severe ... with a slightly menacing presence'. His frequent reprimands were balanced by his kindness in giving each of them an egg and a half-crown at Easter.[73] Waterfield's educational experience was soon seen in the various improvements for the care and education of the choristers.[74] He was a strict disciplinarian in his rule of the cathedral and had little contact with the parishes.[75]

There was a determined effort at this time to improve the environs of the cathedral. The town council's suggestion of placing seats in the Close was rejected, as the chapter felt that they 'might encourage picnicing and general untidyness in what, after all, is an old graveyard'. In 1927, however, the council agreed to pay half the cost of repairing the paths in the Close, and seats were eventually permitted

71. Ibid., pp. 51, 58, 2 April, 13 November 1919.
72. A. L. Moir, *Deans of Hereford* (Hereford, 1968), pp. 54–55.
73. HCA, Barrett (uncatalogued), letter of Michael Morris, 9 February 1996.
74. HCA, 7031/24, pp. 68–134, 6 March, 15 May, 25 June, 11 and 31 December 1920, 12 and 23 September 1921, 25 June 1923.
75. HCA, Barrett, letter of Blackler, 28 February 1996.

in the north-west corner in 1936.[76] Through the generosity of Colonel Heywood, four old houses in Broad Street at the west end of the Close were demolished in 1935, thus opening up the cathedral to the city.[77]

1926 was a notable year in Hereford. In the summer there were great services to mark the 1250th anniversary of the diocese. Among the special preachers were Archbishop Davidson and Hensley Henson, by then bishop of Durham.[78] In the autumn Alban Moore retired after having served as sexton and verger for fifty-two years. He was succeeded by James Poulter. Poulter was 'small, rotund, rosy-cheeked and most polite', even lifting his bowler hat to schoolboys in the Close, but autocratic in 'his' cathedral. Like Deans Leigh and Waterfield, he was a Freemason, as were Dr Percy Hull, the cathedral organist, and several of the lay clerks.[79] In the following year a new scheme was introduced by Waterfield and Archdeacon Money-Kyrle by which the parishes of the diocese were prayed for in the cathedral in turn day by day.[80] Other matters which occupied the attention of the chapter at this time included the provisions expected to be included in the proposed Cathedrals Measure and the opening of all the cathedral to visitors without charge. This began at Easter 1931; Canon Streeter made arrangements for the sale of postcards in the cathedral.[81] Consideration was also given to insuring the building against earthquake, a sensible precaution considering the damage which had been caused in 1896.[82]

Waterfield became chairman of the Cathedrals Commission set up by the Cathedrals Measure of 1931. Hereford, like every other cathedral, was required to revise its statutes.[83] The new statutes, confirmed by Order in Council on 8 June 1937, were the first significant revision of the government of the cathedral since the Laudian statutes of 1636. The number of residentiary canons remained at four, but for the first time it was required that all the dignitaries were to be members of the administrative chapter, thus effectively making it impossible for a non-residentiary to hold one of these posts. Lilley, as holder of the golden prebend and a residentiary, was not replaced on his retirement in 1936, and from then until 1982, when the archdeacon of Hereford became a residentiary, the admin-istrative chapter consisted of the dean, precentor, treasurer and chancellor, with

76. HCA, 7031/24, pp. 173, 191, 340, 345, chapter acts, 1 July 1926, 2 July 1927, 10 October 1935, 4 January 1936.

77. Ibid., pp. 316, 319, 321, 327, 333, 26 June, 8 August, 8 October 1934, 9 January, 6 April 1935.

78. Moir, *Deans of Hereford*, p. 56; see HCA, 7031/24, p. 170, chapter acts, 24 March 1926.

79. HCA, Barrett (uncatalogued), letter of Morris, 9 February 1996.

80. HCA, 7031/24, pp. 197, 199, chapter acts, 10 November, 8 December 1927.

81. Ibid., pp. 217, 225, 255, 262, 268, 270, 29 September, 8 November 1928, 11 November, 30 December 1930, 24 March, 24 June 1931.

82. Ibid., p. 248, 24 June 1930.

83. Ibid., pp. 273, 278, 292, 2 November 1931, 23 February, 10 November 1932; see Moir, *Deans of Hereford*, p. 56.

the fourth canonry in abeyance. Other changes in the statutes included the financial arrangements, to reflect modern practices. But the greatest historic change was the dissolution of the college of vicars choral. Its property was transferred to the dean and chapter, and the college fund was to be administered by them for the upkeep of the college buildings, and the stipends of the remaining vicars choral and the lay clerks. Any surplus was to be used in the first instance to meet the cost of the organist, the choir and the music.[84]

In 1932 Lennox Lee, a notable benefactor of the cathedral, suggested to the dean that a body of Friends of the cathedral should be established, following the successful example of Canterbury a few years earlier. Twenty-five people attended the initial meeting and set up a provisional committee.[85] In their constitution, the Friends included among their objects 'to maintain or assist in maintaining the fabric and furnishing of the Cathedral', and 'to undertake any such work as shall in the opinion of the Council ... tend to improve and beautify the Cathedral and its precincts'.[86] Since their foundation the Friends have provided valuable financial assistance and support for numerous projects, including cleaning and treatment of the shrine of St Thomas Cantilupe and the tomb of Bishop Peter of Aigueblanche, the removal of houses at the west end of the Close, new cathedral lighting and sound systems, repairs to the organ and stained glass, choral bursaries, and the silver-gilt corona in memory of Bishop John Eastaugh.[87]

H. A. V. Moreton succeeded to the canonry held by Streeter in 1935. A youthful man with a young family, and a pronounced Anglo-Catholic, he was thought by some to bring an element of fresh air into the chapter, whom he persuaded to wear coloured stoles at communion services.[88] An accomplished historian, he had a French doctorate and was actively engaged in ecumenical work, especially with the church in France. In the following year, C. E. Warner replaced Canon Bannister as precentor, and Archdeacon Dixon succeeded Canon H. A. Moore, who had been treasurer since 1929. Warner came to the cathedral after thirty-eight years in three incumbencies in the diocese. A faithful priest and pastor, he took a keen interest in education, serving on several committees, and organised crowded ecumenical occasions in Hereford where he was also rural dean.[89] An experienced parish priest before he became archdeacon of Ludlow, Dixon was a man of wide theological sympathies, a well-read patristic scholar and an enthusiastic sportsman with a gift for friendship.[90] In 1937 T. O. D. Steel was appointed joint chapter

84. HCA, 7044/27, statutes, 1937.
85. HCA, 7031/24, pp. 279, 286, 291, chapter acts, 23 February, 4 July, 24 September 1932.
86. *FHC*, 1 (1933), pp. 12–13.
87. For list of work undertaken, see *FHC*,

6–14, 46, 65 (1938–46, 1980, 1999).
88. HCA, Barrett, Morris and Blackler letters.
89. *Hereford Diocesan Messenger*, 48 (1945), pp. 82–83.
90. Ibid., 42 (1939), p. 56–57.

clerk with his father, A. D. Steel.[91] A further change occurred at the beginning of the war when Archdeacon Dixon died suddenly and was replaced in 1940 by Canon Jordan.

In May 1938 Bishop Lisle Carr conducted a visitation of the cathedral.[92] Some interesting facts about the cathedral's life on the eve of the Second World War may be found in his charge. The average attendance on Sundays was forty-five at 8 a.m., 100–150 at matins, and 75–100 at evensong, with more in the summer. Only about nine communicants came to the 12.15 p.m. said celebration after matins. 'I find it particularly distressing at ordinations', said the bishop, 'to leave the Choir of the Cathedral and pass into the Nave, where the quite numerous congregation at the beginning of the service is reduced to a mere sprinkling.' There were five or six communicants at weekday communions, but even fewer attended sung matins and evensong on weekdays. He praised the 'jealous care' and 'cleanliness and order' shown by the dean and chapter in maintaining the building but criticised the eastern transepts: 'It is hard to believe that they are parts of the House of God and not of a provincial museum'. He praised the cathedral choir and suggested several additional activities. Much could be achieved at the cathedral, he believed, with initiative and 'restless imagination'.

The Second World War caused the cathedral even more problems than its predecessor. Once again military service reduced the number of cathedral personnel. Both Philip Wilson, a lay clerk, and Walter Gittens, then the college gardener, were called up in 1941.[93] Waterfield moved out of the deanery into the cloisters, so that the building might become a military headquarters: it was damaged when American troops were subsequently billeted there.[94] By the summer of 1943, Canon Moreton was also absent on active service, leaving Canons Jordan and Warner to divide the months of residence between them. A former Salisbury lay clerk was given an honorarium for singing in the cathedral choir while stationed locally with the RAF, and the cathedral fire-watchers were given keys to those parts of the cathedral normally kept locked.[95] By the autumn of 1944 the normal administration of the cathedral had virtually collapsed: there were no chapter meetings between November 1944 and March 1945. Dean Waterfield was nearly eighty; Canon Warner had died, leaving Canon Jordan as the only effective member of the chapter until Archdeacon A. J. Winnington-Ingram, son of E. H., was installed to

91. HCA, 7031/24, p. 369, chapter acts, 3 July 1937.
92. Ibid., pp. 377–84, 21 and 29 March, 29 June, 4 October 1938; for the bishop's charge, see *Primary Visitation of Lisle, Bishop of Hereford, May 1938* (Hereford, 1938).
93. HCA, 7031/24, pp. 401–2, chapter acts, 2 April, 30 June 1941.
94. Moir, *Deans of Hereford*, pp. 55–56.
95. HCA, 7031/24, p. 432, chapter acts, 5 July 1943.

replace Warner. Canon Moreton returned in time for the July chapter meeting, when the minutes of such chapter meetings as had occurred in the whole of the previous year were read.

Waterfield retired in 1946 and was succeeded by Hedley Burrows, who came to Hereford from Winchester, where he was archdeacon as well as canon residentiary after four incumbencies. He lived in the college cloisters, as the old deanery had been let to the cathedral school. It was immediately apparent that Hereford had gained a dean of tremendous energy and vitality. Within a week of his installation, he persuaded the chapter to agree to the use of vestments and obtained £10,000 from the Pilgrim Trust for restoration work. He introduced monthly chapter meetings on the last Tuesday of each month, following a pattern which he knew at Winchester, as well as informal chapter meetings. He obtained from the chapter their consent for him to deal with any emergency matter and to 'amend or curtail' details in the regular cathedral services. The chapter also endorsed his plans to use honorary chaplains, led by Prebendary Beattie, to welcome visitors to the cathedral. Arrangements were made with the Ecclesiastical Commissioners to take over the cathedral's endowments, with a capital value of £228,253 1s. 5d. The canonical residences were valued at £110 10s. 5d. In return they paid the dean and chapter annually the sum of £6618 18s. 8d.[96]

For his first Christmas at Hereford, Burrows obtained a thirty-foot Christmas tree from Lennox Lee, to act as a focus for gifts of money for 'Save Europe Now', the local Red Cross and 'Christian Reconstruction in Europe'.[97] A new quarterly publication, *Hereford Cathedral News*, was launched early in 1948. The new spirit in the cathedral did not, however, extend to ecumenical matters. In August 1948 the chapter refused to allow the Salvation Army to give a concert in the cathedral, as 'it was undesirable to grant such facilities to any one denomination other than the Church of England at the present time'.[98] There was a broadcast from the cathedral on the morning of Easter Day 1948 and the Friends' festival was enlivened by three one-act plays in the college cloisters.[99] Burrows's autumn engagements in 1948 included sixteen harvest festival sermons, as well as visits to three parishes in Shropshire, four schools and three nonconformist churches.[100]

Burrows continued to show immense vigour throughout his fourteen years at

96. Ibid., pp. 476–88, 1 May, 27 May, 24 June, 29 July 1947.

97. Ibid., p. 495, 30 December 1947. In later years the collections were given to the Save the Children Fund.

98. HCA, 7031/25, p. 11, chapter acts, 31 August 1948. The band played in the cathedral for the first time at the united service on Good Friday 1948, *Hereford*

Times, 27 March and 3 April 1948.

99. *Hereford Cathedral News*, no. 2 (Summer 1948), p. 4; no. 3 (Michaelmas 1948), p. 7. There was a further broadcast on 5 March 1950, HCA, 7031/25, p. 47, chapter acts, 29 December 1949, and a Children's Hour on 2 March 1958, *Hereford Cathedral News*, no. 40 (April-June 1958), p. 8.

100. Ibid., no. 4 (Christmas 1948), pp. 6–7.

Hereford. He refurnished the Lady chapel with financial support from Lennox Lee.[101] When the south wall of the south transept was found to be in an alarming state, he quickly raised the necessary funds for its urgent restoration.[102] But he is chiefly remembered for his great gift of arranging impressive special services at the cathedral. The catalyst for these was the Festival of Britain in 1951. An agricultural service was held in May with a packed congregation, at which lessons were read by the president of the Free Church Council and the Minister of Agriculture; Women's Institute choirs were placed at strategic points to coordinate the singing, and the service culminated with a procession of agricultural implements to be offered at the altar, including a tractor and plough placed under the tower.[103] Other 'glorious' services that year included those for the Mothers' Union, the Royal and Ancient Order of Buffaloes, and the first county harvest festival. This quickly became an annual event, with participation by the National Farmers' Union, the Young Farmers' Clubs, the National Union of Agricultural Workers, as well as the Free Churches. A Rogationtide service in 1952 was broadcast and another in 1955 was televised.[104] Burrows had extensive links with the gentry of the diocese and encouraged them to support the cathedral, especially on great occasions. The highlight of Burrows's time as dean came in 1957, when the Queen and the Duke of Edinburgh visited the cathedral on a sunny spring day. The visit, which lasted only twenty-five minutes, enabled the Queen to tour the cathedral, inspect its treasures, and meet many of its staff. She sat in King Stephen's Chair while the choir sang the carol *This Joyful Eastertide* (fig. 50).[105]

The early 1950s saw several breaks with the past as well as new appointments. James Poulter retired as senior verger in 1950 after fifty years' service to the cathedral. His 'rare store of memories' extended well back into the nineteenth century when he was a servant in the household of Canon Musgrave. He was completely devoted to the cathedral and a highly esteemed local character.[106] Miss Maude Bull, who lived at Harley House, died in December of that year. A bell-ringer and sub-librarian, her death ended a family connection with the Close

---

101. HCA, 7031/25, pp. 36, 86, chapter acts, 2 August 1949, 29 May 1951; see also *Hereford Cathedral News*, no. 7 (Michaelmas 1949), pp. 5–6; for its consecration, see *Hereford Cathedral News*, no. 14 (Summer 1951), p. 10.

102. HCA, 7031/25, pp. 130, 134, chapter acts, 27 October 1953, 3 March 1954; see also *Hereford Cathedral News*, nos 26, pp. 5–6; 27, pp. 6–7; 28, p. 11; 30, p. 7; 31, p. 12; 34, p. 9 (Summer, Autumn and Christmas 1954; Summer 1955; Autumn 1955; Summer 1956).

103. *Hereford Cathedral News*, no. 14 (Summer 1951), pp. 3–5.

104. Information supplied by Mr George Johnson. Another televised service was held on 13 March 1960, HCA 7031/25, p. 260, chapter acts, 23 February 1960.

105. *Hereford Cathedral News*, no. 38 (Summer 1957), pp. 1–5.

106. Ibid., no. 10 (Summer 1950), pp. 5–8; no. 30 (Summer 1955), pp. 10–11; see HCA, 7031/25, p. 149, chapter acts, 29 March 1955.

Fig. 50. Royal visit, April 1957.
Left to right: Sir Richard
Cotterell, lord lieutenant;
Prince Philip; Bishop Tom
Longworth; the Queen; Dean
Hedley Burrows.

that had lasted for a century.[107] Walter Davis, clerk of the works since 1936, died a few months later. Edwin Preston became a minor canon in 1951 and chaplain to the cathedral school. Cyril Jones, known to later generations as 'Jones the Mower', was appointed Close keeper and college gardener in 1956.

Burrows' years at Hereford had been unusually free from changes in the chapter, but towards the end of his time new faces began to appear. Canon Jordan died suddenly in August 1959, aged seventy-seven. Two years later, Tom Randolph, who had recently succeeded A. J. Winnington-Ingram as archdeacon of Hereford, also succeeded to his canonry. The autumn of 1961 saw Burrows's own retirement as dean. He left Hereford with the cathedral reinvigorated and with a final word of thanks to his secretary, Miss Esther Poole-Hughes: 'What I owe to her goodness, skill and judgement is more than I can put into words'.[108]

107. *Hereford Cathedral News*, no. 17 (April-June 1952), pp. 12–13; for Miss Leila Bull, see ibid., no. 40 (April-June 1958), p. 11.

108. Ibid., no. 53 (Autumn 1961), p. 11. For a memorial tribute to him by Bishop John Poole-Hughes, see *FHC*, 50 (1984), pp. 10–13.

The next dean, Robin Peel Price, came to Hereford from Christchurch where he had been vicar of its historic priory church for sixteen years. A chaplain to the Queen, he had previously been Burrows's curate in Bournemouth, but he was very different in manner, being described as a shy man, but a notable preacher and after-dinner speaker. He was also very musical with a strong sense of humour. In 1964 Eric Eyden, previously vicar of Shepton Mallet in Somerset, was appointed precentor. He was 'a fine old-fashioned tractarian parish priest, who, wherever he had served, had had a thriving parish communion, and was a notable preacher who was much involved in the College of Preachers'. Canon Moreton retired in 1965 after thirty years as chancellor. His successor, Murray Irvine, came to Hereford after work as a college chaplain in Cambridge and a selection secretary for ordinands in London. With his young wife and growing family, Irvine was well suited to encourage ordinands and junior clergy in the diocese with warm and generous hospitality in his home.[109]

The removal of the choir screen was the outstanding event of the 1960s. This caused a considerable local and national controversy. Having previously considered its removal in the 1930s, the chapter's decision in October 1964 was 'on aesthetic grounds and in view of the heavy expenditure necessary for its cleaning and repair'. There was opposition from both the Cathedrals Advisory Committee and the Royal Fine Art Commission.[110] Peter Fleetwood-Hesketh, the architectural correspondent of the *Daily Telegraph*, called its proposed removal 'one of the most senseless acts of contemporary iconoclasm'.[111] Others who urged its retention included Professor Nikolaus Pevsner, John Betjeman, and Jane Fawcett, the secretary of the Victorian Society. Dean Seiriol Evans of Gloucester said it made 'architectural and ritual nonsense of a cathedral to turn it into one large room for the occasional large service'. But Canon Dawson, who had instigated the removal of the screen at Salisbury, condemned the Hereford screen's 'spiky, blatant vulgarity'. Robin Price told *The Times* that the main reason for its removal was 'the incongruity and over-obtrusiveness of this large Victorian-Gothic work in a Norman Cathedral'. He told the Friends that it was 'thoroughly dilapidated and corroded and spreads an atmosphere of gloom and decay'. The Friends agreed that 'the cathedral would gain spiritually, artistically and aesthetically' from its removal, and contributed to

109. HCA, Barrett (uncatalogued), Murray Irvine, 'Hereford 1965' (MS); Paul Chappell, 'Recollections of Hereford Cathedral, 1967–71' (MS).

110. HCA, 7031/25, pp. 376, 397, 411, chapter acts, 27 October 1964, 27 June 1965, 22 February 1966; *The Times*, 25 February

1966; *Hereford Times*, 4 March 1966.

111. *Daily Telegraph*, 16 August 1965. A Liverpool architect prophetically wrote to this newspaper: 'there is a growing disquiet that autocracy in our cathedrals cannot be trusted so far as fabrics and fittings are concerned'.

the cost of its transfer to the Herbert Art Gallery at Coventry.[112] The screen was removed in February 1967, when Canon Eyden emphasised that

> the cathedral is a centre of worship, not a museum, and liturgical considerations must be given full weight. Most of those who worship regularly in the cathedral find the screen a distraction … In a small cathedral like Hereford the linking of nave and choir makes an effective setting for diocesan and county services.[113]

While this debate was in progress, the cathedral received some new statutes in 1966. They included the provision that the chapter was not to alienate 'any object of historic or artistic importance' without the consent of the Visitor: previously it had been necessary to receive permission from the Ecclesiastical Commission (by 1966 the Church Commissioners). The new statutes also required two of the residentiary canons to be engaged exclusively on cathedral duties.[114] Soon after the removal of the screen Robin Price resigned, and Archdeacon Randolph paid tribute to

> his unfailing courtesy and kindness; his outstanding gift of leading in worship; his deeply sincere and readily understood sermons; his well constructed and amusing speeches … No 'dignitary' was at the same time so dignified in his office, and yet so humble and unassuming in all his ways.[115]

The new dean, Norman Rathbone, came to Hereford in May 1969 from Lincoln where he had been chancellor for ten years, after substantial parochial experience at Coventry. His English brand of Catholicism, founded on medieval principles and expressed through the dignified language and ceremonial of the Prayer Book, made him seem rather conservative in the radical climate of the 1960s, but his radiant holiness, fine preaching and deep scholarship, allied to a delightful sense of humour, gradually established him and enabled him to grace his office with distinction and dignity.[116] He was not, however, the man to tackle the cathedral's mounting financial problems. Soon there were further changes among the cathedral clergy. Tom Randolph retired as archdeacon and was succeeded by John Lewis, formerly archdeacon of Ludlow. Lewis was a breezy and colourful character in the Close, but made no secret that he preferred the diocesan part of his work.[117] Paul Chappell, vicar choral 1967–71, had also been

112. *FHC*, 31 (1965), pp. 7–8; see HCA, 5891/1, for newspaper reports.
113. *The Times*, 15 February 1967.
114. HCA, 7044/35.
115. *FHC*, 34 (1968), p. 9.
116. P. L. S. Barrett, 'The Very Reverend Norman Rathbone, Dean of Hereford, 1969–1982', *FHC*, 62 (1996), pp. 14–17.
117. Memorial address by Norman Rathbone, 9 March 1984, *FHC*, 50 (1984), pp. 14–19; HCA, Barrett, Irvine, 'Hereford, 1965', p. 7.

appointed chaplain to the congregation and had pioneered a more active pastoral element in the cathedral's ministry, with links with some 150 families and growing youth and children's work.[118] A new appointment in 1972 was Laurence Reading, who became the first non-residentiary canon. Although his responsibilities in the cathedral were not large, Reading's expertise in group dynamics and his shrewd comments and questions were invaluable gifts, both at formal meetings and in the general life of the Close.[119]

In 1975 when T. O. D. Steel retired as chapter clerk after thirty-six years service, the chapter recorded their appreciation, not only of 'his great services to the cathedral', but of the 135 years in office of members of his family. Group Captain A. W. Caswell, formerly the diocesan secretary, was appointed to the new office of honorary administrator.[120] Another significant development in 1975 was the creation of a cathedral shop, situated in the north nave aisle, of which Dick Ankerson was the first manager.[121] Allan Shaw, the new precentor, was particularly keen to improve the cathedral's efficiency and circulated a plain-speaking memorandum to his colleagues in May 1976. The cathedral office was created in 1977 in an outbuilding of his house in St John Street. Group Captain Caswell was based there and was soon joined by Miss Eilene Hassall, who had recently retired as the bishop's secretary. The office gradually expanded into three interconnected rooms as the staff increased. In addition to the monthly chapter meetings, staff meetings began to be held from the mid 1970s, attended by all the cathedral clergy, the administrator, organist and head verger. A weekly duplicated notice sheet was produced and the cathedral's ministry to visitors was developed by the introduction of blue gown stewards in 1978 and the serving of refreshments from a trolley in the cloisters. Dean Rathbone told the general chapter in 1979 that the teams of voluntary helpers had all grown in strength: 'The support they give us is helping very noticeably in the friendly atmosphere, commented upon by visitors, and in the increase in giving by those visitors'.[122] Clergy from the diocese once again began to minister to visitors to the cathedral during summer months and led the intercessions at evensong. A series of visits by the foundation to different churches began in 1979 with evensong at Ludlow, followed by visits to Condover, Bridgnorth, Bromyard and Ross-on-Wye.[123] In 1980 a treasury was opened in the crypt, organised in conjunction with a flower festival by the Diocesan Community Trust.

118. M. P. Chappell 'Some Thoughts on the Twentieth-century Witness of the Cathedral', *FHC*, 35 (1969), pp. 12–14.
119. HCA, 7031/26, p. 63, chapter acts, 5 May 1972.
120. Ibid., pp. 132, 156, 6 January, 26 June 1975.
121. Ibid., pp. 148, 150, 167, 3 March, 7 April, 5 May, 8 September 1975; see R. Ankerson, 'Early Days of the Hereford Cathedral Shop', *FHC*, 63 (1997), pp. 9–11.
122. HCA, 7031/26, p. 342, chapter acts, 22 June 1979.
123. *FHC*, 46 (1980), p. 6; HCA, 7031/26, p. 400, chapter acts, 24 June 1980.

Facilities for visitors to light candles and leave intercessions were also introduced about this time.[124]

The cathedral was becoming increasingly used for concerts, plays and exhibitions. There were protracted negotiations with the Hereford Choral Society in 1972 over their use of the cathedral for concerts on Saturday evenings, in the teeth of strong disapproval by the vergers.[125] Shaw took a leading part in the extensive diocesan festival which was held in 1976 to commemorate the 1300th anniversary of the foundation of the diocese.[126] The highlight was the visit by the Queen and the Duke of Edinburgh to distribute the Royal Maundy, but it was altogether a remarkable year, with concerts, plays, exhibitions, special services and many other events at the cathedral.

John Lewis retired from his archdeaconry and canonry early in 1977 and was succeeded by Tom Barfett. A chaplain to the Queen with considerable financial expertise, he was greatly occupied with central church work in London. Further changes occurred in 1978. Murray Irvine became provost of Southwell after thirteen years at Hereford and was succeeded in 1979 by Prebendary Russell Acheson, vicar of Much Wenlock. Both Walter Gittens and Cyril Jones died suddenly. Ted Pannell, for several years Gittens' assistant, succeeded him as head verger (fig. 143).[127]

The 1970s were a time of mounting inflation and the dean and chapter struggled desperately to control the cathedral's finances. This was not easy: it was only once in a while that one could launch a special appeal, and something had already been done back in 1967, when £145,000 was asked for as part of a diocesan appeal, following the fall of some stones from the tower two years before.[128] In 1973 there were delays in the annual revision of salaries at the cathedral, and a finance committee was appointed under the chairmanship of Sir Humphrey Mynors.[129] In 1975 Dean Rathbone warned the general chapter that there was no room for financial complacency, and Group Captain Caswell was authorised by the chapter a few days later to arrange overdraft facilities of up to £35,000. A special committee was established to find ways of increasing income, and through the initiative of Allan Shaw a cathedral stewardship committee was formed. This doubled the income from the cathedral congregation. In September 1977, Tom Barfett obtained £10,000 from the Diocesan Community Trust, with a promise of further grants

124. HCA, 7031/26, pp. 301, 319, 400, chapter acts, 4 September 1978, 8 January 1979, 24 June 1980.
125. Ibid., pp. 55, 58, 59, 65, 73, 4 January, 1 February, 8 March, 12 June, 3 October 1972.
126. *FHC*, 43 (1977), pp. 7–12.
127. Ibid., 42 (1976), p. 10; 54 (1988), pp. 17–19; HCA, Barrett, Chappell, 'Recollections of

Hereford Cathedral, 1967–71'; Irvine, 'Hereford, 1965'.
128. HCA, 7031/25, pp. 392, 410, 416, 444, chapter acts, 1 June 1965, 22 February, 31 May 1966, 29 August 1967; *FHC*, 34 (1968), p. 5.
129. HCA, 7031/26, pp. 90, 138, chapter acts, 1 May 1973, 3 February 1975.

of £50,000, but thereafter the cathedral would be left to launch its own appeal. The budgeted deficit rose from £20,000 in 1977 to £85,000 a year later. Lay stipends were raised by 73 per cent between 1977 and 1981. The projected capital expenditure rose from £350,000 in 1974 to £800,000 in 1978, and to £1,500,000 in April 1981. Two months later Tom Barfett told the chapter that the need for additional funds was 'a vital and immediate question'. By September 1981 the dean and chapter decided 'that there is now a clear necessity for a cathedral capital appeal as an independent issue'.[130]

In 1981 the Deans' and Provosts' Conference was held at Hereford, and in the following year Norman Rathbone, Tom Barfett and Laurence Reading all retired, while Allan Shaw became dean of Ely. Group Captain Caswell retired as administrator and was succeeded by Alfred Plews, a former solicitor. Much had been achieved during Rathbone's time as dean, but the need for additional funds was undeniably urgent, and a further appeal was essential. Although 1982 was dominated by the Cantilupe festival, it was also a year of substantial change. A largely new chapter began to take responsibility for the next phase of the cathedral's history.

130. Ibid., pp. 158–473, passim, 7 July 1975–11 September 1981.

7

The Closing Years of the Second Millennium

John Tiller

The two final decades of the twentieth century at Hereford Cathedral, as at most other ancient English cathedrals, have been dominated by two themes: finance and tourism. Of course the two are inevitably linked, since skilful encouragement of the latter can help to solve problems of the former. Yet they are far from being two sides of the same coin. Deans and chapters would have to struggle with the enormous burdens of the maintenance of vast buildings, whether anyone wished to visit them or not. And while lively public interest in visiting cathedrals might appear to be a godsend for the fabric fund, in practice the invasion of the tourists is far from being an unmixed blessing.

First, proper provision has to be made for receiving the visitors. This involves capital expenditure in the shape of restaurants, shops, toilets; a proper explanation of what is on view, entailing exhibitions, notices and trained staff; together with meeting ever increasing expectations of facilities and interpretations for the disabled. Ongoing costs include greater security arrangements, insurance and the employment of extra staff, involving the cathedral authorities in the far-reaching requirements of employment legislation, contracts and pension schemes.

Then there are the problems resulting from the very success in attracting visitors: wear and tear to the fabric actually increases, so more maintenance is necessary. And then there is the question of whether admission charges should be imposed at a building consecrated for prayer. On the other hand, in many places it has been felt necessary to take special measures to preserve some degree of peace and calm, either by limiting the number of visitors or by setting apart spaces for prayer and meditation. For the chapters concerned, theological questions have been raised of how coping with visitors is related to the mission, ministry and liturgy of the Christian faith.

It is all a far cry from the remote, tranquil world which the cathedral Close and buildings have traditionally been thought to encompass. The successful management and marketing of assets and direction of a diverse staff have become daily responsibilities of frequently ill-prepared clergy. From the perspective of Hereford at least, as will be shown below, these twenty or so years have witnessed perhaps the greatest ever change and development in the way the cathedral is operated.

In the twenty months between the end of January 1982 and the end of September 1983 the entire existing administrative chapter left. Replacements were not completed until December 1984. One result of this high turnover was that at the Three Choirs Festival in 1985 no member of chapter was present who had attended the previous one in Hereford. In these circumstances the continuity of the vicar choral in making the arrangements became crucial.

Dean Rathbone retired at the end of January 1982, followed by Archdeacon Barfett in May. The chapter then decided to petition the bishop for the restoration of the fourth residentiary canonry.[1] At the general chapter in June it was announced that the precentor, Allan Shaw, would be leaving to become dean of Ely. The new archdeacon of Hereford, Andrew Woodhouse, and a new residentiary canon, the Reverend Austin Masters, SSM, joined the chapter in September. The archdeacon was appointed treasurer, and Canon Masters became acting precentor on Canon Shaw's departure in November. In the same month the chancellor, Russell Acheson, announced his retirement in September 1983.

The new dean, Peter Haynes, formerly archdeacon of Wells, was installed on 18 December 1982. In the following month he took the chapter and the vicar choral away for a day to consider various matters of cathedral policy, including liturgical arrangements, budgeting, staffing and better use of dean and chapter properties.[2]

In October 1983 the Reverend Paul Iles, FRCO, an incumbent from Oxford, took up his appointment as canon residentiary and precentor. At a July meeting of the chapter it had been agreed that the remaining canon when appointed should hold the office of chancellor and be wholly occupied in cathedral duties (that is, be the second of the two commissioners' canons), as the archdeacon and Canon Masters both had extensive diocesan responsibilities.[3] In the meantime Canon Masters became acting chancellor until the arrival of Canon John Tiller, previously chief secretary of the Advisory Council for the Church's Ministry, in December 1984. Before that, Prebendary Leonard Moss was made canon non-residentiary, as provided in the statutes, combining this with the appointment of bishop's social responsibility officer. In March 1985 Canon Masters took on the title of treasurer from the archdeacon.

1. HCA, 7031/27, chapter acts, 7 June 1982. 3. Ibid., 4 July 1983.
2. Ibid., 7 February 1983.

These changes were then followed by a lengthy period of stability on the chapter, enduring through the controversy over the proposed sale of Mappa Mundi. In March 1991 John Tiller became diocesan director of training. He retained his residentiary canonry and the offices of chancellor and master of the library, but Canon Masters undertook the additional residence responsibilities of a commissioners' canon in his place. Andrew Woodhouse retired in the following September and Canon Moss became the new archdeacon of Hereford. So even these adjustments were internal to the chapter. It was not until the retirement of Dean Haynes in April 1992, therefore, that the first major change took place in the chapter for over seven years.

Meanwhile it had been decided, on the departure of the Reverend Philip Barrett in 1986 to be rector of Compton and Otterbourne in the diocese of Winchester, not to continue the appointment of a vicar choral, thus ending at least for the time being an office of ancient significance in the history of Hereford Cathedral. Following the dissolution of the college, a succession of minor canons had perpetuated the title, but to have a single senior priest on the staff who was not a member of chapter was no longer appropriate. After considerable discussions between the chapter, the organist and the bishop, it was decided that in future the duties of a singing priest at the cathedral should be given to someone who had been in orders for two or three years and who wished to spend up to three more gaining experience at a cathedral before moving to a more permanent post.[4] The new title was to be succentor, and it was held by the Reverend Paul Brophy from 1988 to 1990, and by the Reverend Michael Gill from 1990 to 1993. The post was then combined with the chaplaincy of the cathedral junior school and held by the Reverend Andrew Hutchinson from 1994 to 1997, followed by the Reverend Geoffrey Howell.

The new dean, Robert Willis, formerly vicar of Sherborne, was installed in November 1992. Canon Masters retired three months later, having held every dignity on the chapter including that of acting dean. James Butterworth, formerly team rector of Bridgnorth, was installed as the new commissioners' canon and treasurer a year later, and given particular responsibilities for visitors and for pastoral care of the congregation. There was then no further change until Archdeacon Moss retired in August 1997, when he was succeeded by Prebendary Michael Hooper, team rector of Leominster (fig. 51).[5]

There had been an honorary, part-time administrator at the cathedral (Group

4. HCA, 7031/28, chapter acts, 6 July 1987, 3 August 1987, 14 September 1987.

5. The Revd Anthony Osborne was non-residentiary canon and social responsibility officer from 1992 until 1997, when the Revd Brian Chave, bishop's staff officer and diocesan communications officer, succeeded him as the non-residentiary canon.

Fig. 51. Chapter meeting, summer 1999. Left to right: Canon B. Chave; Canon J. Tiller, chancellor; the Very Revd R. A. Willis, dean; Canon P. R. Iles, precentor; the Ven. M. W. Hooper, archdeacon of Hereford; Lt. Col. A. K. Eames, chapter clerk.

Captain Caswell, formerly diocesan secretary) since 1975. He was succeeded by Alfred Plews, a retired solicitor, in 1982. When the chapter clerk, Anthony Weston, resigned in October 1984 the chapter resolved that 'in order to comply with the statutes, the cathedral administrator be now referred to as the chapter clerk'.⁶ This was a significant change, taking the duties of recording the chapter acts and other business away from the office of a local solicitor and bringing them into the cathedral office. Alfred Plews was a qualified solicitor himself, but he died suddenly in the following March and his successor, Raymond Kingsley-Taylor, was not so qualified. Although the dean and chapter therefore had to obtain legal advice from elsewhere as and when necessary, under Raymond Kingsley-Taylor the administration of the cathedral developed out of all recognition into something resembling a modern office. He was succeeded by Lieutenant-Colonel Andrew Eames, RM in 1995.

These administrative changes were far-reaching and indicative of an institution where lay involvement was moving from chapter dependence on voluntary helpers or external advice, to professional and contractual appointments. Thus in the accounts office, in 1982 one cashier was working a twenty-hour week at £4 per

6. HCA, 7031/27, chapter acts, 3 December 1984.

hour under the direction of a volunteer honorary accountant, managing a budget of under £200,000. By 1993 the cathedral employed two full-time and one part-time staff in accounts, with an annual budget of over £600,000. The office itself had in 1982 an unpaid, part-time administrator assisted by one secretary, Miss Eilene Hassall, former bishop's secretary, who was paid for twenty hours a week but probably averaged more like forty. By 1993 computerisation had arrived and there were three full-time secretaries meeting the needs of the clergy and the chapter clerk.

A cathedral steward was appointed in 1987 to keep the diary and make arrangements for booked parties of visitors and concerts and other special events in the cathedral. At first combined with the post of dean's verger, it became a separate, full-time appointment when Douglas Harding took office in June 1990. The library, too, which had survived with an honorary librarian, an honorary archivist and a battered typewriter, had by 1990 acquired a salaried librarian and a part-time paid secretary; a part-time paid archivist was appointed in 1997. In 1992 a commercial company, Mappa Mundi Ltd, was set up to manage the trading activities of the cathedral. It is wholly owned by the dean and chapter and has three departmental heads, the shop, restaurant and exhibition managers, each with paid staff and voluntary helpers.

All in all, the payroll of the cathedral (not counting the clergy, or the two organists and six lay clerks) increased from twelve in 1984 to fifty-one in the summer of 1998. It is understandable that some of the most dedicated voluntary helpers watched these changes with disquiet. But the scale of operations at Hereford, as at many other cathedrals, was simply growing beyond what could reasonably depend upon volunteers whose assistance could be withdrawn without notice. In 1985, for example, the 'restaurant' was a trolley serving tea and biscuits; five years later, it was providing hot meals. The trading figures speak for themselves: in 1985 the net income from trading activities was £6484 and was declining, but in 1993, the first year of Mappa Mundi Ltd, the net profit paid over to the general fund of the dean and chapter was £72,000. The extra staff more than paid for themselves.

Many may regret the passing of the 'age of the volunteer' at our cathedrals. In most cases the ministry to visitors would not have taken off without this preliminary stage. At Hereford a movable shop had been opened in 1975, the refreshment trolley in 1979, and the 'blue gown' stewards at the door began in 1978. At its peak some 300 people gave varying amounts of time each week to staff these facilities, as well as the chained library and the treasury. In reality, volunteers continue to play a vital part as guides, welcomers and assistants in shop, restaurant and exhibition, as well as serving as flower arrangers and broderers. The church is essentially a voluntary organisation. But the very success of their commercial operations has forced the major tourist cathedrals to move on.

At its first meeting in 1982 the chapter received a draft budget from its administrator. He identified a worsening financial position which was attributed to three factors: the increasing demands of major restoration work; continued inflation without corresponding increases in normal income; and the failure of expected contributions in the previous year from the Hereford Diocesan Community Trust. No new restoration work was proposed for the coming year. Even without this he forecast that there would be an anticipated further deficit of £20,000 in 1982. An appeal for capital would clearly have to be undertaken as soon as practicable.[7]

In the following month the chapter received the support of the bishop and the lords lieutenant for Herefordshire and Shropshire for the launch of an appeal. It is symptomatic that an offer of a £52,000 grant from the Department of the Environment at this time for the refurbishment of the college cloisters had to be refused because of the chapter's inability to find the balance of £88,000 required.[8] The general chapter in June was told that a public appeal for £2–3,000,000 would have to be made.

Very much in line with the administrator's forecast, an increase of £20,000 in the cathedral's overdraft facility had to be negotiated at the beginning of 1983. At this time the cost of hiring the cathedral for an event such as a concert was £7; it was now increased to £50. The solitary cashier's hours were increased to twenty-five a week. A feasibility study was begun on the use of dean and chapter properties.[9]

It was hoped to launch the appeal in October 1984. On professional advice it was to be limited to £1,000,000 and was dedicated to the needs of the fabric alone, not the costs of the choir as well (as had originally been proposed).[10] The architect, Michael Reardon, appointed in 1983, drew up a schedule of urgent restoration work which could be achieved for one million. The Hereford Diocesan Community Trust set things going with a contribution of £25,000. In the event the launch took place on 9 April 1985 in the presence of the Prince and Princess of Wales.

The dean and chapter were already considering the sale of 'an important object' to help the appeal. Meanwhile donations did little to ease the immediate cash flow problems and £60,000 had to be borrowed from the diocesan board of finance to service the overdraft. On the brighter side, the appeal almost reached half its target by the end of the first six months. By the end of 1986 it was three-quarters of the way to £1,000,000. Then response slowed down, although by the time it was eventually wound up, at the end of 1991, the appeal had exceeded its target by £60,000.[11]

7. HCA, 7031/27, chapter acts, 25 January 1982.

8. Ibid., 1 February 1982.

9. Ibid., 7 March 1983.

10. Ibid., 25 June 1984, 14 April 1986.

11. Ibid., 4 February 1985, 4 March 1985, 4 November 1985, 1 December 1986; chapter acts, 16 December 1991.

All of this money was for the fabric. It did not prevent a continuing operating deficit for every year down to and including 1989, by which time the accumulated deficit for seven years amounted to £220,558. The overdraft at the bank at the beginning of December 1989 was £161,751.[12]

It is not surprising that before this, in September 1986, the chapter had accepted help from a major firm of accountants in producing a financial report on the cathedral's needs. Its conclusions were received in the following April, when it was understood that a capital injection of £7,000,000 was required to secure the future of the cathedral and enable the chapter to develop its assets properly by such means as a better use of its properties, a proper presentation of its treasures, and an adequate endowment of the choir.[13]

In February 1986 Sotheby's had been invited to do a valuation of the cathedral's treasures towards enabling the chapter to identify a possible object for sale to help the appeal.[14] However, the immediate result was to increase the problems because it became clear that the dean and chapter were seriously deficient in their responsibilities for conserving, insuring and displaying the major treasures in their possession, in particular the chained library. This outstanding survival, described by Christopher de Hamel of Sotheby's as 'of the highest possible importance', and its manuscripts as comprising 'by far the greatest untouched pre-renaissance secular cathedral library', could only be reached up a narrow spiral staircase which became dangerously crowded at busy times. It was housed in a poorly lit room which was capable of containing no more than half the collection. Furthermore, before any scholar could consult a medieval manuscript it had to be carried out of doors to the working library. There were no means whatever of protecting or rescuing the books in case of fire. Yet the items in the library were valued by Sotheby's in 1986 as well in excess of £10,000,000 and possibly £14,000,000, not allowing for their collective identity as the historic library of Hereford Cathedral.[15] Clearly, the proper care of such a treasure required a large capital investment in its own right.

Such an investment was part of the calculated £7,000,000 in the financial report of 1987. By the beginning of 1988 the chapter had identified Mappa Mundi as the one object of sufficient value to meet the requirements. Unlike the chained library, it was thought not to be integral to the history of Hereford Cathedral.[16] Rather, it was regarded as an important medieval manuscript, having long-standing but obscure links with Hereford, which could be seen and studied better elsewhere than hanging, as it then did, in a dark corner of the cathedral.

---

12. Ibid., 18 December 1989.
13. HCA, 7031/27, 28, chapter acts, 1 September 1986, 6 April 1987.
14. HCA, 7031/27, 3 February 1986.

15. C. de Hamel, 'Hereford Cathedral Library Medieval Manuscripts', unpublished report, 17 February 1986.
16. HCA, 7031/28, chapter acts, 11 January 1988.

This view did not go unchallenged. Claims were later made in parliament about it having 'hung undisturbed for some 700 years'; what is actually known of its history suggests far otherwise.[17] It was also claimed by some who criticised this decision that the theological character of the map required it to be studied in a cathedral, an argument which would have to be extended to putting almost every surviving medieval artefact inside a sacred building, and certainly by removing many valuable books from the British Library.[18] It is also true to say that research done since the chapter made its critical decision has pointed to possible ways in which the map may have more fundamental links with Hereford than were thought at the time.[19] On 11 January 1988 the chapter unanimously agreed to 'instruct Sotheby's to negotiate the sale of Mappa Mundi on the understanding that it is the intention of the dean and chapter to set aside a substantial part of the proceeds of the sale towards the provision of a new building for the secure housing of the chained library and its worthy display to the public'.

At that date it was still within the power of the dean and chapter to make such a decision, subject to the agreement of the Visitor, in this case the diocesan bishop. Cathedrals were and are exempt from the exercise of the Faculty Jurisdiction, which controls what happens to the art and architecture of parish churches. However, a new Care of Cathedrals Measure was already making its way through the General Synod. When it became law in 1990, the Cathedrals Advisory Commission was replaced with the Cathedrals Fabric Commission for England, a body with statutory powers equivalent to the Faculty Jurisdiction. Until then, deans and chapters had as much legal right as any private owner of an art treasure to dispose of their property.

In February 1988 a deputation from the National Heritage Memorial Fund visited Hereford to look at the problems of housing the chained library, but with no tangible result.[20] By September the chapter had decided upon a public auction of the map.[21] Preparations were made to announce their intentions at the beginning of December, having first informed those who would need to be in the picture before anything appeared in the papers.[22] However, on 16 November both the *Guardian* and the *Independent* newspapers carried reports of the proposed sale (fig. 52). The latter stated that the proceeds were needed to 'clear an overdraft, repair the fabric, endow the choral foundation, provide adequate staffing and build premises to house the medieval chained library'.

17. Reported in *Hereford Times*, 19 July 1990. The earliest recorded date for the map's presence in Hereford is *c.* 1682, and evidence shows that it has been disturbed many times since then; indeed, it is remarkable that it has not suffered greater damage.

18. Letter to *Times*, 28 November 1988.
19. See below, note 31.
20. HCA, 7031/28, chapter acts, 15 February 1988.
21. Ibid., 26 September 1988.
22. Ibid., 14 October 1988.

Fig. 52. Proposed sale of
Mappa Mundi: Dean Peter
Haynes (left) and Lord Gowrie,
chairman of Sotheby's, with a
copy of the nineteenth-century
facsimile of Mappa Mundi,
16 November 1988.

On the following day the *Times* reported that 'Lord Gowrie, chairman of
Sotheby's and a former Minister for the Arts, told a press conference in Hereford
yesterday that he had been trying for more than a year to negotiate a private sale
to the nation of all the cathedral's treasures'. Four days later a letter from Gowrie
appeared in the *Daily Telegraph* explaining the course of these negotiations. He
'suggested that the best solution might be for the British Library to open a branch
at Hereford which would house the chained library'. His opinion was that 'we
have not yet decided, as a nation, how we might separate the curatorial from the
pastoral role of some of our great ecclesiastical institutions. If we want them to
act as heritage bodies we must will them the means to do so'.[23]

Public reaction to news of the impending sale was enormous and not limited
to the United Kingdom. Although British visitors to the United States know how
seldom events in this country receive any mention in the American news service,
Mappa Mundi gained major coverage. In Moscow, a Hereford businessman attending

23. *Daily Telegraph*, 21 November 1988.

a trade fair met a Russian named Alexei Petrov who had heard the news. Petrov gave him his private stamp collection, all featuring maps, with the words: 'Let it be my humble Christian and Christmas gift to the Church of England for saving Mappa Mundi'.

Opposition came from two main quarters. There were those who regarded the idea of the alienation of a national treasure as sacrilege. Sir Roy Strong resigned from the cathedral's appeal committee, commenting: 'This is one of the most terrible and vulgar ideas I have ever come across'.[24] Secondly, there was a multitude of Herefordians who felt affronted that the dean and chapter should propose to get rid of what they regarded as part of their heritage without consulting them. On 16 February 1989 the *Hereford Times* carried a picture of local councillor George Hyde presenting the dean with a petition against the sale containing 11,000 signatures.

Soon it was realised that Hereford was in some sense the tip of an iceberg. Journalists got busy and discovered that around the country cathedrals were currently appealing for £47,000,000, with another three about to ask for a further £8,000,000.[25] Questions were asked about how the nation proposed to safeguard this huge element of our heritage and, in particular, why English Heritage should make grants available to parish churches but not to cathedrals. Virginia Bottomley, Under-Secretary of State for the Environment, explained in the Commons on 20 December that when state aid for historic churches had been introduced in 1977 the Church of England had taken the view that cathedrals 'were better placed than churches to raise large sums from the public and other private sources'.[26]

Speaking in the Lords a day later, Lord Blake continued to put his faith in public appeals, accusing the dean and chapter of Hereford of taking 'a lazy way out'.[27] But others could see that this would no longer do, and within two years English Heritage had announced a programme of grants for cathedral repairs. More immediately, the National Heritage Memorial Fund (NHMF) offered the dean and chapter the sum of £1,000,000 gift aided from an anonymous private source to create a building to house the map and the chained library, conditional upon their ownership being transferred to a body of trustees to be appointed jointly by NHMF, the bishop and the chapter. Further, they would make a grant of £2,000,000 available to the trustees as a capital sum from which income could be used for the upkeep of the treasures, the fabric and other cathedral purposes.[28]

Meanwhile the nation developed a fascination with Mappa Mundi as an object of mystery and delight. It acquired an international reputation. Buses and railway

24. *Daily Express*, 19 November 1988.
25. *Observer*, 27 November 1988.
26. *Times*, 21 December 1988.
27. *Times*, 22 December 1988.
28. HCA, 7031/28, chapter acts, 20 February 1989.

engines were named after it. Curiously, just before the crisis broke, the Heart of England Tourist Board had prepared a report on the weaknesses of tourism in Herefordshire, including the 'lack of a major, nationally known attraction'.[29] Hereford clearly now had an asset ripe for development.

Further excitement was caused by the researches of Martin Bailey of the *Observer*. He drew attention to a drawing in the British Library dating from the late eighteenth century depicting the map as the centrepiece of a triptych, with Gabriel and the Virgin on the side panels. In the summer of 1989 a frame corresponding to this was discovered buried under junk in the cathedral stables, but with the side panels missing. Carbon dating by Professor Edward Hall of Oxford established that the frame contained medieval woodwork and could have been the original housing for the map. Bailey developed a theory that the map had been used as an altar-piece.[30] Later, in a lecture to the Royal Historical Society in 1997, Professor Valerie Flint of Hull proposed a link between the map and the cult of St Thomas Cantilupe.[31]

An early example of 'mappa thinking', in the spring of 1989, was the idea of a group of city businessmen in London to float shares in Mappa Mundi on the stock market, to raise the funds needed by the cathedral. Plans were prepared in secret under the codename anagram 'Madam Pinup'. An attempt was made to sell 7500 shares for £1000 each. The prospect of a dividend was slight but the share certificate, in the shape of a magnificent reproduction of the map, was confidently described as the grandest ever offered. The issue failed: by the closure date only just on 1000 people had subscribed. But in fact this was probably a record in raising £1,000,000 for a cathedral in forty days by public appeal. About a quarter of the subscribers were content to leave their money with the cathedral as a donation.[32]

By November 1989 negotiations had led to agreement between the dean and chapter and NHMF along the lines already described.[33] The anonymous benefactor was disclosed as J. Paul Getty, Jnr, now Sir Paul Getty. On 21 May 1990 the map was returned to Hereford from the British Library, where it had been on view since its withdrawal from auction, into a new air-conditioned case in an exhibition in the crypt of the cathedral. The Mappa Mundi Trustees had come into existence in January 1990 under the chairmanship of Sir John Cotterell. They now set to work on their brief to make a new home for the map and the chained library.

29. *Hereford Times*, 26 January 1989.
30. *Observer*, 13 August 1989, 20 August 1989, 3 September 1989, 5 November 1989.
31. V. I. J. Flint, 'The Hereford Map: Its Author(s), Two Scenes and a Border', *Transactions of the Royal Historical Society*, sixth series, 8 (1998), pp. 19–43.
32. HCA, 7031/28, chapter acts, 24 February 1989, 22 May 1989, 5 June 1989; *Sunday Telegraph*, 19 March 1989; *Hereford Times*, 23 March 1989, 30 March 1989; *Financial Times*, 12 May 1989; *Daily Telegraph*, 31 May 1989; *Independent*, 2 June 1989.
33. Chapter acts, 2 October 1989, 6 November 1989.

The notice in the *Times* of the map's return pointed out that, while the map had been saved, it had not solved the cathedral's financial problems.[34] Only part of the £7,000,000 needed had been achieved, and that was to be spent in the first instance on care of the treasures. At the end of 1989 the overdraft reached a new high.

In fact for the next four years there was an operating surplus. This was due in part to a large increase in the number of visitors attracted by the chance to see the now famous map. Partly, too, it was because at first the Mappa Mundi Trustees were able to help the cathedral out of their endowment income, before the start of the new building consumed all their resources until 1998, when they were once more in a position to resume supporting other cathedral needs. And largely, the arrival of English Heritage grants at a level of 70 per cent meant that at last the fabric fund had realistic support. By the end of 1993 there was in fact a small accumulated surplus in the accounts for the whole preceding decade. But then the Church Commissioners began a systematic reduction in support for cathedrals which, in the case of Hereford, amounted to 50 per cent over three years. This coincided with the period when the Mappa Trustees were fully committed to funding the new building, so from 1994 the accumulation of a deficit began again.

Dean Willis reacted to the worsening situation by proposing a Perpetual Trust for the cathedral, which would replace the old-style appeal with a body which would campaign continuously on the cathedral's behalf.[35] It was established in 1995, with Lady Alexandra Cotterell in the chair and Mrs Sue Embrey as its director, and it set its sights initially on producing matching funds to ensure the cathedral could claim the available grants from English Heritage; and, secondly, on creating an endowment for the choral foundation. In its first three years it enabled over £500,000 of restoration work and put aside in excess of £100,000 capital for the benefit of the choir.

Meanwhile the Mappa Trustees commissioned Whitfield Partners to design the new library building. It is described elsewhere in this book. It will be sufficient here to mention that the trustees and their architects encountered every possible obstruction to begin with but, in the end, created a building which has won universal praise and a number of awards, including the Building of the Year Award for 1997 from the Royal Fine Art Commission (fig. 92). It was officially opened by the Queen on 3 May 1996 (plate XV.). It brings together under one roof Mappa Mundi and the chained library, each in its own room (the latter with the book presses in their original layout for the first time for 150 years); the working library in a splendid reading room above them; and a basement archive store. An accompanying exhibition, designed by Ivor Heal, introduces visitors to the treasures

---

34. *Times*, 22 May 1990.
35. Chapter acts, 29 November 1993, 11 April 1994, 15 August 1994, 3 April 1995, 22 May 1995.

as they walk through the refurbished south cloister on their way to the new building. The dean and chapter owe a great deal to those who have served as Mappa Trustees for their unstinting efforts and for the experienced management of the resources at their disposal.

In 1994 the neighbouring parish church of All Saints appealed to be allowed to sell its parochial chained library in order to raise funds for a restoration programme, including the internal reordering of the medieval building and the installation of a restaurant. Curiously, there was no outcry at this further proposal to dispose of a Hereford treasure. Following a consistory court on 28 October, permission for the sale was given. A few people appreciated the loss to Hereford of this interesting library. Led by Anthony Hobson, for many years a member of the cathedral's library advisory committee, and the late George Clive, funds were raised to buy it and place it in the new exhibition at the cathedral. As a result, the two historic Hereford libraries are now together, the cathedral and the parochial, a unique survival in one place.[36]

So it is possible to record how, with the help of a number of able people both locally and nationally, the Mappa Mundi crisis worked as a catalyst for the ultimate benefit of Hereford and of cathedrals generally. That may not justify, in some people's eyes, the actions of the dean and chapter in the first place. In the minds of the press they will always be tainted with scandal. The *Times* of 6 November 1996, reporting on the reforms of cathedral government being introduced in response to the report of the Howe Commission, *Heritage and Renewal*, said that the reforms had arisen 'out of a concern about the damage done to the image of the church by the Trollopean internecine troubles at cathedrals such as Hereford and Lincoln'. Whatever folly the Hereford dean and chapter of 1988 may be guilty of, it ought to be noted that they acted throughout in good conscience, in complete harmony and in a spirit of prayerful responsibility for what had been committed to their charge. Not everyone shared their priorities, as summed up by Canon Moss in a speech to the General Synod on 8 July 1989: 'The Mappa Mundi is a great treasure, but the cathedral is a greater treasure. The really important treasures committed to our care are the people we are called to serve. We care about Mappa; we care more about the cathedral; we care most about the mission of the church as it witnesses to the priorities of God.'[37]

It might be thought that preoccupations with finance and treasures and the media would have left the chapter with little time for other things, including those things which they held as priorities. In fact a number of other significant developments

---

36. Ibid., 11 April 1994, 25 April 1994, 4 July 1994, 18 July 1994, 19 September 1994, 31 October 1994.
37. *General Synod Report of Proceedings*, 20 (1989), p. 546.

took place during this period. A cathedral council was established and consulted regularly over matters of congregational life. Already at Easter 1984 an important liturgical change had been introduced with a principal choral cathedral eucharist with sermon on Sundays celebrated at 10 a.m. at the altar under the tower crossing. This amalgamated a choral celebration without sermon and a congregational one with sermon. Choral matins was moved to 11.30 a.m., at a time when many visitors were entering the cathedral during the summer.[38]

Then in 1988 the chapter agreed to install, with financial help from the Friends of Hereford Cathedral, a permanent platform under the tower, covered in mosaic tiles. This made Hereford one of the first medieval cathedrals to have a permanent central position for the celebration of the liturgy. A new wooden altar table was placed on the platform in 1991 with matching detachable communion rails on three sides round the platform. In December 1992, a magnificent silver-gilt corona was hung above it, designed and made by Simon Beer and commissioned by the Friends in memory of Bishop John Eastaugh (fig. 53).[39] Another liturgical change was the introduction of lay assistants for the administration of holy communion. During the same period a strong team of teachers was recruited for a Sunday school which was growing in numbers. Altogether this was a period of increasing strength in the congregational aspect of the cathedral's life.[40]

The Friends were ably chaired during this period by Sir Roger Mynors until 1988, then John Champion until his tragic illness in 1993, followed by Brian Beves. Joan Bookham ended twenty years' service as their honorary secretary in 1993 and was succeeded by June Chase. In addition to the help already mentioned, the Friends performed a great service in 1994, the year of their Diamond Jubilee, by funding the installation of a decent sound system. Frequent references in the chapter acts over many years bear testimony to the enduring nature of this problem, which no tinkering with cost-cutting ideas had solved. Sometimes a note of humour can be detected, as when the administrator was asked by the chapter to install an extra speaker 'so that sermons could be heard clearly in the bishop's throne', but in general the lack of adequate sound amplification and distribution had caused continuing frustration over many years.[41]

As a result of these improvements the cathedral became a splendid setting for the great occasions. The diocese celebrated the 1200th anniversary of St Ethelbert in 1994, when Princess Margaret attended a special service in the cathedral on

38. HCA, 7031/27, chapter acts, 2 April 1984, 7 May 1984.
39. Ibid., 3 November 1986; 7031/28, 9 November 1987, 7 March 1988, 2 May 1988; chapter acts, 22 January 1990, 3 September 1990, 8 October 1990, 9 September 1991, 21 October 1991; *FHC*, 59 (1993), pp. 23–25.
40. HCA, 7031/27, 28, chapter acts, 1 December 1986, 1 June 1987, 5 October 1987.
41. Ibid., 5 April 1982; chapter acts, 28 November 1994; *FHC*, 60 (1994), p. 7.

Fig. 53. Bishop John Oliver celebrating the 10.00 a.m. eucharist at the tower crossing on Whitsunday 1999; showing the modern platform, communion table and corona.

20 May. Another remarkable occasion was the ordination service for the first women priests. At the end of the millennium the building is geared to meet the expectations of the ever-increasing number of people who enter its doors day by day. The crypt has been refurbished as a place of quiet. The Cantilupe shrine has been restored and the surrounding area in the north transept cleared to make it a focus for pilgrimage and prayer. Scaffolding has come off the tower, for the first time in thirty years, and the delicate task of restoring the Lady chapel has begun. Everything has been done to enhance Hereford Cathedral's special combination of intimacy and transcendence and to ensure its continuing accessibility for the future.

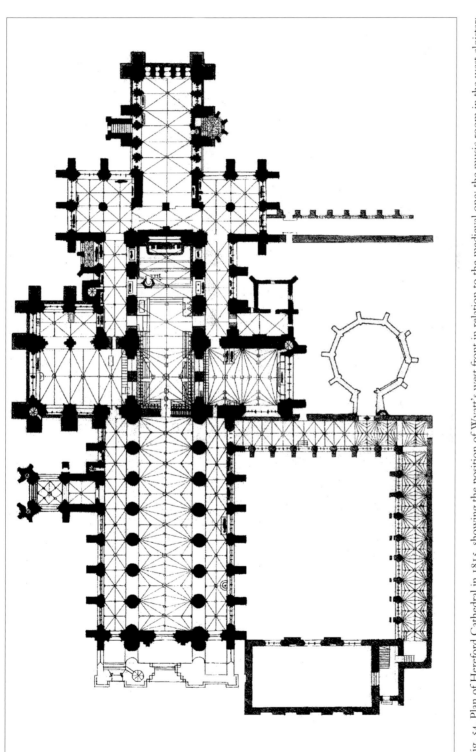

Fig. 54. Plan of Hereford Cathedral in 1815, showing the position of Wyatt's west front in relation to the medieval one; the music room in the west cloister; the medieval pulpitum and choir stalls, and the choir as remodelled in the eighteenth century. Adapted by G. W. Taylor from the plan drawn by T. Garbett and printed in J. and H. S. Storer, *The History and Antiquities of the Cathedral Church of Hereford* (London, [1815]).

PART II

Architecture and Furnishings

The Architectural History
of the Medieval Cathedral Church

R. K. Morris

Hereford Cathedral stands on the north bank of the River Wye, where a cathedral church has been sited since at least the ninth century.[1] It is essentially a twelfth-century Romanesque church to which several high quality set-pieces have been added: notably the glorious north transept, and also the Lady chapel, the Stanbury and Audley chapels, and the Booth porch. The remnants of its Romanesque fabric are of exceptional art historical significance, and both the layout and forms of its Gothic architecture and sculpture bear vivid testimony to the influence of saint cults on the development of a medieval great church.

The cathedral is already well provided with writings on its medieval architectural history. Besides the contributions of nineteenth-century authorities such as Britton, Willis and Scott, in the twentieth century Hereford is one of the very few English cathedrals to have received a description by the Royal Commission on Historical Monuments.[2] In 1951 George Marshall published his monograph on the architectural history, remarkably modern for its relatively early date,[3] and more recently Malcolm Thurlby has made a special study of the Romanesque architecture and sculpture in a series of articles.[4]

1. R. Stone and N. Appleton-Fox, *A View from Hereford's Past* (Hereford, 1996), pp. 4–9; see also above, Chapter 1, pp. 4–5.
2. RCHME, *Herefordshire*, i, pp. 90–120.
3. Marshall, *Hereford Cathedral*; also citing, *inter alia*, the works by Britton, Scott and Willis, p. 14. This chapter will not always agree with Marshall's views, but readers are referred to his book for more information and detailed illustrations than this chapter can provide.

4. M. Thurlby, 'A Note on the Romanesque Sculpture at Hereford Cathedral and the Herefordshire School of Sculpture', *Burlington Magazine*, 126 (1984), pp. 233–34; M. Thurlby, 'The Former Romanesque High Vault in the Presbytery of Hereford Cathedral', *Journal of the Society of Architectural Historians*, 47 (1988), pp. 185–89; and especially M. Thurlby, 'Hereford Cathedral: The Romanesque Fabric', in Whitehead, *Medieval Art at Hereford*, pp. 15–28.

Many visitors and worshippers will be interested to know how the cathedral came to assume its present shape, and therefore the opening pages are concerned with this story, told as far as possible from the evidence of the fabric still visible today. Function, in the form of the liturgy, the cult of saints and other aspects of ecclesiastical usage, was a key factor in fine-tuning the standard cruciform basilican plan which forms the basis of most great churches. In the case of Hereford, very little relevant documentation exists before the late thirteenth century, the period in which most of the main forms of its church were established. Even in the later middle ages, uncertainties remain about the locations of various altars and chantries known through documents. Nonetheless, some progress can be made with the help of contextual knowledge from other cathedrals whose history is better understood, such as Winchester.[5]

The core of the cathedral's plan and structure is made up of the fabric of the new Romanesque cathedral built between about 1107 and 1148.[6] Nothing survives from its predecessors, but it is generally assumed that Bishop Athelstan's pre-Conquest church lay between the present cathedral and the former bishop's chapel to the south.[7] However, as nothing is known for certain about its location, we should keep an open mind and entertain the probability that more than one church or chapel existed in the complex, as at pre-Conquest Worcester and Winchester.[8] Romanesque Hereford is essentially an example of one of the standard plan-types favoured by the Normans: a cruciform church with crossing tower, a nave of eight bays, and a shorter eastern arm terminating in three separate chapels (fig. 55). More significant for our purpose is where the scheme differed from the norm, in three areas: around the south transept, at the west end of the nave and around the high altar.

The Norman south transept is very unusual in having no eastern chapel or extension in which to place an altar (fig. 6). Instead we find the present vestry on the site which was documented in use as a treasury by the fifteenth century and doubtless served the same purpose earlier in the middle ages (fig. 55).[9] Its two

note 4 continued

Whitehead's volume is a valuable collection of essays on other aspects of the cathedral as well. Part of the aim of this chapter is to pick up on ideas and research not represented in the existing literature.

5. J. Crook, ed., *Winchester Cathedral: 900 Years* (Chichester, 1993).

6. There is no definite evidence in the fabric for the earlier start date of *c.* 1080 suggested in some books, eg. Marshall, *Hereford Cathedral*, p. 35, and the latest guidebook, *Hereford Cathedral* (Norwich,

1998), p. 13.

7. R. Shoesmith, *Hereford City Excavations*, ii, *Excavations on and Close to the Defences*, Council for British Archaeology Research Report, 46 (London, 1982), pp. 74–95; also Stone and Appleton-Fox, *View from Hereford's Past*, pp. 4–9.

8. See P. Barker, *A Short Architectural History of Worcester Cathedral* (Worcester, 1994), pp. 10–11; and B. Kjølbye-Biddle, 'Old Minster, St Swithun's Day 1093', in Crook, *Winchester Cathedral*, pp. 13–15.

9. Marshall, *Hereford Cathedral*, pp. 42–43.

Dean John of Aigueblanche
Bishop Peter of Aigueblanche
Bishop James Atlay
Bishop Robert Bennett
Dean George Benson
Bishop Robert de Béthune
Joanna de Bohun
Bishop Charles Booth
Bishop Giles de Braose
Bishop Thomas Cantilupe
Bishop Lewis Charlton
Bishop Thomas Charlton
Bishop George Coke
Bishop Herbert Croft
Dean Richard Dawes

Alexander and Anne Denton
Bishop Robert Foliot
Peter de Grandisson
Bishop Augustine Lindsell
Bishop Robert the Lotharingian
Bishop Richard Mayew
Bishop Robert de Melun
Sir Richard Pembridge
Bishop Reinhelm
Bishop John Stanbury
Precentor John Swinfield
Bishop Richard Swinfield
Bishop John Trefnant
Bishop William de Vere
Bishop Herbert Westfaling

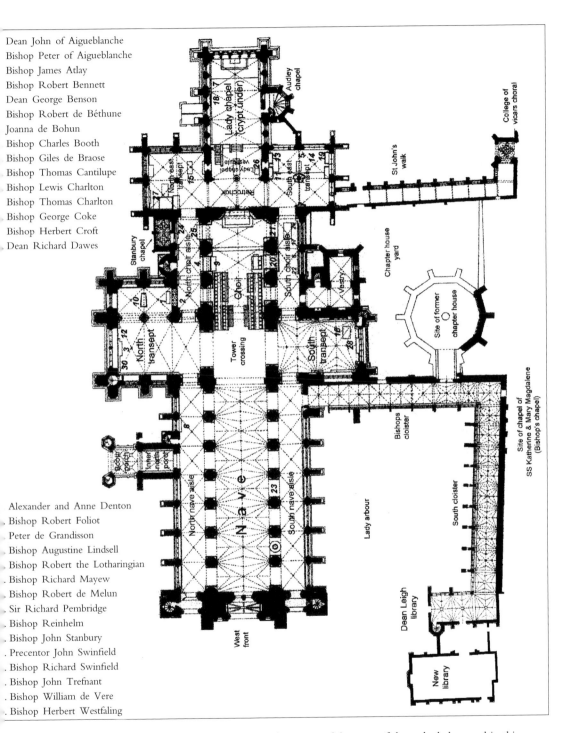

Fig. 55. Plan of Hereford Cathedral, 1999, giving the names of the parts of the cathedral as used in this volume, and the location of the principal tombs and monuments. Adapted from several sources by G. W. Taylor.

original Norman bays are groin-vaulted in stone, very appropriate considering the pillage and burning of the Welsh raid in 1055; and its elaborately carved stringcourse implies a room of some significance.[10] However, a treasury could have been located elsewhere in the Norman cathedral so as not to preclude the provision of an eastern chapel off the south transept. This suggests that the 'treasury' might incorporate an earlier site of some religious significance, perhaps pre-Conquest; loosely analogous to the early chapel off the south choir aisle at Lichfield Cathedral, used as a sacristy and treasury in modern times.[11] If so, we have found another piece in the puzzle of the religious topography of Anglo-Saxon Hereford.

Secondly, we can be virtually certain from scrutiny of old views of the cathedral that the single axial tower which stood at the west end of the nave until 1786 was an original Romanesque feature, and not a fourteenth-century addition; it was only heightened in the latter period (figs 33, 37).[12] This is a rare feature for the west front of a Norman great church, more usually found in conjunction with a west transept as at Ely and Bury St Edmunds, and examples are also known to have existed in the late Saxon period.[13] However, axial west towers are more frequently encountered on the near Continent in France, the Low Countries and the lower Rhineland:[14] an area with strong religious and architectural ties to Anglo-Saxon England at the time of the monastic reforms of the tenth century.[15] Thus there is at least a suspicion that the employment of an axial tower at Hereford may be explained by lingering traditions of architectural forms known

10. Stringcourse illustrated in Marshall, *Hereford Cathedral*, pl. 3; though of the twelfth century, rather than Anglo-Saxon as implied, p. 45.
11. See W. Rodwell, 'Archaeology and the Standing Fabric: Recent Studies at Lichfield Cathedral', *Antiquity*, 63 (1989), pp. 285–88. The earliest known building on the site is late twelfth-century (idem, 'A Note on Archaeological Recording Carried out in the Consistory Court, Lichfield Cathedral, in August 1992', unpublished report to the Dean and Chapter of Lichfield, p. 1), thus predating the Gothic rebuilding of the present cathedral. The chapel became the locus for the late medieval cult of St Chad's head: by analogy, it is conceivable that the Hereford treasury site had some connection with the cult of St Ethelbert.
12. Thurlby, 'Hereford Cathedral: Romanesque Fabric', p. 22.

13. J. P. McAleer, 'The West Front of the Abbey Church', in A. Gransden, ed., *Bury St Edmunds: Medieval Art, Architecture, Archaeology and Economy*, British Archaeological Association Conference Transactions, 20 (Leeds, 1998), pp. 28–29.
14. For example, Lobbes and Soignies in Belgium, St-Riquier in northern France, and the key Lotharingian monument of St Maximin at Trier. See X. Barrel y Altet, *Belgique romane* (La Pierre-qui-Vire, 1989); W. Sanderson, 'Monastic Reform in Lorraine and the Architecture of the Outer Crypt, 950–1100', *Transactions of the American Philosophical Society*, new series, 61, part 6 (1971), pp. 32–34; E. C. Fernie, *The Architecture of the Anglo Saxons* (London, 1983); pp. 82–83.
15. See further A. Klukas, 'Liturgy and Architecture: Deerhurst Priory as an Expression of the *Regularis Concordia*', *Viator*, 15 (1984), pp. 81–98.

to the Lotharingian bishops of Hereford in the later eleventh century, Walter and Robert.[16]

This supposition is strengthened by the former existence of smaller towers over the east bay of each of the choir aisles of the Romanesque cathedral, flanking the sanctuary.[17] One of their purposes may have been symbolic, to give external emphasis to the most sacred area of the church, and perhaps to provide an ecclesiastical counterpoint to the Norman castle directly to the east: an image of a heavenly city. Double eastern towers are no longer thought to be so unusual in Norman England, in that modern scholarship has argued for their former existence at Winchester, Durham and Canterbury Cathedrals, for example, and, closer to hand, at St John's, Chester.[18] Their usage also has a wide distribution on the Continent, and north of the Alps is concentrated in Lotharingia from the mid tenth century, perhaps taking its lead from the key monastic reform church of St Maximin at Trier.[19] The incorporation of tribune chapels into some of these towers is a common link between English and continental examples,[20] and it could be the Lotharingian precedent which helps to explain why this particular form of east end found favour at Hereford. There is a clue in a later document that the first-floor chamber of one of the Hereford towers might have contained an altar. A popular dedication was to the archangel Michael, most commonly for a west tower, as noted for a number of churches in Lotharingia,[21] but perhaps found in the south-east tower at Hereford. For St Michael is one of two dedications recorded in the south-east transept in 1364,[22] and the most likely explanation is that space was made for it at ground floor level in the early thirteenth century, when the

16. See above, Chapter 2, p. 23. Reinhelm, in whose episcopate the present Romanesque cathedral was begun, may well have been a Lotharingian too, but firm evidence is lacking (personal communication from Dr J. Barrow).

17. For the evidence for these, see RCHME, *Herefordshire*, i , pp. 92–93.

18. For an overview of English and continental examples, see Thurlby, 'Hereford Cathedral: Romanesque Fabric', p. 19; and M. G. Jarrett and H. Mason, '"Greater and More Splendid": Some Aspects of Romanesque Durham Cathedral', *Antiquaries Journal*, 75 (1995), pp. 212–21, fig. 4. For St John's, Chester, see R. D. H. Gem, 'Romanesque Architecture in Chester, *c.* 1075–1117', in A. Thacker, ed., *Chester: Medieval Archaeology, Art and Architecture*, British Archaeological Association Conference Transactions, 22 (Leeds, 2000).

19. C. B. McClendon, *The Imperial Abbey of Farfa: Architectural Currents in the Early Middle Ages* (New Haven, 1987), pp. 88–89.

20. See Klukas, 'Liturgy and Architecture', pp. 85–94, 'Chapels at Upper Levels'; idem, 'The Continuity of Anglo-Saxon Liturgical Tradition in Post-Conquest England', in J. Pouilloux, ed., *Les mutations socio-culturelles au tournant des XIe-XIIe siecles* (Paris, 1984), pp. 111–24.

21. See Sanderson, 'Monastic Reform', pp. 33–34.

22. Capes, *Charters*, pp. 231–32.

east transept was first built and the tower was reduced in height or demolished. It has been suggested that the north-east tower may have housed a bell.[23]

The first major change to the Romanesque cathedral was the extension and remodelling of the eastern arm. The evidence from the architectural fabric clearly indicates that the work was executed in two main phases, the first producing the new eastern transepts, including the bays now called the 'retrochoir' and 'Lady chapel vestibule' (figs 55, 15); and reasonably attributed to the episcopate of Bishop William de Vere (1186–98).[24] Then apparently a break occurred until about 1220 when the crypt and the Lady chapel above were built, with the last stages of this work carrying on into a remodelling of the upper parts of the chancel in the 1230s, providing it with a new Gothic vault and clerestory. However, we do not know whether the eastern extension was designed as one scheme, nor indeed what existed on its site before work commenced. It seems likely that the new retrochoir was always intended to lead into a projecting eastern chapel, and we should not discount the possibility that an earlier chapel of some significance was standing there. If it was detached, then de Vere's work could have been devised to link it to the main church, before it was subsequently decided to rebuild it on a grander scale. But it might have been physically part of the church already, for the length and liturgical arrangement of the central chapel of the Romanesque cathedral is unknown.[25] Scott was probably correct in thinking that the chapel extended at least one bay east of the present sanctuary arch (fig. 56),[26] but in fact its eastern limits are unrecorded and it could have continued considerably further like that at Romanesque Winchester.[27]

The purpose of the above speculation is not just to open new windows of enquiry for their own sake, but to introduce the problems of explaining the functions of the new Lady chapel and its crypt. Marshall presented the scheme as providing an improved physical setting for the cult of St Ethelbert, being promoted in the late twelfth century by *The Life* written by Gerald of Wales and by the quest for new relics of the saint.[28] We need look no further than the competition

23. Jarrett and Mason, 'Romanesque Durham Cathedral', p. 219; the function as bell towers is also noted by McClendon, *Abbey of Farfa*, pp. 86–89.

24. Leland noted the inscription '. . . multa edificia egregia construxit . . .' on de Vere's tomb; Bannister, *The Cathedral Church of Hereford*, p. 41.

25. The altar arrangement in Marshall, *Hereford Cathedral*, p. 28, is entirely speculative: a high altar dedicated jointly to St Mary and St Ethelbert is another

possibility.

26. G. G. Scott, 'Hereford Cathedral', *Archaeological Journal*, 34 (1877), pp. 326–27; see also G. M. Hills, 'The Architectural History of Hereford Cathedral', *Journal of the British Archaeological Association*, 27 (1871), p. 503, for evidence of the foundations of the side walls.

27. See J. Crook, 'Bishop Walkelin's Cathedral', in Crook, *Winchester Cathedral*, pp. 23–25.

28. Marshall, *Hereford Cathedral*, pp. 52–53.

Fig. 56. Gilbert Scott's reconstruction of the Romanesque choir. *The Building News* (August 1878). (HCL, B.4.153, neg. 137.)

from neighbouring ecclesiastical rivals, particularly Worcester, to understand the significance of attempting to revive this royal saint's cult at this time. The east end of the cathedral priory church at Worcester was being vastly enlarged in the first half of the thirteenth century following the canonisation of St Wulfstan (1202) and the burial there of King John (1216). Marshall suggested that the crypt was intended as a place where pilgrims could venerate relics of St Ethelbert.[29] However, recent research relating to the cult of St Swithun at Winchester Cathedral should warn us against assuming that the provision of new space for a relic was the rationale for many of the eastern extensions to great churches in the early Gothic period. The east arm at Winchester (*c.* 1200–35) is an important early example of the fashion for decorating architecture with foiled figures (or medallions), providing an association with precious metalwork and contemporary shrines; and this idea is

29. Ibid., p. 64.

taken up in the Lady chapel at Hereford (fig. 24). Nonetheless, Crook has demonstrated that the shrine of St Swithun at Winchester was not moved into the new retrochoir in the thirteenth century, but remained firmly behind the high altar until 1476.[30] Likewise at Worcester, the shrines of Saints Oswald and Wulfstan were set up by the high altar; and the pre-existing Romanesque crypt was apparently liturgically down-graded, judging by its physical mutilation to enable the new work.[31] At Hereford therefore, any relic or shrine of St Ethelbert may well have remained adjacent to the high altar, where the *locus* of the cult was definitely centred in the late middle ages; and we should explore other possible explanations for the commissioning of the eastern extension.

Hereford has the last crypt new-built in any English cathedral, a frequently quoted but rather misleading statistic (fig. 57). In fact old St Paul's Cathedral, destroyed in the great fire of London, had an enormous new Gothic crypt added to its smaller Norman one between about 1258 and 1265, the western half of which housed the parish of St Faith, whose church had been demolished to make way for the eastward extension of the cathedral.[32] Herein lies the germ of a possible hypothesis for Hereford's crypt: that it provided space for worship for the cathedral parish of St John the Baptist. By the late fourteenth century, the 'church' of St John the Baptist was established in the cathedral nave, because complaints arose in 1394 and later of interference with the services of the dean and canons (fig. 25, no. 17).[33] However, this need not preclude a different location for the parish altar in the thirteenth century, and siting it in the new crypt would provide an alternative explanation for the provision of the external access by way of the north door like old St Paul's, if the idea of a relic cult in the crypt is rejected (fig. 54).[34]

Of course, the most obvious justification for the eastern extension is as a response to the fashionable devotion to the Virgin and its physical manifestation in a new Lady chapel.[35] There appears to be no early record of the dedication the chapel

30. J. Crook, 'St Swithun of Winchester', in Crook, *Winchester Cathedral*, p. 61. For an overview of the context, see N. Coldstream, 'Cui Bono? The Saint, the Clergy and the New Work at St Albans', in P. Crossley and E. Fernie, eds, *Medieval Architecture and its Intellectual Context* (London, 1990), chapter 14.

31. Barker, *Worcester Cathedral*, pp. 30–31, though the disfigurement of the Worcester crypt was forced by structural problems.

32. G. H. Cook, *Old St Paul's Cathedral* (London, 1955), pp. 36–37; fig. V shows a north external stair in the west bay.

33. Marshall, *Hereford Cathedral*, pp. 173–74.

34. Duncumb noted in 1804 a tradition that the crypt had been the parochial church of St John the Baptist, but assumed instead that the crypt had been designed as a charnel house; cited in R. Shoesmith, 'The Crypt under the Lady Chapel' (unpublished interim report to the dean and chapter, February 1998), p. 7.

35. For the general context regarding 'Lady' chapels, see P. Draper, ' "Seeing that it was Done in All the Noble Churches in England" ', in Crossley and Fernie, *Medieval Architecture*, chapter 13.

Fig. 57. Crypt interior, looking south west.

to the Virgin, so it must be treated as an assumption, albeit a reasonable one.[36] A later document implies the crypt had a chapel of St Anne, the mother of the Virgin.[37] However, a crypt was not a necessary attribute for a Lady chapel, and this brings us back to considering whether the unusual two-storey arrangement of the Gothic extension was not predetermined by an earlier building which stood somewhere on its site; perhaps some sort of outer crypt of the kind found in the tenth and eleventh centuries in the area of Lotharingian reform on the Continent.[38] A number of these so-called 'crypts' were of two stories, and typically incorporated altars to the Virgin and the Trinity, especially to the latter in the eleventh-century examples.[39] With regard to Hereford, there is record of an altar of the Trinity in the thirteenth century, which Marshall proposed to site in the Gothic crypt, albeit

36. An early reference to the chapel's dedication to the Virgin is contained in the account of Cantilupe's first miracle of 1287: see R. C. Finucane, 'Cantilupe as Thaumaturge: Pilgrims and their "Miracles"', in M. Jancey, ed., *St Thomas Cantilupe, Bishop of Hereford: Essays in his Honour* (Hereford, 1982), p. 137.

37. A mortmain licence of 1381 refers to the

chapel of St Anne *below* the shrine of St Thomas of Hereford, which by then stood in the Lady chapel: *Calendar of the Patent Rolls, Richard II* (6 vols, London, 1895–1909), ii, p. 50. I owe this reference to David Lepine.

38. For a list of examples, see Sanderson, 'Monastic Reform', pp. 5–16.

39. Ibid., pp. 14–15, 34.

on rather circumstantial evidence.[40] Thus, some grounds exist for speculating that a chapel with altars to the Virgin and the Trinity existed at the east end of the Norman cathedral, perhaps physically connected to the main church and perhaps already incorporating a crypt; and that it would most likely be the work of one of the Lotharingian bishops, Walter or Robert, or built under the influence of continental ideas they brought to Hereford.[41] This formed the direct model for the new Gothic Lady chapel with crypt. Outer crypts were associated with burial and salvation, so the likelihood of a cemetery east of the cathedral church, and a longstanding tradition of calling the Hereford crypt 'Golgotha',[42] provide helpful context for this hypothesis. The tradition is usually connected with the later medieval and post-medieval uses of the crypt as a charnel house, but this function could develop naturally out of the earlier medieval associations with an outer crypt.

It is evident on stylistic grounds that the rebuilding of the chancel clerestory must have followed very closely on the completion of the Lady chapel, if not actually overlapping with it. What is particularly impressive is how the ornate carved motifs of the Lady chapel – medallions, arcading and deeply carved window arch mouldings – are continued on the exterior and interior wall surfaces of the clerestory (fig. 76). Most authorities agree that the Romanesque chancel was vaulted (fig. 56), so Marshall's proposal can be discounted that the work was undertaken primarily to provide the chancel with its first stone vault.[43] The most practical explanation for the work is probably that the first vault had become unsound, given the amount of subsidence and distortion noted by Willis in the east arch of the Romanesque crossing.[44] It is unlikely that even the special regional technique of Romanesque vaulting, in which much of the vault webbing was independent of the walls,[45] could withstand this amount of settlement without cracking. Nevertheless, the opportunity was taken in the new chancel work to provide conformity with the Gothic aesthetic of the new eastern extension, including the piercing of lateral windows for the first time in the east clerestory bay of the chancel by removing the north-east and south-east towers over the choir aisles.

To summarise the development of the eastern arm up to *c.* 1240, the setting of the revived cult of St Ethelbert was enhanced by the increased space and rich

40. Marshall, *Hereford Cathedral*, p. 63. The record that it was a 'new made' altar need not preclude the possibility that it was the revamping of an old altar.

41. Most clearly exemplified in Bishop Robert's episcopal chapel. See R. Gem, 'The Bishop's Chapel at Hereford: The Roles of Patron and Craftsman', in S. Macready and F. H. Thompson, eds, *Art and Patronage in the English Romanesque*

(London, 1986), pp. 87–96; see also below, Chapter 11, pp. 294–96.

42. See further Shoesmith, 'The Crypt', p. 7.

43. Marshall, *Hereford Cathedral*, p. 67. For the vault, see Thurlby, 'Romanesque Vault', pp. 185–89.

44. R. Willis, *Report of a Survey of the Dilapidated Portions of Hereford Cathedral in the Year 1841* (Hereford, 1842), p. 17.

45. Thurlby, 'Romanesque Vault', pp. 185–87.

architectural ornamentation of the Gothic works. The new retrochoir provided an impressive processional path behind the high altar, which was now complemented by additional altars at main floor level in the eastern transepts. The plan is comparable to better known contemporary schemes like Salisbury (begun 1220) and Worcester (begun 1224), but significantly is earlier than either; and the general inspiration for them all was doubtless the rebuilding of the east arm of Canterbury Cathedral (1175–84) after the martyrdom of Thomas Becket. At Hereford it is proposed that any relics of St Ethelbert remained in the vicinity of the high altar, which may explain the opening up of clerestory windows in the sanctuary bay and the smart Gothic remodelling of the upper parts of the chancel (fig. 58). Thus the provision of a new site for the cult is unlikely to be the explanation for the new Lady chapel and crypt, and we should not discount the possibility that they may represent the enlargement and rebuilding of some sort of outer crypt chapel which formerly stood at the east end of the Romanesque cathedral. However, a specific reason for the crypt is probably to provide a church for the parish of St John, in which case it is speculated that the three eastern altars were dedicated to St John the Baptist, the Trinity and St Anne. The Lady chapel above was probably commissioned as such from the start.

The next significant work was the rebuilding of the north transept during the eventful episcopate of the wealthy French bishop, Peter of Aigueblanche. Transepts

Fig. 58. Choir interior, looking north east.

in English great churches are frequently forgettable, a mishmash of odds and ends, but the north transept at Hereford is an outstanding design, dominantly of one period: the finest architectural set-piece in the present cathedral (fig. 59). The lack of any obvious vestiges of Romanesque fabric led Marshall to the erroneous assumption that the north arm of the Norman cathedral was never finished.[46] Rather we see at Hereford the product of wealthy ecclesiastical patronage typical of the age, like that of Bishop Northwold at Ely (responsible for the new east arm of his cathedral church, 1234–52) or of Archbishop de Gray at York (1216–55). The latter is an especially appropriate role model, promoting the building of the Gothic south transept at York on the site of a smaller Romanesque predecessor, and being commemorated by a fine canopied tomb in the new work, like Aigueblanche a decade later (fig. 11).[47]

The main clue in the fabric at Hereford that a Romanesque north transept once existed is that the present north arm is longer north to south than the Romanesque south transept, by approximately the thickness of a medieval wall. We may surmise that the north wall of Aigueblanche's new work was erected outside the Norman transept, and that the east wall of the new aisle also lay east of it. Thus his work could proceed to the equivalent height of the aisle wall on the north and east sides before the main parts of the old transept needed to be demolished. The latter was most likely of the standard Norman plan, with a single eastern apsidal chapel, as may still be seen in the south transept at Tewkesbury Abbey (*c.* 1100). Consequently the north and south arms of the Hereford transept differed in plan, and probably in their eastern elevations too, because of the existence of the 'treasury' adjoining the south transept (fig. 6).

The style of the new transept is the closest copy in England of King Henry III's French-inspired rebuilding of Westminster Abbey, begun in 1245. The close relationship between the two works hints strongly at the pivotal role of Bishop Aigueblanche, and it seems likely that the structure was essentially complete by his death in 1268. The Sugwas version of Aigueblanche's will in November 1268 records no major contributions to the cathedral or mention of the fabric.[48] The main stylistic connections lie with the eastern parts of Westminster (1245–59), and the 'triplet' window traceries (fig. 59) relate to building projects begun in the mid

46. Marshall, *Hereford Cathedral*, pp. 44, 71.
47. For de Gray's involvement with the transept, see H. G. Ramm and others, 'The Tombs of Archbishops Walter de Gray (1216–55) and Godfrey de Ludham (1258–65) in York Minster, and their Contents', *Archaeologia*, 103 (1971), pp. 104–5; also E. A. Gee, 'Architectural History until 1290', in G. Aylmer and R. Cant, eds, *A History of*

York Minster (Oxford, 1977), pp. 111–48. For the international context for Aigueblanche's patronage, see J. Gardner, 'The Tomb of Bishop Peter of Aquablanca in Hereford Cathedral', in Whitehead, *Medieval Art at Hereford*, pp. 105–10.
48. C. E. Woodruff, 'The Will of Peter of Aigueblanche, Bishop of Hereford', *Camden Miscellany*, 14 (1926), pp. x, 2.

Fig. 59. North transept interior, looking north east.

1250s and 1260s, like the new east arm of old St Paul's Cathedral, London.[49] Stylistic comparisons also suggest that masons formerly engaged on the Hereford transept moved on to build the new church at Tintern Abbey, started in 1269. Valuable evidence is provided by a recently discovered indulgence in Worcester Cathedral records, dated 1 March 1257, for those making donations to 'sumptuous works' replacing old fabric at Hereford Cathedral.[50] This can only relate to the transept works and, taken together with the presence of Bishop Aigueblanche in England for a few months in 1255–56 and his generally good relations with the chapter at this time,[51] indicates fairly conclusively that building had begun in earnest.

The new north transept would have appeared stunningly modern and French

49. See R. K. Morris, 'The "New Work" at Old St Paul's Cathedral and its Place in English Thirteenth-Century Architecture', in L. Grant, ed., *Medieval Art, Archaeology and Architecture in London*, British Archaeological Association Conference Transactions, 10 (Leeds, 1990), pp. 87–88.

50. P. M. Hoskin, ed., *English Episcopal Acta, xiii, Worcester, 1216–1268* (Oxford 1997), p. 89, no. 111. I am grateful to Alexandrina Buchanan for drawing my attention to this reference.

51. Bannister, *The Cathedral Church of Hereford*, pp. 52–53.

to a contemporary audience, in contrast even to the recent Early English Gothic works at the cathedral (figs 24, 59). It is tempting to see the new transept as a personal statement by Bishop Aigueblanche, symbolising the dominance at Hereford of the new bishop and his Burgundian clergy. However, we should beware of reading more into the style than an appreciation of northern French architectural fashion which was to sweep England in the second half of the thirteenth century, especially in the form of large bar tracery windows. Moreover the funding was not solely – nor, perhaps, mainly – from Aigueblanche's generosity, if we may judge from the document of 1246 enforcing payments by canons towards the expenses of the fabric.[52] Indeed, this document may indicate that advance planning for the new transept goes back to the 1240s at least.

The question remains as to why just one transept arm was rebuilt. The eastern arm of the cathedral was newly extended and remodelled, so we can understand why his attentions would focus on another part of the church. There is no evidence that the work was part of a more general remodelling of the Norman cathedral, as at York or Lichfield, where both transept arms were rebuilt more or less simultaneously in this period. It is likely that the Romanesque north transept had suffered some degree of structural failure, but Willis's analysis of the crossing arches suggests that subsidence was a problem on the south side as well.[53] Yet the south transept waited for another century, until a piecemeal updating by bishops Trefnant (1389–1404) and Spofford (1421–1448), restricted to new windows and a vault (fig. 60).[54] So the answer may lie in Bishop Aigueblanche's perception of the scheme. From his viewpoint, the transept would provide a smart new setting for his burial, like his collegiate foundation of 1258 at Aiguebelle in Savoy, and it would appear that he was making architectural provision for his death whether it occurred in this country or away on service in southern Europe. Up to about 1257, he was concentrating on the Hereford site, but thereafter he also developed the continental option. It would be the east aisle of the transept which would interest the bishop most specifically, as providing the chapels adjoining his monument (like Archbishop de Gray at York), and it is a pity that the dedications of their altars are not recorded.

Two snippets of information point to the possibility that, beyond his own burial, Aigueblanche had in mind a more general association of the new work with the authority and sanctity of episcopal office. First, it is generally taken to be on his initiative that the *Consuetudines* of Hereford Cathedral were drawn up *c.* 1246–64.[55]

---

52. Marshall, *Hereford Cathedral*, p. 72; Capes, *Charters*, p. 80.
53. Willis, *Survey of Hereford Cathedral*, pp. 11–18.
54. Marshall, *Hereford Cathedral*, pp. 128–29.
55. Bannister, *The Cathedral Church of Hereford*, pp. 47–48, 55–58. See also above, Chapter 2, pp. 43–47, and below, Appendix 1.

Fig. 60. South transept interior, looking south.

Secondly, it is interesting to note that at Aiguebelle he tried to obtain permission to transfer the remains of an archbishop, Herluin of Tarentaise 'of blessed memory', to add status to his new foundation.[56] We may surmise that he had something similar in mind for the north transept, perhaps with the establishment of the cult of a suitable predecessor such as Bishop Robert de Béthune (1131–48). One valid reason for copying the architecture of Westminster Abbey would be as a setting for a saint's cult, as happened with the cult of St Hugh of Lincoln in the Westminster-inspired Angel Choir at Lincoln Minster (1256–80).[57] The diaper pattern carved above the gallery arcades of the Hereford transept is a motif derived ultimately from precious metalwork such as shrines, by way of Westminster.[58] Clear indications of a revival of interest in Bishop de Béthune do not appear until the early fourteenth century, with a collecting box and assertions that some

56. Gardner, 'Tomb of Aquablanca', pp. 106–7.
57. See, for example, V. Glenn, 'The Sculpture of the Angel Choir at Lincoln', in T. A. Heslop and V. A. Sekules, eds, *Medieval Art and Architecture at Lincoln Cathedral*, British Archaeological Association Conference Transactions, 8 (Leeds, 1986), pp. 102–8.
58. See, for example, C. Wilson and others, *Westminster Abbey*, New Bell's Cathedral Guides (London, 1986), pp. 53–56.

of the Cantilupe miracles parallel events in de Béthune's life.[59] Possibly the idea stems back to the mid thirteenth century, but came to nothing then. Certainly the north transept is a very appropriate architectural setting for a saint's cult, and within twenty years of Aigueblanche's death, it was to receive the saintly remains of a bishop.

The translation of the bones of Bishop Thomas Cantilupe (d. 1282) to the north transept in Holy Week 1287, and the resulting pilgrimage, provided the chapter with an enormous if short-lived boost to the fabric fund.[60] The monies were mainly put towards an ambitious architectural updating of the cathedral church, with the aims of producing a modern setting for the pilgrim route, promoting the status of the bishopric, and creating an eye-catching skyline of towers to help proclaim these functions.[61] The effect of the excitement generated by the cult and the new works can also still be appreciated in the rebuilding of parts of numerous local churches at this time, combined with the promotion of religious attractions in the diocese, such as the statue of the Virgin at Madley and the relic of the True Cross at Abbey Dore.[62]

The main effect on the cathedral was the insertion of Gothic rib vaults and large new windows throughout the aisles of nave and choir between about 1290 and 1310, replacing the dark mural spaces of the Norman church (fig. 74). Some appreciation of the new translucence may be gleaned from the fragments of original canopies and grisaille glass in the two surviving early fourteenth-century windows in the south choir aisle and north-east transept.[63] Evidence for the dating of the aisles comes primarily from the fabric roll of 1290–91 which mentions 'eight windows', and the papal commissioners' report of 1307 noting two new 'naves', i.e. aisles.[64] The style of tracery is the same in all the windows, but differences in their mouldings suggest that the nave north aisle was done first, followed by the

59. See HCA, 2412, 2413, 1437 (David Lepine, personal communication). For the shared miracle, see R. C. Finucane, 'The Cantilupe-Pecham Controversy', in Jancey, ed., *St Thomas Cantilupe*, p. 122.

60. W. N. Yates, 'The Fabric Rolls of Hereford Cathedral', *National Library of Wales Journal*, 18 (1973), pp. 79–86. For details of the cult and relics, see the essays in Jancey, ed., *St Thomas Cantilupe*; for the 'shrine' in the north transept, see below, Chapter 14, pp. 328–30.

61. See further P. E. Morgan, 'The Effect of the Pilgrim Cult of St Thomas Cantilupe on Hereford Cathedral', in Jancey, ed., *St Thomas Cantilupe*, pp. 145–53.

62. S. Brown, 'The Fourteenth-Century Stained Glass of Madley', in Whitehead, *Medieval Art at Hereford*, pp. 122–30; J. Hillaby, 'Cults, Patrons and Sepulture', in R. Shoesmith and R. Richardson, eds, *A Definitive History of Dore Abbey* (Almeley, 1997), chapter 9. The chapter of Hereford was the patron of the living at Madley.

63. See further F. C. Morgan, *Hereford Cathedral Church Glass* (3rd edn, Hereford, 1979), pp. 11, 15; the glass in these two windows was found in boxes and placed there in 1864.

64. The 1290–91 roll is in Capes, *Charters*, pp. 163–65; the 1307 report is cited in P. E. Morgan, 'Pilgrim Cult', p. 149.

choir aisles together with the north-east transept.[65] The nave aisle was given priority as the public route between the north porch and Cantilupe's monument in the north transept (fig. 55). The function and precise dating of the nave south aisle is less obvious, but it helps complete the updating of the nave. The presence in its wall of a Decorated tomb recess, which has close similarities to the mouldings of the book room door in the cloister at Tintern Abbey, tends to confirm a date no later than *c.* 1300.[66]

The choir aisles are a second phase, designed to symbolise the longevity and status of episcopal office through a display of posthumous effigies of ten bishops of Hereford from 1079 to 1219 (fig. 23): the physical fulfilment of a scheme which perhaps had been in the air since Bishop Aigueblanche's time.[67] The series of effigies culminates in the tombs of Bishop Richard Swinfield (1282–1317), in whose episcopate all these works were executed, and two of his nephews in the north-east transept and Lady chapel vestibule.[68] Their recesses, like those of some of the posthumous effigies (fig. 5), are carved with ballflower ornament, implying a date early in the fourteenth century and contemporary with the new towers. Another justification for remodelling the choir aisles is suggested by the fact that Bishop Swinfield, the promoter of Cantilupe's cult, chose to be buried away from his former master's tomb in the north transept. Presumably he and his nephews were anticipating early in the fourteenth century the canonisation of Cantilupe and the translation of his relics to the Lady chapel, even though ultimately both events took place after Swinfield's death.

Two other interesting architectural features are to be associated with the Cantilupe cult. First, what is now the inner north porch was the point of entry for pilgrims to his tomb, and their symbolic association is suggested by the way in which the cinquefoil design of the tomb-chest arcading is repeated on a monumental scale in the porch doorway (figs 96, 61). There has been considerable discussion over the date of the porch, but it fits best as contemporary with the Cantilupe tomb in the 1280s.[69] The complex carvings jammed into the three orders of the outer arch of the porch surely refer to Cantilupe and his cult, through the figure of a pilgrim and several busts of a mitred figure (fig. 62); though perhaps set within a

65. R. K. Morris, 'The Remodelling of the Hereford Aisles', *British Archaeological Association Journal*, 38 (1974), pp. 22–25.

66. The recess, in the second bay from the east, thus predates the effigy in it, usually identified as Dean Ledbury (1320–52). The Tintern door is illustrated in D. M. Robinson, *Tintern Abbey*, Cadw Official Guide (3rd edn, Cardiff, 1995), p. 54, where it is probably dated slightly too late.

67. See further P. G. Lindley, 'Retrospective Effigies, the Past and Lies', in Whitehead, *Medieval Art at Hereford*, pp. 111–21.

68. For the identifications, see Marshall, *Hereford Cathedral*, pp. 92–93.

69. Morris, 'Hereford Aisles', pp. 22–23; Marshall, *Hereford Cathedral*, p. 87, dates the comparative work in the piscina at Grosmont too early.

Fig. 61. Inner north porch doorway.

wider frame of references to the cathedral's older saints, St Ethelbert (the figure of a king) and the Virgin Mary (a Tree of Jesse).[70]

The second feature is the prominent spiral staircase in the north choir aisle, which provides the only access to the eastern gallery of the north transept and the choir north gallery. It may have been built only with access to the latter in mind, because the link passage through to the transept gallery appears to be an afterthought. In Bishop Aigueblanche's time, the intention seems to have been to approach the gallery from the spiral staircase in the north-west corner of the north transept, across a bridge in the north wall; hence the elevated passage openings still to be seen in this area (fig. 59). This scheme seems to have been abandoned during construction of the transept, when the form of the north window tracery was finalised, leaving the transept gallery as a functionless space in terms of religious usage, as it is at Westminster Abbey too. We may surmise that the circumstance which gave it new purpose, and caused the new access to be created, was the enormous quantity of offerings made at the shrine and shown to the papal commissioners in 1307: 107 model ships, 100 silver images of persons, and so on.[71] Thus the transept gallery became a storage area and treasury, probably in conjunction with the choir north gallery. This could explain why the latter was retained in the remodelling, whereas on the south side of the choir the floor of the Romanesque gallery was removed to permit taller aisle windows.

The other major architectural investments made at the height of the Cantilupe cult were the two new towers at the crossing and at the west end, replacing Romanesque towers which had either been built or were planned in these positions. To the outside world they proclaimed the greatness of the shrine and the church

---

70. See Marshall, *Hereford Cathedral*, p. 88, for a catalogue of the carvings; his observations that the carvings are in good condition and deserve a close study remain equally valid

today. The altar to the Virgin Mary in the porch upper room was a fourteenth-century development, see further below.

71. Cited in Yates, 'Fabric Rolls', p. 80.

Fig. 62. Inner north porch, arch sculpture detail.

which housed it, and to the approaching pilgrim their ornate forms must have appeared like the towers of some celestial city (fig. 33). Both were decorated with thousands of ballflowers, a new ornament which resembles a stylised rosebud or a bell on animal collars, which dematerialises the solidity of the fabric and is thus highly appropriate for the architectural setting for a new saint. The Hereford towers are amongst the earliest examples of the use of ballflower in England, as we know from the papal commission that by 1307 the 'great tower' was partly constructed.[72] This must have been the crossing tower, for Hugh le Barber's evidence to the same commission calls it the great 'bell-tower'.[73] As it is likely that its predecessor had to be taken down for structural reasons, the provision of a new working bell-tower was of crucial importance for the liturgical functioning of the cathedral and the audible impression made on visitors at feast days and festivities.[74] Work continued after 1307 to complete the crossing tower, and then to undertake the west tower, which looks to have been the later of the two because of its more clearly articulated exterior form (fig. 37).

Unfortunately, architectural ambition was allowed to override a past record of poor foundations and movement of the fabric. In 1319 the chapter had to appeal

72. Capes, *Charters*, p. lv; P. E. Morgan, 'Pilgrim Cult', p. 149.

73. M. Jancey, 'A Servant Speaks of his Master: Hugh le Barber's Evidence in 1307', in Jancey, ed., *St Thomas Cantilupe*, p. 201.

74. For consideration of an earlier tower and its demolition, see Marshall, *Hereford Cathedral*, pp. 48–49.

to Pope John XXII for financial assistance, claiming that they had spent large sums of money on 'superstructures' of sumptuous workmanship, which now threatened ruin.[75] This could refer to either of the towers, both of which gave considerable trouble subsequently. Ultimately the west one collapsed in 1786, though brought about in part by later medieval insertions (the west window) and eighteenth-century removals (the west cloister).[76] However, the crossing tower was the more likely subject of concern in 1319.

The claim in the petition that the fabric would have to be rebuilt from the foundations was presumably calculated rhetoric to remind the papal curia that Cantilupe's canonisation process had still not been completed.[77] For there can be little doubt that the present crossing tower is the one erected before 1319, and not a rebuild after *c.* 1320 as argued by Hills and Scott (fig. 63).[78] The main reinforcement work following the success of the petition was directed at the arcades adjoining the north-west crossing pier, and did not extend to the tower itself (fig. 64).[79]

Cantilupe was finally canonised in 1320, and preparations were put in hand for the translation of his relics to the Lady chapel, especially the commissioning of a new metalwork shrine. However, for various reasons which reflect on the waning popularity of the cult, the event was postponed in 1321.[80] It was not until 1349, following the first visitation of the Black Death, that Bishop Trillek had the saint's relics moved to the Lady chapel; though it should be noted that by the fifteenth century his skull was apparently back in the north transept, venerated in a head shrine.[81] Material evidence for the various intentions and postponements can be plotted in the location of various medieval tombs in the cathedral. As we have seen, Bishop Swinfield (d. 1317) was buried in the north-east transept in anticipation of the move, whereas Bishop Thomas Charlton (d. 1344), the next bishop interred at Hereford, chose the north transept because the relics had remained there (fig. 55, no. 12).

75. P. E. Morgan, 'Pilgrim Cult', p. 149; Capes, *Charters*, pp. 184–86, for the papal bull of 1320 in response.

76. See further below, Chapter 9, pp. 258–62, and D. Whitehead, 'A Goth among Greeks: The Architecture of Hereford Cathedral in the Eighteenth Century', *FHC*, 57 (1991), pp. 33–38.

77. See further P. H. Daley, 'The Process of Canonization in the Thirteenth and Fourteenth Centuries', in Jancey, ed., *St Thomas Cantilupe*, pp. 133–35.

78. Hills, 'Hereford Cathedral', p. 73; Scott, 'Hereford Cathedral', pp. 341–45.

79. Willis, *Survey of Hereford Cathedral*, p. 22.

80. See further A. T. Bannister, ed., *The Register of Adam de Orleton, Bishop of Hereford, AD 1317–1327*, Cantilupe Society (Hereford, 1907), p. xxiv.

81. The reference to a separate shrine for St Thomas's head comes from the will of Thomas Chapman (1493) in which he requested burial in the 'north ile before St Thomas' head': PRO, PROB 11/10, fol. 42v. The clavigers' account distinguishes a separate collecting box there 1478–79, a reference also found in a miscellaneous account of 1457–58, HCA, R 369, R 696a. I am indebted to David Lepine for all this information.

Fig. 63. Tower, detail.

Fig. 64. Nave, north arcade, east bay, in 1841. J. Merewether, *A Statement of the Condition and Circumstances of the Cathedral Church of Hereford* (Hereford, 1842). (HCL, neg. 142.)

After the translation, we find the monument of Bishop Lewis Charlton (d. 1369) strategically placed between the Lady chapel vestibule and the south-east transept rebuilt in his episcopate (figs 55, no.11; 15); and that of Sir Peter Grandisson (d. 1358) actually in the Lady chapel in preference to burial at Dore Abbey and its relic of the True Cross.[82] St Thomas Cantilupe figures prominently amongst the statues in his tomb canopy (plate VIb). It is more questionable whether Lady Joanna de Bohun (d. 1327) was buried in the Lady chapel in anticipation of the translation, and more likely that the chapter placed the monument there because of the appropriateness of a Marian setting for a female benefactor (plate VIa).[83] Much later it is equally likely to be devotion to the cult of the Virgin Mary which caused Bishop Audley (1492–1502) to site his two-storey chantry chapel on the south side of the Lady chapel (fig. 19): the centre boss of the upper vault depicts the Assumption of the Virgin.[84]

In this context, it is worth comment that Bishop Trillek (1344–60) chose instead to be buried in the centre of the choir,[85] reminding us that the success of the Cantilupe cult had a knock-on effect on other works and devotions. Trillek is not usually noted as a patron of the fabric,[86] but the most likely explanation for his choice is that he commissioned the new choir fittings, and perhaps encouraged a renewed interest in St Ethelbert. One side-effect of placing Cantilupe's shrine in the western part of the Lady chapel would have been to reaffirm the sanctuary as the focus of devotion to the Anglo-Saxon martyr, and the fine Gothic statue of Ethelbert now to the south of the high altar may bear witness to this development (fig. 1). Its style is mid fourteenth-century and therefore it is very likely to have been commissioned during Trillek's episcopate. We cannot be certain that its present location is correct, but the existence of such a figure in this vicinity later in the middle ages is corroborated by the location of the tomb of Bishop Mayew (d. 1516) to the south of the high altar, 'by the image of St Ethelbert' (fig. 55, no. 21).[87]

Recent research on the bishop's throne and choir stalls has reassigned them on artistic grounds to the period of about 1340–55,[88] in which case Trillek must almost

82. Hillaby, 'Cults', p. 102.
83. See further L. Gee, 'Fourteenth-Century Tombs for Women in Herefordshire', in Whitehead, *Medieval Art at Hereford*, pp. 132–34; and Bannister, *The Cathedral Church of Hereford*, p. 191. Hillaby, 'Cults', pp. 101–2, thinks Joanna was anticipating Cantilupe's imminent translation.
84. See further Marshall, *Hereford Cathedral*, p. 161.
85. His monumental brass, of which the fine figure survives, was moved in the eighteenth century: A. J. Winnington-Ingram,

Monumental Brasses in Hereford Cathedral (Hereford, 1956), p. 16; see also below, Chapter 15, p. 333, and fig. 100.
86. For example, Marshall, *Hereford Cathedral*, makes no mention of Trillek.
87. Cited in A. H. Fisher, *The Cathedral Church of Hereford*, Bell's Cathedral Series (London, 1898), p. 79. The bracket on which the statue now stands appears to be the same date as Mayew's monument.
88. C. Tracy, *English Gothic Choir-Stalls, 1200–1400* (Woodbridge, 1987), pp. 30–33.

I. Hereford Gospels, eighth century: opening page of St John's Gospel (HCL, MS P.I.2, fol. 102r).

IIa. Opening page of the thirteenth-century statutes (HCA, 7044/1, fol. 1r).

IIb. Title page of the Laudian statutes, 1636 (HCA, 7044/7).

IIc. Hereford Cathedral from the south by J.M.W. Turner, 1794.

IIIa. Hereford Cathedral from the headmaster's garden, 21 May 1799: watercolour by James Wathen. The headmaster's house (school house) is on the left.

IIIb. East view of the remains of the old chapter house, 9 July 1799: watercolour by James Wathen.

IVa. Hereford breviary, 1262–68: from the office for the feast of St Ethelbert (HCL, MS P.IX.7, fol. 263r).

IVb. Wycliffite English translation of the Bible, early fifteenth century: the opening of the Book of Genesis (HCL, MS O.VII.1, fol. 14v).

IVc. Late thirteenth-century stained glass in one of the windows on the south side of the Lady chapel.

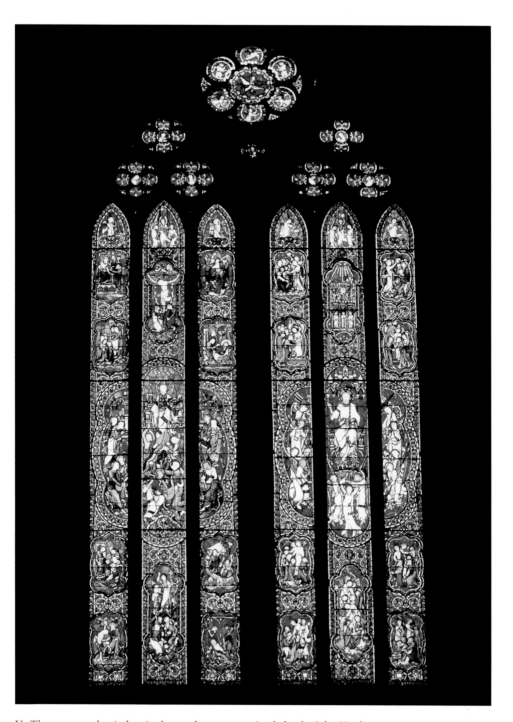

V. The great north window in the north transept: stained glass by John Hardman, 1864.

VIa. Tomb of Joanna de Bohun, died 1327, Lady chapel.

VIb. Tomb attributed to Peter de Grandisson, died 1358, Lady chapel.

VIIa. Tomb of Bishop Charles Booth, died 1535, north nave aisle.

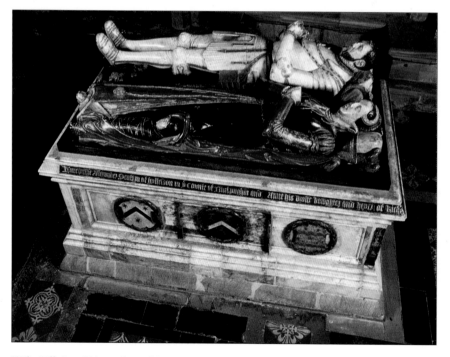

VIIb. Effigies of Alexander and Anne Denton, 1566, south transept.

VIIIa. Medieval manuscript miniature painting: St Mark, winged and with a lion's head, as a medieval scribe, in a twelfth-century gospel book (HCL, MS O.I.8, fol. 45v).

VIIIb. Medieval manuscript miniature: baptism of a child in a large font: fourteenth-century painting in a thirteenth-century law book (HCL, MS P.IX.2, fol. 302r).

VIIIc. Medieval manuscript miniature: deathbed scene, with scribe writing will, in a thirteenth- to fourteenth-century law book (HCL, P.IX.1, fol. 58v).

VIIId. Elaborate marginal decoration by hand in an early printed book: law dictionary by Petrus de Monte, Nuremberg, 1476 (HCL, E.I.1, fol. 4r).

IXa. The cloister of the college of vicars choral from the tower: school house is in the foreground to the left.

IXb. College hall, college of vicars choral.

Xa, b. Tiles of *c.* 1500 and late medieval stained glass in the chapel of St Katherine's Hospital, Ledbury.

Xc. Coloured decoration discovered by the architect L.N. Cottingham on the arch at the end of the south nave aisle leading to the south transept. Reproduced from F.T. Havergal, *Fasti Herefordenses* (Edinburgh, 1869).

XI. Watercolour by Joseph Carless of the nave in 1833, showing the medieval pulpitum and the Renatus Harris organ of 1686.

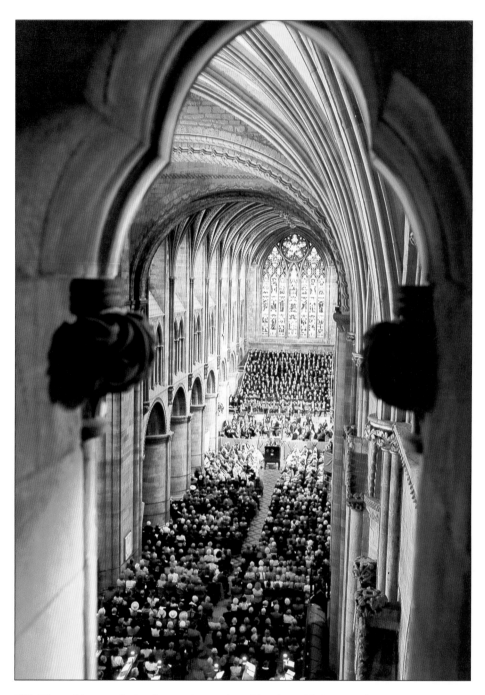

XII. View of the nave during the opening service of the Three Choirs Festival, 18 August 1991.

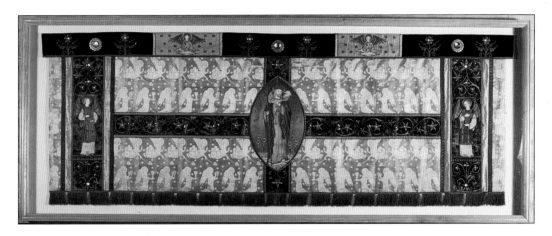

XIIIa. The Gilbert Scott altar frontal, 1873, framed in the Lady chapel.

XIIIb. The Limoges enamel reliquary of Thomas Becket, early
thirteenth century.

XIV. Hereford Cathedral from the north west, summer 1999.

XV. Opening of the new library building, 3 May 1996. Left to right: Sir John Cotterell, chairman of the Mappa Mundi Trust; Her Majesty the Queen; Lord Charteris, chairman of the National Heritage Memorial Fund; J. Paul Getty Jr, now Sir Paul Getty; Mrs Victoria (now Lady) Getty.

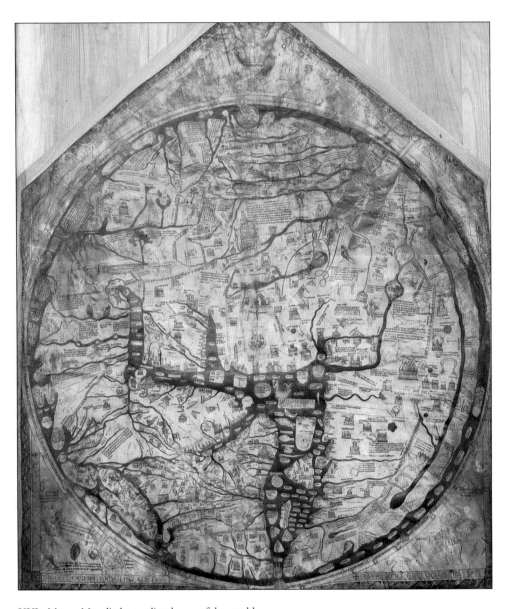

XVI. Mappa Mundi: the medieval map of the world.

certainly have been the patron (fig. 117). The wooden rails of the so-called 'organ loft' in the south choir aisle belong stylistically with these fittings,[89] and to these years also should be attributed the new pulpitum screen, which provided the return for the choir stalls between the western crossing piers and survived *in situ* until 1841 (fig. 25, no. L.).[90] The screen could not be placed further east because the plan of the Romanesque chancel had not been enlarged in any subsequent rebuilding, in contrast to virtually all other secular cathedrals such as Exeter and Lichfield. The commissioning of elaborate stone pulpitum screens was highly fashionable in the Decorated period, with several important examples in the west directly preceding Hereford, such as Exeter (1317–25), Tintern (*c.* 1330) and St David's (*c.* 1340).[91] However, unlike these, Hereford was not of the 'veranda' type, but more comparable to the solid screen still surviving at Wells Cathedral (*c.* 1335). At Hereford, the functions of rood screen and pulpitum were combined, with the altar of the 'Much Cross' set in front of the screen, and another altar of the Holy Cross in the rood-loft (fig. 25, nos 16, 18).[92]

By 1394 the parish altar of St John the Baptist was also located by the pulpitum, to the south of the choir entrance,[93] and we may surmise that at some stage during the fourteenth century the parish had moved out of the crypt and into part of the nave. As late as 1381 there is documentation to imply that an altar to St Anne was still maintained in the crypt,[94] but shortly afterwards the crypt was apparently abandoned to become a charnel house, from which function it was rescued briefly by Andrew Jonis at the end of the fifteenth century.[95] By the start of the fifteenth century, we know that the south transept housed the main chapel of St Anne, because Bishop Trefnant requested burial in her chapel in 1404, and his monument survives today in the south wall of the transept (fig. 60).[96] About 1430 Bishop Spofford added a Perpendicular window in the transept to light the altar of St Anne,

89. Marshall, *Hereford Cathedral*, p. 108, pls 35–36; but he dates the pieces too early, and the interpretation as an organ loft is speculative.
90. Tracy, *Choir-Stalls*, p. 30; for a drawing of the screen before its removal, see pl. XI.
91. See S. A. Harrison, R. K. Morris, D. M. Robinson, 'A Fourteenth-Century Pulpitum Screen at Tintern Abbey, Monmouthshire', *Antiquaries Journal*, 78 (1998), pp. 212, 223, 244.
92. Both altars to the Holy Cross are mentioned in the same list of 1536; see A. T. Bannister, ed., *The Register of Charles Bothe, Bishop of Hereford (1516–1535)*, Cantilupe Society (Hereford, 1921), p. 365 (appendix, Register of Bishop Foxe).
93. This and a subsequent reference of 1414 cited in Marshall, *Hereford Cathedral*, pp. 173–74.
94. See note 37. HCA, 2228, dated 1379, also refers to the same foundation, but does not locate it (David Lepine, personal communication).
95. See Marshall, *Hereford Cathedral*, p. 63; Shoesmith, 'The Crypt', p. 9.
96. Stated in Trefnant's will of 6 March 1404, in Lambeth Palace Library, Reg. Arundel Canterbury, i, fol. 207r (David Lepine, personal communication).

and the stone vault of the transept is generally attributed to him as well on heraldic evidence.[97]

Spofford's commissions typify the nature of the majority of late medieval works at Hereford and most other English cathedral churches: the insertion of smart new windows and rib vaults, usually focused on a part of the building in which the patron had a personal interest. For example, in the 1430s Canon William Lochard (d. 1438), a royal clerk and precentor of Hereford, takes credit for the large six-light west window in the nave and its glass, and contemporaneously founded a chantry chapel of St George at the west end of the cathedral (fig. 37).[98] The window tracery and chapel were destroyed as a result of the fall of the west tower in 1786, but some fifteenth-century glass from this window, or from Spofford's south transept window, is thought to be amongst the fragments reset about 1925 in the west windows of the north transept.[99]

No dates are known for the rib vaults in the nave and under the crossing tower, the former rebuilt in pastiche by Wyatt after 1786 and the latter removed in 1840.[100] Previous authorities have dated them no more precisely than the fifteenth century, but it is not generally recognised that four capitals and three bosses almost certainly from the crossing vault still survive in the stones collection in St John's walk, and on stylistic grounds these date to the early decades of the century (fig. 12).[101] With regard to the nave, it is possible that payment in the fabric roll of 1383–84 for glazing for six nave windows may refer to the new Perpendicular windows inserted in the clerestory,[102] which, if correct, would also provide the most likely period for its vault. This work may be connected with the presence of the parish of St John the Baptist in the nave,[103] and led on to the remodelling of the south transept and crossing, in similar fashion to the comparable works of

97. Marshall, *Hereford Cathedral*, p. 128, though the window may not be the west one in the south wall, as he states (see further below). See D. O'Connor, 'Bishop Spofford's Glass at Ross-on-Wye', in Whitehead, *Medieval Art at Hereford*, pp. 138–43, for Spofford's devotion to the cult of St Anne, and pp. 143–44, for the proposed date of the glass.

98. Marshall, *Hereford Cathedral*, pp. 150–51.

99. O'Connor, 'Bishop Spofford's Glass', p. 142.

100. See further below, Chapter 9, p. 261.

101. N. Drinkwater, 'Hereford Cathedral: The Chapter House', *Archaeological Journal*, 112 (1955), pp. 70–72, incorrectly suggests that

these stones were carved for the chapter house vestibule. The stones were moved from the vestibule to their present location after the Second World War; (personal communication, Arthur Jones, former master mason at the cathedral).

102. I am grateful to David Lepine for spotting this information in HCA, R 621.

103. About 1414 there was an abortive attempt to build a separate chapel apparently for the parish on the south side of the nave: see Marshall, *Hereford Cathedral*, p. 174; and J. H. Harvey, *English Mediaeval Architects: A Biographical Dictionary down to 1550* (revised edn, Gloucester, 1984), p. 80 (entry for Thomas Denyar).

updating at Worcester Cathedral *c.* 1375–80.[104] The employment throughout of a tierceron vault design like that still surviving in the south transept is rather conservative (fig. 60), and presumably reflects the limited funding available to cathedrals like Hereford and Worcester for large-scale works, compared with the elaborate lierne vaulted naves of wealthy sees like Canterbury and Winchester.[105] In contrast, special commissions of a more manageable size could indulge in stylish elaboration, such as the fan vaults of the Stanbury and Audley chapels or the lierne vault of the Booth porch (figs 19, 115).[106]

Almost certainly the earliest building at Hereford to include a decorative vault was the new chapter house, completed *c.* 1370, a reminder that significant architectural works were ongoing beyond the confines of the church.[107] A new chapter house was apparently being contemplated in Bishop Swinfield's time, but the structural problems relating to the crossing tower delayed matters until *c.* 1340, which is the date of the surviving parts of the vestibule and lower walls (fig. 65).[108] The start of work may be implied by the acknowledgement by the dean and chapter in 1337 of funds from Swinfield's executors for 'the fabric and windows of a new chapter house'.[109] Further interruption was caused by visitations of the plague, and it would seem that the contract of 1364 between the dean and chapter and Thomas of Cambridge, mason, finally led to the execution of the vault.[110] Some authorities argue that this feature was of fan vault design, based on the reconstruction drawing by the eighteenth-century antiquary, William Stukeley, and the panelled springer stone surviving on site today (figs 16, 66).[111] However, there are several problems with this reconstruction, not least that the vault had collapsed by the time Stukeley visited in 1721, and that the panelled stone cannot derive from a central springer; indeed there is no archaeological proof that the chapter house had a centre pier.[112] Rather it is as likely that the vault was of a lierne type

104. See R. K. Morris, 'Worcester Nave: From Decorated to Perpendicular', in G. Popper, ed., *Medieval Art and Architecture at Worcester Cathedral*, British Archaeological Association Conference Transactions, 1 (Leeds, 1978), pp. 134–35 and n. 77.

105. Crook, *Winchester Cathedral*, fig. 5.1, for illustration.

106. For the fan vaults, see further W. C. Leedy, *Fan Vaulting: A Study of Form, Technology and Meaning* (London, 1980), pp. 171–73.

107. For ancillary buildings, see further below, Chapter 11, pp. 293–310.

108. The documentary evidence is summarised in Drinkwater, 'Chapter House'. For the stylistic evidence, especially similarities with the tomb recess of Bishop Thomas Charlton (d. 1344), see R. K. Morris, 'Decorated Architecture in Herefordshire: Sources, Workshops and Influence' (unpublished Ph.D. thesis, 2 vols, University of London, 1972), ii, pp. 408–18.

109. Capes, *Charters*, pp. 220–21.

110. For the contract, see ibid., pp. 231–32.

111. Drinkwater, 'Chapter House', pp. 65, 71–72; also J. H. Harvey, *The Perpendicular Style, 1330–1485* (London, 1978), pp. 91–92.

112. See Morris, 'Decorated Architecture in Herefordshire', pp. 430–31; also Leedy, *Fan Vaulting*, p. 172, who arrived independently at the same conclusions as the author.

Fig. 65. Chapter house yard, looking south west across the site of the chapter house to the vestibule.

Fig. 66. Fan-vaulted springer stone on the site of the chapter house.

of single span, perhaps with ribs arranged in radiating patterns like the presbytery vault of Tewkesbury Abbey (*c.* 1340),[113] and perhaps with fan-type springers, if the panelled stone on site derives from a corner springer.[114]

The choice of a decagonal plan for the chapter house was derived from local monastic exemplars, of which the most recent was that at Evesham Abbey (finished by 1317): which, incidentally, was also vaulted without a centre pier.[115] In a national context, Hereford was the latest in a succession of secular chapters to adopt the polygonal chapter house as a fashionable architectural symbol of its corporate identity; others included Lincoln, Salisbury, York, Wells and London. Often the new work spurred the rebuilding of the adjoining cloister, and at Hereford this seems to have been contemplated in the second half of the fourteenth century, though there is no documentary proof of new work under way until 1412.[116] The cloister had a processional function, but the main practical aims were focused on the east walk, to link the chapter house to the church and to provide a first-floor room for chapter records in the bay adjoining the vestibule. This probably explains why parts of the south and west walks were apparently not finished until the late fifteenth century,[117] a situation familiar from the spasmodic rebuilding of some other secular cloisters like Exeter and Wells.

The last major architectural addition to the cathedral is the outer north porch of the nave (fig. 67). Documentary evidence indicates that it was started by Bishop Mayew (d. 1516), and completed in 1518 by his successor, Bishop Booth, whose tomb lies close by in the nave north aisle (plate VIIa) and after whom the 'Booth' porch is usually named.[118] Its distinctive features are the pair of polygonal stair turrets – like a grand Tudor gatehouse – and its wonderfully glazed upper chamber, a combination for which it is difficult to find a parallel in the porches of other cathedrals, except for the Perpendicular porch inserted into the west front of

113. Leedy, *Fan Vaulting*, p. 172; see Morris, 'Decorated Architecture in Herefordshire', pp. 426–42, for a full account of the evidence, though disregarding the attribution to the 'Hereford Master'.

114. It is just possible that the panelled springer stone comes from vaulting in the western parts of the nave, removed after the collapse of 1786; Hearne's drawing (1806) shows fan springers there, reproduced in Thurlby, 'Hereford Cathedral: Romanesque Fabric', pl. 2a.

115. M. Walcott, 'The Mitred Abbey of St Mary, Evesham', *British Archaeological Association Journal*, 32 (1876), p. 19; and D. C. Cox, 'The Building, Destruction and Excavation of Evesham Abbey: A Documentary History', *Worcestershire Archaeological Society Transactions*, 3rd series, 12 (1990), pp. 128–30.

116. For the evidence of the compotus roll of 1412 (HCA, 2369), see Marshall, *Hereford Cathedral*, p. 131, and P. E. Morgan, 'Pilgrim Cult', p. 152. The style of the cloister tracery belongs to *c.* 1370–1400, and may be to the design of Thomas Denyar in the undated contract cited in Capes, *Charters*, pp. 232–33.

117. A full analysis of the cloister development is in Marshall, *Hereford Cathedral*, chapter 16.

118. See ibid., chapter 25, for a full account of the dating evidence.

Fig. 67. Booth porch exterior from the north east.

Peterborough.[119] The common denominator between Hereford and Peterborough is that both provide external access through two staircases to an important upper room, which suggests that functional rather than stylistic parallels should be sought with parish church porches with an upper room used as a chapel, as at Salle (Norfolk), or to house a relic, as at Lapworth (Warwickshire).[120] At Hereford, we know that a chapel of the Virgin Mary had existed over the inner north porch since 1367 at least,[121] which may be the date when its upper chamber was added, and is very likely to be the date of the two image canopies reused in the outer porch chamber. The chapel had become popular, but the only access was by the

119. The connection is suggested in Fisher, *Cathedral Church of Hereford*, p. 28. See most recently L. A. Reilly, *An Architectural History of Peterborough Cathedral* (Oxford, 1997), pp. 116–19, where a liturgical function for the porch is conjectured.

120. For parish church porches, see F. Bond,

Gothic Architecture in England (London, 1906), p. 584; for Lapworth, see N. Pevsner and A. Wedgwood, *Warwickshire*, Buildings of England (Harmondsworth, 1966), p. 331.

121. Bannister, *The Cathedral Church of Hereford*, p. 191; Marshall, *Hereford Cathedral*, p. 163.

single spiral staircase in the nave north aisle, so the outer porch with two new stairs was added to provide direct entry from the exterior to the upper level, and a return route, on the model of a relic cult. At the same time the former north facing window of the inner porch room was converted to a door aperture to link the two upper chambers, probably for the use of a priest.

The chamber of the outer porch is still a fine room, retaining some of its floor tiles and a blue painted ceiling with gold stars, and it deserves to be better known (fig. 116). The liturgical arrangements after 1518 cannot be reconstructed with certainty, but Bishop Booth set up an altar to St Saviour and a Jesus image, both of which are likely to have been in the new outer room; in which case the altar to the Virgin may have remained in the inner chapel (fig. 25, no. 20).[122] A further ground-floor oratory or chantry appears to have been planned directly adjoining the inner porch on its east side, but only a stone door-frame bearing the date 1519 survives.[123] The north window of the outer porch chamber is unusual in having a centre light of double width (fig. 67), an idea found occasionally in a 'feature' window of major churches, such as the east window of the fourteenth-century collegiate church at Edington (Wiltshire).[124] Without doubt, the wider light was reserved for a religious representation of special significance, which in the case of the north porch would probably have been an image of Jesus or the Virgin Mary.

The Booth porch is a work of outstanding quality and demonstrates how the cathedral was a major centre for architectural craftsmanship in the region: a tradition which continues to this day with the employment of firms like Capps and Capps. Occasionally the name of an individual craftsman surfaces from the records: Master Hugh in 1290, John of Evesham in 1359, Thomas of Cambridge in 1364, Thomas Denyar towards 1400 and Thomas Mason in 1414.[125] However, the vast majority of master craftsmen who created the present cathedral remain anonymous today, though they were not so in the middle ages.[126] Sometimes their characters still speak to us through the style and other distinctive traits of the surviving stonework, and the final section of the chapter deals briefly with this aspect. An apology must be given here that space does not permit a consideration of the wooden roofs of

122. I am grateful to David Lepine for discussion of these points.

123. See further Marshall, *Hereford Cathedral*, p. 164.

124. Edington is illustrated in Harvey, *Perpendicular Style*, pl. 18. I am grateful to Michael Reardon and the late Nicholas Moore for discussion of the fabric of the porch window.

125. For all these masons, see the entries in

Harvey, *English Mediaeval Architects*; though he places Thomas Denyar too late and conflates him with Master Thomas of Hereford (p. 80). Miss Morgan has suggested the alternative spelling of 'Deuyas' for 'Denyar': P. E. Morgan, 'Pilgrim Cult', p. 152.

126. For the individuality and status of medieval master craftsmen, see Harvey, *English Mediaeval Architects*, pp. xxxix-lii.

the cathedral church, hidden above the vaults, but there is very little information about them and more research and recording is required. Parts of at least two medieval roofs are known, apparently of the thirteenth century over the Lady chapel, and of the later fourteenth century over the south-east transept.[127]

At times of extensive building activity – for example when the Norman church was constructed or when the aisles were remodelled – the cathedral would have had a masons' lodge, and it is possible from the evidence of the fabric to plot the influence of this workshop in the local area. Moreover, comparison with other major buildings further afield, especially Wells Cathedral, allows us to assess the place of various works at Hereford in a regional and national context. None of the five craftsmen named above are known to have had a high profile career, but the fabric bears witness to significant links at times with the royal works at Westminster and Windsor.

The important role of the cathedral lodge is evident in the first half of the twelfth century, as a centre of employment and artistic interchange for masons of the so-called 'Herefordshire' and 'Dymock' schools of monumental sculpture.[128] Some conventions of figure carving which were to become local characteristics have been noted in the six figure-capitals from the presbytery arch of Reinhelm's church, for example the bulging eyes and cap-like rendition of hair (fig. 7), presaging elements of parish church works of the second quarter of the century, like the tympanum at Rowlstone.[129] As work on the cathedral progressed westward to the crossing and the east bays of the nave in the 1120s and early 1130s, the growing repertoire of geometric and vegetal embellishments was copied at new churches such as Kilpeck and Shobdon (fig. 68).[130] Though almost all the cathedral's Romanesque decoration was recut or replaced in the 1840s under Cottingham,[131] the authenticity of motifs like the rich foliate trails with curly tips can be verified from original carvings removed at this restoration and now stored in St John's Walk (fig. 12). In the

127. C. A. Hewett, *English Cathedral and Monastic Carpentry* (Chichester, 1985), pp. 12–13, 219–20.

128. For a recent short bibliography of these schools, see E. Chwojko and M. Thurlby, 'Gloucester and the Herefordshire School', *British Archaeological Association Journal*, 150 (1997), pp. 24–25 nn. 1–2. Also most recently M. Thurlby, *The Herefordshire School of Romanesque Sculpture* (Almeley, 1999). For the role of architect and patron in eleventh-century Hereford, see Gem, 'The Bishop's Chapel', pp. 87–96.

129. Thurlby, 'Romanesque Sculpture at Hereford Cathedral', pp. 233–34; also Thurlby,

The Herefordshire School, pp. 111–15 for Rowlstone.

130. See further J. F. King, 'The Parish Church at Kilpeck Reassessed', in Whitehead, *Medieval Art at Hereford*, pp. 82–85; and Thurlby, 'Hereford Cathedral: Romanesque Fabric', pp. 21–23.

131. See further D. Whitehead, 'The Mid Nineteenth-Century Restoration of Hereford Cathedral by Lewis Nockalls Cottingham, 1842–1850', in Whitehead, *Medieval Art at Hereford*, pp. 176–86, especially pp. 184–85; also J. Myles, *L. N. Cottingham, 1787–1847: Architect of the Gothic Revival* (London, 1996), pp. 99–103.

Fig. 68. Nave interior, eastern bays.

nave, changes discernible in the arcade arches in the third bay – if they authentically reflect the medieval details – suggest there was a break after two bays were completed, thus releasing masons around 1130 for work elsewhere.

Moving to the Gothic period, we can observe a similar process in the 'Cantilupe cult' works undertaken in Bishop Swinfield's episcopate. The pointed trefoil, the most memorable motif of the new aisle windows of about 1290 (fig. ii), is copied in several local church works like the east window at Dilwyn (before 1305), to be followed by the use of ballflower ornament, which arrived in the cathedral workshop in the first decade of the fourteenth century and which was taken up with great popularity in the diocese and in major churches further afield like St Peter's Abbey, Gloucester (now the cathedral).[132] Of course, the 'source and influence' model is too mechanistic to represent all the subtle interactions of

132. R. K. Morris, 'The Local Influence of Hereford Cathedral in the Decorated Period', *TWNFC*, 41 (1973), pp. 48–67; and idem, 'Ballflower Work in Gloucester and its Vicinity', in T. A. Heslop and V. A. Sekules, eds, *Medieval Art and Architecture at Gloucester and Tewkesbury*, British Archae-ological Association Conference Transactions, 7 (Leeds, 1985), pp. 100–2.

medieval craftsmen at cathedral and local level, but nevertheless the relatively peripheral position of Herefordshire, and the dominance within it of the cathedral city, make it a clearer example of the centrifugal process than is the case at more cosmopolitan centres in the east of England.[133]

We can often be reasonably confident in the Gothic period that the chief designer based his activity at the cathedral lodge, in the sense that his most elaborate work was produced there; and also that we can distinguish other hands with experience of the lodge, like the 'Madley mason', executing parish church works.[134] The contract of 9 April 1359, appointing John of Evesham as cathedral master mason, specifies that he was to live in Hereford and a house was to be let to him.[135] For the Romanesque period, however, the type of evidence is no longer available which is necessary to make such judgements. The building of the Norman cathedral provided an early repository for architectural motifs in the area, but the fact remains that the acknowledged 'masterpieces' of the Herefordshire school are doorways and fonts in small churches like Kilpeck and Castle Frome. This may be due to a modern art-historical bias in favour of figurative sculpture, or to a lack of appropriate survivals at the cathedral – the mutilated Romanesque font being a solitary reminder of what we may have lost (fig. 10).[136] It may, however, also reflect a rather more fragmented pattern of patronage in twelfth-century Herefordshire.

The cathedral lodge did not exist in a vacuum, and most changes of fashion were brought about by the arrival of a master mason with experience of another regional centre or from further afield. For the Romanesque period, artistic connections have recently been recognised between Gloucester and Herefordshire, including the cathedral, and the presence of a sculptor from Old Sarum has been proposed.[137] These are in addition to the better known outside factors which carried the Herefordshire school to maturity, namely the influence of the Cluniac abbey at Reading by way of Leominster Priory (founded 1123) and ideas gleaned from a pilgrimage to Santiago de Compostela in the entourage of Oliver de Merlimond, the founder of Shobdon church;[138] but these seem to have arrived too late to have

133. For regional patterns affecting architectural detail, see R. K. Morris, 'The Development of Later Gothic Mouldings in England, c. 1250–1400, Part II', *Architectural History*, 22 (1979), pp. 32–35.

134. R. K. Morris, 'The Mason of Madley, Allensmore and Eaton Bishop', *TWNFC*, 41 (1974), pp. 180–97.

135. Capes, *Charters*, pp. 230–31.

136. Several Romanesque worked stones, probably from the former west front, were recovered in the 1993 library excavation,

but they added little to our knowledge of the cathedral's repertoire of motifs: the most interesting are a voussoir with triple roll moulding, a piece carved with point-to-point chevron, and a detached nook-shaft of sandstone.

137. Chwojko and Thurlby, 'Gloucester and the Herefordshire School', pp. 17–24; King, 'Kilpeck Reassessed', pp. 85–88.

138. G. Zarnecki, *Later English Romanesque Sculpture, 1140–1210* (London, 1953), pp. 9–15.

had any major effect on the cathedral works. Injections of ideas new to the area can almost always be shown to stem from the initiative of the patron, such as de Merlimond at Shobdon or Bishop Aigueblanche in the thirteenth century for the cathedral's north transept. With regard to the latter, the relationship between the transept and work at Westminster Abbey is so intimate, including details like lateral bead mouldings in the arch profiles, as to leave little doubt that the master mason from Westminster was consulted: presumably Master Henry of Reyns (d. 1253) or his successor, John of Gloucester.[139] Only Bishop Aigueblanche amongst the Hereford clergy was sufficiently well-connected to procure the services of such an architect.

The ability to lure masons with experience of royal works to Hereford continues in evidence in the later middle ages, especially at times when the concept of a 'court style' is strong, as in the reign of Edward I and in the early Tudor period. When the aisles were remodelled from *c.* 1290, the tracery patterns – especially the giant trefoil – reveal a knowledge of smart examples of French Rayonnant architecture like the collegiate church of St-Urbain at Troyes (mainly 1262–66), familiar in English court circles and London.[140] The idea that Bishop Swinfield was in a position to obtain an architect with this sort of knowledge is supported by the royal interest in the Cantilupe cult; and it is likely that he had come from the royal county palatine of Chester, where Burgundian and Savoyard masons were present in the later thirteenth century in connection with Edward I's castle-building campaigns in north Wales.[141] He may well be the Master Hugh who received the handsome retainer of five pounds in the Hereford fabric accounts of 1290–91, which suggests a mason of status, but unfortunately nothing more has been pieced together of his career.[142]

Another instance where the nature of the patronage and the style of the work bear clear testimony to the presence of a court mason is in the design of Bishop Audley's chantry chapel (*c.* 1500). Audley was a canon of St George's Chapel, Windsor, and became chancellor of the Garter in 1502, so it is no surprise to discover that the elegant star-patterned fan vault of his chantry (fig. 19) is derived

139. For Westminster Abbey, see Wilson, *Westminster Abbey*, pp. 22–31, and fig. 10/4 for lateral bead mouldings. Also J. Bony, *The English Decorated Style: Gothic Architecture Transformed, 1250–1350* (London, 1979), pp. 4–5, for the transept's French sources.

140. Morris, 'Hereford Aisles', pp. 29–31; and idem, 'Old St Paul's', p. 88.

141. Bony, *English Decorated Style*, p. 14. For the stylistic affiliations of the unusual type of sunk chamfer mullion employed in the aisle windows, see R. K. Morris, 'The Development of Later Gothic Mouldings in England, *c.* 1250–1400, Part I', *Architectural History*, 21 (1978), pp. 30–31 and n. 40.

142. See Harvey, *English Mediaeval Architects*, pp. 152 (Hugh the Mason III), 252–53 (Hugh de Reyns). Harvey's speculation that he may be Hugh de Reyns is unhelpful, and it might be more profitable to consider an identification with Hugh de Boudon or Hugh Tichemers (p. 369, Key to Christian Names).

from vault designs in the new St George's Chapel, begun as a royal mausoleum by Edward IV and continued by the early Tudors.[143] The moulding profiles corroborate a very precise link with Windsor,[144] and though Audley's architect has not been identified, the elegance of design and detail contrasts with the more indigenous style of Bishop Stanbury's fan-vaulted chantry chapel (before 1492) and the almost identical vault of the entrance porch to the college of vicars choral (fig. 115).[145] When Audley was translated to Salisbury, he commissioned another fan-vaulted chantry there in about 1516 which took the latest royal work as its model, Henry VII's chapel at Westminster Abbey.[146]

In general, affiliations with a variety of provincial workshops predominate in the later middle ages. For example, Evesham Abbey is likely to have provided the main inspiration for the decagonal chapter house at Hereford, and it may well be that the contract of 1359 with Master John of Evesham continued a link established earlier in the fourteenth century: some have even seen him as the designer of the upper parts of the chapter house, completed by Thomas of Cambridge after 1364.[147] By the start of the fifteenth century the blind tracery around Bishop Trefnant's tomb in the south transept, and the large window in its west wall, relate to works in the north Cotswolds and Oxford (figs ii, 60).[148] Whereas the gridiron tracery pattern of the south window clearly represents a change of plan, perhaps to be attributed to Bishop Spofford, and suggests affiliations with workshops in the north midlands and beyond; perhaps reflecting Spofford's Yorkshire origins and the proposed source for his stained glass (fig. 60).[149] A century later, the fussy sub-reticulated Perpendicular tracery of the Booth porch, and the pattern of its lierne vault, hint at the presence of a master from the Bristol area, familiar with the great city church of St Mary Redcliffe and reworking motifs from the earlier Perpendicular

143. Leedy, *Fan Vaulting*, p. 171.
144. For example, the minor mullion of the blind tracery of the screen to the Audley chapel is from the same template as mullions of Edward IV's first-floor chantry at Windsor.
145. Leedy, *Fan Vaulting*, pp. 172–73. Leedy relates these to a late fifteenth-century chantry at Great Malvern (p. 170). The ultimate source of this style of fan vault in the west midlands is the cloister at Gloucester.
146. Leedy, *Fan Vaulting*, pp. 14, 198. The completion of the chapel at Hereford after 1502 was apparently overseen by James Bromwich, canon and chancellor (1494–1524), hence the initials 'IB' on the screen: see P. E. Morgan, 'The Audley Chapel',

FHC, 39 (1973), pp. 11–12.
147. Harvey, *English Mediaeval Architects*, p. 104. The decagonal plan and lack of central column at Evesham chapter house (complete by 1319) has been confirmed by a geophysical survey done for Hereford and Worcester County Council in 1994; I am grateful to David Kendrick for this information.
148. For example, work in the north transept of Merton College chapel, Oxford: Harvey, *Perpendicular Style*, pl. 126.
149. O'Connor, 'Bishop Spofford's Glass', pp. 141–44. The sequence of work in the Hereford south transept is clearly more complicated than is generally presented, e.g. Marshall, *Hereford Cathedral*, pp. 128–29.

period in the south west (fig. 67). Overall, the Perpendicular architecture is the least studied period of the medieval cathedral, and deserves more research.

The regional workshop which had most influence on Hereford was that centred on Wells. The building of a completely new Gothic cathedral church there from *c.* 1175, in what had previously been a backwater, produced a lodge which was to revolutionise the architecture of the south west, west midlands and south Wales (to which the term 'west country' has been loosely applied), taking the lead from older Romanesque centres like Gloucester.[150] The creative genius of various masters at this lodge continued through to the later fourteenth century at least, backed by an unbroken supply of excellent Doulting freestone.[151] The part of Hereford Cathedral which first reveals general influence from the west country school is the retrochoir and 'Lady chapel vestibule' in the late twelfth century, with ogee keel mouldings and vault ribs with lozenge-chevron decoration (fig. 15),[152] but design ideas specifically from Wells appear in the Lady chapel proper. This is most obvious in the east elevation of the Lady chapel exterior, in the way in which the feature of the tall windows alternating with pairs of stacked-up niches is an adaptation of the centrepiece of Wells west facade (fig. 78).[153] The connection is validated by the employment in the Lady chapel of groups of neat roll mouldings interspersed with semi-circular hollows and fillets, which are a 'trademark' of Wells work and first appeared there in the west bays of the nave. There seems little doubt, then, that a mason with personal experience of the Wells lodge in the time of Master Adam Lock (fl. *c.* 1215–29) was in charge of at least the later stages of the Lady chapel work.[154]

In the first decade of the fourteenth century, another mason from Wells appears to be in charge of the second phase of the remodelling of the aisles and the construction of the new towers. The evidence lies in the employment of moulding profiles closely related to ones in use at Wells in the last quarter of the thirteenth

150. The seminal study is H. Brakspear, 'A West Country School of Masons', *Archaeologia*, 81 (1931), pp. 1–18.

151. See further L. S. Colchester, ed., *Wells Cathedral: A History* (Shepton Mallet, 1982), especially pp. 98–101.

152. These features relate to work at other late twelfth-century centres of the school, like Glastonbury, though lozenge-chevron had made an early appearance in the Romanesque work. See Thurlby, 'Hereford Cathedral: Romanesque Fabric', pp. 19, 24; and idem, 'The Lady Chapel of Glastonbury Abbey', *Antiquaries Journal*, 75 (1995), pp. 107–70.

153. Colchester, *Wells Cathedral*, pl. 24, for the Wells facade. The authenticity of the relevant features of the Lady chapel facade before Cottingham's intervention is vouched for in various antiquarian engravings, of which the most reliable is T. Garbett, *A Brief Enquiry into the Ancient and Present State of Hereford Cathedral* (Hereford, 1827), pl. 8 (fig. 78); I am grateful to David Whitehead for advice on this point.

154. For Adam Lock and his successor, Thomas Norreys, see most recently J. Sampson, *Wells Cathedral West Front* (Gloucester, 1998), pp. 46–55.

century, and of ballflower ornament, which seems to have made its first appearance in the west in the main chamber of Wells chapter house (*c.* 1295–1306).[155] This brings us to consider ballflower, the architectural ornament of the Decorated period (*c.* 1300–*c.* 1330) for which Hereford is well known, and to unravel the relationship of the crossing tower to other ballflower-studded cathedral towers of the same period at Salisbury, Lincoln and Lichfield (fig. ii). We know that the Hereford tower was at least partly erected by 1307, and the dating of the others is extremely close – Salisbury probably begun in the decade *c.* 1300–10 and the Lichfield west towers by *c.* 1310, with the Lincoln crossing tower documented as planned and built 1307–11.[156] We are clearly observing a decorative motif which spread like a craze, not just for towers but for other works like the nave aisle at Gloucester and the Lady chapel at St Albans, and which fell from popularity equally rapidly.[157] It almost certainly had a lost source in the royal works,[158] but within the tight chronology of extant early examples, it is still possible to maintain that Hereford derived the idea from Wells, and from then on assumed an important position in its further distribution; which is most likely to be explained by the short-lived surge of enthusiasm for the Cantilupe cult. At Lincoln and Lichfield, the ballflower appears part of the way up the fabric, which may represent an acknowledgement of Hereford's influence after work had commenced.

The closest comparisons of architectural detail are between the crossing towers at Hereford and Salisbury, together with the chapter house at Wells.[159] The sequence of events is likely to be that the lower stage of the Hereford tower was started before Salisbury and built by *c.* 1307, employing ballflower and moulding ideas derived from Wells. In the meantime, work on the much more ambitious tower at Salisbury had begun, indebted both to Wells and Hereford for some features, and subsequently the design for Hereford was adapted in some details in the upper stage (between *c.* 1310 and 1319) to take account of further fashionable refinements made at Salisbury. These are seen in the sub-cusped tracery of the window heads, not found in the lower windows, and the horizontal band of cusped lozenges

---

155. Morris, 'Hereford Aisles', pp. 32–36.
156. R. K. Morris, 'The Style and Buttressing of Salisbury Tower', in L. Keen, ed., *Medieval Art and Architecture at Salisbury Cathedral*, British Archaeological Association Conference Transactions, 17 (Leeds, 1996), pp. 46–47, 55–56; J. Maddison, 'Building at Lichfield Cathedral during the Episcopate of Walter Langton', in J. Maddison, ed., *Medieval Archaeology and Architecture at Lichfield*, British Archaeological Association Conference Transactions, 12 (Leeds,

1993), pp. 79–80.
157. Morris, 'Ballflower in Gloucester', pp. 99–100, for a brief overview.
158. Possibly in one of the lost Eleanor Crosses; see Morris, 'Ballflower in Gloucester', p. 99 and n. 3, and Maddison, 'Building at Lichfield', p. 79.
159. Morris, 'Decorated Architecture in Herefordshire', i, pp. 172–75 and figs 18–21, for comparative details; idem, 'Salisbury Cathedral Tower', pp. 46–47, for chronology.

between the stages (fig. 63). A further reminder of these links was discovered during conservation work on the tower in 1985, when the pinnacles and upper courses of masonry were removed from the south-west corner. This revealed that the original arrangement at each corner, since encased in later masonry, was for two elegant freestanding pinnacles of triangular plan, a distinctive type also employed at Salisbury to cap flying buttress piers connected with the tower work, and ultimately derived from the buttress pinnacles of Wells chapter house.[160] No evidence has come to light that Hereford was intended to have a stone spire like Salisbury, nor is it likely, but old views show a modest timber spire of unknown date on the crossing tower, until it was taken down in Wyatt's time (fig. 33).[161]

The exchange of ideas about tower construction continues with Wells between the 1320s and 1340s, but this time mainly in the reverse direction. A new crossing tower had been erected at Wells Cathedral (*c.* 1315–22) which makes no attempt to use ballflower ornament, an early sign of the waning of the costly craze and also, perhaps, of fervour for the Cantilupe cult. By 1338 the Wells tower was causing serious structural problems, and it is not surprising to find that the Wells masons, under Master William Joy, undertook some structural reinforcements of a kind already familiar at Hereford.[162] One of these was to insert a rectilinear grid of stone inside the lower part of the upper stage, the medieval equivalent of modern concrete ring-beams. At Hereford a similar ingenious grid of masonry had been built inside the tower from the start and was presumably designed to reduce the load on the piers below (fig. 117), hence the statement in 1319 that 'skilled masons had considered the old foundations to be sound'.[163] Clearly the masons at Hereford were aware of the foundation problems, but in the event had still underestimated them. To help rectify the situation, the arcade arches of the east bay of the nave were rebuilt, apparently after 1319, in the ballflower style of Hereford, but employing round arches to accommodate the Romanesque elevation, and these were still visible until removal by Cottingham.[164] At Wells, the same type of underpinning was undertaken in the nave arcades adjoining the crossing, in a style sympathetic to the earlier Gothic elevation, at some time between 1322 and 1338, and following the structurally successful precedent at Hereford.

160. Morris, 'Salisbury Cathedral Tower', p. 47, and pls 14c-d.
161. See further below, Chapter 9, pp. 256, 262.
162. Colchester, *Wells Cathedral*, pp. 87–89. See also P. Draper, 'The Sequence and Dating of the Decorated Work at Wells', in P. Draper and N. Coldstream, eds, *Medieval Art and Architecture at Wells and Glastonbury*, British Archaeological Association Conference Transactions, 4 (Leeds,

1981), pp. 18–29.
163. P. E. Morgan, 'Pilgrim Cult', p. 149.
164. Willis, *Survey of Hereford Cathedral*, p. 22. It is evident that the arches under the west tower had been rebuilt in the same fashion: see J. Merewether, *A Statement of the Condition and Circumstances of the Cathedral Church of Hereford* (Hereford, 1842), pls 10, 11, reproduced in Myles, *L. N. Cottingham*, pls 53, 54.

Thus, Hereford's reputation amongst architectural historians as one of the 'also-rans' amongst English medieval cathedrals is misleading. Despite the amount of damage and restoration since the middle ages, its medieval fabric remains a fascinating and rewarding subject for study, with much yet to be discovered and set in context. Even today the fine south-easterly aspect of Hereford seen from across the River Wye is the envy of many more famous cathedrals and a poignant reminder of the great age of St Thomas Cantilupe (plate IIc).

9

The Architectural History of the Cathedral since the Reformation

David Whitehead

Bishop Booth's porch brings to a close the medieval enrichment of Hereford Cathedral (fig. 67). The work had been done well and John Leland decided in about 1530 that the cathedral was 'very strongly built' – admittedly after a rather cursory glance.[1] Henceforward, the dean and chapter and its craftsmen struggled to maintain an immense structure, designed for a catholic liturgy, with an increasing number of obsolete features. Their work was denigrated by nineteenth-century restorers, but through their assiduous attention to roof and wall, they brought the cathedral through the twin crises of Reformation and Civil War into an age when its antique character began to be appreciated. Unfortunately, as we now know from Robert Willis's *Report of a Survey of the Dilapidated Portions of Hereford Cathedral* (1842), the Romanesque fabric was fatally flawed. The great tower was provided with insufficient foundations and its powerful thrust ultimately pushed over the west tower in 1786 (fig. 69).

The condition of the fabric during and immediately after the Reformation can only be dimly perceived from the poor documentation available. As a secular cathedral the full impact of the Reformation was deferred until the 1540s.[2] The dissolution of the chantries in 1548 threw the maintenance of several chapels of delicate construction – Stanbury, Audley, SS. Katherine and Mary Magdalene – upon the already overstretched resources of the fabric fund. An analysis based upon the *Valor ecclesiasticus* shows that only Chichester among English cathedrals

1. L. Toulmin Smith, ed., *The Itinerary of John Leland* (5 vols, London, 1906–10; repr. 1964), iii, p. 48. Gilbert Scott regarded Booth's porch as a final 'very beautiful addition' to the medieval fabric whilst all subsequent alterations were 'rather works

of deterioration than improvement', G. G. Scott, 'Hereford Cathedral', *Archaeological Journal*, 34 (1877), p. 346.
2. T. Cocke and P. Kidson, *Salisbury Cathedral: Perspectives in Architectural History* (London, 1993), p. 15.

Fig. 69. Watercolour of 1731, showing the medieval cathedral, complete with west tower and spire. (Hereford City Library, Top. print, 914.244 Hereford.)

had less income than Hereford.[3] The palace chapel of SS. Katherine and Mary Magdalene was especially well endowed and Mary I's sympathy for the old order did not prevent her from granting away its lands in 1556.[4] The chapel was soon in difficulty and in the fabric roll of 1593 the master noted that the ruinous condition of the cloister adjoining 'the Katherines' was due to the decay of the roof of the chapel.[5]

Apart from the destruction of the Cantilupe shrine and the defacing of the mourning knights on his tomb chest (fig. 96), there appears to have been little deliberate vandalism at Hereford.[6] The *Letters and Papers of Henry VIII* in 1538

3. Stanford E. Lehmberg, *The Reformation of Cathedrals* (Princeton, 1988), p. 26.
4. *Calendar of the Patent Rolls Philip and Mary* (4 vols, London, 1936–39), iii, p. 272.
5. HCA, R 592.
6. G. Marshall, 'The Shrine of St Thomas de Cantilupe in Hereford Cathedral', *TWNFC*, 28 (1930), pp. 43–44.

refer to a holy water stoup and an image of the Trinity being removed and a further letter in 1547 required the removal of all images including stained glass.[7]

Elizabeth's reign marked a more stable period for the cathedral and the first series of fabric rolls between 1587 and 1592 provides a detailed insight into the maintenance of the fabric. The work is very routine. Lead is brought from Bristol to repair the north pitch of the Lady chapel roof for which the plumber John Morgan receives £22 12s. 6d. The outside of the choir is repointed with lime and stone by Martin Taylor and some new casements are provided for the chapter house. The 'newe library' in the Lady chapel requires 'bordes for the windowes' and other timber and in 1593 the 'upper most part of one of the south windows in the bodie of the church' is replaced by Martin Taylor. The most important job of this year was (white) 'washing' the choir, which took John Pole, and another labourer, twenty-eight days for which they were paid 40s. 7d.[8] Thus, in Dean Merewether's words, 'the spreading plague which mars the beauty of our ecclesiastical fabrics' was already being laid on thick with a mixture of Forest of Dean lime and hair.[9]

The same Protestant sensibilities which brought whitewash into the choir also kept the cathedral carpenter, Simon Geoffrey, well employed in 'making seates in the bodie of the church for more convenient hearing of sermons' (1588). He added further seats to the choir, and was paid in total £29 10s. 9d., but the following year he returned reducing the back of one of the new seats 'made for the gentlemen of the citie' so that other people could see the pulpit and hear better.[10] The colonisation of the cathedral during this era by the gentry is exemplified by the fine monument to Alexander Denton and his wife (1566) in the south transept (pl. VIIb). There is no doubt that the dean and chapter were very conscious of their public image. Hence the considerable sums spent upon the bells, chimes and clock, which were a constant reminder of the cathedral's presence in the community. Similarly the paths in the Close regularly received fresh gravel and repairs were carried out to the school in 1590.[11] The statutes of 1583 dedicated £5 from each of the resident canons towards the fabric and a further sixth of their income was also to be spent on repairs to their common property 'so long as it be necessary'.[12]

The complete fabric roll of 1615–16 shows that the master of the fabric had

7. J. S. Brewer, J. Gairdner and R. H. Brodie, eds, *Letters and Papers of the Reign of Henry VIII* (23 vols in 38, London, 1862–1932), xiii, pt 2, no. 1208; Lehmberg, *Reformation of Cathedrals*, p. 72.

8. HCA, R 588, R 592–93.

9. J. Merewether, *A Statement of the Condition and Circumstances of the Cathedral Church of Hereford* (Hereford, 1842), p. 7.

10. HCA, R 588, also quoted in Lehmberg, *Reformation of Cathedrals*, p. 161. Simon Geoffrey was also employed on the master's house of St Katherine's Hospital, Ledbury, *TWNFC*, 34 (1953), pp. 111, 114.

11. HCA, R 588, R 592–93.

12. Quoted in Bannister, *The Cathedral Church of Hereford*, p. 89.

£73 4s. 3d. in his account, derived from the Shinfield and Swallowfield tithes and several small rents for properties around the Close.[13] There were also burial fees: sixteen persons at 3s. 4d. each were buried in the Lady arbour; eight in the cloister at 6s. 8d. and two in the cathedral for £1 each. The total expenditure for the year was £81 19s. 9d. and the masters, John Best and John Benson, claimed the excess from the chapter. These accounts were well kept and although money was not 'thrown' at the fabric, that which was required was found. There was a formal fee of 40s. for the master of the fabric whilst the church carpenter, Richard Rogers, also received a similar sum. The keeper of the clock and the plumber received 13s. 4d. each.

The early seventeenth century was a period of enrichment for many English cathedrals when expenditure upon the fabric moved beyond simple mainten-ance.[14] Although the fabric rolls for Hereford are incomplete, this seems to be supported. In 1617 there was a major campaign to reglaze the windows. Ironwork was provided for the 'newe glazed' north and east windows but the latter had timber mullions, which were sawn and shaped by Hugh Davies. Bishop Robert Bennett (1603–17) left £40 for the fabric in his will, which was used to provide new seats and desks for the choir made by a joiner called Rowland. These were probably the 'miserable square panelled pews' discarded by Cottingham in the 1840s.[15] Together with Rogers, Rowland also made some new seats for the south side of the middle aisle and others beneath the pulpit, which may also have been made at this time albeit there is no reference in this particular account (fig. 32). A little earlier, in 1611, Rogers also refitted the library in the Lady chapel, following the instructions of Dr Thomas Thornton, outbidding a joiner from Oxford (fig. 146).[16] This was admired in 1634 by the three educated soldiers who were proudly shown the cathedral by a 'portly' alderman of the city. Within the new library they noticed the Cantilupe shrine and what remained of the 'neat little' Lady chapel with its 'curiously cut and carv'd works'. The chapter house they thought 'very fayre, and not much shortt of any wee yet saw' (fig. 16). They commented on the 'Antique worke in good colours' which adorned the walls.[17] The chapter house also impressed John Speede: it dominates the perspective of the cathedral on his plan of the city of 1610. There is no suggestion at this date that

13. HCA, R 601.
14. G. W. O. Addleshaw and F. Etchells, *The Architectural Setting of Anglican Worship* (London, 1945), pp. 136–38. For William Laud's innovations and repairs at Gloucester see D. Welander, *Gloucester Cathedral* (Stroud, 1991), pp. 353–57.
15. HCA, R 601 (1617–18); J. Myles,

L. N. Cottingham, 1787–1847: Architect of the Gothic Revival (London, 1996), pp. 101–2.
16. F. C. and P. E. Morgan, *Hereford Cathedral Libraries and Muniments* (2nd edn, Hereford, 1975), p. 7.
17. H. Reade, 'Tours and Tourists in Seven-teenth-Century Herefordshire', *TWNFC*, 26 (1924), p. 34.

the chapter house was being abandoned, for unspecified work is mentioned in every surviving fabric roll. Other routine work during this period (1616–19) included the cleaning of the gutters in the cloister; repointing in various places; chipping a hole in the vault of the choir to remove birds' nests; lead-work on the steeple; pins to hold the pinnacles on the tower; and replacing the brass 'scutcheon' on 'Fisher's tombe'. There was also much gravelling, and paving around the communion table in 1618. The lack of rolls for the 1630s means that it is not possible to pin-point the arrival of the altar rails – 'heavy and discordant' according to a nineteenth-century commentator. The Laudian statutes have little to say about the fabric and this suggests that all was in good order.[18]

Between 1615 and 1618 the average annual expenditure on the fabric was just over £74 but the next fabric roll of 1640 shows it had declined to £23 7s. 1d. and in 1645 to £9 0s. 5d.[19] The Swallowfield tithes, small rents and burial fees are still being received but the contributions from the canons via the chapter have disappeared either because the community has been dispersed or because the national emergency provided an excellent opportunity for non-payment. The gentry had certainly not deserted the cathedral and in 1645 Sir Samuel Aubrey of Clehonger and the child of Sir Henry Lingen were buried there. The church carpenter, now promoted to surveyor of the fabric, and the clock keeper, continued to receive small salaries and tallow lights were bought for services. The only sign of the dramatic events of that year, which saw the city besieged by the Scottish army, is the reference to the burials of 'Mr Adams, his man killed in the seege' and 'Captain Tailoures wife' – presumably the notorious sequestration commissioner, Silas Taylor. James Jaggard, the plumber, seems to be the only craftsman at work on the fabric, whilst Probin, the smith, serviced the bells.

Neglect and not wilful damage posed the greatest threat to the fabric between 1645 and 1660. There are no fabric rolls surviving from this period during which the cathedral became the 'meeting house' for the city on the abolition of the dean and chapter in 1649. The puritan survey of 1642 had suggested it be demolished but the city preacher, Richard Delamaine, and his four ministers provided regular services which continued to be attended by the mayor and gentlemen of the city. Delamaine had difficulty in obtaining money from the Protectorate government for the fabric, and as there were no arrears of rents when the rolls recommence in 1660, the income was obviously still being collected but diverted from its purpose.[20]

18. T. Garbett, *A Brief Enquiry into the Ancient and Present State of Hereford Cathedral* (Hereford, 1827), p. 69.

19. HCA, R 606–7.

20. H. W. Phillott, *Diocesan Histories: Hereford* (London, 1888), p. 213; J. and T. W. Webb, *Memorials of the Civil War as it Affected Herefordshire* (2 vols, London, 1879), ii, p. 316; Bannister, *The Cathedral Church of Hereford*, pp. 99–100; *The Compact Edition of the DNB* (2 vols, London, 1975), i, p. 522.

Rawlinson, writing in 1717, says that in 1645 the cathedral was 'profaned by the Scots Army, some of the effigies of Bishops defaced and near a hundred gravestones deprived of their Brasses by the sacrilegious hands of those Rebels'. This was clearly wrong as the city was successfully defended by the royalists and it seems most likely that the 'sacrilegious hands' were those of the desperate defenders. Indeed, Rawlinson reluctantly acknowledges that 'In the general Havock, this Church did not entirely escape, but I think met with better Quarter from Scottish covenanters, than most of our Cathedrals'.[21] The only casualty of the era was the chapter house, 'being beat down in the Rebellion' and subsequently stripped of its remaining lead by Colonel Birch to make the castle habitable (plate IIIb).[22]

At the Restoration one of the first acts of the claviger of the newly established cathedral chapter was to spend £3 15s. 0d. 'for getting and carrying records from London', whilst Dr Benson, the master of the fabric, made an appeal to the local gentry to support the restoration of the fabric.[23] He also persuaded the dean and canons 'considering the present ruines and wants of the said Cathedral Church' to contribute to the fund.[24] Dr Benson provided an important element of continuity – as a minor canon he had signed the last fabric accounts in the 1640s. His first account after the Restoration was a model of good order; the many minor rents for properties around the churchyard are carefully recorded and correspond almost exactly with the last account of 1645. Benson's talent for fundraising is demonstrated in the section headed 'Extraordinary Receipts', where five new canons paid £5 each to the fabric on admission to the cathedral and several new appointments to livings in the diocese 'granted by the King' were encouraged to make contributions up to £25. From this source alone Benson augmented the fund by £124 4s. 3d. Finally, there was an important windfall of £80 received as a fine for the renewal of a lease for Cannwood.[25] Altogether, Benson raised £235 17s. 1d. but in this account spent £295 15s. 8d. As the deficit is not carried forward, it seems the master of the fabric put his hand in his own pocket. This is confirmed in 1664 when the chapter reimbursed him with a £120 grant for his trouble.[26] Unfortunately the expenditure in 1660–61 is not itemised but the sum was no doubt sufficient to expunge the odour of puritanism from the cathedral and begin to put the fabric in good order.

21. R. Rawlinson, *The History and Antiquities of the City and Cathedral-Church of Hereford* (London, 1717), pp. vii, 4. In 1722 Elizabeth Barlow was accused of stealing brasses from the cathedral, W. D. Macray, *Catalogue and Index to MS Papers etc. from the Municipal Archives of the City of Hereford* (Hereford, 1894), p. 8.

22. Webb, *Memorials*, ii, p. 421; J. Price, *An Historical Account of the City of Hereford* (Hereford, 1796), p. 135.

23. HCA, R 610.

24. HCA, 7031/3, p. 233.

25. HCA, 2379.

26. HCA, R 610.

During the next two years – 1661–62 and 1662–63 – expenditure was reduced to £53 and £57 respectively, but rose soon after this as the gifts from the gentry began to be credited to the accounts. Those for 1664–65 show £180 from this source, including £100 from Viscount Scudamore, £50 from the bishop, £15 from John Kyrle and several smaller gifts from the minor gentry and clergy of the county.[27] Further contributions are credited to the accounts during the following years and it seems from a small payment to the 'collectors of money' in Worcester that the appeal went beyond the diocese. Viscount Scudamore, who was also high steward of the cathedral, provided a gift of timber in 1665.[28] Once again the exact character of the work is tantalisingly obscure but the climax of the restoration came in 1666 when £470 0s. 4d. was spent upon 'reparations' – a sum not exceeded until the emergency repairs to the west end in the late eighteenth century.[29] Specific items of expenditure included £25 upon 'mending, adorning, colouring and varnishing' the choir; £22 to James Jaggard for glazing and mending the church windows; and a small sum to the carpenter, John Symonds, for 'setting upright ye steeple'.[30] The largest payments were credited to the joiner, Rowland Andrews, who received in all £124 for unspecified work between 1663 and 1666. Andrews was the master of the fellowship of joiners in the city and probably the craftsman principally responsible for restoring the Anglican setting of the choir.[31] At about this time John Aubrey (1626–97), the antiquarian, visited Hereford and admired the intersecting arches – probably in the chancel – which are referred to in his unpublished 'Chronologia Architectonica'.[32] We also have an eyewitness description of the cathedral during this era in Richard Rawlinson who apologises for the deficiencies in his book caused by 'the Scaffold and Disorder the church was in when the survey was first taken at the time it was Beautifying'.[33]

With the emergency over, it seems that some eyes looked enviously at the burgeoning fabric fund, which was frequently £150–200 in credit. Rumours that some of this increment was to be appropriated came to the notice of Bishop Croft, who in a letter to chapter in 1683 warned the chapter about contemplating the alienation of the Shinfield and Swallowfield fines 'from ancient use to your own private profits'. It would, he said, be 'little better than sacrilege'. The warning seems to have had the desired effect, although occasionally the claviger can be seen dipping into the fabric fund for his general expenses.[34]

From the 1680s onwards it is possible to identify a small group of craftsmen

27. HCA, 2380–82.
28. HCA, 2384, R 610.
29. HCA, R 610.
30. HCA, R 610.
31. HRO, transcripts of city archives, sacks 24–27, fol. 289.
32. T. Cocke, 'Rediscovery of the Romanesque', *English Romanesque Art, 1066–1200* (London, 1994), p. 361.
33. Rawlinson, *History and Antiquities*, p. 4.
34. HCA, 7031/3, pp. 411–12.

who were constantly employed upon routine work around the cathedral. They were under the direction of John Silvester the sexton, a carpenter and joiner by trade.[35] In an informal sense, Silvester was the surveyor of the fabric, the eyes and ears of the master of the fabric to whom the chapter addressed its more general concern for the structure of the cathedral. In November 1697 Dr William Johnson, archdeacon as well as master of the fabric, was instructed to 'take care to repair the roof over the Quire'. The work was duly carried out by the church plumber, William Griffiths, who received £60 9s. 7d. Two years later 'the Rodd Isle and Great Cloyster' were to be viewed and similarly repaired and in 1704 it was the turn of the 'Australis partis' (southern part – south transept?). The Laudian statutes of 1636 had urged the master of the fabric to take care that the 'arches, walls and windows, and the whole church be cleaned annually'. In this period this was the annual work of Barnaby Sayse. For example, in 1704 he was paid £2 10s. 0d for 'sweeping and cleaning the Roofe of the church and walls'.[36] Between 1706 and 1736 three successive deans – Tyler, Clavering and Harris – were concurrently bishops of Llandaff. Their absence provided an opportunity for the energetic bishop, Philip Bisse (1713–21), to improve rather than simply maintain the cathedral. Setting aside the necessary work at the Restoration, this was the first initiative in this direction since the early sixteenth century. The new bishop was a cultivated man of some discernment, a fellow of the Royal Society and well connected at court.[37] His refined taste can be admired in the great hall of the palace, which, if not in detail, at least in substance, is essentially Bisse's creation. While his energy is also reflected in the series of acts concerning the improvement of the canonical houses in the Close, it was the cathedral church which received Bisse's closest attention. At the bishop's first visitation in 1713 a new set of orders were drafted to clarify the earlier statutes. Two of these deal directly with the fabric and reflect the bishop's eagerness to improve the cathedral and, conversely, the chapter's reluctance to carry the expenditure. Nos 8 and 9 state: 'That no officer or workman shall make any repairs or provide any materials for the church without order and direction of the Hebdomadary or the Master of the Fabrick'; and 'that the Master of the Fabrick shall not undertake any unnecessary reparation, the chardg of which shall exceed the sum of £10 without first acquainting the Chapter with the same and having their consent thereto'.[38]

Large bills soon followed. Edward Davies and James Pearce were ordered in 1713 to whitewash the body and the aisles of the church as well as the library,

35. *TWNFC*, 11 (1884), pp. 161–64. John Silvester and Rowland Andrews made the case for the new organ in 1686. See W. Shaw, *Organists and Organs of Hereford Cathedral* (Hereford, 1976), p. 36.

36. HCA, 7031/3, pp. 517, 527, 556; HCA, 7020/2/1, 1698–99, fabric accounts.

37. A. L. Moir, *The Bishops of Hereford* (Hereford, 1964), pp. 54–56; *DNB* (1975), p. 162.

38. HCA, 7031/4, p. 24.

which cost the chapter £45. Timber was being felled during these years (1713–21) at Cannwood, Ridgehill and the Frith for 'the repair of the Cathedral Church'. Presumably with this work in mind, the chapter formally appointed Samuel Roycroft 'Church carpenter' in 1720. His stay in Hereford was short-lived and he was soon replaced by Thomas Willim, whose contribution to the cathedral was to be much more substantial. Robert Willis believed that Bisse was responsible for the oxeye masonry, which filled the north and south tower arches. Each had a pierced opening at the centre 'in the form of an ancient *vesica piscis*, called by workmen an oxeye' (fig. 40). As there is no sign of expenditure upon this work in the accounts, this rather futile attempt at stabilising the great tower was probably erected at the Restoration. It appears on Browne Willis's plan of 1727.[39]

The chapter acts are silent on the bishop's great work in the choir but the accounts provide some important detail. The years of relative inactivity had produced a handsome surplus on the accounts. The receipts in 1720, including £365 19s. 3d. previously lent to the claviger, came to £460. This healthy situation was aided by £150 fine paid for the Shinfield tithes in 1717 and a gift of £50 from James Brydges, duke of Chandos. Such a gift was unusual in this period and, although its purpose is not specifically revealed, it can only have been directed towards Bisse's new choir. Chandos had close connections with the cathedral. In the 1690s he leased the deanery whilst looking for a *pied à terre* in the county of his birth. He had also recently succeeded Lord Scudamore as high steward of the cathedral.[40]

Chandos, the builder of Cannons, the most prodigious house erected in the early eighteenth century, may well have had some influence upon the choice of John Paty as the craftsman employed by Bisse to provide the new altarpiece for the choir. James Paty (fl. 1721–46) was the senior member of a family of wood and stone carvers who practised in Bristol during the eighteenth century.[41] James and his son Thomas (?) were employed at various times by the architects John Wood and John Strachen who, in their turn, were consulted by Chandos over the development of his property in Bath.[42] This connection would certainly explain how this 'foreign' craftsman appeared in Hereford in 1720.

For £67 2s. 0d. Paty provided a reredos for the cathedral similar to those which exist (or existed) in several Bristol churches such as St Nicholas and St Thomas,

39. R. Willis, *On the Present State of the Cathedral Church of Hereford* (London, 1841), p. 31.

40. C. H. Collins-Baker, *The Life and Circumstances of James Brydges, First Duke of Chandos* (Oxford, 1949), pp. 7, 9, 21, 33, 173, 362 n. 4, 411.

41. For the Paty family see G. Beard, *Craftsmen and Interior Decoration in England, 1660–1820* (Edinburgh, 1981), p. 274; R. Gunnis, *Dictionary of British Sculptors, 1660–1851* (London, 1962), pp. 294–95; W. Ison, *The Georgian Buildings of Bristol* (Bristol, 1952), pp. 39–43.

42. Collins-Baker, *Chandos*, chapter 13.

which may well have been his work.[43] Under a broken pediment supported by twin columns, the centrepiece contained the Ten Commandments painted by a local artist, William Fisher. On either side there were further fluted columns framing empty niches, and above, pedimented tabernacles with two more niches designed for statuary. The fine woodwork continued on either side with pedimented panels which filled the first north and south bays of the choir (fig 70). This was provided by Edward Barrow, a Hereford joiner, who was paid £54. The whole scheme was given unity by being placed upon a boldly panelled dado and plinth. Above the woodwork in the eastern gable of the choir a perpendicular window was flanked with curtains, including tassels, painted on panels in an illusionist fashion. The Laudian altar rails of *c.* 1636 with their turned balusters were allowed to remain, enclosing the setting on three sides.

Nineteenth-century commentators spewed venom upon this 'wretched' composition but in the eighteenth century it was highly praised.[44] Browne Willis, one of the earliest authoritative observers upon cathedrals, described it as 'a most magnificent Altar piece ... one of the stateliest and loftiest in England'.[45] Even John Price, writing in 1795, at the very moment when Richard Gough was articulating his disgust for such additions in the *Gentleman's Magazine*, found the altar-piece 'sumptuous and elegant' (fig. 71).[46]

Bishop Bisse made his choir more cosy by erecting high galleries on the south and north, above the prebendal and choir stalls, which were occupied by the cathedral staff, the households of the canons and the mayor and corporation, who paid the cathedral carpenter Thomas Willim £21 9s. 4d. for their gallery in 1724.[47] Westwards the choir extended under the tower, terminating in a massive late fourteenth-century stone screen which stretched between the western piers of the crossing and upon which stood the organ. The doors beneath were renewed by Willim in 1726 and the whole area of the choir was repaved by Batty Edwards for £21 9s. 4d. The comfort of the new choir soon attracted the parishioners of St John, who petitioned the dean and chapter to be allowed to move their services from the north transept to the new altar. This was agreed as long as they paid the sexton ten shillings a year 'for the more than ordinary trouble he will have in cleaning the Chore'. Bisse had thus created an oasis of classical order in the heart of the Gothic cathedral.

Bisse set a good example which was followed by the dean and chapter. But improvements were expensive and in 1731 the first of many loans was raised on the credit of the Shinfield tithes – £100 was borrowed from Thomas Smith a

43. C. F. W. Dening, *The Eighteenth-Century Arch-itecture of Bristol* (Bristol, 1923), pp. 126–31.
44. Myles, *Cottingham*, p. 100.

45. Willis, *Survey of the Cathedrals*, pp. 505, 530.
46. Price, *Historical Account of the City of Here-ford*, p. 91.

Fig. 70. Bishop Bisse's choir panelling: illustration possibly from a sale catalogue of *c.* 1840. (Hereford City Library, Pilley Collection, 2267, p. 12.)

Fig. 71. The east end of the choir *c.* 1841, showing Bishop Bisse's altarpiece of 1721 and the stained glass window of 1823 portraying Benjamin West's *The Last Supper.* J. Merewether, *A Statement of the Condition and Circumstances of the Cathedral Church of Hereford* (Hereford, 1842). (HCL, neg. 138.)

local mercer at 5 per cent. The fabric accounts reflect greater activity in all parts
of the cathedral with a greater proportion of income being devoted to substantial
repairs. The lead and timber spire on the central tower was probably erected in
the fifteenth century but it had received little attention before 1726 when a Mr
Merrick, an unknown surveyor, was paid two guineas for 'drawing a model of
the spire'. During the next four years carpenters, masons and, especially, plumbers
and smiths received regular payments for 'work upon the steeple'. The timber
sub-structure was repaired, new laths were fixed and great quantities of lead were
laid upon the frame. In all, two plumbers, William Griffiths and Richard Cubberley,
were paid the large sum of £213 – including materials and labour. The immense
weight of the new lead must have added considerably to the burden carried by
the fragile tower: the spire itself was 'extremely crooked' when Francis Grose
(1731–91), the antiquarian, viewed it from Castle Green in 1774.[48] The 1730s also
saw a concentrated campaign to repair the windows of the cathedral. Several
unspecified windows were repainted in 1734 and reglazed by William Reese in
1736. Reese was designated 'church plumber' and worked on the fabric for the
next forty-eight years.[49] On 7 August 1735 the chapter agreed with:

> Avery Hunt of Ross for the taking down of the great window at the west
> end of the church and setting up a new one in its place and stead thereof and
> did empower Mr Richard Pyle their Chapter Clerk to article with him in
> writing for the work, in the manner and according to the measures and
> propositions of severall parts or materials thereof, which were now agreed upon
> between him and the Chapter.[50]

Hunt was an iron founder and recommended a cast iron window. This was
discovered ready to be erected by Browne Willis on a visit to the cathedral. He
claimed he persuaded the dean and chapter to set this aside and repair the window
in stone.[51] As a result they called upon the services of Francis Smith of Warwick,
the most celebrated architect practising in the midlands at this date. He was
pre-eminently a country house builder but was also experienced as a surveyor of
ecclesiastical fabric and had been consulted by the chapter of Lichfield Cathedral
between 1715 and 1721. He had given advice on the repair of the south transept
of Worcester Cathedral in 1725 and, rather conveniently, in 1735 was remodelling
the nave of Monmouth church.[52]

47. HRO, Hereford City Council Minute
Book, 1708–53, fol. 463.

48. G. M. Hills, 'The Architectural History of
Hereford Cathedral', *Journal of the British
Archaeological Association*, 27 (1871), pp. 496–
513, at 509.

49. HRO, Hereford City Council Minute
Book, 1696–1736, fol. 590; obituary in
Hereford Journal, 12 April 1781.

50. HCA, 7031/4, p. 164.

51. Hills, 'Architectural History', p. 508.

52. H. Colvin, *A Biographical Dictionary of British*

Smith's schedule of work for the west window included taking out and reusing the old stone work, reglazing with 607 feet of glass in lead squares braced by three-quarter inch thick iron bars (fig. 72). There was no mention of the medieval coloured glass but the account of William Reese, the glazier, allows him interest on the glass which the chapter had reserved for themselves. This may suggest that the old glass, perhaps traditionally the property of the glazier, was being kept by the dean and chapter. Smith's estimate for the work 'for pulling down and rebuilding the large window at the west end of collegiate church at Hereford' came to £96 9s. 10d.[53] The fabric accounts confirm this expenditure in payment of Hunt, Reese and the carpenter Thomas Hope who provided the props and the scaffolding. Smith also examined the roof of the north aisle and found it moving away from the wall of the nave. This required remedial work by Thomas Hope and Richard Cubberley, the plumber, in 1736–37. The report makes no mention of the intrinsic weaknesses of the tower and the west

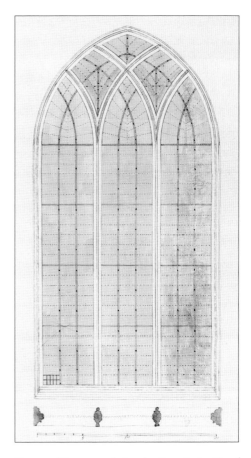

Fig. 72. The 1735 design by Francis Smith of Warwick for a new west window with cast iron tracery. (HCA, 3982.)

end. He assumed, perhaps, that by strengthening the stone tracery with iron bars, the west window would provide a better brace for the whole structure.[54]

The restoration work of the 1730s had a detrimental affect upon the fabric account which only just remained in credit by 4s. 6d. in 1738. The chapter had already placed a brake upon repairs, ordering in the previous June 'that the workmen

Architects, 1600–1840 (3rd edn, London, 1995), pp. 885–86; Worcester Cathedral Library, Treasurer's Book, 1725.

53. HCA, 3982/1.
54. An engraved print of the west front of the cathedral drawn by a local artist, James Wathen, as the first of a set 'celebrating' the fall in 1786 (fig. 37), shows the grill-like effect of the new tracery and contrasts with earlier engravings of the west front, e.g. Willis, *Survey of the Cathedrals* (1727).

shall proceed no further this Summer on the repairs of the North Cross Isle of the church, but only to cover and make good so much of it as has already been uncovered and to keep the rest of it dry'. In 1738 £250 was borrowed for 'the use of the church' and old sources of income were reviewed. The fabric account once again drifted into deficit between 1743 and 1746. It was balanced again between 1747 and 1750 but in debt between 1751 and 1753. Further sums were borrowed from St Katherine's Hospital, Ledbury, which was repaid from the fine of the Shinfield tithes when this was received in 1760. The effect of this mid century retrenchment was severely to restrict work upon the fabric, so that in the 1740s and 1750s less was spent upon the cathedral than in the previous two decades.[55]

The chapter, which had hitherto only paid spasmodic attention to the fabric at its meetings, now issued a series of directives which tightened up the procedure for carrying out routine work. In 1752 'alterations and repairs intended to be made at the west end of this Cathedral Church be from time to time carried out under the direction of the Master of the Fabric according to the Plan and in a manner approved and agreed by the Chapter'. In the event two pinnacles were replaced. Equally unnecessary, perhaps, was the £55 9s. 3d. spent in 1752 on gilding and repainting Bisse's choir. The work was carried out by Daniel Mansfield, possibly the son of the royal plasterer, Isaac Mansfield.[56]

A further act of 1753 restricted the initiative of the craftsmen even more severely. It was ordered that:

all orders to be given to workmen employed in work in and about the Fabrick shall be putt in writing and signed by the Residentiary or Master of the Fabrick and delivered to the Surveyor of the Fabrick Works, before such work shall be entered upon or taken in hand. In which orders shall be particularly expressed what work is to be done in what part of the Fabrick and the said Surveyor is hereby ordered to keep and preserve all such written orders safe, to be returned to the said Claviger or Master of the Fabrick when they or either of them shall call upon him for the same. And to take all due care that this order be in all respects strictly observed and complyd with according to the true intent and meaning thereof.[57]

There were certain difficulties in complying with this directive as the claviger and

---

55. The 1750s and 1760s saw a general decline in building activity throughout England. For Worcester see D. White-head, 'Urban Renewal and Suburban Growth: The Shaping of Georgian Worcester', *Worcester Historical Society* *Occasional Publications*, 5 (1989), pp. 32–33.

56. For Isaac and Samuel Mansfield (but no sign of Daniel) see Beard, *Craftsmen and Interior Decoration*, p. 270.

57. HCA, 7031/4, p. 269.

master of the fabric were both career churchmen and often absent from Hereford; whilst the surveyor, despite his professional title, was not always a craftsman and frequently just one of the cathedral staff whose basic qualification seems to have been that he was on the spot. Earlier in the period the surveyor was usually one of the sextons. John Silvester was well qualified as both a surveyor and a craftsman but Richard Adams, who figures prominently in the 1730s and 1740s, and the cathedral lecturer, Mr Wishaw, who acted in a similar capacity, seem to have been neither. Similarly John Morgan, who was chosen in 1759 as surveyor 'in the room of the said James Rawlinson deceased', remains an anonymous figure. This dangerous dichotomy between amateur surveyor and skilled craftsmen led to a serious situation in 1761 when:

> James Garbett the Church Carpenter having without order taken upon him to repair and amend the work about the Bells which not right understanding he has actually spoiled and thereby putt the Master of the Fabrick to a great and unnecessary Expense.[58]

Garbett was discharged of his office of church carpenter. As he had worked at the cathedral since 1742 and was replaced by Philip Evans, a craftsman with no previous track record in Hereford, this must have further diminished the effectiveness of the cathedral workforce. Most of Evans's time, it seems, was spent supervising the felling and sale of timber from the chapter's woods rather than working upon the cathedral, with the result that very little was done to the fabric during the 1750s and 1760s.

In 1762 Richard Hawkins, the mason, was paid the large sum of £77 8s. 10d. for work in the south-west cloister. The sources are not very explicit but he was paid for rebuilding two buttresses, taking down the cross in the centre of Lady arbour and providing an unspecified amount of stone from his quarry at Withington. The work represented the demolition of the western range of the south-west cloister and the construction of a purpose-built schoolroom which doubled as a concert hall during the music festivals. Most of the work was paid for by public subscription but the chapter was left with the problem of patching up the rest of the cloister 'now in danger of falling'. This was done 'forthwith', hence Hawkins's bill, but within a few months the full implications of the alterations became apparent. It was ordered, on 19 April 1763, 'That the north west end of the Church be supported by some temporary prop till the chapter can be advised what will be the best methods of compleating the effectual reparation thereof'. Rather late in the day, it seems, the chapter realised that the cloister provided a prop for

58. Ibid., p. 401.

the west end.[59] An engraving made a little later by the local artist, James Wathen, shows a sinister crack at the north-west corner of the west front, produced, no doubt, as the masonry began to slump towards the south west (fig. 37).[60]

Temporary wooden props were provided by Philip Evans from the woods at Pipe but these were replaced in May 1763 with some buttresses 'in a manner expressed in the estimate delivered by the mason', Richard Hawkins. Four months later the problem thrust itself forward again and a different solution was suggested by the church mason, who submitted an estimate 'of the charge of building a wall inside the west end of the Church over the little door there for securing the Building'. As it turned out, this was the last task carried out by Hawkins and in December 1764 he was ordered to surrender the lease to Caplar quarry. He and his son had been caught red-handed raising 'a large quantity of stone' for their own use. William Hergest replaced him at the cathedral but he was not formally appointed church mason until 1768. He was clearly related to John Hergest who had been active around the fabric between 1719 and 1731. The chapter was also unfortunate in losing its ironmonger, Michael Brampton, who 'left off business' in November 1766. Thus the guardianship of the cathedral in these last crucial decades was, to begin with, in the hands of a relatively inexperienced group of craftsmen.

Bishop James Beauclerk made a visitation in 1765–66. Suspecting, perhaps, that the fabric fund was being mishandled, he urged the dean and chapter to be more diligent in their accounting and to use the rents and fines, especially from Shinfield and Swallowfield, 'wholly upon the fabric'. He also suggested that £100 should be raised on the credit of the leases and invested in stock presumably to establish a more up-to-date endowment. Nevertheless, he supported the ancient practice of the chapter dividing the fines from the properties not specifically reserved for the fabric between themselves at the annual audit. He even thought that the Shinfield and Swallowfield fines could be directed elsewhere if 'some urgent cause shall happen'.[61]

The fabric account soon began to display a healthier balance and the chapter decided to embellish Bisse's choir. Thomas Symonds, a mason whose yard adjoined the churchyard, was invited to provide an estimate for a new floor of 'white stone dotted with black marble'. The work was duly completed in 1774 and cost £92.

59. Canon Clutton, who campaigned against Dean Merewether's alterations to the fabric in the 1830s drew an unflattering parallel between the dean's probing and stripping, and 'the nasty and incautious meddling with walls and pillars' which precipitated the fall in 1786. HCA, 7031/19, 31 May 1837.

60. See note 54 above.
61. HCA, 7031/4: the record of the visitation is at the back of the volume. The chapter's finances during the last decade before the fall are explored by B. Trueman, 'The Administration of Hereford Cathedral, 1776–1786', *FHC*, 42 (1976), pp. 26–36.

Rather generously, the chapter gave Symonds an extra £10 over and above his bill 'on account of the loss he sustained in doing that work'. Symonds' father had for many years been the churchyard 'pitcher', but the son was a skilled statuary whose marble monuments, sometimes enhanced with portrait medallions, as at Sellack, can be seen in churches throughout the county.[62]

The lack of a qualified surveyor began to trouble the dean and chapter and in November 1775 they decided to seek 'the opinion of the most eminent Architect ... respecting the state of the West Tower and other parts of the Cathedral'.[63] In the accounts, James Pears received £21 6s. 0d. for 'surveying the fabric'. Pears was by no stretch of the imagination an 'eminent Architect'. He was an Oxford builder who knew his way around ancient structures and was probably invited to Hereford by Dean Wetherell, master of University College. He was later well known to James Wyatt, executing his alterations to New College between 1789 and 1793, but in 1776 he was relatively unknown in Oxford and had only become a freeman of the city in that year.[64] The chapter was clearly seeking inexpensive advice.

Sadly, his report does not survive, but from the act book and the accounts we can guess at his recommendations. The lack of a qualified surveyor obviously concerned him and on 4 September 1777 the act book records:

> Thomas Symonds be appointed Surveyor of the Fabric with an annual salary of £3 6s. 8d. in recompense for his trouble in frequently surveying the same, and that he have power from time to time to order the necessary repairs to be done and lay out a sum not exceeding £2 for which he is to account regularly at the next quarterly chapter, and to make a report of the State of the Fabrick at the general chapter. All bills respecting reparations to be signed by the said Surveyor.[65]

In Symonds the chapter probably got the most qualified local advice available at the time. His craft as a statuary provided him with the design skills necessary to launch a career as an architect and surveyor, a path followed by many provincial stone carvers in the eighteenth century. In 1775 he is to be found acting as clerk of the works for Richard Payne Knight at Downton Castle and major schemes were to follow at the county gaol, the infirmary, Allensmore Court and The Lodge, near Ludlow.[66] Symonds, presumably following the recommendations of Pears, collected his craftsmen in 1776, erected scaffold and partitioned off the west end of the cathedral. Large bills were paid to Philip Evans (£15 9s. 0d.), William Hergest (£33 5s. 6d.), Phillip Williams, the new smith (£50) and William Parker

62. Gunnis, *Dictionary of Sculptors*, p. 379.
63. HCA, 7031/5, p. 134.
64. Colvin, *Biographical Dictionary*, p. 746.
65. HCA, 7031/5, p. 154.

66. Colvin, *Biographical Dictionary*, p. 945–46. See also *Country Life*, 12 January 1989, p. 112, and 21 October 1989, pp. 210–12.

(£100 6s. 1d.). Ten guineas were also credited to Symonds for 'his extraordinary trouble in and about the reparation of the Cathedral'. William Parker was a significant addition to the team as he had also made the transition from artisan to architect and was the surveyor to the Hereford Improvement Commission.[67]

According to the act book, earlier in 1777 Symonds had also raised scaffold to 'repair the Pannels of the Groins of the Roof of the Nave'. In the following spring he delivered a 'memorial of repairs necessary to be done to the West Tower', but time passed and it was not until 1781 that the chapter made a determined effort to save it. In August workmen were ordered to raise 'not less than 200 tons' of stone at Caplar quarry. This cost £216 6s. 0d. excluding £49 9s. 0d. for Mr Pearce, the barge owner, for transport up the Wye to Hereford. Francis Thomas was instructed to fell trees at Ridge Hill and Symonds presented his second memorandum. He was directed in November 1781 'to repair the Tower at the West End of the Church agreeably to the Plan exhibited by him at an expense not exceeding £200 exclusive of Iron Work and the original price of Stone at the Quarry'. It seems, according to Garbett, that Symonds completed the work begun by Hawkins in 1777, underfilling the aisle arcades nearest the west end, tying in the new stones with iron clamps and providing the sort of support the west tower should have been given in the fourteenth century. This of course did not go to the root of the problem: the lateral pressure being exerted by the central tower. With the benefit of hindsight Garbett thought that new buttresses, outside the cathedral, would have been more suitable. He decided that Symonds was 'injudicious and unskilful'.[68] Disbursements in the fabric fund achieve an all time record in the next five years: 1781–82, £414; 1782–83, £244; 1783–84, £328; 1784–85, £510; and 1785–86, £481. Many more workmen were now involved and substantial payments were made to William Williams, the smith, newly appointed in 1781. The dean and chapter seem to have been pleased with its surveyor's endeavours and in 1783 he received an ex gratia payment of £18 7s. 0d. 'for superintending the work at the West End of the Church'.

The accounts suggest that everything that could humanly be done to secure the tower had been done. In September 1783 all discussion of the fabric disappears from the act book and for two and a half years discussion focused upon the routine management of the cathedral – appointments, services, the choir, leases. There was an eerie silence almost as if the chapter felt that the future of the tower was firmly in the hands of the Almighty. Indeed, the silence continued even after Easter Monday, 17 April 1786, when it all came crashing down. It was only broken on

67. HRO, Guildhall Collection, 1/550, Improvement Commissioners' Minute Book; Hereford City Library, pamphlets 34, F200; *Hereford Journal*, 29 August 1782

68. Garbett, *Brief Enquiry*, p. 19.

13 June when the church carpenter was asked to erect 'a screen at the west end of the Choir in order that the choir service may be renewed'.

The antiquarian John Britton believed 'the fall of the western end of Hereford Cathedral is the most remarkable event of modern times in the history of English Cathedrals'.[69] The event was first presented to the world by local artist James Wathen, who provided a rough sketch for the *Gentleman's Magazine*, and later the sublime views of the shattered nave by Wathen and Thomas Hearne were widely circulated (figs 73, 38, 160). John Byng visited Hereford about a month later and had no hesitation in attributing the blame to 'the woeful idleness and neglect of the canons of the see'. Soon the *Gentleman's Magazine* was railing against 'the barbarous indolence of the chapter'.[70]

To a degree the blame was well placed. The fabric fund was regularly in deficit in the decades before the fall, even though the general income from the chapter estates was increasing. The real problem lay, however, with the Laudian statutes which made no provision for the fundamental weaknesses of the cathedral structure which had been apparent for centuries.[71] The chapter was not inactive and the resident canon immediately organised thirty labourers to sort out the stone, guard the lead and seal off the choir, where services for the parish of St John were recommenced in June. Architects of 'character and ability' were already being consulted with instructions to rebuild 'instead of a tower, a west end which is to correspond with the stile of the church and to be nearly the same as the original west end before the tower was added to the church'. Already the decision had been taken to reduce the aisles of the church to make the building 'more uniform than when the tower was standing'.[72]

Anthony Keck, a local architect with an extensive country house practice in Herefordshire and Gloucestershire, was the first on the scene, but his small fee of eight guineas suggests that he recognised the project was beyond his competence.[73] In the summer Thomas Hardwick, who was supervising the rebuilding of the All Saints' church spire at the other end of Broad Street, was also paid £19 2s. 6d. for a survey but he too backed away. However, his contractor at All Saints, Richard Dyche of Stratford, Essex, had more confidence and produced detailed plans, elevations and an estimate of £15,000 for the new west end.[74]

69. J. Britton, *The History and Antiquities of the Cathedral Church of Hereford* (London, 1831), p. 46.
70. G. L. Gomme, ed., *The Gentleman's Magazine Library* (London, 1894), p. 181; C. B. Andrews, ed., *The Torrington Diaries* (4 vols, London, 1934–38), i, p. 314.
71. Trueman, 'The Administration of Hereford

Cathedral, 1776–1786', pp. 33–34.
72. HCA, 7031/5, fos 239, 242.
73. Colvin, *Biographical Dictionary*, pp. 569–70; HCA, 7031/5, fol. 241 and 5695/10.
74. Colvin, *Biographical Dictionary*, pp. 458–60; HCA, 7020/2/2, p. 195; *Hereford Journal*, 28 September 1786; HCA, 5695/30–31.

Fig. 73. View of the ruined west end of Hereford Cathedral 'as it appeared in 1786 and 1788', drawn by James Wathen.

Dyche's self-assurance contrasted with the reticence of two experienced architects emphasises the novelty of the situation. Hitherto, the cathedral had been maintained by a group of local artisans, under the supervision of the surveyor of the fabric – generally a more superior artisan – with the occasional intervention of a national architect or mason for a specific problem. The surveyor, Thomas Symonds, had been asked to resign, and therefore the guiding hand of the man most familiar with the quirks of the cathedral had been removed. Moreover, educated opinion in late Georgian England was becoming increasingly self-conscious about the nation's 'ancient edifices'. This was moulded by vigorous preservationists like John Carter and Richard Gough, who corresponded via the *Gentleman's Magazine*. Keck and Hardwick, it seems, sensed the dangers whilst Dyche, an artisan, ignored them and was ready to get on with the job.[75]

The dean and chapter was reluctant to trust an untried craftsman and haggled over Dyche's fee of £172 4s. 3d. Bishop Beauclerk also held up progress. He was

75. J. M. Frew, 'Richard Gough, James Wyatt and Late Eighteenth-Century Preservation', *Journal of the Society of Architectural Historians*, 38 (1979), pp. 366–74; J. Mordaunt Crook, *John Carter and the Mind of the Gothic Revival* (London, 1995).

unhappy about the chapter's assumption that the nave should be shortened; he asked for an opportunity to examine the fabric accounts and hesitated about giving his backing to a public subscription.[76] The deadlock was broken by his death in November 1787 and the appointment of John Butler as bishop in February 1788. Since 1777 he had been bishop of Oxford where the dean of Hereford, Nathan Wetherell, was master of University College. Oxford craftsmen had appeared in Hereford in the past and with the new bishop came James Wyatt, already well respected for his work on several Oxford colleges. Moreover, he was also surveyor of the fabric at Westminster Abbey and already involved, on paper at least, with major work at Lichfield and Salisbury Cathedrals. He was one of the most prominent Gothic architects of his day and very well qualified to meet the challenges at Hereford.[77]

His first survey was presented on 2 June 1788. As far as possible, he hoped to preserve the major part of the nave by supporting it with external flying buttresses. This was necessary because the key source of weakness in the cathedral was, as Wyatt recognised, the central tower, which was exerting lateral pressure upon all the other parts of the fabric, particularly the nave, pushing all its piers out of vertical. It seemed that the Romanesque triforium was to be saved. Work finally began on 2 September 1788, when Bishop Butler laid the foundation stone.[78]

Wyatt's modest estimate was £6500, which clearly indicated that he intended to 'patch and mend'. Work progressed along these lines until February 1790, when 'several yards' of the roof collapsed, killing at least two workmen. The result seems to have been a reappraisal of the contract. A new memorandum speaks of taking down 'the present Groins as far as the organ' and rebuilding 'the side walls which are now standing as well as those which are already down'. A decision had also been taken by the dean and chapter completely to reroof the cathedral in slate, lowering the pitch of the roof and repairing the decayed parapet walls. In the nave new vaults were to be made in lath and plaster, fixed to a wych elm frame. Wyatt's timber roof survives today and provides an efficient but lightweight brace for the structure, which held the central tower firm and prevented further subsidence (fig. 74). As an additional prop, flying buttresses were provided for the choir, Lady chapel and south transept.[79]

At Salisbury and Lichfield Wyatt, with the encouragement of the deans and chapters, lengthened the choir by removing the altar-piece and putting an arch

76. HCA, 7031/5, fos 246–48.
77. HCA, 5695/1; Moir, *The Bishops of Here-ford*, p. 59; A. L. Moir, *The Deans of Hereford* (Hereford, 1968), pp. 45–47; Colvin, *Dictionary*, pp. 1107–21; Frew, 'Richard Gough', pp. 368–69.
78. HCA, 5695/1–3, reprinted by A. J. Winnington Ingram, 'The Rebuilding of Hereford Cathedral, 1786–1796', *TWNFC*, 34 (1954), pp. 51–53.
79. *Hereford Journal*, 3 February 1790; R. Willis, *Report of a Survey of the Dilapidated Portions of Hereford Cathedral in the Year 1841* (London, 1842), p. 13.

Fig. 74. The south aisle of the nave showing Wyatt's plaster vault.

under the choir window. Something similar, according to the local antiquarian Garbett, was proposed at Hereford but never undertaken, presumably because Wyatt realised the importance of the retrochoir wall as a further support for the tower. Iron clamps were placed around the crossing piers high up in the tower and clustered shafts added both strength and beauty to the nave piers. Finally, the leaden spire and two stair turrets at the angles of the tower were removed and replaced with battlements.[80]

By this work Wyatt secured Hereford Cathedral for nearly half a century. When the scholar and structural engineer, Robert Willis, surveyed the fabric in 1841, he found 'scarcely a vertical wall or pier in the whole building [except] the new work of Mr Wyatt [which] remains perfectly upright'.[81] Local commentators were generally complimentary about the work. For the *Hereford Journal* it was a 'building of elegant simplicity' while John Duncumb felt that 'Mr Wyatt has perhaps never been under the necessity of completing so extensive an undertaking at so limited an expense'. They generally liked the new west front and were excited by the prospect of William Eginton's new stained glass window, for which a subscription had been raised from the local gentry.[82] For Richard Gough and John Carter, however, it was 'poor, meaningless, insipid and shallow', a wretched piece of Batty Langley's perverse Gothic. They did not appreciate its picturesque qualities and cried out for an archaeological reproduction.[83] Less ardent commentators recognised that it had something of the west front of Winchester, with quotations from the other pointed parts of Hereford (fig. 75). It did indeed correspond with much of the 'stile' of

80. J. Frew, 'James Wyatt's Choir Screen at Salisbury Cathedral Reconsidered', *Architectural History*, 27 (1984), p. 482; Garbett, *Brief Enquiry*, pp. 63–65.

81. Willis, *Report of a Survey*, p. 6.

82. Price, *Historical Account*, p. 89; J. Duncumb, *Collections Towards the History and Antiquities of the County of Hereford* (8 vols, Hereford and London, 1804–1915), i, pp. 529–30.

83. Frew, 'Richard Gough', p. 373.

Fig. 75. View of the cathedral from the south west *c.* 1840, showing Wyatt's west front and the scars on the tower created by lowering the roof. (HCL, B.3.50.)

the existing church, which externally, at least, was pointed and not Romanesque. It worked well at a distance and, later, the basic ingredients were combined to make a forceful entrance at Fonthill. Garbett, writing in 1827, still found it 'a well proportioned and graceful composition', but four years later John Britton refused to include a view of it in his *The History and Antiquities of the Cathedral Church of Hereford*, using in its place Hearne's print of the ruined nave to remind his readers of the perfidy of James Wyatt.[84] Britton railed against Wyatt's workmanship in the nave, its 'flimsy columns, poor mean mouldings, all the dressings equally insipid and wholly discordant to the original work'.[85] He wondered why Wyatt had not rebuilt 'in conformity with the old work'. Unlike the local observer Garbett, he conveniently forgot that the Romanesque clerestory had already been destroyed by the introduction of Gothic lights (fig. 135). The Romanesque work

84. W. Rees, *The Hereford Guide* (Hereford, 1827), p. 141; Garbett, *Brief Enquiry*, p. 22; Hereford City Library, FLC, 726.6, Thomas Garbett's letters to John Britton, August to October 1728.

85. Britton, *Hereford Cathedral*, pp. 37, 45.

Fig. 76. View of the cathedral from the north east in 1833, showing Wyatt's battlements on the Lady chapel and north transept, also the scars on the tower. (HCL, B.4.147.)

on the west front had also been diluted long before the fall; indeed, the 'esteemed' west window was a reconstruction of 1736.[86] As Wyatt's work continued to be grossly denigrated by the purists, Garbett's appreciation of the restored nave, 'the magnitude of the work, the chastity of its style and the harmony and proportion of its several parts', was ignored and forgotten.[87]

Even Garbett, however, found it difficult to excuse the alterations to the cathedral's roof-scape and the imposition of a uniform battlemented parapet, which led to the destruction of a great deal of significant surface detail (fig. 76). A window disappeared in the gable of the south transept; drip stones and side mouldings were erased; pinnacles, clustered columns and ancient carved work were removed from the Lady chapel. Finally, the lowering of the roof to take slate left several prominent scars on the four sides of the tower which were visible for several decades (figs 75, 76).[88] In mitigation, Willis suggested that the choir gable had probably been already ruinous before Wyatt started work. Moreover, Wyatt's preference for battlements was very much in tune with contemporary views. No less an authority

86. D. Whitehead, 'A Goth among the Greeks: The Architecture of Hereford Cathedral in the Eighteenth Century',

FHC, 57 (1991), pp. 30–31.
87. Garbett, *Brief Enquiry*, pp. 21, 23.
88. Ibid., pp. 24–25, 28.

than Uvedale Price of Foxley, a subscriber to the restoration, noted in one of his *Essays* the many picturesque advantages of a battlemented tower.[89]

Rightly or wrongly, Wyatt had very little control over the day to day supervision of the project, which was in the hands of his collaborator, Joseph Potter of Lichfield. As the clerk of the works, Potter was responsible for the many minor decisions which had to be taken as the work progressed. Wyatt's last recorded appearance in the archive is January 1791. After that date he received infrequent payments being still owed £400 when he died in 1813.[90] If Potter's men were allowed to 'gouge rather than nibble', this was partly the fault of the dean and chapter, who failed to appoint a resident surveyor to replace Thomas Symonds. Such an official would have kept an eye on the stained glass, the brasses and monuments which, according to popular fables, were said to have been sold or destroyed, adding further undeserved calumnies to the reputation of James Wyatt.

Notwithstanding Wyatt's work at the cathedral, discriminating visitors were disgusted by the general dereliction of the interior. In 1809 there were 'broken pavements, monuments uncared for, the grand Norman pillars buried in coats of whitewash' (fig. 77). A few years later, in 1813, Malcolm found the presbytery 'defiled with filth', clustered pillars in the north transept broken, the Lady chapel 'little better than a lumber room' and the choir so deranged that it was beyond description.[91] Externally, the pinnacles designed by Wyatt for the tower were still missing and antiquarians with books to illustrate published views with them in place even though this did not occur in reality until 1830. Nevertheless, during the 1820s some work was done. The choir stalls and episcopal throne were stripped of their paint; the Laudian railings were removed from the choir and, after some heart-searching, a new gallery was erected in the north transept for the parishioners of St John's (fig. 40).[92]

The process was accelerated with the arrival of John Merewether as dean in 1832. As an active antiquary, he was not pleased with the state of Hereford Cathedral and inaugurated a wholesale programme of restoration. The process is recorded, stage by stage, in his *Statement of the Condition and Circumstances of the Cathedral Church of Hereford* (1842), which reads like an antiquarian discourse upon the architecture of the cathedral but fails to record the dismay with which his investigations were greeted by the chapter.[93] The chapter acts give a completely

89. Willis, *Report of a Survey*, p. 8.
90. HCA, 5695/110; HCA, 7031/5, fol. 312v.
91. F. E. Gretton, *Memory's Harkback Through Half-a-Century, 1808–1858* (London, 1889), pp. 4–5; P. Malcolm, *An Account of Hereford Cathedral* (Hereford, 1813), pp. 99–103.
92. HCA, 7020/2/3, pp. 27–91, fabric accounts, 1817–30, passim; Garbett, *Brief Enquiry*, pp. 69–71.
93. P. Barrett, 'John Merewether, Dean of Hereford, 1832–50', *FHC*, 43 (1977), pp. 23–39.

Fig. 77. A sketch of the south choir aisle in 1819, showing the pavement made uneven by a multitude of indents. (HCL, B.3.25.)

different impression. At first there was a spirit of cooperation. The Lady arbour was landscaped following the removal of the old school in 1835; the adjoining cloisters were repaired; all the external pinnacles were investigated and strengthened; and the mullions of the great south window were restored. But Merewether's enthusiasm lay with 'the once majestic and beautiful decoration' which he believed lay neglected and hidden behind the eighteenth-century panelling in the choir. He petitioned the chapter in 1835, seeking its support to 'open up the Saxon arch' behind the altar. There was no clear decision but the dean went ahead anyway and was 'charmed by the appearance of a stone apparently forming part of the architrave of an arch, which bore traces of Norman ornaments'. Out of his own pocket, he restored the capitals of the adjoining pillars and hoped that the result would encourage the chapter to support further investigations. He drew attention to the healthy state of the fabric fund, and suggested a public subscription, but the chapter was uninterested.[94] The Georgian chancel that Merewether was dismantling had recently been substantially beautified. Its centrepiece was a representation of Christ carrying the Cross copied from an original in Magdalen College in 1816. Above, masking the east window, was a reproduction in Munich glass of Benjamin West's *Last Supper*, which had cost £2000 in 1823 (fig. 71). The dean left the chapter in no doubt that he intended to remove the 'whole incongruous covering of the east end'.[95]

Canon Clutton, who had held office for many years, was his most outspoken opponent. Notwithstanding the dean's efforts to exclude his statements from the act book, Clutton poured withering scorn upon the dean's 'effusions of taste'. He recorded:

> How astounded some of us were at finding on a sudden part of the cathedral covered with rubbish and the rest with dust and filth, upon a large wall behind the altar being pulled down: the ruinated appearance of which drew this exclamation from a zealous visitor at our music meeting 'What! Are the heathen come into the Lord's inheritance? His holy temple have they defiled and made a heap of stones!'

He remembered how 'the premature fall of the noble tower at the west end [was] caused by hasty and incautious meddling with the walls and pillars' and saw the possibility of 'a similar catastrophe from a similar cause'. But the dean was not at all mortified and with his 'miners' in 1837 changed the location of his campaign. He 'chanced to espy an old doorway in the crypt' and began to excavate in the dark, ten to twelve yards under the pavement of the Lady ante-chapel, almost

94. HCA, 7031/19, chapter acts, 1834–44, pp. 44–45, 56, 62, 70–71, 75–78.

95. Whitehead, 'A Goth among the Greeks', pp. 25–27; Rees, *Hereford Guide*, p. 159.

Fig. 78. The unrestored Lady
chapel. T. Garbett, *A Brief
Enquiry into the Ancient and
Present State of Hereford
Cathedral* (London and
Hereford, 1827). (HCL, B.3.40.)

breaking into the family grave of a 'very respectable residentiary'. Clutton tolerated
'the damp and pestiferous vapours', which made morning prayers disagreeable for
a few winter months but, with the dean absent at court, he blocked up the
'Golgothean nuisance' with brick. Merewether returned, and tried to have the
rebellious canon removed, but the bishop intervened and a temporary truce was
arranged. Clutton died in 1838.[96]

It was the dilapidations of the Lady chapel which provided an issue around which
a new consensus emerged. Philip Hardwick, the architect recently consulted by the
bishop about improvements to the bishop's palace, casually remarked to the dean
in 1840 that 'If you do not take care you will surely have that beautiful building
down' (fig. 78).[97] Cracks were revealed inside and, as a result, the exterior walls
were immediately propped up and the chapter began the laborious task of removing

96. HCA, 7031/19, pp. 105–6, 152, 187–88,
    339–40, 431, 462, 467, 484, 494–95, 498,
    500, chapter acts, 1837–41.

97. J. Merewether, *A Statement of the Condition and
    Circumstances of the Cathedral Church of Here-
    ford* (Hereford, 1842), pp. 6–7, 12, 15–17, 48.

the library to the archive room (fig. 79). An architect was required and in February 1842 'Mr Cottingham Archt' was being consulted about 'the best mode of repairing the window at the east end of the cathedral now much dilapidated [and] furnish a plan for its effectual restoration'. The chapter conceded this and asked for two separate estimates – the first for necessary repairs, the second for further work. The architect was also asked to view the 'necessary repairs' for the window disturbed by Merewether's investigations behind the altar.[98]

All thought of restoration work in the Lady chapel and the choir was abandoned when Cottingham and Merewether climbed into the tower and made an 'absolutely appalling discovery'. At each angle of the tower, below the floor of the bell chamber, there were four apertures, two and a half feet in diameter, running through the walls, admitting light from the exterior. The resulting subsidence had shattered and crushed the surrounding stones, creating other fissures and dislocations. Cottingham, close to tears, warned the dean that the 'majestic tower, might be beyond the power of human skill to save'.[99]

Fig. 79. The Lady chapel east wall propped up at the instigation of Dean Merewether. J. Merewether, *A Statement of the Condition and Circumstances of the Cathedral Church of Hereford* (Hereford, 1842). (HCL, B.3.59.)

Merewether had chosen his man well, for Cottingham was probably the only architect in Britain who could save the church. He was a product of the preservationist lobby, which had so maligned the work of Wyatt. John Carter was an early influence, encouraging the young architect to take a serious interest in Gothic architecture and how it worked. Like Merewether, Cottingham was a

98. HCA, 7031/19, pp. 501, 504, 508, 524, 546.
99. Merewether, *Statement*, pp. 21–22.

member of the Oxford Society for Promoting the Study of Gothic Architecture and he had turned his London house into a museum of medieval antiquities only rivalled by the collection of Samuel Rush Meyrick at Goodrich Court, Herefordshire. Indeed, Meyrick may have played a role in bringing Cottingham to Hereford, although he was also known to Philip Hardwick. His recent works had included stabilising the tower of Rochester Cathedral, a thorough restoration of Magdalen College chapel and a major refurbishment of St Alban's Abbey, which like Hereford had suffered a long period of neglect and dilapidation. Cottingham was also an antiquary, using the opportunities that arose as a church restorer to probe and investigate those nooks and crannies created by post-medieval alterations. Long-forgotten tombs at Rochester and the Temple Church in London were discovered in this way and Cottingham was therefore a man close to the heart of Dean Merewether.[100]

Naturally, there was no opposition from the chapter to the restoration of the tower. The dean provided a series of flattering affidavits from Cottingham's recent employers to vouch for his skill. The architect estimated £5719 would be necessary to rebuild the tower and the dean toured the diocese appealing to the gentry for support. His moving account of the deficiencies of the cathedral fabric formed the basis of *A Statement of the Condition and Circumstances of the Cathedral Church of Hereford* (1842). Encouraged by the bishop, the chapter sought a second opinion on the state of the fabric from the eminent ecclesiologist Professor Robert Willis, who in general confirmed Cottingham's diagnosis but was more restrained in his recommendations. He thought, for example, that it was only necessary to rebuild the two westerly piers of the crossing, and that the other two should be left alone as 'the repairs are of sufficient antiquity to claim respect'. Such thoughts, however, were out of step with Merewether's and Cottingham's aspirations where 'restoration was the grand object to be achieved – not mending and patching, too much of this has indeed already been permitted'. The tower was to be 'the polar star which will guide us in all we have to do'.[101]

Cottingham's contract, which names John Carline of Shrewsbury as the contractor, is dated 12 May 1843. It refers to eighteen drawings, none of which appear to have survived, and reveals in great detail the architect's working methods. Cottingham personally shored up the first pier – the north-west – to demonstrate the techniques to be employed on the others. Every third course of stone was to be cramped with iron; additional iron ties were to be laid through the piers and 'cogged down' to the ashlar, and the rubble in-fill of each pier was to be raked out and consolidated. For the repointing of the crossing arches, a patent cement

100. Myles, *Cottingham*; Colvin, *Biographical Dictionary*, pp. 271–72.
101. Willis, *Report of a Survey*, pp. 25–33; Merewether, *Statement*, pp. 42–45.

containing iron filings and turnings mixed with urine was employed.[102] Cottingham's work on the crossing piers was an heroic undertaking – 'perhaps the greatest work of church restoration which has been witnessed for many years' – but his sensitivity to the ancient fabric left something to be desired. The contract constantly reiterates his intention to provide 'a faithful restoration of the original work now in existence' or 'the most perfect restoration'. Unfortunately, much of the surviving detail, although capable of being interpreted by the architect's 'modeller', was too imperfect to satisfy the rigorous standards set by Cottingham and Merewether and was therefore removed. They yearned for a 'grand and beautiful design' which excluded any 'deformities'. They created a new crossing where the ornament was 'reinstated in strict conformity with the original work' but it was all recut, exhibiting the talents of the Victorian stone carvers rather than those of the twelfth century. Havergal illustrates a drawing made by Cottingham of the coloured decoration, found by his workmen, after removing several coats of whitewash from the archway of the south transept, leading to the aisle of the nave. 'The varied and brilliant patterns were brought to light in a fair state of preservation' but 'the whole was destroyed, no attempt being made to replace any of the old stonework' (plate Xc). Already a new generation of purists were demanding something more authentic: when the British Archaeological Association visited the cathedral in 1871 it did not appreciate the 'four *quasi* Norman arches' which it noticed had been 'reconstructed' by Cottingham.[103]

The work upon the crossing continued for several years, but with the tower safe, the chapter turned its attention in 1845 to the Lady chapel. The dean was eager to start on the choir, which the *Gentleman's Magazine* noticed in 1843 had already been deprived of its 'wretched' painted window and altarpiece. The first priority, however, was to stabilise the east wall of the chapel, where the cracks were four inches wide. A decision was taken to raise Wyatt's roof so that the high gable could be restored, enhanced by 'an elegant circular window' that had already been illustrated in *A Statement* (1842). Cottingham dutifully produced a full-sized drawing of the window with its mouldings (fig. 80). Once again, inside and out, everything was to be done 'in conformity with the original work' and the modeller was kept busy interpreting the shattered ornament for the carvers. An antiquarian bonus for the dean and his architect was the discovery of the monuments of Joanna de Bohun and 'Humphrey de Bohun' (now thought to be Peter de Grandisson) behind the library panelling. They were, of course, automatically repainted 'in

102. HCA, 7005/7, register of leases, etc., 1841–51, pp. 88ff.

103. Myles, *Cottingham*, pp. 99–103, for a more sympathetic view of Cottingham's work; Hills, 'Architectural History of Hereford Cathedral', p. 503; F. T. Havergal, *Fasti Herefordenses* (Edinburgh, 1869), p. 155.

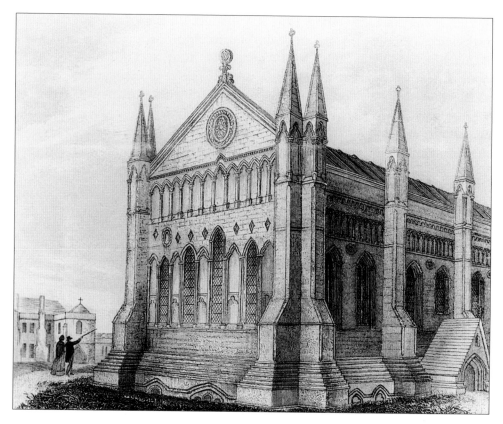

Fig. 80. Merewether's conjectural scheme for the restoration of the Lady chapel. J. Merewether, *A Statement of the Condition and Circumstances of the Cathedral Church of Hereford* (Hereford, 1842). (HCL, B.3.54.)

conformity with the original work'. Work on the enrichment of the Lady chapel was slow and in 1847 the contractor, John Carline, was in dispute with the chapter about a second contract for the chapel. He retired in 1848, complaining that the chapter still owed him £2588.[104]

By this date Cottingham had been joined by his son Nockalls Johnson Cottingham. When the contract for the choir was drawn up, in January 1848, Cottingham senior was already ill. At last, two years before his own death, Merewether's aspirations for the choir were to be fully realised. The finished result, apart from the reredos, follows the scheme published in the *Statement* (1842). It was, he had assured subscribers, 'in precise accordance with the remains developed, [a] sound

104. HCA, 7005/7, pp. 182ff. On John Carline see D. Whitehead, 'The Mid Nineteenth-Century Restoration of Hereford Cathedral by Lewis Nockalls Cottingham, 1842–1850', in Whitehead, *Medieval Art at Hereford*, pp. 182–83.

architectural composition of the highest order'. Nevertheless, once the panelling was removed, much of the Romanesque detail was found to be severely damaged and, according to the contract, 'All the defective ashlar bases, columns, capitals, arches and reveals are to be cut out where directed and the new work to be inserted according to drawings 1–9'. Only the 'jambs at the altar arch [were] found on further examination to be in a much more perfect state than when the contractor first made his estimate' and were therefore spared. No attempt was made to 'reinstate in strict conformity with the original work'. The perpendicular window in the east wall of the choir had already been condemned in the *Statement*, where Merewether decided it should be a 'triplet in the first pointed style'. Cottingham junior worked up the design but, as the British Archaeological Association noticed, he ignored the 'admirable lessons at hand in the sides of the choir clerestory' and, although he chose the right style, 'utterly spoilt the idea in the execution'.[105]

The furnishing of the choir proceeded more slowly. Cottingham senior died soon after being taken ill at a chapter meeting in October 1847. He had already dismantled the fourteenth-century pulpitum when he had worked on the crossing in 1841. The organ, which stood on the screen, had been removed to a temporary site in the south transept; a decision about its permanent position was deferred until 1861. Merewether wanted the pulpitum to be replaced by one of 'Norman character' but this was ignored. The medieval choir stalls were to be restored but those with square backs – presumably dating from the seventeenth century – were discarded to be replaced with more 'appropriate seats with gothic ends'. At the east end of the choir, behind the altar, Merewether illustrated a screen of ornate Romanesque arches above fretwork panels. This was clearly a piece of improvisation and was discarded in 1851 when, with the death of Joseph Bailey, MP, a public subscription raised sufficient funds for the present marble Caen stone reredos, designed by N. J. Cottingham and carved by W. Boulton of Lambeth. The subscription also paid for the completion of the glazing of the eastern triplet window above the new reredos, erected in 1852.[106]

N. J. Cottingham's time at Hereford was less happy than his father's. By the late 1840s public enthusiasm for the restoration of the cathedral had declined and funds from the subscription were slow to materialise. In January 1849, two years after his death, Cottingham senior was publicly accused of 'extravagant misapplication of funds' by a member of the restoration committee. Although these slurs were refuted, Cottingham junior never enjoyed the same independence or the generous

105. Merewether, *Statement*, pp. 46–9; Hills, 'Hereford Cathedral', p. 504.
106. HCA, 7005/7, pp. 288ff; Hereford City Library, Pilley Collection 339, *A Brief*

Description of the Memorials to the Late Very Revd John Merewether, DD and Joseph Bailey Esq. (Hereford, 1852), pp. 10–13.

financial backing as his father.[107] Merewether died in April 1850 and the prime mover in the great endeavour was removed. The restoration committee tried to capitalise upon the event, urging subscribers to view the completion of the Lady chapel as a monument to the dean's memory. In the event, the strategy failed and by 1852 there was only enough money to pay for his memorial window in the east end of the chapel – 'an exquisite example of the first pointed or Early English style'. N. J. Cottingham provided the design for twenty-one subjects on the life of Christ. The author of the memorial appeal (1852) regretted that the 'external dilapidations' of the north and south walls of the Lady chapel had yet to receive attention. The details of the ornate panelling, windows and parapets were in a 'rapid state of decay', whilst the Audley chapel, 'the leading feature of the interior', was also in a ruinous condition with its fine details 'fast crumbling away': yet the architect had estimated a mere £700 for its restoration.[108]

Three years earlier, funds were still sufficiently available for the younger Cottingham to sign a contract for the restoration of the nave in April 1849. Presumably much of the work had already been planned by Cottingham senior and included the reinstatement of the double semi-shafts on the nave piers. Evidence for this feature had been found when the base of the piers had been investigated. Wyatt was blamed for their removal, although it was far more likely that this had happened in the fifteenth century when the nave was reroofed. After some debate about the purpose of reinstating a non-functioning feature as ornament, this 'very rare feature' was reproduced on each pier even though the piers failed to connect with Wyatt's triple vaulting shafts which supported the new roof. The 1849 contract also refers to a new tiled pavement in the nave and new groining for the ceiling with a stencilled design. The north and south aisle walls were to be underpinned and Wyatt's plaster mouldings on the two arches abutting the west end were to be cut out and restored 'in exact accordance with such two of the ancient arches existing'. Finally, the doors of the Booth porch were to be lengthened and covered with ironwork designed by Potter of London. The work continued until 1851, when the subscription again ran out.[109] The author of the Bailey memorial made an earnest appeal for more subscribers, reiterating the letter sent out to the gentry of the county in 1847 by Robert Biddulph Phillips of Longworth. N. J. Cottingham found himself unemployed and announced his intention of writing a new architectural guide to the cathedral, but again this depended upon public subscription. He was paid in full in 1853 but absconded with the money contributed by the Misses Rushout for an eagle lectern that he had designed. Enquiries were made by the chapter via the architect William Eden Nesfield, who found in 1855 that

107. *Hereford Times*, 20 January 1849, 27 January 1849.

108. *A Brief Description* (1852), pp. 6–8.

109. HCA, 7005/7, pp. 389ff.

the lectern was on loan to Boston church, Lincolnshire, and confirmed that the errant Cottingham, 'a disgrace to his profession in every way and this is not the only swindling transaction he has been guilty of', was rumoured to have embarked for America but was lost at sea when his ship, the *Arctic*, foundered. Eventually a new subscription was raised, to which a major contribution was made by Canon Phillott, and a new lectern was purchased in the 1870s.[110]

George Gilbert Scott (1811–78) and his contractor, Messrs Ruddle and Thompson of Peterborough, signed their extensive contract with the chapter on 8 October 1858.[111] Scott was at the climax of his career and was already actively repairing cathedrals at Lichfield, Ely and Peterborough. Eventually, only three British cathedrals escaped his attentions. Cathedral restoration was a minefield for a successful architect and, although he inherited Cottingham's mantle in this field, Scott was aware that his predecessor's work was already under scrutiny and had been found wanting. Scott was very scrupulous about his cathedral work and wrote about it at length in his memoir *Personal and Professional Recollections* (1879). The modern editor of this work believes that his cathedral restorations 'may be regarded as the most impressive and valuable part of his achievement'.[112]

His interest in Hereford Cathedral predated 1858, for in December 1855 Scott had written to the antiquarian, the Revd Francis Havergal, on the subject of the choir.[113] He was pleased to hear 'that the opening of the choir produces so striking an effect. I have no doubt the choir must look very noble'. He urged the chapter to complete the restoration but was puzzled over Merewether's intentions: in his letter he sketched three alternative suggestions for the original design of the east end of the Romanesque choir. The letter seems to have been ignored by the chapter but his correspondent, for one, was not happy with Cottingham junior's enrichment of the choir and felt that the Bailey reredos was too high, intercepting the view of the Lady chapel. Moreover, the designs for the choir windows were 'too minute a character'. Scott too, in an unguarded moment, thought that Cottingham senior's work was 'founded upon utility rather that history'.[114]

In 1858 the choir was still unfinished. The medieval stalls, injured by being 'hastily and carelessly taken down', had been stowed away in the crypt by Cottingham senior and mouldered there for twenty years. The 'fragmentary pieces' were fitted together but new 'miseres' (misericords) of a consistent character were

110. *A Brief Description* (1852), pp. 15–16; HRO, C71/II/9, Havergal Correspondence; Myles, *Cottingham*, p. 103.
111. HCA, 7005/7, pp. 389ff.
112. D. Cole, *The Work of Gilbert Scott* (London, 1980), p. 64; G. Scott, *Personal and Professional Recollections: A Facsimile of the Original Edition*, ed. G. G. Stamp (Stamford, 1995), pp. f–g.
113. HCA, 5760.
114. HRO, C71/III/22, Havergal correspondence; Scott, *Recollections*, p. 479.

provided by the contractor. Ruddle was separately credited with £220 in the fabric accounts for the woodwork in the choir. The tile pavement, including probably the roundel depicting St Ethelbert, was provided by Messrs Godwin of Lugwardine. The green tiles were especially admired and Scott complimented the firm in *Recollections*, noting that their tiles came closer in texture to the medieval originals than those of the Minton company. The floor cost £600. The organ, which had been taken down from the crossing screen in 1841, was moved into the first archway on the south side of the choir and thoroughly restored at a cost of £1300 raised by public subscription (fig. 138).[115]

Prior to 1841 the choir had extended westwards beneath the crossing, terminating in a fourteenth-century stone pulpitum which had been removed by Cottingham. Scott found no traces of this and firmly believed that it was not an old structure. Influenced by 'violent agitation' and 'fancy', he decided to restrict the choir to the presbytery, returning the crossing to the congregation, who would be able to view the service through 'an open unobstructive screen, capable of uniting the greatest degree of lightness and of beauty'. Similar arrangements had already been carried out by Scott at Ely and Lichfield.[116]

Scott had already collaborated with Francis Skidmore of Coventry over the screen at Lichfield and the latter wanted something to exhibit at the International Exhibition to be held in London in 1862. He was prepared to manufacture the screen to Scott's design for £1500 and, as the appeal document put it, 'at least £1000 less than such a work could be produced for under any other circumstances'. The screen was lauded at the exhibition as 'the greatest and most triumphant achievement of modern architectural art'. Composed of iron, copper, brass, vitreous and other mineral substances in mosaic panels – 50,000 in all – it was an irresistible object (figs 81, 103). The *Appeal* of 1862 promised subscribers that 'When the Screen is placed in its proper position beneath those glorious Norman Arches which support the Tower, it will be satisfactory to see that the productions of modern art may be made to blend harmoniously with the types of beauty furnished by the taste and science of former ages'.[117] There were few voices of dissent but Scott confided in his memoir that he had designed the screen on 'a somewhat massive scale' and that 'Skidmore followed my design somewhat aberrantly' and 'kicked over the traces'. The final product was 'too loud and self-asserting for an English church'. He also regretted reducing the length of the choir and confessed that 'he could not do the same now'. Skidmore received his £1500 in 1863–64

115. HCA, 7005/7, pp. 389ff; HCA, 7020/2/3, pp. 234–55, fabric accounts, 1860–62; Scott, *Recollections*, pp. 224, 290; *An Appeal from the Dean and Chapter of Hereford, for Aid towards the Completion of the Restoration of their* *Cathedral* (Hereford, 1862), pp. 5, 11.

116. Scott, *Recollections*, pp. 290–91; *Appeal* (1862), p. 6. See also chapter 16, p. 339.

117. *Illustrated London News*, 18 September 1852, p. 246; *Appeal* (1862), p. 6.

Fig. 81. The screen by Sir George Gilbert Scott and Francis Skidmore in situ from the south, 1890. (HCL, B.4.157.)

but also provided the cathedral with fittings for gas lighting and an ornamental wrought iron corona which hung from the floor of the bell chamber and illuminated the crossing with a circle of gas twelve feet in diameter.[118]

Scott's principal contribution to the structure of the cathedral involved underpinning the walls, especially beneath the transepts, the choir aisles, the lesser transepts and the north and south walls of the Lady chapel. The walls of the north transept were still bulging as a result of the lateral pressure exerted upon them by the tower and much of the interior detail was in a 'dreadful state'. The clustered columns surrounding the windows were 'sadly broken' and other windows were partly blocked in this 'Magna Carta of gothic architecture'.[119] Scott's specification

---

118. Scott, *Recollections*, pp. 216, 190–91 (and see further below, p. 339); HCA, 7020/2/3, pp. 250–63, fabric accounts, 1862–64; R. J. King, *Handbook to the Cathedrals of England, Western Division: Gloucester,* *Hereford, Worcester, Bristol, Lichfield* (2nd edn, London, 1874), p. 85.

119. Malcolm, *An Account*, p. 103; HRO, C71/III/22, Havergal Correspondence; Marshall, *Hereford Cathedral*, p. 75.

for the work includes the provision of twenty-six detached shafts for the windows in the west side and the reconstruction of much of the wall for which a thousand cubic feet of Caplar stone was required. The new work was to be 'trowelled with slate' and fixed with Portland cement. 'All work was to be made in strict accordance with the original features' and where whitewash remained on the original stone this was to be removed by chemical means. In certain circumstances, under the direction of the architect, the tooling was to be restored. Similarly, if wall paintings were found, these were to be inspected by the architect. Very little internal work was required on the east side of the transept except in the east aisle, where the sills and tracery to the windows were repaired. Under the north window Bishop Charlton's tomb was refurbished with two new pinnacles, four cusps and six crockets. The floor was removed and new Godwin tiles were laid on six inches of cement, whilst the ceiling received fifty feet of new groining and was painted with polychrome decoration by Octavius Hudson. Externally, Scott provided the buttresses with gables, restored the spire to the stair turret in the south-west angle and removed Wyatt's battlements. The windows to the muniment and chained library room over the north transept, which had been blocked up for reasons of security, were reinstated.

Having underpinned the aisle wall from the transept to the Booth porch, the porch itself was also restored. Three hundred cubic feet of new stone was used to replace defective work around the stairs, buttresses, turrets and windows. The original carving was 'carefully restored' but a new cross was placed on the gable. Very little work was done internally to the south transept. On the east side the Norman triforium was restored using specially cut large blocks of stone and two new shafts with their capitals and bases were also required for the lower arcade. Some defective stonework was replaced in the south window and one hundred feet of new ashlar was used for the damaged west wall. The exterior of the transept remained untouched, although the roof was releaded in 1865.[120] Scott paid particular attention to the Denton monument, which he found lying in pieces. Sir Alexander Denton was buried at Hillesden in Buckinghamshire, close to Scott's home, where according to the *Recollections* the young architect had been inspired by the beauty of Gothic architecture. The Hereford tomb was placed as near as possible to its old site but Scott was saddened to see that some of the heraldry had been damaged. He wrote to Lord Leicester, a descendant of Denton, suggesting that he help finance the restoration of the monument, but without success. Eventually, the

120. HCA, 7005/7, pp. 389ff; HCA, 7020/2/3, pp. 228–39, [274–81], fabric accounts, 1859–60, 1867; King, *Handbook*, pp. 91–93, 111, 116; Scott, *Recollections*, pp. 288–89; *Appeal* (1862), pp. 3, 9. On Scott's enthusiasm for the Early English parts of the cathedral see his paper 'Hereford Cathedral', *Archaeological Journal*, 34 (1877), pp. 332–36.

missing heraldry was found in the north-east transept but Scott was still writing about the monument to Havergal in 1873 (plate VIIb).[121]

Scott's men, directed by his clerk of works, William Chick, worked fastidiously along the choir aisles and into the lesser transepts. Most of their work was of a minor character. Some stretches of groining were repaired and, where necessary, defective stones were cut out and replaced in the walls. Wherever possible old stone was reused. Where tombstones were removed from the floor, their position was marked on a plan in case it was decided they should be relaid. The Aigueblanche tomb was cleaned and an attempt was made by 'an amateur' to recolour it, but this was discontinued.[122] The Stanbury chapel was also repaired but, elsewhere, modern mural monuments were removed 'to be re-fixed where directed'. In the north-east transept Scott designed a marble monument for Dean Dawes in 1867 as a tribute to his 'kind and friendly assistance' during his time at Hereford (fig. 44).[123] Traces of wall paintings had been found in the north-east transept and these were 'not to be obliterated in the slightest degree without express permission of the architect'. The south-east transept received a more thorough restoration. The windows in the south wall contained wooden mullions which were removed and replaced with stone ones modelled upon the windows in the east wall.

In the Lady chapel Scott was responsible for the Godwin pavement and for the oak fittings for the parish of St John, which were carved by Thomas Merrick of Hereford. Skidmore provided the ornamental railings between the upper and lower parts of the chapel. The Audley chapel was thoroughly restored, the exterior wall virtually rebuilt, new oak floors laid, incongruous brickwork, patching the screen, removed and the damaged cornice repaired. Most of Scott's attention was directed to the north and south exterior walls of the chapel which were underpinned and substantially rebuilt with the original stone. The blind arcade, which was much decayed, was repaired where necessary with new caps and shafts. The pinnacles on the south side were missing, presumably moved by Cottingham, but were eventually found in the crypt. New ones were carved for the Audley chapel as well as some supremely grotesque gargoyles.[124]

The final phase of the great nineteenth-century restoration of Hereford Cathedral therefore came to an end in June 1863, when the building was officially reopened. Guests from afar were brought to the event by a special train from Gloucester. Scott was well satisfied with his contribution to the cathedral and wrote in the *Recollections* that 'The reparations were carried out with the most scrupulous regard for evidence, and with the least possible displacement of old stone'. He was

121. Scott, *Recollections*, pp. 42, 289–90; HRO, C71/II/63, Havergal Correspondence.
122. King, *Handbook*, p. 97.
123. Scott, *Recollections*, p. 291.

124. HCA, 7005/7, pp. 389ff; Marshall, *Hereford Cathedral*, pp. 56, 123; F. T. Havergal, *The Visitors Hand-Guide to Hereford Cathedral* (2nd edn, Hereford, 1865), pp. 15–18.

particularly pleased with the round windows he had discovered and re-established on the east side of the north transept and also the work of placing the monuments which had been scattered by Cottingham without record. Here he acknowledged the scholarly advice of F. T. Havergal, whose new guide of 1865 was a celebration of their joint endeavours.[125] Locally and nationally the work was well received and contrasted favourably with the work of Wyatt and Cottingham. R. J. King's *Handbook* (published by Murray, 2nd edn, 1874) noted that 'Since the year 1858 the final restoration of Hereford Cathedral has been in the hands of Mr (now Sir) G. G. Scott, and it need hardly be said that the work has been of a very different character. Where reconstruction has been necessary, every stone has been preserved, and, if possible, replaced.' Scott's reputation has remained high in the twentieth century, despite the criticisms of William Morris and his friends. Canon Bannister in 1924 felt that 'what was done under Scott was for the most part done well and carefully, in the spirit not of innovation but of conservative restoration'. More recently, the cathedral mason, Roger Capps, has pointed out that most of Scott's new carving is easy to identify and can be checked for authenticity against the original work. For the contrasting treatment of ornament by Scott and Cottingham one has only to view the former's arcade on the north exterior wall of the Lady chapel where it meets the latter's east front.[126]

Right up until his death in 1878 Scott continued to take an interest in the cathedral. He kept up a long correspondence with F. T. Havergal, urging him to be vigilant against 'attempted vandalism' and relying heavily upon his technical advice for a paper on the architectural history of the cathedral given to the Archaeological Institute in August 1877. Havergal read the draft of the paper before it was published in the *Archaeological Journal* and also provided the plan.[127] Only seven months before he died Scott led two tours, containing a large company of scholars, around the cathedral 'pointing out with great lucidity the various parts of the building'.[128] His final gift to Hereford was William Chick, his clerk of works, who set up practice as an architect in the city, restored many parish churches and eventually became the county surveyor. He remained at hand to supervise some later work at the cathedral, including the releading of the south transept in 1865.[129]

125. Hereford City Library, Pilley Collection, 2265, fol. 22; Scott, *Recollections*, pp. 288–89.

126. King, *Handbook*, p. 72; Bannister, *The Cathedral Church of Hereford*, p. 250; HCL, R. Capps, 'The Cathedral Church of St Mary and St Ethelbert, Hereford' (unpublished Architectural Association Building Conservation thesis, 1986–87), fos 33–36, 55–56.

127. HRO, C71/II/61, 63–66, III/54, 93, 95, 108–9. Scott's paper on 'Hereford Cathedral' was published in the *Archaeological Journal*, 34 (1877), pp. 323–48.

128. *Archaeological Journal*, 34 (1877), pp. 474–501.

129. Cole, *Gilbert Scott*, pp. 112, 189, 193, 236; *Hereford Journal*, 23 November 1889.

Scott did not in any sense regard his work as the completion of the process of restoration at Hereford Cathedral, but little was done in the following thirty years because to finance his work the chapter had borrowed £13,000 in 1857 by act of parliament on the security of its estates, and this had to be paid back within thirty-two years.[130] In 1862 Scott was already aware that a number of important projects were likely to be postponed for some time. These included the external restoration of the tower which was 'rapidly mouldering away', 'deeply cracked' and so friable that 'considerable fragments may readily be removed by hand'. He reflected on the 'very bad state' of the tower in the *Recollections* but regarded it as a 'singularly beautiful design'. Confident of Cottingham's reconstruction, he was ready to approve the hanging of bells in 1862 and even suggested that the leaden spire, removed by Wyatt, should also be replaced as it would 'greatly conduce to the beauty of the entire building'.[131]

Equally high on Scott's agenda was the rebuilding of the west end and the 'amelioration' of Wyatt's windows in the clerestory of the nave, which in 'their present form [were] a disfigurement to throw discredit upon the whole structure'. He was critical of Cottingham's 'offensive decoration' of the ceiling, which, according to Havergal, was 'almost universally condemned'. In his 1877 paper for the *Archaeological Journal* Scott published an 'imaginary reproduction of the ancient west front' based upon various eighteenth-century views – 'the great glory of the cathedral'. He also recommended that the nave be restored to its full length.[132]

Both the tower and the west front were in Dean Herbert's mind when in 1886 he launched a public appeal to raise £30,000 to celebrate Queen Victoria's Golden Jubilee. He reminded the diocese of 'the great stress' placed by Scott on the restoration of the tower and the replacement of the 'meagre', 'tasteless' and 'unworthy' west front. Rather as an afterthought, he also referred to the state of the south-west cloister and the absence of a chapter house (figs 82, 45).[133] In fact, Scott had restored the structure of the cloister and had provided three 'entirely new windows' for the east range. External repairs had also been carried out to the entrance to the chapter house from the cloister as well as to the room above. The chapter house yard and the Lady arbour were both landscaped. The work on the cloister was completed, however, in 1897 by Sir Arthur Blomfield and paid for from a bequest by Prebendary Powell to establish a library for the benefit of the diocesan clergy. The south range of the cloister was restored and an extension

130. Hereford City Library, Pilley Collection, 2265, fol. 22, R. Dawes, *Appeal Pamphlet* (1860).

131. *Appeal* (1862), p. 8; Scott, *Recollections*, p. 291; HRO, C71/II/61, Havergal Correspondence.

132. *Appeal* (1862), p. 10; Havergal, *Hand-Guide*, p. 28; Scott, 'Hereford Cathedral' (1877), opposite p. 329; also in *Building News*, 16 August 1878.

133. Hereford City Library, Pilley Collection, 2265, fol. 28, *Appeal Pamphlet* (1886).

Fig. 82. A mid nineteenth-century drawing by C. Radclyffe of the Lady arbour, showing the south cloister open at the west end. (HCL, B.5.281.)

built to the west, hinting that the cloister would soon be finally enclosed as, it was assumed, its medieval builders intended. Blomfield also published a design for a new decagonal chapter house 'based upon antique researches' which had a much crocketed roofline and fourteenth-century windows (fig. 83a, b).[134]

Following the Hereford earthquake of 1896, it was reported by Messrs Thompson of Peterborough that Wyatt's west front had been weakened and its central and side pinnacles were in a dangerous state. This provided the excuse for Dean Leigh's appeal for the complete replacement of the much maligned edifice. Even so, the dean admitted, on the passing of Wyatt's work, that it had been 'enthusiastically approved in its day', which is more than can be said for its replacement, designed by Scott's pedestrian and dull second son, Oldrid. Moreover, Scott junior rejected his father's archaeological design for a 'vociferous' composition in the Decorated style. Dean Leigh naturally thought it was 'probably one of the finest in modern days of the fourteenth-century style' but all subsequent commentators have been less than enthusiastic (fig. 47). The choice of a raw Hollington stone from North

134. J. W. Leigh, *Record of Work Done* (Hereford, 1910), p. 6; Hereford City Library, Pilley Collection, 2265, fos. 28, 61, *Appeal Pamphlet* (1896).

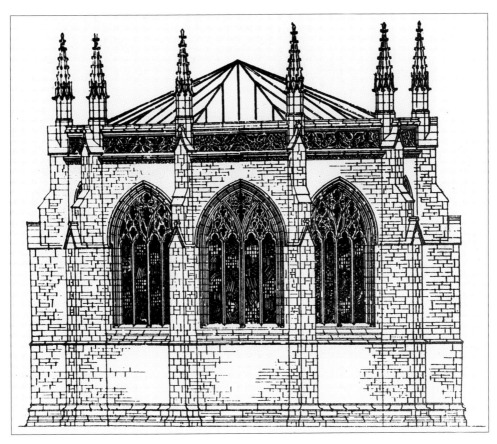

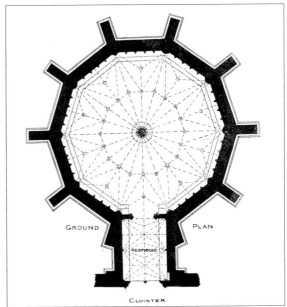

Fig. 83. Plan and elevation of Sir Arthur Blomfield's proposed design for a new chapter house, *c.* 1890. (Hereford City Library, Pilley Collection, 2265, p. 61; HCL, neg. 1011.)

Staffordshire, first used by Blomfield for the new library, was especially unfortunate. The work was carried out in four stages and eventually completed in 1908 at a total cost of £15,550. The statuary and carving were carried out by Messrs Baker and Fincher and regarded by Marshall as 'mediocre, better be passed over in silence'. Time will perhaps change our opinion of this work.[135]

At last, in 1923 the chapter turned its attention to the tower and consulted the senior architect to the Church Commissioners, W. R. Caroe (1857–1938), who had repaired the central tower of Canterbury Cathedral and Tom Tower at Christ Church, Oxford.[136] He was thus the natural choice for a similar task at Hereford. He proposed the complete refacing of the tower and recarving all the 26,000 ballflower ornaments. Alarm bells rang in both Hereford and the offices of the Society for the Protection of Ancient Buildings in London. Alfred Watkins, the antiquarian, who was a member of the society, reported that although the ballflower was much decayed the tower was structurally sound. A memorandum among the society archives states that Caroe was trying to convince people that 'it is still possible to repeat the touch of the craftsmen who created this master piece'. Eventually, pressure from the society, and the £16,000 estimate for the work, convinced the chapter and its advisory committee that they should seek alternative advice. When one of the tower pinnacles fell through the nave roof the following year, the master of the fabric, Canon Bannister, wrote to the society stating that the chapter had decided 'the present surface [of the tower], although somewhat worn, is far more beautiful than a brand new tower would be'. The society subsequently carried out its own survey and offered the services of William Weir, who had been experimenting with resin treatment for decaying stonework. In order to retain the surface detail as it stood, Weir advised that the gaps in the stonework should be patched with handmade tiles and made flush with a mortar finish. None of the perished ornament was to be restored and the decaying surfaces were to be treated with syliconester even if experiments with the material had – according to the society itself – proved 'not very satisfactory'. The chapter was delighted with the advice and particularly with Weir's estimate of £3000–£4000. A public appeal was launched for the pinnacles and work started in the spring of 1927. The cathedral architect, W. E. A. Clarke, soon mastered the technique and the chapter quietly disposed of the services of Mr Weir. Bannister reported to the chapter in November 1927 that the work was complete at a total cost of £2942. When major restoration work recommenced in the 1980s the society's patch and mend technique was found to be seriously flawed and had actually accelerated the

135. Leigh, *Work Done*, pp. 7–24; Marshall, *Hereford Cathedral*, p. 170; N. Pevsner, *The Buildings of England: Herefordshire* (Harmondsworth, 1963), p. 153.

136. A. S. Gray, *Edwardian Architecture* (London, 1988), pp. 134–37.

erosion of the tower. It had, however, prevented the tower from being completely resurfaced and made as lifeless as the west front.[137]

Apart from the restoration of the tower, very little major work took place in the early twentieth century. In 1920 the crypt was renovated at the expense of Sir H. Webb by Caroe, as a memorial chapel for the former's son. A new altar and reredos were designed by Sir W. Goscombe John, RA (1860–1952). Part of the south-west cloister was found to be dangerous in 1922 and work was put in hand by Mr Clarke. Over £1000 was spent on repairing the south wall of the south transept in 1928 and £781 on 'urgent' repairs to the Lady chapel in 1934. The roof of the nave was leaded in 1941 and the cathedral was floodlit for the first time during the Three Choirs Festival in August 1930. Inside the cathedral Mr E. T. Long undertook the restoration of the Audley screen in 1934, removing the varnish from the paintings which, it was discovered, were executed in oils. Long also cleaned and treated the remains of the wall paintings in the north-east transept. In 1923 Mr Lennox Lee of How Caple Court, under the impression that Bishop Stanbury had been the provost of Eton College, offered to pay for some new stained glass in the bishop's chantry. Although when the chapter pointed out that this was erroneous the offer was withdrawn, in 1949 Lee paid for Professor Tristram to clean, adorn and refurnish the Lady chapel.[138]

There were ominous rumblings in chapter in 1934 when Canon Streeter proposed the removal of the Skidmore screen. The matter was referred to the Central Advisory Committee of the Church Commissioners and a sub-committee chaired by the dean of Westminster inspected the screen. There was no further discussion until after the Second World War when 'anti-screen fever became infectious' and in 1967, following the removal of the screen at Salisbury, this 'high Victorian monument of the first order' was removed and sent in packing cases to Coventry – where it had been made almost a century before.[139]

137. HCA, 7031/24, pp. 192, 196, chapter acts, 25 June, 10 November 1927; Capps, 'Cathedral Church', appendix viii, fos [74–80], transcripts of the SPAB correspondence.

138. HCA, 7031/24, 1916–48, passim; Hereford City Library, LC 942.44, Newspaper Cutting Books 3 and 4, pp. 59, 149–50. Mr Lee thought that Stanbury was the first provost of Eton, but inquiries established that this was not the case, although as the priest confessor of Henry VI he was certainly closely associated with the foundation: Marshall, *Hereford Cathedral*, p. 155. On the glass, see below, Chapter 13, p. 321.

139. HCA, 7031/24, pp. 313–14, 316; Pevsner, *Herefordshire*, p. 166.

10

The Restoration of the Modern Cathedral

Michael Reardon

An extensive programme of work was carried out in the 1960s and 1970s under the direction of the then cathedral architect, Mr E. A. Roiser. This was precipitated by the fall of masonry from the tower in 1965, and included the replacement of much of the tracery and other masonry of the east, west and south faces of the central tower and the recasting of a great part of the lead of the nave roof. Some of the window tracery of the nave aisles and clerestory was also replaced and all of the south clerestory windows glazed.

The work was financed from a diocesan appeal, and came to a standstill when the money ran out in the late 1970s.[1] Work had by then begun on the north side of the tower where the quatrefoil blind arcade had been cut out and propped but no replacement stone put back. The scaffolding for this work, becoming ever rustier, was to remain in place for many years.

Documentation for the period is sparse but most of the work was carried out by the old established Hereford firm of Blake and Sons using Mottled Hollington stone from Staffordshire. The banker work was probably all done at the quarry and no attempt seems to have been made to record the existing masonry before it was cut out.

In 1983, the dean and chapter decided to appoint a new architect to replace Roiser, then advanced in years, and Michael Reardon took up this post in January 1984. His brief was to review the approach to repair and to advise the chapter on a long-term strategy for the maintenance of the fabric.

In the repairs of the 1960s and 70s all stone had been worked at a quarry far from Hereford, by masons unacquainted with the building. The work captured little of the spirit of the original and much of the carving is dead and characterless. The new architect advised that a masonry workshop be established at the cathedral itself, as would have been the case in the middle ages. He felt that resident masons

1. See above, Chapter 6, p. 182.

would have a greater commitment to the building and would become familiar with the style and peculiarities of the existing carving. Also, a permanent banker workshop at the cathedral would enable apprentices to be trained in the local style of carving and create a pool of skill which would eventually benefit other churches and historic buildings in the Marches. An appeal was launched in April 1985 to raise funds for cathedral restoration under the banner of 'A Helping Hand for Hereford Cathedral'.[2] By October 1988, almost £1,000,000 had been raised, most of it locally.

The new strategy implied that the repair of masonry would be a continuous process, carried out by a small resident team of masons, backed up by single contracts for the work that did not need continuity, such as recasting the lead or reglazing the windows. Competitive tenders for this type of work could be invited from specialist contractors, not necessarily local. As the chapter did not have the expertise necessary to run a building operation, it was decided to look for a contractor with a good record in conservative repair and a sensitive approach, and who would have the resources to carry out operations like sawing stone and slaking lime which could not be done in the cathedral Close. Initially, there was some resistance to the establishment of a masons' shop in the Close from the city planners, who considered such 'industrial activity' unacceptable in a conservation area, but this was overcome and the masons' workshop is now an accepted part of the cathedral's life: a point of interest for visitors which had the ability to attract funds from those who were prompted to 'buy a stone' for the cathedral.

In 1985 four firms were selected to tender for the first project, that of rebuilding the south-west 'sheerwater' buttresses of the central tower. The conditions of tender required the contractor to establish a banker shop on site and to offer advantageous terms for continuing work on the fabric, subject to satisfactory performance. Each stone had to be individually priced and no work would be done on a dayworks or cost plus basis. The first contract was awarded to the Herefordshire firm of Capps and Capps, who have continued to run the cathedral workshop as well as being responsible for the day-to-day maintenance of the building.

Since 1985, five generations of apprentices have passed through the workshops including the present head mason, Richard Powell, who began his apprenticeship on site at the start of the contract. Masons from the cathedral team have worked on the repair of many other historic buildings from Wales to Oxfordshire. Other trades such as glazing and carpentry are also locally based and it is only for large-scale leadwork or sculpture conservation that the chapter has to look outside the Marches (fig. 84).

2. See above, Chapter 7, p. 189.

Fig. 84. Stonemason working
on a ballflower detail for the
tower, 1984.

Because of this continuity, the work on the fabric has become part of the daily life
of the cathedral community and the maintenance of the building dedicated to the
daily worship of God itself part of the cathedral's witness. This has engendered a sense
of belonging to the life of the cathedral amongst the masons themselves; as one of
those who have been there longest remarked, 'it's like being part of a family here'.

The cathedral was built with stone from several sources, each of which decays
in a different way. Several different types of stone are often found in the same
part of the building and so, in order to match these, up to five different stones
may be used in a single area of repair. Because there are no quarries now working
the strata from which the old stone came, the new stone has largely come from
Derbyshire. However, research is now being undertaken into the possibility of
opening up a more local quarry which might provide stone closer in petrology
to the old, but this is unlikely to be achieved before the current work to the
Lady chapel is completed.

The aim of repair is to retain as much of the existing stone as is consistent
with ensuring the structural stability of adjoining masonry, maintaining the visual

coherence of the design, and following, as far as possible, the existing joint pattern. Unfortunately, the condition of much of the cathedral masonry, even that dating from the nineteenth century, is so poor that 75 per cent or occasionally 100 per cent replacement is often unavoidable. Replacement is generally to a depth of 300 mm. or more, but, where the existing material is basically sound, superficial elements such as ballflowers or sections of mouldings are 'plugged in' to the existing stone and fixed with small dowels and resin. Apart from these, materials used in the repairs are those found in the building and only traditional lime mortars.

The repair of English cathedrals has been both facilitated and complicated by the introduction of the English Heritage grant for cathedrals in 1991, following the passing of the Care of Cathedrals Measure in 1990. These have made the thorough recording of existing fabric prior to repair obligatory, and instituted a system of checks and approvals and the involvement of an archaeologist in the process of repair. The Cathedrals Fabric Commission for England, set up under the measure, has been given statutory powers, and every cathedral must now have a Fabric Advisory Committee. On balance, the changes are for the best, but they have resulted in a slow, top-heavy administrative process which can result in contradiction and confusion and it has taken some time to establish sensible working procedures.

The process begins when the architect advises the chapter that a particular repair should now be carried out. This is generally done a year in advance when an application is made to English Heritage for a grant towards the cost of the work. This will be accompanied by the cathedral archaeologist's report on the age and significance of that part of the fabric, and the proposal must have the agreement of the Fabric Advisory Committee. If the proposals are approved, the elements to be repaired are measured and drawn by a team of archaeologists before the architect can decide on the exact extent and nature of replacement or repair. Each stone to be replaced is marked up on the building and on the archaeologists' drawings. The chapter's quantity surveyor uses these to prepare a schedule of work which is priced by the masonry contractor on the basis of the architect's specification. After the tender has been checked by the quantity surveyor and the work approved by the dean and chapter, it is submitted to the Fabric Advisory Committee for approval. If English Heritage is involved, their inspecting architect and quantity surveyor must also approve the proposed repairs. When the repair is in process, it will be inspected by the architect and valued by the quantity surveyor, and inspected periodically by the English Heritage architect.

The first work to be carried out by the present architect was early in 1985, when he reported that one of the 'sheerwater' buttresses of the central tower was in danger of collapse and recommended the closure of the south transept until repairs could be carried out, which critically threatened the success of the imminent

Three Choirs Festival that year. Little money had yet been raised under the new appeal, but a generous grant from the city council saved the day and work began on what has since been a virtually continuous programme of repair.

By 1991 work on the central tower was well advanced. Three of the 'sheerwater' buttresses and one of the corner turrets had been rebuilt, and the north face, which had been propped for more than fifteen years, had been refaced. The roofs of the Lady chapel, the choir and both the south transepts had also been recast and other urgent repairs carried out. The work on the roofs had been done by traditional methods using sand-cast lead by Norman and Underwood of Leicester. The appeal money was now beginning to run out and the work would have been severely curtailed had not the English Heritage cathedral repair grant come into being at that time. By adding 70 per cent to the remaining funds, this enabled the appeal resources to go much further and it was in partnership with English Heritage that the planned repairs to the central tower were completed. In 1997 the chapter held a party to celebrate the removal of scaffolding from the tower after more than thirty years in position.

In 1995 the Hereford Cathedral Perpetual Trust was formed, partly to take responsibility for the funding of future repairs.[3] The money they have raised, with continuing grants from English Heritage, has enabled the programme of repair to continue. The first project funded by the new partnership was the refacing of the east face of the Lady chapel. This had been refaced once already in the 1840s, by L. N. Cottingham, but the stone he chose, from the old Caplar quarry, though hard and fine grained, has weathered very badly. Some replacement had been done out in the early years of this century but most of the remaining surface was now badly decayed. Work, jointly funded by the Perpetual Trust and English Heritage, began in 1997, and it is anticipated that it will be completed in 2003. Reproducing the complex detail, particularly the foliate capitals, has given the cathedral masons an opportunity to produce carving of outstanding quality in a hard Derbyshire sandstone (fig. 85).

The repair of glazing has been a minor element of the work during this period, but the plain windows of the south transept and the Booth porch have been releaded and the medieval glass of the Lady chapel and the fragmentary panels in the north transept have been cleaned, conserved and protected by isothermal panels. For this work we have been fortunate in finding, in Jim Budd, an excellent local craftsman.

In 1999, the conservation of the Cantilupe shrine, first planned in 1996, was finally completed. The work was done by a team of skilled conservators under the direction of Nicholas Quayle of Cliveden Conservation, working with the

3. See above, Chapter 7, pp. 195–96.

Fig. 85. Foliate capital for the Lady chapel, 1999.

cathedral masons, who dismantled and rebuilt the masonry. The north transept has now been cleared of irrelevant clutter so that this masterpiece of medieval sculpture can be seen to advantage.

In 1985 work began on the rationalisation and repair of the fifteenth-century college of vicars choral. This has been another partnership with English Heritage, who partly funded the repairs. The north range of the college has largely been converted into offices for the administrative staff, and the residential accommodation in the east and west ranges has been rationalised. In 1994 the derelict brewhouse was also repaired and made into the new song school.

Other work has been done within the Close, including internal repairs and the repaving of the south range of the south-west cloister, which now houses the introductory exhibition to Mappa Mundi and the chained library. The canonical residence of the chancellor, 3 St John Street, which is of medieval origin, has been extensively repaired, and the windows of the eighteenth-century house occupied by the precentor have been restored.

The work is by no means at an end. When the Lady chapel is completed, it will be necessary to commence the refacing of masonry on the south side of the cathedral, much of which is presently covered with cement render. The roofs of the aisles, the Booth porch, the north transept and St John's walk have still to be recast. The cathedral barn, one of the oldest surviving secular buildings in the city, is in urgent need of repair, and further work is required on the college of vicars choral. A future generation will have to return scaffolding to the central tower and rebuild the three remaining corner turrets. Inside the cathedral, many of the monuments are in need of conservation and the badly worn tile floors will have to be repaired. Over the past decade, for the first time, such work has no longer had to depend on a start-stop programme funded by appeals. Subject to continued help from public funding, it should be possible to sustain regular work to keep one of our most ancient and interesting, yet also one of our most fragile cathedrals in a state of beauty and accessibility for its historic role as a house of God.

11

The Close and its Buildings

Ron Shoesmith

In its earliest form Hereford may well have consisted of a single street running southwards, perhaps on the line of the present Broad Street, towards a ford across the River Wye. The origins of such a road may well have dated back to the Roman period when the river crossing at Hereford might have been part of the Roman military road leading from Chester in the north to Caerleon in south Wales.[1] Archaeological work has not produced any evidence for the original foundation of the cathedral, but it has demonstrated the existence of a monastic establishment in the Castle Green area, with burials dating from the seventh to the eleventh centuries, and for the construction of timber buildings in the Victoria Street and Berrington Street area in the latter part of the eighth century.[2] The late eighth and early ninth centuries were important periods of growth for the city of Hereford. Either Offa, during his long reign as king of Mercia (757–96), or possibly one of the minor kings who followed him, was responsible for the expansion of Hereford from a minor religious centre, with a few scattered houses, to a planned royal town.[3]

This plan still survives in the grid pattern of streets leading northwards from the line of King Street and Castle Street, its extension to the east of the present cathedral Close. The initial construction of a defensive line around the city in the mid ninth century, with gates at the northern end of Broad Street and western end of King Street, fossilised this plan and restricted the area in which the Saxon cathedral could expand. The growth of the post-Conquest Norman new town to the north of the Saxon defences, the building of the castle to the east of the cathedral grounds, and the eventual construction of a bridge across the river,

1. I. D. Margary, *Roman Roads in Britain* (London, 1967), pp. 321–22.
2. R. Shoesmith, *Excavations at Castle Green*, Council for British Archaeology Research Report, 36 (London, 1980); idem, *Excavations on and Close to the Defences*, Council for British Archaeology Research Report, 46 (London, 1982), pp. 28–35.
3. Shoesmith, *Excavations on the Defences*, pp. 88–95.

led to many of the streets in the Saxon town diminishing in importance and to the eventual closure of the section of the original west-east road to the north of the cathedral.

The sites of the several pre-Conquest cathedrals are unknown, but are assumed to be underneath or to the south of the present building. Referring to the Saxon cathedral, John Duncumb wrote: 'Its position is uncertain, but about 1650 Silas Taylor found, "beyond the lines of the present building, and particularly towards the east, near the cloisters of the college, such stupendous foundations, such capitals and pedestals, such well-wrought bases for arches, and such rare engravings, and mouldings of friezes" as left little doubt in his mind that they were the foundations of the cathedral destroyed by Algar and Griffin'.[4] The position as described could well apply to the eastern side of chapter house yard.

The first major post-Conquest development in the cathedral area was the construction of the chapel of SS. Katherine and Mary Magdalene by Robert the Lotharingian, bishop between 1079 and 1095. William of Malmesbury, writing in 1125, records the construction by 'Robertus Lotharingus' of the chapel after the pattern of Aachen in a style seldom found outside the Rhineland.[5] The eighth-century *Doppelkapelle* (double chapel) built by Charlemagne at Aachen was octagonal in shape with ambulatories on two floors surrounding a central octagonal well. It had a tower porch with two circular stair turrets on the west and a rectangular projecting bay on the east which acted as a chancel. Other examples are at Ottmarsheim (built in the second quarter of the eleventh century) and Neuweiler (built around 1060).[6]

Robert the Lotharingian's chapel (the 'bishop's chapel'), which was unique to this country, was destroyed by Bishop Egerton between 1737 and 1746, apart from the north wall. This, serving a secondary purpose as part of the south wall of the south-west cloister, was saved. Fortunately William Stukeley, who visited Hereford in 1721, prepared some drawings and plans of the building; and the Society of Antiquaries, who strongly objected to the proposed demolition, also had a sheet of drawings produced. These, together with a vignette in the border of Taylor's 1757 map of Hereford, provide the initial evidence on which the overall design of the building can be based (fig. 86).

Access to the lower chapel was from the west through a doorway in the rear

4. J. Duncumb, *Collections towards the History and Antiquities of the County of Hereford* (8 vols, Hereford and London, 1804–1915), i, p. 523.

5. R. Gem, 'The Bishop's Chapel at Hereford: the Roles of Patron and Craftsman', in S. Macready and F. H. Thompson, eds, *Art and Patronage in the English Romanesque* (London, 1986), pp. 87–96.

6. N. Drinkwater, 'The Bishop's Chapel of St Katherine and St Mary Magdalene', *Archaeological Journal*, 111 (1954), pp. 129–37, and a shortened version in *TWNFC*, 35 (1955–57), pp. 256–60.

Fig. 86. Plan and elevation of the bishop's chapel, printed London, 1738. (HCL, neg. 120.)

of a deep segmental-headed recess outlined by a stringcourse that continued around the building. The recess, effectively a porch, was of several orders that continued down the jambs, except for the outer and innermost that sprang from monolithic columns apparently with foliated and cushion capitals respectively. In addition to the west door, the building was designed with doorways in both north and south walls. The southern one was of two orders with detached jamb-shafts and cushion capitals. All the windows on the south side had been replaced, apparently in the fifteenth century, by two-light windows in rectangular frames. Originally the lower chapel would have been illuminated by single lights, like those surviving in the north wall; the upper chapel probably had two-light openings similar to the one shown on contemporary illustrations of the west face.

The main part of the building was square with the sides some 43 feet (13 m.) long and the walls 5 feet 6 inches (1.7 m.) thick. There was a descent from all three entrances of some six steps about 4 feet or 1.2 m. into the lower chapel of St Katherine. It was of three by three square bays, defined by four rectangular piers and ashlar cross-arches. Each bay, apart from the central one, was covered with a groined vault. The central well was probably designed to be open, although it is not shown as such on Stukeley's sketches.

The upper chapel, dedicated to St Mary Magdalene, was approached from the lower chapel by a vice in the thickness of the wall to the south of the recessed entrance. There was a similar vice to the north, although it is shown empty on Stukeley's plan. Indeed, Stukeley shows an external stair to the north of the recessed entrance. Was this a makeshift arrangement towards the end of the chapel's life or did it allow the users of the upper chapel a separate entry without having to mix with the servants using the lower chapel?

The four cylindrical piers in the upper chapel were superimposed on the square pillars below. They supported semi-circular arches leading to monolithic columns against the walls. The central well was open to the lantern above, whilst the side vaults contained continuous half barrel vaults from end to end, with the two end bays having barrel vaulting. The lantern was described as 'an odd eight-square cupola upon the four middle pillars'.[7] The surviving north wall is of at least two periods: the original construction of the latter part of the eleventh century; and the alterations which appear to have taken place during the fifteenth century, possibly around the same time that the south-west cloister was built.[8]

The excavation for the basement of the new library building, a short distance north west of the double chapel, exposed a north-south road, presumably the continuation of Broad Street, leading down towards the ford. The road was in use in the latter part of the eleventh century and possibly earlier and the bishop's chapel would have faced it. On the east side of the road, the excavation also exposed a building containing a stone-lined cellar, a very unusual feature for that date (fig. 87).[9] The site of the bishop's chapel is now in the grounds of the bishop's palace, which extend southwards to the river and include the line of the old road leading down to the ford.[10]

The earliest part of the present bishop's palace comprises the great hall built by Bishop William de Vere (1186–98). Now totally obscured by later brickwork, the remains are those of one of the most important medieval secular buildings remaining in England. In its original state it was a four-bay aisled hall with a side porch and an end chamber block of three floors over a basement, facing the river. The hall,

7. See above, note 6.
8. R Shoesmith, 'Hereford Cathedral : The Bishop's Cloister. A Report on the Alterations in Advance of the New Mappa Mundi Exhibition' (unpublished report in the Hereford Archaeology Series, no. 283, July 1996) includes an

updated description based on recent observations.
9. R. Stone and N. Appleton-Fox, *A View from Hereford's Past* (Almeley, 1996), p. 33.
10. A. Watkins, 'The King's Ditch of the City of Hereford', *TWNFC*, 23 (1920), pp. 249–58.

Fig. 87. The stone-lined cellar found during the 1993 excavations on the site of the new library building.

55 feet (16.8 m.) wide and 100 feet (30.5 m.) long and open to the roof, was certainly appropriate for use when the bishop had to entertain the king and his retinue during their frequent visits to Hereford. As with the bishop's chapel, the main front faced west on to what had been the main north-south road leading down to the ford. Alterations to the great hall by Bishop Bisse (1713–21) and his successors have left a mere fragment of this once magnificent hall, but some of the piers, with their colonnettes and scalloped capitals, and part of the arch-braced roof, with nail-head ornamentation, survive. To the rear of the great hall, and linked by a passage or covered way, was another large building. In the late eighteenth century this was described as the 'Mansion-house contiguous [to the chapels of SS. Katherine and Mary Magdalene] belonging to the Chaplains of the said Chapels'. It has every appearance of being a detached chamber block and would originally have contained the bishop's great chamber on the first floor.[11]

Within this quadrant of the city there are several different alignments of buildings and boundary walls, all different from that of the present cathedral. The main alignment is taken from the bishop's chapel, which was built before the present

11. J. Price, *An Historical Account of the City of Hereford* (Hereford, 1796), p. 136; J. Blair, 'The Twelfth-Century Bishop's Palace at Hereford', *Medieval Archaeology*, 31 (1987), pp. 59–72, reassesses earlier articles and presents new evidence for its original plan.

cathedral was started and may well have been aligned with the Anglo-Saxon cathedral. This is the alignment that is followed by the putative bishop's great chamber and by a wall, partly still standing and partly traced as footings underneath the ruined fourteenth-century chapter house. The Royal Commission examined this wall and reported that 'excavation has proved that it continued up to and probably beyond the wall of the vicars' cloister; near this point was found the west splay of a doorway dating from the twelfth or thirteenth century'.[12] This wall separated the palace from the cathedral grounds and left enough space for an ample passageway to the north of the bishop's chapel. Projected westwards, the alignment of this boundary wall was eventually taken up by the inner wall of the early fifteenth-century south cloister. Although the sixteenth-century gatehouse and servants' range to the north west of the bishop's palace follow the alignment of the chapel, the bishop's palace and its stable block are slightly more on the skew, perhaps reflecting a curving road leading down to the ford. In the twelfth century the general aspect of the bishop's grounds must have been strikingly different from what is seen today. The great hall and chapel both faced westwards across an outer court to the old main road. Here there may well have been a gatehouse with a secondary road leading between the hall and the chapel to an inner court flanked on the eastern side by the bishop's great chamber and closed off to the south by a passage.[13]

Once the Normans had established themselves in Hereford they made a start on a completely new cathedral. This was laid out during the time of Bishop Reinhelm (1107–15) with scant regard for the Saxon town plan, for it cuts across the line of the old west-east road represented by King Street and Castle Street. It was this work, coupled with the increasing activity in the king's castle to the east, that began to establish the boundaries of the cathedral grounds as they are known today. With the cathedral centrally placed on the gravel terrace, and the bishop's palace occupying the ground towards the river, the scene was set for canons' houses to be laid out in a grand semi-circle around the new cathedral (endpapers). The positions of the original houses are no longer known with certainty, but it is probable that the present arrangement of large houses around the cathedral reflects these earlier buildings. Some, at least, must have been of substantial size and status, for in 1446 Canon Grene's great hall was being used by the bishop for transacting business. This was one of the two canonical houses that were taken over to provide a site for the new college of the vicars choral in October 1472. The other was the site of Canon Wolston's house which had apparently been burnt down some years earlier.[14]

12. RCHME, *Herefordshire*, i, p. 116.
13. Blair, 'The Twelfth-Century Bishop's Palace at Hereford', p. 71 and figs 6 and 7.

14. A. T. Bannister, 'The College of the Vicars Choral in Hereford Cathedral', *TWNFC*, 23 (1918–20), pp. 82–84.

As the more important of the two, it is suggested that Canon Grene's house occupied a prime site on the gravel terrace overlooking the river. As such, it would have been in a similar situation to the twelfth-century bishop's palace a little further upstream. Given that Canon Grene's house had been in use up to his death in April 1472 and was presumably in good condition only six years earlier, it is likely that it would have been appropriated by the vicars choral for their own use, probably as their new college hall. The diagonal wall which separates the grounds of the bishop's palace from the college grounds is probably earlier than the college. This wall or its predecessor may well have formed a similar separation between the bishop and Canon Grene. Indeed, it may reflect one side of a passageway, similar to the present one leading to Harley Court, leading to Canon Grene's house, with other canonical houses to the east. If this hypothesis is accepted, then the site of Canon Wolston's house could well be in the area of the college chapel and another canonical house could have been on the site of the present school buildings which almost adjoin the north range of the quadrangle. This is a late eighteenth-century brick-faced building with a timber-framed core, probably of seventeenth-century date (fig. 161).

To the north of Castle Street, the old deanery (fig. 164), although a nineteenth-century building, is an obvious site for a canonical house and one can be postulated here with little doubt. Adjoining it to the north is the narrow passage which leads to Harley Court. Most of this building, now two houses, appears early Georgian from the outside, but internally the northern part is timber-framed with a huge central chimney stack which may well be of sixteenth-century origin. Attached on the south side is a fourteenth-century four-bay hall. Although it is relatively small, 36 feet (11 m.) long by 17 feet (5.2 m.) wide, the hall is well-decorated with arch-braced principals and moulded and cambered tie-beams and decorated wall-plates. The wind braces, supporting the single purlins, are handsomely pierced and cusped. Underneath it is a cellar containing medieval stonework and close-studded timberwork.[15] There would seem no doubt that this formed yet another of the canonical houses.

The lane leading to Harley Court has, on its north side, the ample grounds of Harley House. This is a complex building which was refronted in 1739 with stone that is said to have come from the destroyed chapter house. Inside, the inspectors for the Royal Commission considered that the cellars and the lower parts of the south-western block were medieval, but that there had been additions and much rebuilding in the sixteenth and seventeenth centuries.[16] Facing Harley House across St John Street is the appropriately named Canon's House. The roadside part of

15. A. Watkins, 'Three Early Timber Halls in the City of Hereford,' *TWNFC*, 23 (1918–20), pp. 164–71.

16. RCHME, *Herefordshire*, i, p. 141b.

the building to the north of the entry is of sixteenth-century date and was originally jettied. The east front includes two windows with four-centred lights in square heads. This range was extended to the south, probably in the seventeenth century. This sixteenth-century range forms a cross-wing to a fourteenth- or early fifteenth-century hall range. It is of five bays with a heavily restored hammer-beam style roof with curved braces under the collars and strengthened by two rows of cusped wind-braces. In the ground floor there is a fifteenth-century doorway with a four-centred arch in a square head with foliage and trefoils in the spandrels.[17] The name and present use of this building makes it almost a certainty as one of the original sites for a canonical house. When the fourteenth-century hall was built, St John Street would have been a narrow lane (called Milk Lane) no wider than Harley Close. This lane was set against the grounds of Harley House, so there would have been ample room for a boundary wall on the eastern side of the Canon's House.

All the buildings that now face on to the Close are relatively modern with the exception of the half-timbered building directly in front of the Canon's House with its gable facing St John Street (fig. 88). Now merely a barn, this building was originally a hall in its own right with grounds probably extending well into the present close. From the outside it does not look as though it is of any great interest, but a detailed investigation has shown that it is one of the oldest secular buildings in the city, having been built in the latter part of the thirteenth century. In its original state it extended by an additional half-bay into St John Street, had aisles on each side and included an open scissor-braced roof. It was reroofed in the sixteenth century and it may have been then that the aisles were lost and the sides underbuilt in stone. It was probably at the same time that the half-bay that jutted out almost to the middle of St John Street was removed as part of an early street widening exercise.[18]

There are two houses on the north side of the present close, the Archdeacon's House and the Precentor's House. Both are shown on Taylor's 1757 plan (fig. 89), but their histories are vastly different. It is suggested that the easternmost one – the Precentor's House – with its long but narrow garden, was inserted, partly from the grounds of the Canon's House, but also from the grounds of the canonical house that stood in front of the Canon's House (now the barn), during the early eighteenth century. This partition of properties shows particularly well on eighteenth- and nineteenth-century maps and the site is therefore not considered to be that of

17. Ibid., p. 142a, and recent personal observations.
18. First described in an unpublished interim report in the Hereford Archaeology

Series, 62, October 1989. It will be included in R. K. Morriss, *The Timber-Framed Buildings of Hereford* (forthcoming).

Fig. 88. The cathedral barn including the remains of a thirteenth-century hall.

an early canonical house. The late eighteenth-century Archdeacon's House is another matter, for it occupies the corner site between the present Close and Church Street. An early photograph shows that, on the corner, there was a two-storeyed timber-framed building with jetties on the two main fronts and a second timber-framed building to the rear. In the latter part of the nineteenth century, when these buildings were demolished, the front of the Archdeacon's House was extended in matching style and brickwork. It is suggested that this corner site balanced the one still containing the thirteenth-century building at the corner of St John Street and was the site of yet another canonical house, probably with grounds extending well into the present Close.

The similarity goes even further, for the house behind the Archdeacon's House, now 20 Church Street, was also most probably a canonical house, matching the Canon's House in St John Street. Here, a fourteenth-century first-floor hall and

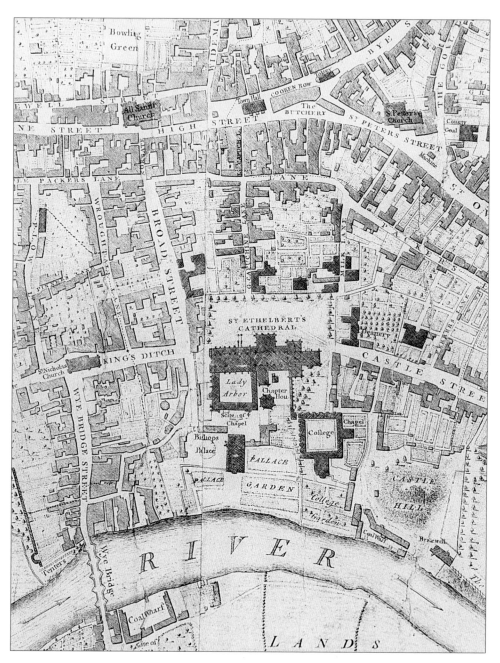

Fig. 89. A section of the plan of Hereford by Isaac Taylor, 1757, showing the cathedral and Close. (HCL.)

Fig. 90. The fourteenth-century first floor hall inside 20 Church Street.

undercroft has recently been restored to its late medieval splendour (fig. 90). This three-bay building includes an almost complete crown-post roof. The clearance has exposed a screens passage with original ogee-headed doorways and a well-preserved timber window of four cusped, ogee-headed lights. In the undercroft is a similar, but undecorated, window. The hall has a central fireplace on the southern wall set into a large external stone stack and a stair tower on the opposite side.[19] Excavations to the north of the hall exposed the foundations of what may have been a detached kitchen.[20]

If the above hypotheses are accepted, it can be inferred that the Close before the eighteenth-century was much smaller than the present one, with the grounds of the canonical houses stretching a considerable distance further south than at present. From the dates of the present buildings, it would appear that in the latter part of the seventeenth century or early in the eighteenth century there was a radical change in the whole appearance of the Close.

In the mid eighteenth century the plot on the western corner of Church Street

19. Hereford Archaeology Series, interim reports 18 (September 1987) and 82, (July 1990), and Morriss, *Timber-Framed*

Buildings.

20. Hereford Archaeology Series, interim reports 99 and 99a (March, May 1991).

and the Close was separated from the plots fronting Broad Street by a narrow passage. On Taylor's 1757 plan this plot was devoid of buildings and was apparently in use as a garden. Although one or two small buildings had been erected on the plot by the mid nineteenth century, there was little overall change. The medieval arrangements of buildings in the area immediately to the west of Church Street are much more difficult to understand now because the whole site was cleared and replaced with a new telephone exchange in 1949.[21] It may well be that a canonical house was lost during the late seventeenth- or early eighteenth-century replanning of the Close described above, leaving only a part of the garden. On the opposite side of the passage and facing Broad Street, the Roman Catholic church of St Francis Xavier and its presbytery, both probably of 1839, and the Post Office, built in 1881, indicate the scale of the changes associated with this corner.

Between the Close and the southern end of Broad Street, and directly facing King Street, was a row of houses of varying date which were demolished following a fire in 1935.[22] Plans, photographs and documentary sources give some impression of the area. The buildings that were demolished all had commercial uses in the nineteenth century. Indeed, one was the Globe tavern, an inn of long standing that was converted to an apartment house in the 1860s.[23] It is evident that if there had been any canonical houses adjoining Broad Street, then they had been cleared and the sites used for alternative commercial purposes, well before the nineteenth century.

There is no specific reason to suppose that Broad Street together with Palace Yard, its continuation leading towards the bishop's palace, limited the area where canonical houses may have been. Indeed, 'The Residence', until the 1950s an attractive Victorian-Gothic stone house with a timber-framed building to the rear, situated on the north-west corner of the junction with King Street, was occupied by the canon residentiary in 1891, becoming a private hotel at a later date.[24]

The Close has been so-called since at least 1389 when a royal licence was given to the dean and chapter to enclose the cemetery and to keep the gates locked after curfew. The reasons stated for the measure were the many dangers and moral scandals, the thefts of church goods, the secret burials of unbaptised infants and the mischief done by swine and other animals that dragged the dead bodies from their resting places in the ground.[25] In the late 1840s, Dean Merewether exhibited a set of keys which were said to be the seven (or eight – the reports are

21. F. C. Morgan, 'Excavations on the Site of the New Telephone Exchange', *TWNFC*, 33 (1951), p. 212.

22. A. Sandford, *Hereford in Old Photographs* (Gloucester, 1987), pp. 112–13.

23. R. Shoesmith, *The Pubs of Hereford City* (Almeley, 1998), p. 56.

24. D. Foxton, *Hereford, Then and Now* (3 vols, Hereford, 1988–97), i, p. 40; ii, p. 82.

25. Capes, *Charters* , p. 84.

contradictory) keys of the ancient gates of the Close at Hereford. They were joined together by an iron bar.[26]

The Close had been the general burial ground for the town from well before 1140, and its exclusive rights over other churches in the city were jealously maintained. There were other problems such as the time when Bishop Robert Foliot (1173–86) protested about a house of an archdeacon which had been built upon the churchyard itself and insisted that it should be immediately removed.[27] Indeed, the uses of the cemetery extended far beyond the town itself. A typical agreement was that made in 1288 between the rector of Hampton Bishop and the chapter. It was agreed that any parishioner whose goods at the time of his death exceeded 6s. in value should be brought to the cathedral cemetery for interment, whilst women and those of lesser means should be buried nearer home.

The constant use of such a limited area for burial meant that, as it was filled and refilled with monuments and coffins, the level of the ground gradually rose. The level then was much greater than it is at present, for various old deeds speak of the ascent to it from different sides. In one, Church Street was described as 'the lane which leads from the Cemetery steps (*scaleriis*) to Caboche lane'. These steps are also described as 'the scalernds at the Broad Cabach lane' in a municipal document of 1520.[28] Steps at the entrance from Castle Street are called 'scallions' in 1699,[29] and others are mentioned leading from Broad Street up into the cemetery.

By the end of the eighteenth century the situation had become so serious that on 11 September 1790 the dean and chapter wrote to the several parishes in the city and suburbs to the effect that:

> The Dean and Chapter ... having very seriously considered the present state of the Minster churchyard and that of the Lady-Arbour (the only places of Interment in this populous City) how greatly crowded they are, and have long been with Bodies ... how great reason there is to apprehend that some contagious Distemper may arise to the endangering the Health and even the Lives of the Inhabitants have found it absolutely necessary to declare, That from and after the twenty fifth day of March 1791 no bodies can be admitted for Sepulture here, except of those who shall happen to die within the Precincts ...[30]

In 1796 it was noted that 'all the tomb-stones and grave-stones in the cathedral yard were levelled and removed, in the presence of an assembled multitude, who could not refrain from venting their grief at this outrage'. This may have been

26. Notes in *Proceedings of the Society of Antiquaries*, 2 (1849–53), p. 6; and *Archaeological Journal*, 6 (1849), p. 199.

27. P. Morgan, 'The Cathedral Close', *FHC*, 42 (1976), pp. 15–19; HCA, 1379.

28. R. Johnson, *The Ancient Customs of the City of Hereford* (London and Hereford, 1868), p. 138.

29. HCA, 7031/3, p. 525.

30. Morgan, 'The Cathedral Close', p. 17.

partly due to the damage done to the countless memorials to the dead during the works following the fall of the western tower in 1786. Burials continued to take place from time to time in the early years of the nineteenth century, presumably of those who 'died within the precincts'.[31] It was not until 1850–51 that the ground level in the Close was lowered, in some places by several feet, and all the tombs and headstones were taken down.[32]

It was not just the parts of the cathedral precinct to the north and east of the cathedral that were used for burial; the area to the west of the cathedral and the Lady arbour was also used. During the archaeological excavation for the new library building adjoining Palace Yard the remains of over 1100 articulated bodies were exhumed, including some 200 from what are assumed to be mid fourteenth-century plague pits.[33]

In 1395 the vicars choral were incorporated as a college with the form and title of *Collegium vicariorum ecclesiae Herefordensis*. The charter that was granted at that time indicates that there were then twenty-seven vicars, of which one was the custos. The vicars already had a communal residence – a building on the south side of Castle Street, parts of which still survive. Set back from the street, and now incorporated into a later complex of buildings (collectively No. 29), are the remains of what was originally a ground-floor hall. It was built of coursed, dressed sandstone and the blocked matching doorways of the screens passage survive at the northern end. In addition, there are the remains of two very tall primary windows, probably each of two lights, on either side of the hall. The roof, of nine quite narrow bays, was clearly once open to the apex. Rows of peg-holes at the ends of the collars indicate the former presence of arch-braces. Above each of the collars a pair of cusped raking struts rises to the principals. The trusses support two tiers of moulded purlins and a ridge-piece. The two rows of wind-braces – paired, triple-cusped and with solid spandrels – form decorative arches. The central cusps have pierced spandrels and are tipped by ornately carved fleurons. There were just two common rafters to each bay, square-sectioned and of thick scantling. There is no obvious sign of a side stack and an open hearth cannot be

31. Burial still occurred in the nineteenth century as the recent archaeological excavation of a depression to the east of the Lady chapel has shown. The work exposed the lower part of an open, brick-lined vault that contained the coffins of Mrs Mary Powell, who died in Chelsea in February 1823, aged ninety-two, and her brother Daniel Powell, who died in 1807. The burials were very shallow and it was apparent that the main reason for the depression was the loss of the stone that originally sealed the vault. Many of the gravestones that were moved at that time were reused to form a pavement in the chapter house yard and it is there that the stone, which originally sealed the vault containing Mary Powell, finally found a resting place.

32. Stone and Appleton-Fox, *A View from Hereford's Past*, p. 13.

33. Ibid., p. 24.

ruled out, especially as the southern portion of the roof has been radically rebuilt. Despite being fairly small in area, the hall was sufficiently tall for first and attic floors to have been inserted into it in the post-medieval period. This building, presumably the communal hall of the college, was probably built during the second half of the fourteenth century.[34]

Some eighty years after their incorporation, the vicars complained to Bishop Stanbury that their dwelling was 'so distant from the church that through fear of evil-doers and the inclemency of the weather, many of them cannot go to the church at midnight to celebrate divine service'. The bishop must have viewed this situation seriously for, on 18 October 1472, he obtained a licence from the king to provide them with a site for a new building.[35] As already mentioned, this was the sites of two canonical houses and it is probable that the great hall of one, that of the late Canon Grene, was incorporated as the new hall for the vicars (endpapers). The construction work was started immediately and was completed in about three years. It is suggested that the eastern range, including a chapel and possibly the eastern part of the southern range, was built in the first season. The northern range followed in the second, and the project was completed in the third year (plate IXa).

The college is built of the local Old Red Sandstone with ashlared external elevations and partially dressed coursed rubblestone to the cloister. Each lodging consisted of a two-bay first-floor hall, open to the apex of the roof, above a smaller ground-floor chamber. The lower chamber was narrower than the room above because the cloistral walk around the garth is incorporated into the ground-floor space. The walk is separated from the lodgings by a timber-framed wall of close-studding. There is an open, stone arcade to the cloister. Each first-floor hall was reached by an internal staircase which was directly behind the door leading off the cloistral walk. Many of the original four-centred doorways have been blocked, but their positions have been apparent since the close-studding was fully exposed in the 1930s. The two external walls of each lodging were of stone, each wall having two windows on the first floor. Those on the courtyard side were of equal size, but the external windows, which flanked the fireplace, were of two sizes – a narrow light illuminating the stairs and a wider one which lit the hall. The ground-floor room had windows only on the external face. Each lodging had fireplaces, in the ground- and first-floor rooms, with four-centred heads with either hollow-chamfered or wave-moulded and stopped decoration. The partition walls between the individual lodgings normally consisted of wide-panelled timber frames carrying a closed roof truss. In each lodging the roof was divided into two bays

34. RCHME, *Herefordshire*, i, p. 141; and Morriss, *Timber-Framed Buildings*.

35. Bannister, 'The College of the Vicars Choral', p. 83.

by an arch-braced truss. A trefoil pattern was created in these trusses by the cusping of the upper portions of the principals and the tops of the collars. The principals sprang from chamfered and moulded timber corbels, with plain or tilting shields, set a little below the wall plates. The roof structure consisted of two tiers of chamfered and stopped purlins braced by cusped, chamfered wind braces. Originally the roof had overhanging eaves and was probably covered in tilestones.[36]

The entrance to the college is in the north-eastern corner, where there is a two-storey entrance porch (fig. 91). There is also an access by a corridor of ten bays from the college to the cathedral south-east transept (fig. 106).[37] The chapter house yard is between this corridor and the bishop's cloister.

The foundations and the lower parts of some of the walls of the decagonal chapter house fill the western part of the yard. Work started on the construction of the chapter house about 1340, but it was probably not completed until about 1370. The delay may well have been due to the plague, for it was not until 1364 that the dean and chapter contracted with Thomas of Cambridge to complete the project. This was fortunate, for Thomas designed a fan-vault of an advanced type, contemporary with that in the cloisters of Gloucester cathedral. The building had ten sides and was 45 feet (13.7 m.) in diameter. It was described in 1634, by an early tourist to Hereford, as being 'very fayre, and not much shortt of any wee yett saw, wherein are ten fayre square built windows of Antique worke in good colours. It is adorned on the walls with forty-six old Pictures, curiously drawne and sett out' (fig. 16).[38]

During the Civil War the lead was removed from the roof for reuse in the castle and was not replaced afterwards. Bishop Bisse (1712–21) then removed some of the windows when restoring his palace, and by 1769 the building was so dangerous that it had to be demolished. Recent clearance has exposed sufficient of the foundations to appreciate the shape and size of the building and the south wall still stands up to window sill level. The chapter house was joined to the bishop's cloister by a two-bay vestibule. Sufficient of the south wall survives to demonstrate that it had a stone vault with wall, diagonal and intermediate ribs. The line of the roof can be seen on the cloister wall (fig. 65).[39]

The south-west cloister or Lady arbour lies to the south of the cathedral nave (fig. 45). The eastern cloister may well have started its life in the twelfth century

36. R. K. Morriss and R. Shoesmith, 'The College of the Vicars Choral in Hereford', in Whitehead, *Medieval Art at Hereford*, pp. 157–72.

37. G. Marshall, 'The Roof of the Vicars' Cloister at Hereford', *TWNFC*, 23 (1918–20), pp. 71–81.

38. N. Drinkwater, 'The Chapter House at Hereford Cathedral', *Archaeological Journal*, 112 (1955), pp. 61–75, and a shortened version in *TWNFC*, 35 (1955–57), pp. 260–65.

39. RCHME, *Herefordshire*, i, p. 116, and Drinkwater, 'The Chapter House at Hereford Cathedral'. See also above, pp. 227–29.

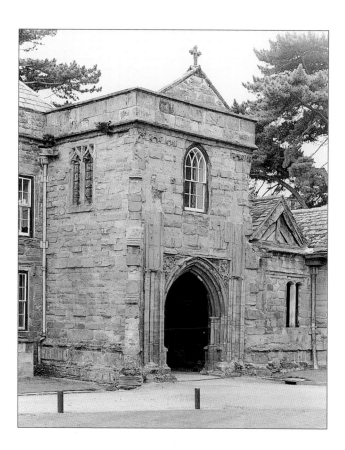

Fig. 91. The entrance porch to
the college of vicars choral.

or even earlier as a corridor or pentise connecting the cathedral with the bishop's
palace and eventually providing a covered link to the fourteenth-century chapter
house. When, in the early fifteenth century, the passageway was radically reconstructed to become the eastern range to the cloister, and the west and south
cloistral ranges were built, the north wall of the eleventh-century bishop's chapel
was incorporated into the new build.

The south cloister is of nine bays excluding those on the angles. Each bay,
except the seventh from the east, has a window of four cinquefoiled lights with
tracery in a four-centred head. The seventh bay contains a central doorway. The
stone vault continues the pattern in the three southern bays of the east cloister
(tierceron stars). Between each bay the vault springs from round shafts with moulded
capitals and bases on the north wall and from head-corbels on the south wall. The
vault has moulded ridge, diagonal, subsidiary and wall ribs with bosses at the
subsidiary intersections and an eight-pointed panel with a carved boss at the main
intersections.[40]

40. See above, note 6.

In 1760 the west range of the cloister, which had been used for a time by the Free Grammar School, was totally demolished. It was replaced by a new, much more spacious Georgian building called the Music Room which was designed for use during the Three Choirs Festival as well as by the School.[41] By 1835 that building had also been demolished and the space was left empty until it was partially filled by the construction of the Dean Leigh library in 1897. The library building, which is of similar style to the rest of the cloistral ranges, was designed to have a northern extension that would join it to the cathedral. In the event, the new library building, completed in 1996, was positioned to the west and parallel to the Dean Leigh building to which it was joined by a wide corridor.

41. Stone and Appleton-Fox, *A View from Hereford's Past*, p. 13.

12

The New Library Building

John Tiller

The terms on which the Mappa Mundi Trust was established required the trustees to make provision for the conservation, security and public display of the map and the historic chained library in Hereford. The problems of erecting a new building in an ancient cathedral Close are such that it needed to be established first whether any existing building in the vicinity could be adapted to meet the purpose. Whitfield Partners were appointed as the consulting architects, and in their first report to the trustees, dated 1 October 1990, they made the following points: first, the chained library and Mappa Mundi should continue to be housed within the cathedral precinct, and should be associated with the whole of the cathedral library, not only for functional convenience but because the continuous nature of the collection is of outstanding importance. This led to the second point, that the chained library and Mappa Mundi should be understood by visitors to be an integral part of the library, and not an isolated tourist attraction. Thirdly, since the implication of the above was for a new building, it should be recognised that its location and design would inevitably generate anxiety and possibly downright opposition on architectural, contextual and archaeological grounds.

The trustees accepted the report. After consideration had been given to several sites, including that of the missing western range of the south-west cloister, a site immediately to the west of the Dean Leigh library, and linked to it, was selected as the most suitable. The size and shape of the new building was determined by the surviving seventeenth-century bookcases of the chained library, which were to be arranged according to their original layout in the Lady chapel. From this starting point a building was developed which housed the map and the chained books in two chambers on the ground floor, with a space for the reading room and modern library above them, and a basement strongroom beneath for the cathedral archives and unchained rare books. The whole was linked to the Dean Leigh building in such a way as to give public access to the historic artefacts through an introductory and interpretative exhibition in the south-west cloister, and at the same time the upper floor of Dean Leigh provided additional shelving and office space for the working library above. Users of the library were to be admitted through a separate entrance to the building, giving access by stairs and lift to the reading room. In this way a considerable area of accommodation was provided without imposing too large a building on the site. Visitors to the exhibition move on a horizontal axis, while the working library operates on a vertical one (fig. 92).

The architectural character of the building derives from a number of factors. Obviously, its close proximity to the west front of the cathedral, the cloister and the Dean Leigh library called for a design that could sit comfortably alongside them without necessarily adopting an over-historical style. Certain requirements such as security and internal environmental control had a profound effect on both the structure of the building and its external appearance; it is from these that the particular pattern of windows and wall surfaces is derived. Essentially, the building is designed to maintain the exacting environmental conditions necessary for the protection of its contents. Only the flow of visitors disturbs this equilibrium, and to cope with this some air conditioning has been introduced. A high level of 'passivity' is ensured by the use of the massive stone walls that are a feature of the building. There is also a highly sophisticated system to protect against fire damage, although neither this nor the air conditioning system are apparent in the rooms containing the map and the chained library (fig. 150).

Fig. 92. New library building, 1996, on the right; the Dean Leigh library, 1897, on the left.

Fig. 93. The reading room in the new library building.

The particular aesthetic of the building was largely prompted by purely practical considerations such as have been mentioned, combined with a wish to use all materials in an honest and, where appropriate, traditional way. Unlike many contemporary buildings, the new library is an expression of the way it is built. The basic materials are traditional: stone from Derbyshire, slate from Westmorland, oak from Herefordshire. The reading room, which lies within the roof structure, takes its character from the fully exposed green oak frame lined with cedar wood, and affords a fine view through the principal window north along Broad Street (fig. 93).

There was a protracted process to obtain the necessary approval for the building from the Cathedrals' Fabric Commission for England, the local planning authority and English Heritage. This was followed by a lengthy and expensive archaeological excavation of the site which uncovered a huge number of human remains including over 1100 articulated skeletons. Finally the new building was opened by Her Majesty The Queen on 3 May 1996 and subsequently received favourable recognition and a number of awards, including that of Building of the Year from the Royal Fine Art Commission in 1997.[1]

1. This chapter is based on personal knowledge, undeposited archival material, and W. Whitfield, 'The Architect's Description of the New Building', *Three Choirs Festival Programme* (Hereford, 1997), pp. 18–19.

13

The Stained Glass

Paul Iles

Describing the cathedral at the beginning of the nineteenth century, the antiquarian John Duncumb reports the absence of stained glass in the building and comments disapprovingly on 'an uninterrupted glare of light' in the nave and aisles.[1] The cathedral is still a light and airy building with a good deal of clear glass in its windows but there is also some impressive stained glass mostly of the nineteenth and first half of the twentieth centuries. Earlier vandalism and destruction during the sixteenth and seventeenth centuries left the cathedral with only fragments of ancient glass. These pieces offer tantalising glimpses of what might have been but sadly there is no detailed information available about the cathedral's medieval glass to help either factual knowledge or imagination.

What may be the oldest glass from the cathedral's medieval windows is no longer in the building itself but is now at the east end of Allensmore church, one of the parish chancels for which historically the dean and chapter has been responsible.[2] The glass dates from the late thirteenth or early fourteenth century and makes up three small panels of great beauty, the central one depicting the crucifixion with the wood of the cross coloured green, *arbor vitae*.

Remnants of fourteenth-century glass are still in the cathedral. The pieces were discovered during the extensive restoration in the middle of the nineteenth century, when the windows were given much needed attention. William Warrington (1796–1869), who was engaged to install new glass in three windows, was particularly interested in ancient glass as well as being a designer and maker of glass. During his work in the cathedral, he found several boxes containing fourteenth-century glass and, in 1864, he restored it and used it in two windows, one in the south choir aisle and another in the north-east transept. The four figures in the first

1. J. Duncumb, *Collections towards the History and Antiquities of the County of Hereford* (8 vols, Hereford and London, 1804–

1915), i, p. 537.
2. F. C. Morgan, *Hereford Cathedral Church Glass* (3rd edn, Hereford, 1979), p. 21.

window (St Mary Magdalene, St Ethelbert, St Augustine and St George) are original, though the figures in the other window (St Katherine, St Michael, St Gregory, St Thomas of Canterbury) are by Warrington. The canopies, spandrels and the surrounding grisaille are all good examples of medieval glass.

Before the old glass was taken out and replaced with new glass in 1737, the large window at the west end of the cathedral almost certainly contained fifteenth-century stained glass.[3] The window was inserted before 1435 by William Lochard, canon residentiary and precentor, whose memorial brass was at the west end of the nave (died 24 September 1438). The brass was lost after the collapse of the west front but it provided information about Lochard's career which included royal service at Windsor, which may explain why the fifteenth-century glass is said to have been made up of a series of royal portraits: Richard II, Henry IV, Henry V, Henry VI, John, duke of Bedford, and Humphrey, duke of Gloucester.[4] In 1737 the chapter deliberately and carefully retained the medieval glass from the window and some of it, together with other fragments, is believed to have made up the two panels of fifteenth-century glass, with its characteristic pale colours and yellow stain, which are now in the north transept. The panels were purchased in 1925 in a sale at Hampton Court, near Leominster, and given to the cathedral. At the top of these panels there is a Madonna and Child; in the left hand panel the main subject may be St Katherine surrounded by saints;[5] and in the right hand panel there are fragments of various scenes: John the Baptist and his mother Elizabeth, a head of the Virgin from an Annunciation scene, the heads of two sleeping soldiers (presumably from a Resurrection scene), and the figures of Judas and one of the chief priests.[6]

More pre-Reformation glass is to be found in the eastern window in the south nave aisle where there are fragments from scenes from the story of Joseph, showing him being let down into the pit and his dream, with the sun, moon and stars, and the wheatsheaves bowing down in his honour. In the Audley chantry (*c.* 1496), in the four upper windows, there are quarries of the late fifteenth or early sixteenth

3. According to the fabric accounts, William Reece was paid £12 17s. 8¼d. 'for Glazing and painting at the West Window from Aug. 13 to Nov. 10th 1737', HCA, 7020/2/1, fabric accounts, 1737–38. I am grateful to the cathedral archivist, Rosalind Caird, for this information.

4. BL, MS Harley 4046. The window is described in Duncumb, *Collections*, i, p. 542, and Marshall, *Hereford Cathedral*, pp. 150–51. For full details of the replacement of this window in 1737 see D. Whitehead, 'A

Goth among the Greeks', *FHC*, 57 (1991), pp. 18–41, at 30–31.

5. Wilfrid Drake, one of the donors, suggested that the figures were the Blessed Virgin Mary and six other virgin saints, Katherine, Barbara, Ursula, Margaret, Lucy and Dorothy.

6. A description of the window by F. S. Eden is in the *Burlington Magazine*, 47 (1925), pp. 115–21. Other pieces of glass from the same window are scattered, some being in Boston, USA: Morgan, *Hereford Cathedral Church Glass*, p. 4, n. 1.

century which include suns, a white rose, a star and roundels with wreaths enclosing the Audley arms and the arms of the Hereford deanery.[7]

The oldest glass at present in the cathedral, however, which is of outstanding quality, is in two windows on the south side of the Lady chapel. They contain grisaille glass and four panels of remarkable late thirteenth-century glass from a Munich workshop. Originally they were in St Peter's church, Hereford, and had been taken out in the 1820s, though it is not yet certain how they got there.[8] A brass tablet below the windows records that the glass was bought for £5 by Robert Biddulph Phillips of Longworth and presented to the cathedral in 1849. Dean Merewether, who included medieval stained glass among his many enthusiasms and who had reassembled the famous fourteenth-century glass in the church at Madley where he was incumbent,[9] proposed to put the Munich panels into the north transept but he died before the work could be carried out. The glass was taken to Betton and Evans's workshop in Shrewsbury, which may be where it acquired some of the unfortunate defects which are now apparent,[10] and it was not inserted into its present position until much later, in 1898, when the work was paid for by W. Henry Barneby, also of Longworth. The iconography of the windows includes a vesica-shaped Majesty with the signs of the four evangelists surrounding it; an Agnus Dei; the Three Marys at the Sepulchre; the Crucifixion, and Christ carrying his cross in which again the green cross is an *arbor vitae* (pl. IVc).

Most of this small collection of remaining medieval glass was not in its present position in the cathedral until the second half of the nineteenth century. During the 1830s, however, antiquarian interest in ancient glass design and manufacture developed rapidly. Locally, in 1832, the firm of Betton and Evans of Shrewsbury began work on the famous fourteenth-century glass in St Lawrence, Ludlow, and its restoration became a major contribution to the revival of interest. Then William Warrington published his *History of Stained Glass* in 1848. Gradually both accurate and reasonably full details of the design of ancient glass became known and, at much the same time, chemical analysis uncovered the technique of how it was

7. Morgan, *Hereford Cathedral Church Glass,* p. 14. The glass was repaired by the Friends of Hereford Cathedral in 1935: *FHC,* 3 (1935), pp. 18, 21–22. Morgan also describes the glass which was in the lower windows of the chantry chapel and which is now lost but was made in the nineteenth century, probably given by John Goss, custos of the college of vicars choral and vicar of St John the Baptist, 1860–77.

8. R. Shoesmith, 'The Medieval Glass in the Lady Chapel: An Interim Report, October 1998' (HCA, Archaeologist's Reports), p. 3.

9. S. Brown, 'The Fourteenth-Century Stained Glass of Madley', in Whitehead, *Medieval Art at Hereford,* pp. 122–31 at 124.

10. I owe this information to Jim Budd of Ross-on-Wye, glassmaker, who was responsible for the most recent work of cleaning and repair of the window, paid for by English Heritage and the Friends of Hereford Cathedral. A report of earlier repairs to this glass, *FHC,* 3 (1935), p. 22, records that previously some 'very pink heads' had been put in.

made. Many new churches were being built after 1840 and, instead of placing memorial plaques and tablets on the walls, it became fashionable for memorial stained glass to be donated and put into church windows. To meet the increased demand for such glass, new companies were founded and many of them became famous. Happily for Hereford, the considerable amount of memorial Victorian glass in the cathedral made after 1850 represents some of the best work of the most important of these firms. Much of the glass is splendid and incidentally records interesting details of the history of the nineteenth-century cathedral.

The earliest memorial window was put in at the east end of the Lady chapel in 1852. The window was designed by N. J. Cottingham, son of L. N. Cottingham, and appropriately it is a memorial to Dean Merewether. The window was made in the London studio of Charles Gibbs with a design which uses narrative scenes from the life of Christ. The design appears to be almost deliberately reminiscent of the famous thirteenth-century glass in the Sainte-Chapelle in Paris and it fits perfectly with the architecture of the cathedral's Lady chapel, built 1220–40. The other glass in the chapel was also designed by Cottingham junior and was made in the Gibbs studio. It fills a series of windows commemorating members of the Morgan family: Charles Morgan, precentor 1771–87; his children Elizabeth, Ann and Hugh, a canon of the cathedral; Hugh Morgan's second wife, their daughter and son (who died aged one month); and, finally, their son Hugh Hanmer Morgan, chancellor of the cathedral, and his wife Helen Mary.

Warrington's three new large windows were installed in time for the reopening of the cathedral in 1863. The first was the window in the north nave aisle above the Booth tomb which includes scenes from the life of St John the Baptist and is a memorial to John Clutton, the father-in-law of Archdeacon Lane Freer, and his wife Mary, who was the daughter of Dean Wetherell. Warrington also designed two other memorial windows: in the south-east transept to George Huntingford, bishop 1815–32, depicting the life of St Peter, and in the north choir aisle to Thomas Musgrave, bishop 1837–47, with scenes based on the life of St Paul.

After 1845, the ecclesiastical metalwork firm of John Hardman of Birmingham was encouraged by Pugin to develop the manufacture of stained glass and he employed Hardman to make many of the windows he designed.[11] But it was not until some years after Pugin died (in 1852) that Hardman made what is perhaps the greatest window in the cathedral: Pevsner says of it, 'a Victorian piece to be proud of' (pl. V).[12] An unusually large window put in the north transept in 1864 at the considerable cost of £1316, it is a memorial to Archdeacon Lane Freer. The huge design divides into two sections with an elaborate and successful narrative

11. P. Stanton, *Pugin* (London, 1971), p. 169.
12. N. Pevsner, *Herefordshire*, The Buildings of England (Harmondsworth, 1962), p. 166.

scheme. On the left hand side the iconography portrays the church militant and on the right hand side the church triumphant. It is a magnificent example of Hardman's work with remarkable colours especially of cobalt blue and ruby red. Later, in 1872, Hardman made the window above the high altar to a design approved by Gilbert Scott, the architect responsible for the later restoration of the cathedral. The centre light shows Christ in majesty and in the three panels below there is another carefully devised theological scheme, bringing together the Sacrifice of Isaac, the Crucifixion and the Supper at Emmaus.

Previously the window at the east end of the choir had undergone a number of changes. Through a benefaction from Dr George Cope (died 1821), it had been glazed in 1825 with Charles Backler's painted glass based on Benjamin West's picture *The Last Supper* (fig. 71). Dean Merewether may at least have considered retaining it during his restoration of the choir, since it did not appear to interfere with the Romanesque arch underneath, which he was determined to open up.[13] Later, however, the plan changed and the whole window was reconstructed demanding new glass. A note in the chapter act book, dated 1 September 1849, states that an anonymous donor had placed £150 in a London bank to provide glass for the new window's central light.[14] At the same time the hope was expressed that in due course the side lights would be filled by other donors. By 1851, however, only the central light had been filled and a proposal was made that the side lights should be glazed as a memorial to Joseph Bailey MP with a design which would have continued and completed the narrative scheme of the Merewether memorial windows in the Lady chapel, which rather oddly ended with the supper in the house of Mary, Martha and Lazarus. Thus the choir windows were to begin with the triumphal entry into Jerusalem and conclude with Our Lord seated in majesty, surrounded by the Apostles.[15] Pevsner (without giving any reference, though the dating is consistent with the claim) stated that Phoebe Stanton had discovered that the window, made by Hardman, was designed by Pugin.[16] Murray's *Handbook*, 1864, says the window was 'filled with stained glass by Hardman; too minute perhaps in design for the height at which it is placed, but very good'.[17] Later, Hugh Fisher in Bell's guide to the cathedral (published in 1898 but based on observations which must have been made before 1871) says, 'the eastern central

13. A sketch showing the window in one of Merewether's conjectural schemes is reproduced in Whitehead, *Medieval Art at Hereford*, pl. XXXIVb.
14. HCA, 7031/20, p. 176, chapter acts, 1 September 1849; Morgan, *Hereford Cathedral Church Glass*, p. 23.
15. Bailey's memorial included the reredos behind the high altar. The whole scheme with details of the windows is given in *A Brief Description of the Memorials of the late Very Revd John Merewether DD and Joseph Bailey Esq.* (Hereford, 1852).
16. Pevsner, *Herefordshire*, p. 165.
17. R. J. King, *A Handbook to Hereford Cathedral* (London, 1864), pp. 16–17.

window of the choir was an anonymous gift in 1851, executed by Hardman. Its beauties are entirely lost at its present height from the ground. The circular medallions are three feet in diameter, the subjects being 1. The Ascension; 2. The Resurrection; 3. The Crucifixion'. There are also four semicircles which show the Descent from the Cross, the Harrowing of Hell, the appearance of Jesus to Mary in the garden and Thomas placing his hand in the side of the risen Christ.[18] Eventually, the chapter engaged Hardman to replace this unsatisfactory window with the present one. The earlier glass of 1851 was placed in the high clerestory windows in the east wall of the south transept where it remains today but where, especially if it was designed by Pugin, regretfully it still cannot be easily seen and appreciated.[19]

Clayton and Bell, another famous studio, was founded in 1855. They put in the window in the north choir aisle with a simple and attractive design of medallions which must represent the early work of the firm (Pevsner calls it 'charmingly humble') to commemorate John Hunt, the young organist who succeeded Wesley and who died in tragic circumstances in 1842 after falling over a food trolley in college cloisters.[20] The windows in the clerestory in the north transept were made by the same firm to commemorate three other famous organists of the cathedral: S. S. Wesley, Townshend Smith and Langdon Colborne.[21] The designs here show King David and St Cecilia and a number of musical instruments, including a double shawm, a psaltery, cymbals, fiddles and portative organs. The rather dull and less successful memorial window to Queen Victoria at the west end of the nave is also by Clayton and Bell (1902) and was put into existing tracery from Wyatt's west front which Oldrid Scott had managed to incorporate into his own design. John Burlison and Thomas Grylls were trained in the studios of Clayton

18. A. H. Fisher, *The Cathedral Church of Hereford: A Description of its Fabric and a Brief History of the Episcopal See*, Bell's Cathedral Series (London, 1898), p. 89.
19. Morgan, in *Hereford Cathedral Church Glass*, p. 18, misidentified one of the windows calling it The Last Supper, though it is in fact The Ascension, or to give it the original title, Our Lord seated in majesty, surrounded by the Apostles, which may have led to the confusion. A minute in the chapter acts states 'the small portions of glass remaining from the windows taken out of the East End of the Choir were granted to Canon Musgrave for use in his Residence House', HCA, 7031/22, p. 21, chapter acts, 25 June 1872. This house was the canonical house in Broad Street occupied later by Streeter. Comparing the reset windows in the transept with their original siting in the choir, it is clear that they have been altered in order to fit their new position and it is not surprising that there were some leftover pieces for disposal.
20. See below, Chapter 22, p. 420.
21. Members of the cathedral choir gave the window to Townshend Smith; Dr G. R. Sinclair, an enthusiast for stained glass, initiated the windows to Wesley, Colborne and Ouseley.

and Bell and in 1868 they founded their own firm. They produced the clerestory window in the choir which commemorates John Jebb (1805–86), praelector and eventually chancellor of the cathedral, who was an important nineteenth-century liturgist. The design shows four angels playing musical instruments: a harp, a portative organ, a violin and a citole.

A large window in the north-east transept was put in by Heaton, Butler and Bayne in 1878, at the request of the college of vicars, and paid for by them in memory of John Goss, vicar choral, custos of the college and vicar of St John the Baptist. The design was accepted by Gilbert Scott the cathedral architect and informally submitted to Mr Thomas Gambier Parry of Highnam, Gloucestershire, for his approval. It shows the Adoration of the Magi and the baptism of Christ.[22]

The firm of C. E. Kempe flourished from 1869 to 1934 and in 1895 they produced the large window in the south transept which commemorates Dean Herbert. The design represents a text from *Te deum laudamus*: 'the glorious company of the apostles praise thee'. Some have called it pedestrian and parochial.[23] Certainly it lacks the grandeur of the Hardman window opposite but at least part of its interest lies in the illustrations of local saints: St Ethelbert, St Thomas of Hereford and St Dubricius.[24]

In the south nave aisle there are three early twentieth-century windows from the London firm of Powell and Sons, which was based at Whitefriars. In 1834 James Powell took over a firm which had been making glass since the seventeenth century and was to continue in production until 1973. The first window has a narrative design showing the visit of King Charles I to the city in September 1645. It includes the principal persons who were in Hereford during the Civil War at the time: King Charles and Prince Maurice, Dean Croft[25] and Barnabas Scudamore who commanded the city during the final siege, the Mayor, William Carter, the town clerk, James Clarke and 'the good lord [John] Scudamore' the chief steward of the city. The next window is in memory of a famous Victorian precentor of the cathedral, Sir Frederick Arthur Gore Ouseley, and includes pictures of Old Testament musicians, Miriam, David, Asaph and Deborah. Finally, the third window by Powell commemorates Frances, the wife of Dean Leigh, and ingeniously incorporates a series of biblical mothers with their children. Mrs Leigh was the daughter of the famous actress 'Fanny' Kemble, who was married to Pierce Butler,

22. HCA, 7031/22, pp. 234, 240, 242, chapter acts, 9 February, 25 March and 2 April 1878.

23. E.g. Pevsner, *Herefordshire*, p. 167.

24. Interestingly Morgan thought less of the Hardman window and more of the one by Kempe, which he said was 'of better design and with softer colouring': an example of changing tastes. [F. C. Morgan], 'Hereford Cathedral Glass', *FHC*, 27 (1961), pp. 14–16, at 15.

25. Unfortunately and inaccurately dressed as a bishop, since Croft did not become bishop of Hereford until after the Restoration in 1660.

an American slave owner. Her mother's efforts to suppress slavery are remembered by the inclusion of a negro child at the top of the window.

In the Stanbury chantry there is a pair of narrative windows designed by Arthur Davies, made by the Bromsgrove Guild and given in 1923 by a number of old Etonians. Three scenes show John Stanbury, priest confessor to Henry VI, at Windsor considering the plans for Eton College; the king granting his royal charter to his new school; and Bishop Stanbury arriving at Hereford and entering the cathedral for his enthronement.[26]

---

26. Morgan, *Hereford Cathedral Church Glass*, p. 10, points out that Stanbury did not approach the cathedral by crossing the Wye bridge, as shown in the window, but walked barefoot from St Guthlac's priory.

14

The Medieval Tombs and the Shrine of Saint Thomas Cantilupe

Nicola Coldstream

Hereford Cathedral has an interesting group of tombs, including a monumental stone shrine base and the tomb of a lay woman – Joanna de Bohun (d. 1327). Although examples exist elsewhere, neither is usual in a secular cathedral. Secular burials in general are uncommon at Hereford: only three tombs of lay people survive, although more are commemorated in brasses, and some have certainly been lost.[1]

The present layout of medieval tombs is a palimpsest, reflecting successive programmes of burial. The architectural remodelling in the years around 1300 destroyed the original tombs of all the earlier bishops except Peter of Aigueblanche (d. 1268) and Thomas Cantilupe (d. 1282), in the north transept. What we have now represents the situation from that period onwards, filtered through an overlay of later destruction and change, rescued to some extent by George Gilbert Scott.

With the acknowledged help of the Revd F. T. Havergal, Scott sought out the tombs 'scattered about in all directions' by Cottingham during his repairs to the

---

1. Not all the tombs can be discussed in detail here. For the tombs generally, see the following works, which should be consulted in conjunction with more specific items in later references: J. G. Nichols, ed., *History from Marble Compiled in the Reign of Charles II by Thomas Dingley*, Camden Society, old series, 94, 97 (2 vols, London, 1867–68), i; R. Gough, *Sepulchral Monuments in Great Britain* (2 vols, London 1786–96), i, pt 2; J. Duncumb, *Collections towards the History and Antiquities of the County of Hereford* (8 vols, Hereford and London, 1804–1915), i; J. Britton, *The History and Antiquities of the Cathedral Church of Hereford* (London, 1831); T. and G. Hollis, *The Monumental Effigies of Great Britain* (London, 1840–41); C. Boutell, 'Tombs and Monumental Sculpture in Hereford Cathedral', *Journal of the British Archaeological Association*, 27 (1871), pp. 191–98; G. M. Hills, 'The Architectural History of Hereford Cathedral', *Journal of the British Archaeological Association*, 27 (1871), pp. 46–84; M. H. Bloxam, 'On Certain Sepulchral Effigies in Hereford Cathedral', *Archaeological Journal*, 34 (1877), pp. 406–24; F. T. Havergal, *Monumental Inscriptions in the Cathedral Church of Hereford* (Hereford, 1881); RCHME, *Herefordshire*, i.

cathedral and replaced 'all that we could identify' in their old places.[2] Correct identification is still a problem, as is clear from the early antiquarian sources, which disagree on both attribution and location.[3] Even today, the two clerics in the south nave aisle have not been certainly identified. In the Lady chapel, the circumstantial evidence for Joanna de Bohun is persuasive,[4] but that for Peter de Grandisson and the member of the Swinfield family is much weaker than the reiteration through the modern literature leads us to suppose.[5]

It was loss of heraldic decoration after the seventeenth century that led to the confusion over Joanna de Bohun.[6] The tomb has since been restored without it, showing that restoration brings its own difficulties (plate VIa). The effigy of Sir Richard Pembridge (d. 1375) in the nave had a damaged right leg, restored in wood with an extra Garter, and subsequently restored, garterless, in stone.[7] The Grandisson tomb has, however, been transformed since the 1940s, when it was unpainted and several figures lacked their heads, to its current appearance, with whole figures and paint that obscures the fine quality of the carving (plate VIb).[8]

Except for Bishop Aigueblanche's tomb, the main focal points for the later medieval burials were the shrines of St Thomas Cantilupe. Cantilupe seems first to have been buried in the Lady chapel, perhaps in a wall recess, before being translated to the tomb/shrine in the north transept in 1287. His process of canonisation began in 1307.[9] At his canonisation in 1320 the authorities commissioned a new reliquary, but his remains were not moved back to the Lady chapel until 1349. In the meantime, Cantilupe's successor, Bishop Swinfield, who was the prime mover in the canonisation project, had remodelled the nave aisles to provide suitable access

2. G. G. Scott, *Personal and Professional Recollections: A Facsimile of the Original Edition*, ed. G. Stamp (Stamford, 1995), pp. 288–89.

3. See differing opinions offered by antiquaries listed in n. 1 above.

4. L. Gee, 'Fourteenth-Century Tombs for Women in Herefordshire', in Whitehead, *Medieval Art at Hereford*, pp. 132–37.

5. Although the attribution was questioned by Gough, *Sepulchral Monuments*, i, pt 2, p. 194, antiquaries continued to attribute the Grandisson tomb to 'Humphrey de Bohun, earl of Hereford', until Havergal changed it to Grandisson in his *Monumental Inscriptions* (plan). Similar confusion occurs between the Swinfield family member and Dean Barowe.

6. Nichols, ed., *History from Marble by Thomas Dingley*, i, p. clxvii; compare J. Merewether,

'An Account of the Opening of the Coffin of Joanna de Bohun, in the Lady Chapel of Hereford Cathedral', *Archaeologia*, 32 (1847), p. 60.

7. Compare Duncumb, *Collections*, i, p. 540, and Bloxam, 'Sepulchral Effigies', p. 410. The stone leg replaced the wooden one in the 1850s. I am grateful to Ron Shoesmith for helping to solve the mystery.

8. C. Blair, 'The Defacement of Monuments: Type and Antitype. Hereford Cathedral and Clehonger Church, Herefordshire', *Bulletin of the International Society for the Study of Church Monuments*, 3 (1980), pp. 58–62.

9. P. Daly, 'The Process of Canonization in the Thirteenth and Early Fourteenth Centuries', in M. Jancey, ed., *St Thomas Cantilupe, Bishop of Hereford: Essays in his Honour* (Hereford, 1982), p. 129.

to the shrine in the transept. He then remodelled the eastern parts of the cathedral, probably from 1307, when he may already have decided to retranslate the relics to the Lady chapel.[10] He established tombs for his displaced predecessors along the walls of the choir aisles; his own tomb was located in the north-east transept; and he provided a tomb for a member of his family in the Lady chapel.[11]

We can perhaps detect two motives here: a desire to found a Swinfield family mausoleum at the east end,[12] and, above all, to celebrate the see of Hereford through an ordered series of tombs of its early bishops, leading to the shrine of its sainted bishop in the Lady chapel, the apex of the building. Until now, although it possessed the relics of St Ethelbert, Hereford, like Salisbury and Exeter, had lacked a major shrine, that is, the remains of a sainted founder that were enshrined behind the high altar to provide a focus second only to the altar itself. At Salisbury attention was given to proficient conduct of the liturgy; at Exeter the clergy were to devise a liturgical focus on the see and its bishops, with elaborate liturgical furnishings to emphasise the importance of the bishops in the liturgy.[13] At Hereford a sainted bishop gave a centre for a celebration of the episcopacy.

Whatever Swinfield's intentions, other tombs support the evidence that Cantilupe's cult was already waning.[14] The burial of Bishop Thomas Charlton (d. 1344) near the shrine in the north transept suggests that there was then little hope of completing the new reliquary and returning the remains to the Lady chapel. But the Black Death seems to have given new impetus:[15] in the 1350s the magnificent tomb attributed to Peter de Grandisson claimed the most important position opposite the newly established shrine in the Lady chapel (plate VIb).

This, then, is the framework for the later medieval tombs in the cathedral. Subsequent burials had to be fitted where there was space: two clergy in niches provided in the south nave aisle, later bishops in both sets of transepts and the choir aisles, until Bishop Booth (d. 1535) was interred in the north aisle of the nave (plate VIIa). Some effigies have been displaced and collected into the eastern transepts. Look beyond the apparently random distribution and there is a pattern that reveals much about medieval attitudes to intercession and the fortunes of the soul.

10. R. K. Morris, 'The Remodelling of the Hereford Aisles', *Journal of the British Archaeological Association*, 37 (1974), pp. 21–39.

11. P. Lindley, 'Retrospective Effigies, the Past and Lies', in Whitehead, *Medieval Art at Hereford*, pp. 111–21; N. Rogers, 'English Episcopal Monuments, 1270–1350', in J. Coales, ed., *The Earliest English Brasses. Patronage, Style and Workshops, 1270–1350* (London, 1987), pp. 53–54, 59.

12. Morris, 'Remodelling', p. 26.

13. V. Sekules, 'The Liturgical Furnishings of the Choir of Exeter Cathedral', in F. Kelly, ed., *Medieval Art and Architecture at Exeter Cathedral*, British Archaeological Association Conference Transactions, 11 (Leeds, 1991), pp. 172–79.

14. R. C. Finucane, 'Cantilupe as Thaumaturge: Pilgrims and their "Miracles"', in Jancey, ed., *St Thomas Cantilupe*, p. 144.

15. Morris, 'Remodelling', p. 27.

Both types of medieval tomb, the freestanding 'altar' tomb and the wall-tomb set within an arched recess, are well represented. Bishop Aigueblanche's tomb, in the south-eastern corner of the north transept, is the earliest surviving tomb in the cathedral. Probably commissioned by his nephew and executor, John of Aigueblanche, it is one of the finest examples in Britain of the freestanding tomb with canopy and sculptured effigy much favoured by mid thirteenth-century bishops (fig. 11).[16] It compares with the lost tomb of Grosseteste of Lincoln (d. 1253) and that of Archbishop Gray of York (d. 1255). Like Gray, Aigueblanche rebuilt the transept, probably with burial in mind, even though he had decided that his remains should be divided between Hereford and his foundation at Aiguebelle in Savoy.[17] The tomb shares with the building clear links to the works at Westminster Abbey: the crucifix carved amid foliage on a finial on the tomb, which survived the Reformation intact, compares closely to sculpture in the north transept at Westminster; and the openwork canopy, with tracery and Purbeck marble colonnettes, resembles other work at Westminster, both contemporary and later.[18]

Apart from John of Aigueblanche next to the bishop,[19] the other notable altar tombs are those of Sir Richard Pembridge (d. 1375), and Bishops Stanbury (d. 1474) (fig. 141) and Mayew (d. 1516). Pembridge's tomb was closely based on the stipulations of his will, although the iron railing round the tomb and his shield hung above it were destroyed by the fall of the nave in 1786.[20] His metal helm, however, survives in the Royal Museum of Scotland.[21] Pembridge's alabaster effigy is in contemporary armour, with its feet on a lurcher. The tomb chest is decorated with shields of arms (fig. 94). Bishops Stanbury and Mayew both have weepers, Stanbury's holding shields of arms, while Mayew's have been identified as saints. Under the choir arcades flanking the high altar, Stanbury's tomb is opposite his chantry chapel; Mayew lies beneath an elaborate canopy with miniature pendant vaults and openwork panels that form part of the choir screen (fig. 95).[22]

The wall tombs typically have a moulded arched recess with head stops and

16. Capes, *Charters*, pp. 188–90; Rogers, 'English Episcopal Monuments', p. 23; J. Gardner, 'The Tomb of Bishop Peter of Aquablanca in Hereford Cathedral', in Whitehead, *Medieval Art at Hereford*, pp. 105–10; P. Williamson, *Gothic Sculpture* (New Haven and London, 1995), p. 211.

17. Gardner, 'Tomb', pp. 106–7; Rogers, 'English Episcopal Monuments', pp. 21–23; Williamson, *Gothic Sculpture*, p. 191.

18. Williamson, *Gothic Sculpture*, p. 211.

19. Capes, *Charters*, p. 186.

20. Nichols, ed., *History from Marble by Thomas Dingley*, i, p. cxliv; R. R. Sharpe, ed.,

Calendar of Wills Proved and Enrolled in the Court of Husting, London, AD 1258 – AD 1688 (2 vols, London 1889–90), ii, p. 188.

21. A. V. B. Norman, *Arms and Armour in the Royal Scottish Museum* (Edinburgh, 1972), no. 3; D. Spalding, 'An Unrecorded English Helm of *c.* 1370', *Journal of the Arms and Armour Society*, 9 (1977), pp. 6–9. For restorations of this tomb see n. 7, above. I am most grateful to Philip Lankester for help with details of the armour on this and the Grandisson tomb.

22. Britton, *History and Antiquities of the Cathedral Church of Hereford*, pp. 59–60.

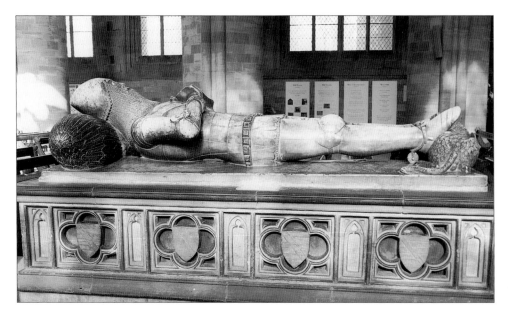

Fig. 94. Tomb of Sir Richard Pembridge, died 1375, south side of nave.

sometimes fleurons and blind tracery (the nave tombs). Most, but not all, were evidently built with the construction of the walls. The sculptured effigies have canopies around their heads, and some tombs have added tracery motifs, foliage or ballflower decoration. The most interesting are undoubtedly those in the east parts of the church.

The rather flat, shallow effigies of the series of bishops (fig. 23) compare with those of ?John Swinfield, precentor, 1294–1311, and John of Aigueblanche, dean, 1282–1320. Their stiff drapery folds, however, are closer in style to those of Bishop Aigueblanche than to the dean and precentor, whose dress is handled in a typically early fourteenth-century manner, with tubular folds and gracefully turned back sleeves.[23]

Precentor Swinfield's tomb arch is appropriately carved with charming pigs amid acorns (fig. 14), and his feet rest on a wild boar. Bishop Swinfield's tomb has similarly beautiful naturalistic vine foliage with grapes. Like Cantilupe, however, the bishop had a commemorative brass rather than an effigy; but on the back wall are the remains of a carved crucifixion scene.[24] This kind of tomb imagery was common across Europe, but few examples survive in this country. Hereford

23. Morris, 'Remodelling', p. 27; Gee, 'Four-teenth-Century Tombs for Women', p. 133; Lindley, 'Retrospective Effigies'.
24. For Cantilupe, see p. 328; Nichols, ed.,

History from Marble by Thomas Dingley, i, p. clxxx; Gough, *Sepulchral Monuments*, i, pt 2, p. 83, gives inscription; Rogers, 'English Episcopal Monuments', pp. 23, 27, 53–54.

Fig. 95. Tomb of Bishop
Richard Mayew, died 1516,
south choir aisle.

has two: paint traces on the back wall of Joanna de Bohun's tomb reveal a
kneeling woman, accompanied by chanting religious figures, offering a church to
the Virgin Mary.[25]

25. Gough, *Sepulchral Monuments*, i, pt 2, p. 194.

More ostentatious by far is the tomb attributed on grounds of style and date to Peter, Lord Grandisson (d. 1358). The 1350s suits the armour and the style of the effigy, which compare to those at Clehonger, Abergavenny and that of Grandisson's wife at Much Marcle.[26] The rectilinear design of the tomb reflects contemporary architecture at Gloucester Cathedral. The restored imagery, including figures of SS John the Baptist, Ethelbert, Thomas Becket and Thomas Cantilupe flanking the Coronation of the Virgin, refers both to the see of Hereford and to Cantilupe's newly installed shrine (plate VIb).[27]

The tomb/shrine of Cantilupe in the north transept is a puzzling structure, and the recent conservation programme has raised as many questions as it has solved (fig. 96).[28] The tomb fits the category of neither altar tomb nor shrine base. Canopies were fitted around tombs rather than, as here, on top; and high shrine bases of this sort would normally be placed behind the high altar.[29] Cantilupe's bones rested here between 1287 and 1349. Judging by the timing of the miracles, Swinfield intended to press for canonisation from the beginning,[30] and we have seen that Swinfield had also probably decided to retranslate the relics to the Lady chapel as early as 1307.

The tomb has a coffin-shaped, tapering base made of local sandstone, carved with soldiers, seated with their feet on various animals, under arcading decorated with naturalistic foliage; a closing slab of Purbeck stone with a matrix for a monumental brass comprising an effigy of St Thomas with two small figures, of which only that of St Ethelbert survives (fig. 99); and a flat-topped, arcaded canopy, also decorated with foliage. It is homogeneous except for the west panel of the canopy, which has fourteenth-century foliage.

The Dingley manuscript records an image of Cantilupe painted on the wall behind the shrine.[31] On the monument itself the foliage includes some identifiable

26. Blair, 'Defacement of Monuments', p. 60; L. Southwick, 'The Armoured Effigy of Prince John of Eltham in Westminster Abbey and Some Closely Related Military Monuments', *Church Monuments*, 2 (1987), pp. 9–21; N. Coldstream, *The English Decorated Style: Architecture and Ornament, 1240–1360* (London, 1994), pp. 150–51; I am grateful to Amanda Simpson for sharing with me her knowledge of these effigies.

27. J. Hillaby, 'Cults, Patrons and Sepulture', in R. Shoesmith and R. Richardson, eds, *A Definitive History of Abbey Dore* (Almeley, 1997), pp. 101–2.

28. F. T. Havergal, *Fasti Herefordenses* (Edinburgh,

1869), pp. 175–76, 178; G. Marshall, 'The Shrine of St Thomas Cantilupe in Hereford Cathedral', *TWNFC*, 27 (1930–32), pp. 34–50; R. Emmerson, 'St Thomas Cantilupe's Tomb and Brass of 1287', *Bulletin of the International Society for the Study of Church Monuments*, 2 (1980), pp. 41–45; Jancey, ed., *St Thomas Cantilupe*; Rogers, 'English Episcopal Monuments', pp. 27, 28, 30–34.

29. N. Coldstream, 'English Decorated Shrine Bases', *Journal of the British Archaeological Association*, 129 (1976), pp. 15–34.

30. Daly, 'Process of Canonization', p. 127.

31. Nichols, ed., *History from Marble by Thomas Dingley*, i, p. clxxxix.

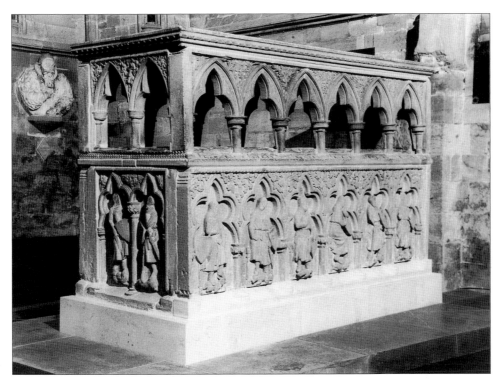

Fig. 96. Shrine of St Thomas Cantilupe, north transept.

flowers and leaves, but compared to the almost contemporary foliage in the chapter house at Southwell, for example, it is very general, giving an impression of reality rather than imitation. It tends, in Jean Givens's words, towards naturalism rather than description.[32] The soldiers, which are the earliest known figures of weepers in this country, may, as suggested, represent Cantilupe's relatives; but they are more likely to be soldiers of Christ, their feet on allegorical beasts, fighting sin.[33] The imagery of Cantilupe's monument is, then, of Paradise: the saint, represented in brass, lies within the Paradise garden, defended against sin by Christ's battalions.

But where were his bones? The structural investigation has shown that it is very unlikely that the bones were originally in the base. Marshall believed that the canopy was an afterthought: it encroaches on the Purbeck slab and to support it

32. J. Givens, 'The *Leaves of Southwell* Revisited', in J. Alexander, ed., *Southwell and Nottinghamshire: Medieval Art, Architecture and Industry*, British Archaeological Association Conference Transactions, 21 (Leeds,

1998), pp. 60–66.
33. E. G. Benson, 'The Cantilupe Indent in Hereford Cathedral', *Transactions of the Monumental Brass Society*, 8 (1949), pp. 329–30.

the base was widened at the west by adding two strips of plain stone. Emmerson argues that the tomb was widened in 1320, when the bones were removed to go into the reliquary, hence also the new foliage for the west panel of the canopy.[34] We now know that the base and the old cross slab on which it is partly built are related in such a way that any widening was impossible. The plain strips were there from the start, presumably with painted decoration. The tomb has not been altered, and the absolute homogeneity of the foliage sculpture and other details argues against any serious afterthoughts. As the tomb was locally made but the Purbeck slab ordered from London, a mistake in the measurements is one possibility.

This means that the bones could not have been extracted from the tomb-base without inflicting great damage, of which there is no evidence, beyond the blocking of the west end of the canopy (which does not allow access to the base). The base itself is unharmed. Marshall believed that the bones were in a reliquary on top of the canopy from the start. As Cantilupe had not yet been canonised this may seem rather irregular, but in the middle ages there was much latitude, especially in areas remote from central authority, and it now seems more likely that Marshall's belief was correct.

Commemorated splendidly though he was in his own personal Paradise, Cantilupe eventually returned, in a new reliquary, to the Lady chapel. Of this we know only Scott's report that Dean Merewether, clearing the library out of the chapel in 1842, found a stone kerb at floor level 'fitted on the inner side to the shape of the shrine and rebated on the outer side for encaustic pavement tiles. Many survive, worn by the feet and knees of pilgrims'.[35] Scott was as interested in the spiritual as in the architectural history of all the buildings in his care. Let us give him the last, as well as the first, words of this short account of Hereford's medieval tombs.

34. Marshall, 'Shrine of St Thomas Cantilupe';   35. G. G. Scott, 'Hereford Cathedral', *Archae-*
    Emmerson, 'St Thomas Cantilupe's Tomb'.   *ological Journal*, 34 (1877), p. 339.

15

The Brasses
and Other Minor Monuments

Sally Badham

From the later middle ages, as a greater spectrum of society aspired to intra-mural burial, floor monuments were laid down in vast numbers. They did not impede the celebration of divine office as a proliferation of tomb chests would and were also cheaper. They were more vulnerable, however, to loss through theft, icono-clasm, neglect and reflooring. Hereford is no exception, but nonetheless retains a larger, more varied collection of minor monuments than most cathedrals. An early type of floor monument was the cross-slab coffin lid. Many were reused as building material: at Hereford, the base of the Cantilupe shrine is cut from a slab of likely twelfth-century date with an expanded arm cross; normally hidden from view, this was exposed during the recent conservation of the shrine. Most of the other survivals here have the cross incised; the most complete example, of likely early fourteenth-century date, has a nimbed, round leaf crosshead with pointed buds (fig. 97). An elaborate relief cross slab of the end of the thirteenth century, though damaged, shows exceptional quality in the design and carving. Above the fleur-de-lis panel at the top, which may derive from the arms of the cathedral, is a blank panel bisected by an incised line, on which was probably originally a painted inscription set out in two lines (fig. 98).

From the thirteenth century onwards, incised slabs often incorporated effigial representation. Two late fourteenth-century examples in the north-east transept, one showing a knight and lady and the other a priest in mass vestments under a canopy, are of a type unique to Herefordshire, involving incised plaster of Paris sections inlaid into sandstone matrices.[1] These inlays have virtually worn smooth,

---

1. For a brief account of these slabs, see F. A. Greenhill, *Incised Effigial Slabs* (2 vols, London, 1976), i, p. 14. Further information on all the incised slabs was provided by John Coales from the unpublished notebooks in the Greenhill archive.

Fig. 97. Early fourteenth-century incised cross slab, north-east transept.

Fig. 98. Relief cross slab, late thirteenth century, north-east transept. Note the blank panel at the top set out for a painted inscription.

though an impression of their original state may be gained from the Herle slab at Allensmore. More visually stunning is the 1497 slab in the crypt to Andrew and Elizabeth Jonis, a product of the Burton-on-Trent alabasterers who dominated incised slab production in England in the fifteenth and sixteenth centuries. The black infilling contrasting with the alabaster displays to advantage details like the elaborate canopy and the cider barrel foot-support.

The wealth of brasses once to be found at Hereford is evidenced by the 170 empty indents recorded in 1717 by Rawlinson, most now gone.[2] The survivals were augmented in 1880 by brasses from the Nichols collection; some non-indigenous plates have been returned to Windsor and Clerkenwell, but others, including a palimpsest Norwich-made merchant's mark of *c.* 1490 from Lowestoft, remain. Most of the medieval brasses in the cathedral were bought from London workshops, complete with their Purbeck marble slabs. A wide variety of workshops was patronised; hence, a good cross-section of London work from the thirteenth to the sixteenth centuries can be seen here. The thirty-six part or complete plates left include a number of minor inscriptions and some fragments, but also fine figure brasses, some of national importance.

Fig. 99. Figure of St Ethelbert from the Ashford series brass, made by 1287, from the indent in the Cantilupe shrine, north transept.

The Cantilupe brass, from which only the figure of St Ethelbert survives, was produced by 1287 by the London-based Ashford workshop; it was one of the earliest brasses in England (fig. 99).[3] From 1350 the majority of medieval English brasses were made in two London workshops, known as B and D, and their successors known as F and G.[4] Bishop Trillek's fine canopied brass, dated 1360, showing him wearing pontificals and holding a crozier, is the earliest surviving London B full-length figure brass in the country (fig. 100). Also from this workshop are brasses to Canon Richard de la Barr, died 1386, and Canon Edmund Ryall, died 1428. The former is a rare partial survival of a cross brass, a type particularly targeted by Reformation iconoclasts, and is one of only ten surviving fourteenth-century brasses depicting a coped ecclesiastic.

The large canopied brass to Richard Delamare, high sheriff of Herefordshire,

2. R. Rawlinson, *The History and Antiquities of the City and Cathedral-Church of Hereford* (London, 1717); for a good modern account of the lost brasses, see P. Heseltine, *The Brasses of Hereford Cathedral* (privately printed, 1982).

3. S. Badham and M. Norris, *Early Incised Slabs and Brasses from the London Marblers* (London, 1999), pp. 32 and 149–51.

4. J. P. C. Kent, 'Monumental Brasses: A New Classification of Military Effigies', *Journal of the British Archaeological Association*, third series, 12 (1949), pp. 70–97.

Fig. 100. London B brass to Bishop John Trillek, died 1360, floor of choir. Only the figure is original medieval work; the remainder of the composition was restored, not totally accurately, in the late nineteenth century.

died 1435, shown in plate armour, and his wife, Elizabeth, with two pet dogs nestling in the folds of her cote-hardi and cloak, both wearing the SS collar denoting allegiance to the Lancastrians, ranks amongst the finest London D products anywhere. Most of the other series D products here are inscription brasses, but the unknown knight of *c.* 1490 with a hound at his feet is an attractive piece of shopwork from the end of the series; formerly part of the Nichols collection, it is unlikely to have come from Hereford. Examples from some of the minor London workshops include the delightful London C civilian of 1394 resting his feet on a dog – this was once part of a cross brass (fig. 101) – and the London E headless coped priest with a largely illegible inscription dated 1434, probably commemorating Dean Stanway.

Series F examples include the civilian figure commemorating John Stockton, mayor of Hereford, died 1480, all that survives of an elaborate composition showing him under a canopy with his merchant's mark; and the 1514 Delabere brass showing Sir Richard, his two wives and their twenty-one children. Only minor products of series G survive at Hereford, the diminutive figure of a priest of *c.* 1520 holding a wafer and chalice being poorly drawn even by the declining standards of the time.

The important series F brass to Archdeacon Richard Rudhale, died 1476, depicts him in a richly decorated cope and wearing the doctor's pileus under a triple canopy populated by saints, including Thomas of Hereford and Ethelbert (fig. 17). The inscription, with oakleaves and beasts separating the words, is especially fine. The 1529 brass to Dean Frowcester is obviously derived from the Rudhale brass in many respects, albeit updated with Renaissance ornament. A key difference between the two brasses lies in the wording of the inscription. The former speaks of the gloomy grave and seeks Christ's intercession for the salvation of Rudhale's soul; such sentiments would have been inadvisable on the eve of the Reformation, hence Frowcester's epitaph is an eulogy of his earthly virtues.[5]

Since the late nineteenth century attempts have been made to rectify earlier neglect. The restoration of the Trillek brass, of which only the figure is original medieval work, lacks accuracy however; the arms on the shields and the wording of the inscription both differ from those recorded in antiquarian sources and the style of lettering is more like early sixteenth-century work. Parts of William Porter's 1424 London F brass, featuring a fine Annunciation in the canopy, were restored to the cathedral by the Friends of Hereford Cathedral in 1932 (fig. 26). The rearrangement of the brasses carried out

Fig. 101. London C brass to unknown civilian, once part of a cross brass: mural on board in south-east transept. A fragment of fillet inscription, mostly now lost, gave the date of death as 1394.

over the past fifty years has been particularly successful, reuniting parts of brasses previously mounted separately, thus presenting a more coherent picture of this valuable collection.[6]

5. For texts see A. J. Winnington-Ingram, *Monumental Brasses in Hereford Cathedral* (3rd edn, Hereford, 1972), pp. 8 and 17.

6. I am grateful to Jerome Bertram, John Coales, Philip Whittemore and Martin Stuchfield for help with various aspects of this chapter.

16

The Decorative Ironwork

Jane Geddes

In terms of decorative ironwork, Hereford Cathedral is probably more notorious for the choir screen it has removed than it is renowned for the items which survive in situ. There are, however, some important medieval survivals and the nineteenth-century revivals are interesting.

There are two chests housed in the south cloister. The first is a plain box, made of poplar wood with a lid of 1930, according to Morgan.[1] The three vertical iron straps on the front and two pairs of corner brackets all end in fleur-de-lis terminals. The main lock plate has concave sides and a circular projection for a nail on each side. This type of poorly defined fleur-de-lis terminal is hard to date, but other examples are found in a twelfth-century context, for instance on the church door at Earl's Croome, Herefordshire. The chest is likely to be a little later, from the thirteenth century, with the lock plate added in the late middle ages. The base of the second chest is also a simple box, but it has a curved lid made from a single piece of wood. Curved lids were particularly suitable for travelling chests, to keep the rain out. In fact, both chests are equipped with rings at each end for inserting carrying poles or ropes. The second chest has plain iron bands but is distinguished by its lock plate which has square leaves splayed to either side of the key hole.[2] It is remarkably like a chest at Little Waldingfield, Suffolk, which also has the plain straps, domed lid and distinctive lock.[3] Both are likely to be fifteenth-century imports from the Netherlands where this type of leafy lock plate was common.

The door on the north side of the presbytery, to the chantry chapel of Bishop Stanbury, is original. The chapel was erected after his death in 1473, and 'newe bylded' in 1491.[4] The lower part of the door is made of wooden panelling but the

1. F. C. Morgan, 'Church Chests of Hereford-shire', *TWNFC*, 32 (1947), pp. 122–43.
2. P. Eames, 'Medieval Furniture', *Furniture History Society*, 13 (1977), pp. 172–75.
3. M. Cautley, *Suffolk Churches and their Treasures* (Ipswich, 1938), pl. 311.
4. N. Pevsner and P. Metcalf, *The Cathedrals of England, Midland, Eastern and Northern England* (London 1985), p. 160; RCHME, *Herefordshire*, i, pl. 106.

Fig. 102. Lock plate of door to
Bishop Audley's chapel.

upper triangle is made from openwork iron tracery bars. This combination of a
door and grille is unusual in England but is also found on the sacristy door at
Rouen Cathedral, from the fifteenth century.[5]

On the highly decorated door to Bishop Audley's chapel is a good example of
a late fifteenth-century fashion in lock design (fig. 102). Edmund Audley uses his
initials EA on either side of the lock plate with his family insignia of the fret and
butterfly. Next to it is the rectangular door handle, already showing suggestions
of a renaissance baluster shape, topped by a crown. Audley was bishop of Hereford
from 1492 to 1502, during which time his chapel was begun. Prior Catton at
Norwich Cathedral used his initials on a lock plate between 1504 and 1529,[6] while

5. H. R. d'Allemagne, *Les anciens maîtres serru-
riers* (2 vols, Paris, 1943), ii, p. xl.

6. J. Geddes, 'The Medieval Decorative

Ironwork', in I. Atherton and others, eds,
*Norwich Cathedral: Church, City and Diocese,
1096–1966* (London, 1996), pp. 431–42.

Sir Reginald Bray used his rebus of the hemp bray on a lock plate at St George's Chapel, Windsor, *c.* 1500.[7]

Bishop Charles Booth, who died in 1535, has sturdy railings installed in front of his tomb in the north aisle (plate VIIa). The crenellated band holding the rails in place is decorated with alternating rosettes and boars' heads, while the stanchions are faced by small shields showing the Booth arms of three boars' heads. In spite of their late date, the railings remain medieval in appearance. Tomb railings decorated with small rosettes and heads first appeared in Canterbury Cathedral between 1376 and 1426, around a variety of tombs ranging from the Black Prince to Archbishop Chichele.[8]

The nineteenth century saw two contrasting approaches to the Gothic revival, both in architectural restoration and ironwork. The Cottingham father and son were punctiliously antiquarian while George Gilbert Scott flexed his imagination within the grammar of Gothic ornament. The north door hinges in the Booth porch were made by Thomas Potter of South Moulton Street, London, from the design by Cottingham junior, between 1849 and 1853.[9] The hinges are elaborated into delicate spiral scrolls ending in stamped foliage terminals.[10] They are closely based on the late thirteenth-century aumbry in Chester Cathedral, and the chapter house doors of York Minster. If Cottingham had not seen these examples himself, he had probably studied Brandon's *Analysis of Gothic Architecture*, recently published in 1847 and illustrating these two models with considerable technical detail.[11]

No information has been found about the designer of the fleur-de-lis hinges on the door in the bishop's cloister, but their antiquarian accuracy suggests it was Cottingham again.[12] They are composed of two C-shaped hinges ending in coarse scrolls. The strap running through the middle of the C ends in three scrolls. The strap crossing the centre of the door ends in fleur-de-lis with distinctive long and thin petals. These are a characteristic feature of local parish churches from the late twelfth to the thirteenth centuries. They are found on church doors at Stoke

7. W. H. St John Hope, *Windsor Castle: An Architectural History* (2 vols, London, 1913), ii, p. 451.

8. J. Geddes, 'Some Tombs in Canterbury Cathedral', in A. Detsicas, ed., *Collectanea Historica: Essays in Memory of Stuart Rigold* (Maidstone, 1981), pp. 66–73.

9. A. Hugh Fisher, *The Cathedral Church of Hereford*, Bell's Cathedral Series (London, 1898), p. 34. The exact payment for this work is not known but in the chapter acts for 2 January 1854 record that Mr Potter applied for payment of £109 6s. 0d. 'for

iron hinges etc.' supplied to the cathedral, HCA, 7031/20, p. 289. The chapter clerk deemed the bill to be exorbitant. He was eventually paid £107 7s. 0d. later in the year, HCA, 7037/4, fabric account, 1854.

10. RCHME, *Herefordshire*, i, pl. 121.

11. R. and J. A. Brandon, *An Analysis of Gothick Architecture* (2 vols, London, 1847), ii, pls 4, 6.

12. The door is on the east wall of the east alley, leading into the chapter house yard. Fisher, *The Cathedral Church of Hereford*, p. 38, says that 'the ironwork of the door is modern by Potter'.

Orchard, Burford (Shropshire), Little Hereford and Madley. It is not possible to say if the cathedral hinges are an authentic replacement of older work. Their design, however, is clearly intended for a single, wide door like that at Little Hereford but the present door is made in two leaves, dividing the strap work illogically down the centre.

Gilbert Scott considered the choir screen which he designed for the cathedral in 1862 to be 'very fine'.[13] It was intended to redefine the liturgical space at the east end of the cathedral, closing off the eastern arm for the choir but allowing the congregation to see through it (figs 103, 81). Reflecting on his work afterwards he wrote: 'Practically, for ordinary purposes, this was a gain; for great diocesan uses it was a loss. From an antiquarian point of view it was an error ... I confess I do not think now I should do the same'.[14] He said he had no evidence for any previous screen so he designed it on a 'somewhat massive scale, thinking that it would thus harmonise better with the heavy architecture of the choir'.[15] The screen consisted of five pointed arches on slender cast iron columns, separating an elaborate cornice from openwork panels at the base. The tracery filling the panels and cornice was a very free interpretation of medieval forms, combining delicate leaves, flowers, geometric patterns and statues. Scott's inspiration came from many medieval sources: the mixture of semi-precious stones, mosaics (to mimic medieval enamel), metal figures and openwork cresting could all be found on house shrines like that of the Three Kings in Cologne Cathedral. The position of Christ and his flanking angels resembles the arrangement of sculpture on north Italian cathedral facades, like that at Siena, while mosaic is used on the facade of Orvieto Cathedral. The clusters of wrought iron, naturalistic foliage derive from the thirteenth-century hinges at Notre Dame, Paris.

For its execution, Scott turned to F. A. Skidmore of Coventry. Skidmore wanted to present a major display for his Art Manufacturers' Company at the International Exhibition of 1862 'and offered to make the screen at a very low price'.[16] As a result, Scott somewhat lost control of the final product as Skidmore 'kicked over the traces [importing] a certain air of eccentricity', producing a 'fine work, but

13. G. G. Scott, *Personal and Professional Recollections*, ed. G. G. Scott (London, 1879), p. 216. For the relationship between Hereford and Scott's other cathedral screens at Lichfield, Ely, Durham, and Worcester, see P. F. Anson, *Fashions in Church Furnishings, 1840–1940* (London, 1960), pp. 143–60.

14. Scott, *Personal and Professional Recollections*, p. 290.

15. Ibid., p. 291. See also above, p. 276.

16. Ibid., p. 291. Scott's drawings were approved by the chapter in December 1861. Skidmore was paid £1500 in 1863 and a further £100 in 1864 for complications during the final installation, HCA, 7031/21, p. 62. An inscription found on the screen in 1967 records that it was erected in 1863 by H. Hodgekinson, foreman, Thomas Barber, carpenter, Abraham Arnold, fitter, HCA, 589.

Fig. 103. The choir screen by Sir George Gilbert Scott and Francis Skidmore. (HCL, B.3.41.)

too loud and self asserting for an English church'.[17] Skidmore only received the drawings in January 1862 and the screen was barely ready for the exhibition four months later. Although he was praised for his vigorous and honest handling of materials,[18] Skidmore took many short cuts, using thin sheet iron and copper plate to encase the cornice which was basically a timber structure. Although some of the bunches of foliage are wrought in the medieval manner, a lot of the decoration is mechanically pressed out of a sheet and then hammered into naturalistic curves. In this way dozens of repetitive forms could be mass produced and swiftly assembled. The subtle use of colour was particularly praised.[19] Skidmore chose

17. Scott, *Personal and Professional Recollections*, pp. 216, 291.

18. 'The iron, which knew how to form shafts that would stand firm and erect in rigid strength, had to be taught to assume that ductile docility which might empower it to realise the varying fantasies of the filigree worker', notabilia of the International Exhibition, 'The Screen at Hereford Cathedral', *The Art Journal*, new series, 1 (1862), p. 205.

19. C. Dressser, *Development of Ornamental Art*

tones of russet-brown, purple and blue green, all of which occurred naturally in iron during the manufacturing process. Unburnished copper, brass, mosaics and semi-precious stones added to the lustre of the monument. The hasty methods of construction, thin but tarnished surface materials attached to a crumbling core, are partly responsible for the current difficulties and expenses involved in restoring the screen.

Contemporary reviews of the screen at the 1862 exhibition were ecstatic. Dresser considered it to be 'undoubtedly one of the finest works of modern times'.[20] It elicited 'the highest eulogiums from the most cultivated minds of the nations'.[21] It was 'the most successful example of modern metalwork that has yet been executed'.[22] It was a 'noble work which knows no compeer amidst the multitudinous gatherings around it, a triumphant expression of living architectural energy'.[23]

The controversy about its removal in 1967 is told elsewhere. A small portion of the screen was retained as the choir aisle gates but the bulk of it then spent sixteen years in crates at the Herbert Art Gallery, Coventry, before reaching the Victoria and Albert Museum in 1984. There, the intention is to make it the majestic focus of the ironwork gallery, visible as a centrepiece from the entrance foyer. Until this work is complete, all that can be seen are a few fragments, attached to a life-size outline of the screen stencilled to the wall.

in the *International Exhibition* (London, 1862), pp. 153–54; *Illustrated London News*, 30 August 1862, p. 246.

20. C. Dresser, *Development of Ornamental Art*, pp. 151–54.

21. *Illustrated London News*, 30 August, 1862 p. 246.

22. *The Art-Journal Illustrated Catalogue of the International Exhibition* (1862), p. 158.

23. 'The Screen at Hereford Cathedral', p. 205.

17

The Bells

John Eisel

While the use of bells in connection with the services of the church is mentioned by Bede *c.* 680, the first mention in connection with Hereford is Robert de Bec's account of the siege of Hereford Castle in 1138, in which he says: 'on the tower, whence they used to hear the sweet and peaceful summons of the bells, they now saw engines erected, and missile weapons thrown against the king's men'.[1] This implies that the low central tower had been completed by this time. The bells would have been moved to a higher level when the central tower was rebuilt in the early fourteenth century. Twelve north-south beams, spanning the tower internally just below the level of the louvres (half of which have since been removed), probably supported the bell frame. The earliest surviving bell, the sixth bell in the present ring of ten bells, is inscribed STEPHANVS BANASTRE ME FECIT and was cast about the middle of the fourteenth century: his name is not otherwise known as a founder.

When the Edwardian inventory was taken *c.* 1552, eight bells were recorded, six of which probably formed a ring (designed to be rung together), and two smaller bells. The treble was cast in London *c.* 1420; this and three more of this ring may be ascribed to John Bird.[2] The two largest bells were cast in Bristol: the fifth bell, *c.* 1480, inscribed WILHELMVS WARWICK CONSTRVXIT ME INSANCTE [*sic*] TRINITATIS HONORE, and the tenor bell, by Thomas Gefferies, *c.* 1500, inscribed SANCTE CUTHBERTE ORA PRO NOBIS.

The present bell frame was probably built *c.* 1640, and is backward-looking in that it is kingposted when other frames constructed in the area at the same period lack kingposts. Remarkably, it was designed to hold eight bells in a hollow-square layout, with pairs of bells swinging mouth-to-mouth along each side. It is most

1. R. Johnson, *Ancient Customs of the City of Hereford* (2nd edn, London, 1882), p. 7.
2. B. S. Stanhope and H. C. Moffatt, *The Church Plate of the County of Hereford* (Westminster and Hereford, 1903), p. 216; BL, Harleian MS 6868, fol. 26a.

likely that the supporting timberwork was built at the same time, raising the frame higher than its predecessor. At this period there were two paid occasions of ringing, the ringers receiving 10s. for ringing on 5 November and on 'ye Kings Inauguration Day'.[3] Despite the number of pits in the frame, when Dingley visited the cathedral c. 1680 there was still only a ring of six bells, the three medieval bells described above and three other bells, since recast. One of these was cast in 1622 by a founder with the initials IP – probably by John Pennington of Monmouth – and another was cast at Leominster, perhaps by a member of the Clibury family of Wellington, working at Leominster c. 1672. The third of these bells had the inscription GLORIA DEO IN EXCELSIS, an inscription much favoured by John Finch, the Hereford bell founder, whose work covers the period 1623–64.[4]

In 1697–98 Abraham Rudhall I of Gloucester completely remodelled the ring and augmented it to one of ten bells, the frame being adapted to hold the extra bells. In the chapter act book of 11 November 1697 it is recorded that the master of the fabric was deputed to treat with 'Mr Abraham Rudhale for the casting of so many of the nyne bells as shall be necessary for the makeing of tunable bells, and for adding of mettle for the makeing of them Tenn ...'[5] The nine bells included the six bells mentioned by Dingley, the Stephen Banastre bell, and perhaps the two small bells in the Edwardian inventory or their successors. Rudhall remodelled the ring of six bells by recasting bells three and four, and replacing the second bell by the Banastre bell which he tuned, and casting four smaller bells to complete the ring of ten bells. The Banastre bell was not recorded by Dingley and may have previously hung in the west tower.

The bells have necessarily received attention from time to time. The chapter act book records that in 1761 James Garbet the 'Church Carpenter' carried out unauthorised repairs to the bells. These were unsuccessful and William Cooke, a bell hanger who worked with Abel Rudhall, was called from Gloucester to put matters right.[6] In 1810 the eighth bell, cast by Rudhall in 1697, which had become cracked, was recast by Thomas Mears of London, and the bells rehung by Thomas Paul of Bristol, who returned to Hereford in the following year and rehung the bells of All Saints.

After the poor state of the piers supporting the central tower was discovered in 1841, the bells were not rung full-circle again until they welcomed the new bishop on 26 April 1848. During the repairs to the tower, the ringing chamber floor in the lantern was removed and the ringing chamber moved to its present position

3. Jebb and Phillott, *The Statutes of the Cathedral Church of Hereford*, p. 88.

4. J. G. Nichols, ed., *History from Marble compiled in the Reign of Charles II by Thomas Dingley*, Camden Society, old series, 94, 97

(2 vols, London, 1867–68), i, p. clxiv.

5. HCA, 7031/3, p. 517, chapter acts, 11 November 1697.

6. HCA, 7031/4, pp. 401, 404, chapter acts, 12 November, 15 December 1761.

just below the bells. However, the bells were in bad repair and, at a meeting on 1 September 1849, the chapter decided that they should not be rung again until they had been properly repaired.[7] Despite this, on 17 August 1863 the bells were rung for the funeral of Archdeacon Richard Lane Freer. During the ringing, the medieval fifth bell, which had been cracked for many years, finally broke. As a consequence, in 1865 this bell was recast by Mears and Stainbank of London, and the bells were rehung by Alfred White and sons of Besselsleigh in 1865–66, being opened on 13 February 1866.[8] A set of rules was printed for the guidance of the new band of ringers.[9]

In 1892 the bells received attention from Messrs Blackbourn and Greenleaf of Salisbury, who repaired the frame.[10] The treble bell was found to be cracked and recast by Mears and Stainbank. During the course of the work certain beams in the centre of the ringing chamber were removed and to improve visibility replaced by cast iron posts. It was not until 1953 that major work to the bells was undertaken. The eighth bell was recast yet again, by Mears and Stainbank, the bells were rehung on ball bearings and the three largest bells were provided with new cast-iron stocks.[11] Apart from the bearings, however, the majority of the fittings of the seven smaller bells remain those provided by Alfred White in 1865. With this the ring took its present form, an individual ring incorporating bells from seven different founders and having, in the tenor bell, the largest medieval bell in the country incorporated in a ring of bells.[12]

Founders of Existing Bells

1	Mears and Stainbank 1892	6	Stephen Banastre *c.* 1350
2	Abraham Rudhall I 1698	7	Abraham Rudhall I 1697
3	Abraham Rudhall I 1698	8	Mears and Stainbank 1953
4	Abraham Rudhall I 1697	9	William Warwick *c.* 1450–80
5	Mears and Stainbank 1865	10	Thomas Gefferies *c.* 1500

7. HCA, 7031/20, p. 177, chapter acts, 1 September 1849.

8. HCA, 7031/21, p. 202, chapter acts, 24 March 1865.

9. Ibid., p. 245, 24 March 1866. The only surviving set appears to be that in Lincoln Cathedral Library. I am indebted to Dr John Ketteringham for communicating a copy.

10. HCA, 7031/23, pp. 146, 148, 152, 154, chapter acts, 13 February, 24 March, 16 and 28 May 1892.

11. HCA, 7031/25, pp. 111, 113, chapter acts, 30 October, 25 November 1952.

12. Fuller accounts of the bells and ringers are to be found in J. C. Eisel, *The Bells of Hereford Cathedral* (Hereford, 1977), and F. Sharpe, *The Church Bells of Herefordshire* (5 vols, Brackley, 1966–75), ii, pp. 182–206.

18

The Woodwork

Philip Dixon

Hereford Cathedral ranks very high among the cathedrals of England for the quality and interest of its woodwork and furniture. Among the most significant pieces is the chair which now stands in the choir, to the north of the high altar (fig. 104). Known as 'King Stephen's Chair', this is a massive piece, measuring some 2 feet 7¾ inches (806 mm.) from side to side, and over 1 foot 9¾ inches (554 mm.) from front to back, and now standing about 3 feet 7¾ inches (1108 mm.) high. The chair is almost entirely made up of pieces of turned oak, very neatly jointed with its tenons turned as dowels. Though at first this seems to be the familiar 'bobbin' turning, the incisions made by the joiner are quite shallow, and only the arms and the top rail of the back have lost much wood in the turning. The four legs have been continued above the top rails to form rounded finials, which are now mutilated. Until the last century some traces remained of vermilion and gold painting at least in the narrow strips between the incised bands of turning.[1]

Some elements are missing: most of the thin uprights which formed the centre panel of the back have been lost, as has the baluster and arches of one of the two double arched openings at the front of the chair. At some point the legs have been shortened fairly roughly by at least 6 inches (150 mm). The original distance of the seat above its base must thus have been almost 28 inches (about 700 mm.), quite high for a chair. Most of the timber seems to be of one date, with the possible exception of the thin oak boards which make up the seat. In general the chair is in excellent condition, after a recent refurbishment.

Its early history is obscure. It was already seen as an ancient piece in the nineteenth century, when the Cambrian Society visited Hereford. For its meeting in 1869 the chair was brought from the cathedral to a lecture room in the city, an event which at the time was thought to be the first occasion on which it had left the church.[2]

1. F. T. Havergal, *Fasti Herefordenses* (Edinburgh, 1869), p. 123.

2. 'Visits', *Proceedings of the Cambrian Society*, 5 (1869).

Leaving the precinct was presumably meant, since the chair had in fact been brought into the cathedral from the bishop's palace at some point before 1827.[3] The opinion of the specialists then gathered to view the chair was that it belonged to the eleventh or twelfth century, a regular view of most of the later writers who have examined it. However, one author, Francis Bond, whose knowledge of churches and church fittings was formidable, simply consigned it to the seventeenth century (saying only 'no doubt [it] is Jacobean'), unfortunately without any explanation.[4] The point is not unreasonable, since almost all the turned work in furniture which can now be seen belongs to the Elizabethan and Jacobean periods. The earlier seventeenth century was, in addition, a period in which a combination of archaising styles and of the reintroduction of classical details led to a considerable popularity in the use of round arches in architecture as in furniture and fireplaces. All this makes one doubt the antiquity of the chair.

In the absence of scientific testing, it is unfortunately not possible to be dogmatic. Several pointers, however, suggest that 'King Stephen's Chair' belongs to an early point in the middle ages. At the front on both sides traces remain of sawn-off tenons, not shown in the published drawings of the chair.[5] The purpose of these was to hold top and bottom rails, which supported a substantial projecting footstool. This is, in other words, a member of a well-known type, a chair of state, a conclusion supported by its considerable width (about 28 inches – 684 mm. – inside its arms). It is very unlikely that a throne would be constructed in the seventeenth century in the turned style of our present example, which has a slightly rustic appearance for that date. In addition, the termination of each of the four main uprights in an upstanding knob is a little unusual in a Jacobean chair, though common enough in the twelfth and thirteenth centuries, with examples (some including turning) from French manuscripts and carvings.[6] A twelfth-century chair which appears to be similar to 'King Stephen's Chair' survives in the Statens Historiska Museet in Stockholm.[7] If we therefore consider that the chair is much more likely to belong to the early middle ages than the Jacobean period, it is possible to be a little more precise about its date. When we look closely at the detail of the surviving arcading at the front, we can see that the combination of rounded arches with turned capitals and a middle strapwork suggests a date at the very end of the twelfth and the beginning of the thirteenth century, and the turned hollow bases of the columns provide a clear link with the style of the crypt of the

3. P. Eames, 'Furniture in England, France and the Netherlands from the Twelfth to the Fifteenth Century', *Furniture History*, 13 (1977), p. 210.

4. F. Bond, *Wood Carving in English Churches*, ii, *Stalls and Tabernacle Work* (London,

1910), p. 115.

5. RCHME, *Herefordshire*, i, p. 107.

6. Eames, 'Furniture in England', pp. 194–95.

7. W. Holmqvist, *Sveriges Forntid och Medeltid* (Malmo, 1949), fig. 391.

Fig. 104. King Stephen's Chair.

Lady chapel, begun early in the thirteenth century. It is quite possible (though without documentary evidence scarcely provable) that the chair was made for the bishop in anticipation of the celebration of the dedication of the east end. It is thus an important example of early furniture, one of only half a dozen surviving specimens. As Penelope Eames points out, 'The chair is one of the most important pieces of medieval furniture in Britain'.[8]

The stalls and throne in the choir are also of considerable importance (fig. 117). In their present arrangement they are the work of Gilbert Scott, who reconstructed the layout of the choir around 1860, and re-erected the medieval stalls, which had been rather roughly cleaned about 1830, and dismantled some ten years later.[9] The choir furniture, like that in Wells and Tewkesbury, is a single-tiered double screen of back stalls and front stalls, with a fine series of three-dimensioned ogee arches

8. Eames, 'Furniture in England', p. 211.
9. F. T. Havergal, *The Visitor's Hand Guide to* *Hereford Cathedral* (3rd edn, Hereford, 1869), pp. 35–36.

nodding forward above the back stalls. In the medieval arrangement there were in all some forty-eight back stalls, and ten more which returned from north to south across the eastern face of the original Norman pulpitum, to the west of the crossing arch of the nave. The reordering, which involved moving the choir eastwards out of the crossing area, meant that only two thirds of the old stalls were now needed, a total of thirty-one stalls, and Scott used some of the old back stalls as front stalls, and introduced new ends at the eastern side. Detailed descriptions of the stalls and the misericords have been given by the Royal Commission on Historical Monuments and in the *corpora* of misericords (fig. 105).[10] The best modern account is that given by Charles Tracy, who shows that the detailed variations in design and carving are likely to represent a single protracted campaign.[11] A comparison with the stalls at Wells (of about 1330–40) and Tewkesbury Abbey (about 1340–44), and with the nodding ogee arches of Gloucester (of about 1350) suggests a date for the Hereford furniture of the later 1340s or early 1350s, at least a generation earlier than generally supposed.[12] The stalls at Hereford, therefore, despite their nineteenth-century reconstruction, are an important link towards the beginning of surviving series of English choir stalls, a development from the simple single-storeyed thirteenth-century seats of Salisbury or Westminster, to the frequent and regular complex arrangements of the late fourteenth and fifteenth centuries. The bishop's throne, which stands at the eastern end of the southern row of stalls, belongs to the same campaign of carving, and is of even greater interest, since it is one of only three great medieval timber thrones to have survived, the others being at Exeter (of *c.* 1312) and St Davids (of the fifteenth century).[13] As is normal, the throne has a central wide seat and two narrower flankers, since the bishop during the office was supported by two chaplains.

In the south-west cloister (formerly in the library) stands a large medieval chest of the type known as a hutch, with framed sides, measuring about 4 feet 6⅜ inches (1 metre 840 mm.) in length. The top is a replacement, but the plain box framed sides and the front, finely carved in shallow relief, are both original. The carving, a series of intersecting arches of developed geometric tracery, dates the piece to around 1310–20, and places it among a small number of such chests which in England belong to the later thirteenth and the early fourteenth centuries.[14]

10. RCHME, *Herefordshire*, i, pp. 113–14; F. C. Morgan, *Hereford Cathedral Church Misericords* (Hereford, 1966); G. L. Remnant, *A Catalogue of Misericords in Great Britain* (Oxford, 1969), pp. 61–62.

11. C. Tracy, *English Gothic Choir-Stalls* (Woodbridge, 1987), pp. 30–33.

12. For example by F. Bond, *Wood Carving in English Churches*, ii, p. 29.

13. F. E. Howard and F. H. Crossley, *English Church Woodwork: A Study in Craftsmanship during the Mediaeval Period, AD 1250–1550* (London, 1917), pp. 192–93.

14. Eames, 'Furniture in England', pp. 140–41.

Fig. 105. Misericord, south side choir stalls, front row: a cat with a viol, and a goat with a lute.

Fig. 106. Detail of the roof of St John's walk.

One final element of the woodwork of Hereford cathedral should be mentioned, though it is not, like the earlier pieces, part of the furniture and fittings. This is the roof of the covered walkway which extends from the south-east transept to the college of vicars choral. The passageway was probably constructed once the courtyard of the college had been completed, perhaps after 1480. The roof is of oak, and is largely original. It is divided into bays by principal rafter trusses consisting of deep plank-like tie beams and king posts. The king posts support moulded ridge pieces, and the principal rafters hold single purlins on each slope. Purlins and ridge pieces carry common rafters, six pairs to each bay. All are dressed with the same delicate mouldings as the main timbers. The timbers of the principal trusses are elaborately carved with intersecting arcading, floral motifs, and with figures and grotesques, many holding emblazoned shields (fig. 106). The whole roof is a splendid example of the carpenter's craft.[15]

15. See G. Marshall, 'The Roof of the Vicars' Cloister at Hereford', *TWNFC*, 35 (1955–57), pp. 260–65.

19

The Post-Reformation Tombs

Roger Bowdler

Most visitors to Hereford Cathedral soon become aware that something rather serious has happened to its monuments. Effigies lie marooned, devoid of their elaborate settings; minor memorials of an early date have all been banished to the cloisters; and to this day the chamber above the former muniment room over the north transept resembles a Golgotha of masonry, with its heaps of fragments of dismantled tombs. Only the Gothic has survived, or been renewed, at Hereford. Fittings from the post-Reformation period have largely been swept away, and something like a third of such tombs no longer exist.[1] This essay seeks to answer two questions: what happened to its tombs? And what is left of note?

The normal explanation for damaged monuments is iconoclasm. There were two major outbursts: during the mid sixteenth-century Reformation, and during the seventeenth-century Civil War. Hereford was indeed captured late in 1645 by the Scottish Presbyterian troops of parliament, and it is customary to attribute the damaged state of the cathedral's older tombs to this event.[2] This explanation does not satisfy, since post-1660 tombs have fared poorly too. The calamitous collapse of 1786 would seem to be a likely alternative explanation, but an examination of an early plan of the cathedral shows how few tombs were affected by the collapse.[3] The truth is actually rather more depressing: most tombs survived these fearful events, only to fall victim to the narrow-mindedness of the Gothic Revival in the middle decades of the nineteenth century. As one commentator remarked in 1827, 'care should be taken not only in making a judicious selection [of monuments for re-erection], but in studiously excluding those of an inferior

---

1. The most thorough study of Hereford-shire's early modern tombs is N. Llewellyn's unpublished Ph.D. thesis 'John Weever and English Funeral Monuments of the Six-teenth and Seventeenth Centuries' (Warburg Institute, University of London,

   1983). Part two is a catalogue of monu-ments in the county from *c.* 1530 to 1660.
2. See, for instance, *The Hereford Guide* (Here-ford, 1806), p. 99.
3. Such as that in Willis, *Survey of the Cathe-drals*, p. 499.

cast'.[4] Alas, such care was duly taken and all too few of the post-Reformation tombs survived the upheavals of Cottingham's and Scott's restorations.

The hero of Hereford monuments, the Revd Francis Tebbs Havergal, wrote heart-rendingly of their forlorn condition in 1853:

> the whole of the inscribed stones were placed outside the South Transept; while thousands of fragments of the most costly monuments were to be seen in hopeless confusion in the Chapter House Yard. The sum of £500 was provided by the Dean and Chapter to effect the present arrangement of the Monuments inside the Cathedral, while several inscriptions have been restored by private assistance.[5]

He went on to lament that 'the sight of such a wreck of Monuments was a truly strange and grievous one. My first care was to rescue this and many other interesting fragments, shields, etc., by placing them inside the Church. The alabaster half-effigy of Bishop Field was exposed on top of this heap ... battered remnants [were] later buried in the churchyard.'[6]

Cottingham died in 1857. Sir George Gilbert Scott, his successor, was later to write that 'the monuments removed by Mr Cottingham were scattered about in all directions, and I could not have recovered their positions had it not been for the aid of the Revd F. T. Havergal'.[7] Some further damage may have happened, but the tide had turned. In 1866 many lesser tablets were refixed in the cloisters, and some of the larger tombs were beginning to be restored. For many monuments, however, such intervention came too late.

The earliest post-Reformation tomb to survive is the elegant alabaster chest with recumbent effigies to Alexander Denton and his first wife, the eighteen-year-old heiress Anne Willison of Sugwas (d. 1566). Medieval in format and hesitantly Renaissance in its decoration, it has been convincingly attributed to the Burton-upon-Trent workshop of Richard Parker (d. 1570).[8] Lying beside Mrs Denton's leg is the fatal baby, swaddled and bound: this monument stands right at the start of the notable tradition of tombs to women who died in childbirth and is of considerable iconographic importance for this reason.[9] The tomb's condition is

4. T. Garbett, *A Brief Enquiry into the Ancient and Present State of Hereford Cathedral* (London and Hereford, 1827), p. 79.

5. F. T. Havergal, *Monumental Inscriptions in the Cathedral Church of Hereford* (London, 1881), p. xiv.

6. Ibid.

7. G. G. Scott, *Personal and Professional Recollections: A Facsimile of the Original Edition*, ed. G. Stamp (Stamford, 1995), p. 289.

8. J. Bayliss, 'Richard Parker "The Alabasterman"', *Church Monuments*, 5 (1990), pp. 42 and 48. The tomb is similar to the Scudamore monument at Holme Lacy of after 1571, Llewellyn, 'John Weever and English Funeral Monuments', pp. 384ff.

9. Judith Hurtig, 'Death in Childbirth: Seventeenth-Century English Tombs and their Place in Contemporary Thought', *Art Bulletin*, 65 (1983), p. 605.

unexpectedly good: Scott restored the dismantled tomb incompletely and reposi-
tioned it within the south transept; it underwent substantial restoration in
1975.[10] Denton remarried and moved to his Buckinghamshire seat at Hillesden,
and it was there that he was buried in 1576: the empty spaces left in the inscription
at Hereford to receive his date of decease were never filled in, a poignant reminder
of his short-lived first marriage (plate VIIb).

Secular memorials like this are rare things within the setting of Hereford Cathedral.
Its medieval episcopal tombs have long been recognised as outstanding, and this
tradition of clerical memorials survived the Reformation. That said, the tombs of
the early seventeenth-century bishops have fared particularly badly and bear scant
resemblance to their original form. Partly this is the result of Presbyterian vandalism
during the Civil War, which especially led to the defacing of a number of effigies;
generally, however, their reduced state is the result of the vicissitudes outlined
earlier.

Bishop Herbert Westfaling (d. 1602) (fig. 28) had the earliest Anglican episcopal
monument in the cathedral.[11] Originally sited in the north-east transept, it was
once an elaborate affair, consisting of a sphinx-borne sarcophagus supporting the
effigy, set within a canopy of Corinthian columns, and the whole protected within
railings. Only the lumpish effigy and a fragment of the strapwork-encrusted
inscription panel (lurking behind the shop till in the cloisters) now remain. Of
local workmanship, it followed Westminster Abbey fashions in format if not in
finesse. Just who carved this and the following episcopal tombs is unknown, but
it would seem likely that some, at least, came from the Stroud (later Gloucester)
workshop of Samuel Baldwin (d. 1645), the most prominent monumental mason
in this part of the country in the Early Stuart period.[12]

The alabaster effigy of Bishop Robert Bennett (d. 1617) lies alongside that of
Bishop Giles de Braose (d. 1215), a testament to the continuity of the see as well
as of the innate conservatism of episcopal portraiture (fig. 107). Bennett left £500
in his will for funeral and monument, and requested that he be depicted in a

10. Scott, *Personal and Professional Recollections*,
    p. 289; Llewellyn, 'John Weever and Eng-
    lish Funeral Monuments', p. 384.
11. See J. G. Nichols, ed., *History from Marble
    Compiled in the Reign of Charles II by Thomas
    Dingley*, Camden Society, old series, 94, 97
    (2 vols, London, 1867–68), i, p. cxxxvii, for
    a seventeenth-century sketch of the tomb,
    along with its inscription. A watercolour of
    c. 1800 by S. Fisher showing its former
    appearance is in the collection of the So-
    ciety of Antiquaries; similar drawings were

made of the Field, Coke, Evans, Bisse,
Tyler, Cornwall, Gomond and Hayward
monuments.
12. None of the Hereford tombs are listed
    among the attributions made by John
    Broome in his 'Samuel Baldwin: Carver of
    Gloucester', *Church Monuments*, 10 (1995),
    pp. 37–54. Their poor condition makes
    firm conclusions as to authorship difficult.
    See Llewellyn, 'John Weever and English
    Funeral Monuments', pp. 257–63 on the
    question of tombs by local masons.

Fig. 107. Effigy of Bishop Robert Bennett, died 1617, with the effigy of Bishop Giles de Braose, died 1215, beyond, north side of choir. See fig. 29.

shroud, a fetchingly macabre fashion in tomb portraits of the day: the request was ignored.[13] Dingley recorded the original monument in one of his sketches, which shows a canopied tomb set behind railings with an elaborate mitre-crowned, obelisk-flanked superstructure which originally stood on the north side of the choir:[14] its former appearance was recorded in a seventeenth-century print (fig. 29).

Among the episcopal effigies, Bishop Theophilus Field's is the most animated. He is depicted in the act of preaching, hand on heart, finger in prayer book: a common way of depicting clerics at this time. The similarity between this figure and the far better-preserved one of the Revd Dr John Hoskyns (d. 1638) at Ledbury again suggests the work of a local workshop.[15] Divorced from its setting ('a canopy lined with ermine, and supported by two angels' according to Duncumb),[16] and awkward in carving, the effigy hardly suggests the cosmopolitan status that Field enjoyed. The sometime chaplain to James I and brother of one of Ben Jonson's

13. Ibid., pp. 404–7.
14. Nichols, ed., *History from Marble by Thomas Dingley*, pp. clxxiii–iv.
15. A further comparison can be made with the tomb at Lugwardine to the Revd John

Best (d. 1637).
16. J. Duncumb and others, *Collections towards the History and Antiquities of the County of Hereford* (8 vols, Hereford and London, 1804–1915), i, pp. 574–75.

principal thespian collaborators,[17] Field was nonetheless commemorated with a distinctly rustic memorial. The same might be said of Bishop Augustine Lindsell's monument: a highly learned man (and associate of the scholar Isaac Casaubon), his symbolically rich tomb (put up after his death in 1634) once had a depiction of the Heavenly City of Jerusalem,[18] as well as reliefs of chained books, a clear allusion to the Cathedral's celebrated library. Tombs at this time were first and foremost indicators of status: they were only just beginning to be displays of artistic sensibility too.

Bishop George Coke's tomb was originally an imposing altar tomb of freestone, the effigy set within an arch framed by Ionic columns of black marble rather in the style of Edward Marshall.[19] A Royalist who died in 1646, his tomb was probably erected after 1660 and survived intact until the 1840s, when disaster struck during Cottingham's restoration and it was dismantled. The effigy has been substantially reworked (fig. 141), and in 1875 a completely new setting, paid for by his descendants, was erected, copied from the monument in Bristol Cathedral to Bishop Paul Bush (d. 1558). So anachronistic a borrowing sums up the Victorian vicissitudes of Hereford's later tombs. So too do the half-effigies of Mary and the Revd William Evans (d. 1659 and 1668) (fig. 108). Currently kept in the masonry store over the north transept, the tomb once stood in the north transept. Mrs Evans died first, and hence holds a skull. One of the few women commemorated in the cathedral, she was remembered with an epitaph which combined posthumous respect with a female version of the *memento mori*:

> All Women shall be, what she is now here;
> But what she was, few Women are, few were.[20]

The eighteenth century is very poorly represented in Hereford's tombs. A number have vanished altogether: Bishop Philip Bisse (d. 1721) had a sumptuous marble monument on the south side of the choir that has virtually disappeared, save for the inscription panels now in the south transept, and which suggest that his monument was a elaborate version of the surviving memorial in the cloisters to Mrs Morgan (d. 1739), with its unusual wrought iron screen. The tomb of James Thomas (d. 1757) has also been broken up, but his bust (fig. 109) and ledger slab remain: the former, now in the new chained library room, has a Hogarthian air of *déshabillé* about it which has led to a long-standing attribution to the great Louis-François

17. See the entry in the *DNB* on Nathaniel Field (1587–1633).

18. This was drawn by John Carter in 1784: BL, MS Add. 29926, fol. 152.

19. R. Rawlinson, *The History and Antiquities*

of the City and Cathedral-Church of Hereford (London, 1717), p. 218.

20. Llewellyn, 'John Weever and English Funeral Monuments', p. 440; N. Llewellyn, *The Art of Death* (London, 1991), pp. 16–17.

Fig. 108. Half effigies of William and Mary Evans, died 1659 and 1668, from their tomb originally in the north transept.

Fig. 109. Bust of James Thomas, died 1757, now in the chained library room in the new library building.

Fig. 110. Gothic monument to
Richard Jones Powell, died
1834, in south cloister.

Roubiliac.[21] Whoever the sculptor, there is no doubting the quality of this portrait.
Other tombs from this period have simply disappeared. The Revd Isaac Donnithorne
(d. 1782) possessed a monument of a weeping woman with an inverted torch,
mourning over an urn; formerly positioned in the nave, no traces remain of this
quintessentially Neoclassical memorial.[22] The only testament to this important era
in tomb sculpture is the allegorical (and unsigned) scene on the east wall of the
cloisters to Colonel John Matthews (d. 1826): 'the subject, "Grief consoled by an
angel", is of some merit, and is carved in Caen stone'.[23]

Of Caen stone too is the engaging tomb of the local worthy Richard Jones
Powell (d. 1834) (fig. 110). Originally in the south choir aisle but removed to the
cloisters in 1861 (the angel was 'considered unsatisfactory'), it was reputedly designed

21. F. T. Havergal, *Visitors' Hand-Guide to the
    Cathedral Church of Hereford* (3rd edn, Here-
    ford, 1869), p. 23. The attribution is not
    accepted in D. Bindman and M. Baker,
    Roubiliac and the Eighteenth-Century

Monument (New Haven and London, 1995).
22. Duncumb, *Collections towards the History of
    the County of Hereford*, i, p. 554.
23. Havergal, *Hand-Guide to the Cathedral
    Church*, p. 40.

by Nockalls Cottingham (1823–54), son of Lewis Cottingham, restorer of the cathedral.[24] A fanciful essay in the Decorated style, reminiscent of tombs designed by Thomas Rickman, it represents the pre-Pugin, pre-archaeologically correct phase of the Gothic Revival, in which Cottingham was a significant figure.

Two of the glories of Hereford's tombs belong to the high and late phases of this movement. Dean Richard Dawes (d. 1867) is commemorated in the north-east transept with a tenderly pious recumbent effigy of Cararra marble, carved by Matthew Noble RA, placed on a rich chest of alabaster and marble by the Messrs Brindley and Richards (fig. 44).[25] Noble had created the monument at York Minster to a former Bishop of Hereford, Thomas Musgrave (d. 1863), which may explain the choice of sculptor. It was a happy one: the dean's fastidious features are offset by the gently interlocked praying hands, and the sacred books below the pillow are a reminder of much earlier clerical tombs at Hereford. Finest of all is the powerful effigy of Bishop James Atlay (d. 1894) by James Forsyth, dated 1897, in the north transept. 'Overbearing and imperious', according to Francis Kilvert,[26] the delicately chiselled figure – a virtuoso display of rendering textures in marble – well expresses the bishop's authority, seriousness and industry. The marks of effort show on his face, and the effigy expresses the release from worldly cares that comes with death (fig. 111). Two small memorials nearby commemorate sons of the bishop, who clearly inculcated a sense of duty into his family: the Revd George Atlay, a missionary, was 'murdered near the shores of Lake Nyasa, by a band of marauding savages' in 1895, and Charles Atlay died of wounds in 1900 while serving with the Imperial Light Horse against the Boers at Ladysmith. The three Atlay memorials form a poignant testament to the religious basis of the imperial ethic.

The last of the opulent memorials to bishops at Hereford is that of John Percival (d. 1917), a marble bas-relief on the south-west pier of the crossing by Allan Wyon, a member of the Wyon dynasty of medallists. Slightly out of character with its setting, this memorial was actually displayed at the 1925 Royal Academy. Later bishops opted for less intrusive memorials, such as the elegant ledger slabs in the crypt to Bishops Carr (d. 1941) and Parsons (d. 1948). Private memorials had fallen out of fashion by this date, and episcopal ostentation was deemed poor form.

Organists too began to be commemorated in the cathedral: not surprisingly,

24. Havergal, *Monumental Inscriptions*, p. xvi. The younger Cottingham designed the reredos of the high altar, also of Caen stone, but was surely too young to have done the Powell tomb. The tomb at Ashbourne, Derbyshire, to Fanny, Lady Boothby (1840) by Cottingham *père* is highly comparable.

25. Havergal, *Monumental Inscriptions*, p. xvii.

26. Quoted in R. W. D. Fenn and J. B. Sinclair, *The Bishops of Hereford and their Palace* (Hereford, 1990), p. 32.

Fig. 111. Detail of the effigy of Bishop James Atlay, died 1894, north transept.

given Hereford's growing reputation for music from the later Victorian period onwards. These began in the 1870s, and culminated in the engaging plaque to George Robertson Sinclair (d. 1917), his portrait in enamel, signed by Fanny Bunn, depicting the director of music at the console of the organ in his gown (fig. 112). The modern tendency towards practical memorials is exemplified by the recent wooden doorway on the north side of the nave, erected in memory of Sir Percy Clarke Hull (d. 1968).

The other distinct group of memorials is that of soldiers: together, they have made a Valhalla of the south nave aisle.[27] Earliest is the large brass of 1875 to men of the 36th (Herefordshire) Regiment, stationed in India from 1863 to 1875, during which time over 350 men died. As was then customary, officers were named but not other ranks; within the Gothic setting, the niches usually reserved for saints now house uniformed figures. Brass plaques to fallen soldiers sprang up around it after the First World War, and at the west end of the nave were erected two seventeenth-century revival alabaster aedicules, one to the Herefordshire Regiment, one to Lieutenant-Colonel Percy Clive (d. 1918). Located not far from the alabaster effigy of Sir Richard Pembridge (d. 1375), these monuments are testaments to the

27. A comparable Parnassus of philanthropic public figures also sprang up, with memorials located at the south end of the west wall of the retrochoir.

Fig. 112. Detail of the enamel portrait from the monument to George Robertson Sinclair, organist, died 1917, south-east crossing pier.

consoling comforts of the traditional way of remembrance, even in an age of high explosive and machine guns.

Hereford's memorials introduce an important human element within the sublime sacred architecture of the cathedral. Many have suffered much; some have disappeared altogether. What remains deserves our attention and demands our respect.

PART III

Music and Worship

20

Music before 1300

John Caldwell

The foundation of the see of Hereford is traditionally placed in 676, when Bishop Putta of Rochester was compelled to vacate his diocese of Rochester and was given a church and a small piece of land in Mercia by Seaxwulf, then sole bishop of the Mercians with his seat at Lichfield.[1] Although Bede is silent on an episcopal role for Putta, whether at Hereford or anywhere else, and although other documentary evidence that Putta (or a Putta) was first in the line of bishops of Hereford has been thought to be of doubtful value, there is good reason not to ignore the presence of this musically skilled, episcopally ordained cleric somewhere in Mercia west of the Severn in the later seventh century.[2] The grant of a church, moreover, implies not just a building but also a going concern, presumably with a body of clergy and an effective administration. We may reasonably think of it as offering a focus for and setting a standard in the performance of divine worship in his day. In this it will have been an important factor in the adoption of Roman custom in western Mercia, where the church at Leominster – a monastic foundation of Celtic origin – had hitherto held sway.[3]

According to Bede, Putta was 'a most skilled exponent of Roman chant, which he had learnt from pupils of blessed Pope Gregory'; and on arrival in Mercia he taught the Roman chant wherever he was asked.[4] It needs to be stressed, however, that two distinct traditions of 'Roman' chant have come down to us, and that neither has a good claim to go back in its extant form to Gregory I. One is that known from the late eighth century onwards as 'Gregorian' (although the earliest

---

1. Bede, *Historia ecclesiastica*, iv, 12. C. Plummer, in his edition of Bede, *Venerabilis Baedae opera historica* (2 vols, Oxford, 1896), ii, p. 222, strongly discounted this as evidence for the establishment of the diocese of Hereford.

2. For the most authoritative review of this whole question see S. Keynes, 'Diocese and Cathedral before 1056', Chapter 1 in the present volume.

3. J. Hillaby, 'Leominster and Hereford: The Origins of the Diocese', in Whitehead, *Medieval Art at Hereford*, pp. 1–14, esp. p. 8.

such description of it occurs in an antiphonary without notation);[5] the other the so-called 'Old Roman', a local form of chant surviving in a small number of Roman manuscripts from the eleventh to the fourteenth centuries. Although this local form of Roman chant is represented only in sources of later date than the Gregorian, it possesses what have been identified as archaic features.

What then was the form of chant that Putta would have been teaching to the Mercians? The fact that he had learnt it from disciples of the blessed Gregory clearly need not mean that it was Gregorian in the usual sense; might it not have been rather the local, archaic form of the chant, supposing that to have been of some antiquity? We cannot, however, make any assumptions as to the antiquity of either repertory as it has come down to us.

It is much more likely that the chant of the Roman Church was in the seventh and eighth centuries still evolving, perhaps growing in sophistication as a succession of Roman cantors sought to impose their own style upon it. But the situation in Rome, with its numerous basilicas and monasteries, was a complex one, and there was doubtless more than one supposedly authoritative source of information to reach England. In 680, soon after Putta went to Mercia, a certain John, *archicantator* (as Bede calls him) of St Peter's in Rome and abbot of the monastery of St Martin, arrived in England to teach the chant, as it was performed at St Peter's, in the north. St Martin's abbey was one of those adjacent to St Peter's and responsible for the maintenance there of the round of daily services; but St Peter's was not, at that date, the church attached to the papal residence.[6]

We do not know from what institution or institutions the pupils of St Gregory who taught Putta came. There are various possibilities, and there can be no certainty that their version of the chant was identical to that propagated by John the archcantor. While we cannot be sure of the nature of the chant taught by Putta, or of his actual role in what was to become the diocese of Hereford, his work is likely to have exercised a formative influence on liturgical custom in Hereford itself, which had become the political as well as the ecclesiastical centre of western Mercia by the end of the seventh century.[7]

There was at that date no fixed rule for communities of secular clergy, and later in the Anglo-Saxon period they gained a reputation for laxity, so much so that several cathedrals were provided with monastic chapters instead. One can get an

4. Bede, *Historia ecclesiastica*, iv, 2: 'maxime autem modulandi in ecclesia more Roman-orum, quem a discipulis beati papae Gregorii didicerat, peritum'; and iv, 12: 'et ubicumque rogabatur, ad docenda ecclesiae carmina diuertens'.

5. D. Hiley, *Western Plainchant: A Handbook* (Oxford, 1993), p. 510. All the earliest sources of 'Gregorian' chant are from Frankish territory (including Monza in north Italy).

6. Bede, *Historia ecclesiastica*, iv, 16. The papal residence was the Lateran palace; its church, St John Lateran, was and is the mother church of Rome.

7. Hillaby, 'Leominster and Hereford', p. 6.

idea of their duties from the *Regula canonicorum* drawn up by Chrodegang, archbishop of Metz, around the middle of the eighth century, even though the direct influence of Frankish reform reached England only later. The most important of these duties was to maintain the daily round of choir offices – matins, lauds, prime, terce, sext, none, vespers and compline. The principal elements of these offices were the psalms, sung through in the course of a week, together with refrains known as antiphons; readings from holy scripture and the Fathers, followed usually by a form known as a responsory; hymns; and prayers. The offices were normally sung, at any rate as regards the psalms with their antiphons and the responsories and hymns, and that mostly by heart, since the music at any rate was not notated; there was also the expense of copying books and of providing light by which to read them in the hours of darkness. It was an onerous task for which a lengthy education was required, the only education that a lucky boy would ever get. The full exercise of this routine cannot have been put into practice at a moment's notice.

It is quite likely that the psalms of the office were sung, in the seventh and eighth centuries, in a manner made familiar by later medieval and more recent practice, namely to one of several very simple 'tones' or melodic formulae that could be adapted to the differing lengths of the psalm verses and which corresponded in tonality to the accompanying antiphons. The antiphons themselves, nothing more than a refrain drawn from the psalm in question, would have been similar to the simpler ones of the later medieval tradition, and the same may be true of the hymn melodies. The responsories, on the other hand, are likely to have been rather more straightforward than they had become by about 900, by which time they were mostly rather complex, even in their refrain sections. Probably they approximated in their musical character more closely to the 'short' responsory of the later middle ages than to the 'prolix' variety.

The principal service as far as the congregation was concerned was the mass on Sundays and other feasts, celebrated by the bishop himself with his clergy in attendance. In Rome and some other places this was a 'stational' liturgy, meaning that it was celebrated in different city churches according to the occasion. It is quite possible that a similar custom existed in English cathedral cities including Hereford, though direct evidence is lacking; in any case the number of churches and the distance between them was usually small. In Hereford itself, while there may have been one or more additional churches or chapels within the cathedral complex, the only other pre-Conquest church of which the existence is certain was St Guthlac, founded by the tenth century at least.[8]

In its Roman form the mass consisted of an introductory rite (entrance song, Kyrie, Gloria and opening prayer), a reading followed by a responsorial chant (the

---

8. I am grateful to Dr Julia Barrow for helpful observations on the liturgical situation in Hereford.

gradual) and an Alleluia (with verse) or tract, the gospel reading, an offertory song and prayer over the gifts, the eucharistic prayer, preceded by the Preface and Sanctus and followed by the *Pater noster* ('Our Father'), the *Agnus dei* to accompany the breaking of the consecrated bread, a communion song, and the final prayer and blessing. The service was in Latin, though perhaps with some vernacular elements such as a bidding prayer and a homily, and mostly chanted, at any rate in a cathedral or collegiate church. The congregation may have joined in with simple responses and in the *Pater noster*, though hardly otherwise.

Some of these chants, and particularly the gradual, Alleluia, and tract, required skilled solo singing, though like the responds of the office they may have been less elaborate in the eighth century than they later became. There seems to be no concrete evidence for professional clerical singing in England at this date, although there was a *schola cantorum* in Rome from the end of the seventh century at least, and the idea spread from there to various parts of Europe. One interesting example comes from Metz, where Chrodegang's successor Angilram (archbishop 768–91) drew up a list of payments for singers and readers. In this, special remuneration was laid down for the deacon and subdeacon on certain occasions; for the soloists who sang particularly important chants; and to the first, second, third and fourth of the *scola* (so spelled).[9] At what stage a system of recognised *stipendia* for musical duties (as opposed to endowed incomes, for which pre-Conquest information is also sparse) came into being in England is unclear, but it will have been difficult to sustain a repertory of elaborate solo chants without it.

When at last notated music first appears in England, in the later tenth and early eleventh centuries, it is the fully-fledged Gregorian repertory, together with tropes and sequences, that the manuscripts transmit. (Tropes are additions before and in between the phrases of an established chant; sequences are extensions to the Alleluia of the mass, sung either to the syllable '-a' or with a text giving one syllable to each note. New texts were often added to existing melismas to form *prosae* or *prosulae*.) Still there is nothing from Hereford itself, but there are possible parallels from non-monastic cathedrals such as Exeter. Amongst them are books given to Exeter Cathedral by Bishop Leofric (1046–72), to which in some places neumes have been added by English scribes in his own day.[10] These are ad hoc additions, but there are other fragments from Exeter that belong to a complete repertory of chants for the mass. The most important of these are from one or more noted

9. The list is printed in J.-B. Pelt, *Etudes sur la cathédrale de Metz*, iv, *La liturgie*, pt i, *Ve–VIIIe siècles* (Metz, 1930), pp. 38–39; he also gives Chrodegang's rule in its original form, pp. 8–28.

10. See e.g. Oxford, Bodleian, MS Bodley 579, fol. 60r, and MS Auct. D.2.16, fol. 29r; facsimiles in E. W. B. Nicholson, *Introduction to the Study of the Oldest Latin Musical Manuscripts in the Bodleian Library, Oxford* (London, 1913), pls 29 and 26 respectively.

missals,[11] a type of book that included the chants as well as the prayers (and sometimes the lessons) of the mass.

Other types of liturgical book with music surviving from before the Norman Conquest – noted breviaries, tropers, and the like – are mostly from the monastic sphere.[12] Undoubtedly the office was sung at Hereford in a form close to that of other secular foundations, but it is not unlikely that a repertory of tropes and sequences for the mass was cultivated, perhaps under the influence of neighbouring Worcester and Gloucester.

None of this music is written down in a form which can be directly read. The neumes of which mention has been made show only the contour of the melody, not the actual notes, and sometimes even the outline is obscure. By now the Gregorian chant had acquired a degree of stability that enables much of this material to be confidently equated with later versions written in staff notation, though it is sometimes clear that they have been altered in minor details. Some parts of the repertory, however, notably many of the tropes or liturgical intercalations, were of only local and temporary currency and did not survive into the period of pitch-specific notation. These are lost for ever, except in vague outline.[13]

Just one other Anglo-Saxon document needs to be mentioned in this connection, though its relevance to the music of the cathedral is unclear. This is the manuscript of the gospels which has belonged to the cathedral since the eleventh century at least, if it was not indeed destined for it in the first place. By that date the lessons of the mass, and of the office in public recitation, were normally sung to a simple melodic formula rather than spoken. The gospel at mass would have been intoned by a deacon, and the Hereford manuscript contains indications of specific passages to be read liturgically. It is not arranged, however, in the order of the gospel

11. Oxford, Bodleian, MS lat. liturg. e. 38 (two fragments, probably from the same book); BL, MS Add. 62104. For further information see S. Rankin, 'From Memory to Record: Musical Notations in Manuscripts from Exeter', *Anglo-Saxon England*, 13 (1984), pp. 97–112.

12. An example of a breviary with musical notation is the so-called *Portiforium Wulstani*, Cambridge, Corpus Christi College, MS 391. This, though apparently copied from books at Winchester, was made for the use of Wulfstan, bishop of Worcester, shortly before the Conquest. The 'Caligula' troper, BL, Cotton MS Caligula A. xiv, fos 1–36, an eleventh-century MS that is followed by a twelfth-century troper possibly from Canterbury, was once associated with Hereford on the strength of the presumed similarity of its paintings to those of Cambridge, Pembroke College, MS 302, an eleventh-century gospel-lectionary that did belong to Hereford. This was ruled out on liturgical grounds by A. Planchart (see next note) and more recently on art-historical grounds by E. C. Teviotdale, 'The "Hereford Troper" and Hereford', in Whitehead, *Medieval Art at Hereford*, pp. 75–81.

13. The major study of English tropes is A. E. Planchart, *The Repertory of Tropes at Winchester* (2 vols, Princeton, 1977). The Old Minster at Winchester was from the later tenth century a monastic foundation.

readings according to the liturgical calendar, nor does it contain any indications that might have assisted a reader in chanting them.[14]

The new minster church built by Athelstan (bishop *c.* 1013–56) provided a suitable context for the greater elaboration that was characteristic of the liturgical music of the period, but its devastation by the Welsh in 1055 will have put an end to inessential adornment. The first Norman bishop, Robert the Lotharingian (bishop 1079–95) built himself a fine chapel, but a new cathedral was finally completed only under Robert de Béthune between 1142 and 1148. It is possible nevertheless that Robert the Lotharingian's chapel fulfilled some of the functions of the damaged minster, while his energetic reorganisation of the cathedral community undoubtedly facilitated the renewal of liturgical music in his day.

There is no specific information as to the course of musical development in the cathedral between the Norman Conquest and the thirteenth century, though there are manuscripts in the cathedral library, such as the twelfth-century gospels (MS O.I.8), that have a bearing on the liturgy.[15] But there is no record that might indicate the cultivation of polyphony, for example, and the few instances of this elsewhere in England before the late thirteenth century are too scattered and isolated to be of significance. Towards the end of that century there are indeed such indications, though they are not specific to Hereford; by and large, however, the music of the cathedrals was restricted to the faithful performance of a repertory of monophonic chant that was in most respects highly traditional.

The main developments were liturgical. Additions to the calendar, some of them universal, others of local significance only, necessitated new music. Much of this, however, was adapted from existing material, and there were reductions as well as additions to the repertory. Many of the earlier tropes, if we may assume that they were adopted at Hereford in the first place, were abandoned; by the later middle ages, at all events, the only remaining vestiges of the practice were the

14. HCL, MS P.I.2. There is little punctuation, and acute accents occur so sporadically as to be of no real significance. I am grateful to Dr Richard Gameson for discussing these details with me; for further information, see his chapter on the gospel manuscript (Chapter 29). The gospel-lectionary mentioned in note 12 above belonged to Hereford, though it did not necessarily originate there, and a pre-Conquest date is not absolutely certain.

15. The twelfth-century pontifical in Oxford, Magdalen College, MS 226, described by W. H. Frere, *Bibliotheca Musico-Liturgica: A Descriptive Handlist of the Musical and Latin Liturgical MSS Preserved in the Libraries of Great Britain and Ireland*, Plainsong and-Medieval Music Society (2 vols, London, 1901 [1894]–1932), i, p. 152, as being 'of Hereford', evidently originated in the diocese of Canterbury and reached Hereford only somewhat later: see H. A. Wilson, ed., *The Magdalen Pontifical*, Henry Bradshaw Society, 39 (London, 1901), pp. vii–ix. None of the twelfth- and thirteenth-century manuscripts (including liturgical homiliaries, a passionale and so on) that originated in Hereford and are still in the cathedral library is of musical significance.

prosulae (verbal expansions) of the Kyrie text, the additions to the *Gloria in excelsis* for Marian masses, and a number of *prosae* (insertions in responsories) for the Office. On the other hand, the repertory of sequences was gradually extended: the printed missal of 1502 contained about eighty.

The thirteenth century was, in fact, the period during which both monastic and secular Uses achieved something like their later medieval form. The monastic Uses need not concern us here, though their significance in England was considerable owing to the fact that Canterbury, the metropolitan cathedral of the southern province, had been monasticised in the tenth century and retained its monastic constitution after the Conquest. Worcester, close to Hereford, was an example of a cathedral priory, as such foundations are generally called. The most widespread of the secular Uses was that of Salisbury, and many cathedrals adopted it with little change. Amongst those that did not were York, the metropolitan cathedral church of the northern English province, and Hereford itself, though their Uses, often clearly labelled as such in manuscripts and always (later) in printed editions, differed from each other in their details rather than in their essentials. The mid thirteenth-century statutes and customs of Hereford Cathedral describe the constitution of twenty-eight prebendal canons, the provision of vicars choral, other clergy and boys, and the allocation of duties in the performance of the services.[16]

It is unfortunate that so little material for the study of the Hereford Use has survived. In particular we possess only one manuscript missal, with some of the chants of the *temporale*, from the fourteenth century,[17] and no gradual or complete collection of chants for the mass. The magnificent noted breviary, a manuscript of 366 folios with all the relevant chants included, dates, however, from the third quarter of the thirteenth century and provides evidence that the distinctive features of the later Use were already in place (plate IVa).[18]

Although the date and significance of the noted breviary have been well known for nearly 170 years, and its text made use of in the modern edition of the Hereford breviary,[19] the manuscript still awaits a full study. It represents the Use

16. See Chapter 21, n. 1, and thereafter for a number of details concerning the organisation of the cathedral duties from this period.

17. This will be considered in Chapter 21.

18. HCL, MS P.IX.7. It is possible that the Hereford Use was brought from Rouen by Bishop Gerard (1096–1100). See Chapter 2, p. 27.

19. *The Hereford Breviary*, iii, pp. lv–lxi. The manuscript, although clearly destined for Hereford in the first instance, seems to have passed to the parish of Mordiford in the deanery of Ross, but its fate at the Reformation is unknown. It was purchased in 1834 from William Hawes, who had bought it from a bookshop in Drury Lane a few years earlier. Proof of the connection with Hereford, and of its date, was supplied to the bishop of Llandaff by the British Museum in a letter dated 1832, now tipped in at the beginning of the manuscript: Mynors and Thomson, *Catalogue*, p. 124.

of the cathedral church, as regards the office, in a pure and uncluttered form, but with all the materials for its performance that could be reasonably required. The main contents are: the *temporale*, in double columns (fos 1r–178v); hymns for the lesser hours, and for the *commune sanctorum*, in one column to the page (fos 179r–182r), with a paschal table on fol. 182v; the calendar (January and February missing, fos 183r–187v); the psalter, with canticles and litany (fos 188r–222r, again in double columns but without music); and the *sanctorale* and *commune*, with the office for the dead, a series of *Venite* settings, and a *tonale* (fos 331r–364v). At the end are two leaves (fos 365–66) devoted to the 'new feast' of Corpus Christi, though this is incomplete; and a few other pages are missing here and there.

At the beginning of the manuscript is a flyleaf of great interest that has received little attention. It is from an antiphonal of the twelfth century with music written in an alphabetic notation of which only a few specimens have survived.[20] The alphabetic series consists of the letters a to p, with a few additional signs but, unlike continental examples, without neumes. Its sequence of items, however, which are for the Trinity season up to 1 August, is unusual and has not been satisfactorily matched up with any known Use, though there are similarities with the cursus of William of Volpiano that was adopted in the Norman monasteries of Fécamp, Mont-Saint-Michel and Jumièges.[21] If the fragment could be accurately placed on liturgical grounds, that might tell us where the Hereford breviary was copied, since it was presumably taken from a discarded manuscript belonging to the scriptorium in which the breviary was produced.

While the breviary itself is not only a unique testimony to the music and text of the Hereford Use in the thirteenth century, it is also a singularly impressive piece of book production. Only a few of its distinctive features can be discussed here. Its music is clearly written on the four-line staff, but with a D-clef instead of an F-clef for the lower-pitched chants (or portions thereof). This is a somewhat

20. It was described, and partly transcribed, in *The Hereford Breviary*, iii, pp. lvi–lvii. There is a facsimile of the verso in W. H. Frere, *Bibliotheca Musico-Liturgica*, i, pl. 2 (the date there given is, however, too early). What is now the verso of the leaf appears originally to have been the recto: it is slightly damaged at the foot. The largest of the known sources of this system of notation is a collection of chants for the mass from Dijon, now Montpellier, Faculté de Médecine, MS H 159. The only other English example known to me is a short passage of polyphonic music, again of the twelfth century, added to a manuscript then at St Augustine's, Canterbury, now Oxford, Bodleian, MS Bodley 572, fol. 49v: Nicholson, *Introduction to the Study of the Oldest Latin Manuscripts*, pl. 16.

21. I am grateful to David Chadd for this observation. For William of Volpiano and his cursus see R. Le Roux, 'Guillaume de Volpiano: son *cursus* liturgique au Mont-Saint-Michel et dans les abbayes normandes', in J. Laporte, ed., *Millénaire monastique du Mont-Saint-Michel*, i, *Histoire et vie monastique* (Paris, 1966); N. Bulst, *Untersuchungen zu den Klosterreform Wilhelms von Dijon, 962–1031*, Pariser Historische Studien, 2 (Bonn, 1973).

unusual feature, though it is also found in the antiphonal produced at nearby Worcester.[22] This might encourage one to believe that the breviary was produced at Worcester itself, but in other ways the music script seems quite different. That would not of course preclude the possibility that the breviary was written in the same scriptorium or in one derived from it.

At the end of the manuscript is a *tonale*, beginning with a diagram of the seven hexachords in the system of Guido of Arezzo, with some traditional mnemonic chants and a summary of the eight modes in a standard form. The main object of a *tonale* was to enable singers to choose the right psalm-tone to go with the antiphons of the office. Such information, for a knowledgeable singer, was obtainable from the formulae appended to the notated chants, but it was found useful to have a summary of the information to be learnt, presumably, by rote.

The contents of the breviary follow standard form, but it is interesting to note the presence of the complete office of St Thomas of Canterbury without mutilation: most English liturgical books have erasures or missing pages, or both, at this point. Perhaps in the obscurity of medieval Mordiford it was possible for the volume to be spirited away and for Thomas Cromwell's command to remove all reference to St Thomas to be ignored.[23] This office occurs, as usual, in the *temporale* – that is to say, the offices for the Sunday cycle and the feasts dependent on it, but including the feasts on calendar dates from Christmas Eve to the octave of the Epiphany, of which the feast of St Thomas on 29 December is one. In the *sanctorale* – containing the feasts of saints other than those of the Christmas season – occurs the feast of St Ethelbert of East Anglia, king and martyr, co-patron of Hereford cathedral, on 20 May.[24]

While the distinctive aspects of the Hereford Use have long been known to liturgists, little work has been done on the local character of the melodies. In many cases the versions recorded in the thirteenth-century breviary differ only superficially, if at all, from those given in contemporary sources such as those of Salisbury Use. The matter awaits further study, and, in the case of the hymns at least, it is clear that the melodies were not transmitted from that quarter. Nor on the other hand is there a connection with the Benedictine form of chant used at Worcester Cathedral. Some chants appear to be unique to Hereford, though they may in the event prove to be adapted from chants known elsewhere. These occur mainly, or perhaps exclusively, in the office for St Ethelbert, in which the

22. Worcester, Chapter Library, MS F.160; facsimile and description published as *Antiphonaire monastique XIIIe siècle: Codex F.160 de la bibliothèque de la cathédrale de Worcester*, Paléographie musicale, first series, 12 (2 vols, Tournai, 1922–25).

23. See above, note 19. The Calendar includes at 4 June in a later hand 'Dedicatio ecclesie parrochialis de mordiford'.

24. For St Ethelbert and his cult in Hereford see E. M. Jancey, *St Ethelbert: Patron Saint of Hereford Cathedral* (Hereford, 1994).

Fig. 113. Hereford breviary, 1262–68: two antiphons for St Ethelbert. (HCL, MS P.IX.7, fos 262r, 264v.)

canticle-antiphons for lauds and vespers may be singled out as especially beautiful. One of these is easily recognised as an adaptation of 'Ave rex gentis anglorum', for St Edmund king and martyr, also an East Anglian saint – though the version of the melody is not quite that of the Barnwell antiphoner, the thirteenth-century source used by W. H. Frere for the greater part of his *Antiphonale Sarisburiense*.[25]

25. W. H. Frere, ed., *Antiphonale Sarisburiense* (London, 1901–24), pl. 597. The manuscript used by Frere, Cambridge University Library, Mm 2.9, is an East Anglian antiphonal of Augustinian provenance, close to Salisbury Use but including material for the non-Sarum feast of St Edmund. The melody is in fact somewhat closer to the version of the antiphon on St Edmund in the Worcester antiphonal. Both texts are related to the much more widespread 'Ave regina celorum, mater regis angelorum'. This may have been the prototype, but in a survey of the evidence M. Bukofzer, *Studies in Medieval and Renaissance Music* (New York, 1950), pp. 18–20, concluded that there could be no certainty on this point, both the Marian and the Edmundian texts being attested from the thirteenth century (he did not know of the text for St Ethelbert); if the Marian text was an adaptation, it will have been made in England and subsequently transmitted to the Continent. See also R. M. Thomson, 'The Music for the Office of St. Edmund King and Martyr', *Music and Letters*, 65 (1984), pp. 189–93 (noting several other adaptations of 'Ave rex' in addition to that for St Ethelbert).

Fig. 114. Modern transcript by J. Caldwell of the two antiphons for St Ethelbert from the Hereford breviary.

The other two canticle-antiphons – 'Tua, martyr ethelberte, frequentet sollempnia' and 'O radix dulcem fusi nectaris stillans liquorem ethelberte' – are illustrated and transcribed here (figs 113 a, b, 114).

The office of St Ethelbert as a whole, a *Historia* based on his life and miracles, has some elements of the typical medieval rhymed office but is not consistently rhymed or even metrical. On the other hand, its melodies are in part ordered by mode, though the complete set of antiphons for matins, for example, would not always be heard in a continuous sequence in the liturgy.[26]

Could polyphony have been used at Hereford Cathedral before 1300? The answer

26. The material for the feast is preceded by a lengthy rubric governing these questions, and it is interspersed with additional smaller such rubrics. Basically the feast had three lessons at matins, but these were expanded to nine when the feast occurred after the Ascension. (Compare the winter and summer versions of the office in *The Hereford Breviary*, ii, pp. 167–82, where the variants from the noted breviary, HCL, P.IX.7, are also given.) For some further comments on this office, and on that of St Mary Magdalene in this manuscript, see Chapter 21, pp. 386–87.

must be speculative. Although it was cultivated at nearby Worcester, the plainchant sources from both venues suggest that there was little musical interaction between them. Certainly some of the Worcester music, perhaps even the greater part of it, was composed elsewhere.[27] The earliest evidence for the cultivation of polyphony in English secular cathedrals – at Exeter, Lincoln and Lichfield, for example – dates only from the fourteenth century. However attractive the idea of a repertory partly shared between the two neighbouring institutions, it is not one supported by the evidence.

The compilation of the Hereford breviary took place during the episcopate of Bishop Peter of Aigueblanche, 1240–68.[28] It is quite likely that he was personally involved in its commissioning and arrangement, even though formal responsibility for the ordering of liturgical worship lay (as it still does) with the dean and chapter. We shall never be able to recreate the decision-making processes that went into the making of so complex a volume: we can only admire the perfection and coherence of the result. The breviary is a supremely impressive symbol of Hereford's concern for musical and liturgical propriety; it is, moreover, practically unique for its date and completeness amongst the records of English secular Uses.[29]

27. E. H. Sanders, ed., *English Music of the Thirteenth and Early Fourteenth Centuries*, Polyphonic Music of the Fourteenth Century, 14 (Monaco, 1979), p. xiii.

28. Mynors and Thomson, *Catalogue*, p. 125, date the manuscript more precisely to between 1262 (obit for Canon Richard de Monte, still alive in 1262, on 3 November), and 1268 (obit for Bishop Peter himself, as 'an early addition' on 27 November).

29. The Scottish noted breviary of Sarum Use, Edinburgh, National Library of Scotland, Advocates' Library, 18.2.13B, dates from *c.* 1300 and is largely complete. See Frere, ed., *Antiphonale Sarisburiense*, p. 81. The Sanctorale of a noted breviary of *c.* 1200, preceded by an incomplete calendar (Oxford, Bodleian, lat. liturg. c. 36) has been described by David Chadd and tentatively assigned to Bath in his 'An English Noted Breviary of *circa* 1200', in S. Rankin and D. Hiley, eds, *Music in the Medieval English Liturgy* (Oxford, 1993), pp. 205–38.

21

Music and Liturgy, 1300–1600

John Harper

The two principal legal instruments of the cathedral foundation are the thirteenth-century statutes and customs,[1] and the Elizabethan statutes of 1583.[2] These mark the broad bounds of the history of music and liturgy in the cathedral from 1300 to 1600, a period which extends from the copying of the late thirteenth-century noted breviary to the organistship of John Bull. So far as they relate to worship, both documents seek to clarify and regulate existing practice. The medieval statutes are particular to Hereford; they include a substantial section on customs in the choir (*consuetudines in choro*),[3] parts of which are amplified or re-expressed in an additional section in some of the sources.[4] The statutes of 1583 are less specific to Hereford; they assimilate much of the mid sixteenth-century royal injunctions which were drawn up as instruments of change in all cathedrals during the decades of Reformation.

What was happening at Hereford during this time was largely typical of other English cathedrals. By 1300 the building, the personnel of the choral body, the statutes, and the texts and music of the liturgy had reached stages of development and stability which provided the framework for a rich pattern of worship in the cathedral until the 1540s. Not that there was stasis thereafter. Additions and alterations continued to be made to the building; the choral body underwent both

1. *Consuetudines et statuta ecclesiae Herefordensis*, printed in Bradshaw and Wordsworth, *Statutes of Lincoln Cathedral*, ii, pp. 36–89; English translation in E. F. H. Dunnicliff, 'Consuetudines et statuta ecclesiasticae cathedralis Herefordensis: A Paraphrase in English' (HCA, typescript, 1962).
2. HCA, 7044/3, a copy belonging to Thomas Thornton, canon 1573–1629. The text has not been edited but is subsumed in the Laudian revision of the statutes found in

Jebb and Phillott, *The Statutes of the Cathedral Church of Hereford*. For a summary of differences between 1583 and 1636 texts, see Bradshaw and Wordsworth, *Statutes of Lincoln Cathedral*, ii, p. 40.
3. Bradshaw and Wordsworth, *Statutes of Lincoln Cathedral*, ii, pp. 61–78; Dunnicliff, 'Paraphrase', pp. 28–51.
4. Bradshaw and Wordsworth, *Statutes of Lincoln Cathedral*, ii, pp. 78–85; Dunnucliff, 'Paraphrase', pp. 52–64.

natural change and considerable expansion; the liturgical aspects of the statutes required interpretation and amplification through the customary, ordinal and chapter acts; and the content and practice of liturgy were subject to accretion, amendment and embellishment.

The principal difficulty in understanding how the liturgy was ordered and celebrated, what affected its conduct, and how it changed between 1300 and 1500, is the lack of evidence. The stages of building can be traced, but there can be no certainty about the impact of building work on regular daily patterns or about the precise use of every part of the cathedral at each stage of alteration. Legal documents record new endowments (often linked to new liturgical observances), but little of the detail of the personnel engaged. There is no customary, an incomplete ordinal,[5] and no chapter acts for this period. Other liturgical books from Hereford or related to the Use of Hereford are few in number by comparison with the Use of Salisbury. The major medieval manuscript source with both texts and music is the famous noted Hereford breviary of the late thirteenth century, specifically written for the cathedral (plate IVa).[6] There are three extant manuscript missals of the Use of Hereford, the earliest of which is the mid fourteenth-century Dewick missal.[7] The best known is that intended for the church of St Dubricius, Whitchurch (now in Gwent), from the fifteenth century;[8] it contains some chants in the temporal, but is not now complete. The largest collection of chant for the mass is found in an incomplete fifteenth-century gradual which awaits full critical examination.[9]

5. BL, Harley MS 2983; *The Hereford Breviary*, iii, pp. lxii–lxvii (description), pp. 65–89 (edition).

6. HCL, MS P.IX.7. Full bibliographical description in Mynors and Thomson, *Catalogue*, pp. 124–25. Other sources for the office are: Worcester Cathedral Library, MS Q.86 (thirteenth-century psalter, with fourteenth-century breviary added), Oxford, University College, MS 7 (fifteenth-century psalter) and Oxford, Balliol College, MS 321 (fourteenth-century collectar). These sources are described in *The Hereford Breviary*, iii, pp. lxi–lxii and lxvii–lxviii; the collectar is edited, iii, pp. 1–30.

7. BL, MS Add. 39675, donated by E. S. Dewick; collated in *The Hereford Breviary*, iii, pp. 253–63.

8. Oxford, University College, MS 78A, here referred to as 'the St Dubricius Missal'; W. H. Frere, ed., *Bibliotheca Musico-Liturgica: A Descriptive Handlist of the Musical and*

Latin Liturgical MSS of the Middle Ages Preserved in the Libraries of Great Britain and Ireland, Plainsong and Medieval Music Society (London, 1901 [1894]–1932; repr. 1967), no. 478 (where it is dated as fourteenth century). The third missal is Worcester Cathedral Library, MS F.161 (late fourteenth century); Frere, *Bibliotheca*, no. 615.

9. BL, MS Harley 3965. The placing of the dedication festival in May and the inclusion of commemorations of St Ethelbert and St Thomas Cantilupe in the kyriale suggest that this may originally have been a cathedral book. Two inscriptions on fol. 140 suggest that it may later have migrated to the church of St Nicholas and then to the church of St Peter, Hereford. Erasure of the sequence of St Thomas of Canterbury in Christmas week (fol. 105v) suggests that the book was still in use after the suppression of that feast by Henry VIII.

Although much is lost, it includes significant parts of the temporal, sanctoral and common, parts of the ordinary, and forty-six sequences (four incomplete and one without music), a number of which (including two for St Ethelbert) are unique to Hereford Use. There is no surviving processional or antiphonal, although the thirteenth-century Magdalen pontifical was apparently intended for a Hereford bishop.[10] The problem of so small a number of sources is exacerbated by the limited amount of research undertaken on them: no large-scale study of the Hereford books has taken place since that of W. H. Frere early in the twentieth century.

From the early sixteenth century there is more evidence. Two printed books of the Use of Hereford were published in Rouen early in the century: *Missal[e] ad usum famose et percelebris ecclesie Helfordensis* (1502),[11] and *Breviarum secundum usum Herfordensis* (2 vols, 1505).[12] Although they lack music,[13] their rubrics go some way to compensate for the absence of customary and ordinal, and details of some processions can be recovered. From 1512 the chapter acts record day-to-day decisions about the conduct of worship and details of the clergy in post.[14] During the Reformation, Hereford was subject to the centralised changes imposed on the church, including the introduction of the English litany in 1534, the royal injunctions for cathedrals in 1547, the dissolution of chantries in 1548, and the new Books of Common Prayer of 1549 and 1552. A reading of the chapter acts gives few indications of the enormity of these changes: little is recorded about their local consequences, or of the subsequent Marian restoration of the Latin rite, or of the Elizabethan settlement. The long-term constitutional impact is embodied in the Elizabethan statutes of 1583, subsequently amended in 1636.

Until the Reformation Hereford Cathedral and diocese enjoyed their own liturgical Use. How distinctive was it? Would a medieval traveller from Paris or Cologne or London have been struck by fundamental differences in the forms, content and conduct of the services? In brief, no. Throughout the western Latin church the daily round of communal prayer consisted of the offices of matins (at midnight), lauds (around dawn), prime, terce, sext, none, vespers and compline (around dusk). Mass was celebrated corporately twice each day, and by individual

---

10. Oxford, Magdalen College, MS 226; Frere, *Bibliotheca*, no. 496.

11. W. G. Henderson, ed., *Missale ad usum percelebris ecclesiae Herfordensis* ([Leeds], 1874; repr. Farnborough, 1969), hereafter *Missale Herefordense*. This is not a critical edition, but there is some comparison with the St Dubricius Missal.

12. *The Hereford Breviary*, i–iii. The edition collates readings from the MS sources.

13. The missal includes the chants sung by the

priest during the mass and at the Easter vigil.

14. There are three MS chapter act books in this period: 1512–66 (HCA, 7031/1), 1572–1603 (HCA, 7031/8), 1566–1600 (draft book, HCA, 7031/2). HCA, MS, P. G. S. Baylis, ed., 'Hereford Cathedral Chapter Act Book Vol. 1' (3 vols, 1969–70) is a transcript of HCA, 7031/1 with numbering of acts (part in draft), hereafter HCA, Baylis.

priests at altars throughout the church. Such was the case in all cathedral, collegiate and monastic churches. Those arriving from Worcester or Winchester Cathedral would have noticed a distinction: there the cathedral was staffed by Benedictine monks,[15] who used the variant form of the office set out in the Rule of St Benedict.[16] At Hereford, as at Salisbury or York,[17] the cathedral was staffed by non-monastic (so-called secular) clergy. The dean and chapter, then as now, had responsibility for and oversight of the worship in the cathedral, but its conduct was largely delegated to the junior clergy. The canons had a rota for residence periods when they were required to be present at services;[18] the bishop or the dean presided only on the most solemn days;[19] otherwise it was the junior clergy – the vicars choral (priests, deacons and subdeacons), clerks in minor orders, and choristers – who formed the permanent core of the choral body chanting the office and celebrating the masses in the cathedral.

The cathedral is best regarded as an agglomeration of spaces for worship, rather than a single church. There were three principal areas where worship was conducted. Of primary importance was the choir and presbytery, which extended from the high altar at the east to the western end of the tower crossing, bounded on each side by the canopied stalls and separated from the nave by a stone screen with gallery above (the pulpitum) and doorway beneath. In the choir the junior clergy, with those senior clergy in residence, chanted the main daily cycle of the office and celebrated high mass. Second in significance was the Lady chapel beyond the high altar. This took the form of a smaller choir and presbytery where the daily mass in honour of the Blessed Virgin Mary was sung. A third area was the 'parish church' of St John the Baptist, intended for the laity living near the cathedral. Originally situated in the north transept, it seems that by the late fourteenth century these services had moved to an altar of St John the Baptist placed on the right-hand side of the pulpitum, on the nave side behind the stall of the dean. Services here sometimes clashed with those in the choir: in 1394 the canons received a mandate from the bishop to forbid this, on account of the rude, dissonant and inept singing

15. As were the cathedrals of Canterbury, Durham, Ely, Norwich and Rochester, as well as Bath (with Wells) and Coventry (with Lichfield). There was an Augustinian cathedral priory at Carlisle. Medieval cathedral monasteries are almost unknown outside England.

16. The Benedictine office includes the same services but their detail varies, especially in the number and distribution of the psalms, and in the number of lessons at matins. See

J. Harper, *The Forms and Orders of Western Liturgy* (Oxford, 1991).

17. Also the secular cathedrals of Chichester, Exeter, Lichfield, Lincoln, London and Wells, as well as Bangor, Llandaff, St Asaph and St David's in Wales.

18. At other times they recited the daily office and celebrated mass privately.

19. Bradshaw and Wordsworth, *Statutes of Lincoln Cathedral*, ii, p. 63; Dunnicliff, 'Paraphrase', p. 30.

of the chaplains, clerks and laity attending at St John's altar which disturbed services in the choir.[20]

In addition to these three areas there was a steadily increasing number of chapels and altars where masses were said and prayers offered for specific intentions, most often for the souls of the benefactors whose endowment provided the income to pay for the priest engaged to recite the services there. There were chapels and altars in the north and south transepts, on either side of the pulpitum in the nave, in the two eastern transepts and in the crypt; there were specially constructed chantry chapels – for instance, those built by Bishop Stanbury (fig. 115) and Bishop Audley (fig. 19) – as well as the episcopal chapels of St Katherine and of St Mary Magdalene above it, located on a site between the cloister and the bishop's palace.[21] By 1517 there was a second Lady chapel above the Booth porch (fig. 116), together with an altar dedicated to the Holy Name of Jesus. These chapels and altars were staffed by chantry priests or chaplains, who normally also sang in the choir.[22]

The daily round consisted of services in the choir at midnight and at regular intervals between about five in the morning and four in the afternoon, sung Lady mass, mass and office of the dead in the Lady chapel, masses at the other altars in the cathedral and adjacent chapels (sometimes several at one altar) especially in the morning, other devotions (including those at the crucifix in the nave, and at the statue of the Blessed Virgin Mary),[23] and processions before mass or at vespers on holy days. To this has to be added the daily presence of those on pilgrimage to the cathedral. A cathedral was a natural place of pilgrimage as mother church of the diocese, but most cathedrals and great abbeys in the middle ages drew pilgrims from a wider area to the shrine of a specific saint: Thomas Becket at Canterbury, Cuthbert at Durham, Alban at St Albans, Etheldreda at Ely. While the shrine of St Ethelbert provided one such focus at Hereford, the canonisation of Bishop Thomas Cantilupe in 1320 stimulated a new fervour for pilgrimage. His body was translated from the tomb in the north transept to a new shrine in the Lady chapel in 1349. Though never rivalling Canterbury, it remained a place for pilgrimage until its destruction in 1538. Hereford Cathedral in the fourteenth and fifteenth centuries was exceptionally busy: a complex pattern of interlocking and

20. '. . . simplices capellani, clerici et layci, psallentes et rudi modo cantantes tantam dissonanciam et ineptum sonitum . . .', W. W. Capes, ed., *Registrum Johannis Trefnant, episcopi Herefordensis, AD MCCCLXXXIX-MCCCCIV*, Canterbury and York Society, 20 (London, 1916), pp. 20–21.

21. See Chapter 11, pp. 294–96, for details of the episcopal chapels.

22. In many instances priests combined appointments as vicar choral and chantry priest (or chaplain). For the locations of chapels, altars and images within the cathedral, see fig. 25.

23. See further below pp. 384ff.

Fig. 115. Stanbury chapel, interior.

overlapping services and devotions in different parts of the church, large numbers
of passing travellers, visitors and pilgrims, and ongoing building works.

The services in the choir, the Lady chapel, the nave, the other chapels and at the
altars required a substantial body of clergy, not only priests but also deacons,
subdeacons, clerks in minor orders and choristers to assist them with duties and
ceremonies in choir and at the chapels and altars. Funds were needed to support
them, most of which came from income derived from endowments of property
and land. Those serving in choir at the time of the medieval statutes included

Fig. 116. Booth porch upper chamber, interior.

four canons' vicars and fourteen 'perpetual vicars'.[24] By 1395, when the college of vicars choral was instituted as a statutory body, their number had increased to twenty-seven.[25] Similarly the number of boy choristers increased from five at the time of the medieval statutes to seven by the sixteenth century.[26] Other clergy attended in choir, including chaplains who were not vicars choral,[27] and those in minor orders.

There was no distinction before the Reformation between those with designated seats in choir and those appointed to sing the office and the mass: all those clergy seated in the choir were also the singing choir. The statutes required all vicars choral to know the psalms, antiphons and hymns by heart within a year:[28] the

24. Bradshaw and Wordsworth, *Statutes of Lincoln Cathedral*, ii, pp. 74–75; Dunnicliff, 'Paraphrase', pp. 45–46.

25. On the college of vicars choral, see below Chapter 23 and P. L. S. Barrett, *The College of Vicars Choral at Hereford Cathedral* (Hereford, 1980).

26. Bradshaw and Wordsworth, *Statutes of Lincoln Cathedral*, ii, p. 83; Dunicliff, 'Paraphrase', p. 60; *Missale Herefordense*, p. 80.

27. At the discretion of the succentor: Bradshaw and Wordsworth, *Statutes of Lincoln Cathedral*, ii, p. 76; Dunnicliff, 'Paraphrase', p. 48.

28. Bradshaw and Wordsworth, *Statutes of Lincoln Cathedral*, ii, pp. 72, 80; Dunnicliff, 'Paraphrase', pp. 42, 54–55.

appointment of William Smythe in 1538 was conditional on his learning the chant within two years.[29] Each cleric had his appointed place. He was only to move when he needed to use a book.[30] As in other secular cathedrals the clergy sat in three rows of stalls on each side of the choir, facing one another. Those in the back row (the third form) had to be canons, vicars choral or priests; those in the middle row (the second form) had to be deacons or subdeacons; the most junior clergy (those in minor orders and the boy choristers) sat on the front row (the first form) (fig. 117).[31]

The care and management of the liturgy, its artefacts and books were delegated by the respective senior canons (the precentor for liturgy and music books, the treasurer for artefacts, the chancellor for other books) to their assistants, appointed from among the vicars choral. The succentor, acting for the precentor, was required to draw up the rota of musical and ceremonial duties according to custom and seniority, to supervise the choir and to arrange processions,[32] to check attendance and to ensure that five juniors or choristers were properly prepared to sing the beginning of antiphons on ferial days or to carry the cross and candlesticks as required.[33] The succentor was responsible for standards of musical performance and reading in choir, specifying those who sang, selecting the singing boys for admission to choir,[34] and regulating the manner of singing the chant and the readings as laid down in the statutes.[35] To this end, he was also in charge of the school.[36]

Under the direction of the treasurer, the sub-treasurer oversaw care and use of the lights, candles, vessels, ornaments and vestments.[37] The statutes do little more than hint at the extent and complexity of these duties, referring rather to other

29. HCA, 7031/1, fol. 81v; HCA, Baylis, no. 590.

30. Bradshaw and Wordsworth, *Statutes of Lincoln Cathedral*, ii, p. 79; Dunnicliff, 'Paraphrase', p. 53. This is a reminder of the small number of books used in choir *c.* 1300.

31. Bradshaw and Wordsworth, *Statutes of Lincoln Cathedral*, ii, pp. 72, 79; Dunnicliff, 'Paraphrase', pp. 41, 53.

32. Bradshaw and Wordsworth, *Statutes of Lincoln Cathedral*, ii, pp. 63, 76–77; Dunnicliff, 'Paraphrase', pp. 30, 48–49.

33. The directions over these last duties occur twice in some MSS of the statutes, first referring to clerks of the first form, 'clericos de scola sua in prima forma' (Bradshaw and Wordsworth, *Statutes of Lincoln Cathedral*, ii, p. 76; Dunnicliff, 'Paraphrase', p. 48); and, secondly, to boy singers, 'pueros, in

puerili uoce cantantes bene, de scola sua' (Bradshaw and Wordsworth, *Statutes of Lincoln Cathedral*, ii, p. 83; Dunnicliff, 'Paraphrase', p. 60). This represents the conflation of two texts rather than provision of two groups of juniors.

34. Bradshaw and Wordsworth, *Statutes of Lincoln Cathedral*, ii, pp. 83; Dunnicliff, 'Paraphrase', p. 60.

35. Bradshaw and Wordsworth, *Statutes of Lincoln Cathedral*, ii, pp. 82–83; Dunnicliff, 'Paraphrase', pp 58–59.

36. See note 28, and Chapter 32, pp. 567–68.

37. Bradshaw and Wordsworth, *Statutes of Lincoln Cathedral*, ii, p. 69; Dunnicliff, 'Paraphrase', p. 38; details of duties, Bradshaw and Wordsworth, *Statutes of Lincoln Cathedral*, ii, pp. 63–70; Dunnicliff, 'Paraphrase', pp. 30–40.

Fig. 117. Choir and
nave, looking west:
medieval bishop's
throne and choir stalls.
In the middle ages the
stalls would have been
further west and the
view broken by
the stone screen.

books now lost.[38] The detailed instructions on lights and candles, however, offer
an insight into the sophisticated protocol which governed one element of the
customs and ceremonies.[39] Otherwise, the brief references to ornamental hangings
around the church at All Saints and Christmas, rushes and ivy at Easter, incense
and the ringing of the tower bells only hint at the total impact of the liturgy on
a principal feast in the cathedral.[40]

The completion of the Lady chapel at the east end of the cathedral in the early
thirteenth century afforded an opportunity to enhance the cathedral liturgy (fig. 24).
The chapel was treated as separate from the cathedral, its affairs overseen by the
warden (*custos*) of the Lady chapel, elected annually.[41] At the time of the medieval

38. Bradshaw and Wordsworth, *Statutes of Lincoln Cathedral*, ii, p. 78; Dunnicliff, 'Paraphrase', p. 51.

39. Bradshaw and Wordsworth, *Statutes of Lincoln Cathedral*, ii, p. 63–69; Dunnicliff, 'Paraphrase', pp. 30–37.

40. Bradshaw and Wordsworth, *Statutes of Lincoln Cathedral*, ii, p. 70; Dunnicliff,

'Paraphrase', pp. 39–40.

41. The accounts of the warden 1356–57, Robert de Henle, survive: HCA, R 690, B. G. Charles and H. D. Emanuel, 'A List of the Hereford Cathedral Account Rolls, Court Rolls, Rentals and Surveys' (HCA, typescript, 1955), p. 82; Capes, *Charters*, pp. 229–30.

statutes one vicar was designated to say Lady mass.[42] In 1330 a substantial bequest made by Joanna de Bohun was used to provide an endowment for ten new vicars (eight priests, a deacon and a subdeacon) with specific duties in the Lady chapel where she lies buried.[43] The bishop, Thomas Charlton, distinguished the simple celebration of Lady mass in a parish church from the solemn celebration appropriate to his cathedral, and observed the current shortage of priests.[44] According to his ordinances, the new vicars were to have good voices and to be competent musicians ('voce sonora et sciencia precipue artis musice sufficienter imbuto'). They were to sing the daily office in choir with the other vicars. Four of the new priest vicars were to celebrate Lady mass solemnly in the Lady chapel, and four were afterwards to say the mass and office of the dead; this was a daily requirement, except on Sundays and major feasts when the duties were to be assigned to a single priest.[45] Charlton enhanced the services in the choir and in the Lady chapel by increasing the number of vicars, and by ensuring that he raised the musical standards by engaging clergy who not only sang well but had musical knowledge. The requirement for solemn celebration of Lady mass has implications for both ceremonial and music; this may perhaps mark a significant development in musical celebration, a time when both improvised and composed polyphony may well have come to greater prominence in the liturgy, especially in the Lady mass.

Throughout the medieval church in the west the basic framework of the mass and the services of the office was consistent. Within this framework of the Latin rite, the texts, their chants and the manner in which the services were conducted varied according to season and feast. The principal features of the calendar of seasons and feasts, and many of the texts, melodies and customs, were shared. But there were significant differences: the distinct forms of the Benedictine office (also used by the Cistercians) are found throughout the west, as are local regional and diocesan variants, referred to as Uses. In the later middle ages, apart from the Benedictine (or monastic) Use, there were three significant regional and diocesan Uses in England and Wales: the Uses of Salisbury, York and Hereford. The Use of Salisbury dominated and came to represent English Use: it was adopted gradually

42. Bradshaw and Wordsworth, *Statutes of Lincoln Cathedral*, ii, p. 75; Dunnicliff, 'Paraphrase', p. 46.

43. The bequest was made in 1327 but converted to this purpose in 1330 on the initiative of Thomas Chandos, archdeacon of Hereford. HCA, 2163, 2165, 3202, B. G. Charles and H. D. Emanuel, 'A Calendar of the Earlier Hereford Cathedral Muniments' (3 vols, HCA, typescript, 1955), pp. 871–72; Capes, *Charters*, pp. 210–15. HCA, 1817, Charles and Emanuel, 'Calendar', p. 873; W. W. Capes, ed., *Registrum Thome de Charlton, episcopi Herefordensis, AD MCCCXXVII-MCCCXLIV*, Canterbury and York Society, 9 (London, 1913), pp. 34–40.

44. Capes, ed., *Registrum Thome de Charlton*, p. 35.

45. Ibid., p. 38.

throughout most of the province of Canterbury (including Wales), and parts of Ireland and Scotland, in non-monastic cathedrals, colleges, parish churches and household chapels, including the chapels royal. The Use of York was prevalent in the north of England in the province of York (the medieval dioceses of York, Durham and Carlisle). Least prolific of the three was the Use of Hereford, largely restricted to the cathedral and diocese of Hereford.

Taken in the wider context of European liturgical practice, the Uses of Hereford, Salisbury and York are closely related and distinctly English.[46] In the early years of the twentieth century the liturgical scholar, Walter Howard Frere, wrote a critical introduction to the formation and contents of the printed breviaries of Hereford, Salisbury and York, and compiled comparative lists of their principal contents.[47] In the absence of more recent research, these indexes remain a valuable source which indicate at a basic level the relationship between the breviaries. In each of the three breviaries over three quarters of the texts of the antiphons, responds, hymns and collects are duplicated in all three Uses.[48] Some items are found in just two of the three breviaries; in these cases Hereford and Salisbury share more items with one another than either shares with York. Other items appear only in a single breviary. The fact that Salisbury has the smallest number of unduplicated items (some 6 per cent of all those items counted) is an indication of its overall dominance.[49] Both Hereford and York contain a larger number of unduplicated items in each category (in each case this represents a little over 10 per cent of all items counted). In the Hereford breviary over a quarter of the collects,[50] and almost a fifth of the hymns,[51] are not found in the other two breviaries; the York breviary has the larger number of unduplicated antiphons and responds (over an eighth of those found in that breviary).

A closer examination of the antiphons and responds found only in the Hereford breviary reveals other features. Some of the unduplicated items are associated with the feasts of saints buried in the cathedral: the East Anglian martyr king, St Ethelbert

46. Based on R.-J. Hesbert's and Knud Otto-sen's studies and interpretations of the ordering and contents of matins responds during Advent found in 800 medieval MSS: R.-J. Hesbert, ed., *Corpus antiphonarium officii*, Rerum ecclesiasticarum documenta, series maior fontes, 7–12 (6 vols, Rome, 1963–79); K. Ottosen, *L'antiphonaire latin au moyen-âge: réorganization des séries de répons de l'Avent classés par R.-J. Hesbert*, Rerum ecclesiasticarum documenta, extra series (Rome, 1986).

47. *The Hereford Breviary*, iii. In the case of the Hereford breviary, Frere includes items from the manuscript sources.

48. The numerical analysis is summarised in Table 1, p. 397.

49. Unduplicated in the sense that they are not found in the Hereford and York breviaries: a comparison with the wider repertory of western liturgical sources has not been attempted here.

50. This number may be inflated because Frere also included collects from the manuscript sources of Hereford Use.

51. Including those proses and sequences used in the office, which are more numerous at Hereford.

(d. 794, patron saint of the cathedral) and St Thomas Cantilupe (bishop of Hereford, 1275–82, found only in liturgical books written after his canonisation in 1320); others are designated for feast days which were widely observed throughout Europe. Particularly prominent among the latter are the feasts of St Mary Magdalene, the Visitation of the Blessed Virgin Mary, her mother, St Anne, and the archangel, St Raphael. The feast of St Mary Magdalene (22 July) has been observed in the west since the eighth century, but assumed greater prominence with the rise of a cult in the eleventh century, a period when Vézelay laid claim to her relics, and led to the composition of new offices in her honour.[52] The office of St Mary Magdalene is found in the thirteenth-century noted breviary complete with chants.[53] Although it is distinct from Salisbury and York, it accords with a number of English Augustinian and Benedictine sources.[54] The other three feasts were established after 1300 and are therefore not included in the thirteenth-century noted breviary kept at the cathedral. The feast of the Visitation of the Blessed Virgin Mary (2 July) was first introduced by the Franciscans in 1263 and extended to the whole church in 1389.[55] The inclusion of the feast in the St Dubricius Missal suggests that the observance may have been introduced in the early fifteenth century at Hereford.[56] Five offices of the Visitation are known.[57] The texts in the printed Hereford breviary are those of the office *Accedunt laudes*,[58] composed in the late fourteenth century by a Benedictine, Cardinal Adam Easton (d. 1397), and widely used in Roman books.[59] The feast of St Anne (26 July) did not become obligatory in England until *c.* 1382, but it was observed in Canterbury and Worcester in the twelfth century,[60] and there was an altar dedicated to St Anne in the cathedral at Hereford by 1319.[61] The introduction of the feast of St Raphael (5 October) can be dated precisely. Both the office and mass of St Raphael were written by Edmund Lacy, who, having been bishop of Hereford (1417–20), was then bishop of Exeter

52. D. H. Farmer, *The Oxford Dictionary of Saints* (4th edn, Oxford, 1997), p. 270.

53. HCL, MS P.IX.7, fol. 279r; *The Hereford Breviary*, ii, pp. 252–58.

54. D. Chadd, 'An English Noted Breviary of *c.* 1200', in S. Rankin and D. Hiley, eds, *Music in the Medieval English Liturgy* (Oxford, 1993), p. 216. Chadd points out that this form is categorised as 'the English Office' in V. Saxer, *Le culte de Marie Madeleine en occident*, Cahiers d'archéologie et d'histoire (Auxerre and Paris, 1959), pp. 309ff.

55. R. W. Pfaff, *New Liturgical Feasts in Later Medieval England* (Oxford, 1970), pp. 41–56.

56. Oxford, University College, MS 78A, fol. 163v; *Missale Herefordense*, pp. 279–81.

57. Pfaff, *New Liturgical Feasts*, p. 44.

58. *The Hereford Breviary*, ii, 223–35.

59. A. Hughes, 'British Rhymed Offices: A Catalogue and Commentary', in Rankin and Hiley, eds, *Music in the Medieval English Liturgy*, pp. 249–50; Pfaff, *New Liturgical Feasts*, p. 44. Pfaff also points out (pp. 50–51) that this office and the office *Colletentur corda fidelium* by the Dominican, Raymond de Vineis (or de Capua), are found in manuscripts belonging to John Leche, canon of Hereford, 1480–*c.* 1489.

60. Farmer, *Dictionary of Saints*, pp. 17–18.

61. HCA, 2100, Charles and Emanuel, 'Calendar', p. 807, endowment of chantry at altar of St Anne.

(1420–55).[62] His letter of 4 June 1445 requests the introduction of the feast at Hereford Cathedral;[63] this was sanctioned by the dean and chapter on 9 September 1445.[64] The evidence of these feasts demonstrates the continuing accretion of new observances in the Hereford calendar in the fourteenth and fifteenth centuries, and the independence of those selecting texts from the influences of the Uses of Salisbury and York.

The offices and masses of the two local saints may well have been written and compiled at Hereford.[65] The office of St Ethelbert is found in the thirteenth-century breviary, complete with music.[66] As with many offices of saints written in the later middle ages, it is in part a rhymed office. In a full rhymed office all the antiphons and responds are composed in rhyming Latin verse; here only the antiphons are rhymed, and some of their chants are organised in modal sequence.[67] The readings at matins are taken from the life of St Ethelbert written by Gerald of Wales (*c.* 1146–1223) who held a canonry at Hereford, and in its rhymed form the office is likely to date from the first half of the thirteenth century. The texts and chants of the office and mass of St Thomas Cantilupe were probably written and compiled in the years leading up to his canonisation in 1320, perhaps by Robert of Gloucester, canon of Hereford Cathedral, 1279–1322.[68] The text of the offices are found in the later manuscript breviary (now at Worcester) and the printed breviary,[69] but only five complete chants (four Magnificat antiphons and a respond) and two fragments (end of a prose and beginning of a respond) are extant.[70] Three of the

62. *The Hereford Breviary*, ii, pp. 354–61; *Missale Herefordense*, pp. 336–38.

63. HCA, 1917, Charles and Emanuel, 'Calendar', p. 1209; A. T. Bannister, ed., *Registrum Thome Spofford, episcopi Herefordensis, AD MCCCCXXII-MCCCCLVIII*, Canterbury and York Society, 23 (London, 1919), pp. 267–79.

64. HCA, 3185, Charles and Emanuel, 'Calendar', p. 1210.

65. In the case of St Ethelbert, the mass propers are largely drawn from the common of a martyr, except for the introit (based on the introit *Gaudeamus* used for a number of feasts, but here adapted for Ethelbert) and the sequence, which is a special composition: *Missale Herefordense*, pp. 258–61. The sequences for the feast and the octave are found in BL, Harley MS 3965, fos 111v–113v.

66. HCL, MS P.IX.7, fol. 261v; *The Hereford Breviary*, ii, pp. 167–82.

67. Hughes, 'British Rhymed Offices',

pp. 263–64.

68. P. Barrett, 'A Saint in the Calendar: The Effect of the Canonization of St Thomas Cantilupe on the Liturgy', in M. Jancey, ed., *St Thomas Cantilupe, Bishop of Hereford: Essays in his Honour* (Hereford, 1982), pp. 153–57; Hughes, 'British Rhymed Offices', p. 278.

69. *The Hereford Breviary*, ii, pp. 309–11 (deposition), 345–54, 361 (feast and octave), 380–83, 385–86 (translation and octave).

70. Gloucester Record Office, fragment 14 prose *Summi regis* (conclusion), Magnificat antiphons *Sicut fragrant, Puer mersus, Salve Thoma*, responds *Hic est Abel, Thomas primus* (beginning); Oxford, Bodleian, MS E Mus. 2, p. 919, Magnificat antiphon, *Lux fulget*; B. Trowell and A. Wathey, 'John Benet's "Lux fulget ex Anglia – O pater pietatis – Salve Thoma"', in Jancey, ed., *St Thomas Cantilupe*, pp. 159–80, including transcription of four chants and Benet's motet, and a facsimile of the Gloucester fragment.

antiphons show distinctive musical characteristics: *Sicut fragrant* employs varied repetitions, with a structural pattern which may be summarised as abab'cdc'ea''; *Puer mersus* uses a large range with strong leaps; and there is a freely treated descending sequence in *Salve Thoma*. The mass texts include some material from the common of saints and some new material.[71]

The cult of St Thomas Cantilupe had a considerable impact on the liturgy at Hereford after 1320.[72] There were the main feast of St Thomas Cantilupe (2 October), a principal feast in the cathedral observed with an octave, and the feast of the Deposition of St Thomas, marking the day of his death (25 August). To these was added the feast of the Translation of St Thomas (25 October) following his removal to the new shrine in the Lady chapel in 1349, again a principal feast with octave. By the time of the printed Hereford missal, a mass in honour of St Thomas Cantilupe was said on Thursday as part of the weekly cycle at morrow mass, the day of the mass of the Holy Spirit according to the earlier manuscript missal.[73]

A single polyphonic motet in honour of St Thomas is extant.[74] Composed for three voices by John Benet (fl. *c.* 1420–50), whose works are found alongside those of Dunstable and Power, the motet sets seven antiphon texts from the office of St Thomas, and uses the melody of another (*Salve Thoma*) as *cantus firmus*. This may be an indication of the manner in which his feast was celebrated (though not necessarily at Hereford), or it may have been written to mark a special occasion: Brian Trowell and Andrew Wathey argue that Bishop Edmund Lacy may have commissioned the work for the centenary of Cantilupe's canonisation (1420).[75] The fact that the superius begins with the text 'Lux fulget ex Anglia' may even suggest that it was intended to promulgate the feast on the Continent. The decision to move the shrine of St Thomas Cantilupe from the north transept to the Lady chapel brought it to the location where the number of clergy had recently increased

71. *Missale Herefordense*, pp. 314–15 (deposition), 333–36, 338 (feast and octave), 347–50 (translation and octave). The gradual, Alleluia and sequence of the feast are proper, but the offertory and communion come from the common of a confessor bishop, and the introit is again *Gaudeamus*, as on the feasts of St Ethelbert, St Raphael, etc.

72. Barrett, 'A Saint in the Calendar'.

73. *Missale Herefordense*, pp. 403–4. The printed missal includes both masses. Provision for the commemoration of St Thomas Cantilupe is also made in the kyriale of the fifteenth-century Hereford gradual, BL, Harley MS 3965.

74. Modena, Biblioteca Estense, MS *a*.X.1.11, fos 135v–136r; Trowell and Wathey, 'John Benet's "Lux fulget ex Anglia – O pater pietatis – Salve Thoma"', pp. 160–61.

75. Benet's known appointments were in London; there is no evidence of any association with Hereford. However, Lacy's appointments as canon of St George's, Windsor (1401–17), and especially as dean of the Chapel Royal (1414–17) would have brought him into contact with leading musicians. Trowell and Wathey, 'John Benet's "Lux fulget ex Anglia – O pater pietatis – Salve Thoma"', pp. 169–70.

by ten, as a result of the Bohun endowment, and where polyphony was most likely to be regularly sung, perhaps including Benet's motet at some time. The Lady chapel was the part of the cathedral where the cathedral clergy and the laity were in closest regular contact: it served for the cathedral's daily sung Lady mass and the office and mass of the dead, lay devotion to the Blessed Virgin Mary, and lay pilgrimage to the shrine of St Thomas Cantilupe.

The chapter acts, extant from 1512 onwards, add human detail to the general knowledge of worship and life in the cathedral. On the one hand, they document the failings of the community, especially young vicars choral distracted by women and gambling; on the other, they also show how careers progressed and music was managed. By the late middle ages there was a large body of professional practitioners in liturgy, ordained clergy who had received an applied education to qualify them to staff the secular cathedrals and collegiate churches. They were competent in reading, in singing chant and at least some polyphony, and in ceremony. The cathedrals could provide both the training and the career structure, with a natural progression: chorister, clerk in minor orders, chaplain or vicar choral, minor canon. Choristers, clerks in minor orders, subdeacons and deacons were all expected to attend school; for the choristers this was a song school, with an emphasis on applied and practical music skills; for the others it was a grammar school to equip them to conduct the liturgy with understanding.[76] Of the sixteen choristers named in the first volume of the Hereford chapter acts (1512–66) none proceeded all the way from chorister to minor canon; but two progressed to be subdeacon and two to be deacon. Of the fifty-three vicars choral identified in the same book, two are known to have begun in minor orders, three others proceeded from subdeacon and five from deacon.[77] Many appear to have been installed directly as vicars choral, perhaps from chaplaincies elsewhere.

In some cases an appointment may have been made for a specific purpose. John Hichons's admission to a vicarage in 1525 was probably related to his technical skills as an organ builder: it certainly occurred in a year when money was spent on a new organ in choir.[78] His career over nine years at Hereford was turbulent, punctuated by a series of serious disciplinary measures: readmission after suspension (March 1529); resignation but with pay continuing while he repaired an organ

---

76. 23 December 1533: deacons and subdeacons warned to attend the grammar school, HCA, 7031/1, fol. 72v; HCA, Baylis, no. 476.

77. These figures are based on P. E. Morgan, 'Hereford Cathedral: Dean and Chapter Act Book, Liber Primus, 16 July 1512 – 5 July 1566: Index Compiled … from the Transcript Made by P. G. S. Baylis, 1969–70' (HCA, typescript, 1973).

78. '… xiiij. li. de debentis M. Hugonis Grene que exspendabantur super nova organa in choro …', HCA, 7031/1, fol. 36r; HCA, Baylis, no. 240.

(March 1531); dismissal by the custos of the college (September 1532), amended to suspension on full pay to complete a new organ (October 1532); reinstatement conditional on completion of work on two organs (one in choir, the other over the sacristan's room, July 1533); and final deprivation in 1534 for contumacy.[79] Were it not for the wish of the dean and chapter for work on the organs to be finished it seems unlikely that they would have tolerated him for so long.

Two named clergy held the degree of BMus. from Oxford, indicating skills in composition. William Chell (d. 1556) made his entire career at Hereford. He seems to have been local, having been ordained deacon in 1517 to the title of Little Malvern Priory.[80] He had graduated as BMus. by 1524. In the cathedral he gained a deacon's vicarage in 1518, was appointed priest vicar choral in 1520, was succentor by 1526 (probably until 1542), canon in 1533 and installed as precentor in 1554. This is a rare instance of the progression of a vicar choral to a senior canonry; it may have been a temporary expediency following the deprivation of his predecessor, John Barlow, who had married. John Mason (d. 1548) may have been active as a musician when a clerk at Eton College (1501–6), a chaplain and instructor of the choristers at Magdalen College, Oxford (1509–10), and a chaplain in Wolsey's household chapel (1521).[81] Having gained royal preferment to a Mortimer chantry at Chichester Cathedral in 1523, his career thereafter was predominantly ecclesiastical: he acquired a non-residentiary canonry and prebend at Salisbury Cathedral, as well as several rectories in southern England.[82] He was installed as a canon of Hereford in 1525, admitted to full residence in 1526, acted during the vacancy of the deanery in 1529, held the annual office of custos of the Lady chapel six times between 1530 and 1546, and was treasurer from 1545.

Others clearly had considerable musical skills, not least those appointed to play the organs and teach the choristers. No statutory provision was made for these duties before 1583, although a clerk, Giles known as *cissor* ('the tailor'), received a

79. HCA, 7031/1, fos 37r, 37v, 45r, 66r, 68v, 70r, 70v, 71r, 73v; HCA, Baylis, nos. 251, 257, 332, 396, 423, 444, 446, 459, 488.

80. A. T. Bannister, ed., *Registrum Caroli Bothe, episcopi Herefordensis, AD MDXVI-MDXXXV*, Canterbury and York Society, 28 (London, 1921), p. 304. I am grateful to David Lepine for this information.

81. R. Bowers, 'The Cultivation and Promotion of Music in the Household and Orbit of Thomas Wolsey', in S. J. Gunn and P. G. Lindley, eds, *Cardinal Wolsey: Church, State and Art* (Cambridge, 1991), pp. 178–218, esp. pp. 187–88. Bowers's suggestion that John Mason was the 'Dom Mason'

who was chaplain of Christ Church, Oxford, in 1529–30, and acted briefly as instructor of the choristers at Christ Church, Oxford, in 1530 seems unlikely, given the evidence of Mason's residence and duties at Hereford at that time: HCA, 7031/1, fos 46r–48v, 59r–66r; HCA, Baylis, nos 337–90.

82. None of the available biographies is entirely accurate, but the information to 1523 is best in Bowers, 'The Cultivation', supplemented by B. Rose, 'John Mason', in Stanley Sadie, ed., *The New Grove Dictionary of Music and Musicians* (20 vols, London, 1980), xi, p. 752.

generous annual pension of ten marks (£6 13s. 4d.) as *custos organorum* between 1307 and 1318.[83] The next named organist, William Wode (d. 1521), received the same salary on his appointment in 1517.[84] Wode, like his successors, was also engaged to instruct the choristers.[85] Richard Palmer (organist, 1527–38), however, was allowed to delegate these duties to John Slade in 1534.[86] In 1543 a vicar choral, Richard Ledbury, took over responsibility for the choristers from John Hodges (organist, 1538 – c. 1583).[87] Oversight and instruction of the choristers were apparently not always undertaken by the same person. William Burley (or Burghill, d. 1546), chaplain of the new Lady chapel over the Booth porch, 1517–46, was appointed master of the choristers in 1524 with responsibility for their housing and subsistence.[88]

The establishment of the new Lady chapel over the Booth porch appears to mark a period of new liturgical activity and expansion, especially with regard to devotions to the Blessed Virgin Mary. It may also suggest a separation of lay devotion (in the porch chapel) from choral observance (in the eastern Lady chapel). In 1515 Bishop Richard Mayew (d. 1516) bequeathed an organ newly bought and already installed for daily use at Lady mass.[89] In 1517 William Wode was appointed organist of the Lady chapel and instructor of the choristers, in the same year that William Burley took up his post in the porch Lady chapel. There is no reason to doubt that organ players had been appointed throughout the fourteenth and fifteenth centuries. However, the fact that the indenture of Wode's appointment is copied into the chapter acts may indicate a change or development of the post-holder's duties. He was required to play the organ daily at the morning mass in the Lady chapel and on feast days in the main choir. Hereford, like other cathedral, collegiate

83. Records of payments in 1307, 1309, 1315, 1318: HCA, 2750, 2594, 2601 and 2680; Charles and Emanuel, 'Calendar', pp. 709, 719, 754 and 801. On the basis of evidence from elsewhere 'keeper' implies both playing and routine maintenance of the organs.

84. HCA, 7031/1, fol. 10r; HCA, Baylis, no. 98.

85. Wode already held the lay office of verger (from 1514, initially jointly), a post later filled by two other organists: Palmer (1528–38), and Hodges (as deputy in 1550 and formally from 1551). Thomas Heywarde (1521–28) succeeded Wode as verger, but it is not clear who served as organist 1521–27.

86. HCA, 7031/1, fol. 73v; HCA, Baylis, no. 487.

87. HCA, 7031/1, fol. 90r; HCA, Baylis, no. 686.

88. HCA, 7031/1, fol. 36r; HCA, Baylis, no. 231; another payment in 1530, HCA, 7031/1, fol. 65r; HCA, Baylis, no. 379. By the 1524 act, choristers were only to lodge here. However, two acts of 1526 suggest that a canon's chorister continued to live in the canon's house, HCA, 7031/1, fol. 37v; HCA, Baylis, nos. 256, 258.

89. 'Item do et lego ad usum cotidiane misse beate Marie virginis, ad honorem ipsius domine Marie et gloriosi Thome confessoris, organa mea noviter empta situanda in capella eorumdem infra ecclesiam meam cathedralem Herefordensem', A. T. Bannister, ed., *Registrum Ricardi Mayew, episcopi Herefordensis, AD MDIV-MDXVI*, Canterbury and York Society, 27 (London, 1921), p. viii.

and monastic churches at this time (and larger parish churches, such as Ludlow), had at least two organs, one in the Lady chapel and one in the main choir.[90] There is no precise information about the use of the organ within specific services. The surviving repertory of liturgical organ music from elsewhere suggests, however, that as a minimum the organ may have been played during the offertory at Lady mass, in alternate verses of the hymns at first vespers, matins, lauds and second vespers on Sundays and major feasts (those in choir singing the intervening verses); and in similar fashion during *Te deum laudamus* on principal feasts and important occasions, such as the arrival of a bishop or prince.[91] It may also have been used at compline on Sunday and major feast days. There is no indication before the Reformation that the organ was to accompany voices.

At Hereford, as in comparable foundations, Lady mass was no doubt sung by the choristers and chaplains with polyphony, whether improvised (descant, faburden and square note) or written-down (pricksong).[92] Written-down polyphony was undoubtedly sung in the main choir on feast days.[93] There is nothing to tell us what polyphonic works were sung at Hereford; it is a matter of looking at the repertories of contemporary choirbooks and part-books,[94] and asking whether music of this kind might have been sung at Hereford. Certainly the sources include works by lay and ordained composers who held office in secular cathedrals, not least by John Mason, whom Roger Bowers uncompromisingly judges to be 'a respectable second-division composer of fair talent'.[95] Four works are attributed to Mason in the Henrician set of part-books preserved at Peterhouse, Cambridge.[96] All are

90. Hichons worked on an organ above the sacristan's room, but this may have been an instrument for teaching the choristers, rather than for the liturgy.

91. The principal source, BL, MS Add. 29996, may possibly have connections with Wales or the Marches, J. Harper, 'Philip ap Rhys and his Liturgical Organ Music Revisited', *Welsh Music History*, 2 (1997), pp. 126–48. For editions of the repertory, see J. Caldwell, ed., *Early Tudor Organ Music*, i, *Music for the Office*, Early English Church Music, 6 (London, [1966]); and D. Stevens, ed., *Early Tudor Organ Music*, ii, *Music for the Mass*, Early English Church Music, 10 (London, [1969]). On the wider subject, see J. Harper, *Sacred Pipes and Voices: The Relationship of Organs, Choirs and the Liturgy in England, 1480–1680* (Oxford, forthcoming).

92. Bishop Charlton's ordinance (1330)

required the Lady chapel priests to be good singers and competent musicians. See above, p. 384.

93. On 25 June 1522, David Orton, vicar choral of the Lady chapel, was admonished for absence from choir on feast days when the song commonly called pricksong was sung ('quando cantus vulgariter nuncupatus *prykkydsong* ibidem cantabatur', HCA, 7031/1, fol. 30r; HCA, Baylis, no. 190).

94. H. Benham, *Latin Church Music in England, c. 1460–1575* (London, 1977); J. Caldwell, *The Oxford History of English Music*, i (Oxford, 1991), pp. 174–276; F. L. Harrison, *Music in Medieval Britain* (London, 1958; 4th edn, Buren, 1980).

95. Bowers, 'The Cultivation', p. 188.

96. N. Sandon, 'The Henrician Partbooks at Peterhouse, Cambridge', *Proceedings of the Royal Musical Association*, 103 (1976–77), pp. 106–40.

antiphons scored for five voices – two Mary antiphons (*Ave Maria ave fuit primus salus*; *Quales sumus O miseri properantes*), a Jesus antiphon (*Vae nobis miseris*) and an antiphon for *Nunc dimittis* at compline in Lent (*O rex gloriose*).[97] In the part-books Mason is described as being of Chichester (*Cicerstriensis* [sic; for *Cicestrensis*]); the works themselves, or the exemplar from which they were copied, may therefore date from the years when he held a Mortimer chantry in Chichester Cathedral from 1523 to about 1525, just before his appointment to the canonry at Hereford. Such a repertory would have been equally appropriate and performable at Hereford.

The role of boy choristers in cathedral and collegiate foundations was transformed from liturgical dogsbody and servant in the canon's household in the thirteenth century to skilled polyphonic singer by the end of the fifteenth century.[98] This may account for the need for a post of instructor of choristers at Hereford specified by indenture in 1517 (and later assimilated into the statutes). The fact that this post was coupled with the organist of the Lady chapel suggests that the principal musical duties of the choristers at this time may have been comparable: performance at the daily Lady mass and in choir on feast days. New arrangements in 1525 extended the duties of the choristers further: the instructor or master of the choristers was required to go with the boys daily after compline to fulfil two observances.[99] First they went to the crucifix in the nave, there prostrating themselves devoutly, to sing the Jesus antiphon *Sancte deus*; thereafter they proceeded to the statue of the Blessed Virgin Mary at the west end of the nave to sing an antiphon of Our Lady with an appropriate versicle and collect, and the psalm *De profundis* ('Out of the deep') and a collect for the dead.[100] These arrangements are typical of practice elsewhere in Britain at this time, and indicate the increasing use of music for devotion in the people's part of the cathedral. Further accretions were introduced in 1530, when the chapter directed that there were to be processions on all feasts of the Blessed Virgin Mary.[101]

The chapter acts give only a few indications of the impact of the Reformation on the cathedral's worship and clergy.[102] John George, who succeeded William

---

97. Benham suggests that although this is a ritual antiphon it is also appropriate as a Jesus antiphon: Benham, *Latin Church Music*, pp. 160–61.

98. Roger Bowers has explored this transition in a number of his writings.

99. HCA, 7031/1, fol. 37r; HCA, Baylis, no. 253.

100. Near the burial place of the former precentor, William Porter (d. 1524), who had endowed this observance.

101. HCA, 7031/1, fol. 66r; HCA, Baylis, no. 395.

102. 3–4 October 1538. Following the dissolution of the Augustinian priory of Llanthony Secunda, Gloucester, John Hodges, formerly master of the Lady chapel there, was appointed organist, and William Browne, formerly one of the canons regular, was admitted as vicar choral on successive days at Hereford: HCA, 7031/1, fol. 82r; HCA, Baylis, nos 595–96.

Chell as succentor in 1542,[103] still held that office in 1563 and presumably arranged the choir duties through every stage of the changes.[104] On the other hand, Richard Ledbury's duties in the Lady chapel ceased during the reign of Edward VI and he resigned his vicarage in 1559.[105] Priests who married during the reign of Edward VI, including Barlow the precentor, were deprived in 1554.

The removal of images and altars from the cathedral is recorded in 1550,[106] as is the introduction of the new service of holy communion in November 1552.[107] Other changes can be deduced from the royal injunctions (1547) and the texts of the English forms of service.[108] From October 1545 the sole English litany displaced the whole repertory of Latin processions on Sundays and feast days; from 1547 it was to be sung kneeling in the choir, without procession.[109] Services in the night were discontinued; matins, now sung at six in the morning,[110] was curtailed from nine to six lessons, and followed by English Bible readings.[111] Lady mass, Jesus mass, masses for the dead, offices of Our Lady, the saints and the dead, and anthems in honour of the Blessed Virgin Mary, were discontinued.[112] The two vernacular Books of Common Prayer (1549 and 1552) rendered the contents of the Latin breviary, missal, antiphonal and gradual redundant.

During the reign of Mary the Latin rite was temporarily restored and altars were re-established for additional masses. The stipend of Robert George was increased in 1556 for celebrating mass before the great cross on the pulpitum.[113] In the same year Roger Caryndyn was admitted to a vicarage and appointed to celebrate mass twice weekly at the altar of St Nicholas;[114] and in January 1558 Henry Mynde undertook to celebrate first mass at the altar of St Nicholas daily.[115] That arrangement was, of course, short-lived. The Elizabethan settlement was introduced rapidly. Although the Elizabethan injunctions for Hereford (1559) largely duplicate the Edwardian injunctions for cathedrals (1547),[116] those for Exeter Cathedral (1559) are more informative: morrow mass was replaced by said prayers, litany and New

103. HCA, 7031/1, fol. 89r; HCA, Baylis, no. 672.
104. HCA, 7031/1, fol. 171v; HCA, Baylis, no. 1149.
105. HCA, 7031/1, fol. 154r; HCA, Baylis, no. 1019.
106. HCA, 7031/1, fos 102v, 105v; HCA, Baylis, nos 794, 805.
107. HCA, 7031/1, fol. 113v; HCA, Baylis, no. 845.
108. 'Royal Injunctions of Edward VI' and 'Royal Injunctions for Cathedrals', in W. H. Frere and W. McC. Kennedy, eds, *Visitation Articles and Injunctions of the Period of the Reformation*, Alcuin Club Collections, 14–16 (3 vols, London, 1910), ii, pp. 114–30, 135–39.

109. G. J. Cuming, *History of Anglican Liturgy* (2nd edn, London, 1982), p. 38.
110. Frere and Kennedy, *Visitation Articles*, ii, p. 138.
111. Ibid., p. 123.
112. P. LeHuray, *Music and the Reformation in England 1549–1660* (2nd edn, Cambridge, 1978), pp. 8–11.
113. HCA, 7031/1, fol. 147v; HCA, Baylis, no. 964.
114. HCA, 7031/1, fol. 148r; HCA, Baylis, no. 970.
115. HCA, 7031/1, fol. 150v; HCA, Baylis, no. 991.
116. Frere and Kennedy, *Visitation Articles*, iii, pp. 47–48.

Testament reading at six o'clock, morning prayer was sung in choir at a quarter to eight, at nine on weekdays the singing of *Veni creator* was followed by a lecture or reading, and holy communion was sung at ten.[117] Evening prayer took place around three in the afternoon.[118] By 1565 at Rochester Cathedral the holy communion was celebrated only once in three weeks on Sunday, and on a very limited number of holy days.[119] In spite of Queen Elizabeth's sympathy for music in the liturgy, expressed in her royal injunctions (1559),[120] the surviving choral music with English texts is modest. The old plainsong tones served for the singing of English psalms.[121] Many organs fell into disuse and disrepair, or were dismantled by the 1570s. The revival came at the end of the sixteenth and the beginning of the seventeenth centuries.[122]

One can only guess at the fortitude and equanimity of priests like the succentor, John George, or the organist, John Hodges, who served throughout this period of constitutional, liturgical, theological and musical change. Out of it came the cathedral's most distinguished musical son, John Bull (fig. 118). Born in about 1563, probably near Old Radnor (in Wales, but in the diocese of Hereford),[123] admitted as a chorister in the cathedral on 31 August 1573,[124] appointed organist on 24 December 1582,[125] and master of the choristers on 21 January 1583,[126] Bull was an outstanding keyboard performer and composer. He ended his career at Antwerp Cathedral, having previously worked in the royal courts of Prince Henry and James I in London and the Archduke Albert in Brussels. It is impossible to know whether any of his keyboard settings of plainsong hymns were written at Hereford.[127] His tenure at the cathedral was brief, and the year 1585 was unsatisfactory, no doubt as he laid the ground for his move to London where he

---

117. Ibid., p. 41–43.
118. For comparable arrangements at Lincoln Cathedral, see R. Bowers, 'Music and Worship to 1640', in D. Owen, ed., *A History of Lincoln Minster* (Cambridge, 1994), pp. 77–111, esp. p. 64.
119. Frere and Kennedy, *Visitation Articles*, iii, p. 152.
120. Ibid., p. 22–23.
121. Metrical psalms were sung before or after the divine service, but did not displace those prescribed in the Book of Common Prayer.
122. I. Payne, *The Provision and Practice of Sacred Music at Cambridge Colleges and Selected Cathedrals, c. 1547 – c. 1646* (New York and London, 1993). This includes Hereford.
123. S. Jeans, 'John Bull', in Sadie, ed., *The New*

Grove, ii, p. 438.
124. HCA, 7031/2, fol. 12. Bull may thereafter have been taken into the choir of the Chapel Royal as a chorister, where he appears to have been a pupil of John Blitheman (often erroneously identified as William). Through the lord chamberlain, the earl of Sussex, he became an apprentice in the Merchant Taylors' Company in 1578, and he was recommended to be organist at Hereford by Sussex's brother-in-law, Henry Sidney, president of the Marches.
125. HCA, 7031/8, fol. 104v.
126. Ibid., fol. 104v.
127. This repertory is reviewed in W. Cunningham, *The Keyboard Music of John Bull*, Studies in Musicology, 71 (Ann Arbor, Michigan, 1984), pp. 77–118.

Fig. 118. Portrait of John Bull,
organist 1582–86.

become a gentleman (and subsequently an organist) of the Chapel Royal early in
1586.[128] He was nevertheless the first to hold a statutory post as organist and
master of the choristers when the Elizabethan statutes were delivered in 1583.[129]
No doubt these statutes regulated a status quo which had emerged gradually
following the disruption of endowments and personnel occasioned by the Chantries
Act (1548). The choral body was reduced to twelve vicars choral (four of whom
were minor canons),[130] four subcanons (including the organist and master of the
choristers) and seven choristers. The subcanons took the place of the former
deacons and subdeacons.[131] In the early seventeenth century, Canon Thomas
Thornton amended his copy of the statutes to read *canonicos laicos* (lay
canons).[132] Until 1590, however, the subcanons continued to be deacons and a
subdeacon: only the organist was a layman, although there is evidence of some

128. E. F. Rimbault, ed., *The Old Cheque Book
of the Chapel Royal*, Camden Society, new
series, 3 (London, 1872, reprinted New
York, 1966), p. 4.

129. On these statutes, see note 2 above.

130. An arrangement not followed at any other
medieval secular cathedral.

131. Jebb and Phillott, *The Statutes of the Cathedral Church of Hereford*, pp. 40–41.

132. HCA, 7044/3.

supernumerary lay singers in the 1580s.[133] By contrast with the expansion of liturgical observances and clergy during the fourteenth century, the later sixteenth century represents a somewhat contracted choral body, but sufficiently stable to sustain the more modest pattern of worship and music of the cathedral in succeeding centuries.

TABLE I

Summary of the numbers of liturgical antiphons, responds, hymns and collects found in the early sixteenth-century breviaries of Hereford, Salisbury and York based on the indexes in *The Hereford Breviary*, iii (1915)

Breviary	Antiphons	Responds	Collects	Hymns	Proses and sequences	Total of all items
Items included in all three breviaries						
HSY	1505	673	304	108	3	2593
Items included in two of the three breviaries						
HS	147	74	52	7	2	282
HY	60	31	25	4	2	122
SY	54	36	23	5	0	118
Items found in only one breviary						
H	175	78	147	17	12	429
S	124	69	78	6	5	282
Y	261	117	42	13	8	441
Total of items in each breviary						
H	1887	856	528	136	19	3426
S	1830	852	457	126	10	3275
Y	1880	857	394	130	13	3274
Total of all items listed						
All	2326	1078	671	160	32	4267

H = Hereford breviary
S = Salisbury breviary
Y = York breviary

Other greater responds are listed.
All the lists relate to texts, not to chants.

133. I. Payne, 'The Choral Force at Hereford Cathedral 1536–1641', in his *The Provision and Practice*, pp. 181–84.

22

Music and Liturgy since 1600

Paul Iles

The musical establishment provided for the cathedral by the Elizabethan statutes (1583) remained in place during the seventeenth century until the choral services stopped some time after December 1645. The terminology of the various offices held by cathedral musicians is ambiguous and can be misleading. Usage is always particular and sometimes unique in each cathedral. At Hereford, the twelve vicars choral were members of their college and had to be in priests orders. They elected their own custos and appointed four of their number, usually the seniors, to be minor canons who sang the priest's part and read the lessons at morning and evening prayer in rotation. One vicar was appointed subchanter (often called succentor) by the precentor to act as his deputy. Together they provided the lower parts in the choir. In addition, there were four subcanons who could be laymen, one of whom was appointed organist and master of choristers. The accounts show that, at least occasionally, the other three men received payments for singing in the choir. Sometimes they are designated sextons, which may reflect the duties of the pre-Reformation deacons and subdeacons. Occasional payments were also made to supernumerary singers.[1]

The adult musicians received a stipend and accommodation from the college and shared a common board, for which they had to discharge both singing duties in the cathedral choir and the corporate parochial duties of the college. Two choristers were paid for out of college income and they may have been housed and cared for by the college when necessary.[2] The chapter paid for the other five

1. I. Payne, *The Provision and Practice of Sacred Music at Cambridge Colleges and Selected Cathedrals c. 1547–c. 1646* (New York and London, 1993), pp. 181–84, 225–27.
2. In some cathedrals, houses were set aside for board and lodging where the boys lived 'in common' with a master in charge. In others, the children sometimes lodged with various members of the chapter or with the organist, while at Hereford the chapter boys probably lived at home with their families, who received the payments made to their child for his singing duties.

boys, made additional contributions to the organist's stipend and provided and maintained the organ and the music books.

The clavigers' accounts records regular annual payments for clothing the five chapter boys, for their tuition, and for wages and pensions: twelve yards of broad cloth at 7s. 4d. per yard to make five gowns; twenty-three yards of white cotton (for surplices presumably); seventeen yards of grey frize (for capes or cloaks perhaps); five hose, stiffenings, pairs of shoes; their wages for the whole year 40s.; for their teaching 53s. 4d.; the pensions for the choristers £3 10s. 6d. There are also payments to the deacons and subdeacons for their service in the choir £10, and to Nicholas Traherne for blowing the organs the whole year 20s.[3]

The choristers sat on the lowest bench of the stalls in the choir, together with the junior clergy. New choristers were selected carefully and elected at chapter meetings, usually at the age of nine. The boys were taught music in the cathedral and grammar in the school. The singing room at one time may have been the room next to the entrance to the college but by the seventeenth century it is believed to have been in 'ye lower chamber behind ye hall next to the saffron garden'.[4] The statutes directed the chapter to accept responsibility for the children in their care seriously and to prepare them for adult life. Each boy had to be provided with the necessary books or instruments for instruction 'in the art of writing, or in Arithmetic, or in the practice of the harp, or Virginals, or in some other liberal employment not unworthy of a respectable man, and suited to earn his livelihood hereafter'.[5] When their voices broke, departing choristers benefited from a bequest left to the cathedral in 1619 by Richard Tomson.[6]

Little detailed information remains about the early seventeenth-century organists and masters of choristers at Hereford. In some cathedrals the two posts were separated but William Inglott, admitted organist on 1 October 1597, appears to have held both, receiving payments each year at Michaelmas 'for teaching the choristers'.[7] In the seventeenth century there were no regular choir practices as understood today; instead the organist was required to teach the boys music, which included instrumental tuition, singing and general musicianship.[8] Thus prepared, the boys (and the adults who were also required to be trained musicians before

3. HCA, R 600, clavigers' accounts, 1612–13.

4. R. K. Morriss and R. Shoesmith, 'The College of the Vicars Choral in Hereford', in Whitehead, *Medieval Art at Hereford*, pp. 160, 169.

5. Jebb and Phillott, *The Statutes of the Cathedral Church of Hereford*, p. 43.

6. HCA, 3957, will of Richard Lane Tomson, 1619. In the nineteenth century the charity was used for apprentice fees and was much sought after by parents as a valuable donation at the beginning of their son's employment (see below, p. 646). In February 1976 the charity was redefined to provide bursaries for the boys while they are singing.

7. HCA, R 595, clavigers' accounts, 1608–9.

8. Organists usually concentrated on instrumental teaching and left the teaching of singing to the subchanter.

their appointment) were expected to sing the choir music used in the liturgy virtually at sight.

Before he came to Hereford, Inglott may have been a chorister and then organist at Norwich Cathedral; if so, sometime before 1611, he resumed his previous post.[9] Hugh Davis had been admitted to the college on 25 June 1604 and thus was one of the singers. While giving information about his membership of New College, Oxford, and his degree, however, Anthony Wood describes him as 'organist of the Cathedral Church of Hereford', which suggests that he became organist when Inglott left in 1610.[10] The only specific reference to Davis in the cathedral archives is an entry in the vicars choral act book on 7 July 1630 which reconciles his singing duties with those of organist: 'the Custos and Vicars now at his request do agree that Mr Hugh Davis be daily spared out of the choir and not be pricked but accounted as present at the psalmody and *Gloria Patri* so that he be ready in the organ loft to play before the reading of the first lesson every morning and evening prayer and attend his duty there'.[11] In 1637 Davis was elected custos of the college and on 6 April 1644 the act book records the election of a new custos in place of 'Mr Hugh Davis, deceased'.[12] There is no further mention of an organist until after the Restoration.

The essential element in the choir service was 'chanting' the daily offices from the Prayer Book, which meant intoning the opening sentences, confession and absolution, the responses and collects, the psalms, and the litany. Chanting could be simply a monotone or singing the remnants of a plainsong melody. Usually it was elaborated with harmony surrounding the chant, the origin of the characteristic Anglican chant. The canticles at morning and evening prayer were sung to a chant or sometimes to a setting, simple or as complex as the choir could manage and the number of singers available permitted. The musical climax of the service was the anthem, which usually demanded considerable skill from both singers and organist. Frequently however the anthem was omitted, contrary to rubric, which became a primary cause of complaint from all who strove to maintain the choral services in the cathedral.[13] In Hereford there was the added difficulty that generally the vicars were not available to sing at the Sunday morning services because of their parochial duties. Whatever level of competence the singers possessed, which

9. Payne, *Provision and Practice of Sacred Music*, p. 236, states that he left Hereford in March 1610.

10. A. Wood, *Athenae Oxoniensis* (2 vols, London, 1691–92), i, col. 844.

11. HCA, 7003/1/1, p. 196, vicars choral acts, 7 July 1630. This implies that the organ was not used to accompany the psalms.

The custom of playing an organ voluntary between the psalms and the first lesson (the middle voluntary) may have replaced the antiphons sung in the pre-Reformation liturgy.

12. Ibid., p. 225, 6 April 1644.

13. On Sundays, Wednesdays and Fridays the anthem was regularly replaced by the litany.

must have varied from time to time, at Hereford it was their availability which hindered the cathedral's music remorselessly until the end of the nineteenth century.

The Hereford chapter regularly resisted episcopal visitations on the (spurious) grounds that the bishop was not the Visitor and therefore only welcome in the cathedral as Father-in-God. However, two disciples of Laud, Bishop Lindsell and Bishop Wren, initiated visitation procedures in 1634/5. The majority of the prebendaries and vicars absented themselves but the answers of two members of the chapter, Dr William Skynner, a residentiary, and Dr Francis Kerry, the treasurer, remain.[14] Skynner declared that 'Morning prayer was said in the prescribed form'; the litany was said 'regularly on the specified days'; the full number of vicars was present and they had been 'chosen with care'; the behaviour of the choristers was 'orderly'; 'there were sufficient song books'; the master of choristers was teaching 'both men and children'; the communion table was properly furnished with 'a Turkey-Carpett' and with sufficient plate; though, said Dr Skynner, 'we have neither Epistoler, Gospeller or Copes'.

The Laudian statutes (1636) did not change the numerical strength of the choir but they enacted discipline among the cathedral's musicians, especially in their daily attendance, to ensure that there would always be enough singers adequately to perform the choral services. Each cathedral shared much the same repertory of music, which is partly known through the collection of cathedral music published in 1641 by John Barnard. Whether Hereford bought a set of Barnard's part-books at this time is not certain. More probably the cathedral acquired the famous set of ten part-books after the Restoration.[15] Part-books were constantly being copied for daily use: for example in the claviger's accounts for 1644, very close to the time when the choir was disbanded, payments were still being made 'to Mr Brode for pricking: 10s.'.[16]

In October 1642 a soldier serving in the New Model Army commanded by the earl of Essex visited the cathedral and gave a record of some of the music and liturgy. Nehemiah Wharton, who was a London apprentice, wrote home saying that on 'Sabbath day, about the time of morning prayer, we went to the Minster,

14. HCA, 1558 and 1559.
15. The Hereford set of Barnard's part-books was among the cathedral's most valued possessions and became famous because by the nineteenth century no complete set remained anywhere. Although Hereford still possessed only eight, it was the least imperfect set to survive. In 1862 the Sacred Harmonic Society, which held copies of the missing books, allowed the cathedral to copy the parts they lacked. The chapter sold their completed set to Christ Church, Oxford, in 1917 for £100 (HCA, 5823). Dr Percy Hull knew the books in Hereford as a chorister and organist and, when he returned from his internment during the First World War in 1918 and looked for them, he discovered that they had been sold the year before. It is said that he never trusted the dean and chapter again.

16. HCA, 2384, claviger's accounts, 1644–45.

when the pipes played and the puppets sang so sweetly that some of our soldiers could not forbeare dauncinge in the holie quire; whereat the Baalists were sore displeased. The anthem ended, they fell to prayer.'[17]

Herbert Croft was appointed dean in 1644. After the execution of Laud in January 1645, the Prayer Book was declared illegal and *A Directory for the Public Worship of God* was put in its place. Nevertheless, Dean Croft and the chapter maintained the traditional music and liturgy for some months. When Charles I entered the city, on 4 September 1645, he stayed in the bishop's palace and attended service in the cathedral. He may have heard the chorister who (according to the records of Tomson's Charity) 'went out in ye beginning of ye warre & songe ye last anthem in ye Chore before King Charles ye first'.[18]

Just before Christmas, Colonel Birch captured the city and the destruction of the cathedral began. How much was saved and how much was lost will never be known exactly. Dean Croft's heroism and Birch's ability to restrain his troops are well recorded and rightly famous.[19] The clergy were ejected from their houses and the choral services came to an end. Episcopacy was abolished in October 1646 and earlier in the same year an ordinance was passed 'for the setting and maintaining of able preachers and godly orthodox ministers in the city and county of Hereford'. Three of these, with an annual stipend of £150 and lodgings in the deanery, were to preach regularly in the cathedral.[20] In 1647 the vicars were pitched out of their college. They sent a petition to the Committee for Sequestration pleading destitution and seeking help, which was not forthcoming.[21] In April 1649, an Act abolishing deans and chapters was passed, ordering the sale of their lands.

The cathedral became a 'meeting house' where sermons and unaccompanied psalm-singing were heard. Ministers 'preached the gospel each morning in the cathedral between 7.00 and 8.00' and gave the usual weekly lecture on Tuesdays.[22] Dean Croft seems to have been a reluctant admirer of the puritan regime established in the cathedral, leading him to a concern for greater unity in the church.[23] The Interregnum became wilderness years for those whose livelihood and work had been to provide the music of the cathedral; but, although things were never the same again, seeds of new ideas in music and liturgy, as well as in political

17. Bannister, *The Cathedral Church of Hereford*, p. 97, quoting *Archaeologia*, 35 (1853), pp. 309–34, at 331–34; see above, Chapter 4, p. 100 n. 42.

18. S. Lehmberg, *Cathedrals under Siege* (Exeter, 1997), p. 166; HCA, 7031/3, p. 224, chapter acts, 22 September 1662.

19. See above, Chapter 4, pp. 101–2.

20. See above, Chapter 4, p. 106.

21. P. Barrett, *The College of Vicars Choral at Hereford Cathedral* (Hereford, 1980), p. 21.

22. The lectures were given in the college chapel and were the responsibility of the praelector; they continued in various forms until the present day.

23. D. Whitehead, 'A Goth among the Greeks', *FHC*, 57 (1991), pp. 18–41, at 21.

thought, literature and art, were sown at the time which would mature in the years ahead.[24]

During February and March 1660 church bells were already being rung in some places and the Prayer Book was again being used openly. On 28 March the seven surviving members of the college reassembled and held their first meeting.[25] The chapter reconvened on 8 August.[26] Quickly they set about the task of restoring the cathedral's worship. The celebration of holy communion required by the statutes on the first Sunday of the month and on holy days had recommenced by Christmas Day. On 27 September the chapter made up the number of singers by appointing five new members of the college, one of whom, John Badham, took up the duties of organist immediately. At Michaelmas the following year six pounds were paid 'to Mr Badham the organist by consent of the Chapter by reason of his poverty and necessity'.[27] In 1665 Badham concluded a lengthy negotiation with the college, which exempted him from parochial duties, enabling him to work solely as organist. He composed some choir music, and in the accounts presented at Michaelmas 1666 there is a note that during the year he had been paid 'for incouragement for making an anthem: 10s.'.[28] Three anthems by Badham are known: *Praise the Lord*; *O Lord thou hast Searched me out and Known me*; *How doth the City sit Sorrowfully*.[29]

It appears a small organ was borrowed for use in the cathedral and, unlike several other cathedrals, the number of choristers was not reduced. New choristers were selected in January 1661.[30] The boys were beginners and had to be taught the music from scratch. While the choristers were learning their part, instruments helped to sustain their line and sometimes entirely replaced them. How long it took for the boys to be confident enough to sing without instruments varied from choir to choir. Under the expert tuition of Captain Henry Cooke at the Chapel Royal it took less than a year.[31] In Hereford the chapter made a special payment to the boys, giving them 2s. 6d. each, 'when they began to sing alone in ye chore,

---

24. Especially the formation of a new and bracing language which produced the 'auditory' church, for example the Harleys' church at Brampton Bryan, built in 1656, and the cathedral itself when Bishop Bisse made his alterations to the choir.

25. See below, Chapter 23, p. 452.

26. See above, Chapter 5, pp. 109–10.

27. HCA, R 609, clavigers' accounts, 1660–61. Payments were made annually at Michaelmas, but in arrears. This payment made by the chapter was in addition to the

stipend he received from the college. Later, in 1662, the chapter raised its contribution to £12 a year.

28. HCA, R 611, cathedral accounts, 1665–66.

29. I. Cheverton, 'English Church Music of the Early Renaissance Period, 1660 to c. 1676' (unpublished dissertation, Cardiff University, 1984), pp. 622–23.

30. Lehmberg, *Cathedrals under Siege*, pp. 71, 158.

31. C. Dearnley, *English Church Music, 1650–1750* (London, 1970), p. 28.

for their Incouragement'.[32] Another payment was made (probably for singing a solo) to 'Davis ye chorister when he sang alone: 2s.'.[33] In May 1666 Cooke may have visited Hereford in search of suitable choristers.[34]

The act books give a few details of the boy's families. The father of one chorister was a bookseller, another a glover and another an apothecary. There are shreds of information about what happened to the boys when they left the choir. One boy went to London, although we do not know whether it was for further study or employment. Another boy joined the college, and there is an unusual record of one boy, Rowland Pearce, who was admitted to the choir in place of his elder brother who had died.[35]

The adult singers, with the statutory requirement to be in priest's orders and members of the college, may have been more difficult to recruit. Marriage was not forbidden but, since no married accommodation was provided, celibacy was implied. The dean and chapter made a visitation of the cathedral in 1663, and one matter of enquiry was 'whether any of the [vicars] be swearers, blasphemers of God, Atheists, Sorcerers, and such like. Also be known or vehemently suspected to frequent or without a most just and necessary occasion to go into Alehouses or Taverns either in City or Country; Also or be known to be Raylers, Scoffers, Sowers of dischord amongst brethren or others, common gamesters at unlawful games, to use excess in appareil either themselves, their wives, their family or no'. In addition they wanted to know if 'any of the aforementioned persons be known or suspected to live incontinently or no. Are any women at any unreasonable times received or entertained in any ones chamber or lodging?' One of the vicars, William Allen, replied, 'I know no such person amongst us. If there be, God amend him'.[36]

New music books were bought and a large part of the earlier repertory recovered. At the same time a considerable amount of new music was being written.[37] The choice of music used in the services was often haphazard and left to the last minute, and the general conduct of the services was very different from today. The singers wore black gowns in the week and, on Sundays, saints days and their eves, open-fronted surplices rather like a dust sheet over their ordinary clothes. There are many references in the act books to the need for cleanliness, tidiness and punctuality. There was no procession into the stalls. Instead the choir and clergy entered in their own time and waited for the clock to strike the hour, which became the signal that the service should begin.

32. Lehmberg, *Cathedrals under Siege*, p. 160.
33. HCA, R 610, cathedral accounts, 1660–65.
34. R. King, *Henry Purcell* (London, 1994), p. 48.
35. HCA, 7031/3, p. 196, chapter acts, 24

January 1661; Lehmberg, *Cathedrals under Siege*, p. 161.
36. HCA, 3399.
37. I. Spink, *Restoration Cathedral Music* (Oxford, 1995).

Bishop Croft's first official visitation of the cathedral began in July 1677.[38] A year later he gave two specific instructions about the music. He directed the organist (Badham) to 'be diligent in performing his Duty; all books necessary for the Quire to be provided and fairly pricked by some careful Person who is skilful in Musick; to be speedily appointed by the Dean and Chapter for that Purpose'.[39] To carry out these instructions, on 27 June 1679 the chapter elected Henry Hall to be Badham's assistant. He was already well known as a musician and composer (fig. 119).[40] At first he was not admitted to membership of the college (probably because there was no vacancy at the time) but he was given rooms and a share in the common table. Not being a member, he was not paid from the college income. Therefore the chapter gave him a grant of £20 a year, for 'assisting the organist, instructing the choristers thrice a week and also singing in the choir according to the instructions which shall be given

Fig. 119. Organ book in the hand of Henry Hall, organist 1688–1707. (HCL, Music MS 30.B.2, fol. 39v.)

him'.[41] Fairly quickly, though, he was made priest and on 27 December 1679 'Henry Hall *clericus*' was fully admitted to the college. His perpetuation as vicar choral on 21 January 1681 is also recorded, and on 3 June there is a note in the act book to say 'that Mr Dean will allow to Mr Henry Hall organist five pounds and that the Canons will allow him three pounds'.[42]

On Sundays the chapter expected the vicars to return to the city from their parishes in time to sing evening prayer. Few did, although none was allowed to

38. See above, Chapter 5, pp. 117–18.
39. HCA, 1579.
40. R. Thompson, *The Glory of the Temple and the Stage* (London, 1995), pp. 7–10.
41. HCA, 7031/3, p. 372, chapter acts, 27 June 1679.
42. HCA, 7003/1/3, p. 90, vicars choral acts,

21 January 1681; 7031/3, pp. 378, 389, chapter acts, 27 December 1679, 3 June 1680. Presumably these sums replaced the original grant of £20 a year made to him before he entered the college and they supplemented his income from the college.

hold livings more than seven miles outside the city.[43] In 1680 the number of vicars attending on Sunday evenings gave the chapter cause for concern and an act dated 3 June required that on 'every Lords day at evening service in the Choir shall constantly be three vicars of a side in the Choir, beginning with the senior first, under the penalty of six pence to be paid each time by each one who shall make default, to be required by the Hebdomadary'.[44] The following year, the first addition beyond the provision of the Elizabethan statutes was made to the choir in an attempt to help maintain sufficient numbers. A thirteenth vicar was appointed, owing to 'severall defects in the Quire and vacancies by reason of infirmities of body'.[45]

There were still only seven choristers. Croft's injunctions reaffirmed the chapter's duty to ensure the boys were properly taught music and grammar. Their singing instruction was now the responsibility of Hall. The five chapter choristers received an annual fee of £1 each and the clavigers' accounts show that clothes were also provided. During the year 1685–86 their gowns cost £5, clothes £3 2s. 11d., making them 15s., hats 17s., stockings 8s. 4d. and shoes 17s. 6d.[46] The conduct of the choristers though was not always acceptable. In 1683 the chapter agreed that one 'William Roberts chorister shall continue in his place untill Michaelmas next unless he be found guilty of drinking, swearing, cursing, fighting or neglecting his duty in the church, and upon any miscarriage the Hebdomadary to out him'.[47] Answers returned by the vicars choral to the dean and chapter after a visitation of the college in 1694 shed more light. Edward Broad asserted, 'Our Choristers are not taught in singing or Grammar as they ought to be', whereas Thomas Gwillim pointed out that 'whether ye Queristers go constantly to schoole or whether they are well instructed when there does not ... concern us but their Masters of Grammar and Musick; one of which I know to be skillfull in what he professes and ye other, I believe thinks himself so'. Henry Hall, the master responsible for teaching them music, told the chapter, 'They have heretofore bin neglected, but of late I'm sure they are taught as they ought to be, I mean to sing only'. The chapter appreciated the work of Hall and on 15 September 1688, after the departure of John Badham (who probably had died), they appointed him organist.[48]

No convincing evidence has been found to suggest that Hall felt isolated in Hereford, regretting its remoteness from London. On the contrary, he lived happily

43. Jebb and Phillott, *The Statutes of the Cathedral Church of Hereford*, p. 115.

44. HCA, 7031/3, p. 389, chapter acts, 3 June 1680.

45. Ibid., p. 400; an instruction added that in future only graduates were to be admitted.

46. HCA, R 616, clavigers' accounts, 1685–86.

47. HCA, 7031/3, p. 416, chapter acts, 25 June 1683.

48. HCA, 3396, visitation of college, 1694; HCA, 7031/3, p. 470, 15 September 1688.

with his wife and at least two children, William and Henry, enjoying the musical life of both the cathedral and the city. He took a full part in the social life of the college and wrote secular music for the evening concerts of the vicars which were popular and held regularly in the college hall after it had been refurbished following the decay of the buildings during the interregnum.[49]

Both Henry Hall's sons were musicians. William was a violinist, who from 1692 until his death in 1700 was a musician in ordinary to the king, and the younger Henry lived to succeed his father as organist of the cathedral. Hall died on 30 March 1707 in his fifty-first year, and was buried in the college cloister. Henry Hall junior (as he is referred to in the MS music part-books in the library) was appointed on 5 June 1707. The chapter act describes him as *nunc vel nuper oppidi de Ludlow* which suggests he had been organist there. Unlike his father he is supposed 'to have composed little or no music, applying himself to verse-making', and his creations were dismissed by some as 'trifles without his father's ability'.[50] The younger Hall, however, did compose at least two services for the cathedral which were still being sung in the nineteenth century: a complete service in F and a setting of the evening canticles in A minor. Quite possibly, during a visit to Gloucester in 1709, Hall discussed with his colleague the organist William Hine the idea of an annual Three Choirs Festival.[51] He died on 21 January 1714, aged twenty-seven, and was buried in the vicars choral cloister near his father.

Travelling through 'the whole island of Great Britain', Daniel Defoe came to Hereford in 1725 and described the cathedral and its choir (by which he meant the stalls not the singers): 'The great church is a magnificent building, however ancient, the spire is not high, but handsome, and there is a fine tower at the west end, over the great door or entrance. The choir is very fine, though plain, and there is a very good organ'.[52] The cathedral organ had been repaired in 1707 and at the time of Defoe's visit there was a new organist, Henry Swarbrick, appointed in 1720 after Edward Thompson had left two years earlier for the organ loft at Salisbury.[53] He was the nephew of the midlands organ builder, Thomas Swarbrick.

Philip Bisse became bishop in 1713. While the deans were also occupied as bishops of Llandaff, he was able to take charge of the cathedral's affairs with a

49. A. Boden, *Three Choirs* (Gloucester, 1992), p. 7.

50. E.g. *All in the Land of Cider, Catch on the Vigo Expedition*, published in *The Grove: or A Collection of Original Poems, Translations* (London, 1721), pp. 98–101, 126.

51. Boden, *Three Choirs*, pp. 9–10.

52. D. Defoe, *A Tour through the Whole Island of Great Britain* (Harmondsworth, 1971), p. 374.

53. HCA, 7031/4, p. 65, chapter acts, 10 November 1720. Nothing is known of an organist between 1718 and 1720, possibly because the organ was not played while Bisse's alterations within the choir were taking place.

firm hand and initiate considerable changes in the area of the choir where the
daily services were sung. The driving force for his alterations was a new approach
to liturgy and worship rather than a new approach to architecture.[54] Whatever
Bisse was doing by giving the cathedral his Grecian choir, he was not attempting
to create 'a cosy drawing room' as some have called it.

First, the altar: having accepted it should stand against the east wall, the bishop
wanted it to have the most gracious setting possible. The altar should be a place
where ministers and congregation could gather for worship and receive holy
communion in spacious dignity. The cathedral's Laudian rails were still in place
and behind the holy table were the usual boards with scripture texts written up,
which displayed the ten commandments.[55] Sometimes a canopy was placed above
the altar or a highly decorated ceiling, sometimes both. The altar itself was furnished
with a decent covering, with two large candles and a handsome almsdish, and
with well-bound books, either a Bible in two volumes or a Bible and a Book of
Common Prayer.[56]

Bisse's second objective was to provide a single open space, large enough for
all taking part in worship – ministers, singers and congregation – to assemble
together without any division or separation caused by rank, class or ecclesiastical
role. In the eighteenth century the sense of mystery in worship gave way to the
demands of audibility and visibility. All present should be able to hear the Word
read and preached,[57] and to see the manual acts of the minister at the sacrament
as he followed the rubrics in the Prayer Book. The ministers' chairs were set at
the side of the altar facing west. The celebrant stood at the north end so that his
hands could be seen, and the reader (or readers when there was an epistoler and
gospeller) stood at the south end. To accommodate all in one place, Bisse increased
the number of seats in the choir and high galleries were put up above the prebendal
stalls for the use of the cathedral staff, the households of the canons and the mayor
and corporation. The area of the choir still extended westwards under the tower
as far as the pulpitum, with its doors renewed by Willim in 1726 and the whole
area repaved by Batty Edwards for £21 9s. 4d. Thus an auditory room was created,
at the centre of a Romanesque cathedral, where the whole cathedral community
together with representatives of the city could share worship (figs 70, 71).

Although eighteenth-century cathedral music has often been dismissed as second
rate and derivative, it had many champions at the time, one of whom was the
younger brother of Bishop Bisse. Thomas Bisse was made chancellor of the cathedral

---

54. N. Yates, *Buildings, Faith and Worship* (Oxford, 1991), pp. 66 and 77.

55. Whitehead, 'A Goth among the Greeks', p. 26.

56. G. W. O. Addleshaw and F. Etchells, *The*

Architectural Setting of Anglican Worship (London, 1948), pp. 155–73.

57. The pulpit was moved from the nave and placed on the north side of the sanctuary steps.

in 1716, remaining until his death in
1731 (fig. 120). He would have welcomed his brother's changes to the choir
for he believed passionately that music
was still a chief adornment in worship,
especially cathedral worship, and that
the setting in which it took place was
vital for its evangelical purpose. 'Musick
is allow'd to sit among, or rather above
human pleasures, as a refiner: it raises
the mind and its desires above their low
level, drives out carnal thoughts and
inclinations as dross, and leaves it like
pure Gold.'[58] Bisse preached a series
of sermons during the Three Choirs
Festivals which were all printed and
'published at the request of the audience'. The one most widely read was
*A Rationale on Cathedral Worship or
Choir-Service* (1720), quoted above. In

Fig. 120. Thomas Bisse, chancellor 1716–31.
(HCL, B.3.65.)

Decency and Order in Public Worship Recommended (1723) he brought together the
work of worship with the demands of charity, to show the practical outcome on
earth of human involvement with the worship of heaven. His sermon in 1726,
Musick the Delight of the Sons of Men, was dedicated to William Croft. In the last
of his festival sermons, Bisse again emphasised the practical outcome of music used
in worship through its 'tending to the furtherance of God's glory, in the exaltation
of His holy worship, to the improvement of our choirs, the credit of our foundations;
to the benefit of our cities, the comfort of the fatherless; to the delight of mankind,
of ourselves, and all that come nigh'.[59]

By the 1740s the cathedral possessed a room of genuine beauty with a high
doctrine of its purpose. A series of brief notes in the act books reveals the attempts
of the chapter to make the cathedral services measure up to this vision. Details
about the conduct of the choristers, the care of song-books and the purchase of
new music to be sung by the choir may read as a mundane list, but their aim
was to order the worship as decently as possible. For example it was

Ordered that the choristers do come to church on Sundays and holy days and

58. T. Bisse, *A Rationale on Cathedral Worship
    or Choir-Service: Sermon Preached in the Ca-
    thedral Church of Hereford, 7 September 1720*

(2nd edn, London, 1721), p. 17.
59. Idem, *A Sermon Preach'd in the Cathedral
    Church of Hereford, 1729* (London, 1729).

on the Eves of the said days in Surplices and all other days in black Gowns; and that their Surplices be washed the First Week of every second Month.

Ordered that four Quarto Common prayer books be provided for the use of the vicars choral in the Choir; and that the Choristers' prayer books be chained to their Desks.

Ordered that six new Quarto Common prayer books be bought by Mr Dean for the use of the Vicars choral.

Thomas David of Bristol waxchandler having proposed to supply the choir with wax candles at 2*s*. 8*d*. per pound for the white and 2*s*. 6*d*. for the yellow (credit 1 penny per pound discount for ready money) the Chapter accepted of his proposal and agreed to buy of him when they shall have occasion.[60]

Two collections of choir music which extended the repertory were bought by the cathedral, Croft's *Musica sacra* (1724) and Maurice Greene's *Forty Select Anthems* (1743). Greene's book became influential and was reprinted more often than any other collection, which led him to attempt a larger project. He aimed to collect and publish a comprehensive collection of the best cathedral music available, but his health failed before he could finish it. He died in 1755 and directed in his will that the material should be passed to his pupil William Boyce so that the work of editing and publishing might be completed. When Boyce began to publish his volumes they too were ordered for the choir.[61] Because music books, whether published editions or manuscript copies, were expensive, they needed to be kept carefully. They were the responsibility of the subchanter who was required to keep a regular check on them: 'Ordered that the musick books belonging to the choir be collected together and entrusted to the care of the Subchanter and that no one be permitted to take a book out of the choir without his leave and that only for a reasonable time, he first taking a promissory note for the redelivering thereof'.[62]

In the middle of the eighteenth century a shift in the priorities of many cathedral musicians seems to have taken place. Making music in secular surroundings had been a popular recreation with both organists and singers since the end of the seventeenth century. Now many began to prefer it to the duties of the cathedral service.[63] Hereford's musicians were no exception. Perhaps this interest in secular

60. HCA, 7031/4, p. 195; 7031/5, pp. 33, 54, 129; chapter acts 7 November 1742, 31 August 1769, 8 November 1770, 7 August 1775.
61. HCA, 7031/4, p. 387, chapter acts, 13 November 1760.
62. HCA, 7031/5, p. 128, chapter acts, 7 August 1775.
63. N. Thistlethwaite, 'Music and Worship, 1660–1980', in D. Owen, ed., *A History of Lincoln Minster* (Cambridge, 1994), p. 91; J. Brewer, *The Pleasures of the Imagination* (London, 1997), chapter 14.

music and the growing demands of the Three Choirs Festivals sapped their energy, but few of the cathedral's musicians had the confidence of the chapter. In April 1758 the new dean, Francis Webber, complained to the college about the choral services: 'I am fully persuaded, upon enquiry, that there is no cathedral choir in England so much neglected in this respect as that of Hereford, and when the number of vicars provided for that service in our church is considered such neglect must appear so much the more inexcusable'. He added a reference to 'the indecency of seeing the Psalms and Hymns so often left to be chanted by the boys only'.[64]

Henry Swarbrick died on 23 June 1754. In less than two weeks, Richard Clack was appointed organist on 6 July.[65] Two particular complaints were made regularly against cathedral organists: they did not always attend their duties in the organ loft 'in person' and frequently neglected to instruct the choristers in music. Instead, at least during the week, they spent their time in private teaching through which they supplemented their inadequate income. In Hereford for example, on 9 November 1764, the chapter admonished Clack for negligence in teaching the choristers. Eighteen months later, on 24 March 1766, he received an instruction: 'to attend personally divine service every day in the week except Wednesdays and Fridays as his predecessors have done and teach the choristers of the said church three times a week a least'.[66] Clack heeded his warnings and on 14 July 1769 'it was also unanimously agreed that Mr Richard Clack organist of this church be elected one of the vicars of the College of vicars founded in the Choir of the said church in the room of Richard Waring, Clerk, late, one of the said Vicars Choral deceased'.[67] Clack was duly perpetuated a year later.[68] His membership of the college would have provided a regular income, giving him some freedom from the demands of private teaching. He remained organist for another ten years, finally attending chapter in person on 11 November 1779 to hand in his resignation.[69]

William Perry was appointed organist at the same meeting and eventually he too began to fail in his duties. Just before Christmas in 1785 the chapter 'ordered that the Chapter Clerk do give notice to the organist that if in future he neglects to instruct the choristers on the Tuesdays and Thursdays in every week he shall be mulct 2*s*. 6*d*. a time for every neglect, to be stopped out of his salary'.[70] Perry

64. HCA, 7003/1/4, p. 154, vicars choral acts, April 1758.

65. HCA, 7031/4, p. 282, chapter acts, 6 July 1754.

66. Ibid., p. 450, 24 March 1766.

67. HCA, 7031/5, p. 31, chapter acts, 14 July 1769.

68. HCA, 7003/1/4, p. 203, vicars choral acts, 26 July 1770.

69. HCA, 7031/5, p. 176, chapter acts, 11 November 1779. According to Duncumb, his burial took place later in the same year: J. Duncumb, *Collections towards the History and Antiquities of the County of Hereford* (8 vols, Hereford and London, 1804–1915), i, p. 556.

70. HCA, 7031/5, fol. 238, chapter acts, 23 December 1785.

lived through Hereford's *annus horribilis* when the west tower collapsed on Easter Monday 17 April 1786, which brought the choral services to a halt. Significantly the first mention of the disaster in the act books is not until 13 June, when the chapter was anxious that the choral services should begin again. They 'Ordered that the Church Carpenter be employed immediately to Erect a Screen at the West end of the Choir in order that the Choir Service may be renewed'. The carpenter must have worked quickly, for on 15 June the *Hereford Journal* announced, 'It is with pleasure we are authorised to say that the cathedral will be perfectly prepared for the celebration of the usual services on Sunday next'.[71]

After the work of rebuilding the nave had begun in September 1788 and winter approached, Perry's health began to decline and he was unable to perform his duties. The chapter recognised the difficulties and on 9 December 'ordered that the organist (on account of his bad state of health) be excused his attendance at choir on Wednesdays and Fridays during the winter months'.[72] Perry suffered only one winter of bad health and on 24 March 1789 the act book records: 'Mr Miles Coyle was this day appointed organist of this Cathedral in the room or place of the late Mr William Perry deceased'.[73]

In 1789, after a distinguished academic career at Oxford, John Napleton was appointed to the golden prebend by Bishop Butler.[74] Napleton believed that the choral service 'considered as a devotional entertainment was essential to a Cathedral church and likely to attract many to divine worship'.[75] He was determined to put his zeal and skill for reform to work for the music and liturgy of the cathedral. At first little succeeding, when the situation became almost intolerable he drew up new standing regulations 'respecting the Service of the Choir' which were accepted and put into practice at the audit meeting of 1800:

> Two vicars shall attend the choir at Evening Service on all Sundays and Christmas Day and one Vicar shall attend at Morning Service to assist at the altar if required by the Dean or Hebdomadary.
>
> The organist shall play a Voluntary before the Morning and Evening service on all Sundays and Christmas Day and before Morning Service on all State Holidays and Days of the Bishop's Visitation and Confirmation when the Bishop Dean Hebdomadary, or other presiding residentiary enters the Choir and on the Days of Assize when the Judges enter.
>
> The Subchanter is desired to assign on some one day in every Week the

71. Ibid., fol. 239v, 13 June 1786; *Hereford Journal*, 15 June 1786.
72. HCA, 7031/5, fol. 264, chapter acts, 9 December 1788.
73. Ibid., fol. 265, 24 March 1789.
74. See above, Chapter 5, p. 150.
75. HCA, 7003/1/5, p. 24, letter from Napleton, 30 June 1792.

Anthems for the Week ensuing; subject to such Alteration as he may afterwards think proper.

If any Member of the Church desire the use of a Music Book, he shall enter his name in a Book kept for that purpose by the Subchanter, and return it safe within a time by Him limited.

No Chorister shall leave his place during Divine Service except to distribute the Anthem Books at the usual time; or by the Direction of the Dean, Hebdomadary, or other residentiary; or of the Subchanter or the Vicar who supplies his place.[76]

Matters improved and while things were more settled the chapter 'ordered that an Augmentation of Fourteen pounds per annum be made to the Organist's Salary to continue during the Dean and chapters pleasure only'.[77] Coyle however was elderly and on 27 August 1805 the chapter 'ordered that an Advertisement be inserted in two reputable London papers signifying the vacancy of the place of Organist by the resignation of Mr Coyle'.[78] This was the first time the vacancy had been advertised in such a way and as a result the new organist came from London. Charles Dare was assistant organist at Westminster Abbey and organist to the Margaret Street Chapel. On the day of his election the chapter included an instruction that he should play between the third collect and the litany on Sunday mornings, which was the place where the Prayer Book rubric directs an anthem to be sung.[79]

The Sunday service then consisted of morning prayer followed by the litany and ante-communion, concluding with a sermon and a congregational psalm; on the first Sunday of the month, holy communion followed. Until 1811 this long service was held at 8.00 a.m. on Sundays and holy days but then the chapter decided to separate it into two parts.[80] The first service, at 8.00 a.m. in the winter and 7.00 a.m. in the summer, was sung by the full choir and finished at the third collect, without an anthem. The 'second service', as it came to be called, was at 11.00 a.m. and began with the litany. The choristers alone sang the music while the vicars went to their parochial duties.[81]

In spite of Dare's illustrious pedigree and earlier career, when he settled in Hereford his conduct as organist became notorious.[82] At the audit meeting of 1813

76. HCA, 7031/5, fos 351v–52, chapter acts, 13 November 1800; P. Barrett, 'Hereford Cathedral in the Nineteenth Century', *FHC*, 52 (1986), pp. 12–37, at 18–19.

77. HCA, 7031/6, p. 117, chapter acts, 11 November 1802.

78. Ibid., p. 151, 27 August 1805. Coyle died later the same year.

79. Ibid., p. 156, 26 November 1805.

80. P. Barrett, *Barchester: English Cathedral Life in the Nineteenth Century* (London, 1993), pp. 115ff.

81. J. S. Bumpus, *A History of English Cathedral Music, 1549–1889* (2 vols, London, [1908]), ii, pp. 374–75.

82. F. E. Gretton, *Memory's Harkback through Half-a-Century, 1808–1858* (London, 1889), p. 8.

he was ordered to be more efficient in his playing and instructing the choristers.[83] Fines were imposed in an attempt to discipline him, but Dare refused to pay and appealed to the chapter:

> The Dean and Chapter having taken into consideration the organist's application for a remission of the fine laid upon him for neglect at the last chapter – have resolved in consequence of his promise to be more attentive to his Duty in future to recall the said fine – but at the same time determine in the event of any future neglect that the organist be removed without further notice. And the Chapter ordered that no person unconnected with the duties of the organ loft be admitted therein.[84]

Dare continued to break his promises, yet still the chapter withheld their threat of dismissal and instead removed more of his stipend in an attempt to bring him to heel: 'Resolved that the augmentation of 40 pounds to the organist be withdrawn until he shall perform his Duty or provide an assistant to be approved of by the Chapter'.[85] The organist's misconduct eventually became intolerable and resulted in his dismissal on 13 November 1817. Dare died in 1820.

The chapter hoped for better times with Aaron Hayter. He came from Salisbury, where he had been a chorister and pupil under A. T. Corfe. He was appointed with unanimous enthusiasm and to some extent he managed to improve the singing and to enlarge the repertory of items used in the services, adding a setting of his own of the evening canticles in E flat. Now the famous Maria Hackett first visited Hereford. Her particular concern was that the boys should be receiving the standard of education to which she believed they were entitled by their appointment as choristers. She reported that at Hereford most of the boys' education was free, though the children had to pay fees for lessons in writing and arithmetic. These were the two subjects which according to the statutes the boys had to be taught, even if they could not enter the grammar school.[86]

Although Hayter believed that the choir had improved,[87] still the chapter regularly noticed 'a very thin Attendance of Vicars in general and a long absence of particular individuals as recorded in the Pricker's Bill: and in some few of those who so attend, a very manifest Disregard of the Duty which belongs to them of Chaunting-in-Turns'.[88] Then something went disastrously wrong. In 1820 two fires occurred

83. HCA, 7031/6, p. 145, chapter acts, 16 November 1813.
84. Ibid., p. 154, 10 November 1814.
85. Ibid., p. 201, 14 January 1817.
86. [M. Hackett], *A Brief Account of Cathedral and Collegiate Schools, with an Abstract of their Statutes and Endowments* (London, 1824),

pp. 34–35.
87. HCA, 5979, Hayter's letter to the chapter, 24 May 1820.
88. HCA, 7031/18, p. 147, chapter acts, 11 November 1819. 'Chaunting-in-turns' is the custom of antiphonal singing which requires not less than six adult singers.

in the college, and somehow in the second, on Easter Sunday, Hayter was implicated. Whether or not he deserved any blame, the chapter had to decide if he should continue. He wrote a long and pleading letter humbly asking for their 'patient and humane Consideration'.[89] After two adjournments, the meeting took place on 26 June and an answer was delivered: 'The Chapter Clerk is directed to inform Mr Hayter that after mature deliberation the Dean and Chapter have no further occasion for his Services as organist of the Cathedral and as Teacher of the Choristers there – and also to pay him his Salary to midsummer'.[90]

Following a series of unsuccessful organists, in an attempt to rescue the situation, the chapter chose a distinguished, widely known and highly respected professional musician to be organist. John Clarke-Whitfeld was fifty years old with a long experience of cathedral music. Noticeably no complaints were lodged against him by act and when his health declined in old age he retained the full support and goodwill of both the chapter and the vicars. The number of choristers had remained the same since Elizabethan times and the chapter warned Clarke-Whitfeld of 'the neglected state of the Choristers with respect to their choral Qualifications'.[91] In November 1821 one of the residentiaries, Dr George Cope, left money to the cathedral in his will to provide an eighth chorister. A month afterwards 'Charles Woodward son of John Woodward aged eleven years was elected the Eighth Chorister – such election to be considered as taking place from Christmas next'.[92]

Only a handful of settings and anthems were being used in the services at some cathedrals.[93] Clarke-Whitfeld's first task was to enlarge the choir's repertory. To improve the choral services, he needed a balanced choir with an equal number of voices to the parts. A letter from the chapter clerk to the college dated 13 November 1823 asks that 'as the vicars are now twelve in numbers, an equal number of counter-tenors, tenors and basses be on each side of the choir and that their attendance on Sunday evenings be more numerous'.[94] Clarke-Whitfeld was an accepted composer as well as an organist,[95] and he wrote a complete *Service in C* for the cathedral which shows the sections of the liturgy which were sung in a choral service: *Te deum, Jubilate, Kyrie eleison, Sanctus, Nicene Creed* (in that order), *Magnificat, Nunc dimittis*. His *Service in E flat*, written between 19 May and 5 June 1826, is evidence that he enjoyed a happy relationship with his singers: 'This morning and evening service is Inscribed to his kind Friends the Custos and Vicars of the College, Hereford by J. Clarke-Whitfeld'. He also

89. HCA, 5979.

90. HCA, 7031/18, p. 153, chapter acts, 26 June 1820.

91. Ibid., p. 170, 10 April 1821.

92. Ibid., p. 184, 9 November 1821.

93. B. Rainbow, *The Choral Revival in the Anglican Church, 1839–1872* (Oxford, 1970), p. 244.

94. HCA, 5643.

95. To commemorate this fact, a new piece, the Clarke-Whitfeld commission, is performed during the Three Choirs Festival each year it is held in Hereford.

wrote three settings of the communion service for two treble voices 'to meet an emergency' when the vicars were absent.[96]

Clarke-Whitfeld remained popular, but poor health dogged him almost constantly until it seriously undermined his work. In his later years the choral services went from bad to disgraceful. The election of choristers became more frequent, suggesting that boys either withdrew or were withdrawn by their parents from the choir. Discipline among the boys began to break down and the attendance of the vicars almost collapsed altogether. At the beginning of 1832, in a final effort to restore the college to some sort of order, the chapter sent a notice to the custos containing details of members' attendance over the past eight years with the message:

> The Dean and Chapter desire to call the attention of the Custos and Vicars to the enclosed account of their attendance on their choral Duties. They will perceive how greatly their attendance has been diminished for some time past and the Dean and Chapter trust that it will not be again necessary to bring this subject to the Notice of the Custos and Vicars.[97]

A gathering storm broke with unexpected ferocity on the cathedral's musicians when John Merewether, chaplain to William IV, was appointed dean.[98] Clarke-Whitfeld's ill health finally defeated him on the day of Merewether's installation when, because of an attack of paralysis, a resolution was taken at chapter:

> In consequence of the long and increasing deterioration in the choral services of the Cathedral proceeding as they are aware from Dr Whitfeld's infirm state of health which has for a long period experienced the forbearance of the Chapter, the Dean and Chapter now feel it to be their indispensable duty to communicate their decision that the office of organist will be vacant at Mid-summer next. Should it be a matter of convenience to Dr Whitfeld to be relieved from his responsibility at any earlier period the Dean and Chapter will be ready to concur in any suitable arrangement.[99]

Many were saddened by the decision and some wrote in support of Clarke-Whitfeld, but the chapter was firm and therefore among his first tasks Merewether had to find a new organist. This took him less than a month and, although the new dean was not himself present at the meeting, on 10 July:

> Mr Wesley the organist of Hampton Church near London was elected to

96. HCL, Music MSS C.9.13, pp. 1–6; 30.B.3, pp. 186, 202–13.
97. HCA, 7031/18, p. 337, chapter acts, 14 February 1832.
98. P. Barrett, 'John Merewether, Dean of

Hereford, 1832–50', *FHC*, 43 (1977), pp. 23–39.
99. HCA, 7031/18, pp. 355–56, chapter acts, 16 June 1832.

succeed Dr Whitfeld as Organist of this Cathedral on a Salary of Fifty two pounds (and eight pounds paid by the Custos and Vicars) and the addition of Forty pounds to take place after the decease of Dr Whitfeld.[100]

Samuel Sebastian Wesley was only twenty-one years of age, the son of Samuel Wesley the composer and grandson of Charles Wesley the evangelist and hymn writer (fig. 121). As a boy he had been a chorister of the Chapel Royal and at Brighton attracted the attention and favours of George IV. Wesley was already known to Merewether through their mutual association with both Hampton and the royal court. Like his predecessors, Wesley discovered immediately how much he needed to supplement his income by private teaching, an occupation he disliked and felt was unworthy of a cathedral organist. At the time the cathedral organ was in the hands of the builders and Wesley was unable to take up his post until November. Once the organ was in use, the dean supported Wesley as he attempted to raise the standard of the choral music. After his first Easter services, knowing the vicars were generally absent in their parishes on Sunday mornings, Merewether took advantage of the statutes: to ensure the attendance of at least two adult singers he appointed Edward Jones and Richard Barrett, two

Fig. 121. Samuel Sebastian Wesley, organist 1832–35: portrait *c.* 1835, attributed to the circle of John Jackson.

lay singing men from Hampton, to be 'Deacons to take part in the Musical Services of the Choir on Sundays, festivals, State Days and at the Audit on the Morning and Evening Services of those days'.[101]

Events the following Easter Day, 30 March 1834, produced a scandal which became the final provocation of Merewether's wrath, wanting as he did to transform the cathedral's ill-disciplined choir into an efficient one. There is a

100. Ibid., p. 365, 10 July 1832. Much to his irritation, Wesley never did receive his full stipend of £100 per year, since Clarke-Whitfeld lived at Holmer until his death in 1836, aged sixty-five, after Wesley had gone to Exeter.

101. HCA, 7031/18, p. 404, chapter acts, 7 June 1833.

record of the chapter meeting on 21 April which indicates something of what had happened:

> The Chapter Clerk is directed by The Dean and Chapter to express their surprize at Mr Jones having taken no notice of the Dean's message to him requiring his attendance as Deacon at the Cathedral on Easter Sunday and to inform Mr Jones that his attendance will be required to be regular and that in case of any neglect in his attendance the Dean and Chapter will thereupon declare his situation void and proceed to elect a successor.[102]

Wesley had rescued the difficulties on Easter Sunday 1834 by writing an anthem which became both famous and popular, *Blessed be the God and Father*, although looking back on it Wesley said, 'I assure you I view it merely as a sort of showy sketch, or a little thing just made to stop a gap, and never meant for publication'.[103] A summer of hot dispute followed. When no vicars attended evensong on 19 July, Merewether fined them 2s. 6d. each. Then he tackled the succentor who had been absent for three weeks. Merewether received the reply that it had never been the custom for a member of the college to ask permission from the dean and chapter to be absent. The dean could not accept this presumption and stated forcefully that harmony in the cathedral would only be achieved if all members performed their duties diligently. The clear instructions he gave about how the choral services should be performed reveal how far the music had collapsed. In the mornings, on litany days (Sundays, Wednesdays and Fridays), the canticles were to be sung to a proper setting and not a chant. In the evening the canticles had to be sung to a setting and the anthem never omitted, and Merewether added, 'The Dean further directs the attention of the Succentor to the propriety of setting whole anthems and not parts of anthems [and] of not changing them when once set'. Only on Tuesdays, when a sermon was preached, could the anthem be omitted.[104]

The quarrel between the dean and the succentor continued unabated through the autumn. Merewether charged him with a 'rude and unbecoming manner' and

---

102. Ibid., p. 427, 21 April 1834.
103. *Musical Times*, 36 (1895), p. 407. This suggests that Wesley wrote it quickly (after the morning service perhaps, at which there would have been no anthem), once he suspected that Jones and Barrett would not be present at the afternoon service when an anthem was required. It was written for the choristers and a single bass, usually believed to have been Merewether's butler. Since choirs were expected to sing anthems at sight, Wesley's anthem may well indicate the standard of sight-reading which was usual at the time.

104. HCA, 7031/18, p. 441, chapter acts, 9 August 1834; pp. 454–55, 465, letters of 30 July and 6 August 1834. To make sure an anthem was performed regularly, Merewether provided a notice board for the door of the pulpitum on which the succentor was instructed to display a fortnightly music list.

said he had seen him 'loitering at a distance from his brethren and not going into choir till they had taken their places', which he regarded as 'a premeditated defiance of authority and obstinate contumacy'. In December Merewether, having continued to fine the vicars for their absences, wrote to each one demanding he observe the statutes strictly. He also wrote to the parents of the choristers requiring them to inform him if their boy was ill at any time.[105]

The never-ending dispute between the dean and the singers could not have helped Wesley's natural tendency to depression and a move from Hereford would have been a relief. Early in 1835 Wesley applied for the post of organist at St George's Chapel, Windsor. Disappointingly Elvey, an even younger man than he, was preferred and appointed. On 4 May, however, a happy event took place, though not without its own particular hazards: Wesley married Marianne Merewether, the dean's sister. Wesley had known Merewether for some time before coming to Hereford and it is entirely possible that he already knew the dean's sister. Several unanswered questions about the marriage provide something of a puzzle. The ceremony was not held in the cathedral as might have been expected but instead at Ewyas Harold, a parish church then in the diocese of St David's and outside the jurisdiction of the bishop of Hereford, which suggests the bride and groom feared it might have been prohibited. The witnesses who signed the church register were the vicar's son, William Bowen junior, and John Parry, which indicates the wedding was kept secret. Neither the dean, his two brothers (Henry and Francis), nor the bride's father (who was still alive until 1847) attended the service, which makes it clear her family did not support the marriage.

Marianne was Merewether's only sister, eleven years younger than he was and the youngest member of the family. She was marrying a man three years younger than herself, and a musician (still not entirely a respectable profession). In spite of Wesley's distinguished family pedigree, almost certainly Merewether believed his own family to be more distinguished. Wesley was recognised as a brilliant and promising man but he was known to suffer from severe depression. He was the natural son of 'old' Samuel Wesley, who had had a terrible accident which had left him with permanent brain damage. While Wesley's father was respected and well known as a highly original and able composer, he had converted to Roman Catholicism. All this makes Merewether's anxious protection of his sister understandable and explains his anger when she refused it. Happily, though, we know the couple enjoyed a long-lasting and happy marriage. Merewether subsequently baptised his nephew, Francis Gwynne, at Exeter in February 1841. Clearly any breach he had with the couple was not permanent.

---

105. HCA, 7031/18, pp. 467, 478–80, letters of 16 and 27 October and 1 December 1834.

Wesley's desire to move away from a troubled cathedral community was fulfilled when he was appointed organist at Exeter early in September. He sent his letter of resignation to the chapter and did not wait long before leaving. On 22 September, at a special meeting of the chapter, the Hebdomadary reported that 'the organ was not played on Saturday evening, the whole of Sunday and on Monday morning last'. Then 'Mills the organ player, was sent for to the Chapter and engaged at One Guinea per week to play the organ from michaelmas to the time when a new organist shall be appointed and in attendance to take to his Duty'.[106]

Having left, Wesley would not let financial matters rest. He engaged an attorney to write to the chapter claiming that his stipend ought to have been £100 a year besides 'a place of abode', whereas, because he had had to contribute to Clarke-Whitfeld's pension, he had only been paid £52, and from that he had paid £30 for lodgings each year. Wesley's sense of injustice sounds reasonable, but the chapter stuck to its written contract and in their reply made it clear that they would not accept any further correspondence on the matter.

The new organist, chosen from seven applicants, arrived before November. John Hunt came from Lichfield where has was a lay vicar. Merewether continued his struggle to make the choir 'efficient', a word fashionable among those pledged to reform in the Church of England. When Merewether used it, his first and major concern was to secure the numerical strength of the choir. In 1840 the Cathedrals Act seriously threatened the future of the cathedral's music. The college was to be reduced by half, not by dismissing its members but by not filling vacancies as they occurred.[107] The cathedral seemed to some to be falling about their ears, since at much the same time Merewether began his vast enterprise of restoring the fabric. The cathedral was closed from August 1841 until April 1850 and the choral services took place first in college hall, then in the college chapel and after 1844 in All Saints church.

John Hunt was the victim of a tragic accident in 1842. On 17 November on his way home after the annual audit dinner he fell over a trolley filled with glass and crockery, which had been left in a dark corner of the college quadrangle, and died. Hunt's nephew, James, who was a chorister, was so shocked that he too collapsed and died three days later.

The post of organist was becoming more prestigious and sought after among professional musicians. George Townshend Smith was selected from forty-two candidates and arrived in time to support Merewether in his radical reform of the choir (fig. 122). When the services moved to All Saints church, the cathedral

106. HCA, 7031/19, p. 32, chapter acts, 22 September 1835.
107. O. Chadwick, *The Victorian Church* (2 vols, London, 1966–70), i, pp. 137–38.

statutes no longer applied and both dean and organist seized the opportunity to appoint a group of lay singers for the daily services. This was entirely satisfactory for the time being but, looking ahead to the time when the cathedral would reopen, Merewether knew that if the choral services were to survive he would have to tackle the decline in the number of vicars, imposed by parliament. When the Cathedrals Act had taken its full toll there would be only six adult singers left. Given the disastrous record of attendance among the vicars, he could see that there would not be enough people in the stalls to sing the parts in the choral services. Merewether formulated a plan to save the choir and presented it first to the college, then to the residentiaries and prebendaries, and finally to the bishop. At the midsummer chapter of 1846, 'The dean called the

Fig. 122. George Townshend Smith, organist 1843–77: tinted photograph by T. E. Seed, 1875, in the song school.

attention of the Chapter to the present very inefficient state of the Choir, and to the necessity of making such permanent arrangements with the College as would ensure the due and effective celebration of the Choral Service for the future'.[108]

Merewether had always hoped to set a choir of lay clerks in place. Although he did not live to see his plan fulfilled, he took the first steps towards it. In October 1846 he dismissed the deacons from the college and began to grasp the difficulty of how to finance the singers. The commissioners were appropriating any income they could to build new churches. Merewether believed he would have to 'resort to Parliament' if his reforms were to be effective. He sent a long statement to the Ecclesiastical Commissioners claiming that the cathedral needed to retain the income from the college, however many members it admitted in the future, in order to provide for the musicians employed in the choral services:

The efficiency of the Choir of Hereford Cathedral being crippled by the operation of the Ecclesiastical Commission Acts 3 & 4 Vict. c. 113 & 45 & 93 and the Age of the members in general being such as to render it improbable that the Service in the Cathedral can be duly performed even now much less

108. HCA, 7031/20, p. 75, chapter acts, 25 June 1846.

when the Cathedral shall be completed, It is the wish of the Chapter to record their opinion that it is necessary to present the same to the Bishop of the Diocese as Visitor of the Cathedral Church with a view to initiate proceedings which may secure and preserve to this Cathedral the whole Proceeds of the College which is the Endowment of the Choral Services of this Church and at once effect such requisite Provision and Reparation that the Cathedral when finished may not be destitute of such adequate Service as such an Endowment and Establishment imperatively demand.[109]

Merewether's concern for the choir was distracted for a time while he opposed the appointment of Bishop Hampden in 1848. After an unsuccessful battle with the prime minister, his previous imperative returned. Boldly but imprudently, and regardless of the 1840 legislation, in 1849 he declared five vacancies in the college, advertised the posts and on 28 September brought the candidates to Hereford for interview. The college resolutely (and rightly) refused to admit any new members even if the dean appointed them. Quickly Merewether had to reconsider his plan. The men were sent home with their expenses paid and a promise to pay future expenses when they were summoned again after the difficulties had been sorted out. Sadly Merewether was able to make no further moves in his strategy because his health collapsed and he died at his vicarage at Madley on Thursday 4 April 1850 'after a severe and painful illness'. The dean's funeral was held on 9 April. Although not yet fully restored, the cathedral was full for the service.

At midsummer, Tuesday 25 June, Dean Richard Dawes was installed. He continued Merewether's efforts to reform the choir and in time for his first Easter, 20 April 1851, he appointed the first lay clerks. The choir had been rescued and the *Hereford Journal* reported:

> We understand that the gentlemen recently appointed lay vicars of our cathedral, whose effective services on Sunday week (Assize Sunday) were so much admired and enjoyed by the very large congregation assembled within the walls of the sacred fabric, will enter upon the regular performance of their duties on Easter Sunday.[110]

Everyone noticed the improvement in the standard of performance at the cathedral services. There was a weekly practice on Saturday afternoons after evensong. From May 1851, details of the music sung in the cathedral services were published each week in the local papers and the earliest music list to survive is dated 11–24 August 1851 (fig. 123). Signed by Edward Howells, subchanter, among the services listed are *Aldrich in A & G*, *Patrick in G*, *Travers in D*, *Gibbons in F*, *King in D*, *Dare*

109. Ibid., pp. 83–84, 12–14 November 1846.   110. *Hereford Journal*, 2 April 1851.

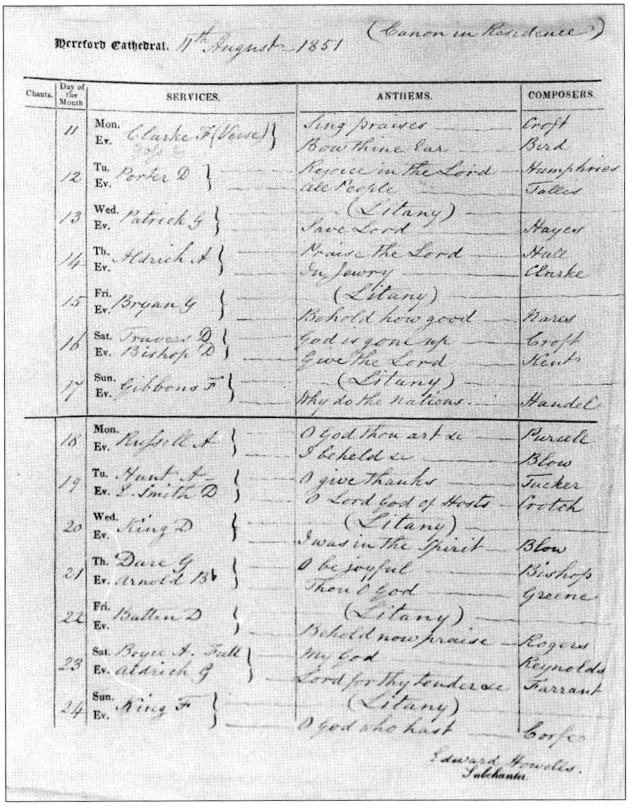

Hereford Cathedral. 11th August 1851 (Canon in Residence)

Chants.	Day of the Month	SERVICES.	ANTHEMS.	COMPOSERS.
	11	Mon. Ev. Clarke F (Verse)	Sing praises	Croft
			Bow thine ear	Bird
	12	Tu. Ev. Porter D	Rejoice in the Lord	Humphries
			all People	Talles
	13	Wed. Ev. Patrick G	(Litany)	
			Save Lord	Hayes
	14	Th. Ev. Aldrich A	Praise the Lord	Hall
			In Jewry	Clarke
	15	Fri. Ev. Bryan G	(Litany)	
			Behold how good	Nares
	16	Sat. Travers D	God is gone up	Croft
		Ev. Bishop D	Give the Lord	Kent
	17	Sun. Ev. Gibbons F	(Litany)	
			Why do the nations	Handel
	18	Mon. Ev. Russell A	O God thou art &c	Purcell
			I beheld &c	Blow
	19	Tu. Hunt A	O give thanks	Tucker
		Ev. S. Smith D	O Lord God of Hosts	Crotch
	20	Wed. Ev. King D	(Litany)	
			I was in the Spirit	Blow
	21	Th. Dare G	O be joyful	Bishops
		Ev. Arnold B♭	Thou O God	Greene
	22	Fri. Ev. Batten D	(Litany)	
			Behold now praise	Rogers
	23	Sat. Boyce A. Full	My God	Reynolds
		Ev. Aldrich G	Lord for thy tender &c	Farrant
	24	Sun. Ev. King F	(Litany)	
			O God who hast	Corfe

Edward Howells.
Subchanter

Fig. 123. The earliest surviving music scheme, 1851. (HCA, RS 6/DP/1/1/1.)

in G, Batten in D and *Arnold in B flat*, with anthems by Croft, Humphries, Henry Hall, Purcell, Blow and Greene. The times of the services on Sundays were changed, partly at the request of the city who wanted the whole service at 11.00 a.m. 'to ensure a large congregation of the inhabitants'. The evening service was changed from 5.00 p.m. to 3.00 p.m.[111]

A new problem began to emerge which would cause a good deal of trouble in a few years time. Choristers were being taken away from the choir before their voices broke. Becoming a chorister not only offered a free education but also, more importantly at this period, when a boy stopped singing it provided a valuable apprenticeship fee from the Tomson Charity. Parents used the opportunity to secure a future for their children, in some cases the sooner the better. The chapter made a strict rule that no chorister should leave the choir before his voice had broken:

> An application from the father of Frederick Rock for the usual apprentice Fee on his withdrawing his son at this time from the Choir was declined on the

111. HCA, RS 6/DP/1/1/1. After 1863 the time of the evening service was changed back to 5.00 p.m. to accommodate the parish evening service held at 3.30 p.m. in the Lady chapel.

ground that the Dean and Chapter consider the removal of choristers just at the time they are becoming useful very inconvenient and also unfair towards the Organist.[112]

In February 1855 the death of the precentor, Thomas Huntingford, created the first vacancy among the residentiaries since the Cathedrals Act 1840, which had laid down a reduction in the number of residentiaries. The vacancy therefore was due not to be filled. Bishop Hampden believed it was important to preserve the appointment of precentor and have it 'worthily embodied in some living Person'. Also he knew the right man for the post: someone who would be as dedicated to developing the highest standards of music in the liturgy as Merewether had been. Hampden wrote to Sir Frederick Arthur Gore Ouseley on 1 March 1855 inviting him to become precentor. The bishop approved of Ouseley's scheme for a college at Tenbury and liked the man. In his letter he explained that the Ecclesiastical Commissioners had appropriated the revenues of the canonry. Nevertheless, Ouseley accepted and was installed to 'the Dignity and Office of Precentor' on 5 June 1855 but without being appointed a residentiary and almost certainly without a stipend. Hampden made sure that Ouseley was, however, assigned 'the stall in the Choir and place and voice in the Chapter to the said Precentorship belonging', specifically stating so in his mandate to the chapter (fig. 124).[113]

Through Merewether's determination and Townshend Smith's hard work, the choir at Hereford was rather better than some other cathedral choirs. Ouseley entered into 'a goodly heritage'. In July 1857 he made his initial report about the choir to the chapter. The choristers, he said, were not up to the required standard for a cathedral choral service and he recommended that one person (he preferred a clergyman) should be put in charge of them, both in the cathedral and in the school, and that they should board in his house so that he would have the complete moral, religious and musical oversight of the boys. Ouseley wanted their education to achieve three things: to 'improve' their local accents for the purposes of singing; to help them understand the psalms better; and to give them a sufficient grasp of the rudiments of music to make them good sight-readers.

Townshend Smith tried to implement these principles but he faced a difficult situation because still too often the boys were taken away from the choir by their parents before their voices broke, in order to obtain the valuable apprentice fee as early as possible. The organist reported to the chapter in 1859 that:

boy after boy has left long before the loss of voice; in the present year the

---

112. HCA, 7031/20, p. 337, chapter acts, 24 March 1855.
113. Ibid., p. 339, 5 June 1855.

Fig. 124. Sir Frederick Arthur Gore Ouseley, precentor 1855–89.

two Seniors thus quitting have made it very difficult to provide for the service although I have practised them almost daily and with the Lay Clerks on Saturday and at the Choral Society on Wednesday.[114]

In the middle of the nineteenth century many cathedral organists began to complain that their choirs were too small. Generally it was agreed that there were insufficient singing men to safeguard against illness. Nor were the resources adequate to perform music for double choir which had always been a strong feature of English cathedral music, or to sing the psalms antiphonally.[115] Townshend Smith wanted to recruit additional singers, especially on Sundays. He told the chapter:

My suggestion as to the Choir is to allow six of the most respectable members of the Choral Society giving preference to old Choristers to attend on Sundays; to provide them with Surplices, to let them occupy the Seats where the Vicars

114. Ibid., pp. 479–80, Townshend Smith's report, 10 November 1859; HCA, 7003/1/6, pp. 148–152, Ouseley's report, 21 July 1857.

115. P. Barrett, 'English Cathedral Choirs in the Nineteenth Century', *Journal of Ecclesiastical History*, 25 (1974), pp. 15–37, at 15–16.

sit, the latter would find due accommodation in the same Row as the Capitular Members and I think the Congregation would hear the Minor Canons better than at present.[116]

In 1863 the cathedral was fully restored, including Scott's refitting of the choir with its new screen (fig. 138). The cathedral was back in full use, but life in a cathedral community never stays settled for long. Dissension between the college and the chapter became acrimonious and unpleasant. Members of the college had never fully accepted the lay clerks and in 1865 three of the vicars (John Goss,[117] Francis Havergal and George Custance) wrote a long and testy letter to the chapter with which they tried to force the chapter's hand to remove the lay singers, threatening to make its contents public if it was ignored. They stated (without acknowledging that it was only their opinion) that both the lay clerks and the boys were inadequate singers. Goss had implanted in his colleagues' minds the mistaken notion that the choir was the responsibility of the college and came under their direct control because the largest share of the costs of the music came out of their income. He wanted to see the lay clerks dismissed, vicars reappointed in their place and the corporate life of the college revived after the reductions imposed by the Cathedrals Act. At first the chapter resisted. They knew only too well how much improvement to the services the lay clerks had brought. Dean Dawes died in 1867 and Dean Herbert was installed on 23 May, inheriting the task of establishing harmony between the chapter and the college.[118]

A small committee was set up under the chairmanship of Ouseley to hold an official visitation of the college and to find a way forward. Unfortunately, the chapter made a misjudgement and in an attempt to be conciliatory they proposed a compromise. Two assistant vicars were appointed in 1867 and in the following year three of the lay clerks were dismissed. There had never been 'assistant' vicars in the history of the college and the only advantage to the choir was a modest one. John Taylor, one of the new assistant vicars, and his wife took chorister boarders into their home in Castle Street, which fulfilled one of Ouseley's original suggestions. Next the college tried the tactic of 'he who pays the piper calls the tune' and 'informed' the chapter that they would no longer pay the lay clerks' stipends. The situation went from bad to worse and in May 1870 Herbert wrote a long letter to the custos, basing his remarks on earlier correspondence

116. HCA, 7031/20, p. 480, 10 November 1859.

117. Goss had been one of the applicants for the post of vicar choral in September 1849 while Merewether was still alive. Without being appointed, he stayed in Hereford and sang at Dawes's installation, although he was not admitted to the college until 24 March 1853. He was custos from 1873 until his death in 1877.

118. HCA, 7031/21, pp. 224–28, letter dated 1 November 1865, chapter acts, 7 November 1865; pp. 279–80, 23 May 1867, installation of Dean Herbert.

between Merewether and the college which had set out the basic financial agreement between the chapter and the college whereby the choir was paid for out of college income. He added the hope that a new scheme would 'place the assistants of the College in a position of security, remove all existing abuses, promote unity in the College itself, secure harmony in the relations of the College with the Chapter, and render permanently efficient the Cathedral Choir'.[119]

Earlier Ouseley had introduced a procession into and out of the stalls at each service while an organ voluntary was played. This became another source of dissension between the college and the chapter because it raised the trivial but delicate question of precedence. The members of the college were prepared to sit and walk in procession with the boys and singing men when they were on duty, but they believed they had the right to sit in the prebendal stalls and walk with the senior clergy when they were not on singing duty. The chapter resolutely refused to accept this and on one occasion the dean spoke loudly and in public to a member of the college telling him to go to his place in procession with the singing men. For a week stormy letters were exchanged demanding an apology. The vicars threatened not to walk in procession at all but to return to the traditional custom of assembling in the stalls informally. The dispute led to the publication of a new set of bye laws for the conduct of worship in 1874.[120]

Gradually through the nineteenth century greater respect was paid to the profession of organist. His work as performer was more widely recognised, primarily through the pioneering of Wesley and Ouseley, both of whom were accepted as outstanding players, especially in the art of improvisation, but the man's task as master of choristers was still regarded as a fairly menial one. During 1874 there were only two lay clerks left, an alto who had been appointed in 1851 and whose voice had gone, and another who then left for Peterborough (perhaps because of the constant trouble with the college). The chapter was determined to appoint again a full complement of clerks and by 1877, in spite of the college, the necessary six AATTBB were in post.

Townshend Smith died suddenly and unexpectedly on 3 August 1877. When his successor, Langdon Colborne (fig. 125), arrived the choir consisted of eight choristers and four probationers, six lay clerks, six vicars choral and four assistant vicars. The succentor, John Taylor, was still in charge of the choir and chose the music for the services. Colborne and Taylor worked well together and with a little too much enthusiasm. The chapter

Resolved that it is desirable that the Musick selected for the *Te Deum, Benedictus*

119. HCA, 7003/1/6, p. 301, printed letter of 31 May 1870, p. 5.
120. HCA, 7031/22, pp. 98–99, chapter acts, 4 July 1874.

and Nicene Creed on Sundays should be of a shorter and less elaborate nature than lately used, and that when Tallis' Litany be used upon Sundays it should only be to the end of the Lord's Prayer, and that this resolution be communicated to the Succentor.[121]

Colborne quickly found both the attendance and the behaviour of the vicars unacceptable. Three of them began to dispute the tempi chosen by the organist and relayed by the succentor and even to argue in choir practices. In the end, Ouseley's authority was needed to sort out the trouble. Colborne faced problems with the boys as well. The succentor and the organist wanted the number of probationers to be increased and the chapter agreed to appoint four more, intending that Colborne should have eight choristers and eight probationers.[122]

Choristers always have to divide their time between cathedral and school. In April 1883 the headmaster sent a proposal to the chapter recommending that the boys should receive four whole days and two half days teaching at school a

Fig. 125. Langdon Colborne, organist 1877–89: photograph in the song school.

week: 'the School hours for the Choristers should be from 11.0 a.m. to 1.0 p.m. upon four days and from 2.0 to 4.30 p.m. on the same days and on the other two days in each week from 11.0 a.m. to 1.0 p.m. which hours were approved'.[123] This necessitated another change in the times of services, and evensong on weekdays was moved from 4.00 p.m. to 5.00 p.m. This proved unacceptable and soon a compromise was reached and evensong was sung at 4.30 p.m.

Colborne's love of oratorio led to a new venture at Christmas 1883 which immediately became very popular and an annual event: 'On Christmas Eve at the afternoon service a selection from Bach's *Christmas Oratorio*, and on Christmas Day a selection from Handel's *Messiah*, was given in place of the anthem'. Dean Herbert introduced special evening services with sermons on Thursdays during Advent and Lent and also each evening in Holy Week (except Easter Eve). Also 'on Good

121. Ibid., p. 248, 12 June 1878.   123. Ibid., p. 416, 28 April 1883.
122. Ibid., p. 328, 11 November 1880.

Friday Evening, after the Sermon, the later part of the Commination Service' was chanted. From 1886 there was a further development: 'On Easter Eve at the Evening Service at 4.30 p.m. the anthem consisted of a selection from Handel's Oratorio *The Messiah*' (sic).

The death of John Jebb,[124] early in 1886, left a vacancy among the residentiaries which was filled by Ouseley on 9 February 1886.[125] For three years Ouseley played his full part as a residentiary, taking his three months' residence during the long vacation in July, August and September. He was elected the cathedral's proctor in Convocation, and took on the regular chapter duty of junior claviger in 1886 and master of the fabric in 1887.

For some years there had been problems with both the quality of the men's voices and the balance between the parts. Great effort had been made to ensure there were sufficient singers to each part with not too many basses. By the time Ouseley took up residence in Hereford and had moved into one of the canonical houses in the Close, the choir was singing at its best. Ouseley's cast of mind was conservative, antiquarian and medievalist and yet, like many Victorians who bent their energies to preserve and establish continuity, he made many far-reaching and now long-established changes: he increased the number of choristers by bringing in probationers, introduced the wearing of cassocks and surplices, processions into and out of the stalls and organ voluntaries, a vestry prayer before and after the service, boarding choristers, an efficient system of education with a definite and hard-working timetable at school, choral celebrations of holy communion weekly and on saints' days, a rudimentary choir benevolent fund at least to help in cases of sickness and the beginnings of a pension fund for the lay clerks. It was also during Ouseley's time that the first choir outings for the boys took place. In chapter on one occasion 'a letter from the Succentor was read in which he asked for the usual "outing" for the Choristers on June 6th under his charge, which was granted'.[126]

Ouseley attended chapter meetings regularly and he was present in the morning on 6 April 1889, the day of his death, which was the day before Passion Sunday. Ouseley died suddenly in the afternoon, aged sixty-three. Previously he had complained of not feeling well but there were no advance signs of his collapse and he had arranged a voice trial of candidates for a probationer place on 9 April

124. Jebb had been prebendary (1858), praelector (1863), residentiary and chancellor (1878). Although more pedantic and unimaginative than Ouseley, he was his considerable ally in the development of the cathedral's music and liturgy: P. M. Young, 'Dr Jebb of Peterstow, 1805–1886', *Three Choirs Festival Programme* (Hereford, 1997), pp. 27–30.

125. It was said by popular acclaim in the diocese; other candidates who were offered the post refused it to make room for Ouseley.

126. HCA, 7031/23, p. 56, chapter acts, 24 May 1888.

at 1.00 p.m. The lay clerks and choristers attended Ouseley's funeral at Tenbury and £3 3s. 0d. was paid to the succentor 'towards the expense of Conveyances for Lay Vicars and Choristers to the funeral of Canon Ouseley'. Later the same year, on 16 September, Langdon Colborne died the day after his fifty-fourth birthday and an era came to an end.[127]

Ouseley's influence on the cathedral's music continued after his death since the new precentor was John Hampton, who had followed Ouseley as warden of St Michael's, and the new organist was one of their pupils at the college, George Robertson Sinclair (figs 139, 112). Although Sinclair was only twenty-six years old, he had already been organist of Truro cathedral for nine years, Ouseley having recommended him to Bishop Benson when he was looking for his first organist for the new cathedral. In appointing him the forward-looking chapter had deliberately sought and found a candidate who would combine three roles in a professional organist which are now taken for granted: performer, choirmaster, and choral and orchestral conductor. More than fifty candidates applied.[128] The college clung to the view that he was paid, largely by themselves, to deliver whatever they wanted. They believed the precentor and succentor (appointed by him from among their own members) still had full control of the choir and the music, which gave them a definite ascendancy over the chapter in the matter. Inevitably the two views led to conflict. An older tradition faced a new one.

When Sinclair arrived in the autumn of 1889, the choir consisted of eight choristers, four probationers and seven lay clerks. There were five vicars in the college. Sinclair brought his own assistant organist with him, Ivor Atkins (his articled pupil) and a new chorister, Alfred Thomas. The times of service were: weekday morning and evening prayer at 10.00 a.m. and 4.30 p.m. and the Sunday services, choral matins and holy communion (fully choral once a month) at 11.00 a.m., the litany at 3.00 p.m. (usually said) and choral evensong and sermon at 6.30 p.m. At Sinclair's first Christmas in 1889, on Christmas Eve he continued the custom at evensong of singing music from Bach's *Christmas Oratorio* instead of an anthem but, fresh from Truro with its service of nine lessons and carols, he added nine carols, including *O Come All Ye Faithful* sung by the whole congregation.

Sinclair's first years were happy ones, but 1892 saw the beginning of more troubles with the college.[129] At first the dispute was internal, but then, claiming

---

127. Ibid., pp. 78, 91, 2 May and 14 October 1889.
128. Among the candidates, one other was nearly appointed: 'The Dean and Chapter cannot in making this appointment help recording their special sense of the very high merit possessed by Mr Brewer, the present organist of St Michael's Coventry', HCA, 7031/23, p. 92, chapter acts, 17 October 1889. Brewer was appointed to Gloucester in 1897.
129. See below, Chapter 23, pp. 458–59.

they were victims of 'a diminished and diminishing income', the college again proposed to stop payments to the lay clerks. The chapter could never accept this and had to insist that the college was still responsible for 'the full performance of the Choral Services'.[130] Not until 1894, when a new tenor lay clerk was appointed from St Albans, did the matter rest. There were also difficulties over the discipline of the choristers. In Truro, Sinclair had undoubtedly forged his own rules, but in Hereford he had to live with a long-standing tradition and the cathedral statutes. They laid down that the succentor was responsible for the behaviour of the boys in the cathedral during services. Sinclair believed it was his responsibility as master of the choristers. A sub-committee was set up to resolve the matter and it had to accept that the statutes were clear. Sinclair's only responsibility was 'the general discipline of the Choristers outside the cathedral'.[131]

Another disagreement arose with the development of choir holidays. Until the beginning of the twentieth century the daily routine of choral services continued throughout the year and absences were fined. Therefore any holiday the singers took (which clearly they did from time to time) had 'to be paid for'. In March 1895 the chapter agreed to give the boys a weekly half holiday on Wednesdays and in 1903 they gave the whole choir three weeks holiday in the summer. The same thing happened in 1904, but this time the college expressed its strong disapproval, restating the argument that because largely they paid for the music it should not cease without their agreement. The organist and the chapter did not give in.[132]

In 1907 the succentor, John Taylor, died and the chapter grasped the opportunity to remove the problems between the organist and the succentor. In a shrewd and unexpected move they appointed Sinclair succentor. This took the college completely by surprise and Duncombe, the custos, dismissed it as 'a mischievous anomaly'. The college made great efforts to reverse the chapter's decision, not all of whom were unanimous in a strategy which seems to have originated with Canon Capes and Archdeacon Oldham, but again the chapter refused to give in and Sinclair's work flourished.[133]

Sinclair arranged special festival services in 1910 to celebrate the centenary of Wesley's birth. He also raised funds to put in memorial windows to both Wesley and Ouseley. In the last year of peace he managed to arrange with the chapter to provide a new song room. He had been holding practices at his house in Church Street in a room known as The Ark, but at the midsummer chapter

130. HCA, 7031/23, pp. 177–206, chapter acts, 26 June 1893 to 3 January 1894.

131. Ibid., p. 223, 4 October 1894.

132. Ibid., pp. 246, 362–63, 368–69, 25 March 1895, 24 March and 10 November 1904.

133. Ibid., pp. 403, 406–7, 2 September and 14 November 1907.

in 1913 it was 'resolved to add two bays of the cloister to the library and to form the next three bays into a room to be assigned until further notice for use as a Music Room'.[134]

During wartime some of the lay clerks volunteered for the army and temporary singing men were appointed. Sinclair is remembered for his 'untiring energy to the Cathedral, its choir, a depleted Music Society ... and his famous organ recitals, which lightened the wartime gloom'.[135] Sinclair had been conductor of the Birmingham Festival Choral Society since 1900. After one rehearsal he was found collapsed in his hotel room. A doctor attended but could not save him. His funeral took place on Saturday 10 February 1917.

Many took it for granted that Sinclair's successor would be Percy Hull who had been a chorister and pupil at the school. He was an articled pupil to Sinclair and acted as his unpaid assistant. To obtain a salary for him, in 1904 he was appointed a subcanon.[136] Unfortunately, he had been interned in Germany throughout the war and in 1917 not all the members of the chapter wanted to leave the post vacant until Hull might (or might not) return. Public support though was strong and included Hull's friend, Edward Elgar, so the chapter's hand was forced. Another of Sinclair's articled pupils, Gordon Brown, played for the services until Hull was released in the spring of 1918 and able to start his probationary year as organist on 11 November.[137]

When the singers came back from the war, Hull's choir consisted of sixteen choristers, nine lay clerks (and two deputies), with effectively only two vicars choral left in the college. The times of services had been rationalised, partly through the effects of the war and partly because since 1917 the dean had taken responsibility for the cathedral parish as its vicar. On weekdays, morning and evening prayer were still at 10.00 a.m. and 4.30 p.m. On Sundays, holy communion was always at 8.00 a.m. (but it alternated between the cathedral and the Lady chapel, which counted as the parish church), with morning prayer, litany and a sermon at 11.00 a.m., followed by a plain celebration of holy communion each week (choral on the first Sunday of the month) and evening prayer and sermon at 6.30 p.m.

Dean Waterfield was appointed in 1919 and now the increased costs of boarding some of the choristers started to present difficulties for the chapter. Eventually the school took them into Langford House, the headmaster's house in Broomy Hill.

134. Ibid., p. 479, 25 June 1913.
135. E. W. Atkins, 'George Robertson Sinclair: A Festival Centenary and his Influence on the Three Choirs, 1891–1912', *Three Choirs Festival Programme* (Hereford, 1991), pp. 27–31, at 31.
136. HCA, 7031/23, p. 367, chapter acts, 10 November 1904. The chapter reinstated this ancient office, suppressed by Merewether in 1846, by appointing four laymen in 1894 when the number of vicars had been reduced.
137. HCA, 7031/24, p. 40, chapter acts, 10 October 1918.

For some time Hull wanted to appoint an assistant organist. He approached the chapter formally in January 1924, but received a firm rejection:

> An application from Dr Hull that a payment should be made to Mr West was declined on the ground that it would be a recognition of the position of Assistant Organist, there being no such Office in the Cathedral, the so-called Assistant Organist being merely a substitute for himself, provided by the Organist, with the assent of the Dean and Chapter, when unable to officiate in person.[138]

Hull changed his tactics and instead of seeking an assistant he began to look for a deputy, which the chapter found more acceptable. They laid down strict conditions for such an appointment and, although they supplemented Hull's salary with a small grant, they required him always to pay for his own deputy. In October 1935, Colin Ross was appointed music librarian and he doubled as assistant organist.[139]

The Hulls were not happy in the organist's house in Church Street. After various attempts to make it more habitable had failed, they decided to buy their own home, The Highlands, in Broomy Hill, moving in 1929. Settled in his more congenial home, Hull's next concern was his hope that the number of choristers could be increased and the boarding arrangements, which he considered to be unsatisfactory and a hindrance to the best interests of the choir, might be abolished: 'A suggestion from Dr Hull the Organist that the number of Choristers would be increased to twenty and that they should all be non-boarders was considered and the Dean was requested to communicate with Dr Crees and ascertain his views of the matter'.[140] Following the consultation between the dean and the headmaster, however, matters remained unchanged.

The pattern of choir holidays was extended and more firmly established. Choral services still continued throughout both Christmas and Easter weeks but in 1934 there was a holiday period from 8 to 13 January, an annual holiday from 23 July to 18 August and a period off after the Three Choirs Festival from 10 to 15 September. Not until 1937, however, was there a holiday period after Easter. During the choir holiday in the summer the services were said in the Lady chapel, and in 1936 visiting choirs from the diocese began to sing the two Sunday services. In 1936 and 1937 choirs came from Leominster, Ross, Kington, Ledbury, Bridgnorth and Church Stretton.[141]

A number of changes in the cathedral services took place. For instance on 11 November 1930 'it was resolved to adopt the *English Hymnal* in lieu of *Hymns Ancient and Modern*, beginning on 1st January, but for a year to give out the

138. Ibid., p. 142, 1 January 1924.
139. Ibid., p. 340, 10 October 1935.
140. Ibid., p. 279, 23 February 1932.
141. *Hereford Diocesan Messenger*, 41 (1938), p. 68.

numbers of the hymns in both books';[142] and 'the question of having certain parts of the service read instead of intoned was considered'.[143] The cathedral was used regularly by the clergy of the city parishes for a united service on Good Friday. The first broadcast evening service from the cathedral took place in 1934.[144]

During the Second World War, four of the lay clerks were away on active service and in 1945 the chapter had to tackle the problem of salaries and recruitment:

> The Dean stated the difficulty of obtaining and sustaining the Services of Lay Clerks now experienced owing to the greater remuneration offered at some other Cathedrals. He proposed that the stipends should be increased at the expense of a reduction in the number of Lay Clerks employed; that there should be only six employed on week-days instead of nine as formerly.[145]

Dean Waterfield retired in 1946 and Hedley Burrows arrived from Winchester as dean in 1947. At his first midsummer chapter meeting, he reported that the choristers needed new surplices. When he had arranged to buy them, he had to add that clothing coupons were required for them.[146]

In the autumn of 1947 Hull arranged to be absent for an extended period during 1948 'to adjudicate in Malta'. He agreed to arrange that Colin Mann should act as deputy. Hull was seventy years old in 1948 and had been a part of the cathedral's daily life probably longer than any other musician in the history of its music and liturgy. Although small of physical stature, he possessed a giant stature in the world of professional musicians and almost singlehandedly rescued the annual Three Choirs Festival when it restarted after the war in 1946, at a time when there was a serious possibility that it would cease altogether. For this and the many contributions he made in the service of music, he was knighted in 1947. In 1949 there was another Three Choirs Festival in Hereford for him to conduct and in November, on the anniversary of his appointment, he retired.[147]

Though it might not have felt so at the time, New Year's Day 1950 may be seen as a watershed for the cathedral's music and musicians. Meredith Davies, appointed from 1 January, and his successors faced problems and difficulties unknown to their predecessors. Some, on the surface, could be dealt with but others were profound

---

142. Dean Herbert had introduced *Hymns Ancient and Modern* into the services on 11 March 1869, another example of Hereford being ahead of the times rather than following behind. St Paul's did not use *Hymns Ancient and Modern* until 1871 and Worcester not until 1882.

143. HCA, 7031/24, p. 255, 11 November 1930.

144. Ibid., p. 304, 24 June 1933. For details of further changes see above, Chapter 6, p. 175.

145. Ibid., p. 463, 17 April 1946.

146. Ibid., pp. 482, 486, 24 June and 29 July 1947.

147. HCA, 7031/24, pp. 490–1, 26 August, 22 October 1947; 7031/25, p. 21, 29 March 1949.

and not easy either to define or recognise. Immediately, among the first: there was no assistant organist in post, no provision for boarding choristers which imposed severe restrictions on the selection of boys, lay clerks were hard to recruit partly because the cathedral's terms and conditions of employment had emerged piecemeal and were antiquated and partly because of the lack of suitable daytime work in the locality. To make matters worse, the chapter had never had any accommodation to offer lay clerks, nor was there a designated organist's house.

Alongside these practical difficulties there were others, cultural and financial, which went deep and could not be so easily resolved.[148] Both the secular world and the church were emerging from the trauma of a generation of war which had almost annihilated confidence, imagination and hope in human beings and their capacity to worship. There was also an inbuilt separation between the church and the arts, inherited from the struggles of the nineteenth century, which had the result that artists, including musicians and composers, no longer looked to the church and its Christian heritage either for inspiration or patronage.[149] Cathedral worship, however glorious to those who took part in it or who had a particular enthusiasm for it, was precarious because it was of such little interest to the rest.[150]

Dean Burrows and his organist nevertheless tackled the task of post-war reconstruction with energy and skill. During the first months of 1950, at every chapter meeting, things moved forward. The times of the services remained unchanged for the time being. On Sundays, matins with a sermon was sung at 11.00 a.m., followed by a said holy communion at 12.15 (except on the first Sunday of each month and on holy days when it was choral) and evensong with a sermon was sung at 6.30 p.m. During the week, though, daily matins became a said service at 10.00 a.m. and choral evensong was at 4.30 p.m.[151] A new assistant organist, Ross Fink from St Michael's Tenbury, who had been interviewed informally before Davies arrived, was appointed on 31 January at a salary of £150 a year. At the same meeting the chapter reduced the number of choral services each week from eleven to nine, agreeing with the organist that one of the two periods should be used for a full

148. For the financial crisis which developed in the cathedral after 1950, see above, Chapter 6, pp. 182–83, and Chapter 7, pp. 189–90.

149. A handful of distinguished people tried to heal the breach; in cathedrals, Walter Hussey, Anthony Bridge, Basil Spence, George Pace, Herbert Howells, William Mathias and others. Some brilliant modern art, music and architecture has been produced for the church and its influence should not be underestimated. At last, at the end of the twentieth century, it is beginning to

receive the recognition it deserves.

150. Cathedral music was dismissed by many in the church as well, who regarded it as an expensive indulgence, out of touch and a minority preserve.

151. Later, weekday choral evensong was changed to 5.15 p.m. (though for a period, from October 1964 to Easter 1973, on Saturdays it was sung at 4.00 p.m.). Sunday evensong was moved to 3.30 p.m. in 1973. With the arrival of Roy Massey daily evensong was again changed, to 5.30 p.m., with a choir practice beforehand.

practice. After centuries, the middle voluntary before the first lesson was omitted. An office hymn was sung before *Magnificat*. A small grant was made from the college fund to buy new music for the choir. At the February meeting, a scheme for pensions was put in place for the organist and the lay clerks, and the organist was authorised to appoint up to six boarder choristers, the first two to be selected in 1950. Happily, in March 'The Dean was authorised to provide the necessary cricket kit for the Cathedral Choir'.[152] Then in April, Meredith Davies sought permission to close the cathedral and hold a choir practice after evensong each Saturday in preparation for the Sunday services. The chapter however only 'agreed to the shepherding of the Public during Choir Practice to the west of the crossing from the North Porch'.[153] A service for the admission and valediction of choristers was approved and, in June, the choristers went to Porthcawl for a summer outing at a cost of £20 (for which donations were invited from 'the generous-minded').

The number of lay clerks in the choir was a problem for Davies throughout his time as organist. He had to rely for help on several voluntary singers. There were two alto lay clerks, Wilson and Fitzjohn, and two basses, Boot and Brook, but the tenor line was virtually non-existent. After James and Dodgson had left in 1946 and 1947, Aiken was the only tenor. He had been singing since 1912 and his health began seriously to hinder him. The organist put a notice in the *Cathedral News*:

> The Choir has for some time been short of its full complement of Lay Clerks – a situation still further aggravated by the unfortunate recent illness of Mr Aiken. As it is almost impossible to fill such a vacancy in these days, without providing some living accommodation, we appeal to anyone who hears of an unfurnished flat or house to let, to pass on the information with all urgency to the Dean, the Precentor, or the Organist.[154]

Whereas the other lay clerks had been singing for many years, the tenors were constantly changing. Ward sang for two years, Gage for four, Smith for less than a year and Wright for five years. In 1953 there were more changes in the choir: Fitzjohn and Brook retired, Gage left for a post at Manchester, Isaac, who had helped out, went to the Royal College of Music, and Fink the assistant organist was replaced by Michael Illman. In spite of the insecurity, the choir extended its repertory and took part successfully in a series of recitals, concerts and broadcasts. The first television transmission was broadcast on 15 May 1955 and was one of Burrows's much loved Rogation Sunday services.

---

152. HCA, 7031/25, p. 56, chapter acts, 28 March 1950.

153. Ibid., p. 57, 25 April 1950.

154. 'A Word to the Watchful from the Cathedral Organist', *Hereford Cathedral News*, no. 10 (Summer 1950), p. 5.

Meredith Davies had come to Hereford from St Albans partly because of the challenge of conducting at the annual Three Choirs Festivals and in 1954 he was given three months leave of absence to attend a conducting course in Rome. He went to Rome again in 1956, and left Hereford after the Gloucester Festival that year, moving first to New College, Oxford, and later becoming a professional conductor at Covent Garden, Sadler's Wells and the Royal Choral Society.

Melville Cook arrived in Hereford in time for Christmas 1956 after nineteen years in Yorkshire, at Leeds Parish Church and with the Halifax Choral Society. He knew Herefordshire because he had been born in Gloucester and was a chorister under Herbert Brewer, a pupil of Herbert Sumsion and then his assistant.

Before he retired in 1961, Burrows put in place a new set of bye laws for the conduct of the services. The hymns were to be chosen by the precentor. Candles were to be lit on the altar 'at celebrations and choir offices on Sundays and Feast Days'. The office was to begin with 'O Lord open thou our lips'. The prayers after the third collect were to be said and not chanted. Variations permitted by the 1928 Prayer Book were accepted, including the revised prayer for the church, the observance of black letter saints' days, the use of the proper prefaces, the use of the summary of the law or the threefold kyrie in place of the ten commandments, the shortening of the words of administration, the omission of Creed and Gloria during Holy Week, and the omission of the bracketed verses in the psalms and the *Gloria patri* after each section of psalm 119.[155]

While Robert Price was dean (1961–69), the cathedral school was still a small direct grant school and only took boys at eleven years, which hampered the choir by curtailing the singing career of the choristers now boys' voices were breaking earlier. In 1964 new arrangements were made and it was agreed that younger boys, aged eight or nine, should be admitted to the choir and attend the nearby cathedral preparatory school.[156] In the 1960s, at least partly in an attempt to regain confidence within a modern culture, the Church of England Liturgical Commission provided new texts for the holy communion service and gradually the eucharist replaced the daily offices as the central focus in Anglican worship. The dean persuaded the cathedral to use Series Two (in addition to the Prayer Book rite) and, having attended the consecration service at the new Coventry Cathedral in 1962 and subsequently preached there on a Sunday morning, he looked for a way to make a cathedral eucharist the main service on a Sunday morning at Hereford. Sadly it eluded him and the cathedral did not have a principal eucharist with preaching and choir regularly on a Sunday morning until 1984.[157] Instead a compromise proposal was accepted and an extra service was added on Sunday

155. HCA, 7031/25, pp. 238–39, 246–47, chapter acts, 21 April and 29 June 1959.

156. Ibid., pp. 372–73, 25 August 1964.

157. See above, Chapter 7, p. 197.

mornings, a family communion at 9.45 a.m., with a sermon but without the choir. To use the spaces in the cathedral more easily and create an open setting for worship, Dean Price bravely led the chapter in the controversial task of removing the Skidmore screen.[158]

Melville Cook resigned and moved to Canada in 1966 and Richard Lloyd, the assistant organist at Salisbury Cathedral, was appointed, taking up his duties on 1 October 1966. Immediately, he faced the difficulty which had hindered the choir since 1950. Among the lay clerks, the tenor line was still insecure. G. C. Lund had been appointed in September 1956, just before Cook arrived, but by 1967 he was the only tenor left. Rather curiously (but considerately) the chapter agreed to increase his salary by 50 per cent while he remained the sole tenor, which lasted until Barnes took over from him in 1969. Briefly, Bilton became the second tenor until Knowles, who had been a lay clerk at Salisbury, came to Hereford in 1970.

The choir made its first recording in 1972 and a reviewer, giving it high praise, coincidentally remarked how close the sound of the choir was to the famous King's sound. Richard Lloyd had absorbed what might be called 'the Willcocks sound' while he worked with the Salisbury choir. He developed it at Hereford, where it admirably suited the cathedral's remarkable acoustic. Lloyd, although successful, popular and much loved, was not settled in Hereford, and (rather like Wesley in 1835) was pleased when he was given another appointment. He became organist at Durham Cathedral in 1974 and the present organist, Dr Roy Massey MBE, was appointed. Almost at once Massey persuaded the chapter to raise the lay clerk's stipend to £485 a year. He carefully extended Lloyd's hard work, giving meticulous attention to the daily singing of the psalms and managing to maintain a well-balanced choir of eighteen choristers and six lay clerks, which is counted among the best cathedral choirs in the country (fig. 126).[159]

Dean Rathbone introduced a number of services not in the Prayer Book. He drew on material from Hereford's medieval liturgies and in his own way anticipated the additions to the calendar and the liturgical texts published in the two books *Lent, Holy Week and Easter*, and *The Promise of his Glory*.[160] In the 1970s the Easter services included an Easter vigil, the singing of the Passion and Veneration of the Cross on Good Friday, a Chrism Eucharist on Maundy Thursday and a Palm Sunday procession which entered by the west doors and used the gallery above to great effect. At Christmas, there was an Advent Carol Service as well as the

158. See above, Chapter 6, pp. 179–80.
159. Paul Iles, 'Dr Roy Massey', *FHC*, 57 (1991), pp. 14–16.
160. *Lent, Holy Week and Easter: Services and Prayers Commended by the House of Bishops of the General Synod of the Church of* England (London, 1984); *The Promise of his Glory: Services and Prayers for the Season from All Saints to Candlemas Commended by the House of Bishops of the General Synod of the Church of England* (London, 1991).

Fig. 126. Dr Roy Massey, organist and master of the choristers since 1974, rehearsing with the choristers in the song school, 1999.

usual Service of Nine Lessons and Carols and a celebration of Candlemas. In 1980 the *Alternative Service Book* was authorised for general use, and gradually the cathedral integrated the new material into its liturgy, deliberately making use of all the available rites for holy communion from time to time, while continuing to sing evensong using the Book of Common Prayer. These decisions meant that the choir music sung in worship was not much changed by the introduction of the new book, although the repertory was enlarged.[161]

At the end of the twentieth century, music in the cathedral still fulfils its traditional role as the handmaid of worship, but cathedral finances are so fragile that the future employment of the cathedral's musicians, without whom the high standard of performance could never be achieved, can no longer be taken for granted. Thankfully at Hereford new money is being found to secure the future

161. Recently a good deal of music has been specially written for the choir, for example by Howells, Mathias, Lloyd, Shephard, Vann and Sanders, some of which has been recorded on CD.

Fig. 127. The choir in the choir stalls during the 10.00 a.m. eucharist, Whitsunday 1999.

of the choir and, along with significant suggestions about future developments for cathedral music,[162] many are beginning again to believe that cathedral music is a civilising voice in a bleak culture and a treasured and essential part of humanity's heritage in a violent world.

162. See for example *Heritage and Renewal: The Report of the Archbishops' Commission on Cathedrals* (London, 1994), chapter 5.

23

The College of Vicars Choral

Philip Barrett

The earliest firm references to junior clergy in English cathedrals are found in the late twelfth century.[1] The emergence of a group of vicars at Hereford reflects this general trend. In 1174 x 1180, David de Aqua, a canon of Hereford, granted in frankalmoign to the church of the Blessed Virgin Mary and St Athebert (sic) of Hereford, with the consent of the bishop, all the tithes of a certain piece of land which the grantor had bought from Robert de Chandos to augment his prebend. The grant was made so that simnel cakes could be made annually on the feast of the Blessed Milburga, for distribution to the canons and vicars of the cathedral and priests in Hereford.[2]

Bishop Ralph de Maidstone gave the church of Diddlebury to the dean and chapter in 1237. From the revenues of this church, twenty marks were to provide

1. For examples at Lincoln, see R. Bowers, 'Music and Worship to 1640', in D. Owen, ed., *A History of Lincoln Minster* (Cambridge, 1994), p. 49; cf. also D. Greenway, 'Orders and Rank in the Cathedral of Old Sarum', in W. J. Sheils and D. Woods, eds, *The Ministry: Clerical and Lay*, Studies in Church History, 26 (Oxford, 1989), pp. 55–63, at 57; contrast K. Edwards, *The English Secular Cathedrals in the Middle Ages* (2nd edn, Manchester, 1967), p. 263. For Exeter, see N. Orme, *The Minor Clergy of Exeter Cathedral* (Exeter, 1980), p. xiv, and Edwards, *The English Secular Cathedrals*, pp. 259–61. For St Paul's, see Edwards, *The English Secular Cathedrals*, pp. 260–62. The first known evidence for vicars choral at both Lichfield and St Paul's comes from the end of the twelfth century, Edwards, *The English Secular Cathedrals*, p. 263. For continental examples, see J. Barrow, 'Vicars Choral and Chaplains in Northern European Cathedrals, 1100–1250', in Sheils and Wood, eds, *The Ministry*, pp. 87–97. Although junior clergy were known at Paris as early as 868, it was again in the twelfth century that they are known to have deputised for absent canons and to have received funds. Often the sixteen clerks of matins were solely responsible for maintaining the night office at Notre Dame, C. Wright, *Music and Ceremony at Notre Dame of Paris, 500–1550* (Cambridge, 1989), pp. 20, 24.

2. HCA, 1383; cf. Capes, *Charters*, p. 24; P. L. S. Barrett, *The College of Vicars Choral at Hereford Cathedral* (Hereford, 1980), pp. 7–8.

the stipends of six vicars.[3] By the time of the earliest *consuetudines* of the cathedral, drawn up by Bishop Peter of Aigueblanche no more than thirty years later, their number had risen to fourteen.[4] These included the four perpetual vicars of the two abbots of the French abbeys of Lire and Cormeilles, who held cathedral prebends, and the perpetual vicar of the dean.[5] In addition, three vicars were appointed by the precentor, treasurer and chancellor to be their official deputies, all of whom had to be present at the services with the other vicars.[6]

Aigueblanche's statutes, promulgated between 1246 and 1268, are the chief source of our information for the daily life of the vicars during the middle ages. Unlike the vicars choral of most of the other English secular cathedrals, they were perpetual vicars, specially endowed by the dean and chapter, rather than the specific financial responsibility of the individual canons.[7] There are traces of canonical responsibility for individual vicars in Aigueblanche's statutes: no priest, deacon or subdeacon was to be admitted into the choir unless the canon who introduced him was responsible for his board and lodging.[8] There is, indeed, a certain amount of repetition in Aigueblanche's statutes which may indicate that they are a revision of an earlier code. They include provisions both for all the vicars choral and also for those who held specific offices. The perpetual vicars were obliged to be present at all the services in the choir, both at night and during the day, and were allowed to

3. Bannister, *The Cathedral Church of Hereford*, p. 164; Capes, *Charters*, pp. 74–75, 123–24; Barrett, *Vicars Choral*, p. 8.

4. Bradshaw and Wordsworth, *Statutes of Lincoln Cathedral*, ii, pp. 36–84; Barrett, *Vicars Choral*, p. 8.

5. Bradshaw and Wordsworth, *Statutes of Lincoln Cathedral*, ii, pp. 60, 62, 72–74. The vicars of the abbots were established in 1195 in the case of Cormeilles and in 1217 in the case of Lire: see above, Chapter 2.

6. Ibid., ii, pp. 63, 69, 71.

7. In 1252 Bishop Aigueblanche claimed that he had the right to nominate them, but it was decided by arbitration that this right belonged to the dean and chapter (Capes, *Charters*, pp. 97, 100). At Hereford the six senior vicars were sometimes known as 'petty canons', a term also employed at St Paul's, Edwards, *The English Secular Cathedrals*, p. 254. Edwards emphasises that 'the exceptional arrangements at Hereford Cathedral were the result of late development, which was closer to French than to English models: four perpetual vicars were attached

to four different altars in the church, and six more, two of them priests, two deacons and two subdeacons, were vicars not of individual canons but of the church', ibid., p. 258. These were the six vicars instituted by Bishop Maidstone, see above, p. 36. The view expressed in Barrett, *Vicars Choral*, that 'the canons, who were often absent from the cathedral on state or papal business, would employ the cantarists as their deputies or vicars to take their place in singing the services in the quire' should therefore be revised. At Exeter, until the vicars acquired their own dwellings in the 1380s, each vicar attended his canon to and from the choir and may well have lodged in his master's house, together with some of the other young clerks attached to the cathedral, Orme, *The Minor Clergy of Exeter Cathedral*, pp. xiv–xv.

8. Aigueblanche's statutes, translated in E. F. H. Dunnicliff, 'Consuetudines et statuta ecclesiasticae cathedralis Herefordensis: A Paraphrase in English' (HCL, typescript, 1962), pp. 41–42.

be absent only with the permission of the dean and chapter for a necessary and urgent reason. They were required to learn by heart the psalms, the antiphonary and the hymnary within a year and a day.[9] The vicars were not allowed to wander abroad from the ringing of the bell for vespers until after compline, unless it was necessary to cross the churchyard, or to set off for or return from a long journey. They were prohibited from frequenting taverns or suspicious or dishonourable places, and from wandering around the city streets at night. Punctuality was especially emphasised. Frequently, at both prime and vespers, the hebdomadary would find himself standing alone in the choir for half an hour or more, without anyone to answer the responses for him, 'waiting for those who ought to be waiting for him'. All the perpetual vicars were therefore admonished to be ready in the choir to perform the offices with the hebdomadary before the bell for prime and vespers had finished ringing. The breviary shows that when the bells were rung and the necessary lamps were lit, the officiant or hebdomadary stood in the choir in his stall; after an interval according to the custom of Hereford, he began vespers.[10]

Certain vicars, when invited to the table of their masters, fed their hosts with idle gossip, 'for all the world as if they were at Herod's banquet dancing with a low woman demanding the head of the prophet, and by this I mean clamouring for the reputation of their neighbours to be beheaded'. Any vicar who made a practice of speaking disparagingly about another brother was to be suspended from the choir for forty days, and to lose his income for the same period. Any vicar who defamed a canon was suspended until the canon who had been wronged interceded for him. The statutes also complained about those 'who haunt the choir, who have no fixed job in the cathedral nor are in dependence upon a canon, but in their own interests use the privilege of the choir'. No one in the choir was allowed to laugh or smile inordinately in a puerile fashion, or indulge in idle conversation. No one was allowed to appear in secular habit in the cathedral or churchyard from the ringing of the small bell for prime until after nones.

As well as these general rules, the statutes also prescribed specific duties for the vicars of the dignitaries, including the dean's vicar and the succentor.[11] As well as these vicars there were also four cantarists, priest-vicars who celebrated at the chantries of the Blessed Virgin Mary and before the crucifix, and for the souls of master Alexander and master Rufus. These vicars were also obliged to be present at all the day and night services.

The fortunes of the vicars choral steadily improved during the fourteenth century.

---

9. For the mnemonic tradition at Paris and other secular cathedrals, see Wright, *Music and Ceremony at Notre Dame*, pp. 325ff.

10. *The Hereford Breviary*, i, pp. 97–98.

11. For details, see Barrett, *Vicars Choral*, pp. 11–12; Wright, *Music and Ceremony at Notre Dame*, pp. 174–75.

In 1327 Joanna de Bohun, whose tomb is on the north side of the Lady chapel in the cathedral, gave to the chapter the living of Lugwardine, together with its dependent chapelries. In 1330, through the generosity of Thomas Chandos, archdeacon of Hereford, the revenues of this church were used to provide a further ten perpetual vicars (eight priests, one deacon and one subdeacon). After his death they were appointed by the dean and chapter. There was clearly a need for an increase in the number of clerks serving the *opus dei*, for the better performance of the cathedral services. In particular, the daily mass of the Blessed Virgin Mary 'was so meagrely endowed that it was no better celebrated than in a parish church'.[12] In 1384 an attempt by some of the vicars to obtain the revenues of the church at Westbury led to a dispute about their right to hold property. This was settled in 1395 when Richard II incorporated the vicars choral as a college, with the form and title of *Collegium vicariorum in choro ecclesiae Herefordensis*. One of their number was to be elected custos; they were empowered to have a common seal and the college was allowed to acquire and hold property. Walter Throleston became the first custos, and there were by this time twenty-seven vicars.[13] The college was situated on the south side of Castle Street, and now forms part of the cathedral school.[14] Bishop Mascall increased the value of the seven poorest vicarages and gave all the vicars additional endowments from the tithes at Westbury.[15] Nearly eighty years after Richards II's charter, the vicars complained to Bishop John Stanbury that they resided 'so distant from the church that through fear of evil-doers, and the inclemency of the weather, many of them cannot go

12. Edwards, *The English Secular Cathedrals*, p. 259; Bannister, *The Cathedral Church of Hereford*, p. 164; Capes, *Charters*, pp. 210–15; HCA, 492, 2163, 3202; W. W. Capes, ed., *The Register of Thomas de Charlton, Bishop of Hereford, AD 1327–44*, Cantilupe Society (Hereford, 1912), pp. 34–40; Barrett, *Vicars Choral*, pp. 8–9.

13. Bannister, *The Cathedral Church of Hereford*, pp. 164–165; Capes, *Charters*, pp. 253–55.

14. Part of the present building, including the fine roof of the former hall, dates from the late fourteenth century. Bannister claimed that the present building includes part of the original chapel and common room, Bannister, *The Cathedral Church of Hereford*, p. 165; cf. RCHME, *Herefordshire*, i, p. 141. See further above, Chapter 11, and R. K. Morriss and R. Shoesmith, 'The College of the Vicars Choral in Hereford', in Whitehead, *Medieval Art at Hereford*,

pp. 157–71. The vicars were in fact living there by 1375. An old, blind vicar was allowed to live there and share their food until he died, provided he paid 20s. a year to their common fund, Edwards, *The English Secular Cathedrals*, p. 277 n. 5, quoting Capes, *Charters*, pp. 237–38. They occupied property in Castle Street for some years before that. In 1336 the chapter granted a mortmain licence for a 'habitation' in Castle Street, *Calendar of the Patent Rolls Preserved in the Public Record Office: Edward III* (16 vols, London, 1891–1916), iii, p. 247: I am grateful to David Lepine for this reference.

15. J. H. Parry and C. Johnson, eds, *The Register of Robert Mascall, Bishop of Hereford, AD 1404–16*, Cantilupe Society (Hereford, 1916), pp. 77–81; Edwards, *The English Secular Cathedrals*, p. 259. There were then twenty-five vicars.

to the church at midnight to celebrate divine service'. In 1472 Stanbury allowed Richard Gardener, the warden,[16] and vicars to build a new college on the site of the canonical houses of the late canons John Grene and Reginald Wolston.[17] The quadrangle now known as the cloisters (or college cloisters) was constructed in about three years (fig. 129; plate IXa). Originally there were twenty-seven small two-roomed houses, a hall with a kitchen, and a chapel. A cloister connected the quadrangle to the south-east transept of the cathedral.[18]

A few glimpses of the college in the early sixteenth century have survived. In a fragmentary paper of presentments dated 1510 x 1520, 'the Koke of the coldg and queer' was accused of forestalling the market by buying cheese, butter, eggs and other victuals.[19] In 1510 Bishop Mayew absolved two vicars for laying violent hands on a priest.[20] In 1517 a vicar called Roger Palmer was charged with incontinence; David May, Richard

Fig. 128. Seal impression of the college of vicars choral, 1413. (HCA, 1495.)

---

16. This term is used in preference to custos.

17. Bannister, *The Cathedral Church of Hereford*, p. 165; J. H. Parry and A. T. Bannister, eds, *The Register of John Stanbury, Bishop of Hereford, 1453–74*, Cantilupe Society (Hereford, 1918), pp. v–vi. Morriss and Shoesmith, 'The College of the Vicars Choral', pp. 159–60, suggest that Grene's house may have become the original college hall.

18. Shortly after the vicars had moved into their new college, they gave their consent to the foundation of one chaplain by the executors of Bishop Stanbury, the new chaplain becoming a member of their college. The sum of £40 was paid for their consent. HCA, 2923 (1246); Parry and Bannister, eds, *Reg. Stanbury*, pp. xi–xiii. In 1487 Pope Innocent VIII allowed the vicars, in consideration of their poverty, to hold other benefices without residing in them, A. T. Bannister, ed., *The Register of Richard Mayew, Bishop of Hereford, 1504–16*, Cantilupe Society (Hereford, 1919), pp. 15–18. In 1509 Bishop Mayew copied into his register a constitution of Archbishop Warham which required chaplains and other stipendiary clergy to attend the choir service of the cathedrals or collegiate churches to which they were attached, on pain of suspension: ibid., pp. 106–7.

19. Historical Manuscripts Commission, *Thirteenth Report, Appendix, Part IV: The Manuscripts of Rye and Hereford Corporations, etc.* (London, 1892), p. 305.

20. Bannister, ed., *Reg. Mayew*, p. 98.

Fig. 129. Cloisters of the college of vicars choral, looking north up the east alley.

Baker, John Hare and William Chell were also indicted. Negligence and absence were also common faults.[21] There is also evidence of unpaid rents owed to the vicars choral in the early sixteenth century.[22] When he died in 1535, Bishop Booth left money to each minor canon, vicar choral and chorister, and to four clerks.[23]

By the early sixteenth century, the number of chantries founded at various altars in the cathedral had increased to twenty-one, fourteen of them being held by vicars choral. In 1517 a vicar choral resigned his stall to become a full-time cantarist.[24] The *Valor ecclesiasticus* reckoned that the annual income of each of the twenty vicars in 1535 was £4 8s. 8¾d. from their common revenues. Besides the fourteen vicars who were also chantry priests, there were six petty canons who each received an extra £3 or £3 10s. 0d. per annum from the dean and chapter.[25] From a writ sent to the crown by Bishop Fox in 1536 we know that there were four minor canons and two others of the Diddlebury foundation, and vicars choral

21. S. E. Lehmberg, *The Reformation of Cathedrals* (Princeton, 1989), p. 220.

22. Historical Manuscripts Commission, *The Manuscripts of Rye and Hereford*, pp. 308, 310.

23. A. T. Bannister, ed., *The Register of Charles Bothe, Bishop of Hereford, 1516–35*, Cantilupe Society (Hereford, 1921), p. x.

24. Lehmberg, *The Reformation of Cathedrals*, p. 23; cf. Edwards, *The English Secular Cathedrals*, pp. 296–97.

25. Edwards, *The English Secular Cathedrals*, p. 259.

who served the following altars: Holy Cross, St Mary, St Nicholas (two), St John the Baptist or Holme Lacy (two), John Stanbury, St Agnes, St Margaret (two), St Stephen, Holy Trinity, Much Cross (two) and St Anne (fig. 25). In addition there were five vacant vicarages (Brayntone, Kyngestone, Gredley, Grenehouse and Philip Rufus), the offices of succentor and sub-treasurer, the chantries of the Blessed Virgin Mary *super portam*, the rectory of the chapel of St Mary Magdalene, and the three chantries of St Katherine. The college also continued to enjoy the revenues of the church at Westbury, and provided a parish priest for the altar of St John the Baptist in the nave.[26] Five years later, when Bishop Skip tried to hold a visitation, the names of twenty-seven vicars are given.[27]

The college survived the dissolution of chantries in 1547, possibly because the custos and vicars, at the time of Henry VIII's survey in 1546, maintained 'that they were and been founded, taken, admitted and allways hath been both reputed and called by the names of the Vicars of the Quyer and not chantries'.[28] But the Reformation substantially altered their duties. In 1547 the royal injunctions for cathedrals ordered that services at night should cease and matins be sung at 6.00 a.m.[29] Following Cardinal Pole's metropolitical visitation of 1556, his commissary, Richard Pates, bishop of Worcester, issued some injunctions for the cathedral. The petty-canons and vicars, as well as the canons, were ordered to avoid the company of heretics 'and other lewd and defamed persons', and to refrain from 'suspicious houses', taverns and ale-houses. They were required to take a servant with them when they went into the town, and had to wear 'decent apparel with a tippet'. They were forbidden from studying during the services or walking about, and must not 'talk jangle or laugh in the choir'. They were ordered to give reverence to the name of Jesus 'with vayling their bonnets and bending their knees', and also at the words *sit nomen domini benedictus* and *et homo factus est*. No women servants were allowed within the precincts except in cases of sickness. The dean and chapter were required to fill the vacant vicarages 'with speed convenient' and not convert their revenues to their own use.[30]

The royal injunctions given to the cathedral in the first year of the reign of

26. *The Register of Edward Foxe, Bishop of Hereford* in Bannister, ed., *Reg. Bothe*, appendix, p. 365.

27. HCL, Theses, P. G. S. Baylis, ed., 'Registrum Johannis Skip, episcopi Herefordensis, 1539–52' (MS, 1968), fol. 43r.

28. HCA, 6450/2, p. 7: 'Herefordshire Chantries and Other Religious Foundations Recorded in the Surveys (of 1546 and 1547)

Preserved in the Public Record Office (PRO, E 301–26)', transcribed by F. C. Morgan, typescript.

29. W. H. Frere and W. McC. Kennedy, eds, *Visitation Articles and Injunctions of the Period of the Reformation*, Alcuin Club Collections, 14–16 (3 vols, London, 1910), ii, pp. 135–39.

30. Ibid., ii, pp. 392–96.

Elizabeth I,[31] largely based on the royal injunctions for cathedrals issued in 1547,[32] included provisions for the vicars as well as the dean and chapter. They were required to be present at the preaching of sermons and the giving of divinity lectures, and were particularly exhorted to avoid having 'any suspect women to resort into any of your houses or chambers'. Suggestions were made about the contents of a library, swearing and blasphemy were forbidden, and those who were bound to offer hospitality were reminded to have a special care for 'such as be poor ministers of this church'. Every day some part of the English Bible was to be read at meal time, so that there should be no other 'slanderous and unfruitful talking'.[33] The revenues of any vacant vicarages were to be divided among the other members of the college.

In 1582 a royal commission was appointed under John Whitgift, then bishop of Worcester, to investigate the affairs of the cathedral and a new code of statutes was published in the following year. The college was reduced to twelve vicars, with four sub-canons or deacons (one of whom was to be the organist).[34] The Protestant reputation of the college was asserted by one of the vicars, Bartholomew Mason, who told the dean and chapter in 1588 that no vicar choral favoured or harboured a Jesuit, seminarist or recusant, or 'prefer the best papist before the worst protestant'. He also assured the chapter that no image of God the Son was painted in the college.[35]

The earliest surviving act book of the college is a late seventeenth-century copy of the original book. It records college meetings from 1575 and affords a vivid glimpse of the Elizabethan college. The longest entry concerns a vicar called Richard Mason, who was seen by three others to have consorted with 'a suspected woman' in his chamber.[36] Several vicars were guilty of intemperate language, especially at meal times.[37] A vicar by the name of William Evans was particularly violent. In

31. Cambridge, Corpus Christi College, MSS vol. cxx, fol. 516, printed in Frere and Kennedy, *Visitation Articles*, iii, pp. 47–48.

32. Frere and Kennedy, *Visitation Articles*, ii, pp. 135–39.

33. In 1588 Bartholomew Mason told the dean and chapter that this was still observed, HCA, 3395.

34. Bannister, *The Cathedral Church of Hereford*, p. 90; cf. HCA, 7044/3 and 4 (contemporary copies of the 1583 statutes).

35. HCA, 3395.

36. HCA, 7003/1/1, pp. 30–31, vicars choral acts, 2 November 1581. A similar incident occurred three years earlier when an aggrieved husband discovered his errant

wife concealed 'in a cole house under a stayer' in one of the chambers, Lehmberg, *The Reformation of Cathedrals*, p. 221 n. 173. In 1584 William Hosier 'was seen in a suspicious place and manner with a lewde woman', and Archbishop Whitgift described this as 'an open scandal', HCA, 4573; for Hosier see Chapter 4, p. 96.

37. HCA, 7003/1/1, pp. 12, 54, 84, 92, 108, vicars choral acts, 25 April 1578, 19 November 1585, 14 February 1593, 21 January 1595, 9 February 1596, 5 January 1598. For a dispute involving Richard Madox in 1579, see Chapter 4, p. 93, and Lehmberg, *The Reformation of Cathedrals*, p. 222.

1597 he hit a servant in the buttery with his key,[38] and the next year he not only uttered 'indecent words', but threw a knife at Thomas Boyce during dinner.[39] Other troublesome vicars included Thomas Howells, George Allen, who muddled the accounts and entertained women in suspicious circumstances, and John Farrant, the organist. He came from Salisbury, where he had tried to murder the dean.[40] Some vicars choral were married. They were fined if their wives were abusive or slanderous. The widows of vicars were given allowances. In 1610 John Boughan was accused of committing adultery with the wife of John Nicholson.[41]

As well as the custos, there were several other college officers. One vicar was appointed 'steward of ye garner', and there were two collectors of rents, two auditors, and two clavigers.[42] The college employed a cook, baker, laundress, porter and brewer, in addition to any personal servants retained by individual vicars.

Various details of the domestic life of the college have survived. The college gates were closed each evening from 9.00 p.m. until the bell for morning prayer was rung on the following day.[43] The vicars were troubled by various boys hanging around the college for scraps of food at meal times.[44] Dogs were not allowed in the college.[45] No vicar could bring a guest to a meal (except a visiting singing man or a college tenant) without informing the kitchen and paying a small fine.[46] In 1581 the brewer was told to brew only beer, not ale. Ten years later, the vicars accepted his ale only if it was four days old. No vicar was served ale or beer before eight o'clock in the morning or three o'clock in the afternoon.[47] Although the cook was allowed to have the college garden and to look after it, together with the hopyard and saffron ground, the vicars were to have all the

38. HCA, 7003/1/1, p. 106, vicars choral acts, 26 July 1597.

39. Ibid., p. 109, 15 September 1598; see also ibid., p. 122, 23 December 1601. Boyce was formerly a vicar choral at Wells. He was promised a place at Hereford in 1593 but incurred the displeasure of his new colleagues in 1596 because 'he did abuse the company by depraving them behind their backs', Lehmberg, *The Reformation of Cathedrals*, p. 185.

40. HCA, 7003/1/1, pp. 84, 113, 129, 130, 138, vicars choral acts, 14 February 1593, 23 June 1599, 31 January 1603, 26 February 1603, 4 December 1604.

41. S. E. Lehmberg, *Cathedrals under Siege* (Exeter, 1996), p. 176, quoting HCA, 7031/3, pp. 79, 131, chapter acts, 25 June 1612, 4 July 1618.

42. HCA, 7003/1/1, p. 15, vicars choral acts,

26 September 1578. From 1585 one of the vicars was elected librarian, HCA, 7003/1/1, p. 52, 24 September 1585.

43. Lehmberg, *Cathedrals under Siege*, p. 170.

44. HCA, 7003/1/1, pp. 21, 32, vicars choral acts, 11 April 1580, 2 November 1581; Lehmberg, *Cathedrals under Siege*, p. 186–87. There are references to boys, some of whom may have been choristers, in the will of Thomas Salte (d. 1569) and Henry Mynde (d. 1580), see Lehmberg, *Cathedrals under Siege*, pp. 192–93.

45. HCA, 7003/1/1, p. 76, vicars choral acts, 16 May 1590.

46. HCA, 7003/1/1, p. 39, vicars choral acts, 28 September 1582. In 1593 the vicars may all have travelled to Lichfield to be entertained by the Lichfield vicars at the Angel, see Lehmberg, *Cathedrals under Siege*, p. 190.

47. Lehmberg, *Cathedrals under Siege*, p. 187.

herbs in it, free entry at all times, and their due portions of the fruits and flowers.[48] In 1596 Thomas Boyce was granted the lower part of the garden on condition that he provided twenty pounds of dried hops annually at All Saints, and that the vicars could have their usual dividends of fruit, apples, pears and plums.[49] From time to time the college fell into debt, 'specially by excessive spending of ale',[50] and economies were ordered. The college maintained two choristers and gave food and money 'to two poor folks that are accustomed to have relief with meat and drink in their college hall during the year'.[51]

In September 1587 they tried to give up their common table on the grounds that the cost of obtaining a new charter from Elizabeth I prevented them from offering hospitality, but the dean and chapter refused to allow this.[52] During Lent 1588 the vicars agreed to have supper in hall on four days a week, 'providing it be very sparingly and not to exceed one dish of fish and another of butter'.[53] In January 1597 they gave up 'beavers' three nights a week so that more money could be given to poor relief during a time of dearth.[54] In 1600 two special dinners, known as 'Barbors feasts', were held on Thursday in Whitsun week and on 4 July.[55] In 1604 they agreed to keep pigs near the pigeon-house,[56] and in 1607 the cook's wages were increased, with feathers as a perquisite, but dripping and suet were 'to be laid up to help to buy candles withall'.[57] As the college contained more dwellings than the twelve ordained vicars choral needed, some were let to prebendaries (who were not allowed to sublet them) and others to those who wished to share their collegiate life. For example, in 1601 they admitted John Jenkins and his wife 'to be as Brother and Sister amongst us according to ye ancient custome of this house … in consideration of eight bushels of mault'.[58] They may well have joined the vicars at their daily evening meal in the hall. Only on Saturdays was this not available (except for a short-lived experiment in 1629–30). Vicars who did not dine were given an allowance of wheat and barley.[59]

48. HCA, 7003/1/1, p. 39, vicars choral acts, 12 November 1582.
49. Ibid., p. 100, 24 September 1596. For Boyce see n. 39 above.
50. HCA, 7003/1/1, p. 38, vicars choral acts, 11 September 1582; see also p. 61, 21 September 1587.
51. Ibid., p. 62, 21 September 1587.
52. Lehmberg, *Cathedrals under Siege*, p. 188.
53. HCA, 7003/1/1, p. 66, vicars choral acts, 25 February 1588; Lehmberg, *Cathedrals under Siege*, p. 188.
54. HCA, 7003/1/1, p. 103, vicars choral acts, 27 January 1597; see also ibid., p. 155, 9 June 1608, and Lehmberg, *Cathedrals under Siege*, p. 170. Drinks or 'cues' were served to the vicars choral several times a day and the butler was obliged to serve them in the buttery in the morning and before and after dinner, HCA, 7003/1/1, pp. 140, 223, 15 March 1605, 16 October 1641.
55. Ibid., p. 116, 4 April 1600.
56. Ibid., p. 137, 8 November 1604.
57. Ibid., p. 151, 2 October 1607.
58. Lehmberg, *Cathedrals under Siege*, pp. 169–70, quoting HCA, 7003/1/1, p. 120, 4 April 1601.
59. Lehmberg, *Cathedrals under Siege*, p. 170, quoting HCA, 7003/1/1, p. 151, 2 October 1607.

In 1634 Lieutenant Hammond and some soldiers visited the college and he left a delightful account of what he saw:

Next came wee into a brave and ancient priviledg'd Place, through the Lady Arbour Cloyster, close by the Chapter House, called the Vicars' Chorall or Colledge Cloyster, where twelve of the Singing Men, all in Orders, most of them Masters in Arts of a gentile Garb, have their convenient severall dwellings, and a fayre Hall, with richly painted windows Colledge-like, wherein they constantly dyet together, and have their Cooke, Butler, and other Officers, with a fayre library to themselves, consisting all of English Bookes.[60]

In 1636 a fresh set of statutes, drawn up by Bishop Matthew Wren, was signed by Archbishop Laud and issued under royal authority on 31 May. These statutes are based on those of Whitgift issued in Elizabeth's reign, but with additions often based on the medieval code.[61] The provisions for the vicars choral allowed the custos to choose only one week a year for saying public prayers 'because he is specially burdened with the very numerous affairs of the college'.[62] The Elizabethan statutes stressed the need for the vicars to study theology and the Laudian statutes reinforced this obligation. One of the vicars in turn was to deliver a theological lecture each quarter, but the later statutes allowed one of the homilies to be read instead.[63] A special provision was made for the organist's stipend,[64] and for the custos to have the power of fining any obstinate or querulous member of the college.[65] The sum of £100 at least was to be laid up and not spent without the bishop's consent in writing.[66] The individual vicarages or 'corpses' were carefully listed and no lease or financial transaction concerning their revenues was allowed without the approval of the custos and the majority of the vicars, and a copy of the indenture lodged in the college archives. The revenues of the other vicarages, which had not survived the pruning in Elizabeth's reign, were assigned to the common fund of the college and to the organist's stipend.[67]

The Civil War led to the suspension of the cathedral foundation and the college. The last entry in the college act book was made on 17 October 1645. In 1647 the vicars choral sent a petition to the Committee for Sequestration, pleading destitution and praying that their stipend might not be included in the general

60. BL, Lansdowne MS 213, fols 332–34; see also Chapter 4, p. 98.
61. Printed in Jebb and Phillott, *The Statutes of the Cathedral Church of Hereford*.
62. Ibid., pp. 110–11.
63. Ibid., pp. 112–13.
64. Ibid., pp. 114–15.
65. Ibid., pp. 118–19.
66. Ibid., pp. 122–23.
67. Ibid., pp. 126–29. Hospitality by the college was limited 'in order that the lavish extravagance, especially in drink, which has so reduced the means of the said College, as almost to exhaust them' could be curtailed: ibid., pp. 120–21.

sequestration of capitular property, they 'having never acted anything prejudicial to the parliament nor being any ways under the notion of delinquency'.[68] The petition was rejected, they were expelled from the college, and the chambers used to lodge poor homeless people.[69] One of the vicars, John Clarke, was even pursued to his living at Norton Canon, where the parliamentary soldiers removed his only hat, so that he was compelled to borrow a bonnet from his female servant whenever he left his house.[70]

When Charles II was restored in 1660, the dean and chapter and the college of vicars choral were also re-established after 'the dispersion', as the college records describe the years when the foundation was in abeyance. Indeed, the college was restored some two months before the monarchy, since the first college meeting took place on 28 March 1660.[71] During the Civil War the buildings of the college had become very dilapidated and decayed, and needed extensive repairs. By 1667, however, when the dean and chapter conducted a visitation of the college, the custos, Richard Cox, reported that 'the college chapel and edifices are in a good condition' (fig. 130).[72] Cox's answers show that the collegiate life was quickly and securely re-established. There were twelve vicars and four 'deacons' who regularly attended the cathedral services, 'and these do orderly sing or read prayers with due reverence and devotion'. He himself attended the monthly communion services, but the other vicars were 'seldom there by reason of their officiating at their cures'. A scriptural reading was a feature of their common meals and the college seal was safely kept in a chest with three locks. Good hospitality, especially to the poor, was practised. Humphrey Fisher was largely responsible for the work on the library and the hall, which was apparently rebuilt and completed in 1676. He also rescued and transcribed old documents belonging to the college, including the act book for 1575–96. His accounts as steward of the buttery include a complete catalogue of household furniture and other possessions of the college.[73]

Around this time the vicars developed a convivial and worldly reputation. Barnabas Alderson, who was elected in 1686, was a regular member of card parties held in the coffee house in Milk Lane (now St John Street), where much money and time were recklessly squandered.[74] Perhaps the most scandalous figure was

68. A. G. Matthews, ed., *Walker Revised* (Oxford, 1948), pp. 8–9.

69. Bannister, *The Cathedral Church of Hereford*, p. 98; see also J. and T. W. Webb, eds, *Military Memoir of Colonel John Birch*, Camden Society, new series, 7 (London, 1873), p. 154 n.

70. HCA, 7003/4/3–4, W. Cooke, 'Biographical Memoirs of the Custos and Vicars'.

71. HCA, 7003/1/1, p. 229, vicars choral acts,

28 March 1660. New vicars choral were appointed in September 1660, Lehmberg, *Cathedrals under Siege*, p. 71, quoting HCA, 7031/3, p. 192, chapter acts, 27 September 1660.

72. HCA, 4621.

73. HCA, 7003/4/3, Cooke, 'Biographical Memoirs', no. 7. For the library of the vicars choral, see below, Chapter 28, p. 532.

74. Ibid., no. 14.

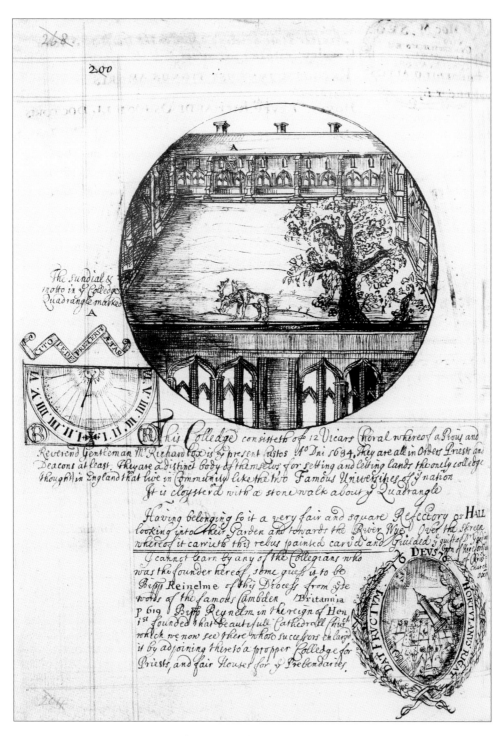

Fig. 130. Drawing and description of the college from Thomas Dingley's 'History from Marble', 1684. (Oxford, Bodleian, MS Top. gen. d. 19, fol. 138v.)

John Broad, who was expelled from the college for a while in 1670 for living incontinently with one Elizabeth Fletcher, who said that he had fathered her child. On 19 April 1670, a girl caused a sensation by bringing a child into college hall during dinner and leaving it near the seat of Broad, saying, 'Mr Broad, here is your child, look to it'.[75] Broad faced proceedings from Bishop Croft for his transgressions in the following year.[76] Several of the chambers in the college were rented by layman, who were elected commoners.[77] The vicars agreed to pay hearth tax for their own chambers in 1664, although they had been told two years earlier that they were not liable.[78] In 1692 they stopped drinking sack at festivals because of its cost, and ceased offering refreshments to guests 'unless it be some substantiall friends or strangers which shall desire to see the Buttry'.[79]

Between 1707 and 1711 no less than six young vicars aged between twenty-six and thirty-three died, as well as two older ones.[80] One of the survivors, Peter Senhouse, was a regular performer in the college musical club, which may have become the nucleus of the Three Choirs Festival.[81] There were seven or eight performers and fifteen or sixteen attenders. They were regaled with ale, cider and tobacco. All the performers gave their services free, except Thomas Woodcock, the leader, who was paid five shillings a night.[82] Woodcock, an excellent violinist, kept a coffee house in the city.[83] The vicars choral were not always perpetuated after their probational year. For example, in 1709 the dean and chapter allowed Francis Astrey to remain living in the college for a while, as they were unwilling 'to load a poor gentleman and master of arts with disgrace or expel him and expose him to hardships; but connive at his stay in the college a little while, to find out some other employment for which he was more fit, being utterly unfit for a choir'.[84]

Custos Richard Waring had 'an increased moroseness of disposition', which was a sore trial to the other vicars. Altogether he was a vicar choral for sixty years.[85] William Crowther had hardly begun his duties in 1711 before he was sent

75. HCA, 7003/1/3, p. 38, vicars choral acts, 29 April 1670.

76. HCA, 6247, p. 37.

77. This practice ceased in 1689; see Lehmberg, *Cathedrals under Siege*, p. 170.

78. Ibid., pp. 170, 203, quoting HCA, 7003/1/3, p. 10, vicars choral acts, 31 October 1664.

79. Lehmberg, *Cathedrals under Siege*, p. 170, quoting HCA, 7003/1/3, p. 155, vicars choral acts, 23 December 1692; cf. HCA, 7003/1/1, p. 140, 15 March 1605.

80. HCA, 7003/4/3, Cooke, 'Biographical Memoirs', no. 32.

81. Ibid., no. 17. This view is accepted in

A. Boden, *Three Choirs: A History of the Festival* (Stroud, 1992), p. 10.

82. D. Lysons and J. Amott, *Origin and Progress of the Meeting of the Three Choirs* (London, 1864), p. 15.

83. J. Hawkins, *A General History of the Science and Practice of Music* (5 vols, London, 1776), v, p. 180. He is not to be confused with two vicars choral by the name of Woodcock.

84. HCA, 7003/4/3, Cooke, 'Biographical Memoirs', no. 29; HCA, 7003/1/3, p. 202, vicars choral acts, 28 March 1710.

85. HCA, 7003/4/3, Cooke, 'Biographical Memoirs', no. 31.

to a lunatic asylum at Droitwich, where he remained for over fifty years.[86] Isaac Donnithorne was a shareholder in Cornish mines, obtaining great wealth through his speculations.[87] Perhaps the most famous vicar choral in the eighteenth century was William Felton (fig. 131). He revived the college concerts about 1749 and transferred them from college hall to the coffee house in St John Street. By extending the range and influence of these subscription concerts, Felton made a considerable contribution to the cultural life of the city and county, building up a substantial body of support. In 1750 college hall was enlarged in time for the evening concerts of the Three Choirs Festival to be held there in 1753 (plate IXb).[88] Felton is chiefly remembered now for

Fig. 131. William Felton, vicar choral 1741–69: portrait in college hall.

his compositions, which include organ and harpsichord concertos and a burial chant written for a funeral service in the cathedral in 1768.

There were many other eccentric vicars choral in the eighteenth century. They included Henry Taswell, who spent hours hitting an octave of bells with drumsticks and refused the attentions of a barber; Thomas Kidley, a vicar choral for over fifty years, who was famous for his brilliant repartee; Thomas Luntley, later a prebendary, who was an able cellist and classical scholar; Richard Underwood, who was a prominent freemason and magistrate, and chaplain to the gaol; and Lewis Maxey, who lost his voice, hearing and sanity during his fifty-one years as a vicar choral (fig. 132).[89]

The life of the college gradually declined during the nineteenth century. Its settled way of life was occasionally challenged by calamities and scandals. New vicars choral had to make certain statutory payments. For example, when Gilbert

86. Ibid., no. 36.
87. Ibid., no. 44. He was neglectful of his duties as a vicar choral, HCA, 5162.
88. HCA, 7003/4/4, Cooke, 'Biographical Memoirs', no. 49; see also HCA, 7003/1/4, p. 114, vicars choral acts, 31 March 1750. The date 1783 in Morriss and Shoesmith,

'The College of the Vicars Choral', p. 168, is a misprint.
89. HCA, 7003/4/4, Cooke, 'Biographical Memoirs', nos. 60–62, 65 and 76; F. E. Gretton, *Memory's Harkback Through Half-a-Century* (London, 1889), pp. 7–8; Barrett, *Vicars Choral*, pp. 24–25.

Fig. 132. Lewis Maxey, vicar choral 1768–1820:
portrait in college hall.

Rice Hancock became a probationary
vicar choral in 1802 he paid 13*s*. 4*d*.
for linen. When he was perpetuated
twelve months later he paid 20*s*. for
eight bushels of wheat and fourteen
bushels of barley. Hancock proved to
be a particularly troublesome individual
and was eventually dismissed.[90]

In 1820 there were three fires in the
college, the first of which destroyed the
college stables. Arson was suspected but
never proved.[91] On 26 July 1828, however, there was a more serious fire,
when 'a great portion of the building
was materially injured and the buttery,
cellar, larder, kitchen and servants' bed-
rooms totally consumed'. In fact, most
of the south range of the college was
badly damaged. The fire was thought
to be accidental, but John Constable,
the college butler, was killed and some
of the college plate and archives were destroyed (fig. 133).[92]

By about this time the average age of the vicars choral had fallen. Nine of
them, they told the dean and chapter in 1831, were young men 'and three seniors
are not so far advanced in years'.[93] At the end of 1832 one of them even brought
his wife to live in the college, much to his colleagues' consternation. They failed
to come to any agreement with him over 'a proceeding so extraordinary and so

90. HCA, 7003/1/5, pp. 72, 76, vicars choral
    acts, 15 December 1802, 15 December
    1803; HCA, 7031/17, pp. 177–79, 180–87,
    190–91, 194–95, chapter acts, 12 and
    24 November, 1 December 1807,
    5 January, 1 March and 2 April 1808;
    HCA, 7003/1/5, pp. 82–83, 89, 17 August
    1805, 15 August 1807; HCA, 5350. For
    details of collegiate life in the early nine-
    teenth century, see Barrett, *Vicars Choral*,
    p. 26, and HCA, 7003/1/5, pp. 90, 148,
    108, 109, 112, 114, 130, 196, vicars choral
    acts, 30 April 1807 and 15 March 1817
    (dogs); 20 September, 27 October and

22 November 1810 (donation to Nelson's
    column and various purchases); 26 March
    and 6 June 1811 (presents); 24 April and
    30 May 1813 (patent steam kitchen
    and college plate); 27 September 1822
    (rent-collector).

91. See above, Chapter 22, pp. 414–15.

92. HCA, 7003/1/5, pp. 237–38, vicars choral
    acts, 9 August 1828. For further details of
    the fires, see P. L. S. Barrett, 'Hereford Ca-
    thedral in the Nineteenth Century', *FHC*,
    52 (1986), p. 16.

93. HCA, 7003/1/5, p. 252, vicars choral acts,
    30 April 1831.

unprecedented in the annals of the college'. The dispute continued for some time.[94]

In the 1830s the vicars choral, together with the rest of the foundation, experienced the determined efforts of Dean John Merewether to improve the life and witness of the cathedral.[95] When the restoration and repair of the cathedral was begun in 1841, the services were transferred to the college chapel for a while, and the books of the cathedral library were stored in the college until 1855.[96] In 1848 Dean Merewether told the Ecclesiastical Commissioners that all eight vicars were either elderly (the oldest, Robert Pearce, was seventy-eight) or in bad health, or resident out of the city.[97]

Two years later the vicars choral were experiencing financial difficulties

Fig. 133. John Constable, butler to the college 1783–1828: portrait in college hall.

because they had been obliged to reduce the rent paid by their tenants for various properties.[98] In fact, the college's income recovered in the early 1850s. The annual amount for each year between 1846 and 1852 shows that the income in 1852 was almost back to the 1846 figure.[99] Dean Dawes told the Ecclesiastical Commission in 1851 that the property of the college ought to be vested in the dean and chapter: 'the property is ill-managed and might be improved – the greater part of the college buildings entirely useless'.[100] In the same year the college leased the

94. Ibid., pp. 273–78, 1 May 1833. In November 1834 Mrs Henry Pearce told Dean Merewether that her sick husband had not received a farthing from the college since the previous April. He was faced with walking to his parish as he could not afford to ride: HCA, 7031/18, p. 477, chapter acts, 1814–34, appendix.

95. See above, Chapter 6, pp. 157–60.

96. HCA, 7031/19, pp. 512, 584, chapter acts, 14 August 1841, 15 January 1844; London, Church of England Record Centre, Church Commissioners' Files, 3208; J. E. West, *Cathedral Organists Past and*

Present (London, 1899), p. 43; F. C. Morgan and P. E. Morgan, *Hereford Cathedral Libraries and Muniments* (Hereford, 1970), pp. 10–12.

97. HCA, 7031/20, p. 137, chapter acts, 26 June 1848.

98. Ibid., pp. 208–9, 14 November 1850.

99. HCA, 7003/1/6, p. 131, vicars choral acts, 2 July 1853. For details see P. L. S. Barrett, *Barchester: English Cathedral Life in the Nineteenth Century* (London, 1993), p. 92.

100. London, Church of England Record Centre, Church Commissioners' Files, 3208.

north-east corner of the quadrangle to the cathedral school, which occupied it for the next twenty-five years. A bridge connected it with school house.[101]

In 1865–66 the dean and chapter held a formal visitation of the college. This led to a revival of monthly college meetings in 1868 and to new regulations governing the life of the college in 1870.[102] In the following year the vicars agreed to eat meals regularly together in the hall. No meals were served in the private rooms of the vicars (apart from tea) except in cases of ill-health or by permission.[103]

The next few years saw several disputes between the vicars choral and the dean and chapter. In 1872 they demanded an apology from Dean Herbert for speaking rudely to one of them.[104] In 1873, John Goss, the custos, reminded the dean and chapter that it had been agreed that the vicars could have their own mace to precede them in procession.[105] But Dean Herbert disapproved, even though they had been given a splendid mace by Sir Frederick Ouseley.[106] In 1874 the chapter objected to the presence of a married vicar choral living with his children in the college.[107] In 1885 they objected to the five assistant lay vicars taking part in 'smoking concerts' at the Green Dragon Hotel and insisted that in future they must not appear at any establishment where intoxicating liquors were sold.[108]

The irregular attendance of the vicars choral continued to cause problems.[109] Perhaps the most notorious matter affecting the college in the late nineteenth century was the case of Dr W. R. Innes. He became a vicar choral in 1887, and brought an action in the King's Bench in 1893 in an attempt to get an equal share of the college income.[110] Later his attendance at cathedral services became very casual. After being admonished by the dean and chapter, following a judgement against him in the appeal court, he appealed to the bishop as visitor. In August

101. HCA, 7003/4/4, Cooke, 'Biographical Memoirs', no. 85; W. T. Carless, _A Short History of Hereford Cathedral School_ (Hereford, 1914), p. 41. About one hundred years earlier, the singing-school and adjoining chamber in the north-west corner of the college were leased to the school: HCA, 7003/1/4, p. 161, vicars choral acts, 19 July 1760.
102. HCA, 7003/1/6, pp. 240–47, 303–6, 310–15, vicars choral acts, 7 December 1865, 4 January 1866, 3 October 1870, 4 April 1871.
103. Ibid., pp. 316–17, 12 August 1871. The common table was discontinued in 1875, never to be revived: ibid., p. 380, 6 March 1875.
104. HCA, 7031/22, pp. 30, 33–35, chapter acts,

4 and 7 December 1872.
105. HCA, 7003/1/6, pp. 335–37, vicars choral acts, 16 June 1873.
106. The subject was revived in 1904, when the chapter agreed to let the vicars choral have their own verger if they paid for him themselves: HCA, 7003/1/7, pp. 172–73, 175, vicars choral acts, 15 February and 20 June 1904.
107. HCA, 7031/22, pp. 110–11, chapter acts, 12 November 1874.
108. Ibid., pp. 482–83, 7 December 1885.
109. HCA, 7031/21, pp. 397–98, 405, chapter acts, 24 March, 4 and 20 April 1870; 7031/22, pp. 25, 195, 24 October 1872, 9 November 1876.
110. W. J. Humfreys, _Memories of Old Hereford_ (Hereford, [c. 1925]), p. 19.

1897 Bishop Percival heard the case, with his chancellor sitting with him as assessor. Innes admitted that he had refused to chant the litany and to read prayers, but claimed that he and his fellow Diddlebury vicar were not responsible for this. Percival dismissed his appeal and upheld the dean and chapter in his judgement of 23 October 1897. Two years later Innes was still rarely seen at the cathedral.[111]

As the twentieth century began, the seeds of the eventual dissolution of the college were already apparent. Dean Leigh was keen to take over its buildings. He told the secretary of the Ecclesiastical Commissioners in 1898 that they were largely uninhabited and should be put to better use.[112] The friction between the dean and chapter and the college continued, and early in the present century there was a dispute over a proposal by the chapter to discontinue choral services for three weeks during the summer holidays.[113] In 1907 the vicars choral complained bitterly when the chapter gave the appointment of succentor to the organist, George Robertson Sinclair.[114]

In 1909 the college plate and goods were deposited in the bank.[115] After the First World War, the Ecclesiastical Commissioners told the college that they held £15,570 on its behalf. A year later negotiations were in hand with the dean and chapter about suppressing one of the four surviving minor canonries, and by 1923 there were only two left.[116] The Church Assembly established a commission of inquiry into the constitution and revenue of cathedrals in 1924. M. R. James, the great Cambridge antiquary, visited Hereford late in 1925 on behalf of the commission to inquire into the college of vicars choral.[117] It was agreed that the property of the college should be handed over to the Ecclesiastical Commissioners, provided a satisfactory agreement could be achieved. Two years later A. D. Steel, the chapter clerk, said that it was many years since he had last collected the fees payable to the college on the installation of a member of the greater chapter.[118] The last meeting of the college was held on 4 June 1937.

111. HCA, 7031/23, pp. 252–53, 260–61, 317–19, chapter acts, 25 May 1894, 12 October 1895, 24 March 1899; HCA, 5242; *Hereford Journal*, 7 December 1898.

112. London, Church of England Record Centre, Church Commissioners' Files, 37357: J. W. Leigh to A. de Brock Porter, 18 April 1898.

113. HCA, 7003/1/7, pp. 163–67, vicars choral acts, 1 August 1903.

114. Ibid., pp. 208–11, 13 and 25 November 1907. 'We are credibly informed', they said, 'that there is a conspiracy afoot among cathedral organists to bring about a total

exclusion of the clergy from any authority or influence whatever in the regulation of the musical services.'

115. Ibid., p. 224, 3 December 1909.

116. Ibid., p. 294, letter from the chapter clerk, 3 July 1919; HCA, 7031/24, p. 131, chapter acts, 24 March 1923. The money saved by leaving these two offices vacant was devoted to increasing the salaries and pensions of the lay clerks.

117. R. W. Pfaff, *Montague Rhodes James* (London, 1980), p. 370.

118. HCA, 7003/1/7, pp. 337, 340, vicars choral acts, 27 November 1925, 20 May 1927.

Fig. 134. Philip L. S. Barrett, 1947–98, the last vicar choral (1976–86), in the choir stalls.

After the dissolution of the college, under the terms of the Cathedrals Measure 1931, the buildings and goods of the college were taken over by the dean and chapter, who sold much of the plate to repair the cloisters.[119] Two minor canons continued to be part of the cathedral foundation, employed by the dean and chapter but no longer possessing the rights, privileges and liberties of their predecessors. Under the terms of the 1966 cathedral statutes, the title 'minor canon' was dropped in favour of the older title of 'vicar choral'. One of the vicars choral was also chaplain at the cathedral school, an arrangement which lasted until 1979. The author of this chapter was the last to bear the title 'vicar choral' until he moved to a new post in 1986 (fig. 134).

119. For sale catalogue, see HCA, 6025/1, 23 June 1938. The Order in Council abolishing the college is dated 29 October 1936: HCA 7005/14, register of leases, pp. 101–11.

24

The Three Choirs Festival

Anthony Boden

For one week every summer the cities of Gloucester, Hereford and Worcester play host, in turn, to the many hundreds of visitors who attend the oldest non-competitive music festival in the world. 'When did it all begin?' is the question most frequently asked by newcomers, and a precise answer is impossible to give. Having searched diligently, the Revd Daniel Lysons, the first historian of the music meetings of the Three Choirs, was, in 1812, forced to admit that, 'it is in vain that I have endeavoured ... to trace anything like the time of their first establishment'.[1]

The earliest printed evidence of a triennial music meeting in one of the three cities is to be found in a notice in an edition of the *Worcester Postman* dated 14–21 August 1719:

> The members of the yearly Musical Assembly of these parts are desired to take notice, that, by their subscription in September last at Gloucester, they are obliged ... to meet at Worcester, on Monday the last day of this instant August; in order to publick performance, on the Tuesday and Wednesday following.

It is clear from this that an annual event was already established by 1719. Although the numbering of the modern festival is counted from 1715, an approximation decided upon by Sir Ivor Atkins when restarting Three Choirs at Worcester in 1920 following a break caused by the First World War, it is probable that the music meetings began even earlier. In the early years of the eighteenth century the organists of Hereford and Gloucester, Henry Hall junior and William Hine, worked closely together and, unusually, collaborated in the composition of a morning service, 'Hall and Hine in E flat': the *Te deum* is by Hall, the *Jubilate* by

---

1. D. Lysons, *History of the Origins and Progress of the Meeting of the Three Choirs of Gloucester, Worcester and Hereford* (Gloucester, 1812), p. 159. See also A. Boden, *Three Choirs: A History of the Festival* (Stroud, 1992), pp. 1f.

Hine. The earliest meetings were of two days' duration, beginning with matins in the cathedral, and it is possible that Hall and Hine's service was composed with a combined performance by two or more cathedral choirs in mind. The Gloucester Cathedral treasurer's accounts show that on an unspecified date in 1709 he paid £2 to Hall, a large sum which could well have represented a payment for Hereford's participation in a combined service – possibly for 'Hall and Hine in E flat'.

If 1709 did indeed mark a first embryonic music meeting, the timing would fit in perfectly with the three-year cycle of known and documented 1719 Worcester, 1720 Hereford and 1721 Gloucester meetings; and if a meeting took place in sequence at Hereford, at Hall's invitation, there is only one year in which that would have been possible: 1711. Henry Hall died in January 1714 at the age of twenty-seven or twenty-eight. What is certain is that the regular annual music meetings began in music clubs:

> The meetings of the Three Choirs of Gloucester, Hereford and Worcester, originated in a compact entered into by members of certain music clubs or societies in those cities, to make an annual visit to each other in rotation, and continue together two days, for improving themselves in harmony, by the performance of several concerts of music. These clubs consisted chiefly of members of the several choirs, with the addition of a few *amateurs* of music, in the several cities and their immediate neighbourhood.[2]

Music clubs had existed in the three cities before the music meetings began, and the closest link between music club and cathedral was at Hereford. The hall of the college of vicars choral had become the focus for a college music club soon after its completion in 1676: a venue for the performance and enjoyment of secular music which, of course, was banned from the cathedral. The club was, as Lysons pointed out, 'an establishment of little expense: the performances were all *gratis*, except that of Mr Woodcock, their leader, whose nightly pay was five shillings. The members were regaled with ale, cyder and tobacco'.[3] Such was the style of the earliest evening secular concerts at Three Choirs. The music meetings had been inaugurated with purely social rather than charitable ends; but change was soon to come.

In 1716 Dr Philip Bisse, bishop of Hereford, appointed his brother, Thomas, to the chancellorship of the diocese (fig. 120). Thomas, an eloquent preacher with a genuine concern for the wretched condition of so many of his clerical brethren and their families, soon pressed forward the idea that the annual music meetings should embrace a charitable purpose similar to that of the annual service held in

2. Lysons, *History of the Origins and Progress of the Meeting of the Three Choirs*, p. 159.
3. Ibid., p. 161.

London by the Corporation of the Sons of the Clergy: to raise money for the relief of poor clergymen, their widows and orphans. Thomas Bisse's first sermon at Three Choirs was published in 1720, *A Rationale on Cathedral Worship or Choir Service*. He continued to promote the interests of the annual celebrations of music, and in his sermon at the 1724 Gloucester meeting he proposed, for the first time, that a collection be taken up after morning service: 'for placing out, or assisting the education and maintenance of the orphans of the poorer clergy belonging to the dioceses of Gloucester, Worcester, and Hereford, or of members of the three respective choirs'.[4]

In the following two years, first at Worcester and then at Hereford, Bisse persisted in his purpose. His 1726 sermon at Hereford was based upon a text from Ecclesiastes 2:8: 'I gat me men-singers and women-singers, and the delights of the sons of men, as musical instruments, and that of all sorts'. In a note to the sermon, he also wrote: 'having first proposed this charity with success at Gloucester, in 1724, and recommended it at Worcester in 1725, I thought myself obliged to promote it in this way, in the church and diocese to which I belong'. The charity soon proved its effectiveness. In the first year, 1724, the collection amounted to £31 10s. 0d., and it eventually became the custom to take up a collection after every concert. As the festival extended in length from just two days to a week, so the amounts collected increased considerably. The 1985 Hereford festival raised £6500, but since that year the collections have been reduced to those following the opening service, the last concert and at the close of each choral evensong. The festival itself is now a registered charity and the distribution of money taken up in collections is decided by the deans and chapters of the three dioceses; but for over 260 years Three Choirs provided a sizeable annual sum for the relief of the widows and orphans of the poorer clergy.

Details of the music performed at Three Choirs in the first half of the eighteenth century are scanty. Two settings of *Te deum*, one by Purcell and the other by William Croft, are known to have been sung at Gloucester in 1721. Ten years later the *Gloucester Journal* makes its first mention of specific musical items at the meetings – and Purcell was still supreme. By 1736 the name Handel had taken its place alongside that of Purcell, and it was the music of Handel which rapidly rose into a position of absolute command at the music meetings.

Whilst Handel's *Te deums* and anthems were included in the morning services, oratorios such as *Alexander's Feast* and *Samson* were not permitted to be performed in the cathedrals. A clear distinction was drawn between sacred and secular music. Even Handel's *Messiah* was regarded as secular entertainment when first given at Three Choirs in 1757 (at Gloucester) and relegated to a public hall. A breakthrough

4. Hereford City Library, Hopton Collection, 361/3648.

was at last made at Hereford in 1759, the year of Handel's death, and for very practical reasons. The college hall would have been too small for the scale of *Messiah* performances which had drawn great crowds to Gloucester and Worcester in the two preceding years. The only other suitable building in Hereford would have been the Guildhall, but that was in a ruinous state. The prestige of the city, a considerable boost to local business and a high potential income to the festival charity were at stake. The mayor and aldermen recognised that urgent action was necessary. In a documented agreement between them and the citizens of Hereford, they agreed that the Guildhall should be rebuilt, 'upon a more extensive plan ... so as to have a room proper for the reception of the company at the meetings of the Choirs of Hereford, Gloucester and Worcester as well as for the general convenience and use of the said city ... and agree to and with the Lord Bishop of Hereford and his successors that the said room when built ... shall at all times be free for the use of the said meetings'.[5] Three weeks later, notices were placed in the papers advertising that *Messiah* would be performed in the cathedral.

The eighteenth-century music meetings and their attendant attractions – entertainment in private houses, great meals at local hotels, balls and horse-races – provided a focal point in the social calendar of the nobility, gentry and better-off clergy. Timed to follow the annual harvest, the meetings provided an interlude of civic hospitality in late August or early September, before the more serious winter business of hunting began. But there was a price to pay. Large-scale works, such as those by Handel, made it necessary to bring in singers to augment the cathedral choirs and to engage the finest orchestral players and soloists from London, often at such expense that costs far exceeded income. Losses were, at first, met by one and later two stewards, wealthy members of county families who were, in effect, guarantors, and who selflessly agreed to shoulder this financial burden in order that the meetings and the charity which depended upon them should survive. As the century drew to a close, this precarious arrangement seemed certain to collapse.

An exceptionally heavy loss was anticipated in 1798. Britain was at war with France. Many gentlemen were on active service and it seemed extremely unlikely that two stewards could be found to underwrite the risk. On 26 July the worried dean and chapter placed a notice in the *Hereford Journal* asking that the nobility, clergy and gentry consider raising a subscription for the charity in the event that the music meeting should not take place; but the idea was a failure and the subscription unproductive. Fortunately, the duke of Norfolk had gathered a large

---

5. HRO, AE 75. The new Guildhall was not built until 1811, but the Music Room in the west cloister at the cathedral, completed by 1762, provided the venue for some Three Choirs events until its demolition in 1834; see below, Chapter 33, p. 582, and R. Caird, 'The Georgian Music Room at Hereford Cathedral', *Three Choirs Festival Programme* (Hereford, 2000), forthcoming.

number of singers and instrumentalists at his country house at Holme Lacy, all of whom offered their services free at two performances in aid of the charity on 5 and 6 September. When news of this plan was published in the *Hereford Journal* it prompted a meeting of the county gentry, from which pride emerged triumphant. Instead of accepting the artists' benevolent offer, it was decided that the meeting of the Three Choirs should go ahead as usual, but that from then on the number of stewards should be increased. In the event, six stewards accepted office in 1798.

Three Choirs had provided an example for other cities, such as Birmingham, Leeds, Liverpool and Norwich, to follow. In the first half of the nineteenth century, England was steadily changing from a rural to an urban society, and by 1851 more than half of the population lived in towns and cities. Thirty years later the figure had risen

Fig. 135. The nave of Hereford Cathedral during a performance of *Messiah*, 1837. (HCL, B.3.53.)

to 70 per cent. Industrialists and businessmen were founding a new aristocracy, accompanied by a desire to give expression to their status. One symbol of this civic pride, Birmingham Town Hall, opened in 1834 and became, quite naturally, the grand new venue for the Birmingham Festival. Up until this time, all cathedral concerts at Hereford had been performed in the choir, where audiences were often packed to suffocation; evening secular performances had been transferred to the recently built Shirehall in 1819. Now the music meetings faced both competition from Birmingham and the urgent need to ease the crush of ever larger audiences in the cathedral. Under these circumstances, and in the face of regular financial losses, the twenty-four-year-old organist of Hereford Cathedral, S. S. Wesley, sought and obtained approval for the nave of the cathedral to be used for the first time for oratorio performances (fig. 135). A similar arrangement was adopted by Gloucester in the following year and by Worcester in 1842. Three Choirs was expanding to meet increased audience expectations. By 1838, the year following Queen Victoria's accession, the orchestra and chorus had grown to three hundred and the meeting was, as at Birmingham, designated, for the first time, a 'Festival'.

Not all of the problems facing the festival committee in the nineteenth century were financial. Evangelicalism, 'the call to seriousness', had established itself in a dominant position in British Protestantism in the century before the 1830s. For the next forty years evangelicals resisted the reawakening of the Catholic spirit which flourished within the Anglican communion under the impetus of the Oxford Movement. Three Choirs was attacked by those who deplored the use of cathedrals, as they saw it, as opera houses and who, at the same time, were alert to any suspicion of 'popery'. Against this background, the choice of items for performance at the festival became a matter requiring great delicacy. Mozart's *Requiem*, for instance, was adapted under the title *Redemption* for performance in English; Beethoven's *Mass in C* was advertised for some time as the *Service in C* 'to suit Protestant tastes'; even so, when performed at Gloucester in 1850 a large proportion of the audience walked out, 'marking painfully the schism in the High and Low Church'.[6] Dean Dawes was even said to have expressed his hostility to the 'abominable festival' at Hereford in 1858 by taking away the key of the choir, whilst Archdeacon Freer and Lord Saye and Sele, one of the canons, left the city.

Opposition to the festival came to a head in 1875 at Worcester, when the dean and chapter refused to give permission for the cathedral to be used for musical performances unconnected with any religious service. The citizens of Worcester, many of whom stood to suffer financial loss, were dismayed. Only about sixty people turned up for the opening service of what became known as the 'Mock Festival'. No solo performers or orchestra were engaged, no platform was erected in the cathedral, no tickets were sold, no secular concerts were held, only the three cathedral choirs took part and only services were heard. The festival seemed to be doomed.

Fortunately, the mayor of Hereford publicly declared the support of the city council for Three Choirs and invited the civic dignitaries at Gloucester and Worcester to come to Hereford to demonstrate their resolve that the festival should continue as of old. They readily agreed and the three bodies proceeded to the cathedral in state as a gesture of their solidarity. Since 1875 the only interruptions to the otherwise unbroken annual Three Choirs tradition have been those caused by the two world wars, but an element of opposition to the festival continued until well into the twentieth century.

Messiah remained an indispensable favourite at the festival for two hundred years, being performed whole or in part every year until 1963. No other work rivalled its popularity until Mendelssohn's *Elijah* entered the Three Choirs programme in 1847: it remained as an annual feature until 1929. British composers whose work enjoyed some popularity at the festival in the last thirty years of the nineteenth

6. *Illustrated London News*, 14 September 1850.

century included Mackenzie, Stainer, Stanford and Sullivan; but, with the addition of the name Hubert Parry, whose cantata *Prometheus Unbound* was first heard at Gloucester in 1880, English music had, as Sir Henry Hadow put it, 'after many years come again to its own, and it had come with a masterpiece in its hand'. Parry's works were performed regularly at Three Choirs, and his *De profundis*, *Magnificat* and *Ode on the Nativity* were written especially for Hereford.

In 1897, the year of Queen Victoria's Diamond Jubilee, George Robertson Sinclair, the Hereford Cathedral organist, broke with the tradition of an opening service and sermon on Tuesday morning, and followed instead the example set by Worcester in 1881 (fig. 136). An 'immense congregation' was present to hear the festival chorus, drawn for the first time at Hereford entirely from the Three Choirs cities, some of the principal soloists and orchestra take part in a special opening service on Sunday morning, 12 September. Three months earlier, Sinclair's young assistant organist, Percy Hull, had been present when Edward Elgar had visited Sinclair:

Fig. 136. Scene at Hereford Cathedral during the Three Choirs Festival, 1897. (HCL, neg. 1162.)

Fig. 137. Three Choirs Festival, Hereford 1933. Standing, left to right: Sir Ivor Atkins, Dr Percy Hull, Herbert Sumsion, organists of Worcester, Hereford and Gloucester cathedrals; foreground, Sir Edward Elgar. (Photograph in the song school.)

I was privileged to hear Elgar play over his *Festival Te deum and Benedictus* in Sinclair's house to see whether the work would be acceptable for the programme of the festival ... He was as nervous as a kitten and heaved a huge sigh of relief when Sinclair said: 'It is *very very* modern, but I think it will do; you shall play it again after supper when Hull and I will give you our final verdict'. All this in Sinclair's stammering and somewhat patronising fashion.[7]

Elgar's *Te deum and Benedictus* was first heard at the 1897 opening service, and within eight years his compositions had established themselves as unassailable festival favourites (fig. 137). British composers had begun to take centre stage at Three Choirs, and works by Vaughan Williams, Holst, Howells, Finzi, Bliss, Britten, Delius and Walton were soon to feature regularly alongside both traditional

7. *Royal Academy of Music Magazine* (1960), p. 6.

masterpieces and festival commissions. Today's programmes are more innovative than ever before, the success of the modern festival reflected in a demand for tickets which regularly outstrips supply. As Thomas Bisse said in 1729, 'we are now become a *great band*; and a greater we may yet grow'.[8]

8. W. Shaw, *The Three Choirs Festival* (Worcester, 1954), p. 108.

25

The Organs

Roy Massey

It is almost certain that in pre-Reformation times Hereford would have been as well equipped as any other cathedral in the provision of organs for the accompaniment of the elaborate liturgy of the Hereford Use but, unfortunately, records are silent about details of any instruments before the end of the seventeenth century. There is, in the second bay on the south side of the choir, the remains of a gallery about twelve feet high which may have been the site of a medieval organ loft.[1] It is large enough to accommodate a small instrument, and there may well have been another organ on the stone pulpitum at the head of the nave. There are records of payments in 1307 and 1315 to Giles, clerk, called tailor, keeper of the organs, who received from the dean and chapter of the church of Hereford five marks of silver, being the annual salary they owed him for his customary service.[2] A new organ was made early in the sixteenth century and in the 1520s and 1530s payments are listed to a John Hichons for repairs to two organs, payment also being made towards another instrument which he had begun to build.[3] Early in the seventeenth century repairs were carried out by Mr (Robert or Thomas) Dallam.[4] Presumably it was this 'most sweet organ' which the three military officers heard when they visited the cathedral and attended evensong during their tour of twenty-six counties in 1634,[5] and which was soon to be destroyed in the Civil War.

At the Restoration of the monarchy in 1660 it must have taken a considerable time to repair the building and its fittings following the depredations of the years of conflict. In the accounting year ending Michaelmas 1666, a fund of 'Benevolence

---

1. Marshall, *Hereford Cathedral*, p. 108.
2. HCA, 2750, 2601.
3. HCA, 7031/1, fos, 36r, 44v, 66v, 70v, 71r, chapter acts, 14 June 1525, 9 September 1528, 13 March 1531, 30 September and 10 October 1532, 1 July 1533; W. Shaw, *The Organists and Organs of Hereford Cathedral* (2nd edn, Hereford, 1988), p. 28.

See also above, Chapter 21, p. 391–92, and below, Chapter 32, p. 572.

4. HCA, R 600, R 604, clavigers' accounts, 1612–13 and 1629–30; Shaw, *Organists and Organs*, p. 28.
5. BL, Lansdowne MS 213, fos 332–34; see above, Chapter 4, p. 98.

Money' was established for repairing the cathedral and for the making of an organ. Disbursements were made from this of £39, £30 and £5 17s. 6d. 'to the organ maker', probably Robert Taunton of Bristol, who was paid a further 10s. when he came to mend the organ. £6 was given to one Stallard for the loan of his organ.[6]

It was not until 1686 that a new instrument by Renatus Harris was built at a cost of £515, exclusive of the case, which, with gilding, painting and carving cost a further £185 (plate XI). A long parchment headed 'Catalogue of All Benefactors of the Great Organ 1686' names all the subscribers to the organ fund, together with a list of disbursements for lead, scaffolding, iron, canvas, carving, gilding, painting etc., as well as post, letters, horse hire and other necessary expenses, bringing the total cost of the instrument to £720.[7] Renatus came of an organ-building family, his father Thomas Harris having married the daughter of Thomas Dallam. Thomas Harris emigrated to France in the mid 1640s,[8] probably realising that the two ordinances of the Lords and Commons of 9 May 1644, 'for the speedy demolishing of all organs, images, and all matters of superstitious monuments in all Cathedrals, and Collegiate or Parish Churches' would effectively deprive him of his means of livelihood in this country. Renatus was almost certainly born in France and, though trained by his father in the art and craft of organ building, must also have absorbed some influences from the style and tonal qualities of the French organ of that period. He is often referred to as the great rival of the other famous post-Restoration organ builder, Bernard Smith, but being twenty-three years younger than Smith he did not begin to achieve prominence until the 1680s. In 1683 he took over the business from his aged father and began to produce a series of notable organs including those in the cathedrals of Bristol (1685), Hereford (1686), Norwich (1689), Winchester (1693), St Patrick's, Dublin (1696), Christ Church, Dublin (1697), Salisbury (1710) and Cork; five organs in collegiate buildings at the universities, among them King's College Chapel, Cambridge, and over a score of instruments in the City of London and suburban churches. The Hereford organ was placed on the pulpitum in cases facing east and west. No print or painting has been discovered of the east front of the instrument, so we do not know whether the Choir division was accommodated in a 'Chair' case positioned behind the player, as was so often the practice at this period. A print dated Wednesday 27 September 1837, showing a performance of Handel's *Messiah* in the nave, shows a west case which closely resembles the still existing front of the 1685 organ in Bristol Cathedral (fig. 135). As at Bristol, the Hereford case appears to be markedly

6. HCA, R 611, accounts, 1665–66; Shaw, *Organists and Organs*, pp. 28–29.

7. HCA, 6255, formerly on display in the cathedral song school.

8. A. Freeman, 'Renatus Harris', *The Organ*, 6 (1927), p. 160.

architectural in feeling with Corinthian columns on either side of the arch-like openings through which the pipes in the flats are displayed under swags of carved foliage. From the pipes which remain in the present organ we can see that several of the display pipes were handsomely embossed and painted or gilded.

The original specification has not come down to us, but from the evidence of Harris's work elsewhere, there would have been a well-developed Great chorus with independent Tierce and Larigot ranks in the French style, together with a lesser chorus on the Choir organ.[9] Repairs and restoration work became necessary as the years went by; Harris was called back in 1707. In 1729 Thomas Swarbrick of Warwick, whose nephew Henry became cathedral organist in 1720, took over maintenance of the instrument. John Byfield (who was Renatus Harris's son-in-law) and probably Snetzler, Green and Avery, all repaired or maintained the organ during the eighteenth century.[10] What is not clear from the records is when the short compass Swell organ was added, but by the end of the century the specification as noted in the Leffler notebooks was as follows:[11]

Compass: Great and Choir, *AAA – d²* ; Swell, *c – d²*

GREAT ORGAN

1	Open Diapason	[8]	7	Fifteenth	[2]
2	Open Diapason	[8]	8	Tierce	[1⅗]
3	Stopped Diapason	[8]	9	Small Twelfth or Larigot	[1⅓]
4	Principal	[4]	10	Sesquialtera	[III]
5	Principal	[4]	11	Trumpet	[8]
6	Twelfth	[2⅔]	12	Cornet (c – d²)	[IV]

SWELL ORGAN

13	Open Diapason	[8]	15	Cornet	[III]
14	Principal	[4]	16	Trumpet	[8]

CHOIR ORGAN

17	Dulciana (c – d²)	[8]	20	Flute	[4]
18	Stopped Diapason	[8]	21	Fifteenth	[2]
19	Principal	[4]	22	Vox Humana	[8]

9. C. Clutton and A. Niland, *The British Organ* (Ilkley, 1963), p. 77.

10. HCA, 4930; 7031/3, pp. 573, 578, chapter acts, 25 June 1707, 25 June 1708; 7031/5, pp. 77, 89, chapter acts, 23 January, 12

November 1772.

11. Royal College of Music, MS 1161, fol. 47; C. W. Pearce, *Notes on English Organs, 1800–1810* (London, [1912]); Shaw, *Organists and Organs*, p. 31.

A pedal board and pedal pipes were added by Thomas Elliott in 1806, GGG–FF in compass, lacking GGG sharp, a pipe which was added in 1818 during the ill-fated organistship of Charles James Dare.[12] J. C. Bishop took over the maintenance of the instrument in 1832, when a major restoration took place, no doubt influenced by the newly-appointed organist, the young Samuel Sebastian Wesley.[13] This work included the addition of a further fourteen pedal pipes to complete the compass to C, adjustment of the console measurements to facilitate easier pedalling, the provision of a new five-stop Swell division from tenor C, and three of Bishop's patent composition pedals to give greater ease of stop control.[14] Wesley's famous anthem *The Wilderness*, with its elaborate pedal part, was first performed at the reopening of the organ on 6 November 1832.

In 1841 the central tower was found to be in an appallingly insecure condition and, aware of a previous catastrophe in 1786 when the west end tower had collapsed, the dean and chapter, together with L. N. Cottingham their architect, ordered the pulpitum and organ to be hurriedly dismantled to enable structural repairs to begin under the crossing, a work which contemporaries ranked as among the most stupendous engineering feats of the age. Between 1842 and 1850 the cathedral services were transferred to All Saints church, during which time the instrument was removed for safekeeping to the college of the vicars choral.[15] Services were resumed in the nave from Easter 1850, the organ having been temporarily re-erected under the easternmost arch of the north aisle of the nave by J. C. Bishop in 1849, working under the supervision of the organist, G. Townshend Smith.[16] The work cost £420, a sum raised, not without difficulty, by public subscription. The cathedral choir at this time was in a state of dire neglect. A correspondent to the *Hereford Times* on 2 June 1849 wrote:

> No doubt the organ was a good instrument when given by King Charles II [a common misconception at this time] but I happen to know that about seventeen years ago, it had ceased to delight the ears of our worthy citizens and strangers, in as much as most of the stops were not usable – the pipes jostled one another in some places like rows of hop poles, some lying flat, others broken off, and the trackers and connecting rods tied together with thread or mended with sealing wax ... if it is so important, so expedient, so desirable to the Cathedral service that the organ should be re-erected is it not equally so that the broken down choir should be remodelled and reinforced?[17]

12. Shaw, *Organists and Organs*, p. 32.
13. HCA, 7031/18, pp. 365, 372–73, chapter acts, 10 July, 18 September 1832; L. Elvin, *Bishop and Son, Organ Builders* (Lincoln, 1984), p. 167.
14. Elvin, *Bishop and Son*, p. 168; Shaw, *Organists and Organs*, pp. 32–35.
15. J. Merewether, *A Statement of the Condition and Circumstances of the Cathedral Church of Hereford* (Hereford, 1842), pp. 23–24.
16. Elvin, *Bishop and Son*, p. 170.
17. *Hereford Times*, 2 June 1849.

Bishop had the organ ready for the Three Choirs Festival on 11 September and received his fee of £6 6s. 0d. for being in attendance during that time. The organ remained in Bishop's care until 1861, when they lost the contract to another firm at the reopening of the building.[18] Sadly, the Renatus Harris cases seem to have been either lost or consciously dispensed with at this time of uncertainty in the life of the instrument. All that remains of them is a carved wooden lion, over two feet high, crowned and holding between its front paws the royal arms within a cartouche. Sufficient painting and gilding survive on this figure to remind us of the glory that has been lost.

The reopening of the cathedral upon the completion of its restoration necessitated a significant rebuilding and enlargement of the organ. This was done under the direction of the precentor, the Reverend Sir Frederick Arthur Gore Ouseley (fig. 124). Appointed non-residentiary precentor in 1855, Ouseley combined his Hereford duties with those of warden of the college he founded at St Michael's, Tenbury. An authority on organ design, Ouseley rejected proposals received from J. C. Bishop and engaged the firm of Gray and Davison to do the work, using as much of the old pipework as its condition allowed.[19] In Gilbert Scott's reordering, the pulpitum was not replaced, so a new position for the instrument in the westernmost bay of the south side of the choir was adopted. Mr Davison and Scott discussed this on 14 November 1862.[20] The stalls were moved from under the tower into the eastern arm of the building, and the Great organ, bracketed out over the choristers, with the Swell behind over the south aisle, was in a well-nigh ideal position for the accompaniment of the choir. The organist, however, squashed into a little space at floor level behind the prebendal seats, could have heard both his choir in the stalls and the organ above him only very inadequately. The elegant Harris cases were replaced by an organ front to Scott's design with an elaborate wrought iron framework costing £154.[21] The organ took rather longer to build than the dean and chapter had anticipated and several irate letters from the chapter clerk during 1863 urged Gray and Davison to make haste.[22] The instrument was used for the first time on 30 June 1864, the first anniversary of the reopening of the building (fig. 138).[23] Sadly, the organ seems to have given trouble immediately, as on 2 June 1866 a report by Mr Nicholson, organ builder of Worcester, was read to the chapter, from which it appears that the construction of the instrument was

18. Elvin, *Bishop and Son*, p. 170.
19. Shaw, *Organists and Organs*, pp. 35–36.
20. Birmingham, Central Library, British Organ Archive, Gray and Davison ledger, vol. 7.
21. Ibid.
22. HCA, 7031/21, pp. 119–20, 148–49, chapter acts, 16 and 23 February, 3 July, 15 August 1863.
23. See above, Chapter 6, p. 162.

Fig. 138. Contemporary print of the restored choir, *c.* 1863. (HCL, B.4.169a.)

very defective. The chapter clerk was directed to send the purport of such a report to Messrs Gray and Davison, requiring them to fulfil their contract.[24] A further letter, dated 25 June, declined the terms of Gray and Davison for repairs to the pneumatic action. They were informed that the dean and chapter were so dissatisfied with their work that they had determined to employ some other organ builder.[25] The chapter clerk was then ordered to write to Nicholson and ascertain if he was fully acquainted with pneumatic action and if he would undertake to put the cathedral organ thoroughly in order without delay and, if so, to obtain from Mr Nicholson an estimate of the probable cost. Nicholson's estimate was considered the following year but its acceptance postponed until 1868, when the proposals for removing the pneumatic movement from the organ and placing new movements with three new composition pedals were implemented. Nicholson's bill for £100 was not finally settled until November 1870.[26]

The specification was as follows:[27]

Compass: Manuals, CC-f2: Pedals, CCC-F.

Bourdon	16	Twelfth	$2\frac{2}{3}$
Open Diapason	8	Fifteenth	2
Open Diapason	8	Tierce	$1\frac{3}{5}$
Stop Diapason	8	Larigot	$1\frac{1}{3}$
Gamba	8	Furniture	III
Clarabella	8	Mixture	II
Principal	4	Trumpet	8
Principal	4	Clarion	4

Swell to Great

SWELL

Bourdon	16	Fifteenth	2
Open Diapason	8	Mixture	III
Stop Diapason	8	Contra Fagotto	16
Keraulophon	8	(Prepared for)	
(Prepared for)		Cornopean	8
Principal	4	Oboe	8
		Clarion	4

24. HCA, 7031/21, p. 250, chapter acts, 2 June 1866.

25. Ibid., p. 254, 25 June 1866.

26. Ibid., p. 437, 3 December 1870.

27. *Hereford: Cathedral, City and Neighbourhood: A Handbook for Visitors and Residents* (3rd edn, Hereford, 1867), pp. 28–30; Shaw, *Organists and Organs*, pp. 35–36.

CHOIR

Stop Diapason	8	Flute	4
Spitz Flute	8	Principal	4
Dulciana	8	Flageolet	2
		Cremona	8

Swell to Choir

PEDAL

Grand Open Diapason	32	Principal	8
(Prepared for)		Fifteenth	4
Open Diapason	16	Trombone	16
Violone	16	Trumpet	8
Bourdon	16		

Great to Pedal
Swell to Pedal
Choir to Pedal

Pneumatic action for lightening the touch was applied to the Great organ, also to the whole of the drawstop and composition action throughout. It was also intended to blow the instrument by water power, but three handles were used until 1892.

It is not entirely surprising that, before many years had elapsed, moves were afoot to complete the prepared-for stops in the Swell and Pedal departments and to add a fourth manual. In December 1878 a report upon the state of the organ was made to the dean and chapter by the precentor, the succentor and Langdon Colborne, the organist (fig. 125), who recommended the insertion of the Swell Keraulophon and Double Trumpet and the 32 ft Open Diapason on the Pedal. They also recommended the addition of a fourth manual to be called the Solo organ, comprising Harmonic Flutes 8 ft and 4 ft, Orchestral Oboe 8 ft, Clarionet 8 ft and a Tuba Mirabilis 8 ft on heavy wind; also, possibly, a Vox Coelistis on the Swell, to undulate with the Keraulophon and a Vox Humana, together with new couplers Solo to Great and Solo to Pedal. All these additions and improvements it was thought might be added for the sum of £700 exclusive, however, of the reconstruction and repair of the blowing apparatus.[28] At this point Henry Willis, who in 1873 had rebuilt the organ at St Michael's Tenbury for Ouseley and who was rapidly becoming recognised as the leading organ builder in the country, was requested to make a report on the instrument. In his typically thorough and perspicacious manner he wrote as follows:

I critically examined the Hereford organ last Monday. The blowing and bellows are worthless and must be all new. I find that there are facilities for doing all

28. *Hereford Times*, 1 November 1879.

the works specified until we come to the 32 feet Open Wood on the pedals.
I think that £1000 would do what you specify and I will undertake to do it
if you wish; but it appears to me that your scheme does not embrace the most
essential consideration in the improvement of the Hereford organ. I trust,
therefore, that you will permit me to say what I think should be done, bearing
in mind the failure of this and the success of my last three Cathedral organs,
nor should any architectural objection be lightly raised when the importance
of placing the organist well stands in the balance. The organist, as you know,
is placed in the bowels of the instrument, where he hears far more of the
noise of the movements (surpassing a weaving machine) than he does of the
pipes, and as to hearing the choral service it is simply impossible. All this may
be completely reversed and certainly should be the first thing thought of, and
I should proceed in the following manner: 1st. I would elevate the front about
five feet and support it on an arcade. I would elevate the organist until his
head became two feet above the top of the stalls. I would then make good
the organ loft with substantial framing and a stout soffit (organ loft being
approached as at present) and restore the panels of the stalls. I would make an
entirely new disposition of the Great and Choir organs by placing the back
portion over the front one. I would place the Choir organ on the sill (or cill)
of the upper arch, and build the Solo above that sill also. Instead of crowding
in a complete 32 feet Open Wood I would make an effort to dispose of only
twelve notes and derive the remainder from the present 16 feet by that wondrous
pneumatic arrangement so successful for the same purpose at the Royal Albert
hall, which is practically as good and useful as a whole stop without its
inconveniences. There must be new keys, pedals and movements to do even
what you specify, and that horrid pneumatic lever must be extirpated. There
are great facilities for putting new ample and noiseless bellows and their actions,
and this I would do. But such a sweeping improvement (one which would
rid you of all the present annoyances) made in the disposition of the constructive
body of the organ, is not quite all that should be done. There is a good deal
of revoicing in both reeds and flutes that cannot safely be neglected and this
I fear carries your work somewhat above the sum you state as a limit. I do
not think that I could undertake the whole work for less than thirteen hundred
pounds. Of course you would then have one of the finest and most satisfactory
organs in the country; but it appears to me that if you do not improve the
situation of the organist it would be unwise to do more than improve the
wind. The elevation of the front will do no damage to the architecture but
rather improve it, for the stalls will cease to appear to support the organ, whilst
the amount of five feet will hardly be felt in that height or obliterate anything
above. At any rate this is the only thing to concede on the part of the Dean

and Chapter, and if they will do that I am sure you will have no difficulty in raising the money, and I am ready to go into the matter at once; indeed, we should do so to get well away for the festival.[29]

In a second report, dated 16 February and addressed to the dean, Willis said:

My estimate of £1300 is for a total reconstruction of the instrument, with certain important additions, which could not be made except on a redistribution of its several parts. It includes every expense connected with the work, so that you would not have one farthing more than £1300 to pay. The organ loft and its staircase would be provided by me. A floor would be built over the doorway and a staircase for the blowers to ascend would be placed in the passage to the vestry. I have purposed that the front of the organ (which, however, in other respects would remain as it is) should be raised about five feet in order that the head of the organist may be about two feet above the top of the stalls. The organist will then be in the best possible position to hear what everybody is doing and also what he does himself. There is, unfortunately, no middle course, and I advised, if the whole work I proposed cannot be effected, that nothing should be done beyond rectifying the wind apparatus.[30]

It will thus be seen that the extended work proposed by Willis involved the expenditure of a much larger sum than was at first contemplated, but it was considered so desirable that the dean and chapter at once agreed to increase their proposed subscription of £100 to £250. The dean also gave £100 personally, Lord Saye and Sele £50, Canon Musgrave £25 and Lady Saye and Sele £10. The total sums promised by public subscription amounted to £1280 19s. 6d., which left only the small sum of £19 0s. 6d. to be made up. The work was therefore put in hand immediately.[31]

Notwithstanding Willis's assurance to the dean about the fixed price of the contract, he did make a claim for extras over and above the agreed price.[32] The chapter clerk was ordered to write and state the reasons why the dean and chapter objected to pay for them and to withhold any payment to Willis until he withdrew his claim. This matter was satisfactorily resolved in the chapter's favour and Willis was paid on 13 November 1879.[33]

In 1889, George Robertson Sinclair was appointed cathedral organist.[34] At the early age of eight he had entered the Royal Irish Academy of Music in Dublin, where

29. Ibid.
30. Ibid.
31. Ibid.
32. HCA, 7031/22, pp. 290–91, chapter acts,

18 October 1879.
33. Ibid., p. 292, 13 November 1879.
34. HCA, 7031/23, pp. 91–93, chapter acts, 17 October, 14 November 1889.

he had studied under Sir Robert Stewart. He soon, however, left Dublin for St Michael's College, Tenbury, where he became a chorister in 1873 at the age of ten. There he remained for six years, singing in the choir at the daily services, sometimes deputising at the organ, and all the time absorbing the standards and ideals of Ouseley, the college's warden. In May 1879 he moved to Gloucester as pupil-assistant to Dr Harford Lloyd and then, at the age of seventeen, through the influence of Ouseley, became organist of Truro Cathedral, working under the redoubtable Bishop Edward White Benson. In 1887 he was responsible for the music at the consecration of the choir and transepts of Pearson's great building, also supervising the installation of a new four manual organ by Henry Willis.[35]

Hereford felt very rapidly the effects of Sinclair's dynamic personality as he quickly improved the standard of the cathedral choir and began to rejuvenate the repertoire and performances at the Three Choirs Festival. Under his direction the music at Hereford became well known for its excellence. His professional eminence was recognised in 1899 when the archbishop of Canterbury awarded him the Lambeth degree of DMus. He became a great friend of Sir Edward Elgar and he, and his bulldog Dan, are immortalised in the G.R.S. movement of the *Enigma Variations*. Shortly after his appointment, Sinclair drew the attention of the dean and chapter to the shortcomings of the cathedral organ and proposed a major rebuild to bring the instrument up to date.[36] The authorities, though not in a position to finance the work themselves, gave the project their full approval and encouragement and Sinclair set to work to raise the necessary funds himself, with assistance from the dean and several ladies in the cathedral congregation. Sinclair gave eighteen recitals, one special service and two entertainments in the college hall in aid of the required funds; altogether, with the help of a long list of donations, upwards of £2000 was obtained.

Among the defects which worried Sinclair were the short upward compass of the manuals and the fact that the old reeds were so worn that not only had they lost their tone, but they could not be properly tuned. The wind chests were unsound and too small, therefore causing defects such as 'robbing' and 'running' and much of the action was clumsy and noisy, being heard far down the cathedral. Willis proposed new wind chests throughout the instrument together with his latest form of pneumatic action, a new Swell box, new reeds on Great, Swell and Choir organs, extension of the manual compass to top A, some of the Solo stops to be enclosed in a new Swell box, and the whole to be controlled from a new console and blown by means of five hydraulic engines,[37] the water for which had

35. 'Dr G. R. Sinclair, Conductor of the Hereford Music Festival', *Musical Times*, 41 (1900), p. 662.

36. *Hereford Journal*, 26 November 1892.
37. Ibid.

been laid on by the chapter in 1890.[38] Willis produced what was, to all intents and purposes, a new organ, using some of the old pipework but adding a significant amount of new material so that the sound and style of the tonal scheme was unmistakably his own. Most remarkable of all, Sinclair persuaded the builder to install his newly invented all-adjustable combination action which made Hereford's the first cathedral organ in the country to have adjustable pistons. The system consisted of duplicating the drawstop knobs by miniature ones placed on panels above the drawstop jambs. These small control knobs had three positions: off, neutral and on. This perfectly designed and constructed mechanism worked admirably; it was not widely adopted elsewhere because it was expensive. Henry Willis III, grandson of Father Willis, later wrote:

> Dr Sinclair made full use of the adjustables offered to him. It was his custom to set the pistons for the accompaniment of service, and then with a few movements of his agile fingers to reset the combinations on recital lines for his concluding voluntary. Visitors would receive the impression during service that they were listening to a sweet-toned, just adequate, old-world Cathedral organ, and then in the Postlude be well-nigh overwhelmed by a blaze of glorious modern tone.[39]

The specification of the new organ followed the general lines of the period with well-developed Great and Swell departments, an unenclosed Choir organ, a Pedal department based on that of the 1879 instrument, a fourth manual which incorporated a three stop unenclosed Solo together with an enclosed Echo department, its presence due to Sinclair's penchant for delicate colouring.

The organ was reopened on St Cecilia's day, 22 November 1892, with special services commencing with a choral celebration of holy communion at 8.00 a.m. sung to *Smart in F* with the bishop of Hereford as celebrant. Matins at 11.30 a.m. included *Stainer in B* flat, Wesley's *The Wilderness*, Purcell's *O Sing unto the Lord* and Ouseley's *It Came Even to Pass*, with voluntaries by Smart, Guilmant and Mendelssohn. At 7.30 in the evening, festal evensong was sung to *Smart in B flat* with Wesley's *Ascribe unto the Lord*, Walmisley's *If the Lord Himself had Not Been on our Side*, and the *Hallelujah Chorus* from Handel's *Messiah*. Voluntaries during the service were by Mendelssohn, Guilmant and Handel, and Bach's *Fantasia and Fugue in G minor* brought the day to a triumphant conclusion. Collections throughout the day totalled £60 3s. 9d. The celebrations continued two days later with a performance of parts one and two of Haydn's *Creation* together with organ voluntaries and miscellaneous choral and vocal items in the second half of the programme.

38. HCA, 7031/23, pp. 122, 161, chapter acts, 17 November 1890, 10 October 1892.

39. H. Willis, 'Hereford Cathedral Organ', *Rotunda*, 5 (1933–34), pp. 1–9.

The cathedral choir was supplemented by singers from Hereford, Gloucester and Worcester choral societies. Hugh Blair, sub-organist of Worcester Cathedral, conducted while Sinclair played the organ. Thanks to the facilities offered by the railway companies, a large number of visitors from neighbouring towns attended, in spite of the fact that a charge was made for admission. A further collection taken during the concert raised between £35 and £36 for the organ fund.[40]

The specification was as follows:[41]

Compass: Manuals, *CC – a²*; Pedals, *CCC – F*

GREAT ORGAN

1	Double Diapason	16	9	Principal	4
2	Bourdon	16	10	Harmonic Flute	4
3	Open Diapason I	8	11	Twelfth	2⅔
4	Open Diapason II	8	12	Fifteenth	2
5	Open Diapason III	8	13	Mixture	III
6	Gamba	8	14	Double Trumpet	16
7	Stopped Diapason	8	15	Trumpet	8
8	Claribel Flute	8	16	Clarion	4

i Swell to Great
ii Choir to Great
iii Solo to Great

SWELL ORGAN

17	Contra Gamba	16	24	Fifteenth	2
18	Open Diapason	8	25	Mixture	III
19	Stopped Diapason	8	26	Double Trumpet	16
20	Salicional	8	27	Trumpet	8
21	Vox Angelica	8	28	Hautboy	8
22	Principal	4	29	Clarion	4
23	Lieblich Flöte	4	30	Vox Humana	8

iv Swell super-octave
v Swell sub-octave

CHOIR ORGAN

31	Bourdon	16	36	Gemshorn	4
32	Dulciana	8	37	Lieblich Flöte	4
33	Spitzflöte	8	38	Piccolo	2
34	Lieblich Gedackt	8	39	Corno di Bassetto	8
35	Claribel Flute	8			

vi Swell to Choir

40. *Hereford Journal*, 26 November 1892.   41. Willis, 'Hereford Cathedral Organ'.

SOLO ORGAN

40	Harmonic Flute	8	*41*	Harmonic Flute	4
42	Tuba	8			

ECHO ORGAN

(enclosed and played from Solo manual)

43	Viola da Gamba	8	*47*	Orchestral Oboe	8
44	Voix Celeste	8	*48*	Tromba	8
45	Hohl Flute	4	*49*	Glockenspiel	4
46	Clarionet	8			

PEDAL ORGAN

50	Double Diapason (ext. of No. 51)	32	*54*	Violoncello	8
51	Open Diapason	16	*55*	Octave	8
52	Violone (part from No. 1)	16	*56*	Trombone	16
53	Bourdon	16	*57*	Trumpet	8

vii Solo to Pedal
ix Great to Pedal
viii Swell to Pedal
x Choir to Pedal

Accessories

16 composition pistons.	6 composition pedals.
Great pistons to compositions.	Choir pistons to compositions.
Swell pistons to compositions.	Pedal to compositions.
Great to Pedal on & off piston and pedal.	Swell to Great on & off piston.
Solo to Great on & off pedal.	Tremolo pedal to Swell.

The Glockenspiel was described as 'a Mixture of Cymbale type'.

In 1909 a few modifications were made by Henry Willis II under Sinclair's direction (fig. 139). The most important was the addition in the south choir aisle of a 32 ft Bombarde and 16 ft Ophicleide unit of forty-two notes added to the Pedal organ. The pipes had wooden resonators at Sinclair's insistence. The Glockenspiel Mixture was removed and replaced by a set of gongs, similarly labelled, and played from the Choir organ. An 8 ft Cor Anglais by Rolin Frères was added to the Echo department, the Swell Vox Humana replaced with a new one and a Tremulant together with Sub-octave and Unison Off couplers were added to the Solo. In addition, the Clarionet, Orchestral Oboe and Tromba on the Solo were extended downward an octave with a device enabling the player to choose whether to employ these as 8 ft or 16 ft stops.

Fig. 139. George Robertson
Sinclair at the organ in 1909.
The adjustable piston mechanism
can be clearly seen over the
right-hand stop jamb. (*The
Musical Times, 1 September 1909*.)

In 1920 the organ was cleaned and the opportunity taken to replace the wooden
resonators of the 32 ft Bombarde with zinc pipes, a substitution which greatly
improved the sonority of the lower octave.[42]

The organ did daily duty until 1933 when it became obvious that the pneumatic
action was wearing out. The cramped nature of the internal layout of the instrument
made access for maintenance and repair very difficult. It is testimony to the superb
craftsmanship of the Willis firm that the action functioned so well with the
minimum of attention. This could have been a crucial moment in the history of
the Hereford organ: organ building fashion in the 1930s was producing instruments
very different in concept from those of Father Willis. The English organ world
was fascinated by smooth reeds, heavy pressure Diapasons, enclosed Choir organs
and John Compton's totally enclosed instruments built on the extension principle.
Chorus work was often whittled down to a respectable mezzo forte and the full-
throated fire and virility of Willis reeds and bright, ringing upper work was not
appreciated in some quarters. Fortunately the organist at the time, Dr (later Sir)
Percy Hull who had succeeded Sinclair in 1918 and had been a chorister and later

42. Ibid.

assistant organist under him, loved his fine old Willis and was determined, as Sir Walter Alcock had been at Salisbury, not to allow anyone to alter its basic character. As Alcock is reputed to have said, 'How can you improve a Stradivarius?' Hull commissioned Henry Willis III, grandson of the original builder, to rebuild the organ in a conservative fashion with a new electro-pneumatic action and a detached console on the north side of the choir. Money at this period was very tight and Hull costed each item carefully.[43] Willis, on his part, was keen that the instrument should remain under the care of the Willis firm and was as helpful as he could be with his estimate.[44] The tonal changes, such as they were, amplified and sought to give variety to the basic Father Willis scheme. From this rebuild date the Choir Nazard, Tierce and Trumpet, the Dulzian on the Swell in place of Dr Sinclair's replacement Vox Humana which no one liked, and the revoicing and enclosure of the Solo Harmonic Flutes. Willis also did some work on the 32 ft reed, for in a letter to G. Donald Harrison in the USA in 1935, he wrote in answer to a query about such things that 'at Hereford and Salisbury Cathedrals I had the old shorter shallots and naturally left them, the Hereford reed on 16½ inches is superb. Salisbury on 9 inches is not so good, "flabby" on the light pressure.'[45] Willis also revoiced all the Solo pipework, fitting his compensator amplifier which enabled a greater tonal output to be obtained on a higher pressure of wind. A 'Discus' electric blower was fitted, replacing the five hydraulic engines of 1892.

The rebuilt instrument gave admirable daily service until the early 1970s when, once again, it was apparent that some restoration work would soon be necessary. The 1892 leatherwork of the reservoirs and concussion bellows which had not required replacing in 1933 was now showing signs of its age, and wind leakage was becoming apparent. The electric wiring of the console was cotton insulated, in the manner of the 1930s, but as the cotton rotted with age, the wiring was becoming a fire hazard. On one occasion, smoke appeared from beneath the Choir manual during evensong, an ominous sign which had to be taken seriously.[46] During the 1970s the organ world was, once again, experiencing a period of change. The continental and American organ reform movements were influencing tonal concepts and the Downes/Harrison organ in the Royal Festival Hall heralded many new ideals in organ design. There were many for whom the nineteenth-century schemes of Willis and his contemporaries seemed inadequate for the proper performance of the classical repertoire. They looked to the organs on the continent of Europe for their inspiration. A good deal of hard thinking was being done and many fine organs were built inspired by classical ideals. In some cases the baby

43. HCA, 5917, correspondence on organ repairs, 1932–33.
44. Ibid.
45. C. Callahan, *The American Classic Organ* (Richmond, Virginia, 1990), p. 155, letter from H. Willis to G. D. Harrison, 20 December 1935.
46. Summer 1974, personal knowledge.

was lost with the bath water and several splendid Romantic organs were either altered out of all recognition or replaced altogether, sacrificed once again on the altar of changing fashion. Fortunately, and perhaps with hindsight more significantly, the quiet but insistent voice of the conservationist was beginning to make itself heard at this period, urging the British organ world to stop aping the Continent and to take seriously its own rich heritage of fine instruments. There was never any doubt in Hereford that conservation of the Father Willis would be the correct course of action.

The firm of Harrison and Harrison of Durham was commissioned to undertake the work, as they had proved elsewhere their expertise and sensitivity in faithfully restoring distinguished historic instruments. The Willis 1892 tonal scheme would remain intact, but opportunity would be taken to enhance it in the small but significant areas where weaknesses were apparent. This was particularly so in the Pedal department, where new metal ranks at 8 ft and 4 ft together with a four rank Mixture – 19, 22, 26, 29 – were added to complete the chorus and enhance clarity, and a Stopped Flute 8 ft, Open Flute 4 ft and Schalmei 4 ft were also added to give variety to the softer registers. By 1892, Willis was reducing the amount of his Mixture work and only providing one three rank stop on both Great and Swell. To remedy this the Great has gained a four rank Quint Mixture – 19, 22, 26, 29 – which carries up the brilliance of the Willis 4 ft and 2 ft registers, and acts not only as the crown of the chorus, but also as a bridge between the fluework and the splendid family of 16, 8 and 4 ft Trumpets. The Willis three rank Tierce Mixture – 17, 19, 22 – remains unaltered so the Great can still be played exactly as Willis left it. But the new stop does make a wonderful difference to the pleno and the two Mixtures blend together with magnificent effect. The Choir organ has gained immeasurably by being moved from its former buried situation at the back of the chamber to a new position in the centre of the organ case, where the old 1892 console used to stand. The pipes are now just behind the stalls, where their effect is immediate and charming and of immense value when accompanying the cathedral choir. This division has been enhanced by the substitution of a tapered Spitz Flute 2 ft for the old Piccolo, and by the addition of a three rank Mixture – 15, 19, 22 – to replace a 16 ft Bourdon. The Swell organ remains exactly as before, though in order to improve the tonal egress, two additional shutters have been added to the Swell front and a baffle board erected over the box to project the sound forward. The Solo Tuba, which had been in two different positions in the instrument over the years, has now found a commanding home over the Great organ. It was previously located at the back of the Great soundboard where it was not entirely effective. From its new height it peals forth with memorable splendour. The Willis 1933 console has been retained though completely remade and reactioned. Henry Willis III, under the influence of the great American organ builder E. M. Skinner, pioneered the 'standard' Willis console in the 1930s. His famous organs in the Alexandra Palace, Birmingham Town Hall and St George's Hall, Liverpool, to name but a few, had consoles which became renowned for their comfort and for the completeness of control which they offered the player. The Hereford console was a replica of these, being luxurious in its provision of general pistons, reversibles, etc., and having all the aids to registration of a well-equipped concert organ (fig. 140). The action, wind chests, reservoirs, combination and coupling actions were either new or rebuilt as new. All this work was paid for by a wonderfully generous gift from the Hereford-based firm H. P. Bulmer, whose association with the instrument is charmingly commemorated by an illuminated carved woodpecker on the front of the case.

Fig. 140. The present organ console.

Specification of the rebuilt organ

GREAT ORGAN

1	Double Open Diapason	*metal*	16
2	Bourdon	*st'd wood*	16
3	Open Diapason No. 1	*metal*	8
4	Open Diapason No. 2	*metal*	8
5	Open Diapason No. 3	*metal*	4
6	Claribel Flute (open throughout)	*wood*	8
7	Stopped Diapason	*st'd wood*	8
8	Principal No. 1	*metal*	4
9	Principal No. 2	*metal*	4
10	Flute (Harmonic)	*metal*	4
11	Twelfth	*metal*	2⅔
12	Fifteenth	*metal*	2
13	Mixture 17, 19, 22	*metal*	III
14	Mixture 19, 22, 26, 29	*metal*	IV
15	Double Trumpet ⎫	*metal*	16
16	Trumpet ⎬ Heavy wind	*metal*	8
17	Clarion ⎭	*metal*	4

i. Swell to Great   *iv. Choir to Great*   *vii. Solo to Great*
ii. Swell to Great Octave   *v. Choir to Great Octave*   *viii. Solo to Great Octave*
iii. Swell to Great Sub-octave *vi. Choir to Great Sub-octave* *ix. Solo to Great Sub-octave*

SWELL ORGAN

18	Contra Gamba	*st'd wood & metal*	16
19	Open Diapason	*metal*	8
20	Stopped Diapason	*st'd wood & metal*	8
21	Salicional	*metal*	8
22	Vox Angelica (bass from No. 21)	*metal*	8
23	Principal	*metal*	4
24	Lieblich Flute	*st'd metal*	4
25	Fifteenth	*metal*	2
26	Mixture 17, 19, 22	*metal*	III
27	Dulzian	*metal*	16
28	Oboe	*metal*	8
29	Double Trumpet ⎫	*metal*	16
30	Trumpet ⎬ Heavy Wind	*metal*	8
31	Clarion ⎭	*metal*	4

x. Swell Octave   *xii. Swell Unison off*   *xiv. Tremulant*
xi. Swell Sub-octave   *xiii. Solo to Swell*

CHOIR ORGAN

32	Open Diapason	*metal*	8
33	Claribel Flute	*wood*	8
34	Lieblich Gedeckt	*st'd wood & metal*	8
35	Dulciana	*metal*	8
36	Gemshorn	*metal*	4
37	Lieblich Flute	*st'd metal*	4
38	Nazard	*st'd metal*	2⅔
39	Spitz Flute	*metal*	2
40	Tierce	*metal*	1⅗
41	Mixture 15, 19, 22	*metal*	III
42	Trumpet (Harmonic Trebles)	*metal*	8

xv. Choir Octave
xvi. Choir Sub-octave
xvii. Choir Unison off

xviii. Swell to Choir
xix. Swell to Choir Octave
xx. Swell to Choir Sub-octave

xxi. Solo to Choir
xxii. Solo to Choir Octave
xxiii. Solo to Choir Sub-octave

SOLO ORGAN

43	Viol-da-Gamba	*metal*	8
44	Voix Celestes (bass from No. 43)	*metal*	8
45	Harmonic Flute	*metal*	8
46	Concert Flute	*metal*	4
47	Hohl Flute	*wood*	2
48	Clarinet	*metal*	8 or 16
49	Orchestral Oboe	*metal*	8 or 16
50	Cor Anglais	*metal*	8
51	Tromba	*metal*	8 or 16
52	Glockenspiel (A–C)(gongs)(Unenclosed)	*metal*	4
53	Tuba (Unenclosed)(heavywind, harmonic)	*metal*	8

xxiv. Solo Octave
xxv. Solo Sub-octave

xxvi. Solo Unison off
xxvii. Great to Solo

xxviii. Tremulant

PEDAL ORGAN

54	Double Open Bass (ext. No. 55)	*wood*	32
55	Open Bass	*wood*	16
56	Open Diapason (part from No. 1)	*metal*	16
57	Bourdon	*wood*	16
58	Principal	*metal*	8
59	Stopped Flute	*metal*	8
60	Fifteenth	*metal*	4
61	Open Flute	*metal*	4
62	Mixture 19, 22, 26, 29	*metal*	IV
63	Bombarde (ext. No. 64)	*wood & metal*	32

64	Ophicleide	⎫		*wood*	16
65	Trombone	⎬ Heavy wind		*metal*	16
66	Clarion	⎭		*metal*	8
67	Schalmei			*metal*	4

xxix. Swell to Pedal   *xxxii. Choir to Pedal 4 ft.*   *xxxv. Great to Pedal*
xxx. Swell to Pedal 4ft.   *xxxiii. Solo to Pedal*   *xxxvi. Great and Pedal*
xxxi. Choir to Pedal   *xxxiv. Solo to Pedal 4ft.*   *Combs. Coupled*

ACCESSORIES

8 Pistons to Great Organ ⎫
8 Pistons to Swell Organ
8 Pistons to Solo Organ
8 Pistons to Choir Organ   All instantly adjustable
8 Toe Pistons to Pedal Organ   at the console by means
8 'General' pistons controlling   of master locking piston
visibly all stops and couplers
2 Pistons to the couplers ⎭

*★1 Reversible Piston to Great to Pedal Coupler
*★1 Reversible Piston to Swell to Great Coupler
1 Reversible Piston to Choir to Great Coupler
*★1 Reversible Piston to Solo to Great Coupler
1 Reversible Piston to Swell to Pedal Coupler
1 Reversible Piston to Solo to Swell Coupler
1 Reversible Piston to Choir to Pedal Coupler
1 Reversible Piston to Swell to Choir Coupler
1 Reversible Piston to Solo to Choir Coupler
*★1 Reversible Piston to Solo to Pedal Coupler
1 Reversible Piston to Great and Pedal combs. coupled
1 Reversible Piston to Swell Tremulant
1 Reversible Piston to Solo Tremulant
Cancel Pistons to Great, Swell, Choir, Solo and Pedal respectively
1 Coupler cancel piston
1 'Octave coupler cancel' piston,, annulling octave and unison off couplers
General cancel piston annulling visibly all stops and couplers
1 rocking tablet ' Doubles off'
1 rocking tablet ' Pedal Off'
★ (duplicated by toe pistons)

The Festival Organ

In the programme of the 1927 Hereford Three Choirs Festival there is a brief entry: 'New organ built especially for this Festival by Messrs Nicholson & Co., Worcester'. Before 1927 it had been customary to borrow a pipe organ for the Three Choirs, but Percy Hull determined to acquire a permanent organ for festival use. The organ is built on stilts, so that its height accords with the general elevation of the festival platform, and the stilts rest on wooden wheels, making it possible to move the instrument one bay eastward to be level with the orchestral players. The specification reflected Hull's devotion to the music of Elgar which, then as now, is such a distinctive feature of Three Choirs programmes. In his scores Elgar often asks for organ '16, 8 and 4' and the stop list of the Nicholson organ fulfilled this requirement admirably. After some years of neglect, during which the instrument became very dirty and unreliable, it was restored in 1983 through the generosity of the Friends of the Hereford Three Choirs and the cathedral school. There were two spare slides which have now received their long-awaited pipes, and the Swell department, formerly consisting of two 8 ft stops, has been redesigned as a chorus suitable for continuo work. The pipework has all been revoiced and regulated by Dennis Thurlow, the tonal director of Messrs Nicholson & Co., now of Malvern. The specification is as follows:

GREAT		SWELL		PEDAL	
Bourdon	16	Open Flute	8	Open Diapason	16
Open Diapason	8	Principal	4	Bourdon (Gt)	16
Open Diapason	8	Fifteenth	2		
Claribel	8	Super Octave		Great to Pedal	
Principal	4			Swell to Pedal	
Octave	2	Swell to Great		Two combination pedals	
Sub Octave				Balanced Swell Pedal	

Wind pressure 3 inches w.g.
Manual compass C to g‴ 56 notes
Pedal compass C to f′ 30 notes
Tracker action to manuals, pneumatic to pedals

The Lady Chapel Organ

This organ, built by the firm of Hill and Son in the early years of this century for a private house, was presented to the cathedral by Mr and Mrs Lennox Lee in 1951. The instrument was installed by the local firm of Ingram and Co. The specification is as follows:

GREAT		SWELL		PEDAL	
Open Diapason	8	Stop Diapason	8	Bourdon	16
Lieblich Gedact	8	Echo Gamba	8		
Dulciana	8	Voix Celeste	8		
Principal	4	Gemshorn	4		
		Quartane	II		
Great to Pedal					
Swell to Pedal					
Swell to Great		Pneumatic action		Trigger Swell Pedal	

In the year 2001 it is proposed to replace the Hill organ by a new instrument to be built by Peter Collins Ltd of Melton Mowbray with a case designed by Nicholas Plumley of Arundel.

The specification is as follows:

Manual I		Manual II		Pedal	
Open Diapason	8	Chimney Flute	8	Subbass	16
Stopped Diapason	8	Salicional	8	Octave (Gt)	8
Principal	8	Flute	4	Bass Flute (Ext)	8
Fifteenth	4			Fifteenth (Gt)	4

I/Pedal

II/Pedal

II/I (sliding keyboard)

Tracker action

Manuals CC–a 58 notes

Pedal CC–f 30 notes

26

The Ornaments: The Textiles

Wendy Toulson

The textiles at Hereford are not so well documented as those of some other religious foundations, but it is possible to reconstruct their history in outline from the early eighth century to the present day.[1] As with other cathedrals in England, the textiles can be roughly divided into three groups: those used before the Reformation, characterised by a wide variety of vestments and furnishings, liturgical colours, fabrics and jewels; those used from the reign of Elizabeth I until the late nineteenth century – a greatly reduced range of garments and furnishings made from plain fabrics; and those used from the late nineteenth century to the present day, marked by a slow revival of the use of more elaborate furnishings and vestments.[2]

A richly ornamented cross cloth in Hereford Cathedral mentioned in an epigram of Bishop Cuthberht, 736–40, seems to refer to the earliest documented instance of Anglo-Saxon embroidery.[3] Apart from this unusual and important example, Hereford's pre-Reformation textiles conform to the patterns established for other religious foundations. Vestments and altar furnishings were acquired by the cathedral as a result of gifts, bequests and purchase, whether from the coffers of the chapter

1. Documents include the episcopal registers, calendar of obits, clavigers' rolls, miscellaneous receipts and the first part of a late fourteenth-century working inventory, HCA, 4625, largely printed in translation in D. Nicholson, *Symbolism, Colour and Embroidery in Hereford Cathedral* (Hereford, 1983), pp. 52–53. Compare, for example, R. N. Swanson, 'Medieval Liturgy as Theatre: The Props', *Studies in Church History*, 28 (1992), pp. 239–53.

2. W. St J. Hope and E. G. C. F. Atchley, *English Liturgical Colours* (London, 1918); J. Mayo, *A History of Ecclesiastical Dress* (London, 1984); M. Schoeser, *The Watts Book of Embroidery: English Church Embroidery, 1833–1953* (London, 1998).

3. M. Lapidge, 'Some Remnants of Bede's Lost *Liber Epigrammatum*', *English Historical Review*, 93 (1975), pp. 798–820; M. Budny and D. Tweddle, 'The Maaseik Embroideries', *Anglo-Saxon England*, 13 (1984), pp. 89–90.

or from individual cathedral clergy.[4] The sources of textiles are rarely mentioned but, where they are, an English workshop is suggested.[5] The embroidery of aristocratic Anglo-Saxon ladies and of the workshops producing *opus anglicanum* were noted throughout western Europe: patrons would not have had to look beyond England for textiles of the highest quality.[6] Of the raw materials employed, wool and linen cloths could have been locally manufactured and bought; silk and metal thread narrow wares, such as ribbons, laces and tablet woven tapes may well have been of English manufacture; wider woven cloths of silk and metal threads would have been imported into England, often from Italy.[7] Higher value items are likely to have been made up in the London workshops, where the skills of embroiderers, goldsmiths and jewellers could be combined. Some items connected with the cathedral were of considerable value – in 1240 Henry III gave Bishop Aigueblanche a mitre bought for £82, while in 1317 Bishop Orleton received a mitre bought for £40 by Bishop Swinfield. Plainer items appear to have been supplied locally.[8]

Almost nothing survives from the cathedral's pre-Reformation textiles. One exception is the fragment of tablet woven band from Gilbert Swinfield's tomb, *c.* 1299.[9] Fragments of other textiles survive, albeit unseen, in other tombs in the cathedral.[10] A further possible survival is the embroidered orphrey featuring the

4. R. Rawlinson, *The History and Antiquities of the City and Cathedral-Church of Hereford* (London, 1717), appendix (calendar of obits), pp. 9, 16, 17, 20, 24–27, 29, 31; Capes, *Charters*, p. 186; HCA, 4625; R. G. Griffiths and W. W. Capes, eds, *The Register of Thomas de Cantilupe, Bishop of Hereford, AD 1275–1282*, Cantilupe Society (Hereford, 1906), p. 5; A. T. Bannister, ed., *The Register of Adam de Orleton, Bishop of Hereford, AD 1317–1327*, Cantilupe Society (Hereford, 1907), pp. 41–42; A. T. Bannister, ed., *The Register of Thomas Spofford, Bishop of Hereford, AD 1422–1448*, Cantilupe Society (Hereford, 1917), p. 272.

5. Griffiths and Capes, eds, *Register of Thomas de Cantilupe*, p. 223.

6. A. G. I. Christie, *English Medieval Embroidery* (London, 1938), pp. 1, 38–39; Arts Council of Great Britain, *Opus Anglicanum: English Medieval Embroidery. Exhibition Catalogue, Victoria and Albert Museum* (London, 1963).

7. K. Lacey, 'The Production of "Narrow Ware" by Silkwomen in Fourteenth- and Fifteenth-Century England', *Textile History*, 18 (1987), pp. 187–204; S. D. Hogarth, 'Ecclesiastical Vestments and Vestment-makers in York, 1300–1600', *York Historian*, 7 (1986), pp. 2–11.

8. F. Devon, ed., *Issues of the Exchequer* (London, 1837), p. 17; Bannister, ed., *Register of Adam de Orleton*, p. 42; HCA, R 585, fol. 2r, concerning the making of apparelled albs.

9. F. T. Havergal, *Monumental Inscriptions in the Cathedral Church of Hereford* (Hereford, 1881) p. 83, plate III; HCA, 6474/2, inventory no. 18.94.

10. A. T. Bannister, 'Bishop Peter de Aquablanca: His Last Will, his Death and Burial', *TWNFC*, 25 (1924–26), p. 90; J. Merewether, 'Discovery of the Episcopal Rings of John Stanbery and Richard Mayo, Bishops of Hereford, during the Recent Works of Restoration at Hereford Cathedral', *Archaeologia*, 31 (1844), pp. 249–53.

arms of Bishop Robert Parfew/Wharton, 1554–59, now at St Michael's church, Abergavenny.[11]

The Reformation in the church in England formed a watershed in the history of textiles in English cathedrals: the abolition of altars associated with intercessory saints and the replacement of the high altar by a communion table made rich altar furnishings redundant; and changes in the liturgy were accompanied by the abolition of all vestments but the cope, which was preserved for use in the cathedrals.[12] Large numbers of the vestments and altar hangings in Hereford Cathedral are likely to have been sold off, many for conversion into household furnishings.[13] Other textiles, such as the Lenten veil, which contributed to the visual impact of the liturgical year, would also have been disposed of.[14]

It is clear from the pre-Reformation records that the working life of ecclesiastical textiles had always been limited: examples of vestments detailed in the Hereford sources, even those associated with individuals such as Bishop Thomas Cantilupe, Queen Eleanor (of Castile?) and Elizabeth de Burgh, Lady Clare, are rarely more than fifty years old.[15] Wear and tear on textiles were considerable. The missal details the vestments appropriate for each service and procession carried out by cathedral clergy: the treasurer and his appointed deputy would have been responsible for distributing and gathering in the apparel for each occasion.[16] The missal also lays down strict rules for the cleansing or the destruction of textiles accidentally stained with the consecrated wine during the mass – these were to be washed three times: if a stain remained, the marked part was to be cut out and burned, the ashes being kept with the relics.[17] During times of local upheaval textiles kept in the cathedral were vulnerable to damage and theft: the attack on the cathedral in 1055 included the plundering of vestments; in 1140 Geoffrey Talbot entered the cathedral and drove out the ministrants at the altar.[18] Vestments and furnishings were lent to

11. R. H. D'Elboux, 'Pre-Reformation Vestments in Catholic Churches in Monmouthshire', *Archaeological Journal*, 81 (1924), pp. 22–25.

12. M. H. Bloxham, *The Principles of Gothic Architecture* (3 vols, London, 1882), iii, pp. 83–84, 94–97, 101–2, 111, 227–96.

13. B. S. Stanhope and H. C. Moffatt, *The Church Plate of the County of Hereford* (Westminster and Hereford, 1903), p. 216, gives the maddeningly mutilated 1553 inventory of ornaments in the cathedral. For conversion of vestments to household use see G. W. Digby, *Elizabethan Embroidery* (London, 1963), pp. 56, 62.

14. HCA, R 585, fol. 29r: a rare mention of a Lenten veil. W. G. Henderson, ed., *Missale ad usum percelebris ecclesiae Herfordensis* ([Leeds], 1874), p. 85.

15. Bannister, ed., *Register of Adam de Orleton*, p. 42; HCA, 1448; 4625.

16. Henderson, *Missale ad usum percelebris ecclesiae Herfordensis*, pp. xliv, xlvii, 9, 40, 46, 80–81, 87, 90–91, 93–7, 105, 112, 114, 116, 118, 123, 136–37, 158, 237, 353, 437; Bannister, *The Cathedral Church of Hereford*, p. 66.

17. Henderson, *Missale ad usum percelebris ecclesiae Herfordensis*, pp. xxxiii–xxxiv.

18. G. N. Garmonsway, trans., *The Anglo-Saxon Chronicle* (London, 1972), p. 186; K. R. Potter, ed., *Gesta Stephani* (Oxford, 1976), pp. 108–9.

churches in the diocese and certain vestments, such as copes, were exposed to the elements when worn outdoors for processions and for burials, when they might be besmirched with mud and worse.[19] Vestments loaned by the dean and chapter to bishops had a peripatetic existence and were often subject to the perils of the road. Bishop Walter was attacked and robbed in 1060 on leaving Rome with his *pallium*, while Bishop Orleton's ornaments and vestments were seized in 1324, along with the temporalities.[20] The depredations of wear and tear are noted carefully against items listed in the documents. Once vestments or furnishings were of no further use in the cathedral they were disposed of.[21] Fine objects embellished with jewels and gold embroidery were frequently broken up to reclaim the costly materials.[22] Programmes of repair are outlined in the clavigers' accounts from the late fifteenth century.[23] With the reintroduction of vestments in the twentieth century the cathedral Broderers' Guild has taken on this vital work once more.[24]

The visual impact of the Reformation on textiles in the cathedral extended to the garb of the choristers: before the Reformation, choristers were provided annually with new tunics, caps, shoes, and with two cassocks, often brightly coloured – violet, blue, green and russet cloths are all mentioned. The cassocks were fur-lined for Christmas and of lighter weight for summer.[25] By the late sixteenth century choristers received annually a gown, a shirt, breeches, stockings, shoes and a cap, all made from wool and cotton fabrics of grey, black and white.[26]

This monochrome colour scheme was echoed by the cassocks, surplices, chimeres and preaching scarves allowed to the clergy of the cathedral. The 1583 injunctions prescribed the wearing of academic hoods according to the wearer's degree, although this stipulation appears not to have been complied with immediately.[27] By 1635, however, the cathedral seems to have adopted pared down Protestant furnishings: Bishop Wren reported seeing a domestic Turkey carpet on the communion table in the cathedral.[28] There is no hint that Wren's exhortations to replace the carpet

19. HCA, 2875; 7031/1, fol. 19r, chapter acts, April-May 1519; D. Lepine, *Brotherhood of Canons Serving God: English Secular Cathedrals in the Later Middle Ages* (Woodbridge, 1995), p. 115; see also A. T. Bannister, 'Visitation Return of the Diocese of Hereford, 1379', *English Historical Review*, 45 (1930), p. 99.

20. F. Barlow, ed., *Vita Aedwardi Regis qui apud Westmonasterium requiescit* (London, 1962), p. 34: I owe this reference to Mr H. James; R. M. Haines, *The Church and Politics in Fourteenth-Century England: Adam of Orleton* (Cambridge, 1978), p. 51.

21. HCA, 1450, 4625.

22. Archbishop Lanfranc's chasubles and copes were burned in 1371–73, to reclaim the gold from the embroidery threads: J. W. Legg and W. H. St J. Hope, *Inventories of Christchurch, Canterbury* (London, 1902), p. 13.

23. HCA, R 585, fos 2v, 6r, 9v, 12r, 16r, 24r, 24v, 27v, 29v, 31r.

24. *FHC*, 42 (1978), p. 17; 54 (1988), p. 24.

25. HCA, R 696/1, R 369, R 585.

26. HCA, R 587, R 588, R 591–98, R 600, R 601/1, R 602–8, 2384.

27. HCA, 7044/5, p. 32, copy of 1583 statutes; HCA, 4642, fol. 7v.

28. Worcestershire Record Office, BA 2470 (B), 794.093, p. 204: I owe this reference to Dr Kenneth Fincham.

Fig. 141. Medieval and Reformation vestments: effigies of Bishop John Stanbury, died 1474, and of Bishop George Coke, died 1646.

with a paned silk altar frontal and cushions for the service book and the Bible were heeded. The copes sanctioned for continued use in cathedrals were kept repaired in the early seventeenth century, but thereafter they disappear from view (fig. 141).[29]

For the remainder of the seventeenth century, and for the eighteenth and early nineteenth, there are regular entries in the records of payments to the sextons for washing communion table linen and expenditure on clothing for the choristers, sextons and vergers.[30] A pulpit cloth is mentioned in 1663; mats in the choir for the communion were purchased in 1661 and 1666; and in 1761 the chapter discussed rods and curtains for the ladies' seats – but in the main the cathedral's textile furnishings seem to have been meagre.[31]

29. HCA, R 606.
30. HCA, R 598–600, R 601/1, R 602–8, 2384, R 609–12, R 615–20; 7031/3, p. 617, chapter acts, 13 November 1712; 7031/16, p. 287, chapter acts, 15 May 1794; 7031/18, p. 2, chapter acts, 11 November 1814.
31. HCA, 7031/3, p. 226, chapter acts, 22 September 1663; R 610; 7031/12, p. 6, chapter acts, 14 July 1761.

Hereford Cathedral was not in the forefront of the nineteenth-century movement for the reintroduction of vestments. Modest attempts in 1868 by vicars of St John the Baptist to have gold fringes and embroidery added to their stoles were frowned upon.[32] The altar was, however, being more gorgeously arrayed: an embroidered crimson velvet altar cloth was noted in 1867 and by 1882 F. T. Havergal listed four altar cloths. The 'altar cloth used on High Festivals' appears to be the Gilbert Scott frontal: this was manufactured by Louis Grossé of Bruges in 1873, was conserved at the Textile Conservation Centre, Hampton Court Palace, in 1983 and is now displayed on the north wall of the Lady chapel (fig. 142; plate XIIIa).[33] The 'richly embroidered crimson silk frontal; worked by a society of ladies under the direction of Miss Blencow [sic]. Designed by Mr F. Preedy' may well be the 1200th Anniversary frontal, which was restored by the Cathedral Broderers between 1986 and 1991 and is now displayed on the south wall of the nave.[34]

The dean and chapter registered no protest in 1932 when Bishop Carr wished to ordain wearing a cope, but it was not until 1947 that Dean Burrows secured agreement to the reintroduction of vestments into the cathedral. As in the pre-Reformation era, the cathedral's modern holdings of vestments and furnishings have been built up from gifts, bequests and purchase.[35]

In 1535 Bishop Booth left to the cathedral at least one Arras tapestry of the history of David and Nabal.[36] No trace of this legacy remains, but tapestry again became a feature of the cathedral in 1977, when the dean and chapter commissioned three tapestries in commemoration of 1300 years of Christianity in Hereford. The Piper tapestries, depicting the tree of knowledge, the tree of Zion – the deposition –

32. HCA, 7031/21, p. 356, chapter acts, 16 February 1869; 7031/22, p. 6, chapter acts, 18 January 1872.

33. *Hereford Cathedral, City and Neighbourhood: A Handbook for Visitors and Residents* (3rd edn, Hereford, 1867), p. 30, and F. T. Havergal, *The Visitors' Hand Guide to Hereford Cathedral* (6th edn, Hereford, 1882), p. 20, cited in Nicholson, *Symbolism, Colour and Embroidery*, pp. 16–17. Discrepancies between Havergal's description and the actual frontal are explained by Havergal's having described the coloured design for the frontal, rather than the frontal itself. HCA, 6330.

34. Nicholson, *Symbolism, Colour and Embroidery*, pp. 17–19; for the work of Agnes Blencowe see Schoeser, *The Watts Book of Embroidery*, pp. 125–26; *FHC*, 52 (1986), p. 44; 57 (1991), p. 42; 60 (1994), p. 14; 62 (1996), p. 18.

35. HCA, 7031/24, pp. 281, 476, chapter acts, 24 March 1932, 1 May 1947; Nicholson, *Symbolism, Colour and Embroidery*, pp. 19–22; *FHC*, 2 (1936), pp. 25–26; 3 (1937), p. 15; 22 (1956), p. 11; 27 (1961), p. 12; 42 (1976), p. 22; 50 (1984), p. 35; 56 (1990), p. 29.

36. A. T. Bannister, ed., *The Register of Charles Bothe, Bishop of Hereford, 1516–1535*, Cantilupe Society (Hereford, 1921), pp. xiii, 302. For rare fragments of tapestries depicting David and Nabal see H. Chitty, 'Our Tapestries', *Wykehamist*, 497 (February 1912), pp. 463–65.

Fig. 142. Detail of the Gilbert Scott altar frontal, 1873.

and the tree of life, were woven in Namibia and hang on the east wall of the south transept.[37]

37. HCA, 7031/26, pp. 223, 225, 230, 266, 291, 316, 348–50, 382, chapter acts, 6 December 1976 to 4 February 1980; HCA, NS 1/8/1, chapter clerk's papers, Piper tapestries; Nicholson, *Symbolism, Colour and Embroidery*, pp. 23–24; Tate Gallery, *John Piper: Exhibition Catalogue* (London, 1983), pp. 47, 137.

27

The Ornaments: The Plate

Joan Williams

In order to consider all the interesting items of liturgical metalwork associated
with Hereford Cathedral, it is necessary to interpret the term 'church plate'
broadly, to include artefacts in baser metals than gold and silver, and those whose
function was processional, pastoral and devotional as well as those associated purely
with the mass or communion. Many of the significant items in this category which
are currently housed in the cathedral have been recovered in the last two centuries,
through discovery, grave robbery and purchase; and, while Hereford has never
been noted for the value or artistic quality of its plate, many of these treasures
are of particular interest because of the stories attached to them. None of the
cathedral's possessions has been inventoried so often, and to so little avail, as the
plate: while the textiles have been vulnerable on account of their intrinsic suscep-
tibility to wear and tear, as well as for reasons of theological revolution, the plate
has always been at risk because of its innate value, and loss by sale or theft has
continued up to the present day.[1]

Of the riches of metalwork ornament which adorned the cathedral in the later
middle ages, when all the various altars held their own sets of mass vessels, as well
as the glories of St Thomas Cantilupe's shrine, and numerous other reliquaries,
candlesticks and crucifixes, we have only a few tantalising glimpses; no medieval
inventory of the plate survives.[2] The obit book of the late thirteenth century, with

1. Surviving inventories at the cathedral which
include the plate are those of 1765, HCA,
4929; 1857, in HCA, 7007, p. 466; 1947–60,
HCA, 6474/1 and 2; 1978, HCA, 6474/3;
1996, HCA, 6474/4; I am most grateful to
Rosalind Caird, archivist of Hereford Ca-
thedral, for her advice on archival sources.
Accounts of the plate are also included in
B. S. Stanhope and H. C. Moffatt, *The
Church Plate of Herefordshire* (Westminster

and Hereford, 1903), pp. 71–76; RCHME,
Herefordshire, i, p. 113; N. Pevsner, *Hereford-
shire*, The Buildings of England
(Harmondsworth, 1963), p. 168.

2. The imperfect fourteenth-century inventory of 'vestments books and other precious
objects and goods ... of the cathedral of
Hereford' includes only a detailed list of the
textiles: HCA, 4625, translated in D. Nicholson, *Symbolism, Colour and Embroidery*

later additions, includes records of numerous gifts in this category, such as the silver gilt chalice given by Stephen Thornbury, dean *c.* 1234–47, the silver bowl or chalice (*cuppam*) from John Pichart, the chalice and silver cruets given by Canon William de Hay, the large brass or bronze candlestick (*magnum candelabrum ereum*) of Richard de Capella, bishop 1121–27, and the silver gilt chalice given to the altar of St Helen by Nicholas Boteler.[3] Dean John of Aigueblanche bequeathed in 1320 two silver ampullae (phials for holy oil) for use at the high altar.[4] We know that the quality of such objects is likely to have been high, since the wealthy bishops, deans and canons who became the benefactors of secular cathedrals in the medieval period were likely to have been prominent men with sophisticated tastes: we can imagine the quality of such treasures as the silver reliquary in the form of a church given by Bishop Edmund Audley.[5] The thirteenth-century statutes record that the treasurer 'is to keep all the silver and gold vessels and relics also; and he must give an account once a year to the dean and chapter of all these things'.[6] The earliest act book records several cases in the early sixteenth century in which chalices were returned to their appropriate altars, or replaced when lost.[7]

All these riches must have been swept away at the Reformation, although we have no surviving details of how or when. The frustratingly incomplete inventory of church plate in the diocese of 1553 indicates that at least six gilt or parcel gilt chalices remained at the cathedral, together with a silver gilt cross and two silver parcel gilt candlesticks; a pyx, two cruets, a chalice and a censer, all of silver, had already been sold.[8] Enough vessels must have remained to be returned to their original use under Mary I, and in 1555 it is recorded that Edward Baskervile included a silver chalice in his fine for the farm of Preston.[9] But the Protestant Reformation required that there should be only one altar, transforming the requirements in terms of eucharistic vessels. Chalices were converted into communion cups, which had to be larger to accommodate communion in both kinds for the laity; this necessitated also the introduction of flagons. The conversion of chalices took place systematically under Elizabeth I, diocese by diocese, so as not to overload the London goldsmiths with work; Hereford's turn came in 1571.[10]

in *Hereford Cathedral* (Hereford, 1983), pp. 52–53. See above, Chapter 26, p. 494.

3. R. Rawlinson, *The History and Antiquities of the City and Cathedral-Church of Hereford* (London, 1717), appendix, pp. 9, 14, 20.

4. Capes, *Charters*, p. 186.

5. C. Oman, *English Church Plate* (London, 1957), p. 9; Rawlinson, *History and Antiquities*, appendix, p. 21.

6. E. F. H. Dunnicliff, 'Consuetudines et statuta ecclesiasticae cathedralis Herefordensis:

A Paraphrase in English' (HCA, typescript, 1962), p. 37.

7. HCA, MS, P. G. S. Baylis, ed., 'Hereford Cathedral Chapter Act Book Vol. 1' (3 vols, 1969–70), i, pp. 148–49, 309, 390–91.

8. Printed in Stanhope and Moffatt, *Church Plate*, p. 216.

9. HCA, Baylis, ii, no. 947.

10. C. Oman, ed., *Church Plate and Other Art Treasures from the Churches of the Diocese: Hereford Art Gallery, 1958* (Hereford, 1958), p. 3.

We have little record of the plate at the cathedral throughout the interesting period up to the Restoration in 1660; neither the Elizabethan nor the Laudian statutes give any details of communion vessels, beyond the instruction that inventories of all the cathedral's goods are to be kept and reviewed annually.[11] But both give detailed instructions on the provision of candles on specific occasions, so we can assume that candlesticks were also a necessity.[12] The plate makes very infrequent appearances in the chapter acts, and even fewer in the accounts, since such valuable items were usually acquired by gift or exchange. Canon William Skynner's reply to Bishop Wren's visitation of 1635 confirms that the basic essentials of Protestant communion plate were in place: 'one silver-flagon 2 Challices and 2 pattines'. All these disappeared at the 'purging' of Hereford Cathedral early in 1641.[13]

From the late seventeenth century we have a more or less complete picture of the history of the plate. The earliest piece still extant to have a continuous history at the cathedral is the impressive silver (originally silver gilt) dean's mace, dating from the reign of Charles II, which remarkably is still in daily use. It is about three feet long, the bowl crested with linked crosses and fleur-de-lis, and divided into four panels in which are portrayed the arms of the deanery and the see, a Tudor rose crowned and a fleur-de-lis crowned, with four caryatids between them (fig. 143).[14]

There were three important donations of plate over the next seventy years: the gift of two flagons by Egidius (i.e. Giles) Rawlins of London in 1669; two silver gilt pillar candlesticks given by Dean John Tyler in 1719, and two chalices given by Dean Edward Cresset in 1737. These, together with a basin and a salver, comprise the complete collection of plate as recorded in the inventory of 1765: a startling contrast to the medieval situation.[15] On 10 August 1772 the chapter 'ordered that the two Sacramental Cups given by the late Dean Cresset … be exchanged for others of a more convenient size and make, and that the former inscriptions be continued on the new Cups'.[16] The estimate of Charles Wright of London, dated 24 August 1772 and addressed to Mr Mayo, goldsmith at Hereford, includes two flagons, a beaded dish and plate, and two Corinthian pillar candlesticks, as well as the two chalices, all silver gilt.[17] Only the chalices, flagons and an

11. HCA, 7044/6, R. J. W. Bryer, trans., 'The Statutes of the Cathedral Church of Hereford, Promulgated on 26 March 1583' (typescript, 1994), p. 15; Jebb and Phillott, *The Statutes of the Cathedral Church of Hereford*, pp. 94–95.

12. HCA, 7044/6, pp. 7–8; Jebb and Phillott, *The Statutes of the Cathedral Church of Hereford*, pp. 42–45.

13. HCA, 1558, no. 12; J. Eales, *Puritans and Roundheads: The Harleys of Brampton Bryan and the Outbreak of the English Civil War* (Cambridge, 1990), p. 131.

14. Stanhope and Moffatt, *Church Plate*, pp. 73–74; HCA, 6474/4, no. 3.25.1.

15. HCA, 4929.

16. HCA, 7031/5, p. 85.

17. HCA, 5606.

almsdish are known to have been made, Dean Tyler's candlesticks presumably continuing to serve their purpose. Thanks to the copying of the original inscriptions, we still have a record of the Rawlins and Cresset gifts. The 1772 plate is still in regular use for special services.[18] Ten years earlier, in 1762, two silver chalices were commissioned by the vicar and churchwardens of the parish of St John the Baptist, which are also still in the cathedral.[19]

There were few additions to the plate over the next century; in 1831 Henry Huntingford, canon residentiary and prebendary of Colwall from 1817 to 1867, gave a silver tray to hold the spoon at the communion service, 'to be placed length-ways between the two high Cups ... in keeping with the handsome Sacramental Plate, already belonging to the Cathedral'.[20] The list of plate by John Davies, verger, 29 September 1857, recorded in the hebdomadary's book, includes only minimal additions to the 1772 chalices, flagons and almsdish, and the Tyler

Fig. 143. Ted Pannell, head verger 1978–85, with the seventeenth-century dean's mace.

candlesticks.[21] Davies himself gave two patens and a small almsdish, matching the 1772 set, in 1863 and 1869.[22] A pair of candlesticks was given by Canon Jebb in 1871, and a cross by Canon Phillott in 1895, but evidence of the influence of the ritualist movement had to wait for the work of Canon Frederick Mackenzie Williams, whose gift of 'a case containing Communion Plate' in 1897 is recorded after Davies's inventory.[23] This consisted of a chalice and paten, wafer box and spoon. The silver gilt chalice, made in Birmingham in 1866, is in the Gothic style, with six carbuncles set into the hexagonal knop, and diamonds and pearls set into

18. Stanhope and Moffatt, *Church Plate*, pp. 72–73; HCA, 6474/4, nos 3.1.30, 3.3.29, 3.10.3.
19. HCA, 6389; HCA, 6474/4, no. 3.1.61.
20. HCA, 7031/18, p. [325], chapter acts, 10 November 1831.
21. HCA, 7007, p. 466.
22. HCA, 6474/4, nos 3.9.24, 3.10.2.
23. HCA, 7031/21, p. 467; HCA, 7031/23, p. 247; HCA, 7007, p. 466.

the base.[24] Even more ornate is the silver gilt chalice with a large single crystal for a knop, donated by the cathedral communicants at the instigation of Canon Williams in 1902; an appeal for money and jewels was published in the *Hereford Diocesan Messenger*, and it seems that the jewels donated were set directly into the stem and base of the cup. Both these chalices are still in regular Sunday use.[25]

The twentieth century has seen a number of gifts of plate by members of the foundation and the congregation; in some ways this mirrors the medieval situation, although often such gifts are of antique items, enhancing the museum function of the cathedral. In 1980 this was confirmed when, with the aid of a grant from the Goldsmiths Company, the crypt was opened as a treasury, to display the church plate treasures of the diocese as well as the cathedral. Several valuable ornaments, however, remained in their places in the cathedral, including the Tyler candlesticks on the high altar: tragically, these were stolen on the night of 24 June 1983, along with a pair of 1936 silver candlesticks and a silver crucifix. Although the thief was caught and convicted, none of these items was ever recovered. The Tyler candlesticks were valued at the time at £10,000.[26]

The cathedral has no fine examples of modern plate, but it ranks as second to none as the home of craftsmanship in metalwork in the form of the new corona, commissioned from Simon Beer by the Friends of the Cathedral in memory of Bishop John Eastaugh (fig. 53).[27] After the removal of Mappa Mundi from the crypt to the new library building in 1996, the chapter resolved to remove the treasury from the crypt and to restore the latter as a place of worship. This was achieved by August 1997.[28] At the time of writing, therefore, there is no place of display for the historic treasures of the cathedral, other than the chained library and Mappa Mundi, but it is the intention of chapter to find a new place for the treasury in the near future.

The first of the lost medieval treasures to be restored to the cathedral in modern times is the most celebrated of all of them: the exquisite Limoges enamel reliquary which once contained a relic of St Thomas Becket (plate XIIIb). It is now well known to the scholarly world through the work of Simone Caudron, culminating in the exhibition of medieval enamel reliquaries, 'Valérie et Thomas Becket', at Limoges in the summer of 1999, at which the Hereford casket was united with fourteen other of the forty-eight similar Becket reliquaries which survive, whole or in part.[29] The illustrations in the catalogue at last reveal the great variety of

24. Stanhope and Moffatt, *Church Plate*, p. 71.

25. *Hereford Diocesan Messenger*, 5 (1902–3), p. 2; Stanhope and Moffatt, *Church Plate*, p. 72; HCA, 6474/4, no. 3.1.67.

26. HCA, NS 2/1/9.

27. See above, Chapter 7, p. 197.

28. Chapter acts, 10 June 1996.

29. S. Caudron, 'Thomas Becket et l'oeuvre de Limoges', in V. Notin, S. Caudron and G. François, *Valérie et Thomas Becket: de*

these reliquaries: no two are alike, and it would seem that every one was commissioned individually. The large number which survive testify to the popularity of the cult and the effectiveness of the patronage of both the cult and 'l'oeuvre Limoges' by the Plantagenet kings of England. Becket was murdered in 1170 and canonised in 1173; all the reliquaries date from *c.* 1175 to 1220, when production abruptly ceased following the translation of the body of the saint to his new shrine at Canterbury Cathedral, after which the monks at Canterbury were understandably unwilling to distribute any more relics of their profitable saint. None of the actual relics which were housed in the caskets survive; they probably consisted of fragments of his body or his clothing.

Hereford's casket is dated 1200–10, and Simone Caudron proposes that it was commissioned by William de Vere, bishop of Hereford 1186–98, who had known Becket personally.[30] It seems to have been saved from destruction at the Reformation by the Roman Catholic Bodenham family of Rotherwas near Hereford, from whom it was acquired by Thomas Russell, canon of Hereford Cathedral. Russell presented it to the Society of Antiquaries in 1775, proposing that the martyrdom it depicted was that of St Ethelbert, although both the previous owner and the antiquarian Richard Gough were of the opinion that the subject was Becket.[31] Duncumb accepted the Ethelbert suggestion, but F. T. Havergal identified it correctly in 1869.[32] Meanwhile, Canon Russell having died in 1785, the reliquary had been inherited by his nephew, another Canon Thomas Russell, who wrote a description of it, and eventually bequeathed it to the cathedral; it was received by the chapter in November 1831.[33] It has been seen at exhibitions at Gloucester in 1860, London in 1862 and Birmingham in 1934; since 1996 it has been displayed in the showcase in the Mappa Mundi chamber of the new library building, apart from the time of its visit to Limoges in the summer of 1999.

The casket, 8¼ x 7 x 33/8 inches (210 x 178 x 85 mm.), is made of oak, covered with eight copper plates overlaid with enamel in several shades of blue, turquoise, green, yellow and white. The main panel shows the murder of the

---

l'influence des princes Plantagenêt dans l'oeuvre Limoges (Limoges, 1999), pp. 56–68. The Hereford reliquary is no. 18 in this catalogue, described and illustrated pp. 106–7; the works of Simone Caudron are listed in the bibliography, p. 134.

30. Ibid., p. 107. The obit book credits de Vere with the gift of *multa bona in redditibus et ornamentis* to the cathedral: Rawlinson, *History and Antiquities*, appendix, p. 31.

31. Society of Antiquaries of London, MS, 'Minute Book', 14 (1775–76), pp. 170–84.

32. J. Duncumb, *Collections towards the History and Antiquities of the County of Hereford* (8 vols, Hereford and London, 1804–1915), i, pp. 549–52; F. T. Havergal, *Fasti Herefordenses* (Edinburgh, 1869), p. 142.

33. T. Russell, *A Short Description of a Portable Shrine* (Hereford, 1830); HCA, 7031/18, p. 326. A portrait of Canon Thomas Russell the younger (1753–1831) by T. Leeming (copy in the cathedral, HCA, 6474/4, no. 12.3.8) shows him with the reliquary proudly displayed at his side.

archbishop at the altar by three knights with swords; his entombment is portrayed on the panel above. A figure of a standing saint appears at each end, while the back is covered with a repeated design of quatrefoils within squares. A panel at the back, once secured with a key, opens to reveal the chamber which contained the relic; painted on the inner wall of the chamber opposite the opening panel is a red cross of consecration, a feature found in only a few of the similar reliquaries.

The next discoveries took place in the heady days of Dean Merewether and the Cottingham restoration when so many of the medieval antiquities of the cathedral were rediscovered in a newly receptive artistic climate. The first was perhaps the most remarkable. In 1841, when examining the central tower, several medieval items were found among the rubbish in the groining of the vaults, including the heads of two crosses.[34] When Merewether's drawings were printed and described by Havergal, the crosses had been lost again. The one bearing the figure of Christ was eventually bought back for the cathedral in 1911 for £100 by Dean Leigh from A. Langton Douglas, who reported that it had been given or sold by Dean Merewether to the architect L. N. Cottingham, from whom it had been bought by John Fuller Russell, the clerical antiquarian and collector. Douglas had bought the cross from Russell's son.[35] This account was evidently published in the *Hereford Journal*; a letter of 11 July 1911 to Dean Leigh from Merewether's daughter, Emily H. Merewether, denounces the imputation that her father had sold the cross.[36] Russell had exhibited it in 1861 to the Archaeological Institute, describing it as 'a large processional cross of mixed metal, found at Hereford, and formerly in the possession of Dean Merewether. It is probably of English workmanship, date fifteenth century.'[37] It seems that Dean Leigh paid for the cross himself; Moir's assertion that it was bought for the cathedral by Sir Henry Webb is unsubstantiated, although if he is the 'Henry' to whom A. L. Douglas's letter of 22 September 1910 is addressed, he may have been instrumental in bringing the cross to the dean's attention.[38]

Meanwhile, a copy in silver of the other cross discovered by Merewether and illustrated by Havergal had been made and given to the cathedral in 1903; it is still in regular processional use.[39] In 1925, under Dean Hedley Burrows, the medieval cross was mounted on an ebonised staff and put on display in the choir.[40] In 1976 as part of the celebration of the 1300th anniversary of the diocese it achieved a

34. J. Merewether, *A Statement of the Condition and Circumstances of the Cathedral Church of Hereford* (Hereford, 1842), p. 20; Havergal, *Fasti*, p. 147.
35. HCA, 3655.
36. Ibid.
37. *Archaeological Journal*, 18 (1861), p. 77; for

J. F. Russell, 1814–84, see *DNB*.
38. A. L. Moir, *Festival 1976: A Celebration of 1300 Years, 676–1976 AD in Retrospect* (Hereford, 1976), p. 43; HCA, 3655.
39. Havergal, *Fasti*, p. 147 and plate 12.
40. HCA, 7031/24, p. 156, chapter acts, 25 June 1925.

new celebrity when it was chosen to head the Pilgrimage of Prayer through-out the diocese.[41] In 1994 it was again revived as the 'Ethelbert Cross' for the celebration of the 1200th anniversary of the martyrdom of the cathedral's patron saint.

The cross is English and dates from the fifteenth century; it was probably intended both for use on the altar and for processions. The upper part of the cross and the knop are copper; the socket at the base is of brass, and may not be part of the same cross. These two parts are illustrated in Havergal; at the time of its discovery it would seem to have been in two pieces. Since then it has presumably been repaired; the lower part of the stem, including the roundel with the image of a man, is probably a nineteenth-century replacement. The four symbols of the evangelists appear as casts in the roundels at the ends of the arms of the cross, riveted to the centre of each. Stumps on either side of the figure of Christ on the stem may be the remains of

Fig. 144. Processional cross, fifteenth century.

branches which once bore the figures of the Virgin Mary and Saint John. A single rose is engraved on the reverse of each roundel. No trace of silver, gilt or enamelling, which may have been present, remains. Though modest in quality of execution and materials, it is still an awesome object as a rare surviving example of a particular aspect of the medieval liturgical life of the cathedral (fig. 144).[42]

The earliest pieces of plate still at the cathedral are two sets of funerary chalices and accompanying patens. It was the general practice in the middle ages to bury a priest with a chalice and paten, and many examples of surviving medieval plate

41. A. L. Moir, 'The Way of the Cross through the Diocese', *Hereford Diocesan News*, no. 137 (May 1976), p. 3.

42. C. Oman, 'English Medieval Base Metal Church Plate', *Archaeological Journal*, 119 (1962), pp. 195–207 and pl. 17b. I am most grateful to Marian Campbell of the Victoria and Albert Museum for sending me a copy of this article, and for giving her opinion on the date and materials of the cross.

Fig. 145. Silver chalice and paten found in the tomb of Bishop Richard Swinfield, died 1316.

have been brought to light by the opening of tombs.[43] Both chalices and patens are small in size, in the medieval manner. The first set, made of pewter, was found at the opening of the tomb of Chancellor Gilbert Swinfield, who died *c.* 1299, in the north choir aisle in the 1840s; the chalice was placed upright near the right shoulder of the body, still bearing evidence of the wine which it had contained, together with partially burnt tapers in the form of a cross which had been placed across it on a square of silk.[44] The second set is made of silver, dated to the mid thirteenth century, and was taken from the stone coffin of Bishop Richard Swinfield, died 1316, in the north-east transept, which was opened in 1861. It was first described by Havergal, who nonetheless deplored the disturbance of the grave.[45] The chalice is of a simple and elegant design; the paten bears the motif of the *manus dei*, or hand of God, which was a common design in this context (fig. 145).[46] Both sets are in an excellent state of repair, and are probably the most important pieces of historic plate in the cathedral. It is to be hoped that they may soon be able to be seen again by the public.

43. Oman, *English Church Plate*, p. 40 n. 1.
44. Havergal, *Fasti*, p. 198.
45. Ibid., p. 199.

46. Stanhope and Moffatt, *Church Plate*, p. 74; Oman, *English Church Plate*, pp. 299, 304.

PART IV

Library and Archives

The Library

Joan Williams

The histories of most ancient libraries share many common features: a twelfth-century expansion; the first dedicated library room in the fourteenth or fifteenth century; a seventeenth-century revival often associated with a notable benefactor; intermittent periods of neglect; and occasional major disasters by acts of God or man. The history of Hereford Cathedral library includes all these elements, but it is also special in several ways. A significant number of its medieval manuscripts survive in their original or early bindings, constituting what may be 'the richest collection of pre-1500 sewing and binding among the "larger collections" of medieval manuscripts in Britain'.[1] It preserves the largest surviving chained library in the country; it survived both the Reformation and the Civil War apparently without untoward depredations; within the century from 1897 to 1996 it acquired two new library buildings; and it retains to the present day a working theological lending and reference library. All these factors illustrate a common theme of continuity; perhaps uniquely, since the destruction of the cathedral in 1055, the library has suffered no serious depletion by fire, flood, theft or sale of books.

Only one book, the Hereford Gospels, survived the 1055 catastrophe and is still in the library.[2] This book, above all, enacts the theme of continuity: it is regularly on display in the library exhibition and makes special public appearances as an oath book at the enthronements and installations of bishops and deans. Once an object of veneration as a rare embodiment of the Word of God, it is now a source of awe for the heritage generation as the oldest artefact in the cathedral, eloquently demonstrating the persistence of that Word as the continuing essential function of the cathedral (plate I, figs i, 152, 153).

This book, like the only other to survive possibly from the pre-Conquest cathedral, is of course for liturgical use; we do not know what other types of

---

1. M. Gullick, 'The Bindings', in Mynors and Thomson, *Catalogue*, p. xxvi.
2. See below, Chapter 29, pp. 536–43.

book, if any, may have been housed in the Saxon cathedral.[3] The three Anglo-Saxon manuscripts sent to Archbishop Parker by Bishop Scory in 1566 cannot now be identified and of course we do not even know if they originated in Hereford.[4]

The history of the library proper begins at about 1100, the approximate date of the earliest surviving manuscripts known to have been at the cathedral after the Conquest.[5] A large number of the medieval manuscripts still in the library date from the twelfth century, the period at which many ecclesiastical institutions were acquiring their collections of essential texts.[6] Although Hereford at this period was noted as a centre of learning, famously attested to by Simon de Freine writing to Gerald of Wales, this is hardly reflected in the cathedral's books: 'The overwhelming impression is of a practical reference library for the canons: patristics and some more recent theology, biblical studies and canon law'.[7] The largest group from this period is the 'glossed books' (books of the Bible with standard commentary), and remarkable among these are ten of the twelve surviving books from an original gift of twenty by Ralph Foliot, archdeacon of Hereford, c. 1180–98.[8] Ralph was a member of the notable local family who provided two bishops of Hereford in the twelfth century; his gift to the library is the earliest recorded and represents 'the largest cache of manuscripts surviving from any private Romanesque library in Britain'.[9]

The history of the medieval library has been extensively researched by R. M. Thomson.[10] Most of the evidence derives from the books themselves, their marks of previous ownership, of donation, of added titles, lists of contents or valuations; no medieval catalogues survive. Although the library was not large at this time, probably never exceeding the maximum number of 138 of the existing manuscripts, this was roughly typical of an English secular cathedral.[11] Despite this

---

3. Gospel book of *c.* 1050, now Cambridge, Pembroke College, MS 302: see above, Chapter 1, p. 18. For a discussion of the possible Hereford origins of another eleventh-century liturgy, BL, MS Cotton Caligula A. xiv, fos 1–36, see E. C. Teviotdale, 'The "Hereford Troper" and Hereford', in Whitehead, *Medieval Art at Hereford*, pp. 75–81.

4. HCA, 7031/1, fol. 210v, copy of letter from Parker, 20 January 1566, and note of books sent, 8 February 1566, printed in B. H. Streeter, *The Chained Library* (London, 1931), p. 347; HCA, 5756.

5. R. M. Thomson, 'Introduction', in Mynors and Thomson, *Catalogue*, pp. xvii–xviii.

6. Ibid., p. xv; K. Edwards, *The English Secular Cathedrals* (2nd edn, Manchester, 1967), p. 210.

7. Thomson, 'Introduction', in Mynors and Thomson, *Catalogue*, pp. xvii–xviii. For manuscript evidence of scholarship in the Hereford area in the eleventh and twelfth centuries, see C. Burnett, 'Mathematics and Astronomy in Hereford and its Region in the Twelfth Century', in Whitehead, *Medieval Art at Hereford*, pp. 50–59.

8. Thomson, 'Introduction', in Mynors and Thomson, *Catalogue*, p. xviii.

9. C. de Hamel, 'Hereford Cathedral Library Medieval Manuscripts' (HCL, typescript report, 1986).

10. Thomson, 'Introduction', in Mynors and Thomson, *Catalogue*, pp. xv–xxvi.

modest size, the inevitably restricted readership and the paucity of evidence, the status of the library as a source and centre of scholarship has probably never been higher than it was between the twelfth and fifteenth centuries, when a number of distinguished scholars held offices in the cathedral, some of whom are known to have made intensive use of its books, as evidenced by their gifts and annotations, sometimes in pursuance of their studies at Oxford.[12] The cathedral libraries had not yet been overtaken by the university libraries as academic resource centres. Then as later, the secular cathedral libraries in particular were very probably open to members of the literate elite other than the cathedral's own personnel.[13] The story of cathedral libraries in the succeeding centuries tends to be one of modest expansion in size and accessibility, and of a corresponding decline in cultural significance, from which the increase in documentary evidence can easily distract us. But at least the surviving books from the medieval library are now the most treasured and admired part of the library as historic and artistic objects.

There is more external evidence for the life of the library from the thirteenth and fourteenth centuries, as records of gifts of books begin to appear in the obit book and other documents.[14] The earliest cathedral statutes of the mid thirteenth century provide the first evidence for the existence of a working library. The chancellor is charged with the care of the books, both physically in terms of their repair and intellectually in registering their readers and arranging lectures about them.[15]

Notable among the gifts is that of six books of canon law given by Canon Alan de Creppinge, recorded in an ordinance of 1298, and a bequest of six assorted works by Bishop Lewis Charlton in 1369.[16] The latter is of particular interest as it is specified that the books should be chained in the church, presumably to a lectern or stall where they could also be read. There are thirteenth- and fourteenth-century references in two books to cupboards; by implication the books were kept in different places according to use, perhaps by an early division into lending and reference collections.[17] It has been assumed in modern times that books were kept in the three medieval chests which survive in the cathedral, in particular the finely

---

11. Ibid., p. xvii.

12. Ibid., p. xx.

13. T. Kelly, *Early Public Libraries* (London, 1966), p. 25.

14. Oxford, Bodleian, MS Rawlinson B.328, printed in R. Rawlinson, *The History and Antiquities of the City and Cathedral-Church of Hereford* (London, 1717), appendix, pp. 3–31.

15. HCA, 7044/1, fos 10v–11r, printed in Bradshaw and Wordsworth, *Statutes of*

Lincoln Cathedral, ii, p. 71; Thomson, 'Introduction', in Mynors and Thomson, *Catalogue*, p. xxi.

16. HCA, 722; A. B. Emden, *A Biographical Register of the University of Oxford to AD 1500* (Oxford, 1957), p. 392; Thomson, 'Introduction', in Mynors and Thomson, *Catalogue*, p. xx.

17. Thomson, 'Introduction', in Mynors and Thomson, *Catalogue*, p. xxi.

carved fourteenth-century chest with three locks, although it is suggested elsewhere in this book that this more probably housed archival documents.[18]

The fifteenth century saw the first construction of dedicated library rooms in many institutions, presumably the better to accommodate growing collections of books and to provide a suitable environment for their study, but the trend is so marked that fashion and status may well have played a part.[19] Hereford's was an upper room over the west walk of the new cloisters: again, a typical place for one of these early libraries. The room was completed but still new by 1478.[20] Its furniture and arrangement can be deduced from other examples: long lecterns on which the books lay on sloping desks with benches for readers, at right angles to the east and west walls.[21] At Hereford the custom seems to have been for the books to lie with their back covers uppermost, as some books of the late fifteenth and early sixteenth centuries bear horn-covered labels on these covers. One would expect that the books would be chained to these lecterns, although this does not seem to have been done systematically at Hereford at this time.[22]

Donations from the fourteenth century onwards are dominated by law books, reflecting the major professional interests of the canons in this period. The most notable large donations are the thirty books given by Canon Owen Lloyd in 1478, and the bequests of Bishop Charles Booth in 1535 and of Dean Edmund Frowcester in 1529.[23] These consist of printed books as well as manuscripts; they also include some of the most handsome books in the library, suggesting that on the eve of the Reformation it was as active and well-stocked as it had ever been.

Being a secular cathedral, Hereford's library proper does not seem to have suffered any major losses at the time of the Dissolution; on the contrary, it benefited from the subsequent gifts of books removed from monastic institutions in the vicinity. Many of these came in 1555 as the gift of Sir John Prise, who had been involved in the dissolution of many of these houses, and had later

18. Streeter, *Chained Library*, pp. 117–18; Thomson, 'Introduction', in Mynors and Thomson, *Catalogue*, p. xxi; see below, Chapter 30, pp. 545–46.

19. Among secular cathedrals alone the first library rooms were built at e.g. Exeter 1412, Lincoln 1419–26, York *c.* 1420, Wells *c.* 1424, Salisbury 1445: A. Erskine, 'Library and Archives' in M. Swanton, ed., *Exeter Cathedral: A Celebration* (Exeter, 1991), p. 193; Streeter, *Chained Library*, p. 16; C. B. L. Barr, 'The Minster Library', in G. E. Aylmer and R. Cant, eds, *A History of York Minster* (rev. edn, Oxford,

1979), pp. 494–95; R. Birley, 'The Cathedral Library', in L. S. Colchester, ed., *Wells Cathedral: A History* (Shepton Mallet, 1982), p. 205; S. Eward, 'Salisbury Cathedral Library' (HCL, typescript, 1983), p. 2.

20. HCA, R 369; Thomson, 'Introduction', in Mynors and Thomson, *Catalogue*, p. xxi.

21. Streeter, *Chained Library*, pp. 9–23.

22. Thomson, 'Introduction', in Mynors and Thomson, *Catalogue*, p. xxi.

23. Ibid., pp. xxiii–xxiv; N. R. Ker, ed., *Medieval Libraries of Great Britain* (2nd edn, London, 1964), p. 268.

settled in Hereford.[24] Large collections came from the Augustinians of Cirencester, the Hereford Franciscans and St Peter's Abbey, Gloucester (now Gloucester Cathedral): these last are probably to be associated with the large number of medieval documents from St Peter's among the cathedral archives.[25] Thanks to the acquisition of these books, Hereford's current collection of 227 medieval manuscripts is particularly rich (plate VIIIa–d).

Nevertheless, the disruptions of the sixteenth century inevitably took their toll on Hereford's library, as on so many others. Almost all the medieval service books were lost, although these would probably not have been housed in the library room. One of them, the Hereford breviary, made a celebrated return to the cathedral in 1834 (plate IVa).[26] The Injunctions of Edward VI of 1547 demonstrated a concern for cathedral libraries as centres of learning, requiring that they should all contain a minimum of named works of theology, mostly patristics, with Erasmus being the only 'modern' author included.[27]

The Queen's Commission of 1582 nevertheless found the library in a state of neglect, confirming the findings of John Dee, whose account of 1574 provides the first objective report of a visitor to the library.[28] The resulting statutes of 1583 significantly laid down the rules which formed the basis for the care of the library for all its subsequent history. For the first time financial provision was made for the purchase of books by allotting the two pounds installation fee payable by every new canon or prebendary for the purpose. As well as the lists of books to be attached to the end of each desk, their names were also to be entered in two books: the first suggestion of a proper catalogue. One of the residentiary canons was to be appointed annually as master ('custos'); henceforward the character, quality and interests of the master were to be crucial in the development of the library.[29]

There followed the first major migration in the history of the library, when it was moved into the Lady chapel in 1590, releasing the cloister room for the use of the school and enacting the Reformation principle of converting such a chapel to non-liturgical use and leaving only one altar in the church (fig. 146).[30] The

24. N. R. Ker, 'Sir John Prise', *The Library*, 5th series, 10 (1955), pp. 1–24; F. C. Morgan, 'The Will of Sir John Prise of Hereford, 1555', *National Library of Wales Journal*, 9, no. 2 (1955), pp. 1–7.

25. See below, Chapter 30, pp. 546–47.

26. Mynors and Thomson, *Catalogue*, p. 124; see above, Chapter 20, pp. 369–74.

27. W. H. Frere and W. McC. Kennedy, eds, *Visitation Articles and Injunctions of the Period of the Reformation*, Alcuin Club Collections, 14–16 (3 vols, London, 1910),

ii, p. 136.

28. 'Extracts from the Harley Manuscripts in the British Museum, no. 473, Concerning a Visit to Hereford in the Year 1574 AD', *TWNFC*, 34 (1952–54), pp. 23–24; 'John Dee and Hereford Cathedral Library', ibid., 35 (1955–57), p. 193.

29. HCA, 7044/3, fos 3r–3v; 7044/4, pp. 5–6, printed in Streeter, *Chained Library*, pp. 348–51.

30. HCA, 7031/2, fol. 140v, chapter acts, 16 February 1590.

Fig. 146. The chained library in the Lady chapel: drawing *c.* 1841. (HCL, neg. 1).

Fig. 147. Memorial to Thomas
Thornton in Ledbury church.

fabric accounts record the costs involved in this.[31] Security, as ever in library
history, was a prime consideration: a partition was built across the west end of
the chapel (evident in Browne Willis's plan of 1727), and the westernmost windows
on both sides were boarded up to prevent intrusion.[32] Separate accounts for the
library, in accordance with the statutes, appear for the first time for the year
1596–97 and include the first purchase of 'irons and cheines to fasten our Bookes
in the Library' (again fulfilling the provisions of the statutes).[33] Most of the
expenditure was taken up with the huge amount of £39 spent on books, of which
Chrysostom's works in Greek for three pounds are specified.

Clearly a new era has begun. The inspiration undoubtedly came from Thomas
Thornton (*c.* 1541–1629), the first and greatest hero in the history of the library
(fig. 147). An enthusiastic reformer and formidable scholar, he was a student and
then a canon of Christ Church, Oxford, and vice-chancellor of Oxford University
in 1583 and 1599. In 1583 he also first became a canon and precentor of Hereford
(where his continued residence at Oxford brought him into conflict with the rest

31. HCA, R 588, fol. 20.
32. Willis, *Survey of the Cathedrals*, p. 499, plan.

33. HCA, R 593.

of the chapter), being master of the library in 1595–97 and 1610–17.[34] He was zealous in his work for the library: the donors' book, which he instituted in 1611, records some 150 books purchased in 1598 and 1618, at the end of his two periods as master, as well as his own large gifts of chronicles and histories of Britain, reflecting his particular interest (fig. 148).[35] He expended much energy in recovering arrears in the installation fees 'for encrease of bookes in our librarie', and instituted an oath to be taken by readers, modelled on that of Bodley's Library at Oxford, and a set of rules for them.[36]

His abiding legacy, however, was in designing and largely paying for the new chained bookcases, begun in 1611, which remain the chief glory of the library. Evidently inspired by Sir Thomas Bodley's innovation in library design in Duke Humfrey's Library at Oxford in about 1599, he copied this style in the library furniture he installed both at Christ Church and Hereford, at about the same time, the articles of agreement with the joiners or carpenters in both places being closely related.[37] Happily this and a number of other documents at Hereford survive to provide much evidence for this interesting period in the library's history, including details of ironwork, chains and how to attach them, and advice on these matters from experts in Oxford.[38]

The former library furnishings, which must have been moved into the Lady chapel in 1590, were completely replaced by the new cases. Nothing of them remains, unless some of the surviving benches were adapted from the medieval ones.[39] The new cases (which Thornton called 'desks') were set on a raised wooden platform and arranged at right angles to the north and south walls (presumably as the medieval lecterns had been), with a wide aisle between them. Two 'half desks' were set on either side against the east wall; the remainder were double-sided. Each desk was provided with a 'writing table' (which we now call a desk) and detached double seats. According to the draft contract, each desk was to have only four shelves above the table for books, not the nine which exist now and were already in place by the early eighteenth century; probably the draft contract merely

34. A. J. Winnington-Ingram, 'Thomas Thorn-(e)ton', *TWNFC*, 35 (1955–57), pp. 209–11.

35. HCL, MS P.IX.8, pp. 523–25, 621–64. Those purchased in 1618 include at least thirty which had formerly belonged to Edward Doughtie, dean 1608–16, incorporating a minimum of nineteen works which he had acquired from the Jesuit library in Cadiz: P. S. Allen, 'Books Brought from Spain in 1596', *English Historical Review*, 31 (1916), pp. 606–10. See

above, Chapter 4, p. 97.

36. HCA, 1130, 1118, 1124, 1131.

37. HCA, 1135; G. Bill, 'Christ Church and Hereford Cathedral Libraries and the Bodleian', *Bodleian Library Record*, 4 (1952), pp. 145–49.

38. HCA, 1134, 1129, 1121, 1130, 1125, 1126, 1128, 1127.

39. B. G. Charles and H. D. Emanuel, 'Notes on Old Libraries and Books', *National Library of Wales Journal*, 6 (1950), p. 362; Streeter, *Chained Library*, pp. 89–91.

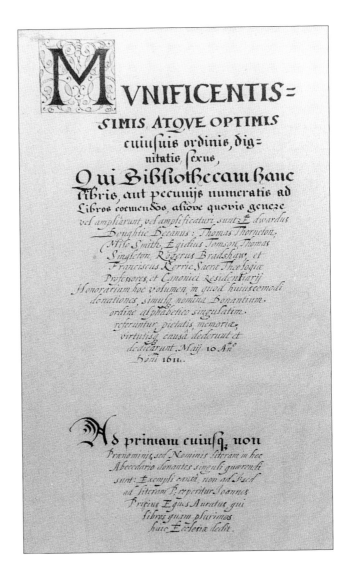

Fig. 148. Title page of the
library donors' book, 1611.
(HCL, P.IX.8, p. 13.)

copied that of Christ Church and was adapted later.[40] We now know that the
first two single and two double cases were provided by Thornton.[41] Three bills
for ironwork in 1625–27 suggest that two more double cases were installed at that
time.[42] The date of the construction of the remaining two double and two single
cases, which formed the complete library in the early eighteenth century according
to the earliest shelf list and the Browne Willis plan, is still unknown.[43]

40. HCA, 1135; Bill, 'Christ Church', p. 147.
41. Charles and Emanuel, 'Notes', p.371;
Winnington-Ingram, 'Thomas Thorn(e)-
ton', p. 214.

42. HCA, 1114, 1136, 1141.
43. HCL, P.IX.8, pp. 669–93; Willis, *Survey of
the Cathedrals*, p. 499, plan.

The chief innovation of the new system was that the books for the first time were placed upright on the shelves, so as to save space. Chaining in this position required that they should be placed with their foredges outwards, so that the chain, which now had to be fastened to the foredge of one cover (usually the front cover at Hereford), would not become tangled when a book was lifted down and placed on the desk for reading.

An arrangement of the books by subject within each bay (i.e. one side of a case) was already in place. A document of about 1612 concerns the painting of subject headings on the face-ends of the cases, although the two subjects specified ('lib Theol' and 'Artium') were not then in the same places as they were by the early eighteenth century.[44] Some of the surviving accounts indicate that the cataloguing specified by the 1583 statutes was being done: Mr Adams, the first named 'keeper' of the library, was paid for writing the registers and lists of books at the end of each case in 1611 and 1612.[45] The answers to Bishop Matthew Wren's enquiries in 1635 indicate that the catalogues were in place.[46] As none of these registers or lists survive, the donors' book and the accounts remain the only records of the books in the library at this period. The 1636 statutes more or less repeat the instructions of 1583; there were now to be three catalogues, the additional one to be kept by the master.[47]

The early seventeenth century was therefore a boom time for the library; it is not impossible that the two additional cases presumed to have been added in about 1625 were required for the large number of additional acquisitions. As well as purchases, the revival of the library attracted many gifts and bequests. Notable among these was that of Miles Smith, bishop of Gloucester and a native and former canon of Hereford, who had been prominently involved in the translation of the Authorised Version of the Bible in 1611, for which he had written the preface.[48] His bequest of 1624 included a number of works in Arabic and Hebrew associated with his translation of the Old Testament, as well as a princely £20 for the purchase of books, which was spent judiciously in London, Oxford and Gloucester, mostly on theological works, numbering in total about sixty volumes.[49] The contents of the library when Thornton first became master must have been barely 300 volumes, including the manuscript codices (although these, being listed separately, seem already to have been considered as of chiefly antiquarian interest); by 1630 this had risen to over 600 volumes.[50] As well as standard works of patristics

44. HCA, 1143.
45. HCA, R 589.
46. HCA, 1558, 1559.
47. Jebb and Phillott, *The Statutes of the Cathedral Church of Hereford*, pp. 26–31.
48. M. Smith, *Sermons* (London, 1632),

pp. [10–11].
49. HCL, P.IX.8, pp. 497–99; Charles and Emanuel, 'Notes', p. 369; HCA, 1117, 1133, 1137, 1119.
50. P. E. Morgan, '[Retrospective Accessions Register]', (2 vols, HCL, manuscript).

and contemporary Protestant theology, the library was enhanced by a number of works of history, geography and general scholarly interest, and a handful of works in English.

The new acquisitions must have necessitated a large programme of binding. The general renewal of interest in the library and its care, and the additional finance available as a result of Thornton's efforts, encouraged a certain amount of rebinding and repair to be included in this, in particular of some of the medieval manuscripts.[51] This was carried out notably by John Cooper in the 1620s.[52] The work included adding clasps to many of the books and manuscripts: 'The impression gained from Cooper's work is that the manuscripts, in contrast to his other work, were cheaply bound, suggesting that they were regarded as less valuable than the printed books.'[53] Tragically, the Hereford Gospels was among those rebound in this way.

For the rest of the seventeenth century the sources of income for the library were the rents from the rectory of Lugwardine and its associated chapels, and the installation fees as specified in the statutes 'unless there be need of them for ornaments of the church'; these had to pay for the salary of the praelector, books for the choir, and candles, communion linen and other 'ornaments', so that often expenditure on specific library purposes is lacking altogether.[54] Although none of the few accounts which survive between 1640 and 1660 include any expenditure on the library, it would seem that its life continued in some form even during these troubled years; intriguingly the clavigers' accounts for 1639–40 include the payment of one shilling 'for carriage of bookes given by Dr Fell to ye Library'.[55] This was presumably Samuel Fell, 1584–1649, dean of Christ Church and father of the more famous John; if the books he gave survive, they have not yet been identified.

Comparing the donors' book with subsequent catalogues, it would seem that, remarkably, the library survived the Civil War without major losses. A small mystery remains. Bannister's statement that the library was plundered probably derives from accounts of the activities of Silas Taylor, a sequestrator for Herefordshire, who after the capture of the city in 1645 'did ransack the library belonging to the Church of Hereford, of most, or at least the best MSS therein'.[56] This is repeated by Rawlinson and Webb.[57] Taylor is know to have acquired

51. Gullick, 'The Bindings', in Mynors and Thomson, *Catalogue*, pp. xxix–xxx.
52. HCA, 1138, 1139, 1140; P. E. Morgan, 'An Unrecorded Seventeenth-Century Hereford Bookbinder', *The Library*, 6th series, 10 (1988), pp. 145–50.
53. Gullick, 'The Bindings', in Mynors and Thomson, *Catalogue*, p. xxx.
54. HCA, 5714, 7036/1, library accounts; Jebb and Phillott, *The Statutes of the Cathedral Church of Hereford*, p. 29.
55. HCA, R 606.
56. Bannister, *The Cathedral Church of Hereford*, p. 98; A. Wood, *Athenae Oxonienses* (2 vols, London, 1691–92), ii, col. 465.
57. Rawlinson, *History*, pp. [viii], vii; J. and T. W. Webb, *Memorials of the Civil War ... as it Affected Herefordshire* (2 vols, London, 1879), ii, p. 310.

only one small manuscript item, 'Brevis relatio de glorioso rege Willelmo', detached from MS P.V.1, which he subsequently gave to the Bodleian Library.[58] Given his antiquarian interests, any 'manuscripts' which he acquired in large numbers almost certainly included archival documents, either those of the cathedral, which at the time were kept in the muniment room over the north transept, or – more probably – those of the college of vicars choral, which may have been in their library, and which would have been much more vulnerable, since the college buildings had apparently been made available to beggars.[59] Since there is no catalogue of either collection of archives at this time, and since Taylor's collections were seized by his creditors after his death, it is now probably impossible to discover what items, if any, he took from Hereford, or what became of them.[60]

After the Restoration the surviving accounts indicate a modest revival of the library: there are payments for cleaning in 1664–65 and for mending chains in 1690, and for the purchase of books in 1688 and 1691, but most expenditure went understandably towards the purchase of new books for the choir.[61] By 1677 installation fees had become the only income.[62]

In 1678 there was a major addition from a surprising source when the books from the dissolved Jesuit College at Cwm were transferred to the cathedral library.[63] Some of the more substantial volumes were chained and added to the bay allotted to Roman Catholic works; the majority, however, were in small formats, bound in limp vellum and unsuitable for chaining, so their original location in the library is unknown. They are not included in the eighteenth-century catalogues but are still housed among the unchained rare books today.[64] Expenditure on the library was minimal in the early years of the eighteenth century, but the references to purchases of books at this period include for the first time the names of the Hereford booksellers Hunt, Broade and Wilde, among others.[65]

There was a new revival during the mastership of Richard Smalbroke, 1713–24, who went on to become bishop successively of St Davids and of Coventry and Lichfield. He transformed the finances of the library; from 1716 all the income from installation fees was devoted to library purposes only. Smalbroke also elicited

58. Mynors and Thomson, *Catalogue*, p. 96.
59. Thomson, 'Introduction', in Mynors and Thomson, *Catalogue*, p. xv; Webb, *Memorials*, ii, p. 310. See also above, Chapter 23, p. 452, and below, p. 532 n. 113.
60. Wood, *Athenae*, ii, col. 465.
61. HCA, 2382, 5714, 7036/1.
62. HCA, 7036/1, library accounts, 1677.
63. *A Short Narrative of the Discovery of a College of Jesuits, at a Place called the Come, in the*

County of Hereford (London, 1679), pp. 4–6.
64. G. Bowen, 'The Jesuit Library in Hereford Cathedral', *Bulletin of the Association of British Theological and Philosophical Libraries*, 20 (February 1965), pp. 13–34; 21 (August 1965), pp. 17–27.
65. HCA, 7020/1/1, last ten folios, accounts of the master of the library, 1699–1730; see F. C. Morgan, 'Herefordshire Printers and Booksellers', *TWNFC*, 30 (1939–41), pp. 106–27.

gifts of money, and raised more by the sale of duplicate books, all of which he spent on new books, which are detailed in the accounts. Some 430 volumes were added during his time as master.[66]

From this period also dates the first catalogue which survives. This is the shelf list, transcribed at the end of the donors' book, which Streeter dates to 1718, with additions to 1734.[67] This gives the first accurate picture not only of the contents of the library (numbering 953 printed volumes, with 123 additions), but also of its arrangement. The bays ('classes') are numbered on the north and south sides from east to west; within them the books are numbered within each numbered shelf ('partitio'). This arrangement was copied into a separate folio volume at some time before 1745, with the books listed in alphabetical order of author within each bay, and with an index. The subject headings for each bay were added to this catalogue.[68] By this time, although not shown in this catalogue, the numerical identification of the bays had been changed to letters: A–G on the north side, H–P on the south. A Mr Fisher was paid 2s. 6d. for painting the letters in 1735–36.[69] Two drafts of a shelf list of this arrangement were drawn up in 1745; James Rawlinson was paid two guineas for making a fair copy of it in 1748–49.[70] This last catalogue, with additions, remained in use until the end of the nineteenth century. Two alphabetical indexes to this arrangement were transcribed by Michael Reynolds in about 1780 and by Mr Spencer in 1781–82.[71] By this time there were over 1200 volumes on the chained library shelves. In 1746–47 Thomas Winston was paid 7s. 0d. for painting the abbreviated subject headings at the top of the face-end of each bay, many of which still survive.[72]

No record of loans survives before 1796, although Kaufman's research into eight other cathedral libraries in the eighteenth century suggests that borrowing from cathedral libraries was quite common.[73] It must be remembered, however, that all Hereford's books were still chained, which must have inhibited such a practice. Loans from 1796 to 1821 are recorded on three pages at the end of the donors' book; only about thirty works are recorded as being borrowed within this period.[74] A separate volume for loans was begun in 1822; this records loans up to 1894, but covers only thirty-eight folios.[75]

Throughout the eighteenth century there continued to be occasional payments

66. Morgan, '[Retrospective Accessions Register]'.

67. HCL, P.IX.8, pp. 669–93; Streeter, *Chained Library*, p. 318.

68. HCL, P.IX.10.

69. HCA, 7020/1/1, clavigers' accounts, 1735–36.

70. HCL, P.IX.15, R.3.2; HCA, 7020/1/1, clavigers' accounts, 1748–49.

71. HCL, P.IX.11, R.3.3.

72. HCA, 7020/1/1, clavigers' accounts, 1746–47.

73. P. Kaufman, 'Reading Vogues at English Cathedral Libraries of the Eighteenth Century', *Bulletin of the New York Public Library*, 67 (1963), pp. 643–72; 68 (1964), pp. 48–64, 110–32, 191–202.

74. HCL, P.IX.8, pp. 708–10.

75. HCA, 7043/3/1.

for chains; books obviously went on being chained at Hereford long after this practice had become obsolete elsewhere. The last books to be chained were some of the Record Commissioners' volumes given to Hereford, as to all other cathedral libraries, in the first half of the nineteenth century. The adoption of the alphabetical identification of the bays implies that there was plenty of space for expansion on the existing shelves, or that the library was not expected to expand any more, as no more bays could be added to the north side without requiring all the south side bays to be relettered. Perhaps Thornton's revolutionary design was already beginning to be seen as an anachronism.

This attitude was certainly acceptable by the early nineteenth century. In 1831 John Britton, after giving an account of the Lady chapel, could comment that 'a stranger, and an admirer of Christian architecture, will lament to learn that this fine room is filled and lumbered with old bookcases'.[76]

It was not for reasons of aesthetic sensibility, however, nor from a liturgically fashionable desire to restore the Lady chapel as a place of worship, which led to the removal of the library, but the discovery of the need for a major restoration of the cathedral, as recorded by Dean John Merewether in 1842.[77] According to Havergal, all the books were moved into upper rooms in part of the vicars choral cloister in 1841 and not moved into the muniment room until 1855; however, it would seem that the latter was at least intended to be their home as early as February 1841, when chapter resolved 'that the Books in the Library, be removed into the Archive Room under the superintendance of the Dean, while the repairs are going on'.[78] Streeter states that the bookcases were dismantled and stored most probably in the crypt, while the benches were converted to pews, but the books were obviously arranged on shelves of some sort in their new home, according to Havergal's account in 1854.[79]

That Dean Merewether took more of an interest in the library than has previously been supposed is also borne out by an entry in the chapter acts for 29 January 1845: 'Ordered that the Catalogue of the Cathedral Library be printed by Mr Vale under the supervision of the Dean, the expense of which to be charged to the Library Fund'.[80] William H. Vale was a printer in Hereford between 1826 and 1855.[81] There seems to be no evidence that this catalogue was ever printed. If it

76. J. Britton, *The History and Antiquities of the Cathedral Church of Hereford* (London, 1831), p. 53.

77. J. Merewether, *A Statement of the Condition and Circumstances of the Cathedral Church of Hereford* (Hereford, 1842), p. 10.

78. HCA, 7043/3/1, fol. 5, manuscript note by F. T. Havergal; HCA, 7031/19, p. 495,

chapter acts, 16 February 1841.

79. Streeter, *Chained Library*, p. 92; HCA, 7031/20, p. 302, letter to chapter from F. T. Havergal, 6 November 1854, read 9 November 1854.

80. HCA, 7031/20, p. 33, chapter acts, 29 January 1845.

81. Morgan, 'Herefordshire Printers', p. 115.

had been, it would have predated any of the other catalogues of cathedral libraries printed in the second half of the nineteenth century.[82]

The Cathedral Commission of 1852 therefore found the library in a relatively sorry state, although the dean and chapter still felt able to report that the library consisted of about 2000 volumes, was financed by installation fees, and was 'accessible to any person obtaining an order from the dean or a canon in residence, and such person is accompanied by some officer of the church'.[83] Even in its exile, it was increasingly becoming an object of fascination. Havergal records in November 1854 that 'The Library has been visited by upwards of two hundred persons during the last six months': a remarkable number, under the circumstances.[84]

Francis Tebbs Havergal is the second great hero in the history of the library (fig. 149). He belonged to a notable clerical and musical family: his father was W. H. Havergal, the composer of church music, and his sister was Frances Ridley Havergal, the hymn writer. Born in 1830, he was first a chorister and then a clerk at New College, Oxford, and became a vicar choral at Hereford in 1853. In 1854 he was appointed deputy librarian. For the next twenty years he worked tirelessly for the library, whose fortunes he undoubtedly transformed.[85] He was perhaps the first to appreciate the historical importance of the manuscripts and early printed books, and provided for their care with both common sense and imagination. The first of his lengthy reports to the dean and chapter, in November 1854, is typical: he was concerned about cleanliness, circulation of air and the provision of heat to reduce humidity during damp weather. He selected certain items in need of repair: 'the original Binding shall as far as possible be always retained'. In all this his attitude was exemplary and far ahead of his time. He noted that the Wycliffite Bible and the Hereford breviary 'deserve especial care on account of their Antiquity and Beauty' (pls IVa, b), and suggested that a showcase be made to display some of the more rare and valuable items: probably the first time that this had been done. He recorded that he had managed to recover several books 'that had been lent out by the late Dean and not duly entered', and lamented that books added since 1780 had not been entered in the catalogue. He had nevertheless put the books in their proper order as far as possible, and had catalogued 'all the Musical Volumes in the Cathedral The same having been made only twice before in 1800 and 1830': these were presumably not in the library. (None of the three catalogues mentioned appears to have survived.)[86]

82. N. R. Ker, 'Cathedral Libraries', *Library History*, 1 (1967), pp. 38–44; reprinted in A. G. Watson, ed., *Books, Collectors and Libraries* (London, 1985), pp. 293–300, at 298.

83. Cathedral Commission, *Appendix to the First Report* (London, 1854), p. 235.

84. HCA, 7031/20, p. 302, Havergal letter, 6 November 1854.

85. Ibid., p. 291, chapter acts, 6 February 1854.

86. Ibid., pp. 301–3, Havergal letter, 6 November 1854.

Fig. 149. Francis Tebbs
Havergal, 1830–90, vicar choral
and deputy librarian. (HCL.)

In 1855 the books and as much of the bookcases as could be assembled were
moved to the muniment room.[87] The cases were restored inaccurately and incompletely, lacking their desks and benches, and they were placed in the middle of
the room, the west wall still being occupied by the archive cupboards (fig. 155).
Havergal's concern however was to provide suitable housing for the books, not to
recreate the chained library. He ensured that the initial unsatisfactory reconstruction
of the cases was improved before placing the books there. He 'carefully removed
all the modern chains and placed the Books as in modern Libraries [spine outwards],
but I have retained the Chains on the MSS and on all antient Books with which
they are in Character'. Turning the spines outwards necessitated the addition of
spine labels, whose absence was so deplored by Botfield; many of these were
provided by Havergal himself, and still survive along with all the repairs he caused
to be effected to so many of the books, as a testimony to his industry.[88] Not the

87. HCA, 7037/4, library account, 1855;
    7043/3/1, fol. 5, notes on the history of
    the library by F. T. Havergal; 7031/20,

    p. 409, letter to chapter from F. T. Haver-
    gal, chapter acts, 12–14 November 1857.
88. HCA, 7031/20, pp. 409–11, letter from

least of Havergal's qualities was his care to record everything he did, in the books he repaired, in the chapter acts, in the notebook he kept on the library; as a result we have a better picture of the life of the library at this time than at almost any other.[89] The continuing importance of his historical publications about the Cathedral, the *Fasti Herefordenses* (1869), and *Monumental Inscriptions* (1881) – and of course the 1872 facsimile of Mappa Mundi which he edited – perpetuate his memory.

There are two brief objective glimpses of the library in this period. The first inkling of a sense of professional self-awareness among cathedral librarians was provided, appropriately at the first annual meeting of the Library Association at Oxford in 1878, in a paper 'Our Cathedral Libraries' by Herbert E. Reynolds, librarian at Exeter Cathedral. Appended to the published transactions is a table giving the answers to Reynolds's questionnaire for all the cathedral libraries in England and Wales. The answers for Hereford, provided by Canon John Jebb (master of the library, 1869–72 and 1877–85) give the impression of modest library activity. The number of 2000 books is taken from the 1854 Cathedral Commission Report. This entry and the comment on gifts – 'Once numerous; now very rare' – confirm that the collection had grown little if at all since its removal from the Lady chapel. There was no artificial light, and no comment on heat, or on opening hours. But it is stated that a catalogue of the manuscripts is in preparation: we have no more information on what became of this project, but it does at least register an awareness of the antiquarian importance of the library, unsurprising considering Jebb's own interests.[90] It may of course refer to Schenkl's catalogue, although this seems unlikely given the date and the fact that none of the other cathedral libraries refer to it.[91] The answers to the Cathedral Commission of 1879 more or less repeat those of 1852–54.[92]

By the end of the century the library's fortunes had spectacularly changed. The first fairy godmother was Caroline, Lady Saye and Sele, widow of the Venerable Lord Saye and Sele, archdeacon of Hereford, and master of the library 1857–63 and 1872–77, who died in 1887. Lady Saye and Sele gave over 200 works to the cathedral from the archdeacon's library. These were largely seventeenth- and eighteenth-century printings but included a number of standard post-Reformation works, for example by Baxter, Bunyan, Comber, Tillotson, and many volumes of

Havergal, November 1857; B. Botfield, *Notes on the Cathedral Libraries of England* (London, 1849), p. 173.

89. HCA, 3592.

90. H. R. Tedder and E. C. Thomas, eds, *Transactions and Proceedings of the First Annual Meeting of the Library Association of the United Kingdom* (London, 1879), pp. 32–43 and appendix 1.

91. H. Schenkl, *Bibliotheca patrum latinorum britannica* (13 vols, Vienna, 1890–1908), iii, pt 2.

92. Cathedral Commission, *Report of Her Majesty's Commissioners for Inquiring into the Condition of Cathedral Churches in England and Wales upon the Cathedral Church of Hereford* (London, 1884), pp. 4–5.

sermons. The gift set the pattern for the cathedral library as a repository for books both historical and theological. In 1895 W. H. Phillott, master 1887–95 and one of the great figures in the study of the history of the cathedral, bequeathed 165 volumes mainly of ecclesiastical history.

It was Phillott who first suggested in chapter in November 1892 that there should be a new library building, although it was undoubtedly the enthusiasm and energy of James Wentworth Leigh, dean 1894–1919 and brother of Lady Saye and Sele, which carried the project to fruition as part of his large programme of restoration of the cathedral.[93] It is fitting that the resulting library building still bears his name. His own succinct account of the origin and progress of the new building can hardly be improved upon:

> This building was erected after designs of the late Sir Arthur Blomfield, ARA, with a legacy bequeathed by the late Canon Powell, of Hinton Court, the object being to provide a suitable home for the Chained Missals and other Valuable Ancient Volumes belonging to the Cathedral. These have been placed in the upper chamber of the new building. The lower part, which forms three bays of a portion of the restored West Cloister, has been utilized for a place of meeting and Modern Library for the benefit of the Clergy and others in the City and Diocese; and in order to obtain more accommodation for this purpose, it was thought expedient to thoroughly restore four bays of the old South Cloister and unite them to the new building. To meet the extra expense incurred, two of the bays were restored as memorials to the late Canon Phillott and the late Prebendary Havergal, former librarians of the Cathedral. Three other bays have also been restored as memorials, one of them being used as a music room for practising the Choir. The New Library was opened by the late Archbishop of Canterbury, April 30th, 1897 (fig. 46).[94]

The new building dragged the library into the real world. Suddenly the limited sources of income (the installation fee had been reduced from £2 to £1 in 1864) had to meet additional charges for gas, water and insurance.[95] New sources of income were found by charging for the use of the lower library for meetings and by a small annual subscription for readers. The new regime established a pattern which, with various improvements and adaptations, is still in place: the historic part of the library is available to tourist visitors in a separate place from the 'modern' lending and reference library, which is open to readers for a modest charge.[96]

93. HCA, 7031/23, p. 163, chapter acts, 10 November 1892.

94. J. W. Leigh, *Hereford Cathedral Church: Record of Work Done* (Hereford, 1910), p. 6.

95. HCA, 7043/1/1/1, library accounts, 1730–1945.

96. J. W. Leigh, 'Regulations', in *Hereford Cathedral Library: Catalogue of Works in the Lower Room* (Hereford, [1897]), p. 3.

Gifts of books began to flood into the newly established library, augmented from 1898 by regular purchases. The 1897 catalogue of the lower library was supplemented in 1899 and 1906, by which time the number of unchained books consisted of some 1750 works in 3200 volumes.[97] Financing this increased activity continued to be a problem. In 1918 the sale of Barnard's *Church Music* (happily the only such sale at Hereford in modern times) raised £100, which was invested in war stock to earn a small annual sum.[98] In 1927 a donation from the Dean Leigh Memorial Fund was spent on the cataloguing; this was the origin of the card catalogue which is still the chief means of access to the library's collections.[99]

The most important benefit received by the library during most of the twentieth century, however, was the time and expertise most generously given by a succession of voluntary and honorary helpers, both professional and non-professional. Langton E. Brown and Maude Bull worked in the library as sub-librarians at the time of the new establishment in 1897; Miss Bull continued working until a few years before her death in 1951, and her achievements in cataloguing and arranging for repairs are still very evident.[100] But the century truly belongs to the Morgans, F. C. and Penelope, father and daughter, both Hereford city librarians at various times, and honorary librarians of the cathedral jointly or separately from 1925 to 1989 (fig. 157). Mr Morgan supervised the cataloguing project of 1927 and thereafter. Both were prominent in the culture of the cathedral and the city and their history, and both were leading lights of the Friends of the Cathedral and of the Woolhope Club, whose publications were greatly enriched by their contributions. Both worked tirelessly in the development of the library during this period.[101] It is to Penelope Morgan that the present writer owes the greatest debt; much of her work in cataloguing, indexing, keeping records and analysing past records remains unpublished and can be appreciated only by her successor. Her most remarkable contribution to the library's history is the two-volume manuscript retrospective accessions register, which assigns a number to every book in the library in putative order of the date of its addition.[102] In writing this chapter I have drawn heavily

97. *Hereford Cathedral Library: Catalogue of the Lower Library* ([Hereford], 1899); *Hereford Cathedral Library: Supplementary Catalogue of the Lower Library* ([Hereford], 1906).

98. F. C. and P. E. Morgan, *Hereford Cathedral Libraries and Muniments* (2nd edn, Hereford, 1975), p. 12; HCA, 5823, 7043/1/1/1, library account, 1918; see above, Chapter 22, p. 401 and n. 15.

99. HCA, 7043/1/1/1, library account, 1927.

100. *Hereford Cathedral Library: Catalogue* (1899), p. [i]; *Hereford Cathedral Library:* *Supplementary Catalogue* (1906), p. [i]; HCA, 7043/4/2, P. E. Morgan, 'Hereford Cathedral Library: A Record of Work Done to 31 March 1979'.

101. See appreciations and obituaries in e.g. *FHC*, 45 (1979), pp. 10–11; ibid., 56 (1990), pp. 23–24; *TWNFC*, 44 pt 1 (1982), pp. 9–11; *TWNFC General Index, 1955–1987* (n.p., n.d.), pp. 1–3.

102. P. E. Morgan, '[Retrospective Accessions Register]'.

on the notes she made towards her own projected history of the library, which she gave me shortly before her death in 1990.

The beginning of F. C. Morgan's involvement with the library witnessed several important developments. As well as the beginning of the cataloguing of the modern books according to professional standards, a catalogue of the manuscripts was at last published in 1927 by Canon Bannister, whose work on the history of the cathedral places him in the tradition of Jebb and Phillott. This catalogue was masterly for its time, superior to other catalogues of cathedral manuscripts produced by scholarly clerics around this period. The Introduction by M. R. James remains a classic.[103]

The restoration of the chained library by B. F. Streeter was the most important event in the history of the library between 1897 and 1993. Streeter was a controversial theologian of some repute but he is still perhaps best remembered in this country for his contribution to library history, based on his researches at Hereford (fig. 48). Although he made some errors, notably in dating the construction of the chained bookcases to 1590 rather than 1611, his work on the early history of libraries remains an indispensable text for students of the subject.[104] The story of the restoration of the chained library which it includes is a remarkable tale of scholarship, inspiration, perspiration and serendipity. As a result of his work the cases were reconstructed as far as possible in their original form, with desks properly attached and seats restored, and the books were rechained and placed correctly on their shelves according to the order set out in the eighteenth-century catalogues. The restoration of the chains was in a sense a retrograde step in terms of the preservation of the historic books, condemning them to a double life as permanent museum objects as well as items of scholarly interest. But this arrangement was already implicit in the separation of the chained library as an object of general curiosity, which is in itself characteristic of the growing role of cathedrals as heritage centres. Given this existing role for the library, it is appropriate that the chained library should be restored to its original order as accurately as possible, as a living example of a seventeenth-century library.

As a result of Streeter's work, there was no longer room for the whole of the restored library in the upper Dean Leigh library. The larger part of it was returned to the old muniment room (now empty of archives), whose floor and ceiling had been restored at the generous expense of Mr H. C. Moffatt, where it was available to visitors, while the 'working' library remained in the Dean Leigh library and south cloister.[105] This arrangement, with the library in two sites, continued until 1996.

---

103. A. T. Bannister, *A Descriptive Catalogue of the Manuscripts in the Hereford Cathedral Library* (Hereford, 1927); Thomson, 'Introduction', in Mynors and Thomson, *Catalogue*, p. xxxiii.
104. Streeter, *Chained Library*.
105. Ibid., p. 94.

During the Second World War the manuscripts, along with Mappa Mundi, were removed for safekeeping, some to Hampton Court, Herefordshire, and others to Bradford on Avon. They returned in 1946.[106] In 1955 the lower Dean Leigh library was converted into a muniment room to receive the archives, which had been sent to the National Library of Wales in 1943.[107] In 1981 the south cloister was restored as a library and reading room with the aid of a grant from the Pilgrim Trust.[108] In 1980 Miss Morgan completed her task of classifying all the post-1800 books according to the Dewey Decimal classification, thus confirming a division in the collections between rare books (on fixed location shelves), and modern reference and lending works.

From 1950, the chained library in the north transept room was open at regular times to visitors. This was made possible by the establishment of a body of enthusiastic volunteers, later to be recruited and trained by Miss Morgan, who also arranged for a small exhibition of manuscripts and early printed books to be on display there in showcases. This exhibition was changed periodically, although the trinity of the Hereford Gospels, the Hereford breviary and the Wycliffite ('Cider') Bible remained the most famous of the library's treasures and were almost permanently on display. The small admission charge, and the sale of a selection of postcards, pamphlets and slides, provided a modest income, which nevertheless, thanks to all the professional and non-professional voluntary labour, enabled the library to be almost totally self-financing in terms of purchase and repair of books and other library functions.[109]

The standard of thoughtful and well-documented repair of books established by Havergal has been happily maintained since his time, first by Maude Bull, whose dedication to this activity in personally transporting volumes for repair to and from the Bodleian Library is recorded in her obituary. Numerous volumes still bear her handwritten labels describing the date, place and nature of the work done.[110] Repairs continued on a regular basis, financed by library funds, until the 1980s, when changing standards in the quality of conservation and the accompanying higher costs of such work necessitated the employment of more specialised conservators and the application to public bodies for funding. The library has benefited greatly in recent years from grants from special funds arranged by the Bibliographical Society from the Getty Fund and the Esmée Fairbairn Memorial Trust. Recent conservation work has concentrated less on the repair of bindings and more on

106. HCA, 7043/1/1/2, p. 2, library accounts, 1946–87; RS 5/1/17, audit accounts, 1945–46; 7043/4/2, Morgan, 'Record of Work Done to 1979'.

107. See below, Chapter 30, pp. 553–54.

108. HCA, 7043/4/1–2, scrapbook compiled by P. E. Morgan, 1975–92; Morgan, 'Record of Work Done to 1979'; NS 4/DCL/1/1, papers of the master of the library, 1981.

109. HCA, 7043/4/2, Morgan, 'Record of Work Done to 1979'; personal knowledge.

110. *The Times*, 8 December 1951, obituaries.

more specialised treatment, in particular to counteract the acidity in the paper of some of the early music part-books.[111]

Several gifts of large collections in the twentieth century effectively doubled the library's stock of rare books, so that there are now as many unchained as chained early books. The first of these was the gift of Paul Henry Foley of Stoke Edith House in 1926, consisting of some 136 works in 242 volumes, dating from the mid sixteenth to the late seventeenth century, chiefly works of Latin theology and patristics.[112]

In 1947 the library of the college of the vicars choral (dissolved in 1937) was transferred to the cathedral library. The vicars choral had had their own library, with its own master appointed annually from an early stage; the first reference to it is found in a reply to the commissioners of 1582.[113] It was housed in a room over the chapel in the east walk of the cloisters.[114] Replies to the dean's visitation of 1588 contain pleas for the replacement of some of the old books by works of modern authors in English,[115] and the donors' book, begun in about 1620, confirms that there was a far greater proportion of secular and English works than in the cathedral library.[116] Many of the books were lost during the Civil War; after the Restoration attempts were made to recover these and to secure them with chains.[117] After the fire of 1828 and the rebuilding of the chapel in 1835, the books were transferred to the vicars' common room, where they remained until their removal to the cathedral library.[118] Many were in a deplorable state through misuse and poor housing conditions in the library's latter years, and an extensive programme of repair was carried out, financed largely by the Friends of the Cathedral. This important collection consists of over 600 volumes, many with detailed donation inscriptions. Together with the donors' book they provide a fascinating glimpse into the life of the college, particularly for the seventeenth century. The inscriptions have also proved useful; that in the lost 1602 edition of Chaucer enabled the book to be identified when it came up for sale in 1984. It was bought back for the library with the aid of a generous gift from Miss Eleanor Hipwell.[119]

111. HCL, current correspondence files; binding register.

112. HCL, 29.B.15, 'Catalogue of Books in the Library at Stoke Edith, Herefordshire, Presented to Hereford Cathedral Library in 1925 by Paul Henry Foley' (manuscript).

113. HCA, 4642. There was a medieval library, of which at least two manuscripts survive, at Dublin and Oxford, Ker, ed., *Medieval Libraries*, pp. 99.

114. J. G. Nichols, ed., *History from Marble Compiled in the Reign of Charles II by Thomas Dingley*, Camden Society, old series, 94, 97 (2 vols, London, 1867–68), i, p. cc.

115. HCA, 3395; see above, p. 96.

116. HCL, R.3.2; part of it is printed in F. C. Morgan, 'Hereford Cathedral: The Vicars Choral Library', *TWNFC*, 35 (1955–57), pp. 222–55.

117. Some were probably plundered by Silas Taylor: see above, p. 522; HCA, 3399, 4621, answers to dean's visitations of 1663 and 1667.

118. HCA, 7003/1/5, reverse p. 58; Morgan, 'The Vicars Choral Library', p. 227.

119. Note in HCL, G.16.11, G. Chaucer, *Workes* (London, 1602); HCA, NS 11/16.

In 1954–55 all the old music books which could be found were collected by the Morgans from the song school, organ loft and choir, and added to the library's historic collections. These numbered some 234 volumes and consisted mainly of many of the manuscript part-books used by the cathedral choir and organist, dating from the early eighteenth century onwards. They also included a number of important printed books, notable among these the cathedral's set of Handel's music, reputedly given by George IV.[120]

In 1978 the historic books of Lady Hawkins School, Kington, along with some of the school's archives, were deposited at the cathedral library.[121] The most recent major acquisition of rare books was the chained library of All Saints church, Hereford, bequeathed to the church in perpetuity by Dr William Brewster in 1715. This was one of the last parish libraries to be chained: Dr Brewster's decision that his books should be so secured was undoubtedly influenced by the example of the nearby cathedral library, although the books, being mostly in smaller formats than the cathedral's books, were less suitable for this practice. The library had survived in the church until 1992, when the books were moved to the Hereford Record Office during the restoration of the church. Following its purchase for the Mappa Mundi Trust, it now graces the exhibition in the new library building, providing an interesting object of comparison with its larger elder sibling.[122]

In recent years there have also been a number of important major gifts to the modern collection. In 1981 the theological section was augmented by the deposit of over 900 volumes by the Hereford Educational Development Centre. In 1982 Miss Morgan gave a large portion of her father's library, chiefly works of local history, to which she continued to add gifts of her own for the rest of her life. Most recently, in 1996, Mr and Mrs Edward Ball bequeathed their large joint personal library to the cathedral library. About one third of the books were retained, greatly augmenting the local, general and church history sections of the reference library; in accordance with the provision of the bequest, the remainder was sold, raising sufficient funds to complete the additional shelving for the modern library in the new library building.[123]

The mastership of Canon John Tiller, since 1984, has seen one of the most eventful and momentous periods in the history of the library. A few important events preceded it: the library advisory committee was established in 1978, and in

120. Botfield, *Notes on the Cathedral Libraries*, p. 187; P. E. Morgan, '[Retrospective Accessions Register]'.
121. HCL, 'Hereford Cathedral Library: Register of Books Deposited on Permanent Loan'.
122. HCL, current correspondence files; F. C. Morgan, 'Catalogue of the Books in All Saints' Church, Hereford' (HCL, typescript, 1964). See above, Chapter 7, p. 196.
123. HCL, 'Register of Books Deposited'; 'Books from the Library of F. C. Morgan and Penelope E. Morgan'; current correspondence files.

the same year the endowment fund was inaugurated, making provision for future financial security, particularly in terms of professional staff.[124] The first full-time paid librarian was appointed in 1990, following Miss Morgan's retirement in 1989. By this time the Mappa Mundi Trust had come into being, and the ownership of all the historic parts of the library transferred to it. The ideal of a new library building, in which the restored chained library could at last be brought together in its original arrangement, thus completing the work of Canon Streeter, was first expressed by Canon Tiller at the advisory committee meeting of 1987.[125] One of the functions of the Mappa Mundi Trust was to make this dream a reality. Happily the site that was eventually chosen was adjacent to the Dean Leigh library, close to the site of the first library in the south-west cloister, and thus maintaining the continuity of the library's history.

In the meantime another long-term project was brought to triumphant fruition. Since the early 1950s Sir Roger Mynors had been working on a new catalogue of the medieval manuscripts. Following his death in 1989, Dr R. M. Thomson of the University of Tasmania, a colleague and friend of Sir Roger, and the author of a similar catalogue for Lincoln Cathedral library, was invited to continue this project.[126] His work on the Hereford manuscripts was completed in a remarkably short time and published in 1993.[127] For the first time the full significance of the manuscripts, in particular their provenance, was revealed, providing an immeasurably valuable resource both for students of the manuscripts and for the library staff.

The new library building, opened by the Queen on 3 May 1996, was sensitively and intelligently designed to accommodate the long-term needs of all aspects of the library's life, according to modern standards of security and environmental conditions.[128] Its greatest achievement was to create a space in which the whole of the chained library could be reconstructed in its original arrangement. The room is beautiful in its own right but not pretentious, either as 'modern' or as a seventeenth-century pastiche: rather it provides a congenial atmosphere for the chained library aesthetically as well as environmentally (fig. 150).

The newly created exhibition department now administers the heritage aspect, while the library department maintains all parts of the collections and makes them available to an appropriate readership during regular opening hours in the handsome reading room over the chained library chamber. The basement strongroom houses the rest of the historic collections, which have included the cathedral archives since 1955. Another important development was the appointment of the first paid archivist

---

124. HCA, 7043/4/2, Morgan, 'Record of Work Done to 1979'.

125. HCL, library advisory committee minutes, tenth annual meeting, 11 September 1987.

126. R. M. Thomson, *Catalogue of the Manuscripts of Lincoln Cathedral Chapter Library* (Cambridge, 1989).

127. Mynors and Thomson, *Catalogue*.

128. See above, Chapter 12, pp. 311–13.

Fig. 150. The chained library in the new library building, 1996.

in 1997. The modern library now consists of some 9000 volumes; the lending
section comprises the largest theological collection in the diocese, while the reference
library also includes enough bibliographical and historical material to serve most
of the needs of those using the historic collections or seeking information on all
aspects of the cathedral's history. Both are inevitably limited by space and financial
resources. As a result of recent developments the library occupies a fittingly
high-profile position in the cathedral's life. It is to be hoped that it will continue
its long tradition of serving the intellectual aspects of the cathedral's witness for
many years to come.

29

The Hereford Gospels

Richard Gameson

The gospel book, MS P.I.2, is the oldest and most valuable of the many treasures in Hereford Cathedral library.[1] It is also the volume that has been at Hereford the longest, its presence in the city being documented from the early eleventh century.[2] The exact date and place of origin of the Hereford Gospels are impossible to establish owing to a lack of evidence, however the manuscript was probably made in the later eighth or earlier ninth century, either in Wales or western England. In the summary discussion that follows,[3] we shall consider in turn the physical fabric of the volume, its text, its script, its decoration and the Anglo-Saxon additions, concluding with some observations on its general significance.

Measuring c. 233 x 170 mm. (9¼ x 6¾ inches) with a written space of c. 170 x 115 mm. (6¾ x 4½ inches), Hereford Cathedral library MS P.I.2 is a fairly small gospel book by any standards (the average early Italian copy, for instance, was c. 300 x 215 mm. or 11¾ x 8½ inches); and it is the smallest of the modestly proportioned Insular and British examples. Yet what it loses in grandeur, it makes up in utility: in contrast to its bigger relatives, it is one of the most easily portable of Insular gospel books, and can comfortably be held open in the hands. Its parchment is of a very modest quality – something which is more typical of books from the 'Celtic' regions of the British Isles than from the Anglo-Saxon

1. Although the commentary on Matthew's gospel, MS P.II.10, flyleaves, is probably older, only two leaves survive.

2. See further below.

3. The present essay is a summary of a fuller study of the manuscript to be published in due course. The essential bibliography on the manuscript to date comprises: W. M. Lindsay, *Early Welsh Script* (Edinburgh, 1912), pp. 41–43; L. J. Hopkin-James, *The Celtic Gospels* (Oxford, 1934), passim; E. A. Lowe, *Codices latini antiquiores* (11 vols plus Supplement with 2nd edn of ii, Oxford, 1934–72), ii, no. 157; P. McGurk, *Latin Gospel Books from AD 400 to AD 800* (Paris, Brussels and elsewhere, 1961), no. 15; J. J. G. Alexander, *Insular Manuscripts 6th to the 9th Century* (London, 1978), cat. 38; and Mynors and Thomson, *Catalogue*, pp. 65–66.

ones.[4] It is also something which, when used for a particularly important text like the gospels, reveals that the manuscript in question was the product of a centre that was not over-endowed with resources. The quires from which the Hereford gospels is constructed are predominantly twelves (that is they comprise twelve folios, twenty-four pages);[5] and this too affiliates the manuscript to the Irish, Celtic and Hiberno-Anglian traditions as opposed to the Italian and Italo-Anglian ones. As was customary in Insular circles, the sheets were folded, not open, when the pricking was done. Unusually, there do not appear to be any vertical rulings; but then the prickings themselves had been positioned at the edge of the written area, and they effectively delineated it. The lack of ruled verticals flanking the text area also reflects the fact that the scribe intended to present the text as a solid block rather than in paragraphs with initials in the margins, and that there was to be no marginal apparatus.[6] In sum, such indications as the physical fabric provides affiliate the manuscript to the Celtic rather than to the Anglo-Saxon tradition of book production, and seem more compatible with an origin in a minor scriptorium than a major one.

The textual content of the volume is limited to the four gospels – there is no ancilliary matter such as prefaces or capitula lists.[7] Many of the very oldest Latin gospel books were similarly 'spare', but from the seventh century onwards this becomes rarer, and thereafter this archaic feature is far more characteristic of Irish copies than of English or continental ones (which generally have a complement of prefatory material). The gospel text itself is not the Vulgate, but rather belongs to a distinctive Irish or Insular recension, with numerous departures from St Jerome's version. Although the Vulgate was introduced into Ireland as early as the sixth century, its text seems to have interacted with, rather than superseded the Old Latin versions that were then current there;[8] while the fact that texts with Old Latin readings were used in Wales in the ninth century is revealed by the biblical quotations in the work of Asser, a monk of Saint David's.[9] The circumstance

---

4. Holes appear within the text block on fos 10, 16, 18, 20, 41, 48–49, 55–46, 61, 88, 90, 97, 114, 122, and 133. Even the *incipit* page to John's gospel (fol. 102r) is pock-marked.

5. There are no quire signatures.

6. Double bounding lines were generally supplied on either side of the text block when section initials were to be placed in the margins, as is the case, for example, in MS O.III.2.

7. The text itself has no section numbers and there are no correspondences marked in the margins.

8. Cf. A. Cordoliani, 'La Vulgate en Irlande du Ve au IXe siècle', *Revue biblique*, 57 (1950), pp. 1–39; and P. Doyle, 'The Latin Bible in Ireland: Its Origins and Growth', in M. McNamar, ed., *Biblical Studies: The Medieval Irish Contribution* (Dublin, 1976), pp. 30–45, esp. pp. 34–37. A well-known Irish manuscript with a strong Old Latin character to its text is Dublin, Trinity College, MS 55 (*Usserianus* I).

9. W. H. Stevenson, ed., *Asser's Life of King Alfred* (Oxford, 1904), pp. 61 and 86 with pp. xciv–xcv.

that around 40 per cent of Hereford's departures from the Vulgate can be paralleled in an Old Latin version echoes this. Furthermore, not only did Insular scribes have idiosyncratic orthographical practices, but they seem also to have treated the biblical text with greater freedom than their continental counterparts, being readier to make minor additions and alterations. Thus in addition to regular variations in spelling and word order, the text of our manuscript sometimes departs from the Vulgate in vocabulary and phraseology. On average more than one word in ten diverges from it in some way. It should be stressed that these verbal changes rarely make a substantial difference to the sense; however, they do strike the reader at once.

Comparison of Hereford's text with that of the other surviving early Latin gospel books enables us to identify its closest surviving relatives. These are the Book of Dimma,[10] written in Ireland, possible at Roscrea in the later eighth or early ninth century; the St Gallen gospels,[11] an Irish manuscript of the second half of the eighth century; the Bern gospels,[12] a 'pocket' gospel book of ninth-century date, and probably of Cornish or south-western British origin; the Lichfield gospels (of which only about half remains) which is probably of early eighth-century date and is of disputed origin (it was in Wales in the ninth century, but had reached Lichfield by the tenth);[13] and the equally fragmentary Rawlinson gospels,[14] an Irish volume of eighth-century date. Textually the closest of these to our manuscript is the Book of Dimma; but even so, in an extensive selection of collations, it only showed an 86 per cent agreement with the text of Hereford. Thus none of these volumes has more than a very general family affinity to the text of our manuscript, which remains singular in detail.

Hereford MS P.I.2 was designed to be used as a gospel lectionary, and its text was marked up with crosses signalling the beginnings of the readings (fig. 151). By far the largest number of such lection marks (forty-one or forty-two) is found in Luke's gospel; then comes John (twenty-one), followed by Matthew (eleven), and finally Mark (three), whose account was generally the least used in early lectionary systems.[15] The choice of readings as a whole is not particularly close to that in any other early manuscript. Considering the content of the passages that

10. Dublin, Trinity College, MS 59: Lowe, *Codices*, ii, no. 275; McGurk, *Latin Gospel Books*, no. 88; Alexander, *Insular Manuscripts*, cat. 48.

11. St Gallen, Stiftsbibliothek, MS 51: Lowe, *Codices*, vii, no. 901; McGurk, *Latin Gospel Books*, no. 117; Alexander, *Insular Manuscripts*, cat. 44.

12. Bern, Burgerbibliothek, MS 671: Lindsay, *Welsh Script*, pp. 10–16 with pls IV–V.

13. Lichfield Cathedral, MS 1: Lowe, *Codices*, ii, no. 159; McGurk, *Latin Gospel Books*, no. 16; Alexander, *Insular Manuscripts*, cat. 21.

14. Oxford, Bodleian, MS Rawlinson G.167: Lowe, *Codices*, ii, no. 256; McGurk, *Latin Gospel Books*, no. 35; Alexander, *Insular Manuscripts*, cat. 43.

15. For an introduction to the genre see A. G. Martimort, *Les lectures liturgiques et leurs livres* (Turnhout, 1992), pp. 22–24.

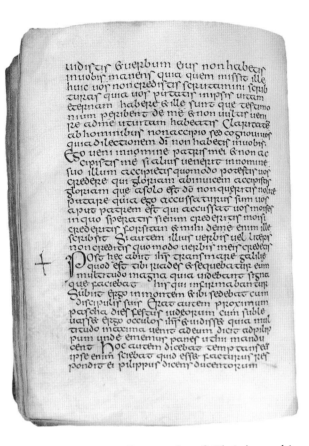

Fig. 151. Hereford Gospels:
page of St John's gospel. (HCL,
MS P.I.2, fol. 109v.)

were thus marked, we find that they are principally a cycle of Christ's teachings and of his statements about himself and the kingdom of heaven; and to some extent they comprise a set of ready-made homilies.

The Hereford Gospels was entirely written by a single scribe in a compact, though not cramped way.[16] The scribe was not unconcerned for the aesthetic of the page – he regularly compressed his work towards the ends of lines to achieve a justified right-hand margin – nevertheless the book was economically rather than expansively produced.[17] The text was set out as a solid block – that is neither in paragraphs, nor *per cola et commata* (i.e. with a new line for each sense unit) – and punctuation *per se* was very sparingly used; however it was subdivided visually and semantically by the deployment of enlarged initials at the beginnings of sentences.[18] The initials were not placed in the margins, but rather within the text block itself

16. As is generally the case in Insular and Anglo-Saxon books, his ink has remained a rich black colour: contrast the much browner tone of that in the Carolingian volume, MS O.III.2.

17. There are several examples on fos 124v–25r, for instance.

18. They are one to two lines high, and are so placed as to extend both above and below their own line.

– another archaic feature. In terms of general accuracy of transcription, the scribe was fairly competent, and corrections – seemingly in his own hand – are few. On the other hand, his spelling (and doubtless that of his exemplar) was far from orthodox. At the end of each gospel, the scribe added an imprecation, thanking God: the first of these (fol. 35v) reads, 'It is finished. Amen. I give thanks to God'. Such formulae, along with the practice of including them immediately after the text without change of ink or script type, are typical of small Irish gospel books.[19]

The script of Hereford is midway between a minuscule and a majuscule, and may best be characterised as a formal Insular minuscule. Moreover, despite a few decorative touches, the letter-forms are generally quite plain. For the couple of lines of text that appear on the *incipit* pages, the scribe enlarged and upgraded his script, which here approximates more closely to Insular half-uncial.[20] Nevertheless, he does not seem wholly comfortable with the half-uncial canon, and the result is really an enlarged, formal minuscule. Although firmly within the Insular tradition of writing, Hereford's script is not particularly close to that of any other extant manuscript. Considered as a whole, the palaeographical evidence implies that the book was produced in an otherwise unattested provincial Insular centre situated to the west rather than to the north or east of Mercia.

The decoration of the Hereford Gospels, which was probably the work of the scribe, is restricted to the *incipits* to the gospels, of which three survive (plate I figs i, 152). In addition, it is highly probable that there was originally a decorated Chi-rho monogram (Matthew 1:18) on the now missing second folio of Matthew's gospel. It is clear that there were never any evangelist portraits, and the main body of the text is entirely unornamented. Although the volume might seem decoratively impoverished in comparison with the more famous Insular gospel books, it should be remembered that the accidents of survival have undoubtedly favoured luxurious copies over humbler ones; and that, even so, other copies conceived at a comparable or lesser grade still remain. Moreover, a high percentage of early Latin gospel books from outside the Insular and Anglo-Saxon worlds had only minimal ornamentation, and no figural decoration.

The three extant *incipits* are intimately related in conception and realisation: in each case the initial monogram is complemented by a simple frame whose dimensions correspond exactly to those of the normal textblock.[21] It is worth stressing that

19. For comparanda see P. McGurk, 'The Irish Pocket Gospel Book', *Sacris Erudiri*, 8 (1956), pp. 249–70, at 255. Most Italian and Anglo-Saxon volumes, by contrast, have a more formal phrase, along the lines of *Explicit euangelium secundum Mattheum* generally written in a different script (sometimes also a different ink) from the gospel text proper, and often more spaciously laid out.

20. Here the script is 4 mm. as opposed to the normal 2–3 mm. high.

21. Merely ornamented with an interlace twist at each corner.

Fig. 152. Hereford Gospels: opening page of St Matthew's gospel. (HCL, MS P.I.2, fol. 1r.)

these *incipits*, although only modestly decorated, are very grand in relation to the size of the book. Such monumentality is most easily paralleled in manuscripts that were produced in an Irish as opposed to an Anglo-Saxon or continental milieu.

Although the ornamental repertoire is limited and the palette restricted, these simple initial monograms reveal a sureness of touch; moreover, each was designed to evoke a cross.[22]

In the first half of the eleventh century, two records were added to previously blank spaces at the end of our manuscript (fos 134–35). Aside from their intrinsic interest, they are crucial witnesses to the fact that the book was then at Hereford. The first document is a remarkably vivid record of a lawsuit which occurred during Cnut's reign (1016–35) (fig. 3).[23] A woman disputed her son's claim to some land, formally disowned him, and granted her possessions to a female relative called Leofflæd. This matter was reported to the shire-court, approved, and then transcribed in the Hereford gospels. The second document,[24] which can be dated to 1043 x 1046, is less colourful, merely recording the purchase of some land by a certain Leofwine; however, it is notable that the individual in question was the brother of the Leofflæd of the previous document. This local family seems to have been particularly alive to the value of having their transactions perpetuated in writing in the Hereford Gospels; correspondingly, one suspects that they enjoyed particularly cordial relations with Bishop Athelstan and his cathedral. The circumstance that by the time of Domesday Book, Hereford Cathedral itself seems to have held one of the two disputed estates of the earlier document is suggestive in this respect.[25]

To sum up, the evidence of codicology, text, script and decoration indicates that our manuscript is more strongly affiliated to the Irish or Celtic tradition of book production than to the Anglo-Saxon one, without being especially close to either. The most obvious hypothesis to account for this phenomenon is that it was produced in a province whose other early books have vanished: Wales. How and when it reached Hereford is unclear; all we know for certain is that it was there by the early eleventh century.

Whether written in Wales or western England, the Hereford Gospels is a key survivor from an area that is drastically under-represented in the corpus of early books; and as such it sheds some light on the extent to which centres in such regions were both linked to, yet at the same time distinct from other Insular scriptoria. It is also an important member of another under-represented class of manuscripts: the non-deluxe gospel book. Ironically, although once far more common, these are now almost rarer than their far more handsome equivalents. The Hereford Gospels gives the impression of being the *magnum opus* of a minor

22. The faded dots within the 'r' of *Liber gener-ationis* on fol. 1r also form a cross.

23. A. J. Robertson, ed., *Anglo-Saxon Charters* (2nd edn, Cambridge, 1956), no. 78; D. Whitelock, ed., *English Historical Documents, c. 500–1042*, English Historical

Documents, 1 (2nd edn, London, 1979), no. 135. See above, Chapter 1, pp. 16–18.

24. Robertson, *Anglo-Saxon Charters*, no. 99.

25. Namely Cradley: F. and C. Thorn, eds, *Domesday Book*, xvii, *Herefordshire* (Chichester, 1983), col. 182a; chapter 2, section 30.

centre – a sacred working book that was made as handsomely as local resources would permit. Equally, it provides valuable insight into the various functions that such an 'ordinary' volume could fulfil: it was a copy of the sacred gospels, a gospel lectionary for use during the divine services, and latterly it became a repository for the land transactions of a Herefordshire family. Whether it was Hereford Cathedral's principal gospel book at that time is unknowable, but it was evidently saved from the conflagration of 1055 which deprived us of other pre-Conquest Hereford books. By the late eleventh century, the Hereford Gospels was a venerable relic that was probably still seeing active use; today, in its battered and worn state, it is an evocative reminder of the continuity of the church in the region for more than a millennium.[26]

26. It is a pleasure to record my gratitude to Hereford Cathedral library and to its invariably helpful staff, who faciliated my study of the manuscript, first in 1989 then again in 1998.

30

The Archives

Brian Smith

Hereford is one of ten English cathedrals with a rich accumulation of archives.[1] These include over 3000 medieval charters of the endowed estates of the dean and chapter, prebends and vicars choral, together with associated estate records and documents issuing from lawsuits in defence of the cathedral's privileges. The charters date from 1132 onwards, many of the earliest relating to the endowments of the hospital of St Ethelbert. By contrast, there are few fabric accounts and the act books of the chapter survive only from 1512 and those of the vicars choral from 1575. After the Reformation the quantity and continuity of the administrative, legal and estate archives increased until the mid nineteenth century, when ecclesiastical reforms deprived cathedrals of their ancient estates and jurisdictions. After that the flow of documents into the archives somewhat abated. Until fifty years ago, however, access to the archives was with rare exceptions restricted to the canons and their officials.[2]

The importance of written evidence was emphasised as early as the mid twelfth century in the wording of three charters of Bishop Robert de Béthune (1131–48), a view echoed in 1793 by James Lane, the chapter clerk, when replying to a correspondent: 'To avoid mistakes arising from verbal Communications it is the practice of the Chapter to transact business by Letter to and from me'.[3] The authenticity of formal documents was established by affixing the dean and chapter's seal, the ultimate mark of corporate identity already in use by about 1190 and

1. I am grateful to Joan Williams, Hereford cathedral librarian, and Marion Roberts and Rosalind Caird, successive cathedral archivists, for guidance among the cathedral archives at Hereford, and to Sally McInnes, assistant archivist, National Library of Wales, for supplying photocopies and information from the National Library of Wales.

2. HCA, 7044/3, fol. 7v, statutes, 1583; 7031/2, fol. 74r, chapter acts, 30 September 1577; 7031/3, fol. 358r, 25 June 1678; 7031/4, p. [498], 29 June 1768; 7031/20, p. 492, 24 March 1860; 7031/21, p. 411, 25 June 1870; 7031/22, pp. 215, 228, 313, 25 June and 5 November 1877, 25 June 1880.

3. *EEA*, vii, p. lxxiii; HCA, 7031/5, fol. 296r, chapter acts, 25 June 1793.

closely resembling the slightly earlier seal of Llandaff Cathedral (fig. 8).[4] By then the practice of the cathedral clergy serving as the bishops' scribes was declining due to the growing complexity and distinction of episcopal and capitular administration.[5] The cathedral's earliest statutes, drawn up by Bishop Peter of Aigueblanche *c.* 1262, laid responsibility upon the chancellor to compose and prepare the documents for sealing and upon the treasurer to ensure the safe custody of the seal.[6] In his scheme for rebuilding the north transept, substantially completed before 1268, Aigueblanche incorporated a chamber above its east aisle which possesses many of the features of medieval muniment rooms and was used for that purpose by the late sixteenth century.[7] This room came to be called the upper archives or muniment room to distinguish it from the lower archives, chapter house or treasury where the most precious capitular archives were stored from at least Aigueblanche's time.[8] The college of vicars choral and St Katherine's Hospital in Ledbury looked after their archives separately and had their own seals, the thirteenth-century seal of the hospital depicting the west front of the cathedral incorporating a figure of St Katherine (fig. 169).[9]

Chests provided the usual medieval storage for archives. In 1276 some episcopal documents stored in the chapter house were in little boxes within a sealed chest.[10] The fifteenth-century chest in which the vicars choral kept their treasures, including some of their archives, is on display in the Mappa Mundi exhibition in the south cloister.[11] The larger, ornately carved and triple-locked mid fourteenth-century chest in the exhibition, described as a bookchest, is probably the chest in which the statutes, royal grants and act books were stored 'fast locked' in the chapter house, and later the chapter room, from at least 1577. Later called 'the great

4. F. C. and P. E. Morgan, *A Concise List of Seals Belonging to the Dean and Chapter of Hereford* (Hereford, 1966), p. 5 and plate II/8; D. H. Williams, *Catalogue of Seals in the National Museum of Wales*, i (Cardiff, 1993), p. 5; D. H. Williams, *Catalogue of Welsh Ecclesiastical Seals as Known Down to AD 1600*, iii, *Capitular Seals*, *Archaeologia Cambrensis*, 135 (1986), plate XIII.

5. *EEA*, vii, pp. liv–lv, cii–cx.

6. HCA, 7044/1; see above, Chapter 2, p. 32, and below Appendix 1, p. 635.

7. RCHME, *Herefordshire*, i, p. 98; Oxford, Bodleian, Oxford University Archives, T. H. Aston's notes on archival furniture for his lecture at the Annual Visitation of the Oxford University Archives in 1973, pp. 2–5; HCA, 7031/2, fol. 74r, chapter acts, 30 September 1577. For the building

of the north transept, see above, Chapter 8, pp. 525–27.

8. Oxford, Bodleian, MS Rawlinson B.328, fol. 48r; HCA, 7031/2, fol. 74v, chapter acts, 30 September 1577; 7041/1–3.

9. A. T. Bannister, 'The Hospital of St Katherine at Ledbury', *TWNFC*, 23 (1918–20), p. 63 n. 9, and plate opposite; Morgan, *Concise List of Seals*, plate II/4; HCA, 7044/3, fos 8v, 11r, 13r; 7031/3, p. 84, chapter acts, 7 November 1612.

10. W. W. Capes and R. D. Griffiths, eds, *The Register of Thomas de Cantilupe, Bishop of Hereford, AD 1275–1282*, Cantilupe Society (Hereford, 1906), pp. 40–41.

11. F. C. Morgan, 'Church Chests of Herefordshire', *TWNFC*, 32 (1947), pp. 132–33; HCA, 7003/1/1, p. 132; 7003/1/3, p. 27, vicars choral acts, 10 June 1603, 3 July 1668.

chest' it remained in use until about 1840, only shortly before the so-called bookchest is first recorded in the muniment room in 1859.[12] By the early fifteenth century Hereford was, like Wells and Winchester, already also keeping archives in lettered lockers (*capsulae*), which have, however, not survived.[13] For easier identification medieval scribes endorsed some of the documents with a brief title. For additional security, selected charters of both the chapter and St Katherine's Hospital were copied into cartularies between the thirteenth and fifteenth centuries, a precaution justified by the subsequent loss of some of the original documents.[14]

Although there are now gaps among the medieval archives, there is no evidence of their wanton destruction. The Reformation caused less change to the cathedral's archives than Tudor administrative developments. There was, however, one remarkable acquisition. Over 230 of the most interesting medieval documents, dating from about 1120 to 1537, relate not to Hereford Cathedral but to the Benedictine abbey of St Peter's, Gloucester.[15] If, as seems probable, the copy of the reissue of Magna Carta in 1217 is one of these, they have been at Hereford since at least about 1720 when it was listed among the cathedral's archives.[16] The likeliest explanation is that they passed through the hands of Sir John Prise, the collector and Welsh historian, who had been the royal visitor to Gloucester Abbey at its dissolution. On his death in 1555, at his home at St Guthlac's Priory in Hereford, he bequeathed to the

12. F. T. Havergal, *Fasti Herefordenses* (Edinburgh, 1869), plate 22; B. H. Streeter, *The Chained Library* (London, 1931), p. 117; F. C. and P. E. Morgan, *Hereford Cathedral Libraries and Muniments* (2nd edn, Hereford, 1975), p. 33; HCA, 7031/2, fol. 74r, chapter acts, 30 September 1577; 7041/1, fos 42r, 44r; 7041/2, fol. 3r, 22 November 1723 and 3 May [1723]; 7041/3, fol. 53r; 7041/5, volume handed to Havergal in 1877 listing documents lent to R. B. Phillipps, 1833–40, including [duplicated] nos 1149–1169, headed 'From the Chapter Room' which at an earlier date are listed as in the great chest.

13. Oxford, Bodleian, MS Rawlinson B.329, fos 1r–120r.

14. G. R. C. Davis, *Medieval Cartularies in Great Britain* (London, 1958), p. 55; A. T. Bannister, 'A Lost Cartulary of Hereford Cathedral', *TWNFC*, 22 (1914–17), pp. 268–77; Oxford, Bodleian, MS Jones 23, partly printed in R. Rawlinson, *The*

History and Antiquities of the City and Cathedral-Church of Hereford (London, 1717), appendix, pp. 32–85; Oxford, Bodleian, MS Rawlinson B.329; HCA, 7018/5. For a comparison of the documents registered in cartularies with those surviving in the cathedral archives see *EEA*, vii, passim.

15. D. Walker, 'Some Charters Relating to St Peter's Abbey, Gloucester', in P. M. Barnes and C. F. Slade, eds, *A Medieval Miscellany for Doris May Stenton*, Pipe Roll Society, new series, 36 (London, 1962), pp. 247–68; R. B. Patterson, ed., *The Acta of St. Peter's Abbey, Gloucester, c. 1122–1263* (Gloucester, 1998).

16. HCA, 7041/3, fol. 17r. The provenance of the 1217 reissue of Magna Carta (HCA, 1516) cannot be attributed to Gloucester Abbey with certainty but the presence of a letter addressed to the sheriff of Gloucestershire announcing the settlement at Runnymede in 1215 (HCA, 2256) makes it likely.

cathedral at least thirty-seven manuscript books taken from Gloucester Abbey and other monasteries.[17]

The post-Reformation cathedral statutes in 1583 underlined the importance of the archives in a society in which literacy and the legal deployment of 'evidences' was widespread. The new statutes confirmed and extended the chapter's existing orders for sealing documents, auditing accounts and making estate surveys. They also created the office of keeper of the archives with responsibility for looking after the papers and instruments, for putting them conveniently into their separate little rooms (*in distinctis cellulis*) and giving him power to levy fines if the relevant injunctions were not carried out.[18] Edward Threlkeld (prebendary of Cublington, 1571–88; vicar of Hope Bowdler, 1569; vicar of Tenbury, 1573) was elected the first keeper of the archives that year, though in practice the chapter clerks continued to exercise day-to-day custody.[19]

Two great presses were erected in the upper archives to contain the records, each measuring some 18 feet 6 inches (5.64 metres) long by 7 feet 6 inches (2.23 metres) high and divided into four rows of ten lockers or 'capsules' (fig. 153). Their dimensions and method of construction are generally similar, one press being some years earlier than the other. They have been dated on stylistic grounds both to the late sixteenth to early seventeenth century and to a full century later. The earlier date is perhaps supported by an entry in the clavigers' accounts for 1630 when David William, joiner, and Henry the smith were paid 15s. and 2s. 4d. respectively for work 'in the Records' and Dr John Best (prebend of Moreton cum Whaddon, 1606; prebend of Moreton Magna, 1607–37) had had the records cleaned and spent 5s. 'for paynting the chests in the Records'. Their design, like that of the library presses for which Best was also responsible under Thomas Thornton's guidance nearly twenty years before, .may have come from Oxford. They are reminiscent of the early sixteenth-century archive cupboards at Magdalen and Corpus Christi Colleges and similar to cupboards fitted in the Bodleian Library in 1613.[20] Other evidence, however, more strongly suggests that the Hereford presses were made in the course of post-Restoration reforms.

17. Information from Miss E. M. Jancey, Hereford cathedral archivist, 1979–96; N. R. Ker, 'Sir John Prise', *The Library*, 5th series, 10 (1955), pp. 1–24; F. C. Morgan, 'The Will of Sir John Prise of Hereford, 1555', *National Library of Wales Journal*, 9, no. 2 (Winter, 1955), pp. 1–7.
18. HCA, 7044/3, fos 7r–8r.
19. HCA, 7031/2, fos 74r, 157v; 7031/3, pp. 82, 358, chapter acts, 30 September 1577, 30 September 1595, 30 December

1612, 25 June 1678.
20. For the earlier dating see HCA, R 604, p. 10; Aston, notes on archival furniture (see note 7 above), p. 10, and the file 'Hereford'; Morgan, *Hereford Cathedral Libraries and Muniments*, pp. 32, 38–39, where the presses are described in detail. Morgan's contention that in the 1583 statutes the location of the archives *in distinctis cellulis* refers to the capsules rather than 'little rooms' is not supported by the

Fig. 153. Detail of the archive capsules in the muniment room in the lower Dean Leigh library, 1970. (HCL, neg. 57.)

The Elizabethan statutes, reinforced by their reissue under royal letters patent in 1636, were timely, for the archives proved essential to the dean and chapter in recovering control of their property and affairs at the Restoration.[21] In 1661 they brought back the archives from London, where they had been transferred under the act of parliament for abolishing deans in 1649.[22] Some contemporary documents, most notably the chapter act book for the period from 1623, were not recovered, probably because they had remained in the hands of those who had been using them.[23] Between 1662 and 1664 a series of chapter acts required the inspection and registration or deposit in the archives of all leases, terriers, rent rolls and

note 20 continued
definition in R. E. Latham, *Dictionary of Medieval Latin from British Sources, Fascicule ii: C* (London, 1981), p. 274. For the later dating see RCHME, *Herefordshire,* i, p. 107; HCA, 7031/2, fol. 74r, chapter acts, 30 September 1577; 7003/1/1,

p. 132, vicars choral acts, 10 June 1603; 7031/3, pp. 84, 99, chapter acts 7 November 1612, 30 March 1614; 7041/1.
21. HCA, 7044/7.
22. HCA, R 609, p. 5; R 610, p. 8.
23. HCA, 7031/2, fos 28r–28v, 29r, chapter acts, December 1570 to January 1571.

audited accounts, the return of unsealed indentures and the holding of new courts of survey to record the chapter's estates. Such acts continued intermittently for another ten years, backed by the threat of fines and accompanied by improvements in record-keeping introduced by Abraham Seward, who held the offices of both auditor and chapter clerk from 1672.[24] Similar steps were taken by the vicars choral, notably by Humphrey Fisher (vicar choral successively of Holmer and Pipe, 1665–1702), who among his other activities transcribed the college act books from 1576. The originals are now missing and presumed destroyed in the fire at the college in 1828.[25]

As part of this recovery the earliest catalogue of the archives was compiled in 1665, its title and arrangement indicating that the storage in numbered presses was a novelty requiring explanation.[26] Certainly, the contents of only about twenty capsules were listed then. By 1717 the first press of forty capsules was almost filled with documents, which by 1722 occupied the second press up to capsule 59.[27] Though subsequently moved twice, the presses were still used to store archives until 1995, when they were set aside in the former chapel of the vicars choral. They are a striking surviving example of early archival furniture.

The experience of the troubled years of the Commonwealth and Restoration remained embedded in the chapter's memory and the practical value of well-ordered archives ensured continuing interest in their care. William Watts, master of the library in 1660, may have been responsible for arranging the archives in the presses in 1665. A little later Dr William Sherborne, keeper of the archives in 1670, and Henry Jones and Richard Pyle, chapter clerks respectively in 1705 and 1710, were instrumental in recovering documents which had gone missing.[28] No one was more active in looking after the archives than Dr Robert Morgan (rector of Ross; prebendary of Cublington, 1702; canon residentiary, 1712), who was keeper of the archives from 1713 to his death in 1745. It must have been he who prompted the chapter acts between 1713 and 1718 setting out new regulations for the proper making and keeping of records. He introduced an accessions and loans register in 1716, probably added the second press of capsules about 1720; certainly he rearranged and listed their contents, and sent an act book to Oxford for rebinding in 1723 (fig. 154).[29]

24. HCA, 7031/3, pp. 202–303 passim, pp. 316, 321, 358, chapter acts, 26 June 1662, 23 July 1674, 26 June 1675, 25 June 1678.

25. HCA, 7003/1/1, pp. 13, 23, 27, vicars choral acts, 5 September 1578, 18 July 1580, 28 July 1581; 7003/4/3, no. 7, W. Cooke, 'Biographical Memoirs'; *Hereford Times*, 30 July 1828.

26. HCA, 7041/1, front cover.

27. HCA, 7041/2, fol. 1v; 7041/3.

28. HCA, 7031/2, fol. 28r; 7031/3, p. 561, chapter acts, 13 January 1571, 8 June 1705; 7041/1, fol. 1r.

29. HCA, 7031/4, pp. 23, 26, 27, 38, 49, and at end reversed pp. 2, 3, 7, chapter acts, 25 March, 25 June, 22 July 1714, 24 March 1716, 27 March 1718; 7041/1–3; 7041/2, fol. 5.

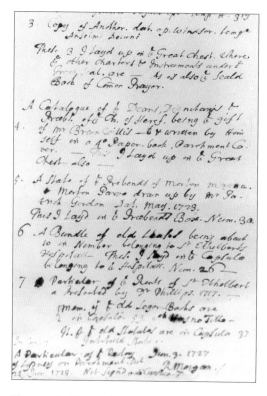

Fig. 154. Archives register, 1665–1751, open at entries
by Dr Robert Morgan, keeper of the archives,
referring to his deposit of the 'leger' or act books and
other documents in the great chest and numbered
capsules. (HCA, 7041/1, fol. 42r.)

Morgan's successors were less active. Although in 1769 James Birt (prebendary of Gorwall and librarian) 'was empowered to employ any person he shall think fit to assist him in putting the writings in the archives in better order', there is a growing impression that the care of the archives was becoming one of the chapter clerk's routine chores.[30] The chapter inspected repairs to the archives in 1780, to the muniment room perhaps rather than to the documents, but otherwise concentrated on ensuring that surveys and maps were drawn up for improved estate management, and accounts and court rolls duplicated for security.[31] The last election of a keeper of the archives occurred in 1783 when the office was held with that of librarian.[32]

No canon, therefore, had special responsibility for the archives throughout the nineteenth century, when unprecedented threats and opportunities arose. Early in the century the archives became weapons not in the defence of the cathedral's rights challenged from outside but in the internal quarrels within the chapter itself. In the long dispute in 1809–14 about the duties of the lecturer, and in the battles of the canons with Dean Gretton in 1814 about the right of the dean also to be an office-holder and with Dean Merewether in 1836–37 about the proper use of the chapter's seal, the archives were extensively searched for precedents.[33] They were also used for the first time for antiquarian research when

30. HCA, 7031/4, p. 367; 7031/5, p. 33, chapter acts, 8 November 1759, 31 August 1769.
31. HCA, 7031/5, pp. 133, 187, fos 237r, 308v, 336v, 351v; 7031/6, pp. 31, 34, 35, chapter acts, 9 November 1775, 26 June 1780, 10 November 1785, 5 May 1795, 24 March 1797, 13 November 1800, 25 March, 14

and 26 November 1805.
32. HCA, 7031/5, fos 214r, 224v, chapter acts, 14 November 1782, 13 November 1783.
33. HCA, 7031/6, pp. 75–103 and 155–84 passim; 7031/19, pp. 87–391 passim, chapter acts, November–December 1809, January–November 1814, February 1837 to November 1838.

between 1833 and 1840 Dean Merewether let Robert Biddulph Phillipps of Longworth borrow batches of 1464 charters in connection with his proposed continuation of John Duncumb's *Collections towards the History and Antiquities of the County of Hereford* and his own antiquarian research.[34] Phillipps repaid the dean and chapter with a catalogue of the charters he examined and by his fund-raising appeal in 1847 for the cathedral's restoration.[35]

Although uniquely Hereford retained the management of some of its estates following the appointment of the Ecclesiastical Commission in 1835, the prebendal estates lapsed to the commissioners, who called in 1847 for relevant documents to be handed over to them.[36] These and other jurisdictional changes irreversibly affected the long-term output of the dean and chapter's records and consequentially affected the amount of space needed for the archives in the muniment room. Already, part of the library had been hastily evacuated there from the unsafe Lady chapel in 1841.[37] Now, following a report by F. T. Havergal (vicar choral, 1853–74; vicar of Pipe and Lyde, 1861; vicar of Upton Bishop, 1874; prebendary of Colwall, 1877–90), the dean and chapter decided in 1855 to move the most valuable books and some library presses into the muniment room.[38]

Havergal was one of Hereford's notable librarians but displayed little interest in the archives. If he used them in compiling his *Fasti Herefordenses* he made no acknowledgement and his proposal in 1854 for the library to occupy the muniment room exclusively put the archives at risk.[39] Fortunately, there was then nowhere else for them to go. For a time, therefore, they remained in their environmentally suitable ancient home where, because parties of visitors were now allowed in to view the chained library, he secured the archives by fitting rods with padlocks across the doors of the capsules in 1860 (fig. 155).[40] The expulsion of the archives

34. Duncumb had published only two volumes, 1804 and 1812; HCA, 7041/2. For Phillipps's scattered notebooks see J. Cooper, 'Herefordshire', in C. R. J. Currie and C. P. Lewis, eds, *English County Histories: A Guide* (Stroud, 1994), p. 182, and HRO, B 56, BC 79, BL 33.

35. HCA, 7041/5, a copy made after 1850; 7031/20, p. 98, chapter acts, 25 June 1847.

36. *Minutes of Evidence and Appendix to the Third Report of the Royal Commission on Public Records Appointed to Inquire into and Report on the State of the Public Records and Local Records of a Public Nature of England and Wales, ii and iii*, Cmd 368, 369 (London,

1919), ii, p. 102 and iii, p. 45; HCA, 7031/20, p. 106, chapter acts, 20 October 1847. The Church Commissioners returned most of the older documents in 1972–76 but retain some nineteenth- and twentieth-century material.

37. HCA, 7031/19, p. 495, chapter acts, 16 February 1841.

38. HCA, 7031/20, p. 301, chapter acts, 9 November 1854; 7037/4, 1855; 7043/3/1, p. 5. For Havergal's achievements as librarian, see above, Chapter 28, pp. 525–27.

39. HCA, 7043/3/1, p. 13.

40. HCA, 7037/4, 1860; 7031/21, p. 318, chapter acts, 24 March 1868.

Fig. 155. The muniment room above the north transept, *c.* 1860, when it housed the chained library cases, the 'great chest' and the archive capsules. Note the bars securing the capsules. F. T. Havergal, *Fasti Herefordenses* (Edinburgh, 1869), plate XXII.

from the muniment room was eventually effected in 1869–70 when, with the cathedral's restoration completed, the Lady arbour room over the bishop's cloister walk was no longer needed by the clerk of the works for storing his architectural plans. The archive presses were dismantled to fit into this inconvenient and unsuitable new home and their contents rearranged.[41] There they remained for nearly a century.

They were rescued from damp and oblivion by William Capes (canon 1904–14), for whom the office of keeper of the archives was revived in 1905 (fig. 156). That year he was also involved in founding the Cantilupe Society for publishing the pre-Reformation registers of the bishops of Hereford. As a gift to the society he published at his own expense his selection of *Charters and Records of Hereford Cathedral* in 1908.[42] His selection has stood the test of time but unfortunately his

41. HCA, 7031/21, p. 385, chapter acts, 17 December 1869; 7037/5, 1869–70; 3483/1.
42. 'Memoir of the Rev. W. W. Capes', in W. W.

Capes ed., *The Register of Thomas Poltone, Bishop of Hereford, AD 1420–1422*, Cantilupe Society (Hereford, 1916), pp. i–xxiii.

Fig. 156. Canon W. W. Capes,
keeper of the archives 1904–14.
(HCL, B.8.16.)

transcriptions, particularly of proper names, have proved unreliable.[43] He commented
that when he began his work the archives did not appear to be in any order, and
he is said to have arranged over half, but it is now difficult to determine what
rearrangement was done either by him or his successor, A. T. Bannister (canon,
keeper of the archives, 1914–35).[44]

The outbreak of war in 1939 obliged the chapter to protect the archives against
air raids. At first in 1940 or 1941 they removed the pre-Reformation charters and
rolls from the Lady arbour room to the crypt, where they suffered from being
stored with damp sandbags, then in 1943 to the National Library of Wales at

43. Z. N. Brooke and C. N. L. Brooke, 'Here-
    ford Cathedral Dignitaries in the Twelfth
    Century', *Cambridge Historical Journal*, 8,
    no. 1 (1944), pp. 3–5, and supplement in
    8, no. 3 (1946), pp. 179–82; many of the
    charters 1079–1234 are correctly transcribed
    in *EEA*, vii.

44. Capes, *Charters*, p. 1; Capes, ed., *The Reg-
    ister of Thomas Poltone*, p. xxi; A. T.
    Bannister, 'A Descriptive Catalogue of
    Manuscripts Dealing with St Katherine's,
    Ledbury', *TWNFC*, 24 (1921–23), p. 23.

Aberystwyth.[45] Although the National Library's offer to catalogue the archives was thwarted by wartime staff shortages, scholars were allowed access to them. After the war it was clear that better permanent arrangements would have to be made for their future care and study.[46] An inspection in 1948 for a report published by the Pilgrim Trust left the dean and chapter in no doubt about the unsuitability of the Lady arbour room.[47] Canon H. A. Moreton (master of the library, 1935–69), who had been responsible for the steps taken to protect the archives during the war, had already engaged F. C. Morgan (Hereford city librarian, 1925–45) as honorary librarian in 1945. When staff returned from wartime service the National Library of Wales was able to begin cleaning, repairing and cataloguing the 4470 medieval documents deposited there. The dean and Canon Moreton resisted the calls for the return of the archives from Aberystwyth until that process had been completed and a better place found for their safekeeping at Hereford.[48]

By 1955 both had been achieved. The catalogue was finished in 1953 and at the cathedral a new muniment room was devised in part of the lower Dean Leigh library and south cloister walk in 1953–55 (fig. 157).[49] Into it were moved the medieval archives from the National Library of Wales; the confused, overcrowded and dust-covered post-Reformation archives from Lady arbour; and, a little later, the diocesan archives which had been housed in the Booth porch since at least 1615.[50] When the diocesan archives were subsequently transferred to the Herefordshire Record Office in 1969, there was space for the estate records to be returned by the Church Commissioners and the archive presses to be re-erected.[51]

45. L. M. Midgley, 'Survey of Ecclesiastical Archives' (typescript, London, Pilgrim Trust, [undated, 1955]), 'Hereford', pp. 18, 19: the inspection of the Hereford archives was carried out in October 1948 and the report written in 1950; Aberystwyth, National Library of Wales, Library archives E 266, general correspondence file He-Hi, 20 January 1935 to 4 August 1947.

46. For example, by J. Conway Davies, who conducted the transfer from Hereford, in 'Ewenny Priory: Some Recently Found Records', *National Library of Wales Journal*, 3, nos 3 and 4 (1944), pp. 107–37, Brooke, 'Hereford Cathedral Dignitaries' (see note 43 above), and D. Walker, 'Hereford Cathedral Charters', *National Library of Wales Journal*, 9, no. 4 (1956), pp. 1–12.

47. Midgley, 'Survey of Ecclesiastical Archives, Hereford', pp. 4–5, 18–19.

48. HCA, 5939; 7031/24, pp. 453, 459;

7031/25, p. 89, chapter acts, 17 July and 19 September 1945, 26 June 1951; information from Mr W. F. Moreton of Wakefield, Canon Moreton's son.

49. B. G. Charles and H. D. Emanuel, 'A Calendar of the Earlier Hereford Cathedral Muniments and A List of Hereford Account Rolls, Court Rolls, Rentals and Surveys' (4 vols, HCA, typescript, 1955); *Hereford Cathedral News*, no. 28 (Christmas, 1954), pp. 8–10; *FHC*, 20 (1954), pp 12–13; 21 (1955), pp. 13–14; HCA, 7031/25, pp. 133, 142, 149, chapter acts, 29 December 1953, 23 September 1954, 29 March 1955.

50. Midgley, 'Survey of Ecclesiastical Archives, Hereford', p. 18; *FHC*, 22 (1956), p. 5; 24 (1958), pp. 12–13; HCA, 7031/3, p. 105, chapter acts, 24 March 1625.

51. Morgan, *Hereford Cathedral Libraries and Muniments*, p. 38; HCA, 7031/25, pp. 489,

Fig. 157. Honorary cathedral librarians Penelope and F. C. Morgan with Canon H. A. V. Moreton, master of the library, in the muniment room established in the lower Dean Leigh library in 1955.

Meanwhile, F. C. Morgan and his daughter, Penelope Morgan (Hereford city librarian, 1949–53; cathedral honorary librarian, 1978–89) set about producing detailed indexes and catalogues.[52]

By this time, though, the confusion of the archives had become institutionalised. The contents of the capsules had been moved about, partly or wholly, over half a dozen times since 1665 and their original archival framework had long collapsed. Even though David Walker had pointed the way in 1956 by detecting traces of an earlier arrangement, it was not until after 1979 that the cathedral's first professional archivist, Meryl Jancey (Herefordshire county archivist, 1959–78; cathedral honorary archivist, 1979–96), began unravelling the confusion.[53] A final removal occurred in 1995–96 when the new library was built and the Mappa Mundi and chained library

491, chapter acts, 14 July and 10 September 1969; NS 11/L/2, library reports from 1957.

52. *FHC*, 42 (1976), p. 20; 52 (1990), pp. 23–24; Morgan, *Hereford Cathedral Libraries and Muniments*, p. 40.

53. Walker, 'Hereford Cathedral Charters'; HCA, 'Handlist of Hereford Cathedral Archives' (typescript, in progress).

exhibition was installed in the south cloister and muniment room. The archives were rehoused in the new building in a purpose-built strongroom constructed in accordance with the current British standard and are available for study in the library's reading room.[54]

---

54. British Standards Institution, *British Standard Recommendations for Storage and Exhibition of Archival Documents: BS 5454: 1989* (2nd edn, London, 1989).

31

Mappa Mundi

P. D. A. Harvey

Its medieval map of the world, or Mappa Mundi, is Hereford Cathedral's best-known possession, an object of national and international importance (plate XVI).[1] Measuring some 5 feet 2 inches by 4 feet 4 inches (1.59 by 1.30 metres), it is the largest survivor of a class of world map produced in western Europe, latterly especially in England, from the twelfth century to the fourteenth. These maps not only showed the geographical outline of the continents and islands; within this outline they provided information on the history, the strange peoples and customs, the extraordinary birds and animals of the far distant lands they showed. They were veritable encyclopedias in map form.

The map is on a single, unusually large and thick, sheet of parchment. Its colours have deteriorated so that it now presents a drab appearance – the seas, once green, are now dark brown – but originally it was brightly coloured, with some lettering and detail in gold which still survives. The geographical outline is contained within a circular frame, and can be seen as a kind of projection: it shows the northern half of what the middle ages knew was a sphere, the half containing all known lands. East is at the top, Jerusalem at the centre. Outside the irregular circle of the continents are the islands of the ocean, from Taphana (Sri Lanka) in the east to Britain in the west. The outline and the rivers derive from lost Roman maps which may well have been reasonably accurate, but successive copying, many

---

1. Full accounts of the map are in W. L. Bevan and H. W. Phillott, *Mediaeval Geography: An Essay in Illustration of the Hereford Mappa Mundi* (London and Hereford, 1873); K. Miller, *Mappaemundi: Die ältesten Weltkarten* (6 vols, Stuttgart, 1895–98), iv; G. R. Crone, *Memoir* accompanying *Reproductions of Early Maps*, iii, *The World Map by Richard of Haldingham in Hereford Cathedral circa AD 1285* (London, 1954); M. Destombes, ed., *Mappemondes, AD 1200–1500* (Amsterdam, 1964); N. Morgan, *Early Gothic Manuscripts*, ii: *1250–1285* (London, 1988), pp. 195–200. The most recent account, P. D. A. Harvey, *Mappa Mundi: The Hereford World Map* (Hereford and London, 1996), needs correction in many details following the analysis of the map's palaeography and art history undertaken by M. B. Parkes and N. Morgan in connection with the Mappa Mundi Conference 1999.

times, by draughtsmen who knew nothing of the true geographical shapes, has produced such distortion that the triangular Sicily is the map's only feature that can be easily recognised.

The continents are named – oddly 'Europa' and 'Affrica' are transposed – and regions and rivers are named throughout the map. Otherwise what is placed within the geographical outline varies from one area to another. Within Europe there are simply places, mostly major cities, but in the Mediterranean there is some more varied information: a swordfish (*miles maris*), the labyrinth on Crete, a picture of St Augustine at Hippo. Further east, events from the Bible appear, all, except the Crucifixion at Jerusalem and the stable at Bethlehem, from Genesis and Exodus: Noah's ark, the tower of Babel, the twisting route of the Exodus itself, and so on. In the extreme east, at the top of the map, is the island of Paradise with, beside it, the expulsion of Adam and Eve. Elsewhere some cities are shown, but mostly we are told of the customs of the inhabitants and the strange creatures of these lands, while in southern Africa we see a series of monstrous races: those with mouth permanently closed so that they can take nourishment only through a straw, those whose face is below their shoulders, and others. This information is drawn from encyclopedias and other works on geography and natural history by late classical and early medieval authors, principally those of Solinus in the third century, Orosius and Martianus Capella in the fifth and Isidore of Seville and Aethicus of Istria in the seventh and eighth, but they in turn relied on some identifiable earlier authors, such as the first-century Pliny the elder and Pomponius Mela. Some of these sources are named on the map.

Outside the map itself are marginal drawings and inscriptions, which have been much discussed as evidence of the mapmaker's perceptions, outlook and intentions. Within the circle round the map twelve puffing heads or figures represent the winds, and outside it are spaced the letters *MORS* (death). At the top is Christ in judgement, dividing the saved from the doomed, while below him the Virgin Mary pleads for those who sought her intercession. Below the map on the left the Emperor Augustus gives a letter to three men ordering them to survey the world; curiously he is wearing the papal triple tiara, and the letter bears a seal of episcopal form. The surveyors are named, and an inscription round the outer border of the parchment tells how Nichodoxus surveyed the east, Policlitus the south and Theodocus the north and west. This inscription identifies the emperor as Julius Caesar instead of Augustus, and the confusion reflects the fact that inscription and picture are based on late and unreliable Latin texts. Still greater difficulties are posed by the enigmatic picture below the map on the right. This shows a man on horseback, hand seemingly raised in greeting to a huntsman, who has bow and arrows and a couple of hounds and who is saying *Passe avant* (go ahead).

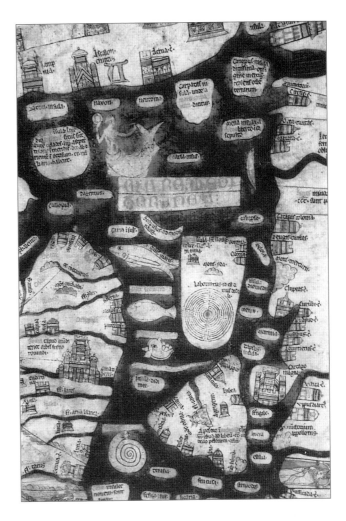

Fig. 158. Detail of Mappa Mundi: the Mediterranean, showing Sicily, Crete with its labyrinth, a swordfish with a sword at its side, and a mermaid.

Very recent research has thrown new light on the map's origin and opens the way to further discoveries. It has long been thought that the map was drawn not at Hereford but at Lincoln, being brought to Hereford soon after it was made. Lincoln is drawn in greater detail than any other town in Britain, with its cathedral or castle on top of the hill and a row of houses leading down to the River Witham, while the map itself tells us, in a note written in French, that its author was Richard of Holdingham (Haldingham) or of Sleaford (Lafford); both are places in Lincolnshire. However, the work of Professor Malcolm Parkes on the map's handwriting suggests strongly that at least the inscriptions were written at Hereford, probably in about 1290–1310. Writing the inscriptions was the last stage of the map's production, but it may well be that the map was produced entirely at Hereford. From his work on the map's pictures, Professor Nigel Morgan reaches the same conclusion on its date: although the cities and some of the animals and birds are drawn in an older style, the leaf ornament of the map's upper borders and the form of Christ on the Cross point to a date after 1290.[2]

Even if the map was executed at Hereford, there can be little doubt that it was copied from an exemplar that came from Lincoln, whether this exemplar took the form of a finished map, a sketched draft, or a series of drawings and notes. This raises two questions: what brought the map from Lincoln to Hereford and what part did Richard of Holdingham play in its creation? Richard of Holdingham has long been identified as Richard of Battle (de Bello), a canon of Lincoln who was prebendary of Sleaford by 1265, and there has been much discussion about whether he could have been the same as the Richard of Battle who, besides other benefices at Salisbury and elsewhere, held a prebend in Hereford Cathedral from 1305 until he died in 1326.[3] Professor Diana Greenway and Professor Valerie Flint have now shown that Richard of Holdingham died in 1278;[4] he cannot have been the prebendary of Salisbury and Hereford, who may, however, have been a nephew or other relation. Richard of Holdingham thus never set eyes on the map that we have: at best he produced or devised its exemplar, in whatever form. Professor Flint in a stimulating paper has, most importantly, interpreted the map against its personal, local and political background. She suggests that the map, designed by Holdingham, was adapted for Hereford by the younger Richard of Battle: in the map's border the rider and huntsman allude to the vindication of hunting rights by Thomas Cantilupe, bishop from 1275 to 1282, and the three surveyors with the emperor are the three supervising collectors of the papal taxation imposed by the 1274 council of Lyons that Cantilupe attended, while the letters RS of MORS are the initials of Richard Swinfield, Cantilupe's successor.[5] In fact, now we know that Richard of Battle, prebendary of Hereford, was not the map's Richard of Holdingham, there is little reason to connect him with the map at all; there were other, more certain, links between Lincoln and Hereford, not least Swinfield himself, who had acted as chancellor of Lincoln Cathedral in 1278–80. It could well have been Swinfield who commissioned a copy of the map by Holdingham that he had seen – in finished form or draft – at Lincoln; this copy might well have incorporated allusions to Cantilupe since Swinfield was then seeking his canonisation.

2. The reports of M. B. Parkes and N. Morgan are to be published in the proceedings of the Mappa Mundi Conference 1999.
3. N. Denholm-Young, 'The Mappa Mundi of Richard of Haldingham at Hereford', *Speculum*, 32 (1957), pp. 307–14; A. B. Emden, *A Biographical Register of the University of Oxford to AD 1500* (3 vols, Oxford, 1957–59), i, p. 556; W. N. Yates, 'The Authorship of the Hereford Mappa Mundi in the Career of Richard de Bello', *TWNFC*, 41 (1974), pp. 165–72; N. Ramsay, 'Richard of Haldingham', in C. S. Nicholls, ed., *DNB: Missing Persons* (Oxford, 1993), pp. 552–53.
4. V. I. J. Flint, 'The Hereford Map: Its Author(s), Two Scenes and a Border', *Transactions of the Royal Historical Society*, 6th series, 8 (1998), p. 26.
5. Flint, 'The Hereford Map', pp. 19–44.

Other research has raised questions about the map's function at Hereford. Before 1948 the map was secured by brass strips round the edge to a wooden panel of more or less the same size and shape as the parchment.[6] Drawings of the 1770s show that this was the centre panel of a triptych; around the map on the central panel was painted a scrolled ornament containing dragons and on the two wings was the Annunciation, the angel on the left and the Virgin on the right. The wings were removed, probably before the end of the eighteenth century, and destroyed or lost; the painted ornament on the central panel was removed at the British Museum when the map was there for conservation in 1855; and when the map was given a new case in 1948 the central part was discarded. It was rediscovered in 1989, when it was realised that the triptych might well throw light on the map's early history and on its original purpose at Hereford. Radio-carbon dating showed that the wood dated from the middle ages.[7] It has been suggested that the map in the triptych was used as an altarpiece, either from the first or at some later period: a representation of God and the whole of his earthly creation in all its variety. This, however, has been seriously questioned. Another possibility is that it played a part in developing the cult of Thomas Cantilupe, canonised in 1320, and was displayed by his tomb; and another is that it was intended for popular instruction, an aid to education or an illustration in preaching.[8]

On the front of the map is a faint signature, 'John Nicolles', in a hand of the early seventeenth century. We might connect this with William Nichols, a vicar choral who died in 1635; John may, perhaps, have been a son or nephew.[9] However, the earliest known reference to the map at Hereford is in about 1680, when a note by a local antiquary, Thomas Dingley, mentions the map in the triptych as being 'Among other curiosity' in the cathedral library.[10] It was still in the library when it was first described in print, by Richard Gough in 1780, as 'a very curious map of the world, inclosed in a case with folding doors'.[11] In 1830 it was moved from the library to the cathedral treasury; the next year a copy was made for the Royal Geographical Society, and from this time its historical importance

6. Bevan and Phillott, *Mediaeval Geography*, photograph following p. xlvii; R. J. King, *A Handbook to Hereford Cathedral* (London, 1864), plate XI.

7. M. Bailey, 'The Mappa Mundi Triptych: The Full Story of the Hereford Cathedral Panel', *Apollo*, 137 (1993), pp. 374–78.

8. Bailey, 'The Mappa Mundi Triptych', p. 377; M. Kupfer, 'Medieval World Maps: Embedded Images, Interpretive Frames', *Word and Image*, 10 (1994), pp. 272–76; Flint, 'The Hereford Map', p. 42.

9. Harvey, *Mappa Mundi*, pp. 14, 17; Professor Morgan, in his analysis of the map's art history (above, note 1), does not accept the suggestion that the signature is in the same ink as the dappling on the horse in the border.

10. J. G. Nichols, ed., *History from Marble Compiled in the Reign of Charles II by Thomas Dingley*, Camden Society, old series, 94, 97 (2 vols, London, 1867–68), i, pp. 35–36, clx.

11. R. Gough, *British Topography* (2 vols, London, 1780), i, pp. 71–76.

became widely appreciated. In 1855 it underwent conservation at the British Museum; in 1862 it was included in an exhibition of works of art at the South Kensington Museum; and from 1863 it was permanently displayed at the cathedral, first in the south choir aisle, then, from the early twentieth century, in the south transept.[12] A coloured lithographic facsimile was published in 1872 and in the following year W. L. Bevan and H. W. Phillott produced a detailed and learned account of the map to accompany the facsimile;[13] this facsimile and book were the basis of much of the subsequent scholarly work on the map.

In the Second World War the map was moved for safety first to Hampton Court, Herefordshire, then to a coal mine at Bradford on Avon. It was then, in 1948, again sent to the British Museum for conservation work at the expense of the Royal Geographical Society, which also provided a new case for its display at Hereford.[14] Some thirty years later it was sent for further conservation by S. M. Cockerell at Grantchester. In 1988 the dean and chapter placed it in the hands of Messrs Sotheby and Co., the London auctioneers, for sale the following summer. Following unexpectedly widespread public protest and debate, it was withdrawn from sale and a way was sought for keeping it at Hereford. Eventually, in 1990, ownership of the map was transferred, along with the chained library, to a new Mappa Mundi Trust, to which the National Heritage Memorial Fund had made a grant, including interest, of £2,270,000.[15] Mr J. Paul Getty Jnr (now Sir Paul Getty) gave a further £1,000,000 for a new building to house the map and the library; this was designed by Whitfield Partners and was opened by the Queen in 1996.

12. Bevan and Phillott, *Mediaeval Geography*, pp. 10–13; Bailey, 'The Mappa Mundi Triptych', p. 377.
13. See note 1 above.
14. *Hereford Cathedral News*, no. 4 (Christmas 1948), pp. 11–12.
15. *National Heritage Memorial Fund Annual Report*, 11 (1991), p. 1.

PART V

The Schools and The Hospitals

32

The Cathedral School before the Reformation

Nicholas Orme

There were schools in England from the time of the conversion of the English to Christianity, usually attached to major churches and primarily concerned, it seems, with training their clergy.[1] By the late eleventh and twelfth centuries there were also schools in the modern sense: free-standing institutions taught by professional masters, open to all who could pay their fees and not requiring their pupils to follow a particular career afterwards. The random nature of early references to schools makes it difficult to know where they were located, but records of them in such places as Brecon and Gloucester by the twelfth century suggest that Hereford too had a school by that date.[2] The Hugh *Gramaticus* whose son Maurice witnessed a grant to Hereford Cathedral in 1132 may have been one of the early teachers.[3]

During the twelfth century, the cathedral became an important centre of learning, distinguished even by national standards.[4] The proportion of its canons recorded

1. This section is an abridged and corrected version of N. Orme, 'The Medieval Schools of Herefordshire', *Nottingham Medieval Studies*, 40 (1996), pp. 47–62.
2. For a map of twelfth- and thirteenth-century English schools, see N. Orme, *Education and Society in Medieval and Renaissance England* (London and Ronceverte, West Virginia, 1989), p. xiv.
3. B. G. Charles and H. D. Emanuel, 'A Calendar of the Earlier Hereford Cathedral Muniments' (3 vols, HCA, typescript, 1955), i, p. 3, no. 1095.
4. The pioneer study of this topic was that of D. Humphreys, 'Some Types of Social Life as Shown in the Works of Gerald of Wales' (unpublished University of Oxford

B.Litt. thesis, 1936), especially pp. 151–66. Other relevant works include R. W. Hunt, 'English Learning in the Late Twelfth Century', *Transactions of the Royal Historical Society*, 4th series, 19 (1936), especially pp. 23–24, 36–37; K. Edwards, *The English Secular Cathedrals in the Middle Ages* (2nd edn, Manchester, 1967), pp. 189–91; most recently and fully, J. Barrow, 'The Bishops of Hereford and their Acta, 1163–1219' (unpublished University of Oxford D.Phil. thesis, 1982), especially pp. 112–18; and Charles Burnett, 'Mathematics and Astronomy in Hereford and its Region in the Twelfth Century', in Whitehead, *Medieval Art at Hereford*, pp. 50–59.

as *magistri*, implying mastery of the liberal arts, rose from a sixth in the second quarter of the century to a half between 1175 and 1225.[5] Roger of Hereford (fl. 1178), though not likely to have been a canon, was a scholar connected with the cathedral or city. He had studied astronomy and astrology at Toledo and wrote Latin works on these subjects including *Theoretica planetarum* and *De quatuor partibus iudiciorum astronomie.* In 1178 he composed a set of astronomical tables, based on the meridian of Hereford.[6] Simon de Freine, certainly a canon between at least 1198 and 1201, shared Roger's interests. In about 1195–97 he addressed a poem in Latin to the scholar Gerald of Wales urging him to visit Hereford, where he would find men of similar tastes and the seven liberal arts being studied and taught more than anywhere in England. The poem enumerates the arts, beginning with grammar, and includes references to astronomy, astrology and geomancy which seem to reflect Roger's studies.[7] Simon also wrote, in Anglo-Norman French, a life of St George and a version of Boethius's *Consolation of Philosophy.*[8] Other scraps of evidence suggest a learned community. In about 1200, the scribe of the earliest English manuscript of *The Prose Salernitan Questions* – a series of enquiries and answers about science and medicine – seems to have come to Hereford, for he mentions three of its clergy in the work.[9] Gerald of Wales, Walter Map and Robert Grosseteste are further writers and scholars known to have visited the city or to have stayed there during this period.[10]

Information of this kind reveals that learning was cultivated rather than how it was taught. Some of the subjects mentioned, being of an advanced nature and involving relatively few people, may have been imparted privately and informally. An organised grammar school, on the other hand, was needed to teach Latin to those who wished to follow these higher studies, as well as to those (the majority) who aimed simply to become clerks or clergy in the diocese. Simon de Freine's allusion to the study of grammar implies a grammar school at Hereford, but the

5. J. Barrow, 'Education and the Recruitment of Cathedral Canons in England and Germany, 1100–1225', *Viator*, 20 (1989), pp. 117–38, especially p. 138.

6. Barrow, 'The Bishops of Hereford', pp. 113–14, 529. Dr Barrow points out to me that there is no record of Roger having been a canon.

7. Hunt, 'English Learning', pp. 36–37. For discussion, see also Barrow, 'The Bishops of Hereford', pp. 114–15.

8. Ibid., pp. 117–18.

9. B. Lawn, ed., *The Prose Salernitan Questions*, British Academy, Auctores Britannici Medii Aevi, 5 (London, 1979), pp. xv–xvi, 6. A marginal note of about the same date in a Hereford Cathedral manuscript of Peter Lombard's *Sentences* names *Magister W. de Burga geometria* and *Magister Raduluus de Wgetot musicam*, who have been conjectured as Hereford men (HCL, MS O.VIII.9, fol. 128v; Mynors and Thomson, *Catalogue*, p. 58.) However, Dr Barrow points out to me that they are not recorded in Hereford sources and that *Wgetot* suggests Wigtoft (Lincolnshire).

10. Barrow, 'The Bishops of Hereford', pp. 116–18.

only reference to any kind of organised school there during this early period occurs in a letter from Gerald of Wales to Master Albinus, canon of Hereford, datable to the years 1208–13. The letter relates to Gerald's quarrel with his nephew Gerald de Barri, and reproaches Albinus for his disloyalty in entertaining men of the nephew's party. Gerald conceded that Albinus was accustomed to deal with many people as a result of 'the teaching of the school which is open to all, annoying and good pupils alike'. But he said that Albinus should not have taken Gerald's enemies as his comrades and even as guests at his table.[11] Was this school the grammar school? Men with the status of canons taught grammar at some English secular cathedrals in the twelfth century, but by 1208 such teaching was probably deputed to professional schoolmasters who were not canons. It is more likely that Albinus was teaching a school of theology for older students, chiefly clergy or clerical trainees. Most of the English secular cathedrals were developing theological schools in this period, and Hereford seems to have had one well before the end of the twelfth century. Nicholas, mentioned as chancellor of the cathedral between 1187 and the mid 1190s, was styled *divinus*, suggesting that he had studied or taught divinity, and three later cathedral clergy were described in records as *theologi* or theologians.[12] Two of these were Simon of Melun, who flourished between about 1190 and 1202, and Peter of Abergavenny, who occurs between about 1201 and 1219. The third was Albinus himself. His career at Hereford stretched from about 1200 to at least 1217, and he ended his life as cathedral chancellor. All this points to him teaching the theology school rather than the school of grammar.

The first clear evidence of formally constituted schools in Hereford comes from the earliest cathedral statutes, apparently drawn up between about 1246 and 1264, and generally assigned to Bishop Peter of Aigueblanche towards the end of that period.[13] By this time there were permanent schools of song, grammar and probably theology. Song, meaning the liturgical music of the cathedral choir, was nominally the responsibility of the cathedral precentor – at Hereford as at the other secular cathedrals. In practice, however, the choral music was supervised by the precentor's deputy and appointee, the succentor, who had to be present at all services in the church by day and night. He was to find five clerks from his school to occupy the first form in the choir and to help sing the antiphons on weekdays and at

11. Gerald of Wales (Giraldus Cambrensis), *Speculum duorum: or A Mirror of Two Men*, ed. Yves Lefèvre and R. B. C. Huygens, University of Wales, Board of Celtic Studies, History and Law Series, 27 (Cardiff, 1974), pp. 156–59.
12. Barrow, 'The Bishops of Hereford', pp. 116, 509–10, 517, 521, 525.
13. Printed in Bradshaw and Wordsworth, *Statutes of Lincoln Cathedral*, ii, pp. 44–85; the date is that suggested by Bannister, *The Cathedral Church of Hereford*, pp. 58–67; see also above, Chapter 2, pp. 43–47, and below, Appendix 1.

funerals.[14] The first form of the choir was the lowest or front rank, and these clerks were what we would call choristers. Hereford's number of five was the lowest of any medieval cathedral and did not increase in number until the later middle ages.[15] The paucity of the group made it slow to develop as an institution. The choristers did not live in a community of their own but were lodged and fed individually in the houses of resident canons. As late as the early sixteenth century, canons who left Hereford on leave were told to board their chorister with another canon,[16] and it was not until 1524 that arrangements were made for common housing.[17] The discipline of the choristers belonged to the succentor, but his power was limited by the cathedral statutes which forbade him to expel them from the choir without the canons' knowledge.[18] That he was expected to find the five 'from his school' is interesting, since it suggests that the succentor's school, the song school, had a larger membership. It may be that the school catered for other boys in the cathedral Close, such as nephews or wards of the canons, and perhaps even for boys coming in from the nearby city. 'Song' in this period was often used as a collective term for the elementary school subjects: learning to read the alphabet, to pronounce Latin words and to sing them according to the rules of plainsong. These were matters which many boys in a community needed to learn.

The second thirteenth-century school was the grammar school. It is implied, but not stated, to exist in the statutes of 1246–64 which declare that the chancellor, the cathedral dignitary who carried out secretarial duties, should appoint 'a regent master in arts' (*magistrum in artibus regentem*). This person was to attend the choir on festival days in the dress of a choirman, designate those who were to read, and listen to them practising their lessons.[19] The regent master referred to must have been the schoolmaster of grammar, although that title is not employed in the passage. A regent master in arts was a university MA, usually a recent graduate who was still engaged in teaching. At Oxford and Cambridge much of the lecturing was carried out by such men as a condition of graduating. The most likely man of this rank in Hereford, other than the canons, was the grammar schoolmaster,

14. Bradshaw and Wordsworth, *Statutes of Lincoln Cathedral*, ii, p. 76. There is some discussion of the choristers' liturgical duties at Hereford in P. Barrett, *The College of Vicars Choral at Hereford Cathedral* (Hereford, 1980), pp. 11–14. Dr Barrow suggests that Nicholas le Chanteur, mentioned in some early thirteenth-century Hereford charters, may have been one of these clerks; he is variously mentioned as living in the precentor's household and as being married with a family.

15. On numbers of choristers, see Edwards, *English Secular Cathedrals*, p. 307.

16. HCA, 7031/1, fol. 37v, chapter acts, 28 June 1526. I am grateful to Dr D. Lepine for this and the references at notes 43 and 57 below.

17. See below, pp. 572–73.

18. Bradshaw and Wordsworth, *Statutes of Lincoln Cathedral*, ii, p. 84.

19. Ibid., ii, p. 71.

and wider comparisons strengthen this conjecture. In all but one of the other eight English secular cathedral cities, the cathedral chancellor was responsible for appointing the local schoolmaster of grammar.[20] This was definitely the case at Hereford in 1384 and is therefore also plausible in the mid thirteenth century.[21] At least three other cathedrals – Lincoln, St Paul's London and York – insisted that their grammar schoolmasters should be graduate masters of arts, suggesting that the Hereford legislators also aimed at the highest standards in this respect.[22]

Cathedral grammar schools and their masters had an equivocal status in medieval times. They were neither fully part of the cathedral body, nor altogether detached from it. This situation was mirrored at Hereford where the statutes give the master some minimal duties in the choir, but only on festival days. The likelihood is that, here as elsewhere, he was not required to be a priest but could be a layman – perhaps even a married man. Cathedral grammar masters sometimes received a small stipend or allowance for teaching members of the cathedral staff: choristers, adolescent clerks and even young adult clergy.[23] But most of their pupils were boys from the outside world, and most of the masters' earnings came from charging these pupils fees. Medieval cathedrals did not usually provide free education to outsiders until the 1540s. Their role was that of a regulating body. The cathedral authorities appointed the grammar schoolmaster of the cathedral city, provided him with a schoolroom and gave him a monopoly of teaching grammar locally. This ensured him an adequate supply of pupils and therefore fees. It is better to envisage his school as the 'grammar school of the cathedral city' rather than the 'cathedral school', because it catered for the general public as well as for the cathedral staff. People called such schools 'the school of the city' or 'the high school' as often as, or more often than, they termed them 'the cathedral school'. The buildings of such schools tended to be sited in the city too, rather than in the cathedral close. This was apparently the case in Hereford. A street in the city was called 'Scholestrete' by about the late thirteenth century, and references occur to an 'Oldescholestrete' in and after 1397: perhaps the same street, from which the school had moved.[24] The latter name seems to refer to a lane near the Close but outside it, towards the north east.[25]

20. The exception was Exeter, where the local archdeacon made the appointment, N. Orme, *Education in the West of England, 1066–1548* (Exeter, 1976), p. 47.

21. See below, p. 575.

22. N. Orme, *English Schools in the Middle Ages* (London, 1973), p. 151.

23. In 1533, those minor clergy at Hereford (such as vicars choral) who were subdeacons and deacons were ordered to attend the grammar school, HCA, 7031/1, fol. 72v, chapter acts, 23 December 1533.

24. *A Descriptive Catalogue of Ancient Deeds in the Public Record Office* (6 vols, London, 1890–1915), vi, p. 257, cf. p. 137; J. W. Tonkin, 'Early Street Names of Hereford', *TWNFC*, 38 (1964–66), p. 245.

25. For the suggested location, see M. D. Lobel, ed., 'Hereford', in *Historic Towns*, i (London and Oxford, 1969), map 3.

The third school likely to have existed in the thirteenth century is the theology school, implied by the presence of the canon theologians already mentioned (fig. 159). All nine English secular cathedrals came to accept the duty of providing teaching in theology or canon law for the local clergy, the responsibility being usually assigned to the cathedral chancellor who had to lecture personally or provide a deputy to do so.[26] There were two exceptions to this arrangement: Chichester, where the task was assigned to the prebendary of Wittering, and Hereford where it came to be linked with the office of penitentiary. Hereford possessed a chancellor by the mid 1190s when Master Nicholas *divinus* held the post, as did Albinus, one of the three recorded *theologi*, in 1217–18. We do not know, however, if Nicholas or Albinus taught theology while they were chancellors, and the other two *theologi* – Peter of Abergavenny and Simon of Melun – are not recorded as having held the office.[27] It is consequently unclear whether the teaching of theology was ever formally linked with the chancellorship at Hereford. If it was, the link was not strong by 1356 when the dean and chapter issued the only recorded statute about the theology school. This provided that the duty of teaching the school should belong to the canon penitentiary who held the prebend known as Episcopi. The statute laid down that no one should be appointed as penitentiary in future unless he were a graduate in theology or in canon law, or at least had studied one or other of these subjects. Thereafter, he was continuously to 'read' (meaning to lecture) and to teach theology or canon law, 'as is observed in cathedral churches'.[28] Unfortunately, this is the only indication that these subjects were taught at Hereford between the early thirteenth century and the Reformation. What we know about the other cathedrals suggests that such teaching could be intermittent. Much depended on the diligence of the officer responsible and on the wish of local clergy to be taught. Of the twenty-two penitentiaries recorded between 1293 and 1558, only five had degrees in theology and three in canon law, though others may have studied these subjects without graduating.[29] All we can safely say about Hereford is that the notion of such teaching survived until the sixteenth century. In 1583, when new statutes were issued for the cathedral, the reading of a lecture on the Bible was reaffirmed or reinstituted, and the duty was again allocated to the prebendary of Episcopi whose predecessors had been the penitentiaries.[30]

Let us now trace the teaching of song and grammar at Hereford in later times, beginning with song. Here, reference must be made to an important musical

26. On this subject see Edwards, *English Secular Cathedrals*, pp. 197–200.
27. Barrow, 'The Bishops of Hereford', pp. 509–10.
28. Capes, *Charters*, p. 228.
29. J. M. Horn, ed., *John Le Neve, Fasti ecclesiae anglicanae, 1300–1541*, ii, *Hereford Diocese* (London, 1962), pp. 22–23; idem., ed., *Fasti, 1300–1541*, xii, *Introduction, Errata and Index* (London, 1967), p. 47.
30. Bannister, *The Cathedral Church of Hereford*, p. 91.

Fig. 159. A medieval teacher with clerical students: miniature painting in a late thirteenth- or early fourteenth-century manuscript in the cathedral library. (HCL, MS O.VIII.2, fol. 59v.)

development at the English cathedrals. During the second half of the fifteenth century, boys' voices came to be used more fully in the polyphonic music of the church, necessitating the training of them in polyphony as well as the traditional plainsong.[31] This established the singing role of cathedral choristers as we now understand it. Some cathedrals – Chichester, Lichfield, and St Paul's London – increased the number of their choristers for the purpose, and the same appears to

---

31. I am grateful to Dr Roger Bowers for dating this development.

have happened at Hereford. In the sole surviving printed edition of the missal according to the Use of Hereford Cathedral, published in 1502, 'seven or five boys' are mentioned singing in the Palm Sunday service at the cathedral.[32] In 1576 we are told directly that the complement of choristers had risen to seven. Five were maintained by the dean and chapter, two by the college of vicars choral, and the number seven was eventually prescribed in the cathedral statutes of 1583.[33] Although most of this evidence is late, the likelihood is that the extra two choristers were added during the period 1450–1500 or thereabouts, in line with developments elsewhere, rather than during the Reformation period.[34] About sixteen choristers are named in the first Hereford chapter act book, between 1512 and 1566. At least four of these are known to have become subdeacons or deacons, indicating an intention to follow careers as clergymen.[35] Others, after leaving the choir, probably went into secular employment, for choirs can be seen as contributing to culture and literacy among the laity, as well as being nurseries of future clergy.

The chief centre of polyphonic activity in cathedrals was the Lady chapel, where the choristers joined some of the adult clergy in performing a cycle of daily services in honour of the Virgin Mary. They also sang antiphons to Jesus and the Virgin elsewhere in the cathedral after compline in the afternoon.[36] This music tended to be directed not by the succentor (whose duties lay in the choir) but by a separate clerk or organist of the Lady chapel who also undertook the training of the choristers in polyphony. At Exeter Cathedral, we can trace how the clerk of the Lady chapel supplanted the succentor as instructor of the boys,[37] and a parallel development evidently took place at Hereford. Here too the succentor was replaced by a new series of officers with respect to the boys. In 1517 the dean and chapter appointed William Wode as instructor of the choristers at a salary of £6 13s. 4d. In addition, he was to play the organ daily at the morning mass in the Lady chapel and to do so on feast days for the whole cathedral choir – implying the siting of organs in both the chapel and the choir.[38] In 1524, William Burley (or Burghill), the chaplain of the new Lady chapel over the Booth porch, was appointed master of the choristers, with responsibility for housing and feeding them. His appointment suggests that Hereford was falling into line with cathedrals elsewhere by centralising the

32. 'Septem vel quinque pueri', W. G. Henderson, ed., *Missale ad usum percelebris ecclesiae Herfordensis* ([Leeds], 1874; repr. Farnborough, 1969), p. 80.

33. For the evidence, see I. C. Payne, *The Provision and Practice of Sacred Music at Cambridge Colleges and Selected Cathedrals, c. 1547–1646* (New York and London, 1993), pp. 181, 184.

34. I owe this suggestion to Dr Bowers.

35. See above, Chapter 2, pp. 389–90.

36. On the music in the Lady chapel, see above, Chapter 21, pp. 383–84.

37. N. Orme, 'The Early Musicians of Exeter Cathedral', *Music and Letters*, 59 (1978), pp. 397–98.

38. On this, and on what follows, see above, Chapter 21, pp. 391–92, an account that now supersedes that of W. Shaw, *The Organists and Organs of Hereford Cathedral* (rev. edn, Hereford, 1988), p. 5.

care of its choristers, but the subject is a complex one, since choristers seem still
to have been living in canons' houses in 1526. Burley's responsibilities did not
necessarily involve teaching, because Richard Palmer (appointed organist in 1527)
was described as instructor of the choristers in the following year, and still had this
function in 1534 when he was allowed to delegate it to John Slade. John Hodges,
who became organist in 1538, was also termed instructor in 1540 and was replaced
in the latter post by Richard Ledbury in 1543.[39] It appears from all this that there
was an office of instructor of the choristers by Henry VIII's reign, usually exercised
in person but potentially by deputy. The office was often held in tandem with the
duty of being organist, and sometimes even with the post of cathedral verger.
Perhaps the small number of boys requiring instruction caused the duty to be
regarded as a modest one, which could be assigned to a variety of appropriate
people.

These early Tudor organist-instructors are obscure men, whose biographies are
difficult to reconstruct. A previous career may be postulated for Hodges, if he is
the same as the John Hogges 'singing man', late of Coventry, who acted as organist
and supervisor of the Lady mass at Lanthony Priory (Gloucester) from 1533 until
its dissolution in 1538.[40] He would have been looking for a new post in that year.
One instructor, Burley, was a cathedral chantry priest,[41] but no record of ordination
or of a church benefice has been found for any of the others, and some may have
been in minor church orders enabling them to marry or to take up lay employment.
They were evidently not musicians of the first rank. None was a graduate in music
and none is associated with a musical composition.[42] Because they are so little
known, we risk underestimating their capabilities which may have been sound in
a practical sense, and we would be unwise to dismiss Hereford Cathedral as
musically unimportant in the early sixteenth century. It had at least two distinguished
musicians as members of its foundation during this period. John Mason, canon
from 1525 and treasurer from 1545 till his death in 1548, was an ex-choirmaster
of Magdalen College, Oxford, and had graduated as a bachelor of music (BMus.)
from Oxford. He composed four five-part motets (which survive) while working
at Chichester in the early 1520s, though he is not known to have been actively
involved with music at Hereford.[43] William Chell, who held the post of succentor

39. Ibid., pp. 5–6.
40. Orme, *Education in the West of England*,
    p. 200.
41. See above, Chapter 21, p. 391; J. Caley, ed.,
    Valor ecclesiasticus tempore Henrici VIII (6 vols,
    London, 1810–24), iii, p. 13.
42. The standard list of known pre-
    Reformation musicians and composers
    is in F. L. Harrison, *Music in Medieval*

Britain (2nd edn, London, 1963),
pp. 434–65.
43. On Mason, see A. B. Emden, *A Biographical
Register of the University of Oxford, AD 1501–
1540* (Oxford, 1974), pp. 386, 657, and
above, pp. 390–93. Dr D. Lepine kindly in-
forms me that Mason was resident at
Hereford from at least 1525–26 until 1540–
41, HCA, R 565–78, R 191–95.

by 1526 and later also the prebend of Eigne,[44] was another Oxford BMus. and transcribed a collection of medieval Latin musical tracts still preserved in Lambeth Palace Library.[45] By Chell's time, however, the existence of a separate instructor of the choristers suggests that the succentor was no longer much involved with their teaching, and it was not until the reign of Elizabeth I that Hereford acquired, in John Bull, a teacher of the choristers who can be called a national figure.

The masters of the cathedral grammar school appear to have had more status. Only two men are definitely known to have held the post before the Reformation, Richard Cornwaille and John Dornell, but three others were teachers of grammar in Hereford and therefore likely to have worked at the cathedral school – the sole public grammar school known to have to have existed in the city. The earliest of the five is John Lelamour, the author of a Middle English translation of what professes to be *De viribus herborum*, a Latin herbal treatise by Macer Floridus.[46] In the unique copy of this work in the British Library, the translation concludes with the statement:

> the whiche boke John Lelamour scolemaister of Herforde Est, they [i.e. though] he unworthy was, in the yer of our lord A[nno] ml ccc lxxiij [i.e. 1373] tournyd into Ynglis [47]

'Herforde Est' or 'East' was a colloquial term for Hereford, used to distinguish it from Haverfordwest (known as 'Herforde West') in Pembrokeshire.[48] John Lelamour was consequently a schoolmaster at Hereford – a conclusion supported by the fact that Middle English texts can now be located fairly precisely through their dialect features, and Lelamour's text contains forms which belong to Hereford or the area immediately south west of it.[49] In turn, this suggests that he was a local man, rather than an immigrant who would have used other dialectical forms. It is not clear that Lelamour's translation is taken from Macer Floridus – it may derive from *Agnus Castus*, a different text – but it is evidently Latin-based and shows that he was fluent in that language. He is therefore likely to have been the master

44. See above, p. 390, and Caley, *Valor ecclesiasticus*, iii, pp. 6, 8, 11–12, 15.
45. On Chell, see the *DNB* (1st edn) article by W. B. Squire, updated in Emden, *Biographical Register of Oxford, 1501–1540*, p. 115, and on his miscellany, Lambeth Palace Library, MS 466, M. R. James and C. Jenkins, *A Descriptive Catalogue of the Manuscripts in the Library of Lambeth Palace* (5 parts, Cambridge, 1930–32), pp. 644–45. Two of the tracts were transcribed in 1526; the miscellany also contains a

fragment of music by the composer John Dunstable, possibly identifiable with the John Dunstavylle who held a canonry of Hereford in the fifteenth century.
46. BL, Sloane MS 5, fos 13r–57r.
47. Ibid., fol. 57r.
48. On this subject, see Orme, 'The Medieval Schools of Herefordshire', pp. 54–55.
49. I am grateful for personal advice on this matter from Professor M. L. Samuels and Dr M. Benskin.

of the cathedral grammar school; indeed 'scolemaister of Herforde' may have been a common way of describing that person.[50]

The next known master of the grammar school was Master Richard Cornwaille, appointed by the bishop of Hereford (John Gilbert) on 26 December 1384. Because Cornwaille's appointment is one of the very few records of the school in the middle ages, some commentators have been tempted to see a special significance in the event, such as a reorganisation of the institution by the bishop. This view is not supported by studying the document or by a wider knowledge of medieval schools. Gilbert makes clear that he was acting only because of failure to do so by the cathedral chancellor to whom the duty belonged. The current chancellor appears to have been Andreas Bontempi, an absentee Italian cardinal,[51] and neither he nor his local representative had bothered to fill the office. The bishop therefore did so, but he respected the chancellor's rights by limiting the appointment to one year.[52] We know nothing of Cornwaille except for his title 'master', and even this is not very helpful. After the Black Death, it was difficult for cathedrals to recruit MAs as grammar masters and some men were allowed to teach with lower qualifications.[53] At the same time, 'master' was becoming applied to non-graduates with some kind of aura or dignity as schoolmasters or scholars, so we cannot be sure of Cornewaille's graduate status. If he secured reappointment, he seems to have gone by 1396 when we hear of a man called Thomas More, 'that was schoolmaster of Hereford', in a legal dispute in Gloucester. The grammar school of that city was controlled by one of the two local Augustinian priories, Lanthony, but its control was disputed by the other, St Oswald's. In 1396 St Oswald's opened a rival grammar school, taught by More, and a legal battle ensued between the two priories and their schoolmasters which lasted until peace was made in 1400. St Oswald's then appears to have abandoned More, but he continued to teach in Gloucester until at least 1409, successfully fighting off legal challenges to his position. Like Lelamour, he is a plausible candidate to have been master of Hereford cathedral school. He was a professional schoolmaster and apparently a tenacious one, in view of his long career. There is something odd about his moving from an established cathedral school to a

50. On the translation, see also G. Frisk, ed., *A Middle English Translation of Macer Floridus de Viribus Herborum*, University of Uppsala, English Institute, Essays and Studies in English Language and Literature, 3 (Uppsala, 1949), p. 16. *Agnus Castus: A Middle English Herbal*, has been edited by G. Brodin, ibid., 6 (Uppsala, 1950).

51. Horn, ed., *Fasti ecclesiae anglicanae, 1300–1541*, ii, p. 12.

52. J. H. Parry, ed., *The Register of John Gilbert, Bishop of Hereford, AD 1375–1389*, Cantilupe Society (Hereford, 1913); Canterbury and York Society, 18 (London, 1915), p. 48.

53. Orme, *English Schools in the Middle Ages*, p. 151.

controversial new one: it almost looks as if he had lost his job and, being unemployed, got involved in starting the rival school in Gloucester.[54]

Two other Hereford grammar masters are known before the Reformation. One is Richard Burgehyll, who died in 1492 and was buried in the cathedral nave beneath a ledger stone inlaid with a memorial brass – a sign of some affluence.[55] The brass included a small effigy, now lost or in private hands, showing a man in layman's dress, wearing a long cloak with a purse or bag hanging from his waist.[56] The Latin inscription beneath it, which is still at the cathedral but in a different place, identifies the figure as Master Richard Burgehyll, 'formerly teacher of grammar of this city' (*quondam instructor gramatice istius civitatis*), and says that he died on 8 November 1492. Brief as it is, the inscription contains three points worth comment. Burgehyll's surname (that of a nearby village) suggests that he was a local man like Lelamour. 'Master', as in the case of Cornewaille, may or may not indicate graduate status, but 'instructor ... of this city' looks like a reference to the cathedral school rather than to any other, especially as Burgehyll's tomb was in the cathedral. The last known pre-Reformation master, Master John Dornell, was confirmed in office by the cathedral chapter on 2 March 1536.[57] He appears to be identical with a man of the same name who was admitted to the law degree of BCL at Oxford on 8 April 1530, having studied in the university for five years.[58] A law degree may seem inappropriate for a schoolmaster, but one or two other instances are known.[59] John Dornell of Oxford was a friend of Robert Joseph, the humanist monk of Evesham Abbey, who evidently met him at university in the late 1520s and added him to the large circle of correspondents to whom he, Joseph, regularly wrote Latin letters. At least one of Joseph's letters to Dornell is extant, dated 1530; in it, the monk discusses Dornell's legal studies, quotes Erasmus and refers to their mutual friend Edmund Field. The letter shows that the Oxford Dornell, and therefore perhaps the Hereford schoolmaster, was a competent Latinist. Moreover, since Joseph was the monastic schoolmaster at

54. On More at Gloucester, see Orme, *Education in the West of England*, pp. 61–3.
55. A. J. Winnington-Ingram, *Monumental Brasses in Hereford Cathedral* (Hereford, 1966), p. 9. I know of only one other brass of a medieval schoolmaster, Orme, *Education in the West of England*, p. 40.
56. J. Duncumb, *Collections towards the History and Antiquities of the County of Hereford* (8 vols, Hereford and London, 1804–1915), i, p. 545; M. Stephenson, *A List of Monumental Brasses in the British Isles* (London, 1926),

pp. 174, 587; M. Clayton, *Victoria and Albert Museum: Catalogue of Rubbings of Brasses and Incised Slabs* (London, 1968), p. 60. Rubbings of the effigy are held by the Society of Antiquaries and the Victoria and Albert Museum London.
57. HCA, 7031/1, fol. 77r, chapter acts, 2 March 1536.
58. Oxford University Archives, Register of Congregation, H.7, fos 211v, 228v.
59. E.g. Orme, *Education in the West of England*, p. 199; cf. p. 146 n. 2.

Evesham and Field the public schoolmaster there, the Oxford Dornell already had links with teachers.[60]

Such scraps as survive about these masters – titles, careers and interests – point to them being professional teachers capable of working to the standards of major schools elsewhere in England. A similar impression is given by the evidence (admittedly rather fragmentary) of what they are likely to have taught. Two manuscripts and one early printed book containing school material have associations with Hereford. Unfortunately, the most informative of these (Oxford, Jesus College, MS 14) has long been lost, and we possess only the brief description made when it was catalogued in 1852.[61] It was a fifteenth-century manuscript and contained a note of ownership by Roger Hygons, who described himself as 'sum tyme clarke of seynt Nycholas paresh in Herford' and could have been an ex-pupil of the cathedral school. The book contained five short texts. The first was a version of the *Accedence* ascribed to John Leland, a widely-used work in English which taught the basic forms of the eight parts of Latin speech. The second was *Dominus que pars?*, a similar elementary work on the parts of speech, but in Latin. The third was part of a treatise in Latin verse on preterites and supines; the fourth a Latin and English vocabulary; and the fifth a Latin prose treatise on heteroclite (i.e. irregular) nouns. The first two texts and the fifth are paralleled in other school manuscripts, and all five are typical of the lower levels of the grammar course in which pupils learnt the forms of the basic parts of speech and mastered vocabulary. The other manuscript is now among the archives of Hereford Cathedral, and is a booklet containing a single quire of twelve leaves written in Latin. It includes a list of books of the Bible with verses to remember them by, some notes on grammar beginning with one concerning verbs, and some extracts from a *Treatise on Dictamen* (i.e. on composing letters) by Simon or Reginald Alcock, written in 1427. This material is a little more advanced than that in Hygons's manuscript, but it yields no evidence (except for its presence in Hereford) to link it with the cathedral school.[62] Finally, in 1517, Jean Gaschet, a French stationer and bookseller operating in Hereford, arranged with a colleague in Rouen (Normandy) for the Rouen printer Eustache Hardy to print for them an edition of *Hortus vocabulorum*, one of the most popular Latin-to-English dictionaries used

60. H. Aveling and W. A. Pantin, eds, *The Letter Book of Robert Joseph*, Oxford Historical Society, new series, 19 (1967), pp. 19–24; cf. pp. 8–9.

61. H. O. Coxe, *Catalogus codicum MSS in collegiis aulisque Oxoniensibus* (2 vols, Oxford, 1852), ii, 'Jesus College', pp. 6–7; D. Thomson, *A Descriptive Catalogue of Middle English Grammatical Texts* (New York and London, 1979), pp. 324–25.

62. HCA, 3169; Mynors and Thomson, *Catalogue*, p. 126. On Alcock, see A. B. Emden, *A Biographical Register of the University of Oxford to AD 1500* (3 vols, Oxford, 1957–59), i, pp. 18–19.

in schools. At this date the London printers were still not able to produce or import printed versions of all the schoolbooks used in the provinces, and Gaschet evidently saw a gap to be filled. One imagines him selling the book to masters and pupils in Herefordshire, and it is worth noting that one surviving fragment of this edition is associated with Lady Hawkins School, Kington, founded in the early seventeenth century.[63]

In England as a whole, the Reformation had an important impact on schools. Those of the monasteries, friaries and nunneries were abolished, along with their houses, between 1536 and 1540. Those attached to monastic cathedrals, collegiate churches and some chantries were refounded by the crown between the 1540s and 1560s. New, uniform primers and grammars were imposed on all schools by the crown between 1538 and 1545.[64] The schools of the nine English secular, or 'old foundation', cathedrals like Hereford experienced least change during the Reformation, as did their parent cathedrals. The governments of Henry VIII and Edward VI aimed to make cathedrals more effective as teaching institutions, but all that was done with regard to the old foundation cathedral schools was to order them to provide free, instead of fee-paying, education. In the summer of 1547 the crown issued royal injunctions to the secular cathedrals ordering them to maintain a free grammar school staffed by a headmaster receiving a salary of £13 6s. 8d. with a house rent-free, and an usher receiving £6 13s. 4d. with a free chamber. By implication, this school was to be free to all local boys who wished to attend. Choristers whose voices had broken and could no longer stay in the song school were to be supported at a grammar school and provided with exhibitions worth £3 6s. 8d. per annum for five years.[65] Hereford cathedral school, as far as we know, was still a fee-paying institution before 1547, but the new injunctions were adopted and were written into the cathedral statutes in 1583.[66] In other respects – appointment of master, school building and methods of teaching – the grammar school probably remained unchanged. The choristers continued to receive tuition in song, and the ancient practice of providing theological lectures was reaffirmed in 1583.[67] The Reformation was therefore a stage in the history of education at Hereford, rather than a watershed.

63. HCL, Kington J.13B; A. W. Pollard and G. R. Redgrave, *A Short-Title Catalogue of Books Printed in England, 1475–1640* (2nd edn., 3 vols, London, 1976–91), i, pp. 601–2 (STC 13833.5).

64. Orme, *English Schools in the Middle Ages*, pp. 258–59.

65. W. H. Frere and W. McC. Kennedy, eds, *Visitation Articles and Injunctions of the Period of the Reformation, 1536–1575*, Alcuin Club Collections, 14–16 (3 vols, London, 1910), ii, pp. 138–39.

66. Bannister, *The Cathedral Church of Hereford*, p. 90.

67. See above, note 30.

The Cathedral School since the Reformation

Egerton Parker

In the early seventeenth century the school received two generous endowments which would be vital for its future alumni. The first benefactor, Charles Langford, dean of Hereford, died in 1607 and in his will left 298 acres of farmland in the parish of Disserth, Radnor, the income from which was to maintain four scholars at the school. The boys were to be born within the city, chosen by the trustees and to attend divine service in the choir of the cathedral clad in gowns and surplices. The income from the property at that time was £30 per annum (out of the same fund four scholars were to be maintained at Ludlow Grammar School). They were sometimes known as dean's scholars, but more usually Langfordians.[1]

The second benefactor was Roger Philpotts, mayor of Hereford, who in 1615 gave a house on the east side of the entrance into the narrow Cabbage Lane (now Church Street) from the High Town, to the dean and chapter towards the maintenance of two of Dean Langford's scholars at Brasenose College, Oxford. At the time the rent from the house was ten pounds per annum, but the funds accumulated, and by 1830 had reached the large sum of £1973 17s. 1d., so that two exhibitions of £35 were able to be paid in that year.[2]

In 1636 the cathedral received from Charles I a new set of statutes, signed by Archbishop Laud. The following is a translation of that section 'Concerning the School':

For disposing that thick darkness of errors and ignorance which we see arise to the injury of most of the people of those places where children are not

1. HCA, 3123, 3128; *Reports of the Commissioners Appointed in Pursuance of Acts of Parliament . . . to Inquire Concerning Charities and Education of the Poor in England and Wales,* *Arranged in Counties*, xiii, *Hereford* (London, 1815–39), pt 2: 'City of Hereford', pp. 9–10.

2. *Reports of the Commissioners Concerning Charities*, pp. 10–11.

educated as they grow up in liberal systems of training and religious principles, we have thought fit to found a school for ever to be governed by a head-Master and Usher, within the precincts of the Cathedral Church ... to be maintained for the future by the Dean and Chapter, as it has been maintained in times past.[3]

The statutes also specified the use by the master of a house and garden situated near the canons' bakehouse. This was on the site of the present school house and the master was ordered to pay 6s. 8d. per annum for rent to the dean and chapter, which continued into the twentieth century, credited to the fabric fund of the cathedral. The annual endowment amounted to £55 6s. 8d. divided up as follows: the master and usher received £20 and £10 respectively, the scholar at Oxford £4, and each of the Langfordian scholars (four at Hereford and four at Ludlow) 13s. 4d. The stipend of the masters remained unchanged therefore from 1583 until the middle of the nineteenth century.

The Civil War had a disastrous effect on the working of the school. The defence of the city was commanded by an old boy at this time, Fitzwilliam Coningsby, MP, who in 1642 was appointed 'Governor of the City and Garrison of Hereford as touching the Militia'.[4] We must presume that the boys from the school played their part, for in a letter written by Sir Barnabas Scudamore to Lord Digby shortly after the raising of the siege he writes: 'we imploy'd our boyes by day and night to steale out and fire their Works'.[5] No doubt they rejoiced when their king and benefactor rode into the city at the raising of the siege and granted the city, as a return for its loyalty, the addition to its coat of arms of two lion supporters and the motto *Invictae fidelitatis praemium*. Unfortunately, shortly after this the city was captured by a ruse and Coningsby had to flee the country. The following years were obviously difficult ones for the school, though there are few records to tell us what was happening. We do know that in 1649 the offices and titles of deans, chapters and prebends belonging to any collegiate church, chapel or cathedral in England or Wales were abolished and their lands and manors confiscated. However, revenue donated to the maintenance of grammar schools was excepted and among the items charged in the accounts presented to parliament of the proceeds of the confiscated estates there were payments for the master and usher of the school, so there is no doubt that education went on.

The Restoration of Charles II was a time of rejoicing for a royalist city and cathedral, but too much damage had been done to be quickly rectified. Something radical was needed to get the school on course again. In 1665 the dean drew up

---

3. Jebb and Phillott, *The Statutes of the Cathedral Church of Hereford*, pp. 30–31.
4. J. and T. W. Webb, *Memorials of the Civil War as it Affected Herefordshire and the Adjacent Counties* (2 vols, London, 1879), i, p. 211.
5. Ibid., ii, p. 387.

fresh regulations for the management of the school. Obviously all was not well: 'Certain disputes and questions have arisen concerning the government of the Grammar school in the City of Hereford'. Because the annual salary of the master was £20 and that of the usher £10 (up until 1773 still referred to as archididascalus and hypodidascalus), 'the school master may demand and require what he thinks fit, not exceeding five shillings for entrance and twenty shillings per annum'. This was only applicable to 'free citizens of the City' and not to those who were 'poor and unable so to do'. The poor were to pay 5s. 0d. on entry and to be left to their own will for the rest; 'as for foreigners [boarders] the school master is left to his own discretion for compounding with them for his salary'. The fees that were collected were to be divided between the master and the usher, but the master could only receive one quarter of the fee of the pupils being taught by the usher. The master had to have 'special regard to the sober and civil demeanour of their scholars as to their good literature, and especially to keep them from that most wicked device, swearing (the epidemical synne of the City)'. The dean and chapter were to settle any disputes between the master and the usher. Finally, 'for the better encouragement of the said Master and Usher, and the advancement of the school, it is agreed … that no Latin Grammar school should be kept within the said city other than the school aforesaid'.[6] The freemen of the city resented strongly the imposition of school fees and the master, Robert Phillips, had to attend the court of Frankpledge. As a new master was appointed the following year, we may guess that the case went against him.

In 1677 Bishop Herbert Croft held a visitation of the cathedral. His question no. 49 was:

> Hath your school an able Master and Usher; are they diligent to instruct the scholars both in the church catechism and in human learning? And are the scholars well trained upon Piety, Sobriety and Modesty, obedience and all good discipline?[7]

This received an affirmative answer, but some obviously were not. In 1683 the son of John Silvester lost his place as a dean's scholar for 'his absenting himself from school and choir since Easter last, breaking the new brick wall, abusing the vergers, and several other miscarriages'.[8] The chapter's glib reply to question no. 49 is belied by their action in 1685, when they ordered that a table be inscribed in the Free School, 'wherein shall be these orders, viz. to introduce the discipline of Westminster School … That there shall be no play days given by the master or usher upon any particular man's request but on Tuesday and Thursday

6. HCA, 1530.
7. HCA, 1575, 1579.

8. HCA, 7031/3, p. 418, chapter acts, 31 October 1683.

in the afternoons except by the appointment of the Bishop or the Dean and Chapter'.[9]

It was just as well that school discipline had been tightened up, for the school now received its finest endowment. By an indenture signed by Sarah, dowager duchess of Somerset, and witnessed by the master of University College, Obadiah Walker, four scholarships were founded at Brasenose College, Oxford, and in 1682 five further scholarships to be held at St John's College, Cambridge, 'for the honour of God and the advancement of good learning'.[10] Scholars were to wear gowns of cloth with open sleeves and square caps without tassels which were provided every two years out of the endowment. In addition to having their chambers and tuition free they were to be paid an allowance of five shillings for their battels. They had to be born in Herefordshire, Somerset or Wiltshire. They could stay for seven years. When the duchess died in 1686 her will augmented her gift; the new scholarships were to be held alternately by scholars of Hereford, Manchester Grammar School and a small Wiltshire school long since closed down, Marlborough Grammar School. In addition she left the living of Wootton Rivers to be presented to a Somerset scholar. The endowment built up so that by the twentieth century the five exhibitions at St John's College, Cambridge were valued at £40–50 per annum and the four Brasenose College, Oxford scholarships at £70 per annum, though later inflation reduced the number of awards and the universities of both Oxford and Cambridge abolished closed scholarships and exhibitions.[11]

The eighteenth century saw a period of much less turbulence and a major expansion and improvement in the school buildings. The old school in the cloisters had become dilapidated and in consequence a much larger building was erected on the site of the original, funds being raised by public subscription on condition that it should be used for the Three Choirs Festival and other public meetings, as well as by the school. For this reason it was sometimes called the Music Room (fig. 160). It was opened in 1762 at a festival concert, and was described as 'a very grand room lately built near the Church'. While it was being erected the school rented two rooms in the north-west corner of the vicars cloisters.[12] In 1775 the chapter agreed that the school room be further enlarged 'by carrying forward the Upper Room, if the present School be found too small'. In 1767 posts were erected 'to prevent the Boys and others from playing at Ball against the Church or School at the west end thereof', and a note of exasperation is detectable in 1797 when the chapter wrote to Mr Squire the headmaster to communicate their unanimous decision that 'in order to preserve the Cathedral Windows ... Your

9. Ibid., p. 443, 11 December 1685.

10. Ibid., p. 142–54, 1682; 7044/17, 20.

11. HCA, 7044/20.

12. HCA, 7003/1/4, p. 161, vicars choral acts, 19 July 1760; W. T. Carless, *A Short History of Hereford School* (Hereford, 1914), pp. 72–74.

Fig. 160. View of the ruined west end of the cathedral in 1786, showing the Music Room on the right, drawn by James Wathen. (HCL, B.3.18.)

Boys ... should be restrained from playing at ball in the Church Yard'. In 1778 the chapter decided to rebuild the master's house on an enlarged site; the dean and residentiary canons personally contributed 100 guineas to this enterprise, to which the Mayor and Corporation added 30 guineas.[13]

The pattern of membership of the school is now clearer: the choristers were not necessarily bright and were local boys, usually sons of small business men from the city, for instance a bookseller, a tailor, an apothecary, a joiner, a shoemaker and a glover. They entered the school as young as seven and stayed until their voices broke, usually at fifteen. The chapter then funded their apprenticeship by means of the Tomson bequest to help 'a poor child who has been a chorister to be an apprentice to some honest trade'. Thus Thomas Diggis and William Phillips in 1695 'shall have Mr Tompson's tenn pounds equally divided betweene them to bind them apprentices'. Diggis and Phillips are also among the first group of choristers of whom we have a record, their names being scribbled on the covers

13. HCA, 7031/5, pp. 133, 467, 166, 169, chapter acts, 9 November 1775, 6 May 1767, 12 November 1778, 1 March 1779; HCA, 1535, letter, 28 July 1797; Carless, *A Short History*, p. 37.

of the volumes of Barnard's *Church Musick* of 1641: 'Thomas Diggis and he is a good boy. Riten 1687'. The final informal list was written in 1731, ending with 'Charles Skyrme – all good but the last he is as great a rogue as gallows did hold'.[14] For the bright chorister, however, there was a rosy future and he could look forward to a Somerset scholarship at Oxford and funding from the Philpotts Charity. Thus in 1763 'Richard Underwood late one of the Choristers of this Church and now a student in Christ Church Colledge in Oxford was admitted to receive henceforwards the Dean and Chapter's allowance of four pounds per annum to their Scholar at that University till further order'.[15] Later he was ordained and came back to teach at his old school. Poor, bright boys from the city could also benefit from Dean Langford's bequest and could win their way to Oxford or Cambridge with the aid of the Somerset awards. These endowments were valuable and parents, especially clergy, used to send their children from the other side of the county to benefit from them. They would join the boarders in the headmaster's house. An advertisement later refers to some very considerable additional building to this house 'for the accommodation of young gentlemen', and points out that 'French, Drawing, Writing, Arithmetic, and the use of globes, are taught by approved masters'.

It is clear that the majority of pupils were sons of the gentry or the clergy, with a syllabus designed for them and the expectation that they would be going on to university. The pressure was on the headmaster to produce results. In 1774 it was ordered 'that the master of the school be directed not to grant any playdays to his Scholars in the future unless the person applying shall pay into his hands the sum of half a guinea to be laid out in books for the use of the School'.[16] The social status of the majority of the pupils is confirmed by a study of Old Herefordian dinners. These started in 1784 when a group of his former pupils was to honour the Reverend Gibbons Bagnall with a dinner at the New Inn, Hereford. He had first been appointed headmaster in 1762 and had had to stand in again when his successor, Abraham Rudd, became bankrupt in 1782. These dinners became annual events, being advertised in the *Hereford Journal*. In 1786 'as many gentlemen, educated with other masters at the same school have expressed a wish to be members of this Society the honour of their company is requested'. Two stewards were appointed each year and from this we can gather their superior social status. Over half were clergymen; most were called Mr or Esquire. One of the stewards

14. HCA, 7031/3, p. 511, chapter acts, 14 November 1695; Oxford, Christ Church Library, MUS 544 533. For Barnard's part-books, see above, Chapter 22, p. 401 and n. 15, and HCA, 5823. The 'Names of Early Choristers Written in These

Volumes' are printed in Carless, *A Short History*, pp. 79–80.

15. HCA, 7031/4, p. 424, chapter acts, 27 July 1763.

16. HCA, 7031/5, p. 122, chapter acts, 10 November 1774.

in 1807, Sir John Geers Cotterell, was a prominent MP and landowner. The forty-eighth and last dinner took place at the Green Dragon on 24 May 1842.[17]

The first half of the nineteenth century was a period of changing fortunes with the number of boys attending the school fluctuating wildly. On the whole, it was a less than distinguished time for all the public schools and for Hereford in particular. A list of the school rules has come down to us from 1808 and gives us a flavour of the time. The boys have to move quietly at all times and wait in silence at the end of the class until dismissed. Rules that were broken were punished by a system of fines. A boy absent from roll call forfeited a penny or three cuts on the hand. A boy dirtying the yard had to pay 3*d.* to the cleaner and 3*d.* to the prize box. Boys writing on the walls, cutting the desk, doors, or rails in the churchyard, were made to copy out a sermon. Bad language was to be punished with a flogging and gentlemanly behaviour was mandatory. Masters had to be saluted by touching the hat. In 1810 the headmaster made all pupils report as an exercise on Monday the sermon they had heard at the cathedral on the previous day. All boys attended the service, choristers and Langfordians sitting in the stalls and the rest of the school in the gallery reserved for them over the south stalls.[18]

When Dr Squire retired in 1803 there were about eighty boys in the school, but in Revd Samuel Picart's first year as headmaster numbers fell dramatically to thirty and a boy died owing to an outbreak of scarlet fever. Fortunately the school then benefited from the arrival in 1807 of Dr Charles Taylor from Ludlow Grammar School, who brought with him an additional ten boys from that school, and numbers were quickly built up. He appointed David Cox as art master between 1817 and 1827, whose almost equally talented son, David Cox the younger, also attended the school. In 1819 Dr Taylor himself published *A Latin Grammar for the Use of the Cathedral School*, which went through several editions. In 1825 he was appointed chancellor of the diocese.

Under his son, another Charles Taylor, who had been head boy of the school and was appointed headmaster at the early age of twenty-three, the school rapidly declined. His heart does not appear to have been in it: even the school register was discontinued at this time. Perhaps he quickly became disenchanted. His request for a playground in 1827 was ignored; it took three years before it was agreed to repair the school roof. The school lost the use of the Music Room, which was pulled down in 1834, and the 'Master of the Cathedral School had to assemble the boys after the recess at his own house'.[19] In 1834 there were twelve choristers: four dean's scholars, twelve pupils paying eight guineas each, and one boarder,

17. I am grateful to Dr J. C. Eisel for his research into this subject.

18. Hereford Cathedral School archives, register, 1808, printed in Carless, *A Short History*, pp. 72–74.

19. HCA, 7031/18, p. 436, chapter acts, 15 July 1834.

named Alfred Salwey, son of the Ludlow MP, who was known to his friends for the rest of his life as 'School'. One reason for the decline was that a dissatisfied usher named Bunning had set up a rival school teaching English subjects and charging only half the fees of the cathedral school. Bishop Edward Grey in the injunctions following his visitation in 1835 included the following:

> that the Dean and Chapter do more minutely enquire into the cause of the falling off of the Cathedral School and report to the Bishop thereon and that they lose no time in providing a suitable School Room in lieu of that pulled down and also a diligent usher.[20]

Perhaps the bishop's prodding did some good. Charles Taylor left to do good work in various parishes, dying in 1892. His successor, William Henry Ley, seems to have started a revival and by the 1840 numbers were up to fifty again. Too strict an adherence to Latin and Greek was damaging the school, and in 1836, after many parental complaints, an English book, Mangnall's *Questions*, was introduced.[21] Throughout this time the headmaster reported each year to the dean and chapter on the books used in the religious instruction given at the school.[22]

We have an outline of the headmaster's duties written for the appointment of Dr Thomas Layng in 1844.[23] He was to be paid £20 per annum with a further 8 guineas for tutoring the Langfordian scholars. Rent however was deducted, leaving him with only £23 3s. 4d. The more private pupils he managed to recruit, of course, the greater his salary: 'There are at present eight day scholars who pay ten guineas each'. The usher was paid £10 per annum by the dean and chapter, but 'any other master would be provided by the headmaster at his own expense'. Dr Layng built up the numbers but there was to be a final blip. After he announced his impending retirement numbers fell to eight, seven boarders and one day pupil, apart from choristers and Langfordians. One problem was that there were in the city at this time seven other schools competing for day boys, and these included the National School in Union Street and the Bluecoat School. Accommodation was also a problem, as the headmaster's house could only take forty boarders. The school room at the back was limited in size, so that the school pressed for rooms in the vicars choral college, for the first time in 1842, in the north-east angle of the college. In 1851 the vicars agreed to lease these premises to the dean and chapter, together with a piece of land for a playground. A bridge was built from the first floor of school house to the college cloisters, so that we know that the

20. HCA, 7031/19, p. 29, chapter acts, injunctions dated 9 July 1835.
21. R. Mangnall, *Historical and Miscellaneous Questions for the Use of Young People* (Stockport, [1800]; 14th edn, London, 1818).
22. E.g. HCA, 7031/19, pp. 4, 38, 219, chapter acts, 13 November 1834, 12 November 1835, 9 November 1837.
23. Hereford Cathedral School archives.

Fig. 161. School house, west front.

headmaster's house had been extended at least up to first floor level on the college
side. In 1859 the roof over the southern section of the house was extended
(fig. 161).[24] A Herefordian's account, written in 1852, reveals 'that the school was
lately at a very low ebb, as low as it could well be, and was only beginning to
rise, owing partly to the closure of a private school called Hayter's and partly to
the energy of the new headmaster'. This was the Reverend Thomas Power.

The second half of the century saw much more positive progress educationally,
not only in the country as a whole but in the cathedral school itself. The numbers
again reached the hundred mark, sixty day boys and forty boarders. The spirit of
reform, so absent in the earlier years of the century, was instigated effectively by
men of the calibre of Dr Arnold of Rugby and Dr Thring of Uppingham. The
Clarendon Commission, leading to the public schools act of 1868, recognised that
these schools were good for the training of character, acknowledged the place of
organised sport and exercise in this, and helped people to control themselves and
govern others: leadership, in fact. The school register shows many boys now going
into the services of the colonies overseas. Two were killed serving in the forces
in the Indian Mutiny, and one became doctor to the emperor of Hawaii. In a

24. HCA, 7003/1/6, pp. 118–19, vicars choral acts, dean's letter and vicars' reply, 17 and 19 April
    1851; 7031/20, pp. 224–25, 462, chapter acts, 9 May 1851, 24 March 1859. This work is described
    by W. E. Vernon Yonge, *Herefordian* (1909), pp. 30–32.

period of thirty years eight leavers became clergymen. Leadership was positively encouraged in the school. The monitors of the year now had to sign a solemn undertaking: 'I the undersigned hereby accept the office and duty of monitor in Hereford School and I promise to do my very best at all times and in every way to maintain the discipline of the school and to put down in other boys everything in which speech and action seems unworthy of a Christian gentleman'.

In August 1865 the school set out its present status and function for the Endowed Schools Commissioners. The replies to their enquiries give a detailed and vivid picture of the school at this period. The intake is clear: 'The parents both of the day boys and boarders are speaking generally professional men (clergymen, medical men, lawyers) and officers residing in the town or County. A few of the leading tradesmen send their sons as day boys, some of the more wealthy farmers theirs as boarders'. Many of the boarders came from a larger distance, attracted no doubt by Somerset scholarships. The dean and four canons governed the school and appointed the headmaster. They received his annual report and he now appointed the usher, 'the stipends both of the Head and Second Masters being very trifling, and the efficient working of the school depending upon the number of non-foundation pupils, and mainly upon the boarders in the Head Master's house'. He paid the stipend of all the other masters and general school expenses. The governors appointed an annual examiner from the university and funded the prizes. The chapter also provided a dwelling house for the master and school rooms. Two separate endowments provides the tuition fees of four foundation scholars and for the partial maintenance of two of their number at university. They stated strongly that the endowment was inadequate.[25] In 1869 the Endowed Schools Act was passed, with the bishops securing the addition of clause twenty-seven requiring the commissioners to inquire into the adequacy of the endowments of cathedral schools. In 1874 its efforts were amalgamated with the work of the Charity Commissioners. In the long run this helped the school; meantime it had to help itself.

The school also now appointed some reforming headmasters. In 1869 the post was advertised nationally for the first time. The response was overwhelming: fifty-seven were shortlisted and the post was offered to the Revd Eric Rudd of Scarborough. His reforms included opening a boarding house in St Owen's Street for the youngest boarders in the care of the Revd James Brown. Fees were raised and the school year was divided into three terms, commencing in January, May and September. Where his salary had been £40 per annum plus fees, that of his successor, the Revd Francis Tatham, who arrived in 1875, was raised sharply to £120 per annum, reflecting no doubt the increasing prosperity of the school. He came from Westminster full of reforming ideas (fig. 162).

25. HCA, 1537, replies to the particulars of inquiry by John Woollam, head master.

Fig. 162. F. H. Tatham,
headmaster 1875–90.
(HCL, B.6.14.)

The immediate problem to be solved was that, as a result of increasing friction between the vicars choral and the dean and chapter, the latter was given a year's notice to end the school's occupation of the college buildings. In 1876 therefore the school moved to its present site, formerly that of the canons' bakehouse, on the corner of Quay Street and Castle Street. A block of buildings was erected consisting of a vestibule and three classrooms on the ground floor and a 'Big School', or hall, above it. The large schoolroom at the back of the headmaster's house was now pulled down. A few years later, owing to increasing numbers, the house was enlarged. The Old Herefordians Club was now founded, with H. W. Apperley as its honorary secretary, its principal event being to dine annually at the Green Dragon hotel, but it also met in London and sometimes at the universities.[26]

26. HCA, 7003/1/6, pp. 374–76, 379, vicars choral acts, 16 November, 24 December 1874, 1 January 1875; 7031/22, pp. 126–27, 4 January 1875.

The annual inspectors' report to the governors in 1876 was positive: 'The school appears to be in a thoroughly satisfactory and efficient condition, the average of work being good and testifying to a good deal of honest industry among the boys … The school is in a thoroughly healthy condition'. A star pupil mentioned by both inspectors was F. E. Weatherly, who was to become a notable QC, but afterwards became much more famous as a songwriter, being the author of the words of *The Holy City*, *Danny Boy* and *Roses of Picardy*. Later he was to write the school song. In his autobiography he wrote of the school: 'What a wonderful new life it was! The masters so kind and clever. The fellows so splendid at cricket and football … But it was the music of the place for which my thanksgiving is deepest'. Contemporaries of his were Philip Wilson Steer, the artist who gained the Order of Merit, and Arthur Machen, the writer.[27]

In 1881 the headmaster raised by subscription the sum of £500 to erect a new library and three classrooms, a porter's lodge and a sick room. These were opened in 1882. He chose this year as the 500th anniversary of the foundation of the school by Bishop Gilbert, which it was not, but it was no doubt a useful weapon to employ in fund-raising. This was followed in 1883 by the development of Wyeside as a games field, the dean and chapter providing £20 towards the rent. Organised games were now becoming a vital part of the school's activity. Rugby was first played against the Hereford militia in 1886 and continued to be played on the barracks' ground. J. A. Bevan played for Cambridge (1887–90) and was the first captain of Wales. Rowing really started with the annual regatta of 1870 and had a spectacular success when the school senior four won the Public Schools Challenge Vase in 1883 at Henley in a boat loaned to them by Eton. Cricket records start in 1878. Tatham's final improvements occurred in 1884 when he built additional dormitories on to his house, the school using premises belonging to the vicars choral. By 1890, when he moved on, not only had the numbers increased and a new boarding house been set up, but he had added German and chemistry to the curriculum and created a much more civilised place. The Gilbert library and the *Herefordian* are his lasting memorials.[28]

In 1893 schemes were at long last approved by the Charity Commissioners under the new Endowed Schools Act of 1889 for the reorganisation of the school's endowments. The Langford foundation was directed to be expended on scholarships in the school, to consist of free tuition and £5 per annum for competition amongst boys in the city elementary schools; the Philpott foundation was directed to be expended on £150 in exhibitions in any university, the scholar to have been at the school for no less than two years. Each exhibition was to be of no more than

27. F. E. Weatherly, *Piano and Gown* (London, 1926), p. 28.

28. HCA, 7031/22, pp. 343, 353, 440, chapter acts, 24 March, 25 June 1881, 12 May 1884.

£50 and to be held for three years. The remainder of the income was to be expended on scholarships within the school similar to the Langford foundation. Thus foundation scholarships were created in the school varying from £10 to £20. As to the school itself, the two yearly sums of £20 and £10 from cathedral funds were voluntarily increased by the dean and chapter to £200 and £73. Most important of all, the Ecclesiastical Commissioners increased the endowment by several thousand pounds. The headmaster's salary was raised to £170, and he was allowed capitation fees ranging from £4 to £8.[29]

Progress was continued under the Reverend William Murray Ragg, who in 1898 established a preparatory school at Harley Court under the charge of Miss Dance and her assistant Miss Thompson. Its origins were modest, being born in an iron shed in the garden of Harley Court, which was at the time the residence of the school's senior master, Mr Sharpley. There were twenty-three in the school, nine being boarders who stayed in Harley Court. When Sharpley left to become headmaster of Louth school, the Revd J. Henderson, by arrangement with the governors, moved the preparatory school into some rooms in the senior school.

The Education Act of 1902, putting into practice the recommendations of the Bryce Commission, brought education under municipal control by establishing local education authorities which replaced school boards and which were given the power to establish new secondary schools where necessary. So Hereford High School was established in 1911. An understanding was reached with the LEA that the cathedral school would maintain its independence and that the new school should not offer a classical education, but would pass on to the cathedral school scholarships for boys desiring such an education. The governors therefore pressed ahead with vital reforms, but they needed funds. They asked the Board of Education if they could raise money by selling part of the Langford foundation scholarship endowment to help purchase additional accommodation. In 1910 the board eventually agreed to the amalgamation of the Langford foundation with that of the cathedral grammar school, so long as the same number of scholarships was offered, and a new governing body was set up to administer the amalgamated foundations, consisting of five governors nominated by the dean and chapter, and one each by the county and the city.

The school now bought 1 Castle Street. This was to be the headmaster's house and a second house for boarders (fig. 163). It was purchased for £5000, half of this being provided by Canon W. W. Capes, a governor, and the other half by the governors, with a further £2000 being raised by the Old Herefordians to equip the building and further improve the facilities.[30] Prebendary Murray Ragg

29. HCA, 1538.
30. HCA, 7031/23, pp. 439–40, chapter acts, 16 April 1910.

Fig. 163. No. 1, Castle Street, former headmaster's house, with the Portman building on the left.

retired, after 'more than fifteen happy years', and in 1913 the Reverend John Henson took over. A strong entry of boarders was wrecked by the outbreak of the First World War, staff as well as pupils leaving hurriedly. Within one month of the OH committee meeting in July, four of its members were fighting and one was already a prisoner. The nadir was reached in September 1915, when not a single boy of seventeen was left in the school who could pass the medical test. Their enthusiasm had no doubt been fired by the success of the school Cadet Corps, formed initially in 1902 but which became in 1908 one of the first units of the OTC with a membership of fifty-five.

In May 1915 the governors enlisted the assistance of the Board of Education. They were pleased to see improvements since the last inspection. Their final comment was: 'Under the present head, the classical education is in excellent hands and the school continues to fulfil a most useful place in the educational scheme of the district'.[31] At this stage there were only sixty-eight boys in the school of whom twenty-nine were boarders and of whom 6 per cent came from elementary schools; only 12 per cent were over sixteen years of age. Each term saw published a new list of killed and wounded – and decorated – old boys. The debating society mirrored the times: 'That this House would rather bayonet a German than shoot

31. Hereford Cathedral School archives, governors' minute book, 1908–21.

him'. At length, the armistice was signed and the war ended. The cost in human life was appalling, and the school had played its part in the sacrifice and the victory. Altogether, 485 OHs had taken part: sixty-five were dead and 311 wounded; thirty-eight had being awarded the Military Cross.

In 1919, after much pressure from Bishop Percival, the Lady chapel of the cathedral was made available for the school's use. Nearby a tablet was erected as a war memorial at which the headmaster and head boy annually place a wreath. In the chapel boys in their mortar boards attended daily prayers, and also matins on Sunday. Dean Leigh gave his stipend as vicar of St John's parish towards the provision of a permanent school chaplain. The following year the school came under the Board of Education and gratefully accepted its grant, which alleviated some of its financial difficulties. Permission was given for an advanced course in classics and provisionally for ones in mathematics and science. It was a time of change. In 1920 the Revd John Henson resigned and was succeeded by Dr J. H. Crees, headmaster of the Crypt School, Gloucester. He brought with him a number of colleagues to fill in the gaps of the cathedral school staff. His appointment also broke a long tradition, for he was not a clergyman. Since 1913 the preparatory school had been taught in school house, but the need for expansion, and the inspectors' pointing out the awkward nature of the arrangement whereby the headmaster ran his own private school within an institution of which he was a headmaster responsible to governors, led to an agreement to move. The governors offered Dr Crees 10s. per annum on his capitation fee if he moved them out, but only if it remained a feeder school for HCS. This proved mutually satisfactory, so in 1925 the preparatory school moved to 28 Castle Street where it remains until this day.[32] In 1929, summing up his ten years as head, Dr Crees noted:

> that there is now a greater demand for a public school education ... that pupils are drawn from a miscellaneous variety of classes ... we are in far closer contact with elementary education by reason of the Board of Education's free places scheme than ever before. Many of those who were educated in Hereford in the past will be surprised at the difference of parentage which may be found here ... ranging from the grandson of a Peer to the son of an engine driver: I cannot say I regret the wider sphere of usefulness which the school has now attained ... nor do I feel its traditions have been lost.

The economic hardship of the 1930s and the declining birthrate during the war years led to a fall in numbers, and in 1932 there was a cut in staff salaries, but the academic standards remained generally high. The 1931 inspection had only three reservations: history was neglected, better laboratories were needed, and

32. Ibid., 1921–45.

geography had only one text book. In fact the governors had backed an appeal to the old boys for £3500 to be associated with the 550th anniversary in 1931. It took hard graft and many years before the laboratories were opened in 1935. Two years later direct grant schools were admitted to the headmasters' conference. In 1939 a number of boys attended the school 'whose parents had been driven from the countries in which they were living owing to racial prejudice ... These boys were possessed of considerable intelligence and took high places in their forms in spite of initial language difficulties'. Dr Crees charged these boys only half fees with the governors' support. Their names were: A. Eisinger, G. Eisinger, H. F. Rothbaum, R. Kimilman, R. Meyer, L. Stogel and G. Berkman. The shadow of war was looming over the school again. Dr Crees's last act before he retired in 1940 was to close Langford House, where choristers had been boarded since 1920. He rented some rooms at 2 Castle Street to take the remaining boarders.

For the entire period of the Second World War, C. Fairfax-Scott, ex-headmaster of Monmouth, Brighton and Taunton, took over the thankless task of running the school. Staff replacements were impossible to find and his tone gets more and more exasperated. Of one teacher he wrote: 'Academically brilliant, very inexpensive but quite incompetent as a school master'. Many of the boys were in no state to learn much in any case; they were part of the dean's squad of fourteen cathedral fire-watchers, up all night. In 1944 the head reported to the governors: 'I have the honour to report that the school is still standing, though in places rather precariously!'[33] The strain was telling. Three of the staff died in the first three weeks of the Christmas term and Fairfax-Scott's wife's health collapsed. He retired in 1945, worn out by his exertions. This also led to the loss of the preparatory school. As he had pointed out, 'the school is my private property and owners of private schools are in dangerous waters these days'. He wanted to sell it to the school, but the governors could not afford it. It went to Robert Thomas, a housemaster from Bedford School. He had already become friends with Mr A. F. J. Hopewell, the new headmaster, who had been exiled to Bedford with Victoria College, Jersey, during the war; an amicable partnership therefore developed easily. The new headmaster, an OH, had already been a member of the staff for five terms when he was appointed.

The Education Act of 1944 set up 'Scheme A' for direct grant schools. To be accepted as an associated school, it was necessary either to abolish tuition fees or to 'grade them to an approved income scale which should provide for total remission if a parent's income requires it'. The LEA should have the right to reserve a number of places, for both day boys and boarders. The number should be settled between the governors and the local authority with reference to the Board of Education,

---

33. Ibid.

Fig. 164. The old deanery.

now to be upgraded to a ministry. The LEA would pay the fees for their pupils. The Ministry of Education would pay a direct grant for the remainder of the pupils. It was advantageous for the school to be part of the scheme, but without enhancing their boarding accommodation and facilities there was 'no hope of recognition'. The dean now made valiant efforts to get the church and the ministry to accept the old deanery as a boarding house: it would take forty-nine boys. It opened in 1945 and the ministry confirmed the direct grant in October (fig. 164).[34] They also finally agreed to apply the Philpott charity funds to build four new classrooms and an art room. These cost over £22,000, and were called the new block, situated at the back of the old deanery.[35] The governing body was now reformed to include not only the dean and chapter but also two representatives from the county council and one from the city council. Relationships were good with the LEA, not least because their members were frequently old boys. They had agreed to pay the fees in respect of free places for all residents in the county, to a maximum of ten, and

34. HCA, 7031/24, pp. 452–53, 456, chapter acts, 17 and 27 July 1945.
35. Hereford Cathedral School archives, Philpott Charity account book, 1894–1968; HCA, 7031/24, p. 497, chapter acts, 27 January 1948.

the headmaster was given precedence over the High School headmaster in choosing pupils: 'a very satisfactory arrangement'.[36]

In 1952 the biology laboratory was finally opened as a war memorial – until then the boys had had to travel to the high school for their lessons – but there was still no gymnasium. Inflation and salary rises were making the financial situation very difficult. More boys were staying on into the fifth and sixth forms than ever before. The foundation had sold securities to provide the new block, so no new entrance scholarships were awarded. When the inspectors demanded a laboratory assistant in 1954, the school paid sixth formers to do it. Mr Hopewell's health suddenly collapsed in 1956 and he had to resign. He had lost a lung while still a schoolboy, but his contribution to the school had been immense, as head boy in 1911, assistant master in 1944 and headmaster in the difficult post-war period. The reaction of the new headmaster, W. J. R. Peebles from Westminster, was: 'Good Staff and top boys of character, but the day boys are not integrated – the Old Block is appalling, and the fees are too low'. He reformed the timetable, revived speech day and began to extend the school facilities. To do this he organised an appeal to develop the old block and to create a new dining room. The Philpotts Foundation was also granted permission to sell 28 High Town to Boots the Chemists for £39,000, but this was selling the family silver and resources were getting dangerously low. In 1967 Peebles died in harness.

His successor, D. M. Richards, was faced by an increasing financial crisis and a strong challenge from the state sector. Hereford County Council had abolished the two local high schools and reorganised its secondary education into a sixth form college and four feeder comprehensive schools. They had no plans to integrate the cathedral school, so the governors resolved to go independent.[37] The headmaster organised a successful appeal to expand the science facilities, and started the junior boarding house in 1 Castle Street. He initiated a parent-teacher association, a day house system and a careers department. His most dramatic reform was the introduction of girls to the school, at first in the sixth form only in 1970, and in the first form from 1973.[38] In 1975 he was appointed headmaster of Portsmouth Grammar School, his place being taken by B. B. Sutton, a housemaster at Wycliffe College. He was immediately faced with the ending of the direct grant and the resultant loss of 'eleven plus' candidates. He therefore felt that his principal task was to raise the profile of the school. Parents had to feel that their children were getting something special from the school community. He was assisted by the dynamism of the new chairman of governors, a layman for the first time, Peter Prior. The girls' intake was extended until the numbers were evenly balanced.

36. Hereford Cathedral School archives, governors' minute book, 1945–81.

37. Ibid.

38. *Herefordian*, 216 (1970), p. 4; 219 (1973), p. 3.

Fig. 165. The interior of the extended Gilbert library, opened 1998.

The buildings were smartened up. A new school appeal was successfully launched to provide scholarships for those being phased out. More importantly, in 1979 the Zimmerman Trustees, administering the fund left by Arthur Ulrich Zimmerman OH, funded an enormous physical expansion of the school, starting with the purchase of 29 Castle Street. The numbers were also boosted by the sudden demise of Lucton School, which enabled the governors to purchase the preparatory school at last. Finally, assisted places were introduced by the new Conservative government in 1979, soon amounting to a third of the entry. In 1987, when Barry Sutton left to become headmaster of Taunton School, Somerset, Dr H. C. Tomlinson from Wellington College was appointed in his place.

The future, as so often in the school's history, is clouded. It has jettisoned many things on the way: fagging and flogging, mortar boards and the school song, boarding and with this the services contingent, those from abroad, OH's children and the South Wales entry. Assisted places have now ended, but the school is larger than it has ever been. Its physical expansion has recently been crowned by the purchase of the old telephone exchange, to be called the Zimmerman Building, thus recognising the Zimmerman Trust's invaluable contribution to the school over the years. The junior school is a flourishing feeder school. There is a Japanese faculty alongside that of classics. The choristers are funded more securely than ever before. *Floreat schola Herefordensis.*[39]

39. Much of the information for this chapter has been taken from the as yet unclassified Hereford Cathedral School archives. Many people, not least past and present pupils and staff of HCS, have assisted me in the preparation of this chapter, but in particular I would like to express my gratitude, for the help and encouragement I have received, to the librarian and archivist of Hereford Cathedral; to Mr R. Croot, Dr J. C. Eisel, Mrs J. Howard-Jones, Dr N. G. F. Scott-Moncrieff, Mr B. B. Sutton, Mr S. Williams and Dr H. C. Tomlinson. Above all I must acknowledge the invaluable assistance I have received from Alan Morris who unhesitatingly placed his indispensable research material at my disposal, without which this chapter could not have been completed.

St Ethelbert's Hospital, Hereford

David Whitehead

In about 1225, during the episcopacy of Hugh Foliot, Elias of Bristol, a canon of Hereford, founded 'a house for the poor' on land that he had recently purchased from Stephen son of Hugh. It was said to be 'next to the cemetery of St Ethelbert's', in other words adjoining the cathedral.[1] Elias was a career churchman, a clerk in the king's service, who had been granted special protection by Richard I in 1198.[2] Naturally, he dedicated the hospital to the memory of the king, his father Henry and his brother John. He owned considerable property in and around the city of Hereford, and some of this he transferred to the hospital but in many cases he simply dedicated a rent charge of a few shillings to his new foundation. The canons of the cathedral also benefited from Elias's generosity and from the beginning there appears to have been some confusion between the land of the hospital and that of the chapter.[3] Bishop Hugh, the archbishop of Canterbury and several other bishops offered indulgences to those who made gifts to the hospital. These added to its endowment and included a yearly delivery of six loads of beans from the abbey of St Augustine at Bristol. Since the foundation deed of the hospital was also signed by the prior of this institution, we can, perhaps, assume that Elias was well known in Bristol. The hospital was clearly welcomed by the citizens of Hereford, who dedicated a tithe of the tolls from their October fair for its support.[4]

The exact character of the institution founded by Elias is uncertain. The archbishop's grant of indulgence in 1226 refers to the 'building of a house for the

1. HCA, 2001, 898; Capes, *Charters*, pp. 57–58, 61–63.
2. HCA, 2256; Capes, *Charters*, pp. 35–36; K. Edwards, *The English Secular Cathedrals in the Middle Ages* (Manchester, 1949), pp. 33–39.
3. HCA, 781, 783, 980, 2001; B. G. Charles and H. D. Emanuel, 'Calendar of the Earlier Hereford Cathedral Muniments' (3 vols, HCA, typescript, 1955), i, fos 174–76; Capes, *Charters*, pp. 57–60.
4. HCA, 898, 998, 2024, 3218; Capes, *Charters*, pp. 56–57, 61–62; Charles and Emanuel, 'Calendar', iii, fol. 1183.

poor next to the church of St Ethelbert' and the building was certainly in existence in 1230 when Master Reginald is referred to as custos. Together with his three brothers (*confratres*) he agreed to receive and maintain three paupers recommended by his special friend Richard who had contributed 20 marks to be invested in land for the support of the three in perpetuity. The hospital was placed under the authority of the dean and chapter, and when in 1252 Bishop Peter of Aigueblanche fell out with them, they were accused of neglecting to provide daily food for one hundred paupers at the hospital. This seems to be an immense number of inmates which suggests, perhaps, that the custos was providing general relief for the poor of the city. Pope Innocent IV in 1250 referred to the 'great multitude of needy' in Hereford but we hear of no further occasion when St Ethelbert's provided such relief, although the tradition that the hospital had once had a more extensive brief for the poor survived until the sixteenth century.[5]

From its foundation, the hospital is traditionally thought to have occupied its present site in Castle Street.[6] While credence is given to this assumption by the several pieces of property that Elias gave to the chapter in this part of the city, the early documents are quite emphatic about the hospital's location next to the cathedral. A moment's reflection would suggest that the Castle Street site was an unlikely location in the thirteenth century when the royal castle was at its zenith and the present site was virtually beneath the great gate of the castle.[7] We have to wait until the early fifteenth century for direct confirmation that the hospital was located in the north-western corner of the Close, between Church Street and Broad Street (fig. 166). In 1406 the mayor of Hereford gave permission to the chapter and the custos, William Peion, to make a stone or wooden step 'in the street called Brodestrete to aid divine worship in the chapel of the almshouse so that a multitude of Christian people may flow there more easily'. The site is confirmed in the boundary clauses of a lease of 1428 that refers to the 'garden of the hospital' to the west of Church Street.[8] A century later, in 1515, Bishop Mayew is found carrying out ordinations in the 'chapel of the St Ethelbert's Almshouse'.[9] It is surprising, given the copious documentary references to the hospital, that there is no other mention of the chapel or its chaplain. However, a chapel was certainly to be expected. St Oswald's in Worcester, which shared an

5. HCA, 994, 1408; Capes, *Charters*, pp. 64, 97.

6. W. W. Capes, 'The Hospital of S. Ethelbert and the Treasurer of the Cathedral', *Some Notes on Old Hereford* (Hereford, *c.* 1910), pp. 5–7.

7. R. A. Brown, H. M. Colvin, A. J. Taylor, eds, *The History of the Kings Works, ii: The Middle Ages* (London, 1963), p. 674.

8. HCA, 2033; Charles and Emanuel, 'Calendar', iii, fol. 1148; A. T Bannister, ed., *The Register of Thomas Spofford, Bishop of Hereford, 1422–1448*, Cantilupe Society (Hereford, 1917), p. 112.

9. A. T. Bannister, ed., *The Register of Richard Mayew, Bishop of Hereford, 1504–1516*, Cantilupe Society (Hereford, 1919), p. 270.

Fig. 166. The north-west corner of the cathedral Close, the site of St Ethelbert's Hospital from 1225 to the mid sixteenth century, now occupied by the post office and the Roman Catholic church of St Francis Xavier.

analogous position to St Ethelbert's vis-à-vis the cathedral, certainly had one; in Hereford, St Giles's in St Owen Street, St John's in Widemarsh Street and probably the leper hospital of St Louis in Eign Street, all had chapels.

In 1520 we obtain further confirmation of the hospital's location and also learn something of its character when Bishop Booth claimed the right of visitation from the chapter of the hospital 'otherwise called the almeshalle by the churchyard of your cathedral church'.[10] The term 'almeshall' suggests that St Ethelbert's conformed to the usual medieval plan for hospital with a great hall – like St Katherine's at Ledbury and St Wulfstan's at Worcester – which combined the functions of a dormitory and refectory, with a chapel attached. At Wells in about 1535 the antiquarian John Leland noticed that at St Saviour's 'The Hospitall and Chapelle is builded al in length under one Roofe'.[11]

10. A. T. Bannister, ed., *The Register of Charles Bothe, Bishop of Hereford, 1516–1535*, Cantilupe Society (Hereford, 1921), pp. 77–79.

11. R. M. Clay, *The Medieval Hospitals of England* (London, 1909), pp. 120–21; J. Hillaby, *The Book of Ledbury* (Buckingham, 1982), pp. 61–62; L. Toulmin Smith, ed., *The Itinerary of John Leland* (5 vols, London, 1906–10, repr. 1964), i, p. 292.

The late fifteenth and early sixteenth centuries were difficult times for almshouses throughout England. Leland noticed many ruined hospitals, like St Michael's at Warwick, its 'buildings sore decayed'. Some suffered as a result of the Dissolution; others, like St Ethelbert's, found their property plundered by career churchmen in an age of diminishing patronage.[12] In 1525, on grounds of poverty, the office of treasurer of the cathedral, held by William Burghill, was combined with the mastership of the hospital.[13] The *Valor ecclesiasticus* shows that the income of St Ethelbert's was £10 1s. 10d. whilst the treasurer's income from lands at Breinton was £6 14s. 5d. Burghill also obtained a residence in place of his ancient house at Breinton which was described as *ruinam*, and now lived next door to the chancellor and archdeacon in Broad Street. The new arrangement was not necessarily disadvantageous to the hospital, as the treasurer had influence in the chapter.[14] In 1542 the treasurer and master, Nicholas Walwen, reserved a 'quarrell of stone upon Capler' – the chapter's quarry on the Wye – for the use of the almshall.[15]

The treasurer lived in some state next to the hospital and we obtain a glimpse of his property in a lease of 1586 whereby the master, Edward Cooper, transferred his 'mansion howse ... called the Allmeshall howse' to Griffyth Lewys, prebendary of Moreton Magna and dean of Gloucester. The almshall itself seems to have disappeared and instead we find an extensive range of buildings with all the features necessary for a genteel life – a great chamber, parlour, great hall 'wyth all chambers and easements' and a garden – all situated on the 'sayde hospitall scite', approached by a great gate from Broad Street. The cathedral school seems to have been here under the master's great chamber, described in 1596 as 'a stone howse ... sometyme a schoolhowse' but there is no sign of the hospital itself.[16]

It seems that the inmates of St Ethelbert's had been scattered and were now occupying single cottages. Some of these may have been in Castle Street on the site of the present almshouses, whilst others may still have been close to the old almshall in Broad Street. The 1583 statutes of the cathedral stated that the inmates of the hospital were to 'live ... in the houses within the city of Hereford belonging to the Hospital', which seems to imply that the community had been dispersed. Elsewhere in England at this date there was a move away from communal life throughout society, evidenced by the disappearance of the great hall in private dwellings. In Exeter the hospital inmates had accommodation called 'cells' as early as the fifteenth century.[17] Once the castle had been abandoned and the great gate

12. Clay, *Medieval Hospitals*, pp. 224–25.
13. Bannister, ed., *Reg. Bothe*, pp. 171–72.
14. J. Caley, ed., *Valor ecclesiasticus tempore Henrici VIII* (6 vols, London, 1810–24), iii, p. 8.

15. Charles and Emanuel, 'Calendar', fol. 1291.
16. HCA, 4494/1.
17. HCA, 7044/6, translation of 1583 statutes, p. 23; Clay, *Medieval Hospitals*, pp. 120–21.

was 'clene downe' – as Leland reported in 1536 – the hospital's property in Castle Street provided an ideal location for the inmates to regroup.[18] The custos, Owen Pole, had purchased an additional plot of land here in 1494, suggesting perhaps an early intention to move the hospital to this site.[19] However, the earliest reference to St Ethelbert's in Castle Street occurs incidentally in a lease of 1589 which records 'the gardens of the almeshouses' on its northern boundary. The grantor of the property is no less than Edward Cooper, who demanded from the lessee 'Twoe wayne loades of Tyle stones towards reparacons of the Almeshouses'. The change of terminology to 'almeshouses' is particularly telling, as is the need for reparations – clearly the houses were not purpose-built. Six years earlier Cooper had secured four oaks from the chapter's woods, also for the hospital.

Sometime in the mid sixteenth century – between 1542 and 1583 – St Ethelbert's hospital had therefore moved from Broad Street to Castle Street. It left the almshall to the treasurer and occupied a series of cottages beneath the castle ramparts. Edward Cooper, who was archdeacon as well as treasurer, and master of St Katherine's hospital at Ledbury where his chaplain said 'He useth the poore better than ever he knewe them used', clearly took St Ethelbert's under his wing and organised the new accommodation. In his will of 1595 he left 40s. to 'the ten poor people inhabiting within the hospital and almshouse of St Ethelbert in the city of Hereford', indicating that the inmates were living together again in the range of buildings marked on Speede's plan of 1610.[20]

Cooper's philanthropy may not have been entirely selfless, for not only did the move to Castle Street give him complete control over the master's house in Broad Street – which as we have seen he disposed of in 1586 – but also the Elizabethan statutes of 1583 placed the hospital for the first time in its history under a set of firm injunctions designed to secure it in the future from rapacious masters.

The statutes insisted that the master should be a resident canon. His income was to be derived from the fines payable on the renewal of leases. He was to keep good accounts on parchment of all transactions involving the hospital's property and was bound by a religious oath to promote the welfare of the institution. There was an acknowledgement that the possessions of the hospital had recently been let out at low rents and the master, aided by the dean, was enjoined to get these annulled and replaced with more economic rents and regular leases of twenty-two years. To enhance the income of the hospital the statutes transferred certain charges and fines to the community; for instance, instead of subscribing to a fund for feast days, the post-Reformation canon was encouraged to contribute £5 to the poor

18. Smith, ed., *Leland*, i, p. 65.
19. HCA, 2022; Charles and Emanuel, 'Calendar', iii, fos 1258–59.

20. HCA, 4491; A. J. Winnington-Ingram, 'Edward Cooper or Cowper 1528–96', *TWNFC*, 32 (1948), pp. xcv–ciii.

of the hospital. Similarly, the fine of £2 levied on a canon absent from his duties was also to be directed towards the hospital.[21]

The dean was ordered to visit the hospital every year and several mandates dating from 1585 to 1604 suggest that this occurred. Four of these documents are endorsed with the names of the inmates: five men and four women in 1588; four men and six women in 1588–89; and two men and eight women in 1590.[22] It is interesting that women already outnumbered men at this early date; and, although men were never officially excluded, by the eighteenth century St Ethelbert's was almost exclusively devoted to the relief of poor women. The inmates were chosen by the dean and the master and had to be of 'venerable age and agreeable manners', and to 'conduct themselves well'. The statutes state that, 'Not withstanding the present shortage of means', the inmates were to receive a loaf of bread 'free of bran and well baked' weighing half a pound every day. This was supplied from the canons' bakery at a cost of £6 10s. 0d. per year. On Sunday a penny was given with the bread, but if an inmate failed to attend daily morning and evening prayers at the cathedral the penny and bread were withheld. The ordinances were repeated almost word for word in the Laudian statutes of 1636.[23]

Although most of the hospital's property seems to have disappeared during the late middle ages, further predations were made during the Civil War. The original site of the almshall in Broad Street was nearly lost when it was sold as dean and chapter property. The master, Richard Delamaine, wrote a long memorandum in 1654 claiming that it should not have been sold, since it belonged to the hospital and not to the dean and chapter, but in 1656 it was in the possession of the notorious parliamentary commissioner, Silas Taylor. After the Restoration the property was recovered and was still referred to as the 'site of the hospital' in a lease of 1725.[24] In 1663 the chapter act book refers to a tenant who 'confesses' he held property from the chapter but 'knows not if it belongs to the hospital'.[25]

The history of the hospital during the eighteenth century was uneventful. The dean and chapter seem to have been reasonably vigilant on the inmates' behalf. After a visitation in 1769, for instance, they pursued the retiring master, Thomas Breton, to Northampton, accusing him of leaving the hospital in a 'dilapidated state'. Several craftsmen were subsequently employed to survey the fabric and carry out basic repairs, and a bill for £29 14s. 10d. was sent to Breton.[26] A book of leases and miscellaneous matters provides some indication of the management of the hospital in the late eighteenth and early nineteenth centuries. In 1805 the

21. HCA, 7044/6, pp. 23–25.
22. HCA, 2031, visitation documents.
23. HCA, 7044/6, p. 23; Jebb and Phillott, *The Statutes of the Cathedral Church of Hereford*, pp. 136–39.

24. HCA, 6442/2, 4494/13. See above, pp. 106–7.
25. HCA, 7031/3, pp. 224–25, chapter acts, 22 September 1663.
26. HCA, 5257.

Fig. 167. The Castle Street façade of the new St Ethelbert's Hospital designed by Robert Jones in 1805.

hospital's property included seventy-six acres of land in the manor of Winaston at Blackmarstone in the suburbs of Hereford; fifty acres at Pipe and Holmer; a small-holding at Clehonger and some miscellaneous properties in Hereford. The total income per annum from these was £29 3s. 8d. Since 1783 the lands had gradually been mapped and surveyed, each tenant being required to produce a 'perfect terrier'. In 1783 and 1798 a subscription had been raised to supply the inmates of the hospital with coal. This raised £350, which Dean Wetherell invested in consolidated annuities. By this means, the ten inhabitants of the almshouses received weekly pay of 3s. 6d. with an extra shilling for the twenty-six weeks beginning the first Friday in October to pay for extra coal. In addition another shilling was provided on Christmas Day for a dinner.[27]

The almshouses were completely rebuilt in 1805 following a visitation by the dean who found them in a 'ruinous state' (fig. 167). The project was financed by gifts from Miss Evans, the executrix of the late master, Joseph Guest, whilst the chapter generously financed any shortfall and provided timber and stone from its estates. Two small houses, part of the hospital's property in Little Castle Street, were also sold. A plan for the new almshouses was provided by Robert Jones, a respected mason and architect of the city, whilst Dr Morgan, the new

27. HCA, 6442/1.

master, acted as clerk of works. During the summer of 1805 ten masons were at work upon the main structure, built of stone from a quarry at Holmer. Some decayed stone was also brought from the chapter house and those pieces with medieval sculpture and mouldings were used to give the building an antique quality that has misled some recent commentators. Paving stone and roof tiles came from St Margarets in west Herefordshire. In September 1805 the craftsmen were treated to a supper at the Catherine Wheel in High Town where Dr Morgan paid the bill of £1 15s. 9d. The seal of St Ethelbert's Hospital, carved in Painswick stone by a local marble mason, Thomas Wood, was set up over the door of the hospital; a well was dug in the garden and a Royal George peach from the Kings Acre Nursery was planted to be trained along the south wall of the building. The new houses were aired and, during a cold spell in January 1806, the inmates were moved in from their temporary accommodation. The total cost of rebuilding was £665 3s. 2d., which provided ten dwellings, each with an upper and lower room with individual entrances at the rear.[28] Contemporaries agreed that the end result was 'a remarkably neat and substantial stone building', 'very appropriate and pleasing'. Indeed, the Gothic style of the building, with its authentic medieval fragments, added another picturesque incident to Castle Green, which was a favourite resort for the citizens of Hereford during this era (fig. 168).[29]

During the early nineteenth century the hospital's income was considerably increased by several legacies, of which the most important was the £500 from Miss Monnington in 1811. It also became the tradition for the master to leave a legacy on retiring: Dr Cope left £200 in 1822, William Russell £433 in 1831 and Dr Clutton £133 in 1834.[30] In the 1830s the Charity Commissioners were delighted with the hospital: 'The whole establishment has an air of cheerfulness and cleanliness which clearly shows that a proper and judicious superintendence has been exercised by those who have the management of its affairs'. It would seem there were no Trollopean skeletons in St Ethelbert's cupboard. The commissioners noticed, however, that the income of the master had increased considerably with the rise in the value of entry fines, so that in 1833 he received £84 10s. 0d. from a new lease of the lands in Holmer parish. Nevertheless, the commissioners recognised that the master was responsible for repairing dilapidations to the almshouses, and this they regarded as a 'considerable liability'.

28. HCA, 7031/17, pp. 142–43, 145, chapter acts, 10 November 1804, 8 January 1805; HCA, 5704, accounts and papers relating to the rebuilding of St Ethelbert's Hospital. For full details see D. Whitehead, 'St Ethelbert's Hospital, Hereford: Its Architecture and Setting', *TWNFC*, 45 (1986), pp. 415–25.

29. *Reports of the Commissioners Appointed in Pursuance of Acts of Parliament to Inquire Concerning Charities and Education of the Poor in England and Wales, Arranged in Counties*, xiii, *Hereford* (London, 1815–39), part 2: 'City of Hereford', p. 7; *The Hereford Guide* (2nd edn, Hereford, 1808), p. 115.

30. HCA, 6442/1; *Reports of the Commissioners Concerning Charities*, xiii, pt 2, p. 8.

Fig. 168. The garden front of the new St Ethelbert's Hospital with the River Wye in the foreground, showing the medieval fragments brought from the old chapter house and set between the upper windows.

The charity continued to prosper and excess income was invested in consols. When the Newport, Abergavenny and Hereford Railway was constructed in the early 1850s, an unspecified sum was raised from the sale of land on the approaches to Hereford. The charity was also able to make a loan of £366, secured by a mortgage, to a local banker, John Holder Matthews of Clehonger, which was retrieved in 1849. The chapter appears to have been a generous with the hospital's assets: when Daniel Davies rebuilt the Mitre Hotel in Broad Street in 1834, his rent was frozen for twenty-four years.[31]

In 1876 an inspector of charities, Mr Hare, made a visit to the cathedral and urged the dean and chapter to draw up a new scheme of management for the almshouse. The large fines being pocketed by the master troubled him and he suggested that this practice be terminated, leaving the chapter to decide upon the details of the new management scheme. This was formally recorded in the register book on 7 July 1876. The renewal of leases for almshouse property was no longer to be conditional on a fine but instead a 'full rack rent' was required. The master, Archdeacon Lord Saye and Sele, gave up his lucrative emoluments for a £50

31. HCA, 7031/20, pp. 442, 168, chapter acts, 30 September 1858, 24 March 1849; HCA, 7031/18, pp. 451–52, 18 October 1834.

stipend per annum but was to be allowed the £545 expected from fines in 1876 and a similar, and final, amount in 1883. He also gave up his traditional right to thirty bushels of wheat per annum from the Almshall estate at Holmer and his dividends from certain 3 per cent annuities. In return, he was no longer held responsible for the repairs and dilapidations of the almshouses in Castle Street. It was anticipated that the scheme would probably generate a surplus and this was to be divided among the 'almsfolk' until their weekly wage reached 10s. The mastership of the hospital was no longer tied to the office of treasurer; henceforward it was usually held by the dean.[32]

The new arrangement quickly ran into trouble. In 1880 the charity required £700 to buy the freehold property, which had become attached to three houses rebuilt in St Ethelbert Street in about 1800 and without which they were untenable. It was proposed to raise the money by selling consols. In 1882 the charity went into debt and sold further consols to cover the deficit of £133. Further deficits followed in subsequent years and, in 1883, to fulfil their commitment to the master, the dean and chapter had to find £545. In May 1889 the Charity Commissioners were consulted again. In a long letter, the chapter outlined the problem. The freehold had still not been purchased for the St Ethelbert Street properties, the almshouses needed repair and the inmates complained about the lack of headroom in the bedchambers, so the roof was to be raised. The chapter proposed a massive increase in the rents for the hospital properties. For two messuages in Clehonger, for example, the rent of £12 per annum was to be raised to £80. Clearly, although the fines had been abandoned, the chapter had been dilatory about raising the rents. The increases were expected to raise an extra £479 per annum, which, it was anticipated, would pay off the deficit, secure the St Ethelbert Street houses and provide £450–500 for the new roof. The commissioners appear to have agreed with the proposal, although they thought the building work should be deferred until the money was in hand – notwithstanding their earnest desire to secure better sleeping accommodation for the inmates. After this, the financial problems of the charity seemed to have been solved. With the guidance of the commissioners the charity raised £651 from the sale of some of its investments in 1898. The chapter tenaciously defended the charity's properties, albeit during the problem years of the 1880s some lessees tried to capitalise on the charity's misfortune by making tempting offers for the outright purchase of their properties.[33]

During the nineteenth century there is little information about the inmates of the almshouses. Their names occur occasionally in the act books: for instance Anne

---

32. HCA, 7031/22, p. 184, chapter acts, 4 July 1876; HCA, 7005/11, pp. 22–23.

33. HCA, 7031/22, pp. 317, 407, 422, chapter acts, 6 August 1880, 21 December 1882, 18 October 1883; HCA, 7031/23, pp. 82–84, 305, chapter acts, 25 May 1889, 24 March 1898.

Harris, a widow and late nurse at the infirmary, was appointed to a vacancy in 1865. Nor is there much information about the fabric of the hospital. We are left to assume that the roof was eventually raised in the 1890s. The dean and chapter's visitation is occasionally mentioned but only to record formally the approval of their good and regular management. They were simply patting themselves on the back.[34]

In the early twentieth century the details of management become much clearer, as more is recorded in the act books. There are no longer any references to deficits and in 1934 £2000 was borrowed from the charity for the fabric fund at 3 per cent interest. By 1942 the loan had risen to £3500, at which point the commissioners stepped in and asked that it be repaid. In 1953 there was a suggestion by the commissioners that the St Katherine's and St Ethelbert's charities should be amalgamated. In 1963 the management of St Ethelbert's was again regulated by the commissioners, this time according to 'normal modern almshouse clauses'. With the expansion of Hereford, the commissioners found it difficult to resist the encroachments of Hereford City Council which, armed with compulsory purchase orders, forced the charity to sell property in St Martin's parish for new housing.[35]

The commissioners also looked after the interests of the inmates. The censor, who looked after the almshouses on behalf of the master, received a salary increase in 1927 from £6 10s. 0d. to £13. Two years earlier the stipend of the inmates had been raised to 17s. 6d. In 1932 the dean submitted a plan for a veranda, which was approved by the commissioners. In 1955 there was a request for bathrooms and modern sanitation, but because the council was reluctant to make an improvement grant, only two bathrooms were eventually built in the following year. Hot water was even more problematic. It was first mooted in February 1964 but the decision to install a central gas boiler 'thermostatically controlled' was deferred until March 1965. The building was comprehensively restored and modernised in 1985.[36]

34. HCA, 7031/21, p. 205, chapter acts, 8 April 1865; HCA, 7031/20, p. 206, chapter acts, 14 November 1850.
35. HCA, 7031/24, pp. 312, 429, chapter acts, 13 February 1934, 9 December 1942; HCA, 7031/25, pp. 96, 119, 357–58, 173, 270, chapter acts, 7 December 1951, 24 February 1953, 29 October 1963, 22 June 1956, 31 May 1960.
36. HCA, 7031/24, pp. 195, 158, 279, chapter acts, 10 November 1927, 30 July 1925, 23 February 1932; HCA, 7031/25, pp. 153–54, 176, 362, 386, chapter acts, 31 May 1955, 25 September 1956, 11 February 1964, 2 March 1965.

St Katherine's Hospital, Ledbury

Joe Hillaby

In 1233 Bishop Foliot entrusted to the dean and chapter of his cathedral the government of the hospital of St Katherine which he had founded at Ledbury. This trust they still exercise. The history of St Katherine's throws a sharp light on periods of crisis for dean and chapter. Long-standing administrative difficulties and problems arising from the Black Death were resolved in 1398 by John Prophete, the greatest of the medieval deans. In 1581, after a legal battle of almost twenty years, dean and chapter successfully resisted the crown's attempt to break its 350-year-old trust. A similarly lengthy legal battle led in 1819 to a revised constitution and the almshouses we see today. In 1962 the Charity Commissioners provided the fourth and final scheme of reform restoring the original jurisdiction, in Foliot's words 'without contradiction of any man'. St Katherine's story is a microcosm of that of dean and chapter over almost eight centuries.

The ideals and thus organisation, architecture and nomenclature of the early English medieval hospital were monastic in origin.[1] Expression of charity as the greatest of the theological virtues was not limited to the monastic orders. It was incumbent on all, especially the bishop as shepherd of his flock, to be, in the words of Job, 'the father of the poor, eyes to the blind, feet to the lame'. At Ledbury, as in each of his manor houses, that saintly bishop of Hereford, the Augustinian Robert de Béthune, provided 'not only a daily ration but the requisite clothes and shoes throughout the year' for a number of paupers. Bishop Hugh

---

1. J. C. Dickinson, *The Origins of the Austin Canons and their Introduction into England* (London, 1950), p. 145; N. Orme and M. Webster, *The English Hospital, 1070–1570* (New Haven, 1995), pp. 69–75; A. T. Bannister, ed., *The Register of Charles Bothe, Bishop of Hereford, 1516–1535*, Cantilupe Society (Hereford, 1921), pp. 185–87; R. W. Eyton, *Antiquities of Shropshire* (12 vols, London, 1854–60), v, pp. 296–99; J. H. Parry, ed., *The Register of John Gilbert, Bishop of Hereford, AD 1375–1379*, Cantilupe Society (Hereford, 1913), pp. 65–66; M. Faraday, *Ludlow, 1085–1660: A Social, Economic and Political History* (Chichester, 1991), pp. 64–69.

Foliot's foundation represents the flowering of an institution already more than a century old. His choice of Ledbury is probably explained by Bishop Gilbert Foliot's belief that here their see had been founded.[2]

Foliot describes the purpose, government and endowments of St Katherine's in two charters. The first, confirmed by Dean Thomas of Bosbury and the chapter in about 1231, declares that he built the hospital dedicated to God and the blessed Katherine for 'the support of wayfarers or pilgrims and the poor', a formula more appropriate to a large institution on a major route. The second, of March 1233, conferring government on dean and chapter, is thus amended to the 'poor and weak lying therein'. Subsequent endowments which specify 'the poor and needy', only occasionally 'the poor and infirm', underline the role of St Katherine's as, in modern parlance, an almshouse not a hospital.[3] Like other medieval hospitals it sought to provide the poor and infirm with 'rest, warmth, cleanliness and an adequate diet'. The use of herbs and blood-letting were common practice but, even if thought appropriate, few hospitals could afford the skills of a professional physician. St Katherine's was dedicated to the salvation of souls, not bodies.[4]

Foundation was not merely an act of charity; the chapel was to be a chantry for the salvation of Foliot's soul. As incentive for its future good government, he provided that prayers be said not only for his predecessors and successors but also for the canons of Hereford; thus a trental, a daily mass for a month, was to be sung on the death of each canon. If, as he hoped, the hospital would in time support two chaplains, the second was to pray for the souls of the living and all benefactors: an incentive for local endowments. Inmates, of whom few if any were

2. H. Wharton, *Anglia sacra* (2 vols, London, 1691), ii, pp. 310–11; J. Hillaby, 'The Saint that Never Slept: Robert de Béthune, Bishop of Hereford 1131–48', *FHC*, 46 (1980), pp. 21–42; idem, 'Presidential Address: The Boroughs of the Bishops of Hereford in the Late Thirteenth Century', *TWNFC*, 40 (1970–72), pp. 10–35. For contemporary views on charity see M. Rubin, *Charity and Community in Medieval Cambridge* (Cambridge, 1987), pp. 58–70; B. Tierney, 'The Decretists and the "Deserving Poor"', *Comparative Studies in Society and History*, 1 (1958–59), pp. 360–73. C. N. L. Brooke, 'The Diocese of Hereford, 676–1200', *TWNFC*, 48 (1994–96), pp. 23–36.

3. HCA, 2175, 1389; *EEA*, vii, pp. 271–72, 278–80, nos 342, 348; Capes, *Charters*, pp. 68–71. The death of Dean Thomas of Bosbury, 29 Sept 1231, provides a *terminus ad quem* for the foundation charter, *EEA*, vii, pp. 304–5. HCA, 3701 (B133) has *ad opus infirmorum* (documents numbered in A. T. Bannister, 'A Descriptive Catalogue of Manuscripts Dealing with St Katherine's, Ledbury', *TWNFC*, 24 (1922–24), pp. 231–53, are given in brackets after the HCA no. with prefix B).

4. M. Carlin, 'Medieval English Hospitals', in L. Granshaw and R. Porter, eds, *The Hospital in History* (London, 1989), p. 31; R. Gilchrist, *Contemplation and Action: The Other Monasticism* (Leicester, 1995), pp. 32–38.

literate, were to participate in these intercessory prayers by recitation of the Paternoster, Ave Maria and possibly the Creed, later often the full Rosary.[5]

Foliot's aspiration was fulfilled before his death in 1234. William of Ockeridge assigned certain tenements 'for the maintenance of an honest and young chaplain' to celebrate mass for his own soul and that of his wife on Sundays forever, a deed inspected by Hugh and witnessed by his brother, Thomas, the cathedral treasurer.[6] Other benefactors were drawn by the religious life of the *familia* and the benefits it would bestow rather than the relief of the poor. A further chaplaincy was founded in 1364 and the chantry continued to attract endowments. As late as 1407 Margery Wynde granted fourteen acres of wood at Tyrells Frith, Little Marcle, for the maintenance of the master and 'certain chaplains to celebrate divine service daily ... according to the primeval foundation', only secondly for 'the support of certain poor persons'.[7]

Foliot was not alone in this enterprise; lay endowment played a major part in medieval hospitals.[8] As he sought ecclesiastical guarantors – the dean and chapter – so also he sought lay support. Walter II de Lacy was the greatest of the barons of the southern march. From strongholds at Ludlow, Weobley, Castle Frome and Ewyas Lacy his family had played a crucial role in local politics since 1075. De Lacy's political, as much as his material, support was an essential element for Foliot in the success of his enterprise. No layman could, apparently, provide firmer guarantees – as well as important endowments.[9]

Walter granted the churches, the advowsons and tithes, of Weston Beggard and Yarkhill and persuaded his tenant, Geoffrey de Longchamp of Wilton, to give Kempley church – adorned with frescoes of *c.* 1150 'as magnificent in conception as the Cluniac paintings of central France'.[10] In 1291 their annual value was £4,

5. R. M. Clay, *The Mediaeval Hospitals of England* (London, 1909), pp. 158–62; Orme and Webster, *The English Hospital*, pp. 50–53. For the role of charity see R. N. Swanson, *Religion and Devotion in Europe, c. 1215 – c. 1515* (Cambridge, 1995), pp. 206–12.

6. HCA, 7018/5/3, pp. 32–33. For Thomas Foliot see *EEA*, vii, pp. xlix, 269–71, 284–85, 289–90, 296–97, 306, nos 341, 355, 360, 367.

7. See below, p. 618 and n. 29. J. M. Kaye, ed., *The Cartulary of God's House, Southampton*, Southampton Record Series, 19, 20 (2 vols, Southampton, 1976), i, pp. xxxiii–iv; HCA, 1888, 3665, 3735 (B85).

8. Granshaw and Porter, eds, *The Hospital in History*, p. 4.

9. For Walter II de Lacy see J. Hillaby, 'Hereford Gold, Part 2: The Clients of the Jewish Community at Hereford, 1179–1253: Four Case Studies', *TWNFC*, 45 (1985–87), pp. 195–239; idem, 'Colonisation, Crisis-Management and Debt: Walter de Lacy and the Lordship of Meath, 1189–1241', *Ríocht na Midhe*, 8, part 4 (1992–93), pp. 1–50. For de Lacy manors in the Frome valley see W. E. Wightman, *The Lacy Family in England and Normandy, 1066–1194* (Oxford, 1966), pp. 118–19.

10. For Longchamp see W. St Clair Baddeley, 'The History of Kempley Manor and Church, Gloucestershire', *Bristol and*

£5 6s. 8d. and £8 respectively. Additionally each was to provide a yearly pension of one pound of incense. Robert, 'dean and rector' of Kempley, who demurred, had in 1234 to appear at the hospital and swear on the gospels in front of the assembled notables, lay and ecclesiastic, that, without deceit or fraud, he would pay the pension annually on the feast of St Ethelbert. Walter de Lacy also gave the manor of Yarkhill. For this he had granted Simon de Clifford annual rents of £30, half in Holme Lacy and half in Meath. His endowment thus totalled almost £40. In the eighteenth century the tithes of Weston and Yarkhill represented a third of St Katherine's rental, excluding fines. The lands at Weston were the last to be sold, in our own day.[11]

Foliot conferred the trusteeship of the hospital on the dean and chapter, to 'keep, maintain and defend its rights and possessions ... to dispose of according to their own will forever and without the contradiction of any man'. A duty of annual inspection is implied by the grant of a yearly fee of 40s. They were to nominate chaplains and brethren and ensure that the chapel's goods and possessions were used only for the benefit of those ministering there. As the charter made no reference to the appointment of the master, this responsibility they assumed. A licence for the celebration of divine service was granted by Hugh's brother, Thomas, and Philip de Braose, as 'rectors' (portionists) of Ledbury.[12]

In practice government lay with master and brethren who were, effectively, a corporation sole. To them were conveyed land and rents and it was they who purchased, leased and exchanged lands. Thus many leases are with the 'unanimous consent' or 'the consent' of the brethren, on occasions joined by the sisters who by 1239, if not at foundation, were members of the *familia*. Two extant thirteenth-century seals, depicting the west front of a major church with St Katherine seated and Bishop Hugh in supplication below, are the formal expressions of this corporate legal identity (fig. 169). The brethren were often allocated specific responsibilities such as the brewhouse or the bakehouse, the larder or the garden, as at Ospringe where they were 'obedientiaries' or 'custodians', whilst the sisters had a nursing

Gloucestershire Archaeological Society Transactions, 36 (1913), pp. 130–49. For the Kempley frescoes see E. W. Tristram, *English Medieval Wall Painting: The Twelfth Century* (London, 1944), pp. 42–44, 134–36.

11. T. Astle, S. Ayscough and J. Caley, eds, *Taxatio ecclesiastica Angliae et Walliae auctoritate P. Nicholai IV, circa AD 1291* (London, 1802), pp. 158, 160–61; HCA, 7018/5/1, p. 50, 3697 (B168); *EEA*, vii, pp. 278–80, no. 348; Capes, *Charters*, pp. 68–70; HCA, 483, 7018/10, rent rolls, 1729, 1762. The demesne tithes of the Lacy manors of Weston and Kempley already belonged to St Guthlac's, Hereford, *EEA*, vii, pp. 23, 149–51, 197–99, nos 22, 204, 260.

12. HCA, 3696 (B105).

Fig. 169. Seal impression of St Katherine's Hospital, Ledbury, thirteenth century. (HCA, 1167; HCL, neg. 1038.)

and domestic role. Early rules show the sexes kept firmly apart, except at work and prayer.[13]

A picture of the hospital, its farm buildings and estates is provided principally by an inventory of 1316.[14] The heart of the institution was the infirmary hall with its eastern chapel. Through a large arch at the eastern end the bedridden had a clear view into the chapel with its altar and lights, enabling participation in all services.[15] Evidence of Foliot's original building can still be seen; the two remaining eastern lancets and one northern lancet are of this period. Books listed in the inventory include various antiphonaries, missals and psalters, an ordinal, a legendary in two volumes and a martyrology with 'the Rule of the House'. The

13. HCA, 1899, 7018/5/3, pp. 91–92, 140, 147, 153, 160; F. C. and P. E. Morgan, *A Concise List of Seals Belonging to the Dean and Chapter of Hereford Cathedral* (Hereford, 1966), p. 6; HCA, 1791, 3730, 7018/5/1, p. 26, and 1841 for the years 1239, 1286, 1423 and 1502 respectively. For brethren and sisters see C. Thomas, B. Sloane and C. Phillpotts, *Excavations at the Priory and Hospital of St Mary Spital, London* (London, 1997), pp. 36–37, 43–44, 52–53, 71–73, 79, 83–84; G. H. Smith, 'The Excavations of the Hospital of St Mary of Ospringe Commonly Called Maison Dieu', *Archaeologia Cantiana*, 95 (1979), pp. 88–89; Clay, *Mediaeval Hospitals*, pp. 145–47, 152–56; Orme and Webster, *The English Hospital*, pp. 80–83. For sisters and women and medicine in medieval society see C. Rawcliffe, *Medicine and Society in Later Medieval England* (Stroud, 1995), pp. 204–13; for St Mary Magdalene, Dudston, see statutes 2 and 23

in E. J. Kealey, *Medieval Medicus: A Social History of Anglo-Norman Medicine* (Baltimore and London, 1981), pp. 108–9, 200–1.

14. HCA, 1658a. The 1316 Ledbury inventory should be compared with St Bartholomew's, Bristol, of 1303, Gloucestershire County Record Office, D340a/T143, printed in R. Price and M. Ponsford, *St Bartholomew's Hospital, Bristol: The Excavations of a Medieval Hospital, 1976–8* (York, 1998), pp. 58–59, and that of the rooms, buildings, lands and tenements of St Mary of Ospringe in 1561, in Smith, 'The Excavations of the Hospital of St Mary of Ospringe', pp. 90–91.

15. For the infirmary-hall plan and the subsequent architectural development of the English hospital and almshouse see W. H. Godfrey, *The English Almshouse* (London, 1955), pp. 20–26ff; E. Prescott, *The English Medieval Hospital, c. 1050–1640* (London, 1992), pp. 5–22ff; Clay, *Mediaeval*

statues of the Blessed Virgin and St Katherine are referred to in a number of deeds. Thus Adam de Strete granted an annual rent of 1*d.* and 5*d.* respectively to keep candles burning before them. As late as 1508–9 Cradley lordship still provided a one-pound wax candle annually to burn before the image of St Katherine, to comfort the inmates through the long nights.[16]

The inventory also provides a valuable glimpse of communal life. In the dormitory were 'a bed for the master and five of the brethren'. One large and two small chests contained a double set of clothing for each, a uniform with a white cross on the breast. In the washhouse the large trough was divided into two sections, one for the brethren and the other for the 'community', underscoring the division between *familia* and *hospitalis*. The hall had four trestle tables, with two long and three short benches.[17]

Hospital and estate buildings were enclosed within a precinct, some 300 by 330 feet, an area today marked out by the car park. Access was through the Great Gate immediately north of the chapel. Later plots were developed along its two street fronts: Bishop (Bye) Street and Middletown (High Street), between the chapel and the Booth Hall, or Hundred House, to its south. Fresh water was ducted from Coneygree Wood in the Bishop's Park, for the parish register records in 1592 that 'whole[some] water was conveyed in new [renewed] lead from the Coninger unto the High Crosse and there to the Hospital gate or conduit there'. The latrines must have flushed either into the stockyard or into the stream flowing down Bye Street as a kennel.[18] Some hospitals had their own burial grounds but

Hospitals, pp. 112–25, and Orme and Webster, *The English Hospital*, pp. 85–92. For *familia* and *hospitalis* see Kaye, ed., *The Cartulary of God's House*, i, pp. xxxii–iii.

16. For inventories of books at God's House in 1362 and 1414–15 see Kaye, ed., *The Cartulary of God's House*, i, pp. xci–xcii; *A Descriptive Catalogue of Ancient Deeds in the Public Record Office* (6 vols, London, 1890–1915), iii, D801, p. 499.

17. HCA, 1658a.

18. HCA, 7018/8, pp. 479–83, register 'B'; HCA, 3692. For hospital precincts, water supply and drains see C. J. Bond, 'Water Management in the Urban Monastery', in R. Gilchrist and H. C. Mytum, eds, *Advances in Monastic Archaeology*, British Archaeological Reports, British Series, 227 (Oxford, 1993), pp. 43–78; R. Gilchrist, 'Christian Bodies and Souls: Archaeology

of Life and Death in Later Medieval Hospitals', in S. Bassett, ed., *Death in Towns* (Leicester, 1993), pp. 101–18; Smith, 'The Excavations of the Hospital of St Mary of Ospringe', pp. 83, 86–87, figs 2 and 3; Thomas, Sloane and Phillpotts, *Excavations at St Mary Spital*, pp. 18–19, 45–46, 50–51, 54, 63, 94, 98–100; Price and Ponsford, *St Bartholomew's Hospital, Bristol*, pp. 84, 108, 110, 125, 222–23; B. Durham, 'The Infirmary and Hall of the Medieval Hospital of St John the Baptist at Oxford', *Oxoniensia*, 56 (1991), pp. 29–34, 66–70. For water supply, etc., at Ledbury see HRO, G 2, J. Lydiard's 'Plan of Ledbury' (1788); HRO, AR 42/1, Ledbury Tithe Map, 1841; HRO, Q/R1/25, Ledbury Enclosure Act, 1813; HRO, K 13/17, Ledbury Improvement Trustees, 'Letter to Subscribers' (November 1820).

there is no evidence of one at St Katherine's. Indeed, the earliest Ledbury parish register records the burial in St Peter's churchyard of 'Thomas Kylynge, priest of the Hospital', in 1558 and 'Gryffyn Foular sometime Chauntry Priest and after Priest of the Hospital' in 1559.[19]

The range of the hospital's estates is indicated by the inventory. Seven boxes and a chest in the sacristy contained 'deeds and writings' for tenements: in Ledbury borough and foreign sixty-eight; Eastnor and Wellington (Heath) thirty; Ockeridge, Massington and Colwall twenty-four; Siddington twenty-three; Donnington twenty; Weston Beggard, Yarkhill, the Hyde and Berrow seventeen; and Kempley eight.[20] The inventory also details income and land use on the demesne (excluding woodland), with the lowland Herefordshire three-season rotation in the open fields of two crops and a fallow, as at Leominster priory.[21]

Hospital deeds, largely undated, show the process of property acquisition. Not all endowments were of land or rents.[22] The *Red Book*, a survey of the episcopal estates, enables us to assess precisely the growth of St Katherine's urban holding about 1288. Foliot's endowment had been one burgage in New Street, one and a half burgages bought from John fitz Gersant and half a burgage from Margaret Frounceys. Now six further burgages were added with four *selde*, market stalls or booths, two curtilages in New Street and a vacant place. Rural property, however, always played the dominant part in the house's finances.[23]

The combination of institutional wealth and virtual corporate independence was not a happy one. Supervision by dean and chapter often appears to have been at best ineffective. The first evidence of maladministration comes in 1322, only six years after the detailed inventory of the hospital's assets had been drawn up, during the mastership of Brother Philip. Pope John XXII appointed the abbot of Wigmore to enquire into the culpable mismanagement of the hospital by master and brethren, in particular the granting of long leases at low rents. Although the leases indicate, pointedly, the brothers' and sisters' 'unanimous consent', they were probably under

---

19. For cemeteries and burial see Thomas, Sloane and Phillpotts, *Excavations at St Mary Spital*, pp. 115–24; Price and Ponsford, *St Bartholomew's Hospital, Bristol*, pp. 81, 107–8, 119, figs 35–37; Smith, 'The Excavations of the Hospital of St Mary of Ospringe', pp. 81, 91, and fig. 2; Clay, *Mediaeval Hospitals*, pp. 199–200; Orme and Webster, *The English Hospital*, p. 106, pl. 16; G. H. Piper and C. H. Mayo, eds, *The Registers of Ledbury*, i, *Baptisms, Marriages and Burials, 1556–1576* (London, 1899), pp. 113, 118. The dedication of Ledbury parish church was changed from St Peter's

to St Michael and All Angels in the mid nineteenth century.

20. HCA, 1658a.

21. J. Price, *An Historical and Topographical Account of Leominster* (Ludlow, 1795), pp. 150–79; J. Hillaby, 'Early Christian and Pre-Conquest Leominster', *TWNFC*, 45 (1985–87), pp. 594–98 discusses the demesne of the four Leominster priory herneys.

22. HCA, 1744. Exchanges include HCA, 3268, 3702, 3703 (B23, 150, 164); HCA, 3695 (B123); HCA, 3666 (B110).

23. HRO, HE/1/133677.

constraint. In 1328 Brother Philip was still in office.[24] The granting in 1330 of a forty-day indulgence to all donating to the hospital or attending masses or offices on certain days suggests a revival – but not for long.

The Black Death swept Herefordshire in 1349. Its impact is glaring in Trillek's register – institutions rose from six a year to 159. At Ledbury the master, Gilbert de Middleton, the parish priest and chaplain of the chantry of the Virgin all died.[25] At Hereford the chapter's income was halved. The effect on St Katherine's estates of the dearth of labour cannot be fully assessed but the Kempley court rolls are indicative. By 1397 the hospital's demesne economy had collapsed; the master had granted all its lands to laymen at farm.[26] He was only following the example set by neighbouring landlords such as the bishop of Worcester and abbot of Westminster, a response due principally to the decline in food prices.[27]

Given depleted clerical ranks, it was difficult to find a suitable replacement for Gilbert de Middleton. His successor, Thomas de Ledbury, was cited by dean and chapter in 1351 to answer charges of wrongdoing and to correct abuses. Failing so to do, he was replaced by Thomas de Bredwardine. In 1353 Trillek had to intervene, urging Bredwardine to correct and amend the errors and excesses of brothers and *conversi* and warning him against such negligence in the future. In June the chapter appointed a commission of enquiry with powers to replace Bredwardine with a suitable person from amongst the brethren. This they did but their appointee, William le Brut, faced problems not of his own making when, in 1354, the bishop's official had to determine a suit between brethren and master over alleged dilapidations to their three churches.[28]

24. M. Rubin, 'Development and Change in English Hospitals, 1100–1500', in Granshaw and Porter, eds, *The Hospital in History*, p. 48; idem, *Charity and Community*, pp. 218–26; HCA, 1822; Capes, *Charters*, p. 199; HCA, 1899, 3272 (B31), 3276 (B36).

25. HCA, 3390 (B37); J. H. Parry, ed., *The Register of John de Trillek, Bishop of Hereford, AD 1344–1361*, Cantilupe Society (Hereford, 1910), pp. 373–84; J. Hillaby, *Ledbury: A Medieval Borough* (2nd edn, Almeley, 1997), pp. 41–42. Figures for the diocese are printed in W. J. Dohar, *The Black Death and Pastoral Leadership: The Diocese of Hereford in the Fourteenth Century* (Philadelphia, 1995), table 2.1.

26. Capes, *Charters*, pp. ix–xi, 168–69; Bannister, *The Cathedral Church of Hereford*, pp. 156–57; HCA, 7018/5/1, pp. 52–54, Kempley court rolls; Bannister, 'Visitation Returns of the Diocese of Hereford in

1397, part III', *English Historical Review*, 45 (1930), p. 93.

27. C. Dyer, *Lords and Peasants in a Changing Society: The Estates of the Bishopric of Worcester, 680–540* (Cambridge, 1980), pp. 145–49, 209–11, 236–39; B. Harvey, *Westminster Abbey and its Estates in the Middle Ages* (Oxford, 1977), pp. 148–51; E. B. Fryde, *Peasants and Landlords in Later Medieval England* (Stroud, 1996), chapters 4 and 5; E. Miller, ed., *Agrarian History of England and Wales*, iii: *1348–1500* (Cambridge, 1991), pp. 444–45, table 5.1 and appendix D, pp. 502–4.

28. J. R. Lumby, ed., *Chronicon Henrici Knighton, vel Cnitthon, monachi Leycestrensis*, Rolls Series, 92 (2 vols, London, 1889–95), ii, p. 63; G. Williams, *The Welsh Church from Conquest to Reformation* (Cardiff, 1962), pp. 147–48; HCA, 3304, 3299; Parry, ed.,

By 1360 the hospital's fortunes began to look up, if temporarily, due to the patronage of the Esegars, a family whose fortune had been made by William Esegar, merchant, one of Ledbury's two representatives at the 1305 parliament. In his will his son, Thomas, left lands to the hospital. In 1364 these formed the endowment of another chaplaincy by Adam de Esegar, Gorwell prebendary 1341–69, a senior member of the chapter and one of the 1353 commissioners. In 1360 he had bought Tyrellsfrith, formerly Roselynesfrith, Little Marcle, from Grimbald Pauncefot of the Hazle, the next year granting it to the chaplains of the hospital.[29]

Adam's gift of Tyrells Wood at the time he was establishing the Esegar chaplaincy suggests this was the source of the timber for St Katherine's splendid roof. An open structural division between hall and chapel, giving a clear view of the altar, now partitioned off, was achieved by a pair of low posts with capitals to carry a truss with tie beam and collar. Thus, as at Beaune, sick and aged participated in services from beds along both walls. The hall itself is divided into five bays with four original open collar trusses strengthened by pairs of curved wind braces. The fifteen-bay roof of the north aisle of the parish church is of similar construction but has no tie beams. The hospital's western bay, with a later roof, was probably part of the service area beyond. Adam's grant thus marks the completion of the fourteenth-century reconstruction of hall and chapel.

The masonry provides further evidence of reconstruction. The chapel's decorated east window of three trefoiled lights and reticulated tracery is the major feature but two other windows are of similar date if simpler design: to the south twin trefoiled lights with tracery above; to the north a single trefoiled light (fig. 170). These had companions in the hall, two on the north, replaced in wood, and another, now blocked, to the south. There are two fourteenth-century doorways on the north, the western probably giving access to the services, and another, now blocked, on the south. Tiles of *c.* 1500 and remnants of late medieval stained glass in the chapel are of especial interest as they hint at local aristocratic patronage (plate Xa, b). The arms of the Grandissons of Ashperton and Stretton appear in the glass and of the Beauchamps of Bronsil in the tiles.

In 1386 renewed evidence of maladministration led to further papal intervention. Urban VI required dean and chapter to ensure that all properties 'wrongfully

note 28 continued
The Register of John de Trillek, pp. 196–97, 240; HCA, 1932, 1730.

29. J. H. Parry, ed., *The Register of Lewis de Charlton, Bishop of Hereford, AD 1361–1369*, Cantilupe Society (Hereford, 1913), pp. 14–17, 1–2, 43–45; W. W. Capes, ed., *The Register of John Trefnant, Bishop of Hereford,*

AD 1389–1404, Cantilupe Society (Hereford, 1914), p. 152; W. W. Capes, ed., *The Register of William de Courtenay, Bishop of Hereford, AD 1370–1375*, Cantilupe Society (Hereford, 1913), pp. 3–4; HCA, 292, 760, 1804, 3256, 3257 (B15–16), 3307–13 (B56, 59, 63, 65, 60, 62), 3315–17 (B61 and 64), 3735 (B85).

Fig. 170. Chapel and hall of St Katherine's Hospital.

alienated by the brethren and their predecessors' were restored. In 1389 the chapter placed the temporalities and spiritualities in the hands of Richard Knight, rector of Eastnor, and their fellow canon, Roger Hore. When the Ledbury jurors gave evidence to Bishop Trefnant at his visitation in 1397 the master was in full control; but his shortcomings had reached crisis point.[30]

St Katherine's was failing in both its roles. In-relief, food for the thirteen inmates, and out-relief, the customary twice weekly distribution to the non-resident needy, had been terminated. To the scandal of the hospital, brothers and inmates were begging their bread on the streets. This, the jurors believed, arose from the granting of the estates at farm to laymen, putting ready cash rather than demesne produce at the master's disposal. Secondly, the daily offices and recitation of intercessory prayers were neglected. The chaplains' conditions were so bad, in terms of food

30. HCA, 2220, 1807; Bannister, 'Visitation Returns', p. 93.

and submission to the master who had assumed arbitrary rights of dismissal, that wherever possible they sought service elsewhere. As early as 1332 Emeric Pauncefot granted the hospital 40s. rent in Cowarne to provide a chaplain to celebrate divine service every Sunday, Wednesday and Friday and all feast days in his chapel at the Hazle. Of the five chaplains there were now only two.[31]

Fundamental reform was the work of John Prophete, an outstanding administrator. As secretary of the privy council, his minutes were a model for future officers. He was the most eminent of Hereford's medieval deans, 1393–1403, yet the cathedral can have seen him but little and Ledbury, where he had been presented to the Overhall portion by Richard II in 1390, even less. Prophete acted swiftly and effectively.[32] His report of 1398 confirmed the jurors' evidence and, by a series of well-judged ordinances, sought observance of the founder's wishes. If residence was inadequate, the master was to be dismissed. The chaplains, now removable solely by dean and chapter, could serve another benefice only by their licence. To ensure that the poor and weak were sufficiently served and suitably maintained, they were to receive weekly at least seven small loaves, each to weigh 1lb. 2oz., baked from good grain. Similar provisions applied to their ale allowance.[33]

Prophete's 1398 ordinances provided firm leadership by improving the quality of the masters. Almost all were now graduates and all but one, John Lye, found promotion, if only to one of the cathedral's prebends. The most outstanding, John Malvern, appointed in 1398, was clearly Prophete's choice for both were prominent in court circles. Malvern's qualifications were remarkable. Doctor of theology and master of physic, he had been an assessor at the trial for heresy at Hereford in 1393 of Walter Brut, the Lollard. He was physician to Henry IV, both as earl of Derby and king. His book, *De remediis spiritualibus et corporalibus contra pestilenciam*, was a standard text.[34] Although absentee and pluralist, Malvern played an active

31. HCA, 1807, 3333; Bannister, 'Visitation Returns', p. 93; *Calendar of the Patent Rolls Preserved in the Public Record Office: Edward III* (16 vols, London, 1891–1916), ii, p. 333.

32. A. B. Emden, *A Biographical Register of the University of Oxford to AD 1500* (3 vols, Oxford, 1957–59), iii, pp. 1521–23; T. F. Tout, *Chapters in Administrative History* (6 vols, Manchester, 1920–33), iii, pp. 466–67, 471–73; J. F. Baldwin, *The King's Council in England during the Middle Ages* (Oxford, 1913; repr. 1969), pp. 149–52, 364–65, 389–91; *Calendar of the Patent Rolls Preserved in the Public Record Office: Richard II* (6 vols, London, 1895–1909), iv, p. 308; *Calendar of the Patent Rolls Preserved in the*

Public Record Office: Henry IV (4 vols, London, 1903–09), ii, p. 327; Capes, ed., *The Register of John Trefnant*, pp. 56–58, 138–40.

33. HCA, 7018/5/1, pp. 36–38. At St Cross, Winchester, *c.* 1136, Bishop Henry de Blois directed that the thirteen poor men have daily 'a good loaf of wheaten bread' and 'drink of good stuff' (strong not small beer), P. Hopewell, *St Cross: England's Oldest Almshouse* (Chichester, 1995), p. 3.

34. Emden, *Biographical Register of the University of Oxford to 1500*, ii, p. 1211; Capes, ed., *The Register of John Trefnant*, p. 360; J. H. Wylie, *History of England under Henry IV* (4 vols, London, 1884–98), iii, p. 231; iv, pp. 153, 171; T. Tanner, *Bibliotheca*

role at St Katherine's. Bells, like cemeteries, infringed parochial rights and thus required a special licence. In 1398 he obtained a papal indult for a bell to be sounded for divine offices, 'even before the celebration in the [parish] church', and 'to have mass celebrated in the chapel, *alta voce*', that is high mass. The present bell, cast in 1696 in memory of Dean George Benson, master 1679–92, probably replaced Malvern's bell. Malvern also secured fourteen more acres of wood in Little Marcle, to maintain 'himself and certain chaplains'.[35]

When Bishop Thomas Spofford arrived in 1424 the diocese, 'at the best of times wild', had effectively been without a bishop for four years. Relations between bishop and chapter were far from cordial. Finding 'transgressions and excesses' at St Katherine's, Spofford threatened to appoint others to visit and reform it if dean and chapter failed to do so before Easter. This reflected little credit on Nicholas Lyney, Malvern's successor, but he retained office until 1428.[36]

In 1483 Bishop Myllyng presented Richard Wycherley to the mastership. A Dominican and doctor of theology, he had represented the English province at the order's general chapter in Rome in 1481. Next year he was consecrated bishop of Olena in the Peloponnese, then part of the Ottoman Empire. Without a see, he was suffragan not only to Myllyng and in all probability to his successors, Audley and Castello, but also at Worcester, 1482–1502. St Katherine's thus provided an ideal base. He was rector of Donnington and administrator of Aylton and Pixley. In Worcester diocese he was rector of Salwarpe and Powicke. He combined these parochial responsibilities and those of suffragan with remarkable skill. Of the twenty ordination services he conducted in the diocese between 1484 and 1492, only five were held at the cathedral. Twelve were held at St Peter's, Ledbury (now known as St Michael and All Angels), the remainder in his own chapel of St Katherine's. Wycherley was buried in 1402 at Worcester Cathedral.[37]

Britannico-Hibernica (London, 1748), p. 505; C. H. Talbot, *Medicine in Medieval England* (London, 1967), p. 168; Wharton, *Anglia sacra*, i, p. 536.

35. Capes, ed., *The Register of John Trefnant*, p. 360; J. H. Parry and C. Johnson, eds, *The Register of Robert Mascall, Bishop of Hereford, AD 1404–1416*, Cantilupe Society (Hereford, 1916), pp. 171, 184; Emden, *Biographical Register of the University of Oxford to 1500*, ii, p. 1211; Wylie, *History of England under Henry IV*, ii, pp. 238–39; iii, p. 231; iv, pp. 153, 171; *Calendar of the Patent Rolls, Henry IV*, iii, pp. 111, 318–19, 343, 461; iv, p. 56; Clay, *Mediaeval Hospitals*, p. 198; W. H. Bliss and others, eds, *Calendar of*

Entries in the Papal Registers Relating to Great Britain and Ireland: Papal Letters, 1198–1492 (18 vols, London and Dublin, 1893–1989), v, *1396–1404*, p. 263.

36. HCA, 1796; A. T. Bannister, ed., *The Register of Thomas Spofford, Bishop of Hereford, AD 1422–1448*, Cantilupe Society (Hereford, 1917), pp. iii–iv, 60–61, 354–56.

37. HCA, 7031/1, fos 175r-v, chapter acts, 11 March 1566; A. T. Bannister, ed., *The Register of Thomas Myllyng, Bishop of Hereford, 1474–1492*, Cantilupe Society (Hereford, 1919), pp. iii and n. 11, 142–43, 169–83, 193, 197; Emden, *Biographical Register of the University of Oxford to 1500*, iii, pp. 2102–3.

The fifteenth century witnessed the first radical change in the character of the community when one of the masters removed himself from the common life to live in his own 'mansion house', now St Katherine's surgery. His large south-facing building conformed to the usual H-shaped plan of the period. An eastern cross-wing formed the service area with buttery and pantry from which a screens passage gave access, through a spere-truss, to a central hall open to the roof. The master's solar, with his chamber above, was in the western cross-wing. The house is said to be of fifteenth-century date on architectural grounds but there is no documentary evidence as to which master broke so overtly with the ideal of the common life.[38]

By the time Wycherley's successor, Thomas Blundell, resigned in 1515, attitudes to hospitals were changing, with public criticism of clerical domination and exploitation of existing institutions.[39] Dissolution of first the smaller and then the greater monasteries raised ominous questions about the future of hospitals. St Leonard's at York, probably England's greatest medieval hospital, and St Wulstan's, Worcester, fell in 1539.[40] The Chantry Acts were a far more serious threat. Hospitals were not listed but, given their chantry function, were very vulnerable.[41] In Ledbury there were other rich ecclesiastical holdings, in addition to the hospital. During this age of plunder all, except St Katherine's, were lost to the church. Possession passed to a small group of lay families, closely linked by blood and economic interests: some, such as the Eltons and Skynners, local; others, such as the Skips and Halls, outsiders. This they achieved by a web of complex transactions, only part of which can now be unravelled. The 'Register' of John Elton, master 1515–47, tells us much of the medieval estates.[42]

38. Swindon, Royal Commission on Historical Monuments, England, National Monuments Record, MS, St Katherine's, Ledbury: Hospital, Inspector's notes, 10 April 1930.

39. HCA, 7031/1, fos 175r-v; *Descriptive Catalogue of Ancient Deeds*, iii, D488, D801; Orme and Webster, *The English Hospital*, pp. 148–50.

40. Clay, *Mediaeval Hospitals*, p. 232; Orme and Webster, *The English Hospital*, p. 163, quoting T. Wright, ed., *Three Chapters of Letters Relating to the Suppression of Monasteries*, Camden Society, old series, 26 (London, 1843), p. 166; Caley, ed., *Valor ecclesiasticus temp. Henr. VIII auctoritate regis institutus* (6 vols, London, 1810–34), iii, pp. 228–29; J. S. Brewer, J. Gairdner and R. H. Brodie, eds, *Letters and Papers, Foreign and Domestic, of the Reign of Henry VIII* (23 vols in 38,

London, 1862–1932), vi, nos 317, 661; vii, no. 1121, p. 59; xv, nos 695, 831, p. 64; xiv, pt 2, nos 113, pp. 2, 6, 13 264, p. 29, 400, p. 140; A. B. Emden, *Biographical Register of the University of Oxford, 1501–1540* (Oxford, 1974), pp. 38–39; *The Victoria History of the Counties of England: Worcestershire* (5 vols, London, 1901–26), ii, p. 176. On survival and change see Orme and Webster, *The English Hospital*, pp. 155–66.

41. *Chantry Acts*, 37 Henry VIII, c. 4; 1 Edward VI, c. 14; A. Kreider, *English Chantries: The Road to Dissolution*, Harvard Historical Studies, 97 (Cambridge, Massachusetts and London, 1979), chapter 7; T. Fuller, *The Church-History of Britain* (6 vols, London, 1655), vi, p. 354.

42. Bannister, ed., *The Register of Charles Bothe*, pp. 68–69, 171–74; S. E. Lehmberg *The Reformation of Cathedrals: Cathedrals in English*

In December 1551 the advowson of St Katherine's was granted to John Skip, Bishop of Hereford (1539–52) and his nephew Richard Willason 'for the next term only'. Skip's death in 1552 thwarted these plans. Scory, his successor, had his own agenda. He persuaded the crown that master, brethren and sisters formed a corporation and that, as a 'deserted or relinquished hospital ... at present concealed and converted to the uses of certain private men of sufficient wealth', it fell under the terms of the 1545 and 1547 Chantry Acts. Thus in 1568 Elizabeth granted the hospital and its possessions to Scory and his successors as masters, appointing as inmates 'twelve honest Poor Men deserving well of the state for their service'.[43] In defence of their rights under Foliot's foundation charter, the chapter, led by Edward Cooper, installed as master in 1562, took the issue to the Star Chamber whence it was referred to the Court of Exchequer.[44]

After eleven years of litigation the court decreed that master, brethren and sisters formed no corporation sole and that freehold and inheritance were in the dean and chapter. All leases granted by the former, as opposed to the chapter, were invalid.[45] Like Dean Prophete, the court sought sound management of the hospital's assets and suitable provision for the poor by the appointment of a well-qualified master and effective supervision by dean and chapter, now 'patrons and owners' of the hospital. A schedule of property and lands showed the total value to be £90 3s. 0d. Annual visitation was to be undertaken by the dean himself, accompanied by at least two of his chapter. The master was to be a canon residentiary, nominated by dean and chapter for life and resident at the hospital for at least four months a year. In addition to the mansion house and demesne lands, he was to have an annual salary, of one-sixth the total value: £13 6s. 8d. Chantry services being abolished as 'blindness and ignorance', there was need for only one chaplain – to read prayers in the chapel on days when there was no service at St Peter's. He was appointed by the master with a salary of £2. Similarly there was now no place for brethren and sisters as religious following a rule. Instead the ten inmates were termed 'brethren' and 'sisters'. Appointed by the master and confirmed by dean and chapter, with at least five from Ledbury, they could be removed only

Society, 1485–1603 (Princeton, 1988), pp. 31–32; HCA, 7031/1, fos 33r, 68v–69v, chapter acts, 3 February 1524, 15 March and 16 May 1532; Jebb and Phillott, *The Statutes of the Cathedral Church of Hereford*, p. 141; Hillaby, *Ledbury*, chapter 10. Elton's register, HCA, 7018/5/2, includes twenty-one court rolls for Berrow 1307–8 to 1536–7, rentals of Edward II's and Richard II's reigns, court rolls for Kempley 1312–13 to 1515–16 and for Hidelow 1318–19 to 1349.

43. *Calendar of the Patent Rolls, Elizabeth I* (7 vols, London 1939–82, in progress), iv, p. 215.

44. A. J. Winnington-Ingram, 'Edward Cooper or Cowper, 1528–1596', *TWNFC*, 32 (1946–48), pp. xciii–civ.

45. HCA, 3575, 3576, 3564 includes a copy of the 1580 exchequer decree and 'Rules to be Observed by Dean and Chapter and Master, Brothers and Sisters'.

by the latter. Their annual salary was to be one-twelfth the total value, £6 13s. 4d. Under Cooper's leadership dean and chapter had successfully resisted the crown's attempt to break its 350-year-old trust. This second scheme of reform was confirmed by statute in 1581. Apart from a brief interruption during the Commonwealth, it remained unaltered for over two centuries until a further act in 1819.[46]

Cooper, who had resigned in 1574, was reinstated. He immediately embarked upon an extensive overhaul of the hospital's buildings. Whilst his accounts, 1584–95, provide a picture of those buildings with details of the source and cost of materials used and of techniques employed, they relate predominantly to the fifteen-year campaign for the repair and modernisation of the master's house. The open hall was divided into ground and first floor. The solar was completely refurbished, being lined with panelling and provided with a fireplace flanked by pilasters and four arcaded panels, similar to that at the Talbot Inn, New Street. On a wooden overmantel above was a painting of Hugh Foliot within a black-letter inscription expounding Cooper's views on episcopal election, the government of the church and the court of Rome (fig. 171). This is now in the chapel. Cooper's initials were carved into the frieze with the year, 1588, when he resigned his prebend to take up permanent residence. As to the chapel and almshouses, there is evidence of slight repair but the ancillary buildings were thoroughly renovated. New facilities included 'kytching' and 'preevie'.[47]

The master's register, 1581–1727, and accounts, 1616–88, record the hospital's progress in the seventeenth century.[48] On the abolition of deans and chapters in 1649, John Tombes was appointed master. Although a native of Bewdley, Tombes had long and honourable connections with this county as vicar of Leominster, 1630–41, and (after a spell at the Temple in London) as rector of Ross from 1646 until his appointment, under the great seal, at Ledbury. In 1654 he begged the incorporation of St Katherine's and the vesting of its lands in himself and two senior brethren. Despite strong objections by the trustees who claimed Tombes had 'almost ruined the hospital', the Lord Protector issued the ordinance for incorporation. With the Restoration of Charles II in 1660 and Dean Herbert Croft a year later, St Katherine's returned to the 1581 regime. All Tombes's leases were excepted from the provisions of the 1660 Act which confirmed leases, etc. of

46. HCA, 3575, 4248, ordinances of 1581 and terrier of estates; *An Act Concerning the Hospitall of Ledburye in the Countye of Hereford*, 23 Elizabeth I.

47. HCA, 7018/6; Winnington-Ingram, 'Edward Cooper', pp. xciii–civ; F. C. Morgan, 'The Accounts of St Katherine's Hospital, Ledbury, 1584–1595', *TWNFC*, 34 (1952–54), pp. 88–132. The overmantel was rediscovered by the determined efforts of the late Sylvia Robinson of Bank Cottage.

48. HCA, 7018/7, St Katherine's register A; HCA, R 643–65, accounts of the masters, 1616–85.

Fig. 171. St Katherine's Hospital: painted overmantel with portrait of Bishop Hugh Foliot, installed above the fireplace in the reconstructed solar by Edward Cooper in 1588; now in the chapel.

colleges and hospitals. One of the chapter's first decisions was to divert St Katherine's money to repair the cathedral's lead spire, work which began only in 1673.[49]

A comparison of the 1581 ordinance with the master's accounts for 1797 indicates remarkable stability but 'augmentations' betray some inflationary tendencies. The yearly pay of brethren and sisters was increased first by 6d. and then by 1s. a week to £10 11s. 4d. While income from his demesne lands had remained static until 1785, the master's salary doubled.[50]

Beneath the apparent calm a severe crisis was looming: the consequence of the ancient and fundamental maladies of inadequate inspection by dean and chapter and non-residence of the master. This is hardly surprising as Dean Wetherell (1771–1808) spent ten months of each year at University College, Oxford. In 1797, prompted by local agitation, the attorney general instituted proceedings in the Exchequer Court against dean, chapter and the master, Canon James Birt. The chapter accepted that 'before Dr Leigh's time [1747–60] residence had been very negligently observed, some masters not residing at all, others for only a few days, occasionally'. However they had 'granted some reasonable indulgence to masters who undertook to reside, making his abode more comfortable and by his personal attention to regulate and improve the Revenue appropriated, to render that Office more desirable and deserving constant attention'.

Birt, appointed in 1785, turned out 'idle tenants and refused to renew undesirable

49. M. A. E. Green, ed., *Calendar of State Papers, Domestic Series, [of the Commonwealth]* (13 vols, London, 1875–86), vii, pp. 170–72, 194, 244–45, 356; G. F. Townsend, *The Town and Borough of Leominster* (Leominster, [1863]), pp. 103, 116–18. The scheme of incorpor-

ation is HCA, 7018/7, pp. 81–85; HCA, 3761; 12 Charles II, c. 31; S. E. Lehmberg, *Cathedrals under Siege: Cathedrals in English Society, 1600–1700* (Exeter, 1996), p. 67.

50. HCA, 7018/10, register D: master's accounts, 1724–97.

leases', in one case increasing rent from £31 10s. 0d. to more than £100. The combination of disgruntled tenants and the disparity in income between master and inmates was explosive. Nevertheless, the chapter submitted that 'as Managers under an Act of Parliament they think that his Income is not larger than the situation calls for and they do not intend to relinquish any part of the right they may have to say what such an income might be'.[51]

In 1800 the problem was referred to the deputy remembrancer, to act 'with all convenient speed'. He reported in 1806: the annual income was £1191 19s. 9d.; one-ninth of the rents should be set aside for repairs, one-sixth of the residue be allowed to the master, the remainder to brethren and sisters as a yearly stipend of £30; leases should be no longer than fourteen years, paying full rent but no entry fine; to prevent improper application of funds the accounts should be approved and signed – not by the dean, but by the bishop – and lodged for public inspection in Ledbury.[52] In a further report in 1818 he recommended that, as annual income had increased to some £1500, Robert Smirke's designs for the new hospital of twenty-four dwellings, at a cost of £5000, be met from existing funds, any shortfall being raised by mortgage on the estate. This the court ratified and, as in 1581, its decree was confirmed by private Act, in 1819.[53] This however took no account of court costs totalling £2036 14s. 10d., with costs for the private Act of £1937 12s. 11d. and £2312 due to the executors of the late master, Dr John Napleton (fig. 41), who had purchased properties in anticipation of the building programme. The dean and chapter had to raise £9000 at 4 per cent per annum, and only the southern wing, with twelve dwellings, and the central tower could be completed in 1822. The builder charged £3553 7s. 10d. and the architect £469 11s. 0d. on which the Charity Commissioner observed in 1837 'nothing in the appearance of the building would lead to the supposition that a metropolitan architect [Robert Smirke] had been employed at such an expense'. The north wing and twelve other dwellings were only completed forty-four years later (fig. 172).[54]

The fourth and final reform of the hospital's administration was made by the Charity Commissioners in 1962. After seven and a half centuries, how far did

51. HCA, 3564, 3764, papers relating to the dispute concerning the building of St Katherine's; HCA, 7010/1, letter book in the case against dean and chapter, 1796–1813; A. T. Bannister, 'The Hospital of St Katherine at Ledbury', *TWNFC*, 23 (1918–20), p. 67.

52. HCA, 7018/3, 'Case Papers: Attorney General v. Dean and Chapter, 1800–13'.

53. HCA, 3564; *An Act ... to Rebuild the Almshouses of St Katherine's Hospital ... and for the Better Regulation of the Affairs of that Charity*, 59 George III, c. 22.

54. HCA, 3564; *Reports of the Commissioners Appointed in Pursuance of Acts of Parliament to Inquire Concerning Charities and Education of the Poor in England and Wales, Arranged in Counties*, xiii, *Herefordshire* (London, 1815–39), p. 115.

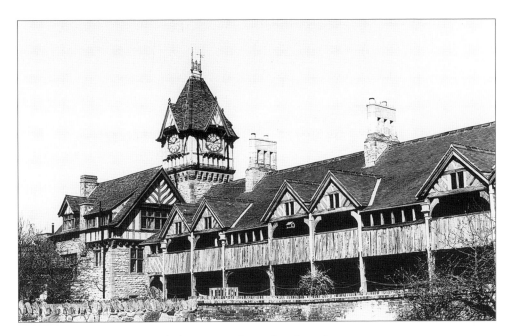

Fig. 172. St Katherine's Hospital: the 1866 northern wing, from the west.

this conform to Foliot's trust? Responsibility and authority was fully restored to dean and chapter as 'body corporate', the annual visitation being retained, now by dean and two colleagues. This was indeed 'without contradiction of any man' for the bishop's supervisory role, introduced by the 1819 Act, was now withdrawn. The perennial problem of non-residence which had so concerned Dean Prophete in 1398 was finally resolved. The master remained accountable for the discipline and care of the almsfolk but no longer had rights in mansion house or demesne. He was to reside within five miles. The arrival of the welfare state, with pensions and new housing standards, was acknowledged. To provide more generous accommodation the mandatory total of twenty-four almsfolk was relaxed. The weekly allowances of the 1581 and 1819 Acts were abolished. Instead a weekly maintenance contribution of 5s. was to be levied. Not only was the charitable role of St Katherine's to be maintained, in a suitably modified form, but its spiritual role was reasserted. Intercessory prayers had disappeared at the Reformation but the newly-defined responsibilities of the corporate body included 'the maintenance of services in the chapel'.[55]

55. *The Charities (St Katherine's Hospital, Ledbury) Order*, Statutory Instrument no. 2807 (1962).

The Present and the Future

John Tiller

At the end of the second millennium of the Christian era Hereford Cathedral is still fulfilling its ancient purpose of being 'the seat of the bishop and a centre of worship and mission'.[1] But the ways in which the building is actually used have changed significantly, and doubtless will change again in the years ahead. The daily round of matins, eucharist and evensong continues, using the sacred space to mark the rhythms of life with a response to a gracious God, but now in a place which does duty also as a concert hall, a museum, an art gallery, an assembly hall, a workplace, an ancient monument, and yes, a market place. No other kind of building is pressed into service for such a variety of uses. The potential for conflict is enormous, and the art of successful management is complex.

Even the religious services are no longer restricted to those of the foundation or of the diocese. At Christmas an increasing list of carol services takes place, including those for local schools, for the fire brigade, for various charities, and for shoppers. Other groups appear at harvest, and for civic occasions commemorating events such as the Battle of Britain. There are St George's Day parades for scouts and guides; there are judges' services. The building is used to make broadcast services, and recordings of the choir for sale on compact discs and tapes. In recent years several films have included scenes inside the cathedral. The local college uses the building for an annual graduation ceremony, in addition to the daily assemblies and annual prizegiving, speeches and commemorations of the cathedral's own senior and junior schools. The choral society uses the building three or four times a year, and on many other evenings there are performances by police choirs, Welsh male voice choirs, travelling choirs from North America or Europe, and various other musical groups. The local sixth form college, and the day centre for the mentally disabled, have performed plays and musicals. All organisations using the cathedral for a production also need rehearsal time. Once in three years the building is

1. As defined by the general principle of the Care of Cathedrals Measure (1990) and the Cathedrals Measure (1999).

taken over for several weeks for the Three Choirs Festival. Each year there is a full programme of organ recitals. There are poetry readings. For one week each year many schools from all over the diocese come to the cathedral for a series of workshops lasting all day. Before the new library building was opened in 1996 it was necessary to close the Mappa Mundi exhibition whenever a wedding, funeral or other service took place during opening times. It remains a common occurrence that groups wish to have tours at times when guides are inaudible because musicians need to practise. There are various fundraising events for good causes, sometimes taking over the whole Close. In the midst of all this time has to be found for the regular floor cleaning, flower arranging, chair moving and organ tuning. And it all takes place against the background noise of a building permanently under repair, with the masons' yard on site.

Such are some of the demands made upon a single space by competing groups: competing, that is, in the sense that there are bound to be times when not everything can be accommodated, and it is all too easy for the attempt to be made to accommodate too much. But in addition to the use made of the cathedral for organised events and by the constant stream of tourists who turn up expecting to be able to gain admission at any time, there is clear evidence that increasingly individuals come into a cathedral seeking space for personal reflection and prayer. This is marked at Hereford, for example, by the large number of candles lit each day beside the Cantilupe shrine and at other points around the building. Many intercessions are recorded on slips of paper and pinned to a board near the shrine, often containing references to poignant or intimate needs. But where in such a place is it possible to find any sense of stillness conducive to a soul doing business with God? As one recent writer has noted: 'For all their size, few cathedrals have spaces where it is possible to be silent, and in the future such sound-proof enclosures may have to be built'.[2] In the absence of any prospect of funding such an addition at Hereford, the crypt has been restored very effectively as a place for quiet prayer.

Any new building in the Close requiring the digging of foundations is an unlikely event in the foreseeable future. The cost of the archaeological investigation when the new library building was planned amounted to nearly 20 per cent of the total expenditure. However, the existing buildings are certain to need some modification if the public is to continue to have access. Gone are the days when we could show visitors our chained library at the top of a narrow spiral flight of fifty-four stone steps. (There were two fatalities on that staircase in its last fifteen years of use.) It is regrettable that the wonderful space at the top of those stairs is unusable as a place, for example, to display the diocesan treasury of plate now removed from the crypt.[3] New regulations concerning access for the disabled will

2. A. Anderson in S. Platten and C. Lewis, eds, *Flagships of the Spirit: Cathedrals in Society* (London, 1998), p. 100.
3. See above, Chapter 27, p. 504.

mean several alterations in the cathedral to doorways and stairs by 2004. Horribly disfiguring green 'fire exit' signs now have to be displayed in the cathedral and inside the new library building. Another kind of modification will be prompted by the development of audio-visual systems. We already take it for granted that a modern cathedral should be equipped with efficient sound amplification; how long will it be before a closed circuit television system, such as gets installed over several days for every Three Choirs Festival, will be a permanent feature available for all occasions when the cathedral is full and many people are presently unable to see what is happening? Such instances are not always predictable, either. The death of Princess Diana in 1997 taught us that at moments of great national emotion cathedrals become a natural resort for impromptu expressions of corporate feeling and may need to respond very quickly to popular demand.

At the turn of the millennium the most far-reaching change which is overtaking all Anglican cathedrals in England is the revision of their constitutions under the Cathedrals Measure (1999). Cathedrals of the 'old foundation', such as Hereford, will perhaps be most affected of all.[4] From the 'parish church' cathedrals will be taken the inclusion of the laity in a shared power of decision making; from the 'new foundation' cathedrals will be taken the bestowal of strong powers of leadership on deans. The corporate accountability of a group of clergy living in close association according to a rule will finally be discarded as unworkable for modern cathedrals. Chapters will have to find a new kind of spirituality, one which is sustaining to a disparate group of clergy and laity, some whole-time and some part-time in their administration of these complex enterprises. Quite what will become of residentiary canons is at present uncertain. It seems likely that in many cathedrals, including Hereford, their offices will become leasehold ones, so that there will be more frequent changes in chapter membership. Deans, however, will continue to possess a freehold. There will be a much clearer definition of the responsibilities of individual canons. Old habits die hard, and the concept of 'residence' will doubtless continue for some time, though it is hard to predict in the longer term what will happen to the dynamics of an administrative chapter where only a minority of its members carry the responsibilities of residence. Chapters are to become accountable in each case to a cathedral council, which will represent not only those who work and worship at the cathedral, but also the wider life of city, county and diocese.

The key question which these new governing bodies will have to face relates to the future role of cathedrals. This has been articulated by David Stancliffe, bishop of Salisbury, as 'whether cathedrals are just institutions which provide an umbrella under which a whole host of different activities take place ... or whether

---

4. See above, Introduction, p. xxxi.

cathedrals consciously embrace and own these different activities as manifestations of their multifarious, but ultimately coherent, life'.[5] In posing such a question, cathedrals are perhaps facing the Church of England with one of its most difficult theological tasks today. Can one church attempt to answer such a question? Does it not raise issues for the whole of Christianity which require an ecumenical response? The very openness of cathedrals (they are literally open for very long hours every day of the year), and their involvement with such a wide variety of elements in the local community, make them a matter of concern to everyone. A student doing a project recently entered Hereford Cathedral and asked the volunteer on the information desk who owned the cathedral. The dean and chapter can only exercise a custodial ownership. The 'church' obviously has an interest in having the bishop's seat there, but the Howe Commission, whose report *Heritage and Renewal* led to the new Cathedrals Measure, did not propose to 'diminish the independence of cathedrals'.[6] It is easy to see that a cathedral has a dimension of Christian mission distinctively different from, and complementary to, that of a parish church. But are these just different arms of a common enterprise, or are cathedrals moving into a separate identity which will need its own rationale, not specifically Anglican, not specifically Christian, not specifically anything?

Returning finally to the particular future of Hereford among cathedrals, the restoration of a separate county of Hereford has addressed one particular issue of identity; but, even then, the diocese of Hereford embraces a large part of Shropshire, and several parishes in Wales, so ecclesiastically there is still a wider constituency. The Friends of the cathedral, now no longer the only ongoing fundraising body for the cathedral, have developed a new role in making links with the deaneries and parishes of the diocese. These are perhaps now stronger than ever, and there are plans to develop an outside worship space in the chapter house yard, so that visiting church groups can make use of this option on summer evenings. That is a secure area, but current concern with standards of behaviour in the Close (not, as readers of this volume will realise, a new problem) have led to consideration of the restoration of railings around the whole precinct. The emphasis is not on exclusion, except late at night, but to serve as a reminder of what it is, an ancient burial ground, and to create a better sense of being in a special place. The cathedral is also engaged with the whole diocese in wider links with the church overseas, particularly with Anglicans in Tanzania and Lutherans in Nuremberg. Clergy from the diocese of Masasi have come on placements at the cathedral, and the choir has visited Nuremberg. There is undoubtedly scope for greater development of a European and a world perspective, but the cathedral's constant window on the

---

5. Platten and Lewis, eds, *Flagships of the Spirit*, p. 53.
6. *Heritage and Renewal: The Report of the Archbishops' Commission on Cathedrals* (London, 1994), p. 6.

world is still Mappa Mundi. It is noteworthy that a place which Hensley Henson once described as 'intensely local in feeling and interest' has witnessed in the final year of the twentieth century a gathering of scholars from thirteen different countries to discuss *mappaemundi*, in the context of a unique exhibition of sixteen such maps.[7] The conference papers when published will demonstrate clearly that the Hereford Map, like the cathedral itself, still has power to stimulate the mind and the imagination of modern enquirers.

7. H. H. Henson, *Retrospect of an Unimportant Life* (3 vols, London, 1942–50), i, p. 271.

Appendix 1

The Constitution of Hereford Cathedral in the Thirteenth Century

Julia Barrow

The establishment of Hereford Cathedral's medieval constitution was a gradual process, which appears to have begun under Bishop Robert the Lotharingian (1079–95). One of the earliest features of the constitution to have been laid down was almost certainly the number of canons, fixed at twenty-nine by Robert, dropping to twenty-five under Robert de Béthune, rising to twenty-seven under Gilbert Foliot and then to twenty-eight under Ralph de Maidstone, with the establishment of the prebend Episcopi for the penitentiary.[1] The number of prebendaries included, or could include, the dean (in the 1291 *Taxatio*, Dean John of Aigueblanche occurs as prebendary of Bullinghope).[2] The establishment of dignitaries also appears to have begun with Robert the Lotharingian, who appointed the first archdeacon and probably also the earliest dean; the dignities of the precentor and the treasurer were probably established before 1131, and the chancellor's dignity was set up only at the end of the twelfth century.[3] The early constitution of the cathedral was probably unwritten. A few of the episcopal acta issued for the chapter in the late twelfth and early thirteenth centuries clearly have the force of statutes: some of them enlarge the common fund,[4] and Giles de Braose confirmed the dean and chapter's powers of jurisdiction.[5] It is obvious that there was a larger body of accepted customs or possibly even written materials from Hugh Foliot's grant to the cathedral dignitaries of the year of grace (the right to a year's revenues after death or transfer into the monastic life) in respect of their dignities, a right already

1. J. Barrow, 'A Lotharingian in Hereford: Bishop Robert's Reorganisation of the Church of Hereford, 1079–1095', in Whitehead, *Medieval Art at Hereford*, pp. 29–49 at 35–37.
2. *Taxatio ecclesiastica Angliae et Walliae auctoritate Papae Nicholai IV, circa AD 1291* (London, 1802), p. 168b.
3. See above, Chapter 2, pp. 23, 31, 35–36.
4. *EEA*, vii, nos 198, 201–02, 254.
5. Ibid., no. 255.

confirmed by his predecessors to prebendaries in respect of their prebends.[6] Then in 1245–46 Bishop Peter of Aigueblanche obtained a series of papal confirmations of statutes of the dean and chapter regulating payment of commons, giving permission for absence for resident canons wishing to go on pilgrimage or to study, and demanding residence at prebendal churches for six months in the year (this would have affected only the prebendaries of Inkberrow, Wellington and Moreton and Whaddon).[7] These papal confirmations precede the first surviving full set of statutes for the cathedral,[8] which date from Peter's pontificate and which must postdate the canonisation on 16 December 1246 of Edmund Rich (archbishop of Canterbury, 1234–40), whose shrine at Pontigny is mentioned.[9] These statutes are divided into two parts, the 'Customs of the Church', outlining the rules on the installation of canons and their residence, and the 'Customs of the Choir', describing the duties of the dignitaries and legislating on behaviour of canons in choir and on the duties of the vicars choral.

At Hereford the bishops were not expected to intervene in the internal workings of the chapter. This emerges not from the cathedral statutes but from disputes between Bishop Peter and the canons in the early years of his episcopate and again in 1320 under Bishop Adam Orleton, whose claim to be able to conduct a visitation was rebuffed.[10] This did not, however, prevent the bishops from exercising considerable influence: they possessed the right to collate to all the prebends.[11] The dean and chapter (and, in decanal vacancies, the chapter on its own) had the right to judge disputes between canons, and breaches of discipline by canons.[12] The dean installed new canons, but in his absence he was replaced by the hebdomadary canon (the canon charged with saying services for that week), an arrangement unusual in English cathedrals and found only at Hereford.[13] Each canon possessed rights of jurisdiction within his own household and on the lands of his own prebend.[14]

New canons, once installed, would be expected to say immediately whether or

6. Ibid., no. 340.
7. W. H. Bliss and J. A. Twemlow, eds, *Calendar of Entries in the Papal Registers Relating to Great Britain and Ireland: Papal Letters 1198–1492* (14 vols, London, 1893–1960), i, pp. 222–23, 229. For Inkberrow see A. Morey and C. N. L. Brooke, eds, *The Letters and Charters of Gilbert Foliot* (Cambridge, 1967), no. 314, p. 375; for Wellington and Moreton and Whaddon see J. Barrow, 'A Lotharingian in Hereford', pp. 37–41.
8. Bradshaw and Wordsworth, *Statutes of Lincoln Cathedral*, ii, pp. 44–85.

9. C. H. Lawrence, *St. Edmund of Abingdon: A Study in Hagiography and History* (Oxford, 1960), pp. 19–20.
10. K. Edwards, *The English Secular Cathedrals in the Middle Ages* (2nd edn, Manchester, 1967), p. 132.
11. Bradshaw and Wordsworth, *Statutes of Lincoln Cathedral*, ii, pp. 44–45, for collation.
12. Ibid., p. 47.
13. Ibid., pp. 45–46; Edwards, *Secular Cathedrals*, p. 151.
14. Bradshaw and Wordsworth, *Statutes of Lincoln Cathedral*, ii, p. 58.

not they proposed to offer residence.[15] Residence entailed spending no more than sixteen weeks in any year outside Hereford, with no period of absence longer than seven weeks, or twelve in exceptional cases; new residentiaries had to perform a period of forty days in residence with no departure from Hereford.[16] Special permission could be given to those canons who had performed a three-year probationary period and who already had some education to go away to study for two years, with a possible extension of a third year. Leave of absence to go on pilgrimage was allowed to resident canons provided that they took no more than three weeks in a year. Each resident canon was permitted only one overseas pilgrimage in his lifetime.[17] The prebendary of Moreton and Whaddon was not allowed to receive either great or small commons, even if he resided, presumably because he was supposed to reside at the churches which formed his prebend, which were situated in Gloucestershire; in any case his was the best-endowed of the Hereford prebends.[18]

To supplement the income from prebends, which was variable, the chapter built up a common fund in the twelfth century from four manors and some churches, which was administered by two or occasionally three canons appointed as chapter bailiffs.[19] Three types of commons payments were supplied to canons: great, small and quotidian. Small commons, consisting of grain and 20s. per year, were paid to all canons. Great commons were paid only to residentiaries: twice a year the chapter bailiffs would make a distribution to all those present, provided that they had fulfilled their residence. This payment would be made in grain. Quotidian commons were paid in bread and ale, or grain in lieu of ale, to canons attending matins, and pence to those attending mass.[20]

The ranking of the dignitaries was as follows: dean, precentor, treasurer and chancellor. The precedence of the treasurer over the chancellor was unusual in English cathedral chapters and can be explained by the late appearance of the dignity of the chancery at Hereford, under Bishop William de Vere (1186–98).[21] The chancellor was expected to appoint the regent master in arts to run the cathedral school, and to draft charters to be issued by the chapter.[22] The chapter seal was kept in the treasury, but keys to the chest in which it was kept were held by the dean and two other canons.[23] The regent master in arts acted as the chancellor's deputy; the precentor and the treasurer each had a vicar (the succentor and the sub-treasurer) to assist them with their duties, and the dean likewise had a vicar, presumably the subdean who occurs in some twelfth- and thirteenth-century

15. Ibid., p. 46.
16. Ibid., pp. 48–50.
17. Ibid., pp. 56–58.
18. Ibid., p. 58.
19. Ibid., p. 50.

20. Ibid., pp. 47–56.
21. See above, Chapter 2, p. 36.
22. Bradshaw and Wordsworth, *Statutes of Lincoln Cathedral*, ii, p. 71.
23. Ibid., p. 69.

charters, who acted as the dean's deputy in his peculiar.[24] The abbots of the Norman abbeys of Lire and Cormeilles, who were honorary prebendaries of the cathedral, had to support two vicars each, who could receive daily distributions of bread and ale like the canons. The abbots themselves could not receive small or great commons, and on their visits to Hereford could only receive quotidian commons if they attended matins. These confraternity arrangements were made in 1195 (in the case of Cormeilles) and between 1216 and 1219 (in the case of Lire).[25]

24. Ibid., pp. 69, 71, 73, 76.
25. Ibid., pp. 59–60; *EEA*, vii, nos 188, 305.

Office Holders at Hereford Cathedral since 1300

Compiled by

G. Aylmer, J. Barrow, R. Caird, D. Lepine and H. Tomlinson

Deans

Gerard	occ. 1085	John Barowe	1446–1462
Leofwin (Liwin)	? Gerard's successor	James Goldwell	1463
Erchemar	occ. 1107 x 1115,	John ap Richard	1462–1463
	d. 1121 x 1127	Richard Pede	1463–1481
Ralph	1134 x 1136–1158	Thomas Chandler	1481–1490
Geoffrey	1158 x 1163–1179 x	Oliver King	1491
	1183	John Hervey	1491–1501
Jordan	1180 x 1184–1187 x	Reginald West	occ. 1503, 1507
	1188	Thomas Wolsey	occ. 1509–1512
Richard Brito	1187 x 1189–1201	Edmund Frowcester	1513–1529
Hugh of Mapenore	1201 x 1202–1216	Gamaliel Clifton	1529–1541
Thomas of Bosbury	1216 x 1218–1231	Hugh Coren	1541–1558
Ralph Maidstone	1231 x 1232–1234	Edmund Daniel	1558–1559
Stephen Thornbury	1234 x 1236–1247	John Ellis	1560–1575
Giles Avenbury	1247–1253	John Watkins	1576–1593
Anselm of Clermont	occ. 1253–1261 x	Charles Langford	1593–1607
	1262	Edward Doughtie	1608–1616
John of Aigueblanche	occ. 1271	Richard Montagu	1616–1617
Giles of Avenbury	occ. 1276, d. 1280	Silvanus Griffiths	1617–1623
John of Aigueblanche	1282–1320	Daniel Price	1624–1631
Stephen Ledbury	1323–1353	John Richardson	1631–1636
Thomas Trillek	1353–1361	Jonathan Brown	1636–1643
William Birmingham	1362–1381	Herbert Croft	1643–1649
John Harold	1381–1393	Herbert Croft	1660–1661
John Prophete	1393–1404	Thomas Hodges	1661–1672
Thomas Felde	1404–1419	George Benson	1672–1692
John Baysham	1419–1429	John Tyler	1692–1724
John Stanway	1430–1434	Robert Clavering	1724–1729
Henry Shelford	1434–1446	John Harris	1729–1736

Edward Cresset	1736–1749		John Merewether	1832–1850
Edmund Castle	1749–1750		Richard Dawes	1850–1867
John Egerton	1750–1756		George Herbert	1867–1894
Francis Webber	1756–1771		James Wentworth Leigh	1894–1919
Nathan Wetherell	1771–1807		Reginald Waterfield	1919–1946
William Leigh	1808		Hedley Burrows	1947–1961
George Gretton	1809–1820		Robert Price	1961–1968
Robert Carr	1820–1826		Norman Rathbone	1969–1982
Edward Mellish	1827–1830		Peter Haynes	1982–1992
Edward Grey	1831–1832		Robert Willis	1992–present

Precentors

Robert	occ. 1132, 1131 x 1137		William Middleham	occ. 1443–1463
William	occ. 1139		John Baily	1463–1479
Gilbert	occ. 1144, d. 1154 x 1157		Thomas Downe	1479–1489
			John Hervey	1489–1491
Reginald	1155 x 1158–1175 x 1186		Robert Kent	?–1515
William Foliot	1186 x 1195–1206 x 1215		William Porter	1515–1524
			Rowland Philippes	1524–1531
William of Kilpeck	1206 x 1216, 1220 x 1223		Thomas Parker	1531–1538
			Richard Benese	1538–1546
Thomas Foliot	occ. 1223		John Barlow	1547–1554
became treasurer	1230 x 1233		William Chell	1554–1556
Robert of Ewerby	occ. 1233, d. 1241		John Parfey	1557–1559
Aimeric of	occ. 1254;		Walter Jones	1559–1573
Aigueblanche	chancellor by 1270		Thomas Thornton	1573–1629
Aymo of Aigueblanche	1270–1271		Mathew Bust	1629–1638
Hervey Borham	1271/2–1275/6		Francis Coke	1638–1649
William Montfort	1276–1294		Francis Coke	1660–1682
John Swinfield	1294–1311		William Brabourn	1682–1684
Richard Havering	1311–1341		Thomas Seddon/	1685
Giles Stamford	1341		Sidney	
Thomas Winchester	1342–1349		William Watts	1686–1722
Walter Elveden	1349–1358		Thomas Whishaw	1722–1756
Ralph Coggeshall	1358–1361		Edward Ballard	1756–1771
Hugh Heremyte	1361–1363		Charles Morgan	1771–1775
William Outy	1363–1364		Henry Beauclerk	1775–1817
William Borstall	1364–1366		Thomas Huntingford	1817–1855
Henry Shipton	1363–1383		Frederick Ouseley	1855–1889
Walter Ramsbury	1383–1406		John Hampton	1891–1916
Henry Myle	1406–1407		Arthur Bannister	1916–1936
Richard Talbot	1407–1412		Charles Warner	1936–1945
Fulk Stafford	1412–1413		James Jordan	1945–1959
Nicholas Colnet	1413		Edward Dunnicliff	1960–1963
Robert Felton	1413–1416		Eric Eyden	1964–1975
John Bridbroke	1416–1432		Allan Shaw	1975–1982
William Lochard	1432–1439		Austin Masters	1983
			Paul Iles	1983–present

Treasurers

Robert of Hereford	early C12	John Wardroper	?–1511
Brientius	occ. 1132, 1144	Richard Judde	1511–1512
Walter	occ. 1148 x 1155	Edmund Frowcester	1512–1513
Ivo	occ. 1163, d. 1181 x 1198	William Goberd	1513–1515
		Henry Martyn	1515–1516
William	occ. 1187 ±, d. –1213	Hugh Pole	1516–1519
Elias of Radnor	1213 x 1215–1230	William Burghill	1519–1526
Thomas Foliot	1230 x 1234–1237 x 1238	Roger Brayne	1526–1527
		Nicholas Walwen	1527–1545
Richard Gravesend	1237 x 1239–1250	John Mason	1545–1547
Giles Avenbury	–1253–1272	Walter Mey	1548–1558
William Rus	1272–1276	William Lewison/Luson	1558–1582
Giles Avenbury	1276–1277	Edward Cooper	1583–1596
Luke Bree	1277–1293	Richard Edes	1596–1604
John Swinfield	1293–1294	Silvanus Griffiths	1604–1606
Roger Sevenoaks	1294–1300	Francis Kerry	1606–1649
Roger Canterbury	1300–1303	Edward Benson	1660–1667
William Gare	1303–1304	Henry Philley	1667–1668
Nicholas Reigate	1304–1308	Thomas Wotton	1668–1711
John Kempsey	1308–1317	Thomas Gwillim	1711–1726
Thomas Pembridge	1317–1329	William Egerton	1726–1731
John Oo/Ewe	1329–?	Samuel Croxall	1731–1732
John Chamber	occ. 1331–1333	William Lane	1732–1745
Thomas Boleie	1333	Rodney Croxall	1746–1754
Henry Shipton	1333–?	William Willim	1754–1760
Richard Sydenhale	?–1348	William Parker	1760–1802
John Boter	1348–1367	Richard Walond	1802–1831
Roger May	1367–1368	Lord Saye and Sele	1831–1892
Robert Upcote	1368–1377	Sidney Smith	1892–1904
Robert Jones	1377–occ. 1385	Charles Palmer	1904–1921
Nicholas Hereford	1397–1417	Edward Winnington-Ingram	1922–1925
William Cave	1417–?		
Richard Rotherham	occ. 1433–1434	Rowland Money-Kyrle	1926–1928
William Middleham	1434– ? occ. 1435	Herbert Moore	1929–1936
Thomas Wassayle	?–1443	Henry Dixon	1936–1939
Richard Rudhale	1443–1446	James Jordan	1940–1945
John Asheby	1446–1460	Arthur Winnington-Ingram	1945–1961
Richard Pede	1460		
John ap Richard	occ. 1462–1463	Thomas Randolph	1961–1970
Robert Geffrey	1463–1464	John Lewis	1970–1976
John Arundel	1464–1476	Thomas Barfett	1977–1982
Simon Stalworth	?–1477	Andrew Woodhouse	1982–1985
Adrian Bardis	1477–1486	Austin Masters	1985–1993
Robert Sherborne	1486–1505	James Butterworth	1994–1999
Owen Pole	1505–1509		

Chancellors

Nicholas *divinus*	c. 1187	John Arundel	1476–1481
Ranulf	? C12th	Ralph Heathcott	1481–1487
Henry de Vere	1195 x 1198–1209 x 1216	Sampson Aleyn	1487–1494
		James Bromwich	?–1524
T(homas of Bosbury)	occ. 1216	William Hulle	1524–1543
Albinus	1217 x 1218–1225 x 1227	John Elton/Baker	1544–1547
		John Compton/Theale	1548–1555
John Foliot	1225 x 1230–1240	Edward Baskerville	1555–1567
Thomas	1241–1243	William Penson	1567
John Foliot	occ. 1247 x 1253	Morgan Powell	1587–1621
Emery of	occ. 1270; d. 1286	Thomas Godwyn	1621–1644
Aigueblanche		Richard Coke	1644–1649
Gilbert Swinfield	1287–1299	Richard Coke	1660–1681
Robert Gloucester	1299–1322	Joseph Harvey	1682–1716
Thomas Orleton	1322–1333	Thomas Bisse	1716–1731
Robert Wynferthing	occ. 1334–1343	William Egerton	1731–1738
Richard	1343–1345	Samuel Croxall	1738–1752
Wymundeswold		Joseph Browne	1752–1754
John Ambresbury	1345–1349	Henry Egerton	1754–1795
Thomas Hacluit	1349–1375	Herbert Hill	1795–1828
Nicholas Hereford	1375	Morgan Cove	1828–1830
Betrand Lagier	?–1381	Hugh Hanmer Morgan	1830–1861
Andreas Bontempi	1381–?	Stall then remained vacant for 7 years	
John Nottingham	1387–1389	Archer Clive	1868–1878
Thomas Hanley	1389–? occ. 1392	John Jebb	1878–1886
Nicholas Hereford	1394–1397	Henry Phillott	1886–1896
Thomas Hanley	Occ. 1399–1417	Henry Bather	1896–1906
Richard Proctor	1417–1425	Herbert Mather	1906–1916
John Castell	1425–1428	John Hampton	1916–1921
Richard Proctor	1428–?	Alfred Lilley	1922 –1936
Richard Rotherham	occ. 1435, 1447	Harold Moreton	1936–1964
John Dylew,	occ. 1449–1460	Murray Irvine	1965–1978
John Asheby	1460–1464	Russell Acheson	1979–1983
Robert Geffrey	1464–1472	Austin Masters	1984
Thomas Yone	1472	John Tiller	1984–present
Simon Tawre	1472–1476		

Archdeacons of Hereford

Heinfrid	occ. 1085, 1101 x 1102; d. before 1115	Alexander of Walton	?1215/16
		William de Ria	1216 x 1219–1224 x 1234
William	occ. 1108 x 1115		
Geoffrey	d. 1120	Henry Bustard	occ. 1231 x 1234; d. 1248 x 1258
Peter	occ. 1127 x 1131; d. 1179 x 1181		
		William of Conflens	1258–1287
Ralph Foliot	1179 x 1181–1198 x 1199	Roger Sevenoaks	1287
		Richard Hertford	1287–1303
William fitzWalter	1200–1215	Henry Schorne	1303–1318

Thomas Chandos, senior	1318–1332
John Barton	1333–?
William Sheynton	1338–1367
John Bedwardine/ Smythes	occ. 1369–1379
Richard Tissington	1379–1380
Richard Kingston	1380–1405
John Loveney	1405–1417
John Hereford	1417–1424
John Barowe	1424–1446
Richard Rudhale	1446–1476
Richard Martin	occ. 1478–1483
Robert Geffrey	occ. 1485–1494
Thomas Morton	occ. 1501–1511
William Webbe	1511–1523
John Booth	1523–1542
John Styrmin	1542–1551
Richard Cheney	1552–1557
John Glazier	1557–1559
Robert Crowley	1560–1565
Edward Cooper	1565–1578
Simon Smith	1578–1606
Silvanus Griffiths	1606–1617
Richard Montagu	1617–1623
John Hughes	1623–1646
George Benson	1660–1684
Samuel Benson	1684–1690
William Johnson	1690–1698
Thomas Fox	1698–1728
John Walker	1729–1741
Robert Breton	1741–1769
John Harley	1769–1787
James Jones	1787–1823
John Lilly	1823–1825
Henry Wetherell	1825–1852
Richard Lane Freer	1852–1863
Lord Saye and Sele	1863–1886
Berkeley Stanhope	1887–1910
Edward Winnington-Ingram	1910–1923
Rowland Money-Kyrle	1923–1928
Geoffrey Iliff	1929–1941
Arthur Winnington-Ingram	1942–1958
Thomas Randolph	1959–1970
John Lewis	1970–1976
Thomas Barfett	1977–1982
Andrew Woodhouse	1982–1991
Leonard Moss	1991–1997
Michael Hooper	1997–present

Archdeacons of Shropshire

Peter le Kauf	occ. 1131 x 1148
Odo	occ. 1144 x 1148
Walter Foliot	occ. 1148 x 1163; d. 1178
Hugh Foliot	1178 x 1186–1219
Nicholas of Wolverhampton	1219 x 1222–1227
Simon Edenbridge	1227–1240
Peter of Aigueblanche	1240
John Foliot	1240 x 1241–1243±
Peter of Radnor	1252
James of Aigueblanche	1253–1269
Peter Radnor	occ. 1272; d. 1276
James of Aigueblanche	occ. 1277–deprived 1280
Adam Fileby	1280–1287
John Bestane	1287–1289
John Swinfield	1289–1293
Roger Canterbury	1293–1300
Philip Talbot	1300–1309
John Ross	1309–1318
William Ross	1318–? occ. 1326
Richard Sydenhale	1333–?
Henry Shipton	occ. 1346–1366
William Borstall	1366–1367
Richard Nowell	1367–?
John Hore	Occ. 1385–1410
John Wells	1410
John Hereford	1410–1417
John Loveney	1417–1422
John Merbury	1422–?
William Laches	1425–1441
Thomas Yone	1441–1472
Robert Geffrey	1472– ?, occ. 1478
Thomas Morton	occ. 1485
John Martyn	?–1504
William Webbe	1504–1511
Arthur Stafford	1511
John Wardroper	occ. 1512–1516
William Goberd	1515–1516
Henry Martyn	1516–1524
Humphrey Ogle	1524–1537

Richard Sparchford	1537–1560
Nicholas Smith	1560–1561
Robert Grenshill	1561–1579
William Greenwich	1580–1631
Morgan Godwin	1631–c. 1644
Thomas Cooke	1660–1669
Stephen Phillips	1669–1684
Francis Wheeler	1684–1686
Adam Ottley	1687–1713
Robert Comyn	1713–1726
Richard Crosse	1727–1732
Samuel Croxall	1732–1738
Robert Breton	1738–1741
Egerton Leigh	1742–1760
John Harley	1760–1769
Robert Clive	1769–1792
Joseph Plymley	1792–1838

William Vickers	1838–1851
William Waring	1851–1877
George Maddison	1877–1892
Henry Bather	1892–1905
Algernon Oldham	1905–1913
Alfred Lilley	1913–1928
Edwin Bartleet	1928–1932
Henry Dixon	1932–1939
Herbert Whatley	1939–1948
Hugh Bevan	1948–1960
John Lewis	1960–1970
Andrew Woodhouse	1970–1982
Mark Wood	1982–1983
Ian Griggs	1984–1987
Richard Lewis	1987–1992
John Saxbee	1992–present

Residentiaries 1583–1937

Edward Cooper	1583–1584
Edward Threlkeld	1583–1588
William Penson	1583–1587
Godfrey Golsborowe	1584–1600
Thomas Thornton	1584–1629
Griffith Lewys	1587–1607
Miles Smith	1587–1624
Gervase Babbington	1589–1596
John Watkyns	1593–1594
Giles Tomson	1596–1612
Thomas Singleton	1605–1614
Roger Brodshawe	1607–1613
Francis Kerry	1607–1649
John Best	1612–1635
George Benson	1614–1649
John Richardson	1624–1631
Thomas Godwyn	1626–1644
William Skynner	1631–1647
Robert Burghill	1635–1641
Henry Rogers	1642–1649
George Benson	1660–1672
Thomas Goods	1660–1678
Stephen Phillips	1660–1667
William Watts	1660–1679
Laurence Seddon	1660–1675
William Sherborne	1667–1679
Daniel Wicherley	1672–1677
Stephen Phillips	1675–1684
Thomas Wotton	1677–1711
Philip Lewis	1678–1684

Walter Rogers	1679–1689
Thomas Seddon/Sidney	1679–1686
Thomas Rogers	1684–1710
William Watts, jr.	1684–1722
Samuel Benson	1686–1690
William Johnson	1689–1698
Adam Ottley	1690–1723
Richard Bulkley	1698–c. 1702
Charles Whiting	1702–1711
Richard Smalbroke	1710–1724
Daniel Phillips	1711–1721
Robert Morgan	1712–1745
Hugh Lewis	1721–1722
John Hoadley	1723–1727
John Evans	1723–1749
Thomas Whishaw	1723–1740
Robert Breton	1724–1768
Daniel Wilson	1727–1743
Samuel Croxall	1740–1752
Humphrey Whishaw	1743–1780
Egerton Leigh	1746–1760
William Lane	1749–1752
John Jones	1752–1768
Joseph Browne	1752–1767
Thomas Russell	1760–1785
William Willim	1767
John Evans	1767–1783
James Birt	1768–1801
John Woodcock	1769–1781
Joseph Guest	1780–1804

Hugh Price	1781–1782	John Jebb	1870–1886
Charles Morgan	1782–1789	Sidney Smith	1877–1904
Gibbons Bagnall	1783–1800	Frederick Ouseley	1886–1889
Hugh Morgan	1785–1809	Henry Phillott	1887–1896
John Napleton	1789–1817	George Whitaker	1889–1892
Thomas Russell, jr	1801–1831	Henry Bather	1892–1905
Henry Ford	1803–1813	Charles Palmer	1892–1910
Thomas Underwood	1804–1839	Frederick Williams	1896–1911
George Cope	1809–1821	William Capes	1904–1915
John Clutton	1813–1838	Algernon Oldham	1905–1909
Andrew Bell	1818–1819	Arthur Bannister	1909–1936
Henry Hobart	1819–1844	Hastings Rashdall	1910–1917
Hugh Hanmer Morgan	1821–1861	Alfred Lilley	1911–1936
Arthur Matthews	1831–1840	Burnett Streeter	1915–1935
Henry Huntingford	1838–1868	Edward Winnington-	1917–1929
Lord Saye and Sele	1840–1887	Ingram	
William Peete	1844–1892	Herbert Moore	1929–1936
Musgrave		Harold Moreton	1935
William Evans	1861–1870	Henry Dixon	1936
William Waring	1867–1877	Charles Warner	1936

Under the terms of the 1937 cathedral statutes residentiaries were to be up to four in number all of whom were also to be dignitaries. Thus the dignitaries, precentor, treasurer and chancellor were the only residentiaries from 1937–1982. From 1945–1985 the treasurer also held the office of archdeacon of Hereford. Since 1985 the archdeacon of Hereford has been an additional residentiary.

Appendix 3

Cathedral Charities

Rosalind Caird

Canons' Dole

The origins of this charity are obscure. According to the thirteenth-century cathedral statutes corn was distributed among the poor annually on 15 January in commemoration of Godiva and Wulviva, the donors of the four chief manors of the cathedral estates, Norton Canon, Canon Pyon, Woolhope and Preston, and on 15 November, the anniversary of the death of Bishop Giles de Braose.[1] By the sixteenth century distribution dates were fixed as the Saturday before Christmas Day and Candlemas.[2] The canons' dole was in the form of bread made from two thirds of rye and one of wheat, baked in the canons' bakehouse, but how it was distributed is not known. The wheat used was a small percentage of that collected by the bakehouse from a large number of cathedral and prebendal estates, whereas all the rye collected was used for the dole, with a small residue being distributed among the residentiaries. The contributors of rye remained fairly constant over the centuries. In 1678 it was collected from Clehonger, Cublington, Holmer, Hunderton, Newton, Tibberton and Withington tithes, Eaton Bishop vicarage and the Mawfield estate, while by 1798 Tibberton and Cublington had been omitted.[3]

In 1664 the chapter decided that the dole should be distributed through parochial machinery.[4] The parishes chosen were the six Hereford parishes and twenty-seven parishes adjacent to the city. In 1835, 4360 loaves were distributed annually to the parishes, each receiving between twenty and 440 loaves. The remaining loaves were distributed among prisoners in the gaol and some cathedral appointments.[5]

1. E. F. H. Dunncliff 'Consuetudines et statuta ecclesiae cathedralis Herefordensis: A Paraphrase In English' (HCA, typescript, 1962), p. 19.
2. HCA, R 641, canons' bakehouse accounts, 1592–93.
3. HCA, 7036/1, audit accounts, 1670–97.
4. HCA, 7031/3, p. 237, chapter acts, 1 December 1664.
5. *Report of the Commissioners Appointed in Pursuance of Acts of Parliament to Inquire Concerning Charities and Education of the Poor in England and Wales, arranged in Counties,* xiii, *Hereford* (London, 1815–39), part 2: 'City of Hereford', p. 14.

The bread dole continued until January 1856 when the chapter 'ordered that distribution of bread from the Canon's Bakehouse be discontinued and the price of such bread be paid to ministers of respective parishes in either money or bread or in aid of any clothing or coal club or parochial school as such ministers may think most convenient to the interests of the poor'.[6] Cathedral appointees also received their share in money. In 1914 those who received payments were the censor of St Ethelbert's Hospital, the verger, pricker, sexton, pitman, organ blower and choristers. This list had been reduced to payments to the censor and the choristers prize fund by the time the charity was wound up.[7]

By 1971 the income from the canons' dole was so low that the chapter decided to distribute it every third year. Only one payment was made on this basis because in February 1974 the chapter decided to accept the county charities officer's suggestion to redeem the canons' dole on a basis of fifteen years' purchase. The dole bread account was closed on 5 April 1975 and a capital payment ranging from £7.50 to £37.50 was paid to each of the participating parishes, with the residue of £26.74 being transferred to the cathedral's general account.[8]

Tomson's Charity

Richard Lane alias Tomson, by his will of 24 July 1619, directed his executors to purchase land which would yield an annual income of £20, and to vest it in the dean and chapter who were to dispose of the revenue as he directed.[9] Two estates were bought, one called Bean's Lands of 39 acres 3 roods 14 perches in Norton Canon, Herefordshire, and the other a farm of 138 acres 2 roods 7 perches, with right of common on Bryngwyn Hill, and the liberty of cutting peat on Rhos Goch Common, in Bryngwyn, Radnorshire. In the 1830s the rent of the former was £46 8s. 11d. a year and of the latter £60.

The original beneficiaries were to be twelve poor people coming to evening prayer in the cathedral every Saturday and each receiving afterwards one penny-loaf of good bread, and 6d. on the vigil of the feast days named; to one deacon of the cathedral 40s. yearly to provide the bread weekly, and to deliver the money; to another deacon 40s. yearly to prick (copy) into books song parts and church services. On his coming half yearly for his wages, he should bring the sub-chanter of the choir to show what he had done in that business, and if he had been negligent, the payment for that time should be given to the same twelve poor

6. HCA, 7031/20, p. 354, chapter acts, 14 January 1856.
7. HCA, 6189/1, 2, dole bread accounts, 1914–75.
8. HCA, 7031/25, p. 25, chapter acts, 5 December 1971; 7031/26, p. 107,117, 4 February, 22 July 1974.
9. HCA, 3957.

people on the following Saturday. The surplus of the £20 rent was to be spent the first year on Maundy Thursday in clothing poor, old, lame and impotent people, or poor, young and fatherless children; the second year, on the same day, in delivering a debtor out of prison, if enough; and the third year, on the same day, used for binding a poor child a chorister in the cathedral, or some other poor child born in the city of Hereford to be an apprentice to an honest trade in England. If there were no debtor, the money was to be used for one of the other stated purposes.

By 1835 the allowances to the twelve poor on the dean and chapter's list consisted of 6d. a week, two four-penny loaves every Tuesday and Saturday, and 6d. on each of the twelve annual vigils per person. The allowance for pricking church music was uncertain, depending on what was needed in the choir. Sometimes for two or three years nothing was paid on this account. Premiums for apprenticeship were not fixed, but were generally from £10 to £15, the choristers having preference. The other allowance for clothing varied depending on circumstances, £37 12s. 0d. being expended in 1835. Nothing had been paid for many years for the relief of imprisoned debtors. The rents having been increased in 1792, a surplus had accumulated amounting in 1835 to £308 1s. 5d., which was lent to the fabric account at 4 per cent interest.[10]

In 1975 4 acres of charity land at Three Elms, Hereford, were sold; the chapter hoped to be able to devote the income derived from investing the purchase price to the use of the music department of the cathedral. This resulted in a new Charity Commission scheme, approved in December 1977, whereby all the income from the charity was to be applied to the provision of establishing and maintaining choral scholarships at the cathedral school after necessary expenses had been taken for the administration and maintenance of the charity's property.[11]

Howells Charity

The will of Mary Howells, spinster of the parish of St Martin, was presented by her executors on 13 November 1712 to the dean and chapter as named trustees of the charitable bequests it contained. £600 was to be used to purchase a freehold property. The trustees were to receive a total annuity of £40 out of the purchased property and twenty-one acres of arable land in the parish of St Martin, and twenty acres in Lugg Meadow, towards the maintenance of ten poor maids 'of a godly and religious life and conversation'. The interest of £100 was to be equally

10. *Report of the Commissioners Concerning Charities*, xiii, part 2, pp. 11–12.
11. HCA, 7031/26, p. 160, chapter acts, 7 July 1975; p. 429, 12 January 1981; HCA, uncatalogued, Charity Commission scheme, 1 December 1977.

divided among six poor women of St Martin's parish, the money to be laid out on good security by her executors. The interest of another £100, laid out on good security, was to be divided between two poor women in each of the other five parishes of Hereford, payable at Christmas and Easter. All women were to be nominated by the dean and chapter. In 1756 the £200 capital sum was used to purchase property yielding two £6 rentcharges.

The charity properties were for many years in the possession of the Donnithorne family, their agent making the payments to the ten poor maids, and the poor women belonging to the parishes, chosen by the dean and chapter. The former had £4 a year each, the six widows of St Martin's 5s. each every quarter, and the ten other widows 6s. each half-yearly. In 1833 property owned by the Donnithorne family was conveyed to Thomas Davis of Hereford, subject to payment of the three rent charges amounting to £52. The property consisted of Meadow's Farm in Preston Wynn in Withington parish. Since then the dean and chapter have taken over the administration of the charity.[12] In 1978 it was amalgamated with Dr Cope's Charity.

Dr Cope's Charity

George Cope, DD, canon residentiary of Hereford, who died in 1821, by his will of 5 April 1820 gave, among other charitable bequests, to the dean and chapter £1000 on trust to pay the interest in ten equal parts to ten old maids or single women of virtuous character whom they chose as they did for a similar charity (presumably Howells), but the same people were not to benefit from both charities. He gave £200 to the master of St Ethelbert's Hospital, the interest to be paid annually to the poor of the hospital at Christmas. The £1000 was lent to the master of the fabric at 4 per cent interest, and £4 a year paid to ten old maids yearly.[13]

By the 1970s the income from the Cope and Howells Charities was so low that it was thought it would be beneficial to rationalise and amalgamate the two charities. Under a Charity Commission scheme of September 1978 they were redefined in two schemes. Cope and Howells Relief In Need Charity amalgamated Cope's Charity and Mary Howells Charity for ten poor maids in Hereford. Under its terms this charity was to apply the income individually or generally to women in need or distress by making grants of money or providing or paying for services or facilities. Mary Howells Charity for Poor Women was to be used for the relief of poor women resident in the area of Hereford and the parish of Grafton either

12. *Report of the Commissioner Concerning Charities*, xiii, part 2, p. 12.
13. Ibid., p. 13.

in gifts in kind or grants of money. This combined the parts of Howells Charity applied to six poor women in St Martin's parish and ten poor women in the remaining five ancient parishes of Hereford.[14]

Dean Langford's Charity

Charles Langford, DD, by his will of 13 October 1607, left his lands in Disserth, Radnorshire, to the three canons residentiary and the treasurer, the revenue of which was to pay eight scholars 53*s.* 4*d.* a year each, four born in the city to be chosen by the trustees from the free school of Hereford, and four born in Ludlow to be chosen by the town bailiffs from poor boys being keen to learn. All eight were to be at least nine years old and to continue in place until they were sixteen.[15]

The endowment consisted of 298 acres 2 roods 20 perches in Disserth with an unlimited right of common on Cornedde-hill. By 1830 the income was £52 10*s.* 0*d.* which was raised in that year to £60, which produced a small surplus for investment. In 1835 £21 6*s.* 8*d.* was paid to Ludlow Corporation by the chapter clerk for distribution among the four boys at Ludlow Grammar School; each of the four boys at the cathedral school of Hereford received £14 2*s.* 8*d.* and clothes worth £8 10*s.* 8*d.*, and the headmaster received eight guineas for their education.[16] In 1893 the endowment of the charity was amalgamated with Philpott's.

Philpotts's Charity

Roger Philpotts by his will, of 24 March 1615, left a house in the city of Hereford, the £10 annual rent of which was to help maintain two of the Langfordians at Brasenose College, Oxford. Although the original trustees did not constitute the dean and chapter, it came into their hands, and they let the house on the same terms as their similar property, that is on a twenty-nine-year lease renewable at the end of nine years. In 1831 the rent was £8 a year and the renewal fine £48. By the beginning of the nineteenth century the fund had not always been applied to, and there was a large accumulating surplus which was being invested. In 1835 the Charity Commissioners found that there had been only seven payments made out of the fund since 1780. Their advice was to advertise more widely the existence of the charity.[17] By the end of the century the charity had not only income from the house in the city and investments in stock, but also mortgages on Orlham farm, Ledbury, and the Hampton Wafer estate.

14. HCA, 7031/26, p. 219, chapter acts, 1 November 1976; p. 265, 5 December 1977; HCA, uncatalogued, Charity Commission scheme, 28 September 1978.

15. HCA, 3123.

16. *Report of the Commissioners Concerning Charities*, xiii, part 2, pp. 9–10.

17. Ibid., p. 10–11.

In 1893 the cathedral school endowments were reorganised under a new scheme making the school responsible to a new governing body made up of nominees of the dean and chapter, Herefordshire County Council and Hereford City Council. Part of the endowments of Langford's and Philpotts's Charities sufficient to raise £2100 3/4 per cent consolidated stock was transferred to Ludlow Grammar School for their separate administration. The new scheme allowed for scholarships from both charities comprising tuition fees and an annual payment of £5. Philpotts's Charity was also to provide three exhibitions to any university of £50 per annum tenable for three years.[18]

Croft's Charity

By his will, of 4 January 1689, Bishop Croft set up a charity to be administered by Joseph Harvey, chancellor, and Thomas Rogers and William Watts, canons residentiary, whereby an annual payment of £14 was made to the curate of Yarpole, £4 to six poor widows of clergymen in the diocese, and a £10 surplus, when accumulated, was to be applied to apprentice some poor minister's son. Vacancies among the trustees were to be filled by a residentiary, dignitary or other minister living in or near Hereford.[19] The income is derived from an estate of 450 acres called the Bury of Luston in the parish of Eye which was purchased with £1200 set aside for the purpose by Bishop Croft's will. The estate was to provide £48 annually to the trustees of the charity.[20] In 1781 the trustees began to invest the trust's surplus in bank annuities to supplement the income given to each widow up to its present level of £8 per annum. Although not intentionally a charity administered by the dean and chapter, in practice all subsequent trustees have been appointed from within the chapter. In 1981 the chapter decided that since 'the trustees are by custom established residentiary canons of the cathedral, the maintenance of the books and accounts will be carried out in the accounts department of the cathedral'.[21]

18. HCA, 1538.
19. HCA, 4936/1, p. 1–6, minute and account book of Croft's Charity, 1746–1824.
20. Ibid., pp. 7–11.
21. HCA, 7031/26, p. 437, chapter acts, 2 March 1891.

Glossary

Antiphonal/antiphoner: liturgical book containing chants for the Office; companion to the breviary.

Ballflower: architectural decoration resembling a ball enclosed in a globular three-petalled flower, generally set into a concave running mould. Particularly popular in the fourteenth century and, since it involved a good deal of labour, an opulent structure.

Battel: account for meals in the college of vicars choral.

Breviary: liturgical book containing material for the daily Office (q.v.).

Canon: ecclesiastical title. Medieval/pre-Reformation: applied to the major clergy of Hereford Cathedral, also known as prebendaries (q.v.). Modern/post-Reformation: at Hereford, the title customarily reserved for residentiary canons (q.v.), as distinct from other prebendaries.

Chancellor *see* **Dignity**

Chantry priest: a medieval priest supported by a private endowment to celebrate mass each day for the soul of the founder of the chantry; such clergy also took part in the duties of the cathedral choir. Chantry chapels were suppressed at the Reformation.s.

Claviger: literally 'key-holder'; one of two officers appointed annually from the residentiary canons to administer general cathedral expenditure other than that on the fabric, which was separately accounted for.

Cogged down: iron ties within the piers notched or morticed into the surface ashlar.

Commons/common fund: income from certain endowments of the cathedral which was shared among the canons, distinct from the endowments of individual dignities or prebends.

Compline *see* **Office**

Consuetudines: the mid thirteenth-century statutes of Hereford Cathedral, preserved in one manuscript, HCA, 7044/1.

Dean *see* **Dignity**

Dignity/dignitary: endowed cathedral chapter office/office-holder. At most secular cathedrals, including Hereford, there were four: the dean in charge of discipline; the precentor in charge of music and services; the treasurer in charge of ornaments and vestments; the chancellor in charge of the school, library and archives.

Evangeliary: a book containing gospel readings in liturgical order.

Evensong: 1. in the medieval church, the alternative name for vespers.
2. in the Church of England since the Reformation, a name for the service of evening prayer.

Ferial: liturgically, applying to weekdays other than special feast days.

Gradual: 1. a psalm or hymn sung between the readings at the eucharist.
2. liturgical book containing all the choral chants for the Proper of the Mass.

Grammar: in medieval education, the study of reading, writing and speaking Latin.

Hebdomadary: the member of chapter on weekly duty to take services.

Hereford Use *see* **Use of Hereford**

Incipit: the opening words of a text in a medieval manuscript.

Insular: belonging to the culture whose heartlands were Ireland and Northumbria in the early middle ages.

Insular half-uncial: the formal bookhand used by Insular scribes.

Lauds *see* **Office**.

Mass pence: money paid to a canon for attending services.

Matins: 1. in the medieval church, the night office (*see* **Office**).

2. in the Church of England since the Reformation, a name for morning prayer.

Neume: a notational sign used in Gregorian chant to indicate pitch and sometimes note length and rhythm.

None *see* **Office**

Obit book: a compilation containing dates for commemorating the deceased on the anniversary of their deaths; the thirteenth-century volume from Hereford Cathedral preserved in Oxford, Bodleian, MS Rawlinson B 328.

Octave: liturgically, the period of eight days beginning with the day of a festival.

Office: the religious services appointed to be said or sung daily: in the medieval church, these consisted of matins (at midnight), lauds (around dawn), prime, terce, sext, none, vespers and compline (around dusk).

Ordinary: 1. liturgically, the invariable parts of the mass or eucharist.

2. the person who has the right of jurisdiction in canon law, not always precisely defined. In Hereford Cathedral, the dean was the ordinary for his peculiar jurisdiction.

Palimpsest brass: a brass which has been reused by being engraved with a new composition on the reverse surface.

Part-book: one of the music books used daily by the singers and organist in the cathedral services, each containing only the particular part to be sung by each vocal section (treble, alto, tenor or bass), or played by the organist.

Peculiar: a place exempt from the ecclesiastical jurisdiction of the bishop of the diocese in which it is situated.

Penitentiary: a cleric charged with the oversight of the administration of the sacrament of penance.

Perpetuation: in the college of vicars choral, the act by which a vicar was confirmed as a full member of the college after a period of probation.

Praelector: the cathedral lecturer: an official appointed to preach at regular times.

Prebend: the portion of the property of the cathedral granted to a prebendary for his maintenance.

Prebendary: the holder of a cathedral benefice, the income for which was derived from an estate whose name was usually attached to his prebendal stall in the cathedral choir.

Precentor *see* **Dignity**

Prime *see* **Office**

Proper: liturgically, the part of the office (such as the psalm) appointed for particular occasions or seasons; the opposite of 'common'.

Pulpitum: screen shutting off the choir from the nave; the fourteenth-century stone screen in Hereford Cathedral, removed in 1841.

Quotidian: daily.

Residence: the obligation of a cleric to reside personally in the place where he was authorised to minister.

Residentiary canon: one of those prebendaries who entered into the obligations of residence (q.v.), fixed at a certain number of weeks in a year. Residentiaries were entitled to a share in the 'commons' (q.v.), in addition to their prebends (q.v.).

Sanctoral(e): the variable parts of the services provided for saints' days; the counterpart of the temporal(e).

Sext *see* **Office**

Spiritualities: ecclesiastical property or revenue held or received in return for spiritual services.

Succentor: the deputy of the precentor, responsible in the medieval period for the choir and choristers, formerly one of the vicars choral.

Syliconester: a synthetic material with high resistance to temperature and water, injected into and bonded with stonework to enhance its preservation.

Synodal: payment made by an ecclesiastical institution to its Visitor at the time of a visitation.

Temporal(e): the variable parts of the services relating to the Christian year, except those provided for saints' days; the counterpart of the sanctoral(e).

Temporalities: material property or revenue of the church or clergy other than that given in return for spiritual services.

Terce *see* **Office**

Tonal(e)/tonary: liturgical book or part of a larger book containing a guide to the rules for church music.

Treasurer *see* **Dignity**

Uncial *see* **Insular half-uncial**

Use of Hereford: the adaptation of the rites of the Latin Church as used at Hereford Cathedral and in the diocese of Hereford in the middle ages, including provision for local saints, e.g. Ethelbert and Thomas Cantilupe.

Vespers *see* **Office**

Visitation: periodic inspection of the temporal and spiritual affairs of a religious foundation by its appointed Visitor, e.g. a bishop or dean.

Index

Page and plate numbers in **bold** indicate illustrations

Abbey Dore *see* Dore Abbey
Abergavenny, Peter of 567, 570
Acheson, Russell, chancellor
    182, 185, 640
Acts of Parliament 281, 402, 626
    (*see also* Cathedrals; Chantry;
    Dean and Chapter;
    Education; Endowed
    Schools; Public Schools;
    Uniformity)
Adams, Mr, library keeper 520
Adams, Richard 255
Adelaide, queen to William IV
    156, 160–61
Æbba *see* Eormenburga
Ælfgar, Earl 18
Ælfric, bishop of Hereford 14
Ælfstan, Ealdorman 12
Ælfryth, daughter of King Offa 9
Æthelbald, king of the
    Mercians 8, 9
Æthelberht *see* Ethelbert
Æthelheard, archbishop of
    Canterbury 10
Æthelred, King 16
Æthelred, king of the Mercians
    4–6
Æthelstan, bishop of Hereford
    see Athelstan
Æthelstan, King 13
Æthelwulf, bishop of Hereford
    14, 16
Aigueblanche, John of, dean
    44, 325–26, 501, 633, 637
Aigueblanche, Peter of, bishop
    of Hereford 20, 34, 38,
    43–49, **44**, 56, 174, 213, 214

and n., 215–20, 235,
    322–23, 325–26, 374, 442,
    494, 545, 567, 600, 634
Albinus, chancellor 567, 570, 640
Alcock, Simon or Reginald 577
Alderson, Barnabas, vicar
    choral 126 and n., 452
Alexander III, Pope 29
Alexander, Master 443
Alfred the Great, King 12
Allen, George, vicar choral 449
Allen, William, vicar choral 404
Allensmore church,
    Herefordshire 314, 332
Almshouses *see* Hereford, city,
    St Ethelbert's Hospital;
    Ledbury, St Katherine's
    Hospital
Alternative Service Book, 1980 439
Andrews, Rowland, joiner 247
Angilram, archbishop of Metz
    366
Anglian peoples 3
'Anglo-Saxons, kingdom of' 12
Aqua, David de, canon 441
Aquablanca, Peter of *see*
    Aigueblanche, Peter of
Arabic science 42
Archaeological Institute 280
Archaeological Journal 280–81
Archbishops of Canterbury
    xxx, 83, 128, 599
    (*see also* Æthelheard; Becket;
    Cranmer; Cuthberht;
    Davidson; Howley; Juxon;
    Lanfranc; Laud; Parker;
    Pecham; Pole; Rich;

Sancroft; Sutton; Temple;
    Theodore; Wake; Wolsey)
Archbishops of York *see* Ealdred
Archenfield 13
Argentine, John, canon 61
Arundel, John, canon 61
Astrey, Francis, vicar choral 454
Athanasian Creed 170–71
Athelstan (Æthelstan), bishop
    of Hereford xxx, 16–19, 22,
    204, 368, 542
    evangeliary 18–19, **18**
Athulf *see* Æthelwulf
Atkins, Sir Ivor 430, 461, **468**
Atlay, Charles 357
Atlay, George 357
Atlay, James, bishop of
    Hereford 357, **358**
Aubrey, John, 'Chronologia
    Architectonica' 247
Aubrey, Sir Samuel 245
Audley, Edmund, bishop of
    Hereford 224, 235–36, 316,
    337, 501, 621
Avenbury, Giles, dean 46, 637
Aylton, Herefordshire 16

Backler, Charles 318
Badham, John, organist 117,
    403–5
Bagnall, Gibbons, canon 139,
    584, 643
Bailey, Joseph, MP 273–75, 318
Bailey, Martin 194
Baker and Fincher 284
Baker, Richard, vicar choral
    445–46

Baldwin, Samuel 352

Ball, Edward, Mr and Mrs 533

Banastre, Stephen, bellfounder 342–44

Bannister, Arthur T., precentor 168, 170, **170**, 174, 280, 284, 530, 553, 638

Barfett, Thomas, archdeacon of Hereford 182–83, 185, 641

Barlow, John, precentor 91, 390, 638

Barnard, John 401 and n., 529

Barneby, W. Henry 316

Barr(e), Richard de la, canon 58n., 333

Barrett, Philip L. S., vicar choral 186, 460, **460**

Barrett, Richard, lay clerk 417 and n.

Barri, Gerald de 567 (*see also* Gerald of Wales)

Barrow, Edward 250

Baskervil(l)e, Edward 58n., 501

Baskervyle, Ralph 53

Bateman, J. **170**

Battle, Richard of, prebendary 560

Beattie, Ernest H. 176

Beauchamp family 618

Beauclerk, James, bishop of Hereford 130–34, 140, 256, 260–61

Bec, Robert de 342

Becket, Thomas, Saint, archbishop of Canterbury 29, 371, 504–6

Beckingham, Thomas, bishop of Bath and Wells **68**

Becknor, Alexander, archbishop of Dublin **74**

Bede, Venerable 5–8, 363–64

Beer, Simon 197, 504

Benet, John 388

Bennett, Robert, bishop of Hereford 96, **97**, 244, 353–53, **353**

Benson, George, dean 113–14, 116, 119–22, 126, 131, 244, 246, 621, 637

Benson, Samuel, archdeacon of Hereford 120, 641

Beonna, bishop of Hereford 12

Berkley, James, canon 65

Bern Gospels 538

Best, John, canon 244, 547, 642

Béthune, Robert de, bishop of Hereford 27, 29, 31–33, 38, 72, **77**, 217–18, 368, 544, 610, 633

Betjeman, John 179

Betton and Evans, Shrewsbury 316

Bevan, William L. 562

Beves, Brian 197

Bible 558
  English 92, 97, 394, 408, 448, 520, 525
  Latin 537–38

Bibliographical Society 531

Birch, Colonel John 100–2, 402

Bird, John, bellfounder 342

Birt, James, canon 550, 625–26, 642

Bishop, J. C., organ builder 473–74

bishops of Hereford xxxii, 6, 14, 19, 21, 25, 38, 39, 54, 55, 67–69, 76, 94–95, 99, 123, 128, 130, 140, 185n., 189, 191, 268, 270, 324, 378, 401, 441, 545, 631, 634
  absenteeism 44
  properties 102
  registers 49, 55, 80
  vacancies 55, 69, 83
  (*see also* Ælfric; Æthelwulf; Aigueblanche; Athelstan; Atlay; Audley; Beauclerk; Bennett; Beonna; Béthune; Bisse; Bonner; Booth; Braose; Butler; Cantilupe; Capella; Carr; Castello; Charlton; Coke; Courtenay; Croft; Cuthberht; Cuthwulf; Ealdred; Eastaugh; Edgar; Egerton; Field; Foliot; Fox; Gerald; Gilbert; Godwin; Grey; Hampden; Harley; Henson; Hoadley; Humphreys; Huntingford; Juxon; Lacy; Leofgar;

Lindsell; Longworth; Lotharingian; Luxmoore; Maidstone; Mapenore; Mascall; Mayew; Melun; Monck; Musgrave; Myllyng; Oliver; Orleton; Parfew; Parsons; Percival; Putta; Reinhelm; Reynolds; Scory; Skip; Smith; Spofford; Stanbury; Swinfield; Tidhelm; Torhthere; Trefnant; Trillek; Tyrhtil; Vere; Walhstod; Walter; Westfaling; Wren; Wulfheard; Wulfhelm; Wulfric)

bishops of Worcester *see* Bosel; Deneberht; Ealdred; Milred; Pates; Whitgift

Bisse, Philip, bishop of Hereford 130–31, 136, 160, 248–51, 256, 297, 308, 354, 407–8, 462

Bisse, Thomas, chancellor 131, 408–9, **409**, 462–63, 469, 640

Black Death, 1348–49 48, 52, 53, 63, 222, 324, 575, 610, 617

Blackbourn and Greenleaf 344

Blackmarstone, Hereford 164, 605

Blake and Sons, Hereford 286

Blake, Robert N. W. Blake, Baron 193

Blomfield, Sir Arthur 281–84, 528

Blundell, Thomas, master of St Katherine's 622

Board of Education 591–95

Bodenham family, Rotherwas 505

Bodley, Sir Thomas 518

Boethius, *Consolation of Philosophy* 42

Bohun, Humphrey de 271

Bohun, Joanna de **pl. VIa**, 224, 271, 322–33, 327, 384, 389, 444

Bond, Francis 346

Bonner, Edmund, bishop of Hereford and of London 88n., 89, 91 and n.

Bontempi, Andreas, chancellor
575, 640
Book of Common Prayer 90,
106, 111, 377, 394, 400,
402–3, 437–39
Book of Dimma 538
Bookham, Joan 197
Booth, Charles, bishop of
Hereford **pl.VIIa**, 48, 49,
76–77, 87, 229–30, 324, 338,
446, 498, 514, 601
Bosbury, Herefordshire 19
Bosbury, Thomas of, dean 611, 637
Bosel, bishop of Worcester 6
Boteler, Nicholas 501
Bottomley, Virginia 193
Boughan, John, vicar choral 449
Boulton, W. 273
Boyce, Thomas, vicar choral
449–50
Boyce, William 410
Bradford on Avon 531, 562
Brampton, Michael 256
Braose, Giles de, bishop of
Hereford 30, 42, 352, **353**,
633, 644
Braose, Philip de 613
Braose, William de 30
Bredwardine, Thomas de,
master of St Katherine's 617
Breinton, Herefordshire 602
Breton, Robert, archdeacon of
Hereford 129, 130, 132, 641
Breton, Thomas, master of St
Ethelbert's 604
Brewster, William 533
Bridwode, John, canon 60
Brindley and Richards 357
Bristol, Elias of *see* Elias of
Bristol
British Archaeological
Association 271, 273
British Library 191, 192, 194
British Museum 561–62
Britton, John 259, 263
Broad, Edward, vicar choral 406
Broad, John, vicar choral
452–54
Bromsgrove Guild 321
Bromyard, Herefordshire 12,
14, 15

Brophy, Paul, succentor 186
Brown, Jonathan, dean 102n., 637
Brown, Langton E.,
sub-librarian 529
Browne, Joseph, chancellor
128–29, 132–33, 640
Browne, William, vicar choral
393n.
Brut, Walter, lollard 49, 620
Brut, William le, master of St
Katherine's 617
Budd, Jim 290, 316n.
Bull, John, organist 96n., 108,
375, 395–96, **396**
Bull, Maude, sub-librarian
177–78, 529
Bulmer, H. P., Holdings,
Hereford 487
Bunn, Fanny 358
Burgehyll, Richard, teacher of
grammar 576
Burghill, William, treasurer
64n., 602, 639
Burley, Simon 58n.
Burley (Burghill), William,
master of the choristers 391,
572–73
Burlison, John 319–20
Burrows, Hedley, dean
176–78, **178**, 434–37, 498,
506, 638
Butler, John, bishop of
Hereford 140, 145, 150, 261,
412
Butterworth, James F.,
treasurer 186, 639
Byfield, John, organ builder 472
Byrhtferth 9

Calkeberge, Ralph de, vicar
choral 37
Calkeberge, Roger de, canon
36
Cambrian Society 345
Cambridge (Cantebrugge),
Thomas of, mason 227, 231,
236, 308
Cambridge, University of
St John's College 582
Canon Pyon, Herefordshire 26,
33, 34, 644

Canterbury, archbishops of *see*
Archbishops of Canterbury
Canterbury, Convocation of 82
Cantilupe Society 552
Cantilupe, Thomas, Saint,
bishop of Hereford 41, 48,
65, 71–76, **72**, 82, 194, 218,
220, 224, 232, 235, 238–39,
240, 320, 328–30, 335,
386–89, 495, 560–61
canonisation 71–73, 83, 219,
222, 323, 330, 379
miracles 218
shrines/tomb xxix, 51, 67,
72–76, 83, 86, 88–89, 174,
198, 218–20, 222, 242,
244, 290–91, 322–24, 326,
328–30, **329**, 331, 333,
333, 379, 388, 500, 629
Canute *see* Cnut
Capel, Alfred, vicar choral 164
Capella, Richard de, bishop of
Hereford 501
Capes, William W., canon
167–68, 431, 552–53, **553**,
591, 643
Caple, William 58n.
Capps and Capps 287
Capps, Roger 280
Care of Cathedrals Measure,
1990 191, 289
Carline, John 270, 272
Caroe, W. R., architect 284–85
Carpenter, Thomas,
prebendary 91
Carr, Charles L., bishop of
Hereford 175, 357, 498
Carr, Robert, dean 150, 638
Carter, John 260, 262, 269
Caryndyn, Roger 394
Castello, Adriano de, bishop of
Hereford 621
Caswell, Gp Capt A. W.,
administrator 181–83, 186–87
Cathedral Commissions, 1852,
1879 525, 527
Cathedrals Act, 1840 424, 426
Cathedrals Advisory
Commission 191
Cathedrals Advisory
Committee 179

Cathedrals Commission 173
Cathedrals Fabric Commission
 for England 191, 289, 313
Cathedrals Measure, 1931 173,
 460
Cathedrals Measure, 1999 xxxi,
 630–31
cathedrals, old foundation xxx,
 22, 34, 37, 54, 93–94,
 364–65, 378, 630
Caudron, Simone 504–6
Cecil, Sir William, Baron
 Burghley 92
Champagne, Bernard of, Prior
 45–46
Champion, John 197
Chandler, Thomas, dean
 66–67, **68**, 637
Chandos, James Brydges, duke
 of 135, 249
Chandos, Robert de 441
Chandos, Thomas, archdeacon
 of Hereford 444, 641
chant 363–67, 376, 400, 414
 and n.
 Anglican 400, 414 and n.
 Gregorian 363–67
 Roman 363–66
Chantry Acts, 1545, 1547
 622–23
Chappell, Paul, vicar choral
 180–81
Charity Commission 588, 590,
 606, 608–10, 626, 646–49
Charles I, King 98, 100, 112,
 320, 402, 579–80
Charles II, King 109, 114, 452,
 473, 502, 580, 624
Charles, Prince of Wales 189
Charlton, Lewis, bishop of
 Hereford 71, 224, 513
Charlton, Thomas, bishop of
 Hereford 222, 278, 324, 384
Charnock, Hugh, canon 64
Charteris of Amisfield, Martin
 M. C. Charteris, Baron
 pl. XV
Chase, June 197
Chaundos, Richard 58n.
Chave, Brian, canon **187**
Chell, William, precentor 67,

92, 390, 393–94, 446,
 573–74, 638
Chick, William, clerk of the
 works 279, 280
Chipman, Thomas, canon 65
Christianity, conversion to 3
Chrodegang, archbishop of
 Metz 365–66
Church Commissioners 180,
 195, 284–85, 554
Church of England 109, 193
 Church Assembly 459
 General Synod xxxi, 191,
 196
Church Times 171
Cirencester, Augustinian abbey
 515
Civil War 87, 100–2, **101**, 105,
 112–13, 245–46, 308, 350,
 352, 451–52, 470, 511, 521,
 532, 580, 604, 624
Clack, Richard, organist 411
Clare, Elizabeth de Burgh,
 Lady 495
Clare, Osbert de 40
Clarendon Commission 587
Clarke, John, vicar choral 452
Clarke, W. E. A., architect
 284–85
Clarke-Whitfeld, John, organist
 157, 415–16, 420
Clavering, Robert, dean 126,
 128, 248, 407, 637
Clayton and Bell 319–20
Clehonger, Herefordshire 605,
 608
Clermont, Anselm of, dean 46,
 637
Clibury family, bellfounders 343
Clifford, de, family 38
Clifford, Simon de 613
Clive, George 196
Clive, Lt-Col. Percy 358
Cliveden Conservation 290
Clofesho, church councils at 8,
 11, 12
Clutton, John, canon 160,
 267–68, 317, 606, 643
Cnut, King 16, 23, 542
Cockerell, S. M. 562
Coenred, king of the Mercians 9

Coke, Francis, precentor 110n.,
 638
Coke, George, bishop of
 Hereford 98–99, 102, 354,
 497
Coke, Richard, chancellor
 110n., 640
Colborne, Langdon, organist
 319, 427–30, **428**, 477
Collins, Peter, Ltd 492
Committee for Sequestration
 402, 451–52
Commonwealth, the xxxi, 87,
 100
Coningsby, Fitzwilliam, MP 580
Constable, John, butler to the
 college 456, **457**
Cook, Melville, organist 437–38
Cooke, Captain Henry 403–4
Cooke, William, bell hanger 343
Cooper, Edward, archdeacon
 of Hereford 602–3, 623–24,
 639, 641
Cooper, John, bookbinder 521
Cope, George, canon 152, 318,
 415, 606, 643, 647
Coren, Hugh, dean 91, 637
Cormeilles Abbey 36, 82, 442,
 636
Cornwaille, Richard,
 schoolmaster 574–75
Cotterell, Alexandra, Lady 195
Cotterell, Sir John **pl. XV**, 194
Cotterell, Sir John Geers 585
Cotterell, Sir Richard **178**
Cottingham, Lewis Nockalls
 160, 232, 239, 244, 269–74,
 275, 276, 279, 280, 281,
 290, 317, 322, 338, 351,
 354, 357, 473, 506
Cottingham, Nockalls Johnson
 272–75, 317, 338, 357
Courtenay, William, bishop of
 Hereford 68
Coventry *see* Herbert Art
 Gallery
Cox, Richard, vicar choral
 452, 453
Coyle, Miles, organist 412–13
Cranmer, Thomas, archbishop
 of Canterbury 63, 87, 91

Crees, J. H., headmaster 433, 593–94
Creppinge, Alan de, canon 51, 513
Cresset, Edward, dean 126–27, 502–3, 638
Croft, Herbert, dean and bishop of Hereford xxx, 87, 100–2, 102n., 110–11, **110**, 114, 116–18, 121–22, 128, 133, 150, 247, 320, 402, 405, 406, 454, 581, 624, 637, 649
Croft, William 409–10
Cromwell, Oliver 87, 100, 106, 140, 624
Crowther, William, vicar choral 454–55
Cubberley, Richard 252–53
Custance, George, vicar choral 426
Cuthberht, bishop of Hereford, archbishop of Canterbury 8, 493
Cuthwulf, bishop of Hereford 12, **13**
Cwenburh, wife to sub-king Milfrith 8
Cwenthryth, queen to King Offa 9
Cwm, Llanrothal, Hereford-shire, Jesuit College 522

Daily Telegraph 179, 192
Dallam, Robert or Thomas, organ builder 470–71
Danes, the 16
Daniel, Edmund, dean 92, 637
Dare, Charles J., organist 413–14, 473
Davidson, Randall T., archbishop of Canterbury xxxii, 173
Davies, Arthur 321
Davies, Daniel 607
Davies, Edward 248
Davies, Hugh 244
Davies, John, prebendary 124
Davies, John, verger 503
Davies, Meredith, organist 434–37

Davis, Hugh, organist 400
Davis, Thomas 647
Davis, Walter, clerk of the works 178
Dawes, Richard, dean 161–63, **163**, 165, 279, 357, 422, 426, 457, 466, 638
De la Barr *see* Barr(e)
De Vere *see* Vere
Dean and Chapter Act, 1840 156
deans and chapters 154, 191
Deans and Provosts Conference 183
Dee, John 515
Defoe, Daniel 407
Delabere, Sir Richard 334
Delabere, William 58n.
Delamaine, Richard, cathedral preacher 106–7, 245, 604
Delamare, Richard, high sheriff 333–34
Deneberht, bishop of Worcester 11
Denton, Alexander **pl. VIIb**, 243, 278, 351–52
Denton, Anne **pl. VIIb**, 278, 351–52
Denyar, Thomas 231
Derbyshire stone 288, 290, 313
Dewick missal 376
Diana, Princess of Wales 189, 630
Diddlebury, Shropshire 36, 441, 446, 459
Dingley, Thomas 328, 343, 353, 453, 561
Directory for Public Worship 106, 402
Disserth, Radnorshire 579, 648
Dixon, Henry, archdeacon of Ludlow (Shropshire) 174–75, 642
Domesday Book 19, 20, 23, 25, 26, 33, 542
Dominican friars 45, 49, 80
Donnithorne family 647
Donnithorne, Isaac, vicar choral 356, 455
Dore Abbey, Herefordshire 218, 224

Dornell, John, schoolmaster 574, 576–77
Doughtie, Edward, dean 97 and n., 518n., 637
Douglas, A. Langton 506
Drokensford, John, bishop of Bath and Wells **74**
Duncumb, John 551
Dyche, Richard 259–60

Eadfrith, Northumbrian priest 4
Ealdred, bishop of Hereford and of Worcester, archbishop of York 20, 23
Eames, Lt-Col. Andrew K., chapter clerk 187, **187**
earthquake, 1896 167, 173, 282
Eastaugh, John R. G., bishop of Hereford 174, 197, 504
Ecclesiastical Commissioners 156, 158, 166, 176, 180, 421–22, 457, 459, 551, 591
Ecclesiastical Revenue Commissioners 155
Edgar, bishop of Hereford 14
Edgar, King 14
Education Act, 1902 591
Education Act, 1944 594
Edward the Confessor, King 22, 23
Edward the Elder, King 12
Edward I, King 235
Edward IV, King 236
Edward VI, King 89, 90, 91, 97, 105, 394, 515, 578
Edwards, Batty 250, 408
Egerton, Henry, bishop of Hereford 294
Egerton, John, dean 126, 127, 134, 638
Eginton, William 262
Eilmar, canon 22, 37
Eleanor of Castile, Queen 495
Elgar, Sir Edward 432, 467–68, **468**, 480, 491
Elias of Bristol, canon 39, 41, 599–600
Elizabeth I, Queen 91, 448, 450–1, 501, 623
Elizabeth II, Queen **pl. XV**, 177, **178**, 182, 195, 313, 534

Elliott, Thomas, organ builder 473

Elton family 622

Elton, John, master of St Katherine's 622

Elyas of Bristol *see* Elias of Bristol

Embrey, Susan 195

Endowed Schools Act, 1869 588

Endowed Schools Act, 1889 590

English Heritage 193, 195, 289, 290, 291, 313

Eormenburga, wife to Merewalh 4

Episcopal lists, Anglo-Saxon 5

Erasmus, Desiderius 92, 576

Erchemar, dean 38, 39, 637

Erchemar, Ranulf fitz, canon 38

Ergyng, Welsh kingdom *see* Archenfield

Esegar, Adam de 618

Esegar family 618

Esmée Fairbairn Memorial Trust 531

Ethelbert (Æthelberht), Saint, king of the East Angles 9, 10, **11**, 22, 40, 65, 76, 197, 208–10, 212, 213, 220, 224, 276, 315, 320, 324, 328, 333, **333**, 335, 371–73, 377, 379, 385–87, 505, 507, 613
statue **11**, 224

Evangelicalism 466

Evans, John, canon 127, 642

Evans, Mary 354, **355**

Evans, Miss 606

Evans, Philip, carpenter 255, 256, 257

Evans, Seiriol, dean of Gloucester 179

Evans, William, prebendary 354, **355**

Evans, William, vicar choral 448–49

Evesham, John of, mason 231, 234, 236

excommunication 53

Exeter Cathedral, medieval music 366

Eyden, Eric, precentor 179, 180, 638

Faculty jurisdiction 191

Fairfax-Scott, C., headmaster 594

Farrant, John, organist 449

Fell, Samuel, dean of Christ Church, Oxford 521

Felton, William, vicar choral 455, **455**

Fernlage, later called Hereford 9

Field, Edmund 576–77

Field, Theophilus, bishop of Hereford 98, 99, 351, 353–54

Finch, John, bellfounder 343

Fink, Ross, assistant organist 435–36

First World War 169, 171–72, 358, 432, 459, 461, 466, 592–93

Fisher, Humphrey, vicar choral 452, 549

Fisher, Mr 523

Fisher, William 250

Flint, Valerie 194

Foley, Paul Henry 532

Foliot family 39 and n., 512

Foliot, Gilbert, bishop of Hereford 29, 33, 38, 40, 42, 43, 611, 633

Foliot, Hugh, bishop of Hereford 25, 30, 31, 33, 41, 599, 610–12, 614, 616, 623–24, **625**, 627, 633

Foliot, Ralph, archdeacon of Hereford 512, 640

Foliot, Robert, bishop of Hereford 29, 30, 36, 305

Foliot, Thomas, treasurer 612–13, 639

Foliot, Walter, archdeacon of Shropshire 39, 641

Ford, Henry, canon 147, 151, 643

Forsyth, James 357

Foular, Gryffyn, priest of St Katherine's 616

Fox, Edward, bishop of Hereford 87, 446

Franciscan friars 45, 49, 80

fraternities 77–78

Fraunceys, Margaret 616

freemasonry 166, 173

Freer, Richard Lane, archdeacon of Hereford 317, 344, 466, 641

Freine, Simon de 30, 40 and n., 42 and nn., 43, 512, 566

French Gothic architecture 214–16, 235

Frere, Walter Howard 385

Frères, Rolin, organ builder 483

Fresne *see* Freine

Friars *see* Dominican friars, Franciscan friars

Friends of Hereford Cathedral 174, 179–80, 197, 335, 504, 529, 532, 631
festival 176

Frisne *see* Freine

Frowcester, Edmund, dean 65, 335, 514, 637

Garbett, James, carpenter 255, 343

Gardener, Richard, vicar choral 445

Gaschet, Jean, bookseller 577–78

Gefferies, Thomas, bellfounder 342, 344

Gentleman's Magazine 142n., 259, 260, 271

Geoffrey, Simon, carpenter 243

Geoffrey, Robert, canon 64

George IV, King 417, 533

George, John, succentor 393–95

George, Robert 394

George, Saint, cult of 40, 76

Gerald, bishop of Hereford 27

Gerald of Wales (Giraldus Cambrensis) 30, 40, 42, 43, 208, 387, 512, 566–67

Gerard, dean 26, 37, 637

Gesant, John fitz 616

Getty Fund 531

Getty, Sir Paul **pl. XV**, xxxi, 194, 562

Getty, Victoria, Lady **pl. XV**

Gibbs, Charles 317

Gilbert, John, bishop of Hereford 575, 590

Giles the tailor 390–91, 470

Gill, Michael, succentor 186

Giraldus Cambrensis *see* Gerald of Wales

Gittens, Walter, verger 175, 182

Glendower *see* Glyndwr

Gloucester Cathedral 233, 234,
    515, 546–47

Gloucester, John of 235

Gloucester, Robert of, canon 387

Gloucester, St Peter's Abbey
    see Gloucester Cathedral

Glyndwr, Owain 49

Godiva 644

Godo, canon 22, 37

Godwin, Francis, bishop of
    Hereford 96–97

Godwin, William, of
    Lugwardine 276, 278, 279

Goldsmiths Company 504

Goodrich Court, Herefordshire
    270

Gore, Charles, bishop of
    Oxford 171

Goss, John, vicar choral 320,
    426, 458

Gough, Richard 250, 260, 262,
    505, 561

Gowrie, Alexander
    P. G. H. Ruthven, Earl of
    192, **192**

Grandisson family 618

Grandisson, Peter de 224, 271,
    323–24, 328

Gray and Davison, organ
    builders 474, 476

Greene, Maurice 410

Gregory I, Pope 363

Grene, John, canon 63,
    298–99, 307, 445

Gretton, Frederick E. 156

Gretton, George, dean 149–50,
    550, 638

Grey, Charles Grey, Earl 156

Grey, Edward, dean and
    bishop of Hereford 150,
    156, 158, 159–60, 586, 638

Griffiths, William, plumber
    120, 248, 252

Grose, Francis 252

Grossé, Louis, of Bruges 498–99

Grosseteste, Robert, bishop of
    Lincoln 42, 566

Gruffudd ap Llywelyn 19, 22

Grylls, Thomas 319–20

Guardian 191

Guest, Joseph, canon, master of
    St Ethelbert's 605, 642

Guy's Hospital 149

Gwillim, Thomas, vicar choral
    406

Hackett, Maria 414

Haldingham *see* Holdingham

Hall, Edward 194

Hall, Frances 115

Hall, Henry I, organist 405–7,
    405

Hall, Henry II, organist 407,
    461–62

Hall, William 407

Hamel, Christopher de 190

Hammond, Lieutenant 98, 108,
    451, 470

Hampden, Renn Dickson,
    bishop of Hereford 160–61,
    161, 343, 422, 424

Hampton Court, Herefordshire
    531, 562

Hampton, John, precentor 430,
    638

Hancock, Gilbert R., vicar
    choral 455–56

Harding, Douglas G., steward 187

Hardman, John 317–19, 320

Hardwick, Philip, architect
    268, 270

Hardwick, Thomas, architect
    259–60

Hare, John, vicar choral 446

Hare, Mr, inspector of charities
    607

Harford, Bridstock 107

Harley, John, bishop of
    Hereford 90–91, 140

Harold II, Godwinson, King
    20, 22, 23

Harris, Anne 609

Harris, John, dean 126, 248,
    407, 637

Harris, Renatus 120, 471–72, 474

Harrison and Harrison, of
    Durham, organ builders 486

Harrison, Richard, cathedral
    preacher 106

Harvey, Joseph, chancellor 121,
    640, 649

Hassall, Eilene 181, 188

Havergal, Francis Tebbs, vicar
    choral 163, 271, 275, 280,
    322, 352, 426, 498, 505–8,
    524–28, **526**, 531, 551

Hawkins, Richard, mason 255,
    256, 258

Hay, William de (la), canon
    52, 501

Haynes, Peter, dean 185, 186,
    192, 638

Hayter, Aaron, organist 414–15

Heal, Ivor 195

Hearne, Thomas 259

Heaton, Butler and Bayne 320

Heinfrid, archdeacon of
    Hereford 24, 37, 640

Henry II, King 599

Henry III, King 43, 214, 494

Henry IV, King 620

Henry VI, King, cult of 76

Henry VIII, King xxx, 49, 82,
    83, 86, 87, 89, 97, 447, 578

Henson, Herbert Hensley,
    bishop of Hereford xxxii,
    166, 169, 171, **172**, 173, 632

Henson, John, headmaster
    592–93

Herbert Art Gallery, Coventry
    180, 285, 341

Herbert, George, dean 162,
    166, 281, 320, 426–28, 458,
    479, 638

Hereford, bishops of *see*
    bishops of Hereford

Hereford breviary **pl. IVa**, 40,
    47, 369–74, **372**, **373**,
    375–76, 385–87, 443, 515,
    525, 531

HEREFORD CATHEDRAL
    **pls IIc, IIIa, XIV, 108,
    142, 242, 263, 264**

administrator 181, 183,
    186–87, 189

almshouses *see* Hereford,
    city, St Ethelbert's
    Hospital; Ledbury, St
    Katherine's Hospital

altar cloths **pl. XIIIa**,
    495–98, **499**

altar rails 245, 250, 265, 408

Hereford Cathedral continued

altarpiece 136, 160, 249–50, **251**, 267, 273, 561

altars 69, 76, 84–85, 90, 197, **198**, 207, 210, 211, 213, 224, 225, 230, 245, 250, 285, 324, 379, 380, 394, 408, 447, 495–98, 501, 515

Anglo-Saxon cathedral(s) 14, 17, 18, 19, 203–4, 206, 293–94, 298, 368, 511–12

destruction, 1055 xxx, 206, 368, 495, 511

anthems 400, 403

appeals, 1886 281; 1927 284; 1960s 286; 1985 182–83, 189, 287, 290

architect 189, 286, 289

archives **pls IIa, b, 13, 17, 33**, 49, **75**, 110, 115–16, 130–33, 522, 534–35, 544–56, **550**, 577

accounts 50, 51, 54, 64, 71, 78, 103–4, 111, 112, 119–20, 135, 218, 226, 242–43, 246, 249, 257, 258, 399, 517, 521

chapter act books 50, 67, 69, 70, 76, 90, 91, 93, 100, 115, 118, 124, 130, 131, 197, 249, 257, 258, 266, 267, 318, 343, 377, 389, 393, 404, 409, 412, 527, 548–49, 572

lockers (capsules) 547–49, **548**, 551, 552, **552**, 554–55

archivist (keeper of the archives) 187, 534–35, 544n., 547, 549–50, 552–53, 556

audit 134–35, 151, 420

Audley chapel **70**, 203, 224, 227, 241, 274, 279, 285, 315–16, 337, 379

bailiffs, chapter 635

bakehouse 34, 54, 580, 589, 604, 644–45

ballflower ornament 219, 221, 233, 238–39, 284

barn 34, 292, 300, **301**

battlements 262–64, 278

bells 81, 136, 221, 243, 245, 255, 281, 342–44, 383, 403, 443

bishop's chapel 24, 204, 241–42, 294–97, **295**, 298, 309, 368, 379, 447

bishop's throne 224, 265, 347–48

books 24, 66, 511–43

law books **pl. VIIId**, 513–14

medieval manuscripts **pls VIIIa–c**, 190, 368, 511–15, 521–22, 525, 534, 536–43, **571**

music/service books 133, 401, 404, **405**, 409–10, 413, 515, 521–22, 525, 533, 646

schoolbooks 577–78, 586

(*see also* library)

bosses **47**, 226, 309

boy bishop 71

brasses 65, 66, **66**, **88**, 113, 246, 265, 322, 326, 328, 333–35, **333**, **334**, **335**, 576

breviary, thirteenth-century *see* Hereford breviary

breviators 78

brewhouse 34

broadcasts, radio and television 176, 177, 434, 436

Broderers' Guild 496, 498

building works 76–78, 81, 140–47

burials 41, 79–80, 125–26, 136, 144–45, 243, 304–6, 322, 324, 331, 507–8

buttresses 261, 278, 289

candles 182, 502, 521, 629

canonical houses 39, 64, 128–29n., 133, 248, 291, 298–304, **301**, **303**, 305, 307

canons 21–23, 25, 26, 30, 31, 33, 34, 36–39, 42–43, 45, 47, 54–61, 159, 216, 245, 378, 381–83, 611, 634, 635

absenteeism 34, 61, 129–30, 169

education 59, 65, 102, 565–66, 568, 570

geographical origins 37–39, 56, 102–3

households 64, 65, 634

houses *see* canonical houses

residentiaries 51, 54, 61–67, 81, 114, 122, 124, 128–30, 134–36, 158, 173, 243, 603, 630, 635

(*see also* residence)

social origins 57–59

wills 64, 65, 67

Cantilupe festival, 1982 183

capitals **31**, **47**, 226, 267, 290, **291**

carpenter 243–45, 247, 249, 253, 255, 412

cathedral council 197, 630

cathedral office 181

chancel *see* choir (architectural)

chancellor 35, 36, 173, 382, 442, 513, 545, 568, 570, 575, 633, 635

chancels, repair of 118

chantries 52, 67, 76, 89–90, 226, 230, 235–36, 241, 443, 446–47

(*see also* chapels)

chapels **84**, 85, 208, 211, 212, 216, 225, 226, 230, 379, 380

(*see also* Audley, bishop's, Lady, Stanbury)

chaplains 25, 36, 37, 176, 181, 379, 380–81, 389–91, 392

chapter *see* dean and chapter

chapter clerk 116, 134, 141, 151, 158, 166, 174–75, 181, 187, 252, 459, 474, 476, 479, 544, 547, 549–50, 648

chapter, general 125, 170

chapter house **pl. IIIb, 62**, 102, 113, 116 and n., 227–29, **228**, 236, 244–46, 281, 282, **283**, 298, 308–9, 545

chapter house yard **228**, 281, 294, 308, 631

chapter meetings 176, **187**

Hereford Cathedral continued
charities
  Canons' Dole 644–45
  Dr Cope's 647–48
  Croft's 147, 649
  Howells 646–47
  Dean Langford's 579–80,
    584–86, 590–91, 648–49
  Philpotts's 147, 579, 584,
    590, 595–96, 648–49
  Tomson's 147, 399, 423,
    583, 645–46
chests 336, 348, 452, 513–14,
  545–46, 635
choir (architectural) xxxii,
  30, 70, 136, 142–43, 160,
  208, **209**, 212, **213**, 243,
  247–51, **251**, 256, 259,
  261, 263, 265, 267, 269,
  271–73, 275–76, 290,
  318–19, 320, 347–48, 354,
  378, **383**, 408, 412, 426,
  443, 465, **475**
  floor 256
choir (choral foundation)
  112, 175, 195, 224,
  380–84, 389–97, 398–440,
  440, 567–68, 570–74
  endowments 190, 376, 380,
    384, 388, 422, 441–42, 444
  recordings 438
  visiting choirs 433
choir aisles 207, 212, 218–19,
  235, 277, 279, 324
  north 220, 317, 319
  south **77**, 225, **266**, 562
choir stalls 224–25, 250, 265,
  273, 275, 347–48, 378,
  382, 399, 443, 474
choristers 65, 96, 112, 156,
  158, 172, 380–81, 389–91,
  392–93, 395–96, 398–400,
  401, 402, 403–7, 409–10,
  411, 413, 414, 415–16,
  423–24, 427–29, 430–38,
  439, 440, 496–97, 568–74,
  578, 583–85, 594, 598,
  645, 646
clavigers 103–4, 111, 119,
  135, 246, 247, 249, 254,
  496, 521, 547

cleaners 171, 248, 629
clergy, lesser 69–70, 170,
  378–79, 380–82, 389–91,
  396, 398, 441
  (*see also* chaplains, vicars
  choral)
clergy, married 91
clerk of the works 178, 265,
  279
clock 243, 244, 245
cloister, south-west **164**, 166,
  222, 229, 242, 244, 245,
  248, 255, 267, 281–82,
  282, 285, 291, 294, 296,
  298, 300, 308–10, 311,
  338–39, 348, 354, 528,
  530, 545, 552, 554, 582
  (*see also* vicars choral, college cloisters)
Close **endpapers**, 39, 62,
  66, 78, 125, 144–46, 165,
  172–73, 174, 177–78, 180,
  243, 248, 291, 293–310,
  302, 600, **601**, 629, 631
common fund 30, 33, 34,
  45, 47, 51, 52, 53, 54, 62,
  71, 105, 634–36, 644
congregation 175, 181, 186,
  480
consistory court 143–44
constitution 48, 50, 633–36
consuetudines *see* statutes,
  1246–68
corona
  Beer 174, 197, **198**, 504
  Skidmore 277
cross cloth 493
cross slabs 331, **332**
crosses, processional 506–7,
  507
crypt 181, 198, 208–13, **211**,
  225, 267, 275, 285, 346,
  357, 379, 504, 524, 553,
  629
dean 21, 26, 35, 54, 63, 93,
  102, 116, 126, 134, 140,
  149–50, 155, 173, 413,
  432, 479, 604, 608, 630,
  633, 635
  peculiar jurisdiction 32, 45,
    50, 79, 636

dean and chapter 21, 27,
  30–33, 37, 43, 45, 46, 54,
  67, 68, 73, 82–83, 90, 96,
  97, 102–3, 108, 109, 114,
  115, 118–19, 125, 126,
  128, 140, 144–45, 146–55,
  158–61, 167–71, 175–76,
  182–83, 185–87, 188, 189,
  190, 193, 196, 243, 245,
  246, 248, 250, 253, 254,
  256, 258, 260, 265, 269,
  281, 284, 286, 289, 304,
  344, 351, 378, 398–99,
  401, 403, 404–6, 410,
  414–20, 421, 426–28, 433,
  441–44, 454, 458–59, 470,
  473, 477, 479–80, 502,
  504, 525, 528, 544, 546,
  548, 550, 554, 580–81,
  583, 586, 588–90,
  599–601, 604, 607–9,
  610–13, 616–18, 621,
  623–27, 630–31, 633–35,
  644–49
  jurisdiction 32, 45, 78–80,
    83, 633
  patronage 70
  seal **32, 55**, 159–60, 544–
    45, 550
deanery 160, 175–76, 299,
  595, **595**
deans *see* Aigueblanche;
  Avenbury; Benson;
  Bosbury; Brown;
  Burrows; Carr; Chandler;
  Clavering; Clermont;
  Coren; Cresset; Croft;
  Daniel; Dawes; Doughtie;
  Egerton; Erchemar;
  Frowcester; Gerard;
  Gretton; Grey; Harris;
  Haynes; Herbert; Hodges;
  Langford; Leigh; Leofwin;
  Mapenore; Mellish;
  Merewether; Price;
  Prophete; Ralph;
  Rathbone; Stanway;
  Thornbury; Tyler;
  Waterfield; Webber;
  Wetherell; Willis
dedication of 10

Hereford Cathedral continued

dignitaries 31, 35, 37, 47, 51, 54, 115, 173, 633–35 (*see also* chancellor; dean; precentor; treasurer)

disabled access 629–30

estates 19, 25, 26, 50, 52, 53, 70, 81–82, 104–6, 114–15, 118, 135–36, 147–49, 166, 176, 259, 281, 544, 644

Shinfield and Swallowfield 118nn., 136, 146–47, 149, 151, 243, 245, 247, 249, 250, 254, 256

excavations 296, **297**, 306, 313, 629

exhibition, Mappa Mundi and chained library 188, 195, 291, 534, 545, 555–56

Fabric Advisory Committee 289

fabric fund 72, 76–78, 113, 118, 135, 140–42, 145, 146–47, 189–90, 215–16, 218, 241–89, 580, 609

finance 50–54, 103–6, 135–36, 140–2, 146–47, 180, 182–83, 184–85, 187–91, 193–96, 250

fire-watchers 175, 594

floodlighting 285

font **35**, 234

foundation of 4, 27

gas lighting 277

glass *see* windows

Godwin tiles 276, 278, 279, 292

gospels, eighth-century *see* Hereford Gospels

Gothic architecture 208–40, 263

harvest festival 177

hebdomadary 119, 151, 248, 406, 413, 443, 634

hebdomadary's book 148, 503

high steward 135, 247, 249

Holy Cross 76, 225

holy water stoup 243

hospitals *see* Hereford, city, St Ethelbert's Hospital; Ledbury, St Katherine's Hospital

installation fees 515, 521–22, 525

intercessions 182

international links 631

ironwork 336–41, **337**

joiner 247

King Stephen's Chair 177, 345–47, **347**

Lady arbour **xix**, 144, 145, 160, **164**, 244, 255, 267, 281, **282**, 305–6, 308

Lady chapel **81**, 89, 160, 164, 177, 198, 203, 208, 210, 212, 213, 219, 222, 224, 232, 237, 243, 244, 261, 263, 265, 268–69, **268**, **269**, 271, **272**, 274, 275, 277, 279, 280, 285, 288, 290, 291, 311, 316, 317, 318, 323–24, 328, 330, 378–80, 383–84, 388–89, 391–94, 432, 498, 515–16, **516**, 524, 527, 551, 572, 593

organ 492

roof 243

vestibule 208, 219, 224, 237, 267

Lady chapel, Booth porch **381**, 391, 572

laity 630

lay clerks 159, 171, 173, 175, 417, 421, 422, 425–27, 431–32, 434–36, 438

lectern 274–75

lecturer (praelector) 117, 126, 149, 162, 521, 550

library 66, 93, 97, 116, 117, 123, 144, 167, 269, 281, 311, 511–35, 536, 551

advisory committee 196, 543, 544

bindings 511, 521, 525, 531–32

catalogues 515, 520, 522–25, 527–28

chained xxix, xxxii, 169, 190, 191, 192, 194, 195, 243–44, 278, 311, 354, 504, 511, **516**, 518–24, 528, 530–31, 533–34, **535**, 562, 629

cloister, medieval 514

cloister, 1897–1996 528

Dean Leigh library 166–67, **167**, 281–84, 310, 311–12, **312**, 511, 528, 530, 531, 534, 554

Lady chapel 243–44, 311, 330, 515–24, 527, 551

librarian 187, 529–34

master 111, 123, 163, 515, 520, 522–23, 527–28, 533, 550

new library building 195, 296, 306, 310, 354, 511, 534–35, **535**

sub-librarian 178, 529

(*see also* books)

liturgy and worship 40, 45, 71, 75, 81, 86, 111–12, 117, 119, 133, 157–58, 162, 163, 170–71, 175, 177, 197, 204, 259, 363–460, 628

mace 502, **503**

Mappa Mundi **pl. XVI**, xxix, xxxi, 186, 190–96, 311, 504, 527, 531, 557–62, **559**, 629, 632

facsimile **192**, 527, 562

Mappa Mundi Conference, 1999 557n., 632

Mappa Mundi Ltd 188

masons' workshop 286–88, 290–91, 629

mass pence 34, 52, 62, 90

mill 52, 53

misericords 275, 348, **349**

monuments, tombs **24**, **77**, **121**, 174, 219, 222, 224, 265, 279, 280, 292, 305–6, 322–30, 331–35, 350–59, **355**, **497**

Aigueblanche, P. **44**, 174, 214, 216, 279, 322–23, 325–36

Aigueblanche, J. 325–26

Bennett **97**, 352–53, **353**

Bohun **pl. VIa**, 224, 271–72, 322–23, 327, 444

Booth **pl. VIIa**, 317, 324, 338

Hereford Cathedral continued
  Braose 352, **353**
  Charlton, L. **58**, 224
  Charlton, T. 222, 278
  Dawes **163**, 279, 357
  Denton **pl. VIIb**, 243, 278–
    79, 351–52
  Grandisson **pl. VIb**, 224,
    271–72, 323–24, 328
  Jonis 332
  Mayew 224, 325, **327**
  Pembridge 323, 325, **326**,
    358
  Stanbury 325, **497**
  Swinfield, J. **57**, 219, 323,
    326
  Swinfield, R. 219, 222, 326
  Trefnant 225, 236
  Trillek 224, 333, **334**, 335
  Westfaling **95**, 352
  (*see also* Cantilupe, shrines)
Much Cross 225
muniment room
  north transept 220, 269,
    278, 522, 524–25, 530,
    531, 545–52, **552**
  Dean Leigh library 531,
    548, 554, **555**, 629
music 67, 75, 96, 98, 108,
  112, 117, 174, 363–492,
  646
Music Room 160, 255, 267,
  310, 464n., 582, **583**, 585
nave **pls XI**, **XII**, 144, 162,
  204, **223**, 226, 229,
  232–33, **233**, 239, 253,
  258, 261, 263, 274, 281,
  284, 285, 286, **383**, **465**
nave aisles 218–19, 233, 235,
  253, 259, **262**, 274, 278,
  315, 317, 320, 323, 324,
  358, 473
new library building 195,
  296, 306, 310, 311–13,
  312, **313**, 505, 533,
  534–35, **535**, 555–56, 562,
  629
obit book 20n., 27, 36, 37,
  40, 41, 45, 493n., 500–1,
  513
obits 52, 53, 67, 71

oblations 52, 76
organ loft 225, 470
organist 96, 112, 357–58,
  390–92, 393, 398–400,
  403–7, 411–12, 424, 427,
  430, 432–33, 436–37, 448,
  451, 472–74, 479, 573
  (*see also* Badham; Bull;
    Clack; Clark-Whitfeld;
    Colborne; Cook; Coyle;
    Dare; Davies; Davis; Far-
    rant; Giles; Hall;
    Hayter; Hodges; Hull;
    Hunt; Inglott; Lloyd;
    Massey; Palmer; Perry;
    Sinclair; Smith; Swar-
    brick; Thompson;
    Warrock; Wesley; Wode)
organs **pl. XI**, 112, 114, 120,
  136, 140, 174, 250, 273,
  276, **359**, 389–92, 395,
  399, 403, 407, 417,
  470–92, **475**, **484**, **487**,
  572, 628–29
  specifications 476–77, 482–
    83, 488–90, 491, 492
oven 34
oxeye masonry **143**, 249
pavement 274–76
penitentiary 31, 78, 570, 633
pews *see* seats
pietà 76
pilgrims 41, 63, 72–73, 209,
  218, 219, 220, 330, 379
Piper tapestries 498–99
plans 84, 199, 205
plate 382, 401, 408, 458–60,
  500–8, **503**, **507**, **508**
platform 197, **198**
plumber 243, 244, 245, 248,
  252, 253
porch, Booth 203, 227,
  229–31, **230**, 236, 241,
  274, 278, 290, 292, 338,
  379, **381**, 554
porch, inner north 219–20,
  220, **221**, 230–31
praelector *see* lecturer
preaching cross 255
preaching ministers 106–7, 402
prebendaries 31, 51, 82, 92,

  105, 111, 115, 128, 158,
  171, 633, 634–35, 636
prebends 25, 26, 30, 33, 34,
  38, 70, 104–6, 128,
  441–42, 634, 635
  bishop's/golden prebend
    123, 173
  values 33, 51
precentor 35, 36, 51, 173,
  382, 398, 424, 430, 442,
  567, 633, 635
properties *see* estates
pulpit xxx, 101, **103**, 243,
  244, 408n., 497
pulpitum 225, 250, 273, 276,
  348, 378–79, 394, 470,
  471, 473–74
quantity surveyor 289
refreshments 181, 188
relics 41, 73, 89, 208, 213,
  219, 222, 328–30
reliquary of Thomas Becket
  pl. XIIIb, 504–6
reredos 272–73, 275, 285
  (*see also* altarpiece)
residence 34, 36, 47, 61–67,
  129–30, 630, 635
restoration 160, 162, 163,
  176, 189, 239, 241–45,
  247–48, 281–85, 286
  1660 246–47, 470–71
  Bisse 248–50, 250–59
  Wyatt 261–65
  Cottingham 269–74
  Scott 275–81
  Reardon 286–92
retrochoir **58**, 208, 213, 237,
  262, 358n.
Romanesque architecture **6**,
  27, 30, **31**, **35**, **47**, 203–4,
  206–16, **209**, 217, 220,
  225, 232, 234, 239, 241,
  261, 263–64, 267, 273,
  275, 278, 298–318, 408
roofs 243, 248, 253, 258,
  261, 263, 271, 274, 278,
  280, 284, 285, 286, 290,
  291–92
  wooden 231–32, 261, 349
royal visits **pl. XV**, 177, **178**,
  182, 189, 195, 197

Hereford Cathedral continued

St John the Baptist, parish of 41, 70, 71, 143–44, **143**, 163–65, 210, 213, 225, 226, 250, 259, 265, 279, 378–79, 432, 447, 498, 503, 593

St John's walk 226, 232, 292, 349, **349**

St Katherine, chapel of *see* bishop's chapel

St Mary Magdalene, chapel of *see* bishop's chapel

saints' cults 40, 48, 72–76, 82, 194, 203–4, 208–9, 212, 213, 217–8, 219, 220, 232, 235, 238–39, 324, 388

sanctuary 79

screens 259, 412

Scott/Skidmore xxxii, 276, **277**, 336, 339–41, **340**, 426

removal 179–80, 285, 341, 438

(*see also* pulpitum)

sculpture

medieval **221**, 232–34, 237–38

modern **288**, 290, **291**

seats 243, 244

sermons 107, 117, 243

sextons 144, 145, 173, 248, 255, 497, 645

shop 181, 188

shrines xxix, 51, 63, 67, 72–76, 83, 86, 88–89, 174, 210, 219, 220, 242, 244, 290–91, 322–24, 326, 328–30, **329**, 331, 379, 388, 500, 629

song school 291, 431–32, **439**

medieval 567–68, 570–74

spires 136, 140, 142, 239, 245, 247, 252, 262, 278, 281

staff 187–88

stained glass *see* windows

staircases, spiral 220, 231, 629

Stanbury chapel 90, 203, 227, 236, 241, 279, 285, 321, 325, 336–37, 379, **380**

statutes

1246–68 **pl. IIa**, 20, 34, 36, 43, 45, 46, 47, 61, 216, 243, 375, 380–82, 442–43, 501, 513, 545, 567–68, 634

1583 93–94, 375, 377, 396, 398, 496, 502, 515, 520, 547, 548, 578

1636 **pl. IIb**, 99 and n., 112, 116, 118, 152, 170, 245, 248, 259, 401, 451, 502, 520, 548, 579–80, 604

1937 173–74

1966 180, 460

steward 181, 187

(*see also* high steward)

stewardship 182

subdean 635

sub-treasurer 382, 447, 635

succentor 36, 133, 158, 186, 382, 398, 410, 413, 418, 422, 427, 430, 431, 443, 447, 459, 477, 567–68, 572, 574, 635, 646

Sunday school 197

surveyor of the fabric 245, 248, 255, 257, 260

textiles 401, 493–99, 521

tithes 82, 104, 114, 148, 243, 245, 249–50, 254

tower crossing **198**, 226, 270–71, 273, 276, 357

towers

central/crossing **142**, 197, 218, 220–22, **223**, 227, 237–38, 241, 245, 249, 252, 258, 261, 262–63, 265, 269, 270–71, 281, 284–85, 286, 289–90, 292, 342–44, 473

east 207–8, 212

west 206–7, 218, 220–22, 237, 241, 257, 258

(*see also* west front, fall of)

transept, east 208, 210–13, 277, 279, 324, 379

north-east 219, 222, 279, 285, 320, 357

south-east 224, 232, 279, 290, 308, 317

transept, north 143–44, **143**, 198, 203, 213–19, **215**, 220, 222, 226, 265, 277, 278, 280, 290–91, 317–18, 319, 324–25, 328–30, 357, 378, 379, 388, 545

transept, south **28**, 143–44, 177, 204, 214, 216, **217**, 225–26, 227, 243, 248, 261, 263, 273, 277, 278, 280, 285, 289, 290, 319, 320, 324, 354, 379, 562

treasurer 35, 107, 173, 382, 442, 501, 545, 602–3, 608, 633, 635

treasury 181, 204–5, 214, 220, 504, 545, 635

vaults/vaulting 212, 216, 218, 226, 227–29, 235, 236, **262**, 308, 309

vergers 173, 182, 497, 573, 645

vestments 71, 174, 176, 493–96, 497–98, **497**

vestry 204–5

vicars choral 36, 37, 47, 69, 82, 89–90, 93, 95–96, 98, 112, 117, 119, 123, 125, 133, 156–57, 158–59, 170–71, 174, 180, 185, 186, 299, 378, 381–84, 389–90, 396, 398, 400, 401, 402, 403, 404–7, 411, 414–20, 426–28, 430–32, 441–60, 462, 473, 544–45, 549, 589, 590, 634

act books 448

college cloisters **pl. IXa**, 174, 298–99, 306–8, 402, 445, **446**, **453**, 460, 524, 582, 586, 589

chapel 158, 299, 420, 532

fires, 1820, 1828 414–15, 456, 532, 549

hall **pl. IXb**, 299, 307, 407, 420, 452, 455, 462, 463, 480

porch 236, 308, **309**

restoration 291

endowments *see* choir, endowments

Hereford Cathedral continued
income 457–58
library 96, 452, 522, 532
seal **445**, 452
voluntary helpers 181,
 187–88, 529
wall paintings **pl. Xc**,
 278–79, 285, 328
west front
 medieval 137, **138**, 256,
  258, 281
 fall of, 1786 122, 136,
  137–39, **139**, 222, 226,
  241, 258–59, **260**, 350,
  412, 473, **583**
 Wyatt 142, 261–64, **263**,
  281, 282, 319
 Scott 167, **168**, 282–84,
  312, 319
whitewash 243, 248, 265,
 271, 278
windows 67, 113, 133, 137,
 216, 218–19, 222, 225,
 226, 233, 236, 243, 244,
 247, 252–53, **253**, 264,
 267, 269, 271, 273, 274,
 277–78, 279, 280, 281,
 286, 290, 314–21, 431
stained glass **pls IVc, V**,
 174, 226, 236, 243, **251**,
 253, 262, 265, 267, 285,
 290, 314–21
woodwork 249–50, 276, 279,
 345–49
Hereford Cathedral Junior
 School 437, 591, 593, 594, 598
chaplain 186
Hereford Cathedral News 176
Hereford Cathedral Perpetual
 Trust 195, 290
Hereford Cathedral School 36,
 42, 133, 168, 176, 243, 310,
 382, 389, 414, 428, 432, 437,
 444, 458, 460, 515, 565–98,
 583, 587, 592, 595, 602, 635,
 646, 648–49
chaplain 178, 460, 593
fees 581, 588, 591, 594–95
governors 588, 591–94, 596
grammar school, medieval
 568–69, 574–78

master 568–69
headmaster 139, 428, 432–33,
 578, 579, 580–81, 584,
 586–88, 589–92, 648
library, 590, **597**
masters 567
song school, medieval
 567–68, 570–74
theology, medieval 567, 570,
 578
usher 580–81
Hereford Choral Society 182,
 425
Hereford, city 5, 9, 10, 19, 41,
 78, 106, 119, 125–26, 165,
 243, 293–94, 297–98, 581
All Saints church 259, 343,
 473
 chained library 196, 420, 553
Berrington Street 293
bishop's fee 45
bishop's palace 29, 92, 248,
 268, 296–99, 402
Bluecoat School 586
booksellers 522
bridge 293
Broad Street 173, 293, 296,
 304, 305, 313, 600, 602–4,
 607
 Green Dragon Hotel 458,
  585, 589
 Mitre Hotel 607
castle 293, 298, 342, 600, 602
Castle Green 293, 606
Castle Street 39, 53, 293,
 298, 305, 306, 426, 444,
 591, **592**, 593–94, 596–97,
 600, 602–3, 605, 608
cemetery 305
chapter fee 78
charters 41
Church Street 301–3, **303**,
 305, 431, 433, 579, 600
city council 290, 609, 649
corporation 126, 583
Dominican priory 80
fairs 40, 599
Franciscan friars 515
Frog Lane 80
gates 293
Globe tavern 304

grammar school, medieval
 569, 574–78
guildhall 464 and n.
Harley Close 300
Harley Court 299, 591
Harley House 299, 300
High Town 596
hospitals 601
King Street 293, 298, 304
king's fee 45
mayor 165, 245, 466, 583,
 600
mechanics' institution 165
Milk Street *see* St John Street
mill 52
music clubs 462
National School 586
Palace Yard 306
police 165
poor relief 165
Post Office 304
Residence, the 304
Roman history 293
St Ethelbert Street 608
St Ethelbert's Hospital 41,
 106–7, 133, 160, 544,
 599–609, **605, 607**, 647
 censor 609, 645
 chapel 600
 income 599, 603, 605, 606–
  7, 647
 inmates 604–5, 608–9
 master 602–3, 606–8, 647
 property 599, 603, 604–5,
  608
St Francis Xavier's church 304
St Guthlac's 5, 10, 14, 29,
 365, 546
St John Street 299–301, 452,
 455
 Canon's House 291, 299–
  300
St John the Baptist, parish of
 see Hereford Cathedral, St
 John the Baptist
St Martin's parish 609,
 646–48
St Peter's church 79, 316
shirehall 465
town council 165, 172
Victoria Street 293

Hereford Diocesan Board of
Finance 189
Hereford Diocesan
Community Trust 182, 189
Hereford Diocesan Messenger 504
Hereford, diocese 56, 167, 173,
181, 182, 197, 246, 286, 364,
379, 501, 504, 507, 528, 631
archdeacons 23–24, 173, 633
archives 554
foundation 4–5, 363
plate 629
Hereford Educational
Development Centre 533
Hereford Gospels **pl. I**, **ii**, xxx,
17, **17**, 18, 19, 22, 367–68,
511, 531, 536–43, **539**, **541**
decoration 540–42
script 539–40
text 537–38
Hereford High School 591
Hereford Improvement
Commission 258
Hereford, John, archdeacon of
Hereford 71, 641
Hereford Journal 138, 141, 152,
262, 412, 422, 464–65, 506,
584
Hereford Mappa Mundi Trust
xxxi, 194–96, 311, 533–34,
562
Hereford, Nicholas, chancellor
64, 65, 640
Hereford, Roger of 42, 566
Hereford Times 168, 171, 193,
473
Hereford Use *see* Use of
Hereford
Herefordian 590
Herefordshire 12, 38, 42, 56,
100, 106, 631
county council 596, 649
sheriff 79
Herefordshire Record Office 544
Herefordshire Regiment 358
Hergest, John 256
Hergest, William, mason 256,
257
heriots 51, 52
Heywarde, Thomas, verger
391n.

Heywood, Lt-Col. G. B. 173
Hichons, John, vicar choral
389–90, 392n., 470
Hill and Son, organ builders 492
Hine, William, organist of
Gloucester Cathedral 461–62
Hipwell, Eleanor 532
Hoadley, Benjamin, bishop of
Hereford 123–24, 129
Hoadley, John, canon 123–24,
642
Hobart, Henry, canon 158, 643
Hobson, Anthony H. 196, 533
Hodges, John, organist 391 and
n., 393n., 395, 573
Hodges, Thomas, dean 111–12,
117, 581, 637
Holand, Marjorie 53
Holdingham, Richard of
559–60
Hollington stone 282, 286
Holme Lacy, Herefordshire 465
Holmer, Hereford 33, 605–6,
608
Home, John, canon 66
Hooper, Michael W.,
archdeacon of Hereford 186,
187, 641
Hope, Thomas, carpenter 253
Hopewell, A. F. J., headmaster
594, 596
Hove, Roger, canon 619
Hosier, William, vicar choral
96 and n.
hospitals, medieval 610
(*see also* Hereford, city, St
Ethelbert's Hospital;
Ledbury, St Katherine's
Hospital)
Howe Commission 196, 631
Howell, Geoffrey, succentor 186
Howells, Edward, succentor 422
Howells, Mary 646
Howells, Thomas, vicar choral
449
Howley, William, archbishop
of Canterbury 154
Hudson, Octavius 278
Hugh *Gramaticus* 565
Hugh, Master, mason 231, 235
Huguenots 119, 120

Hull, Sir Percy C., organist
173, 358, 401n., 432–34,
467–68, **468**, 484–85, 491
Humphrey, duke of Gloucester
66
Humphreys, Humphrey,
bishop of Hereford 123,
126, 130–31
Hunt, Avery 252–53
Hunt, John, organist 319, 420
Huntingford, George I., bishop
of Hereford 317
Huntingford, Henry, canon
504, 643
Huntingford, Thomas,
precentor 424, 638
Hutchinson, Andrew,
succentor 186
Hyde, George 193
Hygons, Roger 577

Iles, Paul R., precentor 185,
187, 638
Illman, Michael, assistant
organist 436
Independent 191
indulgences 73, **74**, **75**, 76–78,
83, 86, 215
Inglott, William, organist
399–400
injunctions, royal 375, 447–48
1547 377, 447, 515, 578
1559 92
Inkberrow, Worcestershire 16,
33
Innes, W. R., vicar choral 458–59
Innocent IV, Pope 44, 600
Interregnum, the 87, 100
Irish gospel books 537–38
Irvine, Murray, chancellor 179,
182, 640

Jaggard, James, plumber 245,
247
James I, King 96, 97
James II, King 120
James, Montague Rhodes 459,
530
Jancey, E. Meryl, archivist 555
Jauncey, Francis, prebendary
121n.

Jebb, John, chancellor 162–63,
    320, 429, 503, 527, 529, 640
Jenkins, John 450
Jesuit College, Cwm,
    Herefordshire 522
John XXII, Pope 83, 222, 616
John, King 30, 209, 599
John the archcantor 364
Johnson, William, archdeacon
    of Hereford 248, 641
Jones, Edward, lay clerk 417 and n.
Jones, Henry, chapter clerk 549
Jones, John, canon 134, 642
Jones, Robert, architect 605–6
Jonis, Andrew 225, 332
Jordan, James H., precentor
    175, 178, 638
Joseph, Robert 576–77
Joy, William, mason 239
Juxon, William, bishop of
    Hereford and of London,
    archbishop of Canterbury 98

Keck, Anthony, architect
    259–60
Kemble, Fanny 166, 320–21
Kempe, C. E. 320
Kempley, Gloucestershire
    612–13, 616–17
Kerry, Francis, treasurer 401, 639
Kidley, Thomas, vicar choral 455
Kilpeck, Herefordshire 232, 234
Kingsley-Taylor, Raymond,
    chapter clerk 187
Kington, Herefordshire
    Lady Hawkins School library
    533, 578
Knight, James H., chapter clerk
    166
Knight, Richard 619
Knight, Richard P. 257
Kylynge, Thomas, priest of
    St Katherine's 616
Kyrle, John 247

Lacy, Edmund, bishop of
    Hereford 76, 386–88
Lacy, Walter II de 612–13
Lambeth Palace Library 104, 148
Lane, James, chapter clerk 141,
    151, 544

Lane, Richard *see* Tomson
Lane, Theophilus, chapter clerk
    158–59
Lanfranc, archbishop of
    Canterbury 23, 24
Langford, Charles, dean 96,
    579, 637, 648
Langley, Batty, architectural
    writer 262
Lanthony Priory,
    Gloucestershire 575
Laud, William, archbishop of
    Canterbury 99, 100, 451, 579
Laudian statutes *see* Hereford
    Cathedral, statutes, 1636
Layng, Thomas F., headmaster
    586
Leche, John, canon 64
Ledbury, Herefordshire 5, 610–11
    St Katherine's Hospital **pls
    Xa, b**, 41, 117, 133, 141,
    160, 254, 545–46, 601,
    603, 609, 610–27, **627**
    bells 621
    chapel 614, 618, **619**, 621,
        624, 627
    chaplains 611–12, 616–20
    hall 618
    inmates 611–12, 615, 619–
        20, 623–24, 627
    inventory 1316 614
    mansion house 622, 624, 627
    master 133, 134, 152, 612,
        616, 619–20, 622–27
    master and brethren 613
    property 612–14, 616–19,
        622–23, 625–26
    seal 613, **614**
    St Peter's church (St Michael
        and All Angels) 621
Ledbury, Ralph de, canon 38
Ledbury, Richard 391, 394, 573
Ledbury, Thomas de, master of
    St Katherine's 617
Lee, Lennox B. 174, 176, 177,
    285, 492
Leigh, Egerton, canon 625, 642
Leigh, Frances B. 166, 320–21
Leigh, James W., dean 166–67,
    167, 170–72, 173, 282, 320,
    459, 506, 528–29, 593, 638

Leigh, William, dean 149, 638
Lelamour, John, schoolmaster
    574–75
Leland, John, antiquary 8, 241,
    577, 601–3
Leofgar, bishop of Hereford 20,
    22–23
Leofric, bishop of Exeter 366
Leofwin (Liwin), dean 26, 37, 637
Leominster, Herefordshire 4, 5,
    14, 15
    priory 234, 363, 616
Leominster, Hugh, canon 59
Lewis, Hugh, canon 124, 126,
    642
Lewis, John, archdeacon of
    Hereford 180, 182, 641
Lewys, Clement, vicar choral 93
Lewys, Griffyth, prebendary,
    dean of Gloucester 602
Ley, William H., headmaster
    586
Library Association 527
Lichfield Gospels 538
Liège Cathedral School 23
Lilley, Alfred L., archdeacon of
    Ludlow (Shropshire) 168,
    179, 173, 642
Limoges enamels 504–6
Lincoln 559–60
Lindsell, Augustine, bishop of
    Hereford 98, 99, 354, 401
Lingen, Sir Henry 245
Lire Abbey 36, 82, 442, 636
Liwin *see* Leofwin
Llandaff, deans of Hereford
    bishops of *see* Clavering,
    Harris, Tyler
Llangarron estate 115, 149
Llanthony Priory,
    Monmouthshire 27
Lloyd, Owen, canon 514
Lloyd, Richard, organist 438
Lochard, William, precentor
    67, 226, 315, 638
Lock, Adam, mason 237
lollardy 49, 65
London
    St Paul's Cathedral 210, 215
Long, E. T. 285
Longchamp, Geoffrey de 612

Longworth, Tom, bishop of
    Hereford **178**
Losinga *see* Lotharingian
Lotharingian, Robert the,
    bishop of Hereford 20,
    23–27, **24**, 33, 37, 207, 212,
    294, 368, 633
Lowe, William, cathedral
    preacher 106
Lugwardine, Herefordshire
    444, 521
Luntley, Thomas, vicar choral
    137, 455
Luxmoore, John, bishop of
    Hereford 150
Lydbury North, Shropshire 5
Lye, John, master of St
    Katherine's 620
Lyndwood, William, canon 61
Lyney, Nicholas, master of St
    Katherine's 621
Lysons, Daniel 461

Machen, Arthur 590
Madley, Herefordshire 218, 316
Madox, Richard, vicar choral 93
Magonsætan 3–6
Maidstone, Ralph de, bishop
    of Hereford 30, 31, 33, 36,
    441, 633
Malmesbury Abbey 8
Malmesbury, William of *see*
    William of Malmesbury
Malvern, John, master of St
    Katherine's 620–21
Mann, Colin, deputy organist 434
Mansfield, Daniel 254
Map, Walter 30, 43, 566
Mapenore, Hugh de, dean and
    bishop of Hereford 30, 36,
    38, 39, 42, 637
Mappa Mundi Trust *see*
    Hereford Mappa Mundi Trust
maps, medieval 557
Margaret, Princess 197
Marianus Scotus 25
Marshall, Edward 354
Martin, Richard, canon 61
Martin, Thomas, prebendary 121
Mary I, Queen 90, 91, 97, 242,
    394, 501

Mary II, Queen 120
Mary, Virgin, Saint 210–11,
    220, 224, 230–31, 378, 379,
    389, 391, 393, 394, 443–44,
    447, 572
Mascall, Robert, bishop of
    Hereford 444
Mason, Bartholomew, vicar
    choral 95–96, 448
Mason, John, treasurer 67, 390
    and n., 392–93, 573, 639
Mason, Richard, vicar choral
    448
Mason, Thomas 231
masons
    medieval 231–39
    modern 286–88
Massey, Roy, organist 438,
    439, **440**
Masters, R. Austin, precentor
    185, 186, 638–40
Matthews, Arthur, canon 160,
    643
Matthews, Colonel John 356
Matthews, John H., banker 607
Maurice, Roger fitz, canon 39
Maxey, Lewis, vicar choral
    455, **456**
May, David, vicar choral 445
Mayew, Richard, bishop of
    Hereford 224, 229, 325, 391,
    445, 600
Mayo, of Hereford, goldsmith
    502
Mears and Stainbank,
    bellfounders 344
Mears, Thomas, bellfounder 343
Mellish, Edward, dean 150, 638
Melun, Robert de, bishop of
    Hereford 29
Melun, Simon of 567, 570
Merchelm, ruler of the
    Magonsætan 4
Mercia 4–7, 10, 12, 363, 540
Merewalh, ruler of the
    Magonsætan 4
Merewether, John, dean xxxii,
    140, 155, 156–61, **157**, 165,
    243, 265–74, 275, 304, 316–17,
    318, 330, 416–22, 424, 457,
    506, 524, 550–51, 638

Merewether, Marianne 419
Merlimond, Oliver de 234–35
Merrick, Thomas 279
Meyrick, Samuel R. 270
Middleton, Gilbert de, master
    of St Katherine's 617
Mildburg, Saint, abbess of
    Much Wenlock 4, 441
Mildthryth, Saint, abbess of
    Minster-in-Thanet 4
Milfrith, ruler of the
    Magonsætan 4
Milfrith, sub-king 8
Milred, bishop of Worcester 8
mills 52, 81
Ministry of Education 595
Moffatt, H. C. 530
Monck, Nicholas, bishop of
    Hereford 111
Money-Kyrle, Rowland T. A.,
    archdeacon of Hereford 173,
    641
Monnington, Miss 606
Montagu, Richard, dean,
    bishop of Chichester and of
    Norwich 98 and n., 637
Montfort, Simon de 46
Montvernier, Richard of,
    canon 46
Moore, Alban, verger 173
Moore, Herbert A., treasurer
    174, 639
Moore, Richard, chapter clerk
    132
Mordiford, Herefordshire 40, 371
More, Thomas, schoolmaster
    575
Moreton, Harold A. V.,
    chancellor 174, 175, 176,
    179, 554, **555**, 640
Morgan, Charles, precentor
    317, 638
Morgan, Elizabeth 354
Morgan, Frederick C., librarian
    529–30, 533, 554, 555, **555**
Morgan, Hugh, canon 147,
    149, 605–6, 643
Morgan, Hugh Hanmer,
    chancellor, 317, 640, 643
Morgan, John, plumber 243
Morgan, John, surveyor 255

Morgan, Penelope E., librarian
529–31, 533–34, 555, **555**
Morgan, Robert, canon 124,
147, 549–50, 642
Morris, William 280
Moss, Leonard G., archdeacon
of Hereford 185, 186, 196, 641
Much Wenlock, Shropshire 4
Munich stained glass 316
Murimuth, Adam, canon 65
Musgrave, Thomas, bishop of
Hereford 160, 317, 357
Musgrave, William P., canon
177, 479, 643
Myllyng, Thomas, bishop of
Hereford 621
Mynde, Henry 394
Mynors, Sir Humphrey C. B. 182
Mynors, Sir Roger A. B. 197, 534

names, medieval 37
Napleton, John, canon xxxii,
141, 147, 150–54, **153**, 412,
626, 643
National Heritage Memorial
Fund xxxi, 191, 193, 194, 562
National Library of Wales
553–54
National Mission 171
Nesfield, William E. 274
Nicholas *divinus*, chancellor 36,
567, 570, 640
Nichols, William, vicar choral 561
Nicholson, John, vicar choral 449
Nicholson, of Worcester, organ
builder 474–76, 491
Nicolles, John 561
Noble, Matthew 357
nonconformists 170
Norfolk, Charles Howard,
duke of 465–66
Norman and Underwood, of
Leicester 290
Northampton, Hugh of, canon 38
Norton Canon, Herefordshire
33, 34, 105, 115, 644

Observer 194
Ockeridge, William of 612
Offa, king of the Mercians 9,
293

Offa's Dyke 9
Ogle, Humphrey, canon 60
Old Herefordians 584, 589,
591–93, 597
Oldham, Algernon, archdeacon
of Ludlow (Shropshire) 431,
642
Oliver, John K., bishop of
Hereford **198**
Ordgar, canon 22, 37
Orleton, Adam, bishop of
Hereford 494, 496, 634
Orton, David, vicar choral
392n.
Osfrith, son of Oshelm 8
Ottley, Adam, archdeacon of
Shropshire, bishop of St
Davids 121, 123, 124, 125,
127, 642
Ouseley, Sir Frederick A. G.,
precentor 162–63, 320,
424–30, **425**, 431, 458, 474,
477, 638
Owen, John T. 125–26
Oxford Movement 466
Oxford Society for Promoting
the Study of Gothic
Architecture 270
Oxford, University of 128,
152, 513, 517–18, 547
Bodleian Library 518, 522, 547
Brasenose College 579, 648

Palmer, Richard, organist 391,
573
Palmer, Roger, vicar choral
391 and n., 445
Pannell, Edward A., verger
182, **503**
papacy 43, 83
taxes 43, 51
(*see also* popes)
papal bull *Super cathedram* 80
papal provisions 55, 60
Parfew (or Wharton), Robert,
bishop of Hereford 91 and
n., 92, 495
Parker, Matthew, archbishop of
Canterbury 512
Parker, Richard 351
Parker, William 257–58

Paris, Matthew 43
Parry, Thomas G. 320
Parsons, Richard G., bishop of
Hereford 357
*Passio S. Æthelberhti regis et
martyris* 9
Pates, Richard, bishop of
Worcester 447
Paty, James 249
Paul, Thomas, bell hanger 343
Pauncefot, Emeric 620
Pauncefot, Grimbald 618
Peada, ruler of the Middle
Angles 4
Pearce, James 137, 248
Pearce, Robert, vicar choral 457
Pearce, Rowland, chorister 404
Pears, James 257
Pecham, John, archbishop of
Canterbury xxx
Peebles, W. J. R., headmaster
596
Peion, William, custos of
St Ethelbert's 600
Pember, John, prebendary 110
Pembridge, Sir Richard 323,
325, **326**, 358
Penda, king of the Mercians 4
Pennington, John, bellfounder
343
Percival, John, bishop of
Hereford 167–71, **167**, 357,
459, 593
Perpetual Trust *see* Hereford
Cathedral Perpetual Trust
Perry, William, organist 411–12
Peter, archdeacon of Hereford
39, 640
Peterstow, Herefordshire, vicar
of 53
Petrov, Alexei 193
Pevsner, Nikolaus 179, 318
Philip, Brother, master of
St Ethelbert's 616–17
Philip, Prince, duke of
Edinburgh 177, **178**
Phillips, Robert, headmaster 581
Phillips, Robert Biddulph 274,
316, 551
Phillott, Henry W., chancellor
275, 503, 528, 530, 562, 640

Philpotts, Roger, mayor of
Hereford 579, 648
Picart, Samuel, headmaster 585
Pichart, John 501
Pilgrim Trust 176, 554
Pipe, Herefordshire 605
Plews, Alfred, administrator
183, 187
Plumley, Nicholas 492
Plummer, Christopher, canon 60
Pole, John 243
Pole, Owen, custos of St
Ethelbert's 603
Pole, Reginald, Cardinal,
archbishop of Canterbury
91, 447
Poole-Hughes, Esther 178
popes see Alexander III;
Gregory I; Innocent IV;
John XXII; Urban VI
Porter, William, precentor 65,
88, 335, 638
Potter, Joseph, clerk of the
works 265
Potter, Thomas 274, 338
Poulter, James, verger 173, 177
Powell, James, and Sons 320
Powell, Richard, mason 287
Powell, Richard J., 356–57, **356**
Powell, William F., prebendary
281, 528
Power, Thomas B., headmaster
587
Prat, John, canon 60
Preston on Wye, Herefordshire
26, 33, 34, 644
Price, John 250
Price, Robert P., dean 179–80,
437–38, 638
Price, Uvedale 263
Primrose, George, cathedral
preacher 106
Prior, Peter 596
Prise, Sir John 514–15, 546–47
Probin, smith 245
proctors 83
Prophete, John, dean 610, 620,
623, 627, 637
Prose Salernitan Questions 42,
566
Public Schools Act, 1868 587

Pugin, Augustus W. N. 317,
318, 319, 357
Puritan Survey, 1642 245
Putta, bishop of Rochester and
of Hereford 5, 6, 363–64
Pyle, Richard, chapter clerk
252, 549
Pyon see Canon Pyon

Quayle, Nicholas 290

Ragg, W. Murray, headmaster
591–92
railways 165, 607
Ralph, dean 29, 31, 32, **33**, 38,
637
Ralph, Earl 18
Randolph, Thomas,
archdeacon of Hereford 178,
180, 641
Ranulf, chancellor 36, 640
Rashdall, Hastings, canon
168–69, 171, 643
Rathbone, Norman, dean
180–83, 185, 438, 638
Rawlins, Giles 502–3
Rawlinson Gospels 538
Rawlinson, James 523
Rawlinson, James, surveyor 255
Rawlinson, Richard 246–47,
333
Reading, Laurence, canon 181,
183
Reardon, Michael, architect
189, 286
Rees, W. J. 150
Reese, William, plumber and
glazier 252–53
Reformation 86, 87, 108,
241–43, 333, 350, 352, 375,
377, 393–94, 447, 495–96,
501, 505, 511, 514–15, 546,
578, 602, 622, 627
Reginald, custos of St
Ethelbert's 600
Regula canonicorum 365
Reinhelm, bishop of Hereford
27, 232, 298
Restoration, 1660 108, 109, 110,
246, 403, 452, 471, 522, 532,
548–49, 580, 604, 624

Revolution, 1688 121–22
Reynes, Henry of 235
Reynolds, Michael 523
Reynolds, Thomas, bishop of
Hereford 91
Rich, Edmund, archbishop of
Canterbury 634
Richard I, King 30, 599
Richard II, King 444, 620
Richards, D. M., headmaster 596
Rickman, Thomas 357
Robert, dean and rector of
Kempley 613
Robert the Lotharingian see
Lotharingian, Robert the
Roberts, William, chorister 406
Rogers, Richard, carpenter 244
Rogers, Thomas, canon 642,
649
Roiser, Ernest A., architect 286
Ross, Colin, assistant organist
433
Roubiliac, Louis-François
354–56
Rouen 27, 377
Rowland, joiner 244
Rowlstone, Herefordshire 232
Royal Commission on
Historical Monuments 203,
298, 299, 348
Royal Fine Art Commission
179, 195, 313
Royal Geographical Society
561–62
Royal Museum of Scotland 325
Roycroft, Samuel, carpenter 249
Rudd, Abraham, headmaster 584
Rudd, Eric J. S., headmaster 588
Ruddle and Thompson 275–76
Rudhale, Richard, archdeacon
of Hereford 65–66, **66**,
334–35, 641
Rudhall, Abraham I,
bellfounder 343–44
Rufus, Master 443
Russell, John F. 506
Russell, John Russell, Earl 160
Russell, Thomas I, canon
132–33, 505, 642
Russell, Thomas II, canon 505,
643

Russell, William, master of St
    Ethelbert's 606
Ryall, Edmund, canon 333

St Gallen Gospels 538
St Ethelbert's Hospital *see*
    Hereford, city, St Ethelbert's
    Hospital
St Katherine's Hospital *see*
    Ledbury, St Katherine's
    Hospital
St Margarets, Herefordshire 606
Salisbury, William of, canon 38
Salvation Army 176
Sancroft, William, archbishop
    of Canterbury 119
Savoyards 46
Saye and Sele, Caroline, Lady
    479, 527–28
Saye and Sele, Frederick
    T.-W.-Fiennes, Baron,
    archdeacon of Hereford 162,
    466, 479, 527, 607–8, 639–41
Sayse, Barnaby 248
science 42
Scory, John, bishop of
    Hereford 91–92, 93, 95, 512,
    623
Scott, Sir George Gilbert
    pl. XIIIa, 162, 208–9, **209**,
    222, 275–81, 282, 318, 320,
    322–23, 330, 336, 347–48,
    351–52, 474, 498–99
    screen xxxii, 179–80, 276,
    277, 285, 336, 339–41,
    340, 426, 438
Scott, J. Oldrid 167, 168, 282, 319
Scudamore, Sir Barnabas 320, 580
Scudamore, John Scudamore,
    Viscount 114, 247, 320
Seaxwulf, bishop of the
    Mercians 5–7, 363
Second World War 175–76,
    285, 434, 466, 531, 553–54,
    562, 594
Sedgwick, John 100
Senhouse, Peter, vicar choral 454
Seward, Abraham, chapter
    clerk 116, 549
Shaw, Allan, precentor 181,
    182, 185, 638

Sherborne, William, canon
    116, 549, 642
Shinfield, Berkshire *see*
    Hereford Cathedral, estates
Shobdon, Herefordshire 232,
    234–35
Side, Roger 79–80
Silvester, John, sexton 120,
    248, 255
Sinclair, George Robertson,
    organist 358, **359**, 430–32,
    459, 467–68, 479–84, **484**
Skidmore, Francis A. 277, 279
    screen xxxii, 179–80,
    276–77, **277**, 285, 336,
    339–41, **340**, 426, 438
Skinner, E. M., organ builder 487
Skip, John, bishop of Hereford
    87, 90, 91, 447, 623
Skynner family 622
Skynner, William, canon 401,
    502, 642
Slade, John 391, 573
Smalbroke, Richard, canon,
    bishop of St Davids 123,
    124, 127, 522–23, 642
Smirke, Robert, architect 626
Smith, Bernard, organ builder
    471
Smith, Francis 252–53
Smith, George Townshend,
    organist 319, 420–21, **421**,
    424–27
Smith, Martin L., bishop of
    Hereford **170**
Smith, Miles, canon, bishop of
    Gloucester 97–98, 520, 642
Smith, Samuel, cathedral
    preacher 106
Smith, T., surveyor 148
Smythe, William, vicar choral 382
Snetzler, Green and Avery,
    organ builders 472
Society for the Protection of
    Ancient Buildings 284
Society of Antiquaries 294, 505
Somerset, Sarah Seymour,
    duchess of 582
Somerset scholarships 582, 584,
    588
Sotheby's 190–91, 192, 562

Speede, John 244, 603
Spencer, Mr 523
Spernore, William 69
Spofford, Thomas, bishop of
    Hereford 56, 68, 216,
    225–26, 236, 621
Squire, Robert D., headmaster
    585
Staffordshire stone 282–83, 286
Stallard, (Richard?) 112 and n.,
    471
Stanbury, John, bishop of
    Hereford 90, 285, 307, 321,
    325, 444–45, **497**
Stanton, Phoebe 318
Stanway, John, dean 334, 637
Steel, Arthur D., chapter clerk
    175, 459
Steel, Thomas O. D., chapter
    clerk 174–75, 181
Steer, Philip W. 590
Stephen, King 29
Stockton, John, mayor of
    Hereford 334
Stokes, William de, canon 33
stonemasons *see* masons
Streeter, Burnett H., canon
    169, **170**, 173, 174, 285, 523,
    530, 534, 643
Strong, Sir Roy 193
Stukeley, William **62**, 227, 294,
    296
Sumsion, Herbert **468**
Sutton, Barry B., headmaster 596
Sutton, Charles M., archbishop
    of Canterbury 149
Swallowfield, Berkshire *see*
    Hereford Cathedral, estates
Swarbrick, organist 407, 411, 472
Swarbrick, Thomas, organ
    builder 472
Swinfield, Gilbert, chancellor
    494, 508, 640
Swinfield, John, precentor **57**,
    219, 323, 326, 638
Swinfield, Richard, bishop of
    Hereford 46, 56, 219, 227,
    232, 235, 323–24, 326, 328,
    494, 508, 560
Swynderby, William 49
syliconester 284

Symonds, John carpenter 247
Symonds, Thomas, surveyor
137, 256–58, 260, 265

Talbot, Geoffrey 29, 495
Taswell, Henry, vicar choral 455
Tatham, Francis H.,
headmaster 588, **589**, 590
Taunton, Robert, organ
builder 471
Taxatio, 1291 51, 72, 633
Taylor, Charles I, headmaster
585
Taylor, Charles II, headmaster
585–86
Taylor, Isaac, map of Hereford,
1757 294, 300, **302**
Taylor, John, succentor
426–27, 431
Taylor, Martin 243
Taylor, Rowland, prebendary 91
Taylor, Silas 107, 115n., 245,
294, 521–22, 604
Temple, Frederick, archbishop
of Canterbury **167**, 528
Theodore, archbishop of
Canterbury 6
Thomas, Alfred, chorister 430
Thomas, James 354–55, **355**
Thompson, Edward, organist
407
Thompson, Messrs, of
Peterborough 282
Thomson, Rodney M. 512, 534
Thornbury, Stephen, dean 501,
637
Thornton, Thomas, precentor
244, 396, 517–21, **517**, 524,
547, 638, 642
Three Choirs Festival **pls XI,
XII**, 142, 150, 285, 290,
310, 407, 409, 411, 433–34,
437, 454–55, 461–69, **465,
467**, 474, 480, 491, 582,
628–30
Threlkeld, Edward, prebendary
547
Thurkil the White 16, 17
Thurlow, Dennis, organ
builder 491
Tidhelm, bishop of Hereford 14

Tiller, John, chancellor 185,
186, **187**, 533–34, 640
Times 179, 191, 195, 196
Tintern Abbey 215, 219, 225
Tombes, John, master of
St Katherine's 624
Tomlinson, Howard C.,
headmaster 597
Tomson, Richard Lane, alias
399, 645
Torhthere, bishop of Hereford
7–8
tourism xxix, 165, 173, 181,
184–85, 188, 195–96, 312,
525, 528, 530–31, 551, 629
Traherne, Nicholas 399
Tree of Jesse 220
Trefnant, John, bishop of
Hereford 56, 67, 216, 225,
236, 619
Tremerig, Welsh bishop 19
Trevenant *see* Trefnant
Trillek, John, bishop of
Hereford 56, 222, 224–25,
334, 617
Tristram, Ernest W. 285
Turner, Joseph M. W. **pl. IIc**
Tyler, John, dean 119n.,
122–27, 134, 248, 407,
502–3, 504, 638
Tyrhtil, bishop of Hereford
6n., 7, 8

Underwood, Richard, vicar
choral 455, 584
Uniformity Act, 1662 107, 112
Urban VI, Pope 618–19
Use of Hereford 27, 46, 48,
369–74, 376, 384–89, 470
missal 369, 376, 388, 495,
572

Vale, William H., printer 524
Valor ecclesiasticus, 1535 51, 52,
53, 69, 71, 76, 79, 83, 241,
446, 602
Vere, Henry de, chancellor 36,
640
Vere, William de, bishop of
Hereford 25, 30, 36, 40, 42,
43, 208, 296, 505, 635

Victoria and Albert Museum
xxxii, 341
Victoria, Queen 160, 319
Victorian Society 179
Visitations
archiepiscopal 83
decanal, of dean's peculiar 79
decanal, of St Ethelbert's
604, 609
decanal, of vicars choral
95–96, 448, 452, 458
episcopal, of cathedral 69,
91, 93, 95–96, 99, 116–18,
130–34, 158, 175, 180,
247, 248, 256, 401, 502
episcopal, of St Katherine's 619
vita communis 22, 26
Voyle, William, cathedral
preacher 106

Wake, William, archbishop of
Canterbury 124
Wales 536–37, 542
Walhstod, bishop of Hereford
7, 8
Walker, David 555
Walker, Obadiah 582
Walter, bishop of Hereford 20,
23, 207, 213, 496
Walwen, Nicholas, treasurer
58n., 602, 639
Waring, Richard, vicar choral
411, 454
Warner, Charles E., precentor
174–76, 638
Warrington, William, maker of
stained glass 314–17
Warrock, Thomas, organist 96n.
Warwick, William, bellfounder
342, 344
Waterfield, Reginald, dean
170, 172–73, 175, 176, 432,
434, 595, 638
Wathen, James 256, 259
drawings and paintings **pls
IIIa, b, 138, 139, 142, 260**
Watkins, Alfred 284
Watts, William, canon 549, 642
Watts, William, precentor 116,
124, 127, 638, 649
Wealdhere, bishop of London 7

Weatherley, Frederick E. 590
Webb, Sir Henry 285, 506
Webbe, William, archdeacon of Hereford 64, 641
Webber, Francis, dean 128, 129, **130**, 132, 149, 411, 638
Weir, William 284
Wells Cathedral 237–39
Welsh bishoprics 127
Welsh, Edward, prebendary 91
Welsh, the 9, 14, 18, 23, 56, 206
Wesley, Charles 417
Wesley, Samuel 417, 419
Wesley, Samuel Sebastian, organist 157, 319, 416–20, **417**, 418n., 427, 431, 438, 465, 473
West, Benjamin **251**, 267, 318
Westbury on Severn, Gloucestershire 444, 447
Westfaling, Herbert, bishop of Hereford 95–96, **95**, 352
Westminster Abbey 214, 217, 220, 235, 236, 325
Weston, Anthony, chapter clerk 187
Wetherell, Nathan, dean 128, 137, 149, 151, 257, 261, 317, 605, 625, 638
Wharton, Nehemiah 100, 401–2
Wharton, Robert, *see* Parfew
Whishaw, Humphrey, canon 129, 132, 133, 255, 642
Whishaw, Thomas, precentor 129, 638
Whitchurch, Gwent
   St Dubricius's church missal 376, 386
White, Alfred, and Sons, bell hangers 344
Whitfield Partners, architects 195, 311, 562
Whitgift, John, bishop of Worcester, archbishop of Canterbury 93, **94**, 448, 451
Wigmore, Herefordshire, abbot of 616
William I, King 23
William III, King 120

William IV, King 156, 416
William, Brother 69
William, canon 41
William, clerk to Bishop Robert the Lotharingian 26
William, David, joiner 547
William of Malmesbury 8, 13, 294
Williams, Frederick M., canon 503–4, 643
Williams, Philip, smith 257
Williams, William, smith 258
Willim, Thomas, carpenter 249, 250, 408
Willis, Browne 123, 125, 127, 249, 250, 252, 517, 519
Willis, Henry I, organ builder ('Father Willis') 477–79, 480–81, 484–85, 486
Willis, Henry II, organ builder 483
Willis, Henry III, organ builder 481, 485–87
Willis, Robert, architectural writer 241, 249, 262–63, 270
Willis, Robert A., dean 186, **187**, 195, 638
Wilson, Philip, lay clerk 175
Winaston, Blackmarstone, Hereford 605
Winberht 9
Windsor Castle
   St George's Chapel 235–36
Winnington-Ingram, Arthur J., archdeacon of Hereford 175–76, 178, 641
Winnington-Ingram, Edward H., archdeacon of Hereford 169, 171, 641
Winston, Thomas 523
Wode, William, organist 391 and n., 572
Wolsey, Thomas, Cardinal, archbishop of York 83
Wolston, Reginald, canon 298–99, 445
woman priests, ordination 198
Wood, Thomas, mason 606
Woodcock, Thomas 454, 462

Woodhouse, Andrew, archdeacon of Hereford and of Shropshire 185, 186, 641–42
Woodward, John, chorister 415
Woolhope, Herefordshire 26, 33, 34, 105, 644
Woolhope Naturalists' Field Club 529
Woollam, John, headmaster 588n.
Wootton Rivers, Wiltshire 582
Worcester, bishops of *see* bishops of Worcester
Worcester Cathedral 209–10, 213, 215, 226, 371, 374
Worcester, city 16
Worcester Postman 462
Wormsley, Herefordshire, prior of 83
Wren, Matthew, bishop of Hereford 98–99, **99**, 401, 451, 496, 502, 520
Wright, Charles 502
Wulfgeat, of Donington 14, 22
Wulfheard, bishop of Hereford 10–12
Wulfhelm, bishop of Hereford 14
Wulfhere, king of the Mercians 4
Wulfric, bishop of Hereford 14
Wulviva 644
Wyatt, James 140–41, 142, 144, 167, 226, 239, 257, 261–65, 269, 271, 274, 278, 280, 281, 282, 319
Wycherley, Richard, master of St Katherine's, bishop of Olena 621
Wyclif, John 49, 65
Wycliffite Bible **pl. IVb**, 525, 531
Wycombe, William de 32, 38
Wye, River 13, 14, 126, 203, 240, 258, 293
Wynde, Margery 612
Wynne-Willson, A. B., prebendary **170**
Wyon, Allan 357

Zimmerman, Arthur U. 597
Zimmerman Trustees 597–98

DATE DUE

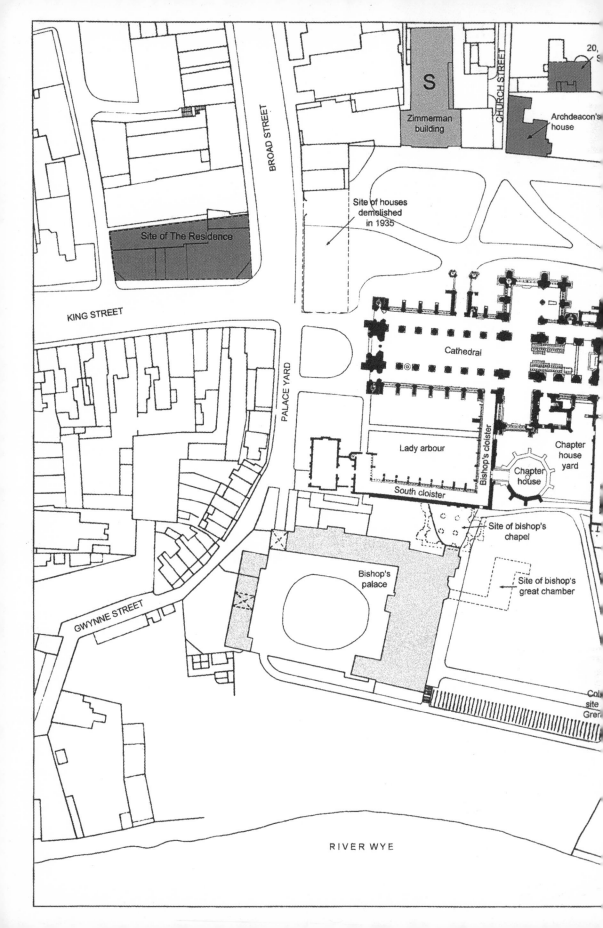

BROAD STREET

S

Zimmerman
building

Archdeacon's
house

20,

Site of houses
demolished
in 1935

Site of The Residence

KING STREET

Cathedral

PALACE YARD

Lady arbour

Bishop's cloister

Chapter
house
yard

Chapter
house

South cloister

Site of bishop's
chapel

GWYNNE STREET

Bishop's
palace

Site of bishop's
great chamber

Col
site
Gre

CHURCH STREET

RIVER WYE